Effective Argument

Effective Argument

A WRITER'S GUIDE WITH READINGS

J. KARL NICHOLAS

JAMES R. NICHOLL

Western Carolina University

ALLYN AND BACON

Boston   London   Toronto   Sydney   Tokyo   Singapore

Executive Editor: Joseph Opiela
Series Editorial Assistant: Amy Capute
Editorial-Production Service: Raeia Maes
Text Designer: Pat Torelli
Cover Administrator: Linda Dickinson
Composition/Manufacturing Buyer: Louise Richardson

Library of Congress Cataloging-in-Publication Data

Nicholas, J. Karl (James Karl)
    Effective argument : a writer's guide with readings / J. Karl Nicholas, James R. Nicholl.
        p.   cm.
    Includes index.
    ISBN 0-205-13063-1
    1. English language—Rhetoric.   2. Persuasion (Rhetoric)
3. College readers.   I. Nicholl, James R.   II. Title.
PE1431.N5   1991
808'.0427—dc20   90-22040
                                                                            CIP

Credits

Dyer, Wayne W., "Your Erroneous Zones." Excerpt from *Your Erroneous Zones* by Wayne W. Dyer (New York: Funk and Wagnalls, 1976, pp. 164–165). Copyright © 1976 by Wayne W. Dyer. Reprinted by permission of Harper Collins Publishers, Inc.

Jackson, Jesse, "Why Blacks Need Affirmative Action." Excerpted from "Why Blacks Need Affirmative Action," *Regulation*, Sept./Oct. 1978. Reprinted with the permission of the American Enterprise for Public Policy Research, Washington, D.C.

The credits continue on the pages following the index. They should be considered an extension of the copyright page.

Printed in the United States of America
10   9   8   7   6   5   4   3   2   1   95   94   93   92   91

For
Marguerite and Ted Nicholas
Lil and Elden Nicholl

Contents

Selected Classic Arguments   385

Appendix   463

Preface

Effective Argument: A Writer's Guide with Readings is, as its name indicates, a combined rhetoric and reader created for use in college-level introductory courses devoted to argumentative and persuasive writing.

We wrote *Effective Argument* in response to the trend to create separate freshman-year courses devoted to argumentative writing, a trend that started in the early 1980s and that continues. We planned the book as a reader, with minimal apparatus, but as we began working on it and examined the competing texts that were beginning to appear, we quickly realized that students would need additional background, training, and practice in argumentation if they were to use the readings successfully as models for writing their own arguments. Consequently, the rhetoric section grew, until it is nearly the size of the readings section, which contains 60 essays.

Effective Argument begins with an introduction that reviews the rhetoric of exposition, the kind of explanatory writing that students typically first attempt in high school and usually continue to practice in their first college writing course. It also discusses the value of learning to write effective argumentation and defines key terms, such as argumentation and persuasion.

The rhetoric section consists of six chapters. Chapter One, "The Argumentation Process," defines and illustrates the notions of claim and support. The next chapter, "Supporting the Claim," details strategies for supporting claims of fact, value, and policy. These two chapters, as do the four following ones, contain a number of illustrative examples of the argumentative techniques they describe by such writers as Loren Eiseley, Jesse Jackson, Phyllis McGinley, and John Steinbeck. Exercises are also placed throughout these chapters, keyed both to their examples and to the model essays in the readings section. This feature, not found in competing texts, provides students immediate and timely opportunities to practice and to test the concepts of argumentative writing while they are learning them; it also encourages students to begin looking closely at a variety of written arguments quite early, and to consider the strategies used by experienced writers.

Chapter Three, "Organizing the Support," treats inductive and deductive strategies in a manner that will seem familiar to most writing instructors; then we introduce the modern logic of the English philosopher Stephen Toulmin. Chapter Four, "Warrants," continues the treatment of modern logic, focusing on the strength of the warrant—its logical, ethical, and emotional appeals.

Chapter Five, "Refutation," divides rebuttals into those that attack the opponents' support of a claim (material fallacies), the argument's form (formal fallacies), and the warrant itself. It also introduces the ironic argument and the reduction to absurdity. (A fuller discussion of fallacies is included separately in "A Short Guide to Material and Formal Fallacies" in the Appendix.)

Chapter Six, "Putting It All Together," focuses on the successive drafts of the argument as students work through the phases of the writing process, on the preparation of effective introductions and conclusions, and on the crucial skills students must develop to document properly the sources they use in supporting the claims of their written arguments.

The readings section of the text begins with an introduction entitled "Reading and Analyzing Arguments," detailing the kinds of careful reading skills that students must develop not only to understand the ensuing essays but also to adapt those essays' techniques for use in their own argumentative writing. To conclude this introduction, we guide students through the analysis of a sample essay.

The readings themselves are divided into four groups: "Speaking Up" (15 essays on various topics), "Taking Sides" (9 pairs of essays with opposing claims), "Varying Voices" (4 groups of 4 or 5 essays each, exploring multiple facets of a single issue), and "Selected Classic Arguments" (10 favorites that are still relevant today). Questions on Content and on Form, plus Suggestions for Writing, are provided for all essays in the readings section. (A separate Instructor's Manual contains answers to these questions as well as additional useful information.)

The book concludes with an Appendix that contains both the guide to fallacies mentioned earlier and a glossary of useful rhetorical and argumentative terms.

Effective Argument owes its existence to the vision, energy, and continuing encouragement of our principal editor at Allyn and Bacon, Joseph Opiela; we are indeed grateful for his patient persistence that helped so much to make this book a reality. We also are glad to have had the professional support of Amy Capute and Rowena Dores at Allyn and Bacon, and we wish to acknowledge in particular the careful copyediting done by Patricia Johnson and the editorial-production service provided by Raeia Maes. The content, organization, and style of the book were immeasurably improved by the thoughtful, incisive criticism our manuscript received at various stages from our field reviewers: Walter Beale, University of North Carolina at Greensboro; Walter Graffin, University of Wisconsin at Kenosha; C. Jeriel Howard, Northeastern Illinois University; David Jolliffe, University of Illinois—Chicago; Nevin Laib, Franklin and Marshall University; Gratia Murphy, Youngstown State University; John O'Bannion, Robert Morris College; Richard Ramsey, Indiana University, Fort Wayne; Mary Saver, Indiana University, Purdue; Judith Stanford, Rivier College; Gail Stygall, Miami University; Lynn Waller, McLennan Community College; Richard Zbracki, Iowa State University. We certainly appreciate the time and effort each person gave in order to help us. We also appreciate the prompt, knowledgeable assistance we got from the entire Reference Staff at Hunter Library, Western Carolina University; without their guidance we would still be struggling to complete the readings section of this book. Laura Cathey, an outstanding senior English major, is someone else who deserves our thanks. She surveyed the interests of a cross-section of local students for us, and her results were very useful in planning the readings section.

Special thanks are due to our families for their support throughout this project; we are sure that Veronica and Kathy will be glad to have us home for supper more often and to know that we can again do our share of the household chores. Our final thanks go to our parents, to whom this book is lovingly dedicated.

J. K. N.
J. R. N.

PART ONE

Effective Argument

Argumentation and the Writing Process

Few human activities are more important or can be more complex than that of persuasion: the art and craft of changing people's minds. When persuasion—or argumentation, if it comes to that—is successful, old beliefs give way to new: our world is understood as round, not flat; it orbits the sun, not vice versa. But when persuasion fails, convictions sometimes clash; then the results can be unpleasant, or even deadly.

For these and other reasons, people began centuries ago to study argumentation, especially in its spoken forms. They wanted to discover what makes some arguments succeed and others fail—which common elements, arrangements, and techniques each includes, and each avoids. The earliest important students of argumentation were the Greeks (such as Aristotle, 384–322 B.C.) and the Romans (such as Cicero, 106–43 B.C.), for in their cultures that skill was especially valued for its immediate influence in their law courts and public assemblies. Scholars of argumentation were called rhetoricians, from *rhetor*, the Greek name for an orator or public speaker. These rhetoricians trained students in the art of effective, persuasive use of language, or rhetoric. To do so, they regularly provided their pupils with samples of successful speeches, helped them to analyze their own and others' techniques, and then coached their novice orators to imitate the successful features of the works they had studied.

This book uses a related approach. Much as Greek and Roman students did, you will study models of effective arguments, learning thereby the most appropriate techniques for changing the minds of an audience. However, we will not be concerned with persuasive

1

public speaking in this book, although sometimes the examples that we include appeared first as speeches. (A familiar example is Patrick Henry's emotionally persuasive phrase, "Give me liberty or give me death!", part of a speech he made shortly before the American Revolution to the legislature of colonial Virginia.) Primarily, we provide examples of effective written arguments—or *rhetorical models.*

You understand, of course, that the models we will provide are unique; other people wrote them for purposes and audiences and times different from ours. But just as, hoping to succeed yourself, you might study and imitate a special technique of an athlete on the court or field, or of an artist in a studio or a musician in a concert hall, so also can you learn from imitation of other writers' successes. In fact, the biographies of notable writers consistently describe how their own work was influenced by reading closely the works of their predecessors and contemporaries.

Of course, you also understand that just as success as an athlete (or musician or scientist or accountant or the like) does not come automatically or without practice or effort, so writing successful persuasive prose requires study, thought, and hard work. No piece of writing in this book sprang instantly and perfectly into being; if you could see this introductory essay as we have gone through the process of piecing it together—with its strike-overs, insertions, scratched-out sentences, revisions in three colors of ink, representing numerous writing and revising sessions—you would readily agree with us that no writer is likely to create a perfect argument on the first attempt, or even sometimes on the second or third or fourth.

That declaration leads to this one: Completed writing projects of much complexity are the result of an extended, recursive (looping) process involving certain phases, and the construction of arguments is no exception. Sometimes a piece of argumentative writing will begin with an assignment from a supervisor or a teacher or some other authority figure; sometimes it starts directly from the heart or the mind (perhaps as an apology or a letter of complaint). In any case, faced with the task, you begin the process. Inevitably that process involves four basic phases, but the process is not usually linear or straightforward. Rather, the phases are often repeated and often overlap, for writing is a messy and plastic activity. Think, for example, of a sculptor working and reworking her mass of clay until she gets a person's facial features into just the form she thinks best. Thus, even though we will describe the phases of the writing process in a 1, 2, 3, 4 progression, we do so for convenience and not because that progression exactly represents the normal reality.

The first phase is devoted to prewriting, a period of time before you actually begin to write and during which you call on all of your resources, bringing them to bear on the issue or proposition you want your audience to accept. It is during this step that you may seek out and examine actual models (such as those in this book or ones in a library or in the files of your organization) of the kind of writing you plan to do. If you plan to write an editorial condemning a sales tax increase or an article proposing stricter drinking laws, it's always a good idea to examine a few such editorials or articles to see what others have done and how they have solved that particular writing problem. You must also consider all the relevant facts that you know and try to find others that you do not know; you will want to think about how best to reach and convince your probable reading audience, tinker with organizational schemes, test your logic, locate possible fallacies; you'll probably, unless you have an exceptional memory, want to jot down useful examples, write yourself notes, even make an outline in some form. In other words, you will immerse yourself in the subject.

Sooner or later, you will have to select the most likely alternative approach of those considered and begin to write. Then you are starting the second phase, the actual writing of the argument. You may be lucky and discover that your initial strategy or organizational plan works smoothly, with its logic unchallengeable and all of the concrete details you earlier jotted down fitting neatly into their supporting slots. But that rarely happens. More often you will have several false starts, perhaps discarding plans whose promise evaporated as you tried to put them into place. Sometimes new and better ideas occur to you as you write. Or maybe you realize that you have forgotten to take proper account of what your intended audience knows—or doesn't know. Sometimes you must toss away everything and start over again, after a break, a meal, or even a good night's sleep (if the paper's due date permits, that is). If you keep going, however, eventually you will complete your first draft. Then your written work is ready for the third phase: revision of your completed first draft. (Of course, you may not in fact complete the whole first draft before you begin revising, especially with a long and complicated piece of writing. And you may even find that you need to return to phase 1, for instance to examine additional related pieces of writing, to gather additional facts, and the like.)

During revision you will continue to consider your purpose, your intended reading audience, and such matters as organization and supporting examples. Now, during this third phase, you will also finally begin to give special attention to style, as well as to grammar, mechanics, and spelling. Quite as important, but often very difficult, is the matter of style. Here the choice is not between the acceptable and the unacceptable; rather, the choice is between several, even many, alternative ways of expressing your ideas and arranging your words, almost all of which are acceptable, but some of which are more effective than others. So you will have to study your sentences to make sure that they say just what you intended in the most effective and most emphatic way. Reading your sentences aloud is one useful strategy at this point. Another is asking peers, at school or on the job, to read and to comment on what you have written. Here, though, you must be sure that those you ask for advice not only understand your writing task, but also that they can give adequate time and serious attention to helping you to revise your work.

With style under reasonable control, it's finally time to make sure that subjects and verbs agree, to insert commas and semicolons, and to check for spelling faults. A standard reference grammar will provide useful guidance in correcting any errors of usage, grammar, and mechanics (such as punctuation) that have slipped into your writing during the preceding step, when you were busily transferring ideas from your mind onto paper. A hardbound dictionary should also be handy in your work area, for ease of reference in answering questions of accurate spelling and appropriate word choice.

As you grow more proficient as a writer, you may find yourself able to juggle more stylistic and grammatical considerations while you write your first draft, pausing momentarily to rearrange a sentence for a better effect, to determine the appropriate case of a pronoun, or to decide whether to use either a semicolon or a period. However, in most cases it is best to avoid conscious or extended concern with revision during phase 2—or any time when you are actually creating a piece of writing. Save some time and your serious attention to revision for phase 3, where it naturally belongs.

The fourth and last phase of the writing process is, of course, the creation of a final copy of your revised piece of writing, one you are ready to submit for the judgment of someone else—such as a supervisor, teacher, editor, or government leader. Here you are going "public" with the latest and best version of your work—publishing it, in a figurative and perhaps even a literal sense. Yet even here you may not be completely finished with the writing process, and may find yourself going back to or through the phases of writing, trying always to improve the expression of your ideas.

It should now be clear that the value of this book lies chiefly in the assistance it offers you in the first two phases of the writing process—prewriting (getting ready to compose your argument) and then writing the first draft. Study of this book provides two very obvious benefits, as well as another more subtle one. Obviously you need to have something to write about, some proposition to argue for or against, and this book's diverse reading selections furnish a kind of launch pad for your persuasive flights by providing interesting, often controversial, materials for your consideration and reactions. In addition, these selections, chosen from the work of professional writers, illustrate a variety of argumentative strategies or organizational plans. The shorter selections illustrate clearly the most common argumentative devices and may serve as models for much of your own writing. The longer ones are perhaps most useful for furnishing the ideas that will eventually grow into your own arguments as you read, ponder, and discuss their subject matter with your classmates and teacher.

More subtly, though, any reading that you do—in this book or elsewhere—will have a lasting effect on your abilities as a writer. Every sentence that you read can add to your subconscious mental storehouse of vocabulary, idioms, organizational devices, and stylistic tactics. Similarly, all arguments that you read heighten your awareness of how they are formulated and presented. The advantage of a book such as *Effective Argument* over random reading lies in the careful choice and arrangement of its selections. The readings ensure your wide exposure to writing that demonstrates accurate word choice, mature and clear style, wise rhetorical strategies, and effective persuasive skills in general.

Modes of Writing

Although this book focuses on the writing of effective arguments, we cannot discuss that subject without occasionally referring to other modes or types of writing which sometimes have a part in the construction of arguments. You likely have already studied and practiced such other writing methods as narrative–descriptive and expository, and perhaps have also done literary and expressive writing. But just to be sure we share the same perspective, let's briefly review the modes that are especially useful in argumentative writing.

In narrative–descriptive writing, the writer strives to make the readers think they see and even experience a scene or a series of actions, either real or imagined. To accomplish this, the writer focuses on specific *details,* especially visual ones, as well as on *qualities* (general traits, such as thin, tall, slow, jagged) and *comparisons* (often using *like* or *as,* following the technique of the poetic simile). News and feature articles, character sketches and biographies, short stories and novels, and travel and historical writing provide typical examples of narrative–descriptive writing.

Expository writing often takes even more account of its intended audience, its writer presuming that readers of the work do not know some or all of a particular piece of information and therefore need it explained to them. Here again details, this time in the form of illustrations or examples, are the writer's most successful means of making the readers understand. These illustrations may be organized in a number of different ways, for instance to form classifications, comparisons, analogies, or cause–effect analyses. Of course, a writer will often find it necessary to use narration and description to present most effectively the information needed by the intended audience. Textbooks, essays and reports, technical manuals, and case studies furnish examples of expository writing. It is the most common type of writing in the majority of school and work situations. And just as it may contain narrative–descriptive elements, it may also use argumentative techniques when its author seeks not just to inform but also to persuade a reading audience.

In argumentation, the writer takes a different approach from the other two modes of writing just mentioned. Here the writer presumes that readers already hold an opinion concerning the subject matter. Argumentation's basic purpose is not merely to add new information, although this is sometimes necessary; rather, its purpose is to discuss known information in a way or ways that will persuade readers to change their minds about that information, and to adopt the writer's opinion on the matter. Here also the writer will present key details, this time to support the proposition whose validity is being debated, and of course she or he will also often use narrative–descriptive and expository techniques. Advertisements, scholarly and scientific treatises, editorials, debates, and political speeches provide examples of this kind of writing.

You need to understand these three divisions—narrative-descriptive, expository, and argumentative—because they will help you answer the most important question that will confront you as a writer: What is my purpose in writing? If you basically want to make your audience see or experience a place, person, or circumstance, you will mainly write in a narrative–descriptive mode and use narrative-descriptive techniques. If you want to inform, to educate, to increase your readers' fund of information, then you will depend most on expository techniques. But if you want to change the minds of your readers, you will write persuasively, using the techniques of argumentation.

Some Key Terms

Although most of you may understand them already, we want to make clear differentiations among three terms that we have already been using, and that we will use even more frequently in the rest of the book. The terms are *persuasion, reasoning,* and *arguing;* we will also briefly discuss some related terms.

"Persuasion" is the broadest of the three main terms, and in fact includes the other two within its general meaning. To persuade is to influence other persons' words or deeds, using virtually any means. People may be persuaded by force (as when they are "coerced"), or perhaps by rewards, including emotional ones (as when they are "induced"). They may be "prevailed upon," here with the sense that someone or something has used pressure or force, physical or otherwise.

Often reasons, presented by means of spoken or written words, are used to influence others regarding the truth or falsity of something; in such cases, when we use declarative statements linked in a convincing or mind-changing way, we are "reasoning" or "arguing." "Reasoning" and "arguing" are thus synonyms, although not exact ones; unlike "reasoning," the term "arguing" has a connotation (secondary emotional meaning) of the existence of conflict or opposing sides. And both terms lie within the bounds of the more inclusive term, "persuasion."

Another related term, "disputing," suggests, as does "arguing," the presence of controversy or opposing sides, just the sort of situation we have observed in a heated dialogue or a debate between persons holding strongly conflicting viewpoints. (Here you might recall the televised debates between presidential candidates that are now a part of the U.S. political scene every four years.) If such a dispute becomes overheated or angry and rude, we may label it a "quarrel"; at that point the element of reasoning by means of words alone tends to fade or disappear, sometimes being replaced by physical threats or even violent acts. Accordingly, our aim is to help you to use reasoning so persuasively that you will not only cause your good ideas to prevail but that you will also be able to avoid quarrels.

You are now ready to begin to examine in detail the standard features of argumentative writing as well as the writing models in this book, studying how professional writers have organized and presented their materials. Then under the guidance of your instructor and *Effective Argument,* you will learn to adapt these techniques for your own written arguments in English class as well as in your other classes, and for use at work as well as in school.

1

The Argumentation Process

Basic Considerations

If we lived in a perfect world, this book would be unnecessary, for all of us would have everything we need and harmony would be universal. Yet even casual observation of simpler forms of life will show us controversy, creatures taking sides against one another: Two ants, perhaps from the same colony, try to tug a beetle's carcass in opposing directions; Garfield the cat tricks Odie the dog out of a comfortable place to rest; one bird species drives another out of a desirable nesting or feeding area. As for us humans, our lives are likewise filled with controversy at home and at school, at work and at play. Sometimes the disputes are relatively trivial, over the last piece of pizza or which television program to watch. But at other times the stakes are much higher, affecting even our survival on this planet, as we argue over mandatory AIDS testing or nuclear weapons control. And as we suggested in the first paragraph of this book's introduction, controversy is as old as humans; presumably, ancient peoples sometimes fought with words or fists over the last piece of mastodon meat, and they argued over whether to share with neighboring clans such valuable innovations as fire or the ability to shape flint into spear and arrow points.

With such a human history and such natural human tendencies (children must be *taught* to share, to wait their turns, and the like), is it any wonder that the Greeks and other earlier humans gave argumentation so much attention? And what would your own life be like if you could not already change others' minds to some extent, or if your ancestors had not been able to do so? Would you be in college, reading this book? Would you have grown up in Ohio rather than in Colorado, or have been reared on a farm rather than in a city's suburb? Would you even exist? How would life be changed for your grandparent or elderly neighbor if Congress had not passed the Social Security Act in the late 1930s, or amended it at intervals since? What if slavery were still legal, or the military draft still existed, or the ten amendments comprising the Bill of Rights had not been added to the U.S. Constitution?

Debating and deciding such issues as those just mentioned is soon to be a responsibility of you and your peers. If you do not learn the basic concepts of argumentation presented in this book, it is likely that you will have little or no influence on the future for yourself and for those who follow you. But presumably you are in college to improve or at least to maintain the quality of life you have experienced so far, and perhaps to try to do the same for others. Furthermore, when you leave college, most of you will go to work.

In your workplace, whether it is in an office, a store, a school, or in a factory, a hospital, or wherever, you will find yourself persuading (and being persuaded) virtually every day, using spoken and written language, sometimes quietly and calmly, sometimes loudly and heatedly. You will get your first job by persuasion, directly or indirectly, and you will keep it by the same means. You will argue often, for or against budget changes, rule interpretations, operating procedures, marketing strategies, or employment practices, among other things. If you argue well, you will thrive; if you argue poorly, you will likely become unsuccessful and unhappy, perhaps even unemployed. Accordingly, we hope by now that you are convinced by *our* argument, that the subject of this book and what it can teach you are crucial to the quality of your life in the future. If so, you will continue to read, to examine with us the argumentative process.

Claims and Support

How many times have you heard people say things like this?

"I know that's so because. . . ."
"I could give you sixteen good reasons why that's so."

Every time that you encounter such declarations, you are face to face with an argument—one that has been stated in its barest possible form. Its bare bones are showing. Let's look more closely.

That's so   Every argument contains at least one of these—an assertion that something is or is not the case, that it is better or worse than something else, or that it should or should not be done. This component of the argument goes by various names: *position, proposition, supposition, premise, conclusion,* or *claim.* Here we will call it a *claim.*

Because   For every claim in an argument, there must be at least one of these—a *because*-clause that tells why a claim is factual, preferable, or advantageous. These *because*-clauses we will call *support.*

Most claims are supported by several *because* statements, and, of course, there may be more than one claim in an argument, each with its supporting statements. What is not always true is that these essential elements will be easy to spot. For instance, examine this argument from Dr. Wayne Dyer's book, *Your Erroneous Zones:*

We are conditioned to look for justice in life and when it   1
doesn't appear, we tend to feel anger, anxiety or frustration. Actually, it would be equally productive to search for the fountain of youth, or some such myth. Justice does not exist. It never has, and it never will. The world is simply not put together that way. Robins eat worms. That's not fair to the worms. Spiders eat flies. That's not fair to the flies. Cougars kill coyotes. Coyotes kill badgers. Badgers kill mice. Mice kill bugs. Bugs . . . You have only to look at nature to realize there is no justice in the world. Tornadoes, floods, tidal waves, droughts are all unfair. It is a mythological concept, this justice business. The world and the people in it go on being unfair every day. You can choose to be happy or unhappy, but it has nothing to do with the lack of justice you see around you.

Our culture promises justice. Politicians refer to it in all of   2
their campaign speeches. "We need equality and justice for all." Yet day after day, century after century, the lack of justice continues. Poverty, war, pestilence, crime, prostitution, dope and murders persist generation after generation in public and private life. And if the history of humanity can be used as a guide they will continue.

The legal system promises justice. "The people demand jus-   3
tice," and some of them even work to make it happen. But it generally doesn't. Those with money are not convicted. Judges and policemen are often bought by the powerful. A President and

Vice-President of the United States are pardoned or wrist-slapped for obvious felonies. The poor fill the jails, and have next to no chance of beating the system. It's not fair. But it's true. Spiro Agnew becomes rich after evading his income taxes. Richard Nixon is exonerated, and his yes-men serve a few months in a minimum security prison, while the poor and members of minority groups rot in jail waiting for trial, waiting for a chance. A visit to any local courthouse or police station will prove that the influential have a separate set of rules, although this is relentlessly denied by the authorities. Where is the justice? Nowhere!

Dr. Dyer's argument about justice quite clearly consists of a combination of claim and because-statements, but these elements are not completely obvious. In the first paragraph, the claim appears: "Justice does not exist." There are no because-clauses following, at least literally, but you can certainly supply the *becauses:* [*Because*] robins eat worms, [and] that's not fair to worms . . . , [*Because*] spiders eat flies, [and] that's not fair to flies . . . , and so on. Dyer's first piece of support deals with the natural world. The next paragraph offers further support, this time from our culture. And the final paragraph furnishes still more support, this time from our legal system.

This example, while it does not announce its essential elements with flashing lights or a drum roll, is certainly easy enough to follow. Locating its basic ingredients did not overload your powers of perception. We do not want to mislead you, however. Not all arguments are so straightforward; therefore, it will serve you well to learn to ferret out the essential pieces—claims and their support—from arguments that you encounter. First of all, this practice will enable you to understand arguments better, and, second, it will help you to write better arguments yourself.

Another thing is worth mentioning at this point: We will be returning to Dr. Dyer's argument from time to time, using it for examples as we discuss the development of argumentative strategies, so you shouldn't allow that brief argument to fade from your memory; it will crop up again. In fact, you would be wise to reread his essay to prepare yourself now. The same use will be made of other arguments that you will encounter later in this chapter, such as the one we will examine next.

Here is an argument made by black political activist and presidential candidate, the Reverend Jesse Jackson. It makes more than one claim. Try to pick out each claim. Then for each claim, list the support.

Let me illustrate the point [this] way, using the familiar ath-   1
letic example, "Runners to your mark, get set, go!" Two world-
class distance runners begin the grueling human test of trying to
run a sub-four-minute mile. Two minutes into the race, officials
observe that one runner, falling far behind, still has running
weights on his ankles. They stop the race, and hold both runners
in their tracks. The weights are removed from the runner far
behind, the officials re-fire the starting gun, and both runners
continue from the points where they were when the race was
stopped. Not surprisingly, the runner who ran the entire race
without the ankle weights comes in with a sizable lead.

The fundamental moral question one could ask about that   2
theoretical race must be, Would anyone call it fair? Again, not
surprisingly, the answer would certainly be a simple and resounding No. If one could devise some means of compensating the
second runner (for example, comparing the runners' times for
the last two laps and projecting them over the entire race), a
more accurate appraisal of each runner's ability and performance
could be made. And if a reasonable means of compensation
could be devised, no one would say that such compensation
constituted "reverse discrimination" against the first runner or
"preferential treatment" for the second. All would agree that
compensation was fair and just.

Everyone can follow this example and see the "reasonable-   3
ness" and morality of the solution because racial attitudes are
not involved. Yet this is similar to the position in which blacks
find themselves in the United States. We have been running the
race with weights on our ankles—weights not of our own choosing. Weights of "no rights that a white must respect," weights of
slavery, of past and present discrimination in jobs, in education,
housing, and health care, and more.

Some argue that there now are laws forbidding discrimina-   4
tion in education, in public accommodations and employment,
in politics, and in housing. But these laws only amount to removing the weights after years of disadvantage. Too often, when
analyzing the race question, the analysts start at the end rather
than at the beginning. To return to the track-meet example, if
one saw only the last part of the race (without knowing about
the first part), the compensation might seem unreasonable, immoral, discriminatory, or a form of preferential treatment. Affirmative action programs (in light of the history and experience of
black people in the United States) are an extremely reasonable,

even conservative, way of compensating us for past and present discrimination. According to a recent publication of the Equal Employment Opportunity Commission (*Black Experience and Black Expectations*, Melvin Humphrey), at the present rate of "progress" it will take forty-three years to end job discrimination—hardly a reasonable timetable.

If our goal is educational and economic equity and parity— and it is—then we need affirmative action to catch up. We are behind as a result of discrimination and denial of opportunity. There is one white attorney for every 680 whites, but only one black attorney for every 4,000 blacks; one white physician for every 649 whites, but only one black physician for every 5,000 blacks; and one white dentist for every 1,900 whites, but only one black dentist for every 8,400 blacks. Less than 1 percent of all engineers—or of all practicing chemists—is black. Cruel and uncompassionate injustice created gaps like these. We need creative justice and compassion to help us close them.

Actually, in the U.S. context, "reverse discrimination" is illogical and a contradiction in terms. Never in the history of mankind has a majority, with power, engaged in programs and written laws that discriminate against itself. The only thing whites are giving up because of affirmative action is unfair advantage—something that was unnecessary in the first place.

Blacks are not making progress at the expense of whites, as news accounts make it seem. There are 49 percent more whites in medical school today and 64 percent more whites in law school than there were when affirmative action programs began some eight years ago.

In a recent column, William Raspberry raised an interesting question. Commenting on the *Bakke* case, he asked, "What if, instead of setting aside 16 of 100 slots, we added 16 slots to the 100?" That, he suggested, would allow blacks to make progress and would not interfere with what whites already have. He then went on to point out that this, in fact, is exactly what has happened in law and medical schools. In 1968, the year before affirmative action programs began to get under way, 9,571 whites and 282 members of minority groups entered U.S. medical schools. In 1976, the figures were 14,213 and 1,400 respectively. Thus, under affirmative action, the number of "white places" actually rose by 49 percent: white access to medical training was not diminished, but substantially increased. The trend was even more marked in law schools. In 1969, the first year for which reliable figures are available, 2,933 minority group members were enrolled; in 1976, the number was up to 8,484. But during the same period, law school enrollment for whites rose from 65,453 to 107,064—an increase of 64 percent. In short, it is a myth that blacks are making progress at white expense.

In analyzing Jackson's essay, to locate its claims and their support, it is useful to *summarize* portions of his argument, stating Jackson's opinions in our own words. The creation of *summaries* is a skill that you will find invaluable as you construct arguments of your own. So bear that in mind as we proceed.

First, notice that Jackson begins with an illustration. It is not clear at the outset exactly what point the hypothetical race is supposed to illustrate, but in the second paragraph he asks whether the race was fair and answers with a No. Here then is a claim: The race was not fair; the support for this claim is obvious from the details of the story. In the third paragraph Jackson makes clear the point his example illustrates: American blacks are like the runner whose ankles had been unfairly weighted; they deserve some just compensation for the unfair treatment they received.

Paragraph 4 contains one of Jackson's most crucial claims: "Affirmative action programs . . . are an extremely reasonable, even conservative, way of compensating us for past and present discrimination." The support for this claim has been established by the comparison with the runner. Simply removing the weights was not enough, in the same way that laws forbidding racial discrimination are not enough.

Paragraph 5 constitutes another statement to support the just-stated claim. It asserts that affirmative action programs are reasonable *because* blacks are measurably behind whites in at least three important professions—and by implication in a great many others, if not all.

In the last three paragraphs, Jackson turns to another claim, one regarding "reverse discrimination," the belief that, as a result of affirmative action programs, whites are now being discriminated against. He states this last claim most clearly in the first sentence of paragraph 7: "Blacks are not making progress at the expense of whites . . ." and repeats it in the sentence that concludes his final paragraph: ". . . it is a myth that blacks are making progress at white expense."

What about the support for this claim? Jackson does two things to support it. First, he cites some statistics showing that whites attend law and medical school in higher numbers than before affirmative action plans were put into effect. Next, he calls upon an authority, syndicated newspaper columnist William Raspberry, who, using other statistics, shows that blacks, as a result of affirmative action, have not encroached upon spaces in professional schools formerly reserved for whites. Rather, what has happened is that seats were added for both blacks and whites. As a result, while increasing numbers of blacks (and whites) have gained medical and law school admission, the imbalance favoring whites has been only minimally reduced.

We might reduce Jackson's argument to the following essentials:

Claim	Support	Location
The race was unfair.	Because the runner's feet were weighted and he was not compensated.	Para. 1–3
Affirmative action plans are needed.	Because laws against racial discrimination do not provide compensation.	Para. 4
	And because blacks are measurably behind whites.	Para. 5
Blacks are not making progress at white expense.	Because more whites are in professional schools now than there were before affirmative action.	Para. 6
	And that is because spaces were added to offset in part those whites lost through affirmative action.	Para. 7–8

To repeat now what you have just seen demonstrated: Every argument consists of two parts: a *claim* and the *support* for that claim. In reading arguments like the two you have just studied, it is obviously important for you to recognize the claims and their support. Why? Being able to recognize the claim and its support enables you to go right to the heart of any argument—to understand it better—and, if you choose, to *summarize* it so that you can use it as a part of an argument of your own. The claim in its barest form will be a statement asserting, or claiming, that something is something else—that is, that X is a Y. Here are some examples of possible claims:

> John Smith is a murderer.
> Geometry is a waste of time.
> *Star Wars* is an excellent movie.
> Carol Stone is a better student than Bill Mudd.
> Women in Literature is a course that should be offered next year.
> Investing in mutual funds is a smart thing to do.

Notice that each of these examples states a position that you could either agree with or disagree with. That is the first condition for a claim: *it can either be affirmed or denied.* It is also easy to see that not all statements of the type X is a Y can be claims, because they do not allow us the option to agree with them or not. Here are some nonarguable claims:

> John Smith is a man.
> Geometry is a branch of mathematics.
> *Star Wars* is a movie directed by George Lucas.
> Carol Stone is a student in English 101.
> Women in Literature is an English course that appears in the college catalog.
> Mutual funds are a type of investment opportunity.

Each of these statements asserts something that no one would care to dispute; such statements are not arguable.

Finding and Stating the Claim

By the same token, just as not all statements that follow the pattern X is a Y turn out to be arguable claims, not all claims are cast in the form X is a Y. The English language furnishes us with a vast array of alternatives; we can make statements in a variety of ways. Each of the claims that were held out as examples could be restated in a form quite different from X is a Y. Here are some possibilities:

> Surely, John Smith murdered Bill Jones in cold blood.
> I can see no practical value in studying geometry.

Star Wars deserved all the Oscars it won.

Carol Stone writes better papers than Bill Mudd.

We should convince the English department chair to include Women in Literature in next year's schedule.

Mutual funds offer a promising investment opportunity.

We know that each of these statements is a suitable claim because it conforms to the two criteria we have established:

1. It is reducible to a statement of the type X is a Y.
2. It can be debated.

Keeping these criteria in mind, you should be able to examine the following list of statements and determine which are legitimate claims and which are not:

1. The Global Ecology course discusses six critical dangers to the earth's ecosystems.
2. Nursing students usually have a more compassionate view of human society than accounting majors do.
3. Bert Biggins has six fingers on his left hand.
4. Allison Edwards really deserves to pass English 102.
5. The Cubs beat the Dodgers yesterday by a score of 9 to 4.
6. The Parkside Restaurant serves the best meals in town.

If you decided that the even-numbered statements represent legitimate claims, or arguable statements, then you were correct. While a little exercise in syntax would render all of the above sentences in the form of X is a Y, only the even-numbered ones pose any possibility for serious debate; the others are just not worth arguing about since their accuracy is so easily verified.

Providing Support

Once you have located the claim, or claims, in an argument, you will need to find the support. As you have noticed in the arguments cited so far, each claim's support is located nearby, and if we reduce the supporting statement to its bare essentials, we discover that the support for any given claim is usually some kind of *because*-statement:

1. Nursing majors usually have a more compassionate view of human society than accounting majors because nurses frequently

work directly with ailing humans, while accountants work with computers and ledger sheets.

2. Allison Edwards deserves to pass English 102 because she completed all the written assignments and most of the homework with passing grades.

3. The Parkside Restaurant is the best restaurant in town because its tables are regularly filled with satisfied clients and because it receives more catering assignments than any other eating establishment in town.

Now you have had some practice in recognizing claims and support, and you have seen that a combination of the claim and its support—stated in barest fashion—makes a pretty good summary of an argument. Here is another argument for you to examine. Locate the claim that it makes, as well as the support for that claim. Set up a table that shows the claim and supporting data, along with their location. Use the table on page 15 as your model.

The Cat Bill Veto

ADLAI STEVENSON

To the Honorable, the Members of the Senate of the Sixty-sixth General Assembly:

I herewith return, without my approval, Senate Bill No. 93 entitled "An Act to Provide Protection to Insectivorous Birds by Restraining Cats." This is the so-called "Cat Bill." I veto and withhold my approval from this bill for the following reasons: 1

It would impose fines on owners or keepers who permitted their cats to run at large off their premises. It would permit any person to capture, or call upon the police to pick up and imprison, cats at large. It would permit the use of traps. The bill would have statewide application—on farms, in villages, and in metropolitan centers.   2

This legislation has been introduced in the past several sessions of the Legislature, and it has, over the years, been the source of much comment—not all of which has been in a serious vein. It may be that the General Assembly has now seen fit to refer it to one who can view it with a fresh outlook. Whatever the reasons for passage at this session, I cannot believe there is a   3 widespread public demand for this law or that it could, as a practical matter, be enforced.

Furthermore, I cannot agree that it should be the declared public policy of Illinois that a cat visiting a neighbor's yard or crossing the highway is a public nuisance. It is in the nature of cats to do a certain amount of unescorted roaming. Many live with their owners in apartments or other restricted premises, and I doubt if we want to make their every brief foray an opportunity for a small game hunt by zealous citizens—with traps or otherwise. I am afraid this bill could only create discord, recrimination and enmity. Also consider the owner's dilemma: To escort a cat abroad on a leash is against the nature of the cat, and to permit it to venture forth for exercise unattended into a night of new dangers is against the nature of the owner. Moreover, cats perform useful service, particularly in rural areas, in combating rodents—work they necessarily perform alone and without regard for property lines.

We are all interested in protecting certain varieties of birds. That cats destroy some birds, I well know, but I believe this legislation would further but little the worthy cause to which its proponents give such unselfish effort. The problem of the cat versus the bird is as old as time. If we attempt to resolve it by legislation, who knows but what we may be called upon to take sides as well in the age-old problems of dog versus cat, bird versus bird, or even bird versus worm. In my opinion, the state of Illinois and its local governing bodies already have enough to do without trying to control feline delinquency.

For these reasons, and not because I love birds the less or cats the more, I veto and withhold my approval from Senate Bill No. 93.

Here is our analysis of the claim and support statements contained in the Adlai Stevenson piece, "The Cat Bill Veto." Your analysis may not agree entirely with ours, but there should be some similarity.

Claim	Support	Location
I don't support Senate Bill No. 93	It fines cat owners who allow their cats to run at large.	Para. 2
	It permits the capture of cats that are running at large.	Para. 2

It permits the use of traps.	Para. 2
It extends the prohibition statewide, to farms, villages, and cities.	Para. 2

Stevenson uses the first two paragraphs to remind his audience of the provisions of the Cat Bill. This first set of support statements is little more than a listing of the bill's provisions. As such, you may not want to view them as actually being part of the support for Stevenson's claim that the bill is undesirable. Stevenson sets up his argument this way so that he can make an easy transition to his next set of supporting statements.

Claim	*Support*	*Location*
I don't support Senate Bill No. 93	There is not widespread demand for this law.	Para. 3
	It could not be enforced.	Para. 3
	It is against the nature of cats to be so restricted.	Para. 4
	Unrestrained cats do positive good by controlling rodents.	Para. 4
	Its passage would open the door for laws restricting other species.	Para. 5

Now here is another argument for you to examine; this one makes more than one claim. Proceed as you did before: Locate the claims and their support.

On Playboys and Bunnies

H. M. HEFNER

Playboy's over-all point of view on the male-female relation-   1
ship in society certainly doesn't limit women to the role of Bunnies in The Playboy Club. Essentially, what we are saying, editorially in the magazine, is that men and women should each have *separate* identities—that they are both happiest when their roles complement rather than compete with each other.

Since the turn of the century, there has been a considerable   2 breakdown in the cultural patterns that distinguish the sexes—especially here in America—causing us to drift toward an asexual society, in which it becomes increasingly difficult for either sex to find true satisfaction or fulfillment in its interpersonal relationships with the other. This is one of the two primary causes, I believe—the other being the increasing complexity and automation of our civilization—for the erosion of individual identity that was mentioned earlier.

Since *Playboy* is a magazine for men, it is natural for us to   3
place most of our emphasis on the problem of male identity. *Playboy* stresses a strongly heterosexual concept of society—in which the separate roles of men and women are clearly defined and compatible. Though we are sometimes accused of having a dehumanized view of women, our concept actually offers the female a far more human identity than she has had historically in the Western world.

It is our religious tradition that has tended to look upon   4
woman as a depersonalized object, or possession, by continually associating her with its antagonism toward sex. Sometimes the emphasis has been placed upon the temptation to sin in womankind and sometimes the emphasis has been placed upon feminine purity and chastity; but whether they were considered creatures of the Devil, or placed upon a pedestal, their status in our antisexual society has always been that of an *object*, rather than a *human being*.

Here is our analysis of the H. M. Hefner essay, "On Playboys and Bunnies."

Claim	*Support*	*Location*
The separate identities of men and women should be emphasized.	Those identities have been eroded by the breakdown of clearly defined sex roles in our society, its "drift toward an asexual society."	Para. 1 and 2
	Sexual identities have been eroded by the "increasing complexity and automation of our civilization."	Para. 2

Playboy's view of women is an improvement over the traditional Western view.	Western religions have tended to treat women as objects, as possessions.	Para. 4
	Western religions have treated women as either temptations to sin or as objects of veneration.	Para. 4
	Playboy views women not as objects, but as human beings.	Para. 4

Remember, you are under no obligation to agree with either Stevenson's or Hefner's argument, but you should be able to determine exactly what claims each essay is making and how those claims are supported. Here is why.

Summaries of Arguments

We have emphasized the need for you to be able to locate the claims and support embodied in the arguments that you read because your ability to do so will enable you to understand them and, just as important, to turn them to your use by incorporating them into arguments of your own by summarizing them.

Notice that Adlai Stevenson *summarized* the provisions of the Senate bill, and Jackson did the same with William Raspberry's argument about reverse discrimination, each writer reducing a lengthy statement into a single paragraph and tailoring it to fit his needs— Stevenson to show the public what proposed legislation he was about to veto, and Jackson to show how claims of reverse discrimination arising from affirmative action are groundless.

Like Stevenson and Jackson, you will often find it useful to turn to other sources, usually arguments, to find support for your own claims. And for that reason, one of the skills you will need to master very early is the ability to create a clear, understandable summary of arguments that you read.

We have taken the first step in showing you how to do that by emphasizing the importance of locating the claims, together with their support, in the arguments that you encounter. Claims and support are the bare bones of an argument, and they are the elements that must necessarily appear in any summary of that argument.

It will be useful at this point to try your hand at some summary writing. The following exercises will direct you to the readings that appear in the next section of this book. (That will also be the practice in most of the exercises that follow.) You will notice that the "suggestions for writing" that accompany each of the readings will almost always begin with an assignment to summarize the preceding argument. We have done that because we feel that your ability to read carefully and to prepare summaries of what you have read is the single most important skill a writer of arguments must develop and possess.

EXERCISES

1. Read the article by Gary Turbak, "60 Billion Pounds of Trouble," on p. 135, and complete the first suggestion for writing. You might begin by listing the claims that you locate, along with their suppport, the way we did earlier in this section. Just to get you started, we might suggest that the argument could be divided into the following parts: Paragraphs 1–7, 8–11, and 12–15. You might summarize the first part this way:

   > Plastic has become a menace to the natural environment. Birds and marine life are especially victimized by discarded plastic in the form of fish nets, soft drink holders, and even sandwich or trash bags. Plastic does not break down and thus clogs land fills and pollutes beaches. This pollution is often dangerous to humans, particularly when it includes such contaminated items as disposable diapers, hypodermic syringes, condoms, and tampon applicators.

   Now go ahead and summarize the remaining sections in a similar way, producing two more paragraphs. Then try to combine all three paragraphs (ours and yours) into a single paragraph, one that captures in a brief space Turbak's total message.
2. Next read S. I. Hayakawa's argument, "Sex Is Not a Spectator Sport," p. 138, and complete its first suggestion for writing, which calls for a single paragraph summary. How many parts does his argument contain? State each part as clearly and as briefly as you can; then merge those parts into a single paragraph.

Types of Claims

So far we have seen that claims are statements that must be supported if a satisfactory argument is to be made. We have further seen that they are statements that can be debated. Finally, we have seen that the most straightforward way of stating a claim is to assert that something is (or is not) something else, or, more simply, X is (or is not) Y. We have also demonstrated, by presenting several sample arguments, that claims are seldom stated so straightforwardly; they can and, in fact, do appear in a variety of ways.

Claims of Fact

Recall now the sample claims we discussed in the last section.

1. John Smith is a murderer.
2. Geometry is a waste of time.
3. *Star Wars* is an excellent movie.
4. Carol Stone is a better student than Bill Mudd.
5. Women in Literature is a course that should be offered next year.
6. Investing in mutual funds is a smart thing to do.

We can begin by examining the first two. These we will call *claims of fact* because they deal with subject matter that can be verified. Either the assertions that they make are so, or they are not so. Either John Smith is a murderer, or he is not. Either geometry is useful or it is not. You might reasonably suppose that a person who makes such claims would be prepared to offer evidence to support them.

The kind of evidence that one might use to support a claim of fact normally will be one or more of these four: physical evidence, facts, reports, or statistical evidence.

To prove that John Smith is a murderer, you will need a signed confession or a photograph of Smith at the murder scene clutching the murder weapon. Lacking these, you might present a hatchet smeared with blood and hair identical with the victim's and bearing Smith's fingerprints. This evidence does not actually prove Smith's guilt, but the set of facts it represents will allow an impartial observer to draw appropriate *inferences* or conclusions based upon them.

If you do not have physical evidence of Smith's guilt, you may be fortunate enough to have an eyewitness who will testify to Smith's violent deed. The reliability of the witness can be called into question, so you will want to take some precautions about the reliability of the witness, making sure that she or he is mentally sound, bears no grudge against Smith, and was not in the pay of someone unscrupulous.

Of course, you may discover that you need to define your terms more clearly. Depending on the level of malice or premeditation, there can be several degrees of murder. Smith may not be guilty of first degree (or premeditated) murder. Rather, he may be guilty of only second degree (or unpremeditated) murder; if so, that is precisely the way the claim should be stated.

Certainly the claim about geometry's being a waste of time suffers from a lack of precision. It is obviously useful to surveying and navigation; indeed, it is the basis of these disciplines. On the other hand, it is not very useful for singers, surgeons, or newscasters. What this claim needs is some redefinition.

Perhaps you might claim that geometry is not useful to you. If, for instance, you happen to be a singer, then you can demonstrate that the skills involved in singing, which you will enumerate and present as evidence—such as pitch, tone, breath control, clarity, and volume—do not depend in any way on an understanding of geometry.

You might even be successful with the somewhat broader claim that geometry is not a very useful skill in this modern age. You might present statistics to show that 87 of the top 100 professions today do not rely on geometry. And you might further demonstrate that most of the 13 professions that do require it, such as marine navigation and air-traffic control, now solve their geometric problems automatically by computers, so that knowledge of the underlying principles is the concern of a limited number of professionals.

Another final point about claims of fact was alluded to earlier. Since these claims deal with verifiable situations, the verification must involve some degree of difficulty, or else the claims are nondebatable and noninteresting statements of this sort:

1. John Smith is a man.

2. Geometry is a branch of mathematics.

These two statements are not claims; they are just facts. You may draw inferences from facts if you have enough of them and if they are in a suggestive arrangement (remember the situation with the victim's hair on the bloody hatchet), but you can't debate them.

Let's have a look now at an argument based upon a claim of fact. This one is by the late Loren Eiseley, one of America's foremost anthropologists and writers. It is part of a larger essay entitled "An Evolutionist Looks at Modern Man." Locate the claim, and then try to enumerate the pieces of support.

Some time ago I had a letter from a professional friend of mine   1
commenting upon the education his daughter was receiving at a
polite finishing school. "She has been taught," he wrote to me a
little sadly, "that there are two kinds of people, the tough- and the
tender-minded. Her professor, whose science I will not name,
informed her that the tough-minded would survive."

This archaic remark shook me. I knew it was not the prod-   2
uct of the great selfless masters of the field, but it betrayed an
attitude which demanded an answer. In that answer is contained
the whole uniqueness of man. Man has not really survived by
toughness in a major sense—even the great evolutionists Darwin and Wallace had had trouble with that aspect of man—
instead, he has survived through tenderness. Man in his arro-
gance may boast that the battle is to the strong, that pity and
affection are signs of weakness. Nevertheless, in spite of the
widespread popularity of such ideas, the truth is that if man at
heart were not a tender creature toward his kind, a loving creature in a peculiarly special way, he would long since have left his
bones to the wild dogs that roved the African grasslands where
he first essayed the great adventure of becoming human.

The professor who growled to his class of future mothers   3
about being tough-minded spent a childhood which is among the
most helpless and prolonged of any living creature. If our parents
had actually practiced certain of the philosophies that now flourish among us, or if our remote ancestors had achieved that degree
of sophistication which would have enabled them to discount
their social responsibilities for the day's pleasure, we—you and I
and all of us—would never have enjoyed the experience of living.

Man, in the achievement of a unique gift—a thinking brain   4
capable of weighing stars or atoms—cannot grow that brain in
the nine months before birth. It is, moreover, a peculiarly plastic
brain, intended to receive impressions from the social world
around it. Instinct, unlike the case in the world of animals, is
here reduced to a minimum. This brain must grow and learn, be
able to profit by experience. In man much of that growth and
learning comes after birth. The result is that the human infant
enters the world in a peculiarly helpless and undeveloped condition. His childhood is lengthy because his developing brain must
receive a large store of information and ways of behavior from
the social group into which it is born. It must acquire the complicated tool of speech.

The demands of learning thus placed upon the human off-   5 spring are greater than in any other animal. They have made necessary the existence of a continued family, rather than the casual sex life of many of the lower animals. Although the family differs in many of its minor features in distinct societies, it is always and everywhere marked by its tender and continuing care of the human offspring through the lengthened period of childhood.

The social regulations of all human groups promote the welfare of the young. Man's first normal experience of life involves maternal and paternal care and affection. It continues over the years of childhood. Thus the creature who strives at times to deny the love within himself, to reject the responsibilities to which he owes his own existence, who grows vocal about "tough-mindedness" and "the struggle for existence," is striving to reject his own human heritage. For without the mysteriously increased growth rate of the brain and the correlated willingness of fallible, loving adults to spend years in nursing the helpless offspring they have produced, man would long since have vanished from the earth.

6

Eiseley's claim of fact occurs most clearly in the second paragraph: "Man has not really survived by toughness . . . instead, he has survived through tenderness." The ensuing paragraphs contain the *because*-statements that support this claim. Paragraph 3 might be paraphrased to say that man survives through tenderness because mankind undergoes a prolonged and helpless childhood during which constant care is necessary.

Paragraph 4 asserts that a long childhood is necessary for man's development because the human brain does not develop fully before birth. Eiseley then points out in paragraph 5 that the family unit arises from the need for educating the young during this prolonged period of development, and he concludes in the final paragraph, "The social regulations of all human groups promote the welfare of the young."

Each of these pieces of support—the prolonged childhood, the slowly developing brain, the nuclear family, and the universal attention to child welfare—are facts hardly to be disputed. (Remember those nondebatable claims? They are useful after all.) Arranged as they are, these nondebatable claims form a chain of inference that allows the reader to nod in agreement with Eiseley's claim that tenderness is indeed more crucial to human's development than toughness.

Claims of Value

We live in a world of facts, but we also live in a world of values. This concern with values as well as facts is one of the things that makes us human. We set store by some things and not by others. And quite often we are called upon to justify the evaluations that we make.

One kind of evaluation that no doubt is very much on your mind these days is the one that your instructor will render in your case at the end of this course. According to your performance, you will receive an A, B, C, D, or F. As a rule, students do not challenge instructors to explain themselves over the awarding of an A, but most instructors do brace themselves for certain questions at the end of the term from those who did not make A's: "Why did I flunk?" or more frequently "Why did *you* flunk *me?*" "I thought I deserved better than a C in this course." "Well, what would it have taken to get an A?"

In response to each of these challenges, the beleaguered instructor must make an argument based on *standards* or *criteria.* "You see, there are four things that influence my judgment in assigning grades: the written assignments, class participation, homework, and examinations. You did well on the first two, but as far as . . . ."

It is as though the instructor has *defined* the highest expected level of achievement in terms of these four criteria and then, student by student, measured the performance of each with respect to that highest expected level.

The notion of *definition* is critical to claims of value because in each case, in order to be convincing, the person making the claim, just like the teacher, must define the standards by which the evaluation has been made. At the outset, there's really no other way of organizing support for such a claim. Later on, of course, the teacher may appeal to facts: "You had twelve homework assignments, and you turned in only nine." "You failed to answer two of the questions on the third exam." But when you ask why the third paper received a lower grade than the first one, then the discussion moves right back to standards and criteria again—the kinds of things that are expected to occur in an A paper and which did or did not appear in your papers.

Occasionally, in supporting claims of value such as this one, it is a good idea to appeal to an authority, a lawful source or someone whose judgment is widely known and trusted. The instructor might point to a student handbook that spells out grading policies, especially as they pertain to missed assignments. Or perhaps the instructor might produce a photocopy of an especially good paper, written by a classmate of a complaining student, which exhibits all the qualities of A work.

To review briefly the ways of supporting a claim of value: First, you must ask yourself what the standards are for making such judgments, whether they be about the worth of Porsches, penguins, or pizzas. Once the standards have been identified, the next step is to determine just how the item you are evaluating measures up. For some standards, you may be able to state the facts: Some feature is there, or it isn't. For others, you may not be so absolute: The feature occurs in greater abundance here than there. Finally, you may want to refer to a well-known authority who agrees with your judgment.

Let's look again at the six claims we examined at the beginning of this section.

1. John Smith is a murderer.
2. Geometry is a waste of time.
3. *Star Wars* is an excellent movie.
4. Carol Stone is a better student than Bill Mudd.
5. Women in Literature is a course that should be offered next year.
6. Investing in mutual funds is a smart thing to do.

By now it should be fairly obvious that claims 3 and 4 represent claims of value. It should be equally obvious that such claims can be supported only if "excellent movie" and "better student" are appropriately defined, each with criteria against which this movie and these students may be measured.

Here now is an amusing argument by American novelist and humorist Phyllis McGinley, one that obviously makes a claim of value. Follow the ways that McGinley supports her claim that women drive cars better than men do. Ask yourself, "What standards is she using to make her judgments?"

Women Are Better Drivers

PHYLLIS MCGINLEY

That men are wonderful is a proposition I will defend to the   1
death. Honest, brave, talented, strong and handsome, they are
my favorite gender. Consider the things men can do better than
women—mend the plumbing, cook, invent atom bombs, design
the Empire waistline and run the four-minute mile. They can
throw a ball overhand. They can grow a beard. In fact, I can think
of only two accomplishments at which women excel. Having
babies is one.

The other is driving an automobile.   2

Don't misunderstand me. Some of my best friends are male   3
drivers. And they seldom go to sleep at the wheel or drive 90 on a
45-an-hour road or commit any other of the sins of which statistics accuse them. But insurance companies have been busy as
bees proving that I don't get around among the right people.

New York State—where I live—has even made it expensive   4
to have sons. Car insurance costs much more if there are men in
the family under 25 driving than if there are only women. Obviously the females of the species make the best chauffeurs.

They ought to. They get the most practice. Aside from   5
truck- and taxi-drivers, it is women who really handle the cars of
the nation. For five days of the week they are in command—
slipping cleverly through traffic on their thousand errands, parking neatly in front of the chain stores, ferrying their husbands to
and from commuting trains, driving the young to schools and
dentists and dancing classes and Scout meetings. It is only on
Saturdays and Sundays that men get their innings, not to speak
of their outings, and it is over weekends when most of the catas-
trophes occur.

Not that men are responsible for *all* the accidents. Some are   6
caused by women—by the little blonde on the sidewalk at
whom the driver feels impelled to whistle. Or by the pretty girl
sitting in the front seat for whom he wants to show off his skill,
his eagle eye, and the way he can pull ahead of the fellow in the
red sports car.

But it isn't caution and practice alone which make the differ-   7
ence between the sexes. It's chiefly an attitude of mind. Women—
in my opinion—are the practical people. To them a car is a means
of transportation, a gadget more useful, perhaps, than a dish-
washer or a can opener, but no more romantic. It is something in
which we carry the sheets to the laundry, pick up Johnnie at
kindergarten and lug home those rose bushes.

Men, the dear, sentimental creatures, feel otherwise. Auto-   8
mobiles are more than property. They are their shining chariots,
the objects of their affections. A man loves his car the way the
Lone Ranger loves his horse, and he feels for its honor on the road.
No one must out-weave or out-race him. No one must get off to a
better jack-rabbit start. And no one, but no one, must tell him
anything while he's driving. My own husband, ordinarily the
most good-tempered of men, becomes a tyrant behind the wheel.

"Shouldn't we bear south here?" I inquire meekly on our   9
Saturday trips to the country. Or, "Honey, there's a gray convert-
ible trying to pass."

"Who's driving!" he snarls like Simon Legree, veering stub-   10
bornly north or avoiding, by a hair, being run into.

Women drivers, on the other hand, *take* advice. They are   11
used to taking it, having had it pressed on them all their lives by
their mothers, teachers, beaus, husbands, and eventually their
children. And when they don't know their routes exactly, they
inquire at service stations, from passers-by, from traffic officers.
But men hate to ask and, when they are forced to do so, seldom
listen.

Have you ever overheard a woman taking down directions on   12
the phone? "Yes," she says affably. "I understand. I drive up that
pretty road to the Danbury turn-off. Then I bear left at the little
antique shoppe that used to be a barn—yellow with blue shutters.
Then right at a meadow with two beech trees in it, and a couple of
black cows. Up a little lane, just a tiny way beyond a cornfield,
and that's your place. Yes. With a Tiffany-glass carriage lamp in
front. Fine. I won't have any trouble." Nor does she.

A man has too much pride to take such precautions. "O.K."   13
he says impatiently. "Two point seven miles off the Post Road. A
left, a rotary, another left. Six point three to—oh, never mind. I'll
look it up on the map."

When they don't insist on traveling by car, men travel by   14
chart. I've nothing against road maps, really, except the way they
clutter up the glove compartment where I like to keep tissues
and sun glasses. But men have a furtive passion for them.

When my husband and I are planning a trip, he doesn't rush   15
out like me to buy luggage and a new wardrobe. He shops for
maps. For days ahead of time he studies them dotingly; then *I*
am forced to study them en route. Many a bitter journey have I
taken past the finest scenery in America with my eyes glued to a
collection of black and red squiggles on a road map, instead of on
the forest and canyons we had come all the way across the country to behold.

"Look!" I cry to him as we rush up some burning autumn   16
lane. "Aren't the trees glorious!"

"What does the map say?" he mutters. "I've marked a covered   17
bridge about a quarter of a mile along here. That's where we turn."

If we should ever approach the Pearly Gates together, I know   18
exactly how the conversation will run. "See all the pretty stars,"
I'll be murmuring happily. "And, oh, do look over there! Isn't
that the City of Gold?"

"Never mind your golden cities," he'll warn me sternly, as he   19
nearly collides with a meteor. "Just keep your eye on the map."

You cannot miss McGinley's claim; it's in the title and it forms the entire substance of the second paragraph. But what about her support? Notice what she does in the third paragraph. It's a strategy that is well worth copying. She mentions a couple of criteria—staying awake at the wheel and minding the speed limits—only to dismiss them. Men and women drivers are alike in this regard. Some criteria are shared by all good drivers, and we can thus ignore them so that we can concentrate on the really important (and debatable) ones—the ones McGinley wants to call our attention to.

So just what are those criteria? The first is practice. In paragraph 5, McGinley points out that women, as a rule, drive far more frequently than men. The second is caution. In the next paragraph she suggests that women are less likely to become distracted or to show off. The last criterion she describes is an attitude of mind, and she uses the remainder of the essay to characterize that attitude. Briefly, it is the superior patience women exhibit in taking advice and asking directions. She illustrates this preferred behavior through a series of anecdotes.

We hope that you didn't miss what was going on in the fourth paragraph. McGinley was appealing to a very important authority—the state of New York. She calls attention to the fact that the state in its wisdom has made auto insurance more expensive for male drivers than for women. Quite obviously, the state of New York believes that women are better drivers.

Claims of Policy

We have now examined the kind of argument that makes a factual claim—one that is difficult but provable when all the evidence is examined. We have studied arguments that claim that something is better or worse than something else, and we have noted the standards or criteria that were inevitably produced to support such claims.

Now we turn to the final kind of claim—the claim of policy. In this sort of claim, you are usually urging your audience to adopt some course of action: "Vote for candidate X," or "Purchase this brand of shampoo."

Usually you can predict that support for the claim of policy will come in two steps. First of all, you must point out that a state of affairs exists which prompts you to make this urgent appeal. In the case of candidate X, you will want to describe the grand state of the nation: its economy, defense posture, and general well-being, all resulting from the presence of your candidate in office—that is, if your candidate is the incumbent. Conversely, if your candidate is trying to unseat the incumbent, you'll call attention to the deplorable state of the nation, its economy, and so forth. In either case, you will be expected to furnish evidence to confirm that the situation is either as excellent or as grave as you have asserted; you will need to provide statistics, reports of authorities, or facts from which inferences may be drawn.

In the second step of your support you'll need to cite some advantages that will follow if the plan of action you propose is adopted. A vote for the incumbent will be a vote for continuing the desirable conditions that now exist, or a vote for the challenger will spell relief from the terrible conditions that the voters are now enduring. In either case, the more specific instances of good or bad conditions that you can name, the more apt your audience will be to take your advice.

Even the more trivial case of touting a new shampoo follows the same scheme. First, you must make your readers aware of the frightful condition of their hair: lack of body, dinginess, split ends, dandruff. Then you present the effects that the new product will produce: not only a correction for each defect, but the creation of a head of hair that will be utterly irresistible to members of the opposite sex.

Now that you have discovered this much about claims of policy, look once more at those six original claims that began this section:

1. John Smith is a murderer.
2. Geometry is a waste of time.
3. *Star Wars* is an excellent movie.
4. Carol Stone is a better student than Bill Mudd.
5. Women in Literature is a course that should be offered next year.
6. Investing in mutual funds is a smart thing to do.

It hardly comes as a surprise now that the last two claims are ones of policy. And you are now prepared to support each by completing the two necessary steps:

1. Make the initial claim of fact, describing the situation— either as bad or good.
2. State the recommended policy that will remedy the bad situation or take advantage of the good one.

In these cases, surely the condition of women in literature is a subject that has been neglected lately, and just as surely the financial market place is ripe for just such an investment as mutual funds. There will be benefits arising from each venture: Students will be better informed and less inclined to male chauvinism, and investors will earn sizable dividends.

Recall also the earlier argument contained in Jesse Jackson's argument about affirmative action. It too posed a claim of policy: Affirmative action laws should be enforced. The story about the unfair footrace served to paint the grim situation faced by blacks in today's job market. Enforcement of affirmative action laws would greatly improve that situation without creating reverse discrimination. That is the remainder of Jackson's claim of policy, which he addresses in the last three paragraphs of his argument. It doesn't matter how you stand with regard to this controversial topic. It is the steps that the argument takes that are of interest here, and those steps are worth reviewing.

First, paint the picture of the situation that you urge your audience to support or reject. The situation is a fact, so you can be factual, supplying details, evidence, reports. Next point out the effects that will follow if your policy is adopted. Look for the development of this pattern in the following argument by Ernest Hollings, a U.S. senator from South Carolina.

Should America Revive the Military Draft?

ERNEST HOLLINGS

We need a military draft.   1

No, not the draft of the Vietnam era, where people of means   2
often went to college or Canada and a disproportionate number
of poor and minorities shed their blood in Southeast Asia. What
we need is an equitable draft, where the burden is shared by all
and exemptions are held to a minimum.

There is both a need and a moral obligation.   3

Demographic indicators warn that the pool of 17-to-21-year-   4
old males—the largest grouping of potential recruits—is going
to fall off sharply. The baby boom is history, and the prognosis is
for a rapidly shrinking recruiting pot.

In 1980, there were approximately 11 million males in the   5
17-to-21-year-old category. By 1990, this group is projected to be
less than 9 million while continuing to shrink in future years.
Some estimates show that by 1993 the all-volunteer Army—in
order to meet projected recruiting goals—would have to get one

of every two males of age 19 due to the competition from an improved economy.

Our reserve forces are now seriously in jeopardy. The Selected Reserve is down 50,000. The Individual Ready Reserve is down by as much as 200,000. 6

The defense budget has gone from $314 billion in 1980 to $262.9 billion for 1985. Approximately two-thirds of that amount goes to pay and benefits. Rather than an equal call on all, with the all-volunteer Army we have perpetuated the rich man's undemocratic lie: "We'll pay for it." 7

The fact is we can never pay for it. We can appropriate to cure the pay deficiencies, as we did with the large pay and benefits packages of recent years. But the fact is, these are stop-gap measures that fail to address the long-term need. 8

How will we meet recruiting objectives in light of competition and the demand for one out of two males? You and I both know the answer. It's money. We will once again be on the treadmill of escalating pay and benefits while diminishing arms for our troops and lessening our capability to defend ourselves and honor our commitments abroad. 9

The only reason we have been reaching the recruiting targets in the past few years is that the economy has helped. We had a recession, and our young people needed jobs. It's that simple. Unemployment has been excessively high for our teenagers— particularly young minorities. Where else can these people turn? The all-volunteer Army is often the employer of last resort, a sort of military Job Corps. 10

We need the draft for many reasons. Most importantly, we need it in order to remain true to the ideals that built this country. 11

Early in the 1970s, with America's morale sapped by our involvement in Vietnam, everyone wanted the easy way for America to defend itself without personal sacrifice. So, we instituted the all-volunteer Army. That Army no longer touches every neighborhood. It is forgotten and removed from everyday life in America. 12

One lesson to be learned from Vietnam, is that a nation cannot move without its people. 13

The broader the cross section of America in our armed forces the less likely that our military will be drawn into unnecessary confrontations. Indeed, one wonders what policy would have been in Vietnam if there had been a truly equal draft that did not discriminate on the basis of wealth. And one wonders still what U.S. policy would be in Lebanon and Central America with a fully informed electorate, where defense is everybody's business. 14

Our volunteer forces are sadly unrepresentative of the soci-   15
ety they serve. Over one-quarter of all new recruits are black—
double their proportion in the population. The number of other
minorities is growing.

And it is not just a race problem, it is a class problem. For   16
even white recruits are largely drawn from the poorer and less
educated segments of society.

A free society defended by its least free is a dangerous contra-   17
diction. We all share the benefits of life in America. Is it not the
responsibility of all of us to defend it?

It seems most of us seek painless ways to meet our obliga-   18
tions. Unfortunately, there is no painless way that we can provide for the defense of freedom.

Senator Hollings does something very important in his second
paragraph, something fully as important as the statement of his
claim of policy, which takes up the first paragraph. Hollings uses the
second paragraph to define what he means by *draft*. He wants an
"equitable draft," unlike the draft of the Vietnam era. Defining
terms is quite frequently a necessity in the early parts of many
arguments, a practice that you will frequently observe as you read
arguments.

The third paragraph actually spells out the two steps that support this claim of policy. First, Hollings states, there is a need. Paragraphs 4 through 10 address that need. A draft is needed because the
supply of young, able-bodied males is shrinking, and it will soon be
too expensive, if it isn't already, to sustain a volunteer military.
That's the situation.

Next, Hollings says, there is a moral obligation. And he turns to
this notion in paragraph 11 and continues to develop it through the
remainder of the argument. The obligation to defend the country
whose blessings we enjoy is the moral responsibility of every citizen, regardless of race, wealth, or social standing. He points out that
a true cross section of America in the armed forces will produce
some very desirable effects: we will be less likely to be "drawn into
unnecessary confrontations," and we will feel better about accepting
the benefits of American life if we have earned them—all this in
addition to correcting the basic problem, which is an expensive volunteer force brought about by dwindling manpower.

Now that we have introduced the three types of claims, it will be
useful for you to study some additional examples. Have a look at the
following exercises.

EXERCISES

1. Turn to the readings that begin on p. 135 and reread the first essay, "Sixty Billion Pounds of Trouble." How would you label the claim that is made in this argument? Is it a claim of policy or of fact? If it is a claim of policy, does it contain a claim of fact? State these claims as succinctly as possible.

2. Now also look again at S.I. Hayakawa's "Sex Is Not a Spectator Sport." The main claim embodied in this argument is one of value. Where does Hayakawa state it? What criteria does he use to define the things that he considers to be valuable?

3. Joan Beck's argument, "Art and Politics: Self-Righteousness and Silly Yahooism," p. 141, is based on a claim of policy. Locate the two parts of the argument: the claim of fact and the policy advocated.

4. If you have completed the exercises in the earlier part of this chapter, on p. 23, you have already written brief summaries of the Turbak and Hayakawa articles. Now add a summary of the Beck article to your collection. Since you know it to be based on a claim of policy, you should be better able to organize your summary.

2

Supporting the Claim

In the last chapter we examined the types of claims that you might be obliged to support when you argue: *claims of fact, claims of value,* and *claims of policy.* Each calls for its special supporting strategy. We might diagram those strategies as shown in Figure 2.1. As the diagram shows, supporting the claim of fact is the most straightforward procedure. Such claims are supported by evidence in the form of facts, examples, statistics, or reports of authorities. It is also clear from the diagram that this strategy is repeated in the claim of value, as well as in the claim of policy, once some preliminary organizational matters have been completed.

For claims of value, where the assertion has been made that something is better or worse than something else, the next logical step is to *define* the standards (A, B, and C) by which this kind of evaluation is to be made; that is, we have to know according to what standard, or set of standards, X is better than Y. Once we have determined the standards, then it is a matter of presenting evidence—based on facts, examples, statistics, or reports—to show that X has more of quality A than Y does, more of quality B, and so on.

Similarly, just as the other two sorts of claims do, the strategy for supporting the claim of policy ultimately requires the presentation of factual evidence; however, the organization of the strategy is a little different. Remember that when we claim we should do A about X, we must usually begin with a factual claim about X: That is, X is Y, where X is alleged to be messed up, ineffective, uneconomical, suicidal or the like, and therefore X needs to be changed or corrected. Or maybe X is excellent as it is, and what we should do about X is to preserve it unchanged. Whatever the case, this factual claim gets familiar support: facts, examples, statistics, and reports.

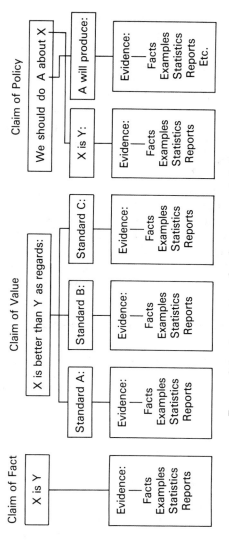

Figure 2.1 *Supporting the three types of claims.*

39

The other step in presenting a claim of policy is to show the benefits that will arise from the recommended course of action. Most often there will be several of these, but for each supposed benefit you will be obliged to show evidence that these kinds of things will indeed occur. The earlier diagram of a claim of policy suggests that factual evidence must be produced in this case also, and that is true. But you cannot avoid the feeling that this situation is just a bit different; these supporting facts are of a different kind— facts that haven't occurred yet, and supporting those kinds of factual claims surely requires something extra.

That felt need is absolutely correct. First of all, claims of fact can often involve speculations about the future. Second, something extra *is* needed to support these claims. The facts, statistics, and reports must be organized so that special kinds of inferences can be drawn—either by making comparisons or by analyzing causes and effects. But that is something we will need to work up to. Let's begin with a closer, more detailed look at our first formulation of factual evidence: facts, examples, statistics, and reports.

Supporting the Claim of Fact

Using Nondebatable Facts as Support

Remember now those earlier sample claims that were judged to be nondebatable and therefore not interesting as claims:

1. John Smith is a man.
2. Geometry is a branch of mathematics.
3. *Star Wars* is a movie directed by George Lucas.
4. Carol Stone is a student in English 101.
5. Women in Literature is an English course that appears in the college catalog.
6. Mutual funds are a type of investment opportunity.

Undebatable as claims, these are the kinds of materials that can be used to support claims, precisely because they are undebatable. They are facts that everyone can agree about, even opponents in an argument. Furthermore, in the event of disagreement, these claims can be verified easily. As such, undebatable facts such as these form the fundamental support for any argument. Let's examine more closely how such factual support can be marshaled in a convincing way.

Recall the claim that Loren Eiseley made in the last chapter: Mankind has survived not by toughness but through tenderness. Now that's debatable. It challenges the familiar notion of the survival of the fittest. Nevertheless, Eiseley presents some nondebatable facts that tend to support the case for tenderness:

1. Humans require a long period of childhood during which they are dependent and helpless.
2. Human brains do not develop fully during the nine months in the womb.
3. The human brain continues to develop during this prolonged childhood.
4. Learned behavior is more important for humans than it is for other animals.
5. All human groups protect their young.

No reasonable person would seriously dispute any of these facts. They are nondebatable. But each in its way supports the debatable claim that the human race has survived through tenderness:

because humans endure a long and helpless childhood, and
because a thinking brain does not develop prenatally, but develops during that extended childhood, and
because survival depends crucially on learning rather than instinct, and
because of all these things, developing humans must be carefully and cautiously protected.

You will use this sort of procedure time and again in formulating support for the claims of your arguments. You will supply nondebatable facts to support your debatable claims.

Remember how Jesse Jackson supported his claim that affirmative action plans were necessary—a very debatable issue. He first pointed to the undeniable fact that laws prohibiting racial discrimination did not provide compensation for the victims of that discrimination. And, second, he focused upon another incontestable fact—that blacks were measurably behind whites in almost all occupations.

Facts, or nondebatable claims, are obviously useful in supporting your claims of fact, and so are *examples.*

Using Examples as Support

There is a subtle difference, by the way, between facts and examples, and you must be aware of it in order to argue most effectively. Eiseley claims that mankind survives through tenderness and points to the long and helpless childhood that every human endures. That long, helpless childhood is a fact, and the reader can easily supply the connection between the claim and the supporting fact. As someone who survived childhood, you know how it is: You don't get through it without someone to look out for you. The connection is immediate, related, and obvious.

On the other hand, Dr. Wayne Dyer claims that justice does not exist and offers the following support: Robins eat worms. Spiders eat flies. Cougars kill coyotes. Coyotes kill badgers. Badgers kill mice. Mice kill bugs. The connection between these killings and a lack of justice is neither immediate nor obvious. The reader needs some help to recognize the connection—to understand, that is, the aptness of these *examples,* specifically that the slaughter of worms by robins is not fair to the worms. Each case is an example of a repeated injustice. It is a fact that robins eat worms, and in this case this fact also serves as an example. But while it is a fact that humans have a long and helpless childhood, that is just a supporting fact, not an example. The killing of worms is, however, an *example* of an injustice, and the overall effect of this listing of examples of injustice is to make believable Dyer's claim: Justice does not exist in the face of so many examples to the contrary.

Sometimes examples are numerous, as they were in Dyer's argument. Sometimes they are few. Sometimes it is even necessary to appeal to an example that has never really existed—a hypothetical or fictional example—to illustrate and thus support a claim. That is what Jesse Jackson did at the outset of his argument about affirmative action. You will recall that he sketched a situation involving a race in which the ankles of one runner had been weighted so that he labored under a severe handicap. Halfway through the race the unfairness was noted and the weights removed, with each runner resuming the race at the exact spot where action had been suspended.

Jackson's initial claim was that the action taken by the judges was unfair because even though the weights were removed, the afflicted runner was not compensated for the adverse effects the weights had caused.

Jackson's example illustrates a number of other principles, each very important for us here. Unlike the numerous examples in Dyer's argument, this narrative presents only one example. It is, however, an *extended example.* Frequently the connection between supporting example and claim is not as readily discernible as in Dyer's argument; in such cases, you must therefore elaborate and expand the example, making it fit the circumstances. Sometimes you may even have to create the example, as Jackson did, producing a theoretical or hypothetical example.

Finally, we must notice that the force of Dyer's examples comes from their abundant quantity, while the force of Jackson's single example comes from its aptness. He was not so much concerned to demonstrate that the race was unfair because the runner's ankles were weighted and because he received no compensation. Rather, he was concerned with another and similar situation—the plight of American blacks after the institution of civil rights legislation. They were *like* the runner whose weights had been removed. Each of them was still far behind in the race, and nothing was done to compensate for the past injustice.

The name associated with Jackson's special use of example is *analogy*. It is a strong and frequently used explanatory device, relying on our human ability to perceive similarities. We can often come to understand difficult and complicated processes by noting that they are in many ways like commonplace, familiar activities.

Analogy, so useful in explanation, is also compelling as an argumentative strategy, as Jackson has just shown us. Having demonstrated the inequity of the hypothetical race, Jackson goes on to point out the similarity between the hypothetical situation and the very real one endured by blacks in modern America. His implication is very clear: What is unfair in a theoretical example is equally unfair in similar settings of real life.

By now you should understand that Jackson's example is three things: (1) an extended example, (2) a hypothetical example, and (3) an analogy. We don't want to be misleading here. It is clear that this kind of example will have a different sort of effect on an audience than the numerous short examples in Dyer's argument. But we also do not want to give the impression that a writer or speaker can use only a single extended example. Certainly multiple extended examples can be used, so long as they can be located or created, and as far as space permits.

Second, you must understand that not all extended examples are hypothetical or constitute analogies. Such was the special virtue of Jackson's example, but it is not the case with every extended example. Recall now just how Phyllis McGinley concluded her argument favoring women drivers. To demonstrate her contention that women's higher degree of patience enables them to perform better behind the wheel, McGinley offers several episodes or extended examples drawn from her own experiences with her husband, involving his typical impatience with elaborate oral directions and overdependence on maps.

McGinley's examples, although more complicated than any Dyer produced, serve the same sort of purpose as his, for each relates immediately to the claim. He says justice does not exist. She says men drivers lack patience. Nothing hypothetical is used in either case, nor is analogy at work.

Using Statistics for Support

Related to the use of facts and examples are *statistics*. Statistics provide a means of condensing many examples or facts into a very small space. Take, for instance, the situation involving the class that you are in right now. The chances are good that it is a freshman class, but if you wished to test the situation, you could inquire of each student, one by one, the status of each: freshman, sophomore, junior, or senior. As each responded, you could record the results, and you could report those results just as they appeared on your clip board, example by example: Mary Greenbaum is a freshman, Bill Shoop is a freshman, etc. However, chances are that you would not resort to such tactics. Rather, you would state the results something like this: "Of the 25 students in my class, all but one are freshmen," or "Freshmen make up 96 percent of my class."

Because statistics represent in a concise way a fairly significant array of facts, they can be quite convincing. Certainly this is the case in Jesse Jackson's argument, where he demonstrates that the representation of blacks is measurably behind that of whites in a number of professions. Specifically he asserts that there "is one white attorney for every 680 whites, but only one black attorney for every 4000 blacks." He repeats this formula for two other professions—physicians and dentists—and then switches to another mode of statistical presentation, pointing out that fewer than 1 percent of the nation's engineers or chemists are black.

While statistics can and often do present a great array of facts or examples in a brief space, we must always be on guard to ensure that they are reliable and correctly interpreted. One way to safeguard both reliability and correctness is to consider the source.

Using Reports as Support

Very few of us conduct our own statistical research. Instead we rely on authorities to accumulate, study, and report the data. When we appeal to such sources, we are obligated to mention them in our writing for two very good reasons:

1. Failure to do so makes us guilty of the crime of plagiarism— using someone else's research or scholarship as though it were our own.
2. Including the name of each source adds the reputation of that source to the force of our argument.

Thus, when the Reverend Jackson provided statistics to show that blacks were measurably behind whites in a number of critical professions in America, he was careful to state that he derived his statistics from a report made by the Equal Employment Opportunity Commission: *Black Experience and Black Expectations.* He avoided the charge of plagiarism or making up his statistics himself, and he placed the whole reputation of a federal government agency behind his claim.

Similarly, Phyllis McGinley appeals successfully to authority when she points out that auto insurance is cheaper in New York for females under 25 than it is for males of a similar age. The effect is very apparent: It's not just Phyllis McGinley who thinks women are better drivers than men; it's the state of New York's whole insurance industry, which presumably has important economic reasons for carefully determining that this is statistically true.

Sometimes, however, it is not quite so important to reveal the source of one's facts. As a member of the U.S. Senate's Armed Forces Committee, Ernest Hollings surely has access to a great deal of reliable data concerning the armed forces, much of it perhaps classified. We, his readers, are willing to accept certain of his pronouncements simply because we have no cause to doubt a person of his stature, with his special access to reliable factual data. When he says that there were 11 million males of age 17 to 21 in 1980, we probably do not question his numbers, and when he says that "some estimates show" that by 1993 we will need to recruit half of the eligible males in order to have a volunteer army, we suspect that he could produce the actual report or reports if he had to. For Senator Hollings, it is the facts that are important, far more than the authority or reputation of the reports that contained them.

But reputations are important. It makes sense to appeal to authorities who are both knowledgeable and unbiased. Accordingly, however, the speculations of the brilliant physicist Stephen Hawking about religion and philosophy are best viewed as just that: the speculations of a man speaking out of his field—a very wise man to be sure, but one who has ventured beyond his area of expertise.

When Jesse Jackson cites William Raspberry as an authority who supports his claim that blacks are not making progress at the expense of whites, he leaves himself open to the charge that Raspberry, as a popular syndicated newspaper columnist, and not a social scientist, is out of his area of expertise in making such a claim. Furthermore, as a black American, Raspberry is likely to be overly sympathetic with Jackson's claim. In the long run, the worth of Raspberry's testimony will depend on the statistics it contains, facts that he drew from other sources—to which he surely referred in his article—and whose authority and freedom from bias can be subjected to scrutiny.

GIVING CREDIT

With regard to claims of fact that you wish to support, you may use your ingenuity and produce as many facts or examples as you can call to mind, but in the long run, you will often need to resort to outside sources to support your claims. In putting together our own arguments, most of us will need to read a great many arguments just to become familiar enough with a sensitive issue to decide how we really stand. Then we will need to credit those sources that have influenced our judgment, and from which we derive supporting material.

In the last chapter when we emphasized the need for writing summaries, we were also emphasizing the importance of appealing to responsible authorities for both statistics and well-considered opinions. Honest writers do not make up their statistics; neither do they make up the opinions that they use to support their claims. They *borrow* their statistics and their opinions from the reading that they do, they *summarize* that reading, and then they *give credit* to their sources for those borrowings and summaries.

The simplest way to give credit for one's borrowings is to mention the name of the responsible author along with the material that you have borrowed, just as Jesse Jackson did when he summarized the statistics he had found in William Raspberry's column. That is the method most frequently employed by professional writers: they summarize their borrowings and they mention their sources. Sometimes, when the information is especially well-stated, writers will quote directly instead of summarizing, but they seldom, if ever, neglect to mention their sources. Certainly you should follow their practices, as a minimum. At other times, your instructor may require or you may voluntarily provide detailed citations (notes and bibliographies) to your sources. Those practices are discussed in detail in Chapter 6.

EXERCISES

1. Read M. G. Lord's "Frats and Sororities: Greek Rites of Exclusion," p. 206. This argument is based almost entirely on a claim of fact. Try to determine how much of the support for his claims is based on Lord's personal experience and how much is based on reports of authorities. Does Lord give appropriate credit for his borrowed information? Does he employ both summaries and direct quotations?
2. Now summarize Lord's basic claim, together with its supporting evidence, in such a way that you might include it as a single paragraph in a paper of your own dealing with Greek life on today's college campuses. Be careful to give appropriate credit to Lord when you compose your summary.
3. Examine Shannon Brownlee's argument "The Myth of the Student-Athlete," p. 160. It too is based on a claim of fact. What is that claim in its barest form? List the supporting evidence that Brownlee provides. First, illustrate the claim and support in a diagram similar to the one suggested after the Jesse Jackson article on p. 15. Then turn your diagram into a brief summary of not more than two paragraphs.

Supporting the Claim of Value

The most important thing to remember about any claim of value—the claim that something is good or bad, or better or worse than something else—is that such claims must ultimately be converted into claims of fact before support can be provided.

You cannot present support to show that Nolan Ryan is a great baseball pitcher until you have defined what you mean by a "great" pitcher. In other words, you have to *define* the great pitcher by enumerating the characteristics that you believe one must possess: blazing fast ball, history of strikeouts, low earned run average, successful win–loss record, accumulation of no-hit games.

Now that you have established the criteria by which great pitching is to be measured, all that you need to do is present the facts about Ryan with respect to each of them. His fast ball is consistently between 90 and 100 miles per hour, he has struck out over 5000 batters, his lifetime ERA is around 3.00, and he has won over 300 games in a career that has seen six no-hit games. Notice that these supporting data are all nondebatable facts, each supporting the separate subclaims of your overall claim that Ryan is a great pitcher.

Using your criteria, you might even go so far as to show that Nolan Ryan is a better pitcher than Hall of Famer Tom Seaver was, in that Ryan has a consistently faster fast ball, far more strikeouts, a lower earned-run average, more career victories, and more no-hit games. Even Seaver fans could not dispute your facts.

On the other hand, in order to make any progress with the Tom Seaver cause, your opponent will have to take exception to your criteria, charging that you have overlooked some important ones that Seaver exhibited but Ryan does not—things such as complete games, won–lost percentages, effectiveness with men on base, fielding ability, or the prevention of the stolen base. If your man Ryan comes up short on these criteria, it therefore would be wise of you to mention them when you are setting up your standards, stressing that in your estimation these skills are of less importance than the criteria by which you choose to measure great pitching.

Similarly, a careful examination of Phyllis McGinley's argument about women drivers reveals that she too has followed this prescription for supporting a claim of value quite well. She has established three criteria by which she chooses to measure good driving: practice, caution, and patience. Once this has been done, the rest is elementary—just present the facts, examples, statistics, or reports to show that women exhibit more of these than men do. And McGinley does just that.

Women get more practice at driving, she states. But first she carefully and cleverly excepts the legion of male truck and cab drivers. If we don't count these men, then her claim must be judged as true. It would probably be true anyway, since the number of women in the country is certainly greater than the number of males engaged in driving professions, but even so it's good that she points out these fairly obvious groups, if only to discount them.

Next, McGinley presents the facts, or rather the examples, drawing from her experience as a suburban housewife. She asserts that in such circumstances, wives drive five days a week to their husbands' two, completing such driving chores as hauling kids to school, scout meetings, and dance classes, shopping, running errands, and so on. All of these trips are *examples* of the practice that women gain while men are working at nondriving occupations.

Caution is the next criterion, and again McGinley provides examples of men who cause accidents while ogling pretty female pedestrians. This weakness is magnified by the prevailing tendency of men to think of their cars as toys rather than tools, showing off with them rather than using them to transport themselves and their passengers.

Finally, the lack of patience that male drivers exhibit, especially in the matter of taking directions, is the subject of the last third of

McGinley's essay, where she supplies several extended examples of instances involving her own husband's typical behavior in this regard. These examples, besides being illustrative of typical male behavior, are also highly amusing, and therefore increase the sympathy of her audience for her line of reasoning.

You must measure McGinley's success not only by how well she has supported each of the three criteria she has established for measuring good driving, but by how carefully she chose her standards. Once she had those criteria established, it was simply a matter of supporting each one in the only ways possible for claims of value— with facts, examples, statistics, and reports.

EXERCISES

1. Examine Rachel E. Jones' essay, "What's Wrong with Black English," p. 157. In making her claim of value, what exactly is the kind of language that Jones suggests we should esteem? What criteria or standards does she establish against which language should be measured? What sorts of evidence does she use to support her claims?
2. Summarize Jones's position in a brief paragraph, being careful to give her appropriate credit.

Supporting the Claim of Policy

As we mentioned earlier, the support for the claim of policy usually occurs in two steps, with each step ultimately involving the use of facts, examples, statistics, or reports in order to convince the audience that some suggested policy is to be preferred.

Certainly this was what Senator Ernest Hollings did when he argued in favor of restoring the military draft. First of all, he stated that the situation that currently exists is not at all good and is not likely to improve. The available pool of young men is shrinking. That is a fact, and he supplies population figures for the years 1980, 1990, and 1993 to illustrate that shrinkage. The reserve forces, both selected and individual ready reserve, have diminished, another fact that he supports with relevant figures. And the national defense budget, over two-thirds of which is allocated to pay and benefits, is also shrinking according to his statistics, making the continuation of a volunteer military force increasingly difficult. Thus Senator Hollings produces three claims of fact with their supporting statistical evidence to underscore his major claim, also a claim of fact, that the personnel situation of the U.S. armed forces is unsatisfactory.

The second step in his argument is to show the good effects of the policy he wishes to institute, effects that, besides being good in themselves, will ultimately serve to correct this bad situation. Hollings claims that a draft, evenly and fairly administered, will allow all male citizens to participate equally in the defense of their country, thus fulfilling a moral obligation that many now avoid. Another effect of such a draft is that it will create a military that is more representative of the citizenry it protects, containing as it would elements from all classes of society: not just the poor, the less educated and hence less well informed who make up the bulk of today's forces, but also the wealthy, the educated, and the well informed. Beyond these hardly debatable facts, Hollings offers some speculations that, though somewhat debatable, are nevertheless encouraging: Such a representative military, he says, would be "less likely to be drawn into unnecessary confrontations," so that peace is more probable.

Senator Hollings does not, however, explicitly state the most important effect of his suggested policy. Rather, it is *implied* with extreme effectiveness. Notice that Hollings describes, using facts about dwindling manpower and financial resources, a bad situation that spells only a worsening problem: America getting less defense for its money as more and more dollars must be spent to attract and maintain a volunteer military force. After tracing carefully this appalling situation, Hollings needn't state explicitly that a draft, which will not require such huge salaries for its temporary forces, will be far more cost effective. While it is probably true that this desirable effect is more important to his argument than the nobler effects he carefully spells out in his concluding paragraphs, Hollings manages to suggest the cost effectiveness of a draft without actually arguing for it directly. He manages that because his obvious implication is a nondebatable fact, one that everyone who is not a dunce readily recognizes: Involuntary draftees will work for less than volunteers, who expect top dollar.

EXERCISES

1. Have a look at Harry Summers' brief argument on p. 147, "Does ROTC Belong on College Campuses?" Unlike Hollings' claim of policy, in which correction is recommended for a regrettable situation, Summers' claim is just the opposite—that a commendable situation should be preserved. What is the situation that Summers wishes to preserve? What good effects does he point to? What bad ones does he suggest are being avoided? What support does he offer for his claim?

2. Prepare a brief summary of Summers' argument. Be sure to mention him as the source of the information within your summary.

Using Definitions in Supporting Claims

Earlier, we showed that definition often proved to be a valuable tool in the construction of arguments, specifically in the support of claims. But definition shows up most clearly and often in the support of claims of value, where the criteria or standards by which value judgments are made must be listed or defined.

A definition is basically a statement that something is related to something else. More exactly we might put it in the form of the following formula: x is a y that is z, where x is the thing to be defined and where y is a larger, more general class of things to which x belongs. The final term, z, then is simply a characteristic (or more often a list of them) that distinguishes x from all other members of the class of things contained in y. According to this formula we might define a sextant (x) as a nautical instrument (y) that enables navigators to steer by the stars (z). In other words, the sextant belongs to the more general class of nautical instruments, which also contains such devices as compasses, anchors, and rudders. But we hasten to add the distinguishing attribute of this particular nautical instrument, that it enables navigators to steer by the stars, a characteristic not shared by other nautical instruments.

Now you should be able to see clearly just how definitions work in setting up the support for your claims of value. When you argued that Nolan Ryan was a great pitcher or that he was better than Tom Seaver, you were obliged to define what you meant by a "great pitcher": A great pitcher (x) is a ball player (y) who exhibits the following meritorious characteristics (z): blazing fast ball $(z1)$, numerous strikeouts $(z2)$, low earned-run average $(z3)$, impressive won–lost record $(z4)$, and several no-hit games $(z5)$. You could even measure the performance of other pitchers, such as Tom Seaver, against the records established by Ryan with respect to each of these characteristics, determining thereby who is the better pitcher.

Similarly, Phyllis McGinley defined a good driver as one who exhibited the following traits: considerable practice, caution, and patience. Then she went on to show that women drivers demonstrated more of these traits than did their male counterparts. In these cases, as in all arguments involving a claim of value, a definition—and a careful one—must be made so that the assembled facts, examples, and statistics support the (z) element of that definition.

The second use of definition in supporting claims is not quite as central as the one just described, but it is no less important. You must often use definition to make clear the point you are arguing, limiting it in such a way that the supporting facts, examples, and statistics will apply most convincingly. Recall that when we were trying to prove that John Smith was a murderer, we had to determine whether the facts would support the claim of first degree (or premeditated) murder or of second degree murder (where evidence of premeditation is not required). We also saw that it would be foolish to argue that geometry was useless because there is too much evidence to the contrary. Nevertheless, it is possible to restrict or limit the term "useless" in such a way that the claim becomes supportable, and you'll recall that is just what we did when we claimed that geometry was useless to singers.

Similarly, before discussing in some detail his claim that the draft should be revived, Ernest Hollings defined what he meant by the term *draft*. And he began by telling his audience what he did *not* mean by it: ". . . not the draft of the Vietnam era, where people of means often went to college or Canada and a disproportionate number of poor and minorities shed their blood in Southeast Asia." Then he went on to define *draft* in positive terms: ". . . an equitable draft, where the burden is shared by all and exemptions are held to a minimum."

EXERCISES

1. In his argument, "Sex Is Not a Spectator Sport," p. 138, Hayakawa must define what he means by obscenity and pornography. Where does he formulate that definition, and how is it crucial to his argument?
2. In his essay "The Warming of the World," p. 186, Carl Sagan must define what he means by "greenhouse effect." Where exactly does he state that definition? Why is it necessary to the rest of his argument? Is Sagan's purpose in constructing his definition similar to or different from Hayakawa's in "Sex Is Not a Spectator Sport"? Defend your response to this question.
3. You have read our discussion of the criteria that might be used to define a great pitcher and thereby justify the choice of Nolan Ryan over another pitcher. You have seen how S. I. Hayakawa defined pornography in such a way that he could denounce those things that fit his criteria. Now try doing the same thing. In a brief essay, define something of your choosing—a good automobile, a successful television commercial, or an Academy Award-winning performance. Then use your definition to demonstrate that one car, commercial, or performance is better than another.

Using Comparison or Analogy to Support Claims

We have already discussed the way in which claims of value may measure one item against another to determine which was better—or worse. We compared the pitching of Nolan Ryan with that of Tom Seaver by defining what we meant by great pitching—providing a list of several qualities exhibited by big league pitchers—and then went on to examine the performances of each pitcher with respect to the items on that list. That allowed us to make a rather straightforward comparison, point by point; while doing so, we determined who was the most impressive of the two with respect to those points.

This kind of straightforward comparison figures quite prominently in the support of most claims of value, particularly when the relative merits or demerits of several persons or things are being argued: Electrolux versus Hoover vacuum cleaners, Toyotas versus Chevrolets as family cars, Richard Nixon versus Lyndon Johnson as U.S. presidents.

Regardless of the items to be compared, one thing is certain: you will need to supply a number of points that may be compared for the items. So long as the items to be compared are fairly similar—vacuum cleaners, automobiles, or politicians—those points will be fairly easy to determine.

On the other hand, when the items to be compared are not so similar, the comparison becomes more risky. You often hear someone being accused of comparing apples and oranges. You would not get very far comparing Richard Nixon to a Hoover vacuum cleaner or to a Toyota. You certainly would not expect to find many points in common; in fact, finding any at all would likely strain your imagination. And yet it is just such an exercise that often proves extremely fruitful in argumentation. Such farfetched comparisons, as you should recognize from our discussion in the earlier section, Using Examples as Support, pp. 42–44, are called *analogies.*

You might, for instance, claim that Richard Nixon did not exactly sweep his administration's dirt under a rug, but like a Hoover vacuum, kept it contained and concealed very hermetically within the circle of his closest White House associates. Pressed further, you might even claim that Nixon was like a Toyota, in that his reputation has not depreciated very much despite all the mileage and tough treatment it underwent.

While these analogies may not be terribly compelling, they do help to expand our sense of a couple of the former president's characteristics: his secretiveness and his durability.

This human ability to see similarities in essentially unlike things is highly prized. Frequently, in fact, it is a measure of our intelligence. You almost surely will recall being exposed to an "analogies test" at some time in your schooling. You will remember the kind of questions involved: *Dog is to cat as gasoline is to*—and then you are supposed to select one of the following: *fire, whiskey, wood, charcoal.* In order to prevail in this sort of test, you must try to discover the very limited relationship that exists between *dogs* and *cats* that is also shared by *gasoline* and one of the items on the list. This is quite a poser, but you might after a while reason as follows: *Dogs and cats don't mix without trouble; gasoline and fire don't either.*

How, though, is this use of analogy beneficial to those who wish to support claims in an argument? There are two ways.

First of all, analogy is an explanatory device. It helps to make things understandable. That is how the Reverend Jackson used it when he was setting up his argument regarding affirmative action. He realized that his audience was not likely to understand the notion of affirmative action, so he devised a way of explaining it. He used an example, as we noted earlier, but it was a very special kind of example—a hypothetical example of two runners competing in a race. One of the runners, however, was handicapped by heavy weights tied to his ankles. As Jackson recounted this extended example, it became clear that he was doing so for a purpose. The race was like the situation that existed after the passage of civil rights legislation. These laws were like the removal of the weights from the ankles of the handicapped runner, but unless something was done to compensate the runner for the previous handicap, he was still likely to finish last. That, Jackson claims, is the situation of blacks in America. Their handicaps have been declared illegal, but they have not been compensated for the past deprivations they have suffered; consequently, they are still at a disadvantage in competing with whites. He could have stated that claim in just so many words, but its effectiveness is enhanced by the analogy, which says in effect: You may not understand very much about the problems suffered by blacks in America, but you probably are familiar with footraces. Well, if you can understand footraces, you can probably understand this issue. And you can, and you do. Such is the power of analogy.

A second use of analogy occurs quite often in the use of examples. Suppose you were assigned the job of finding a site for a new McDonald's in the area where you live. In order to ensure that the new fast food establishment would be successful, you would probably do some research. You would try to determine just what attributes are shared by successful McDonald's sites. In a nearby town, for instance, there might be a McDonald's that enjoys incredible sales. This store is located near a shopping mall. If, in addition, the successful site sports a sign with a revolving face of Ronald McDonald and if it has a playground with giant bouncy fiberglass hamburgers for children to ride on, you might want to have just such attractions for your new location. And your reasoning would run something like this: The McDonald's in the nearby town is near a shopping mall, it has a revolving Ronald McDonald sign, it has a playground with bouncy hamburgers, and it is successful. Thus there is a chance that if the store I am planning shares these qualities, it too will enjoy success. The principle of analogy used here is simply this: If these stores are alike in a number of key details, then there is the possibility that they will be alike in others as well.

While there is no absolute guarantee that the further key similarity of financial success will materialize, there is certainly a very real possibility that it will. Such is the predictive power of analogy.

EXERCISES

1. To understand better both the explanatory and persuasive power of analogy, turn to "The Case Against Man," by Isaac Asimov, p. 214. What comparison does Asimov make in this essay? What is the effect of that comparison? That is, what does it help you to understand better, and how does it tend to persuade you?
2. In paragraph 7 of his argument, "Flag Burning Isn't the Real Issue," p. 144, Jack Anderson makes several oblique comparisons. What is the effect of these comparisons? How persuasive do you find them? Why? Or why not?
3. In paragraph 6 of his argument, "Let's Return to Regulation of the Airlines," p. 150, William F. Buckley draws a very convincing comparison. What is the purpose of that comparison? He makes another one in paragraph 10. What is it?
4. Create your own analogy in a brief paragraph. It need be no longer or more complicated that the ones Buckley introduced into his argument.

Using Cause and Effect to Support Claims

Recall for a moment the argument set forth by Loren Eiseley concerning the importance of tenderness to mankind's survival. We observed that this claim was debatable, but certain facts that Eiseley presented tended to support it quite convincingly: a long and helpless childhood, a brain undeveloped at birth but continuing to develop during childhood, a store of learned behavior that outweighs

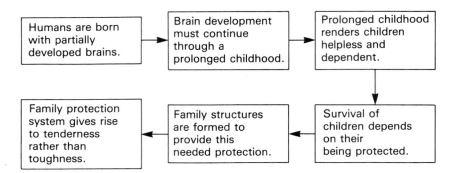

FIGURE 2.2   *A typical causal chain.*

instinct, and a tendency among all humans to protect their offspring. At the time, we said that these facts were clearly related to the claim that Eiseley was making, but we did not explain exactly what that connection was. Now is the time to do that.

The facts that Eiseley presents to support his claim for the importance of tenderness are *causally connected.* They constitute a *chain of causes and effects* leading logically to Eiseley's conclusion. *Because* humans are born with undeveloped brains, brain growth must continue during childhood. *Because* this period of brain development renders children virtually helpless for a long period, they must be protected in order to survive. *Because* adults must protect children over this period of brain development, Eiseley can claim that tenderness is an absolute ingredient in mankind's survival.

To see the chain of causes and effects more clearly, look at Figure 2.2.

The arrangement of facts in this instance to form such a causal chain also serves to highlight another difference between facts and examples. Recall that we observed earlier the connection between facts and the claim that they support, and that we described that connection as immediate, related, and obvious. In other words, the facts are usually *causally* related to the claim that they support. Examples, on the other hand, are not usually so related.

In Dr. Dyer's argument about justice, the examples of spiders killing flies, of mice killings bugs, and of related carnage do not represent either causes or effects of justice or the lack of it; rather they are examples of the kind of things that happen in a world where justice is absent. To put it another way, these killings are not in any way related to one another; one does not cause the other. Neither does a lack of justice bring them about. They are merely bitter facts that serve as examples of a general truth: There is injustice in the world.

Thus we might say that a collection of facts allows one to claim that something resulted because of them. On the other hand, a collection of examples allows one to observe a general truth that each one of the examples illustrates and reinforces.

What we are describing in each of these instances is an argumentative technique known as *inductive proof.* That will be the first subject to examine in the next chapter.

EXERCISES

1. In his argument, "Let's Return to Regulation of the Airlines," p. 150, what does Buckley suggest have been the *effects* of airline deregulation? Does he find those effects desirable or undesirable?
2. On p. 56 we illustrated the chain of causally connected events that Loren Eiseley presented as elements in his proof that toughness rather than tenderness has been the key to man's survival. For another such chain of causally connected events, study Asimov's "Case Against Man," on p. 214, beginning at paragraph 23. Trace the events that Asimov predicts will lead inexorably from one catastrophe to another unless population is brought under control. Now create a schematic diagram to show how these events lead from one to the next.
3. Reread the causal chains in the essays by Eiseley and Asimov; then in a brief paragraph construct one of your own. You can probably discover a suitable topic, but if one eludes you, you might try speculating about the chain of events that could arise from failing a crucial exam.

3

Organizing the Support

Two Classical Approaches

At the conclusion of the last chapter we introduced the notion of *inductive proof.* It is one of two classical methods of arguing; the other is *deductive proof.* Put very simply, to argue *inductively* means to argue *from the particular to the general;* arguing *deductively* is just the opposite, *from the general to the particular.*

Sometimes labeled the scientific method, *inductive proof* begins with the collection of evidence—facts, examples, statistics, or reports—and, using the data, proposes some general principle that the evidence all points to and supports. *Deductive proof,* on the other hand, begins with a general principle and from it derives specific or particular notions, which must be true, provided that the initial principle is true. We might illustrate the two approaches as shown in Figure 3.1. These two classical approaches to argumentation have a long and honored history of use, and for that reason we need to examine them in some detail for what they can show us, especially in light of what we have already learned about claims and support.

Induction

It would be safe to say that almost every argument we have presented so far in this book has been based on an inductive proof. We may need to modify or qualify that statement slightly before we are done, but for the time being it is accurate. Certainly it is the case with the selections written by Dyer and Eiseley.

On first inspection it may not seem immediately obvious that

OUTLINE OF INDUCTIVE PROOF

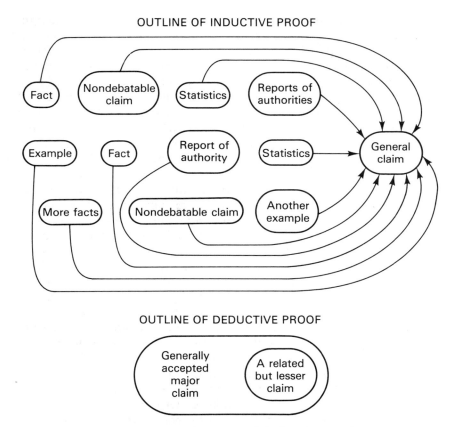

FIGURE 3.1 *Inductive and deductive proofs.*

these writers proceeded from the specific to the general in their arguments. After all, both began with their general claims (Justice does not exist; Mankind has survived through tenderness) and then demonstrated by the presentation of examples or facts that these claims were true. That appears to be a progression from the general to the particular instead of the other way round.

But notice this. In each case, the *claim to be proved* was the general one—not the particular facts that formed the support. In fact, the supporting facts or examples, as we saw, were nondebatable and needed no support. It was only the general claim that was debatable and which, as a result of the supporting evidence provided by the writer, was rendered less debatable and more credible.

To put it another way, it is not really important which comes first in an inductive proof—the supporting evidence or the general claim—as far as the *arrangement* of your argument is concerned. Of course, you will probably need to do some or even a lot of research in order to *locate* the necessary evidence or support before you are entitled and prepared to make your claim. But having done that research, you may begin with the evidence and work up to the claim, or you may proceed as Dyer and Eiseley did, stating the claim and then presenting your evidence. In either case, if the evidence is convincing—that is, if it is nondebatable, accurate, reliable, and of sufficient quantity—then the audience will be obliged to go along with you as you make what has come to be called the *inductive leap* from the specific support to the general claim.

In Dyer's argument, there is sufficient evidence in the form of examples of slaughter in the animal kingdom, with mice eating insects, and cats eating mice, and so on, to convince us that there is injustice there—certainly to insects and mice and other animals ruthlessly devoured. We nod our heads; we begin to agree that these depredations in the animal world represent gross injustice, and it takes only a slight nudge for us to accompany Dr. Dyer in his inductive leap toward the notion that there is an absence of justice elsewhere. Of course, once Dyer has us leaning, he doesn't stop there; he takes us into our own culture, particularly our legal system. There we witness such notables as Spiro Agnew and Richard Nixon getting away with crimes that would have resulted in jail terms for any of us, and again we agree that Dyer's thesis is less debatable than it was at the outset. We have made the inductive leap.

That was the same leap that we agreed to make with Loren Eiseley when we heard his claim that tenderness and not toughness was responsible for the survival of our species. We were dubious at first, but after examining the nondebatable facts that he presented to us, we concluded that humans with their slowly developing brains are perhaps a special case in evolution and that our survival has not been the product of physical fitness but of moral sophistication—in a word, tenderness. Eiseley, like Dyer, has coaxed us into making the inductive leap.

Another brief example will serve to illustrate the inductive strategy. This one is a paragraph excerpted from the Reverend Martin Luther King, Jr.'s "Letter from Birmingham Jail," which he wrote to the white clergy of Birmingham in response to their charge that his direct action campaign for black civil rights in their city was premature and ill-advised.

We have waited for more than 340 years for our constitutional and God-given rights. The nations of Asia and Africa are moving with jetlike speed toward gaining political independence, but we still creep at horse-and-buggy pace toward gaining a cup of coffee at a lunch counter. Perhaps it is easy for those who have never felt the stinging darts of segregation to say, "Wait." But when you have seen vicious mobs lynch your mothers and fathers at will and drown your sisters and brothers at whim; when you have seen hate-filled policemen curse, kick and even kill your black brothers and sisters; when you see the vast majority of your twenty million Negro brothers smothering in an airtight cage of poverty in the midst of an affluent society; when you suddenly find your tongue twisted and your speech stammering as you seek to explain to your six-year-old daughter why she can't go to the public amusement park that has just been advertised on television, and see tears welling up in her eyes when she is told that Funtown is closed to colored children, and see ominous clouds of inferiority beginning to form in her little mental sky, and see her beginning to distort her personality by developing an unconscious bitterness toward white people; when you have to concoct an answer for a five-year-old son who is asking: "Daddy, why do white people treat colored people so mean?"; when you take a cross-country drive and find it necessary to sleep night after night in the uncomfortable corners of your automobile because no motel will accept you; when you are humiliated day in and day out by nagging signs reading "white" and "colored"; when your first name becomes "nigger," your middle name becomes "boy" (however old you are) and your last name becomes "John," and your wife and mother are never given the respected title "Mrs."; when you are harried by day and haunted by night by the fact that you are a Negro, living constantly at tiptoe stance, never quite knowing what to expect next, and are plagued with inner fears and outer resentments; when you are forever fighting a degenerating sense of "nobodiness"—then you will understand why we find it difficult to wait. There comes a time when the cup of endurance runs over, and men are no longer willing to be plunged into the abyss of despair. I hope, sirs, you can understand our legitimate and unavoidable impatience.

To help you understand King's organizational (and rhetorical) strategy, go back through this long paragraph with a pencil and underline each use of the word *when.* Now you can readily see how, with each of the repeated *when*-clauses, King drives home the point of his inductive proof—that waiting is no longer tolerable—for the many reasons he's given, each signaled and emphasized by the repetition of the word *when*.

ORGANIZING THE INDUCTIVE ARGUMENT

It remains now for us to discuss which is the better or more convincing arrangement: to begin with the evidence and then leap to the general truth or claim toward which the induction points, as King did in the preceding example, or to borrow the strategy used by Dyer and Eiseley and state the general principle at the outset and then proceed with the evidence.

We think that in most cases it is more convincing to proceed by first stating the general, debatable concept that you wish your audience to adopt and then presenting the evidence.

However, in making a speech you may gain something by working the other way around; your audience is likely to keep listening, waiting in suspense for the other shoe to drop, for you to announce your general claim. Dr. King's ordering of the support before the claim clearly shows his preference for the oral strategy; he was, after all, one of this century's leading orators. Oral strategies are different from written ones, and listeners often appreciate the flash of insight or revelation as the speaker leaps from evidence to generalization, pausing for effect before delivering the clincher, just as you would hold back the punchline of a joke.

But written strategies differ from spoken ones, and we suspect that if we were to complete a survey of all inductive proof rendered in written form, we would find that the tactics adopted by Dyer and Eiseley would be more common by far. It is simply easier to carry your reader along with you if you state your claim at the outset. In that way each piece of evidence tends to reinforce the initial statement, confirming again and again the general claim, so that its debatability begins to drop away bit by bit as each ensuing piece of evidence or each repeated illustration falls into place.

THE STRENGTH OF THE INDUCTIVE ARGUMENT

The strength of the induction, of course, will always depend on the strength of the evidence. If you supply examples, as Dyer did, then you need appropriate ones and a sufficient number of them. If you present facts, then those facts must point directly to the general claim, either because there is a clear causal correspondence, as was the case with Eiseley's facts, or because there is an emerging pattern that admits to no other interpretation. To use a possibly familiar example, if, in playing the board game *Clue*, all the other parties to the crime, their whereabouts, and their access to murder weapons have been accounted for, then we can confidently conclude that Colonel Mustard committed the crime—in the kitchen—with the pistol.

So far we have seen that inductions depend on two kinds of evidence: (1) nondebatable facts and/or (2) examples. These facts or examples are taken as evidence that points toward a general conclusion, either as *causes* for the general claim or as particular *instances* of a general principle. These are the two most prominent types of inductive evidence. There is, however, another but weaker kind of inductive support—analogy.

Analogy is weaker than the other forms of induction that we have seen because, however well constructed our analogy may be, it represents in actual fact an induction based on only one example. Recall our illustration involving the siting of a new McDonald's. You were tempted to locate your new store near a shopping mall and to equip it with a rotating Ronald McDonald head and a playground with bouncy hamburgers, expecting to enjoy the success of the store with similar features in the next county. If you had studied a bit more closely and discovered that the established store had a parking lot that accommodated 200 cars and a drive-through arrangement equipped with a Dolby sound system, you may have decided to copy those features also. But in doing so you would not have increased the likelihood of your success—at least in terms of an inductive proof.

The number of similarities that you can call attention to makes the *analogy* stronger and more convincing, but it does not make the *induction* stronger. In order to do that, you would need to give examples of several other successful McDonald's restaurants, equipped identically with the one in the next county. Only then would the induction be a true one. Inductions based on analogies do not often go to this extreme, but it is well to remember that they should, if they are to be truly convincing.

LOCATING EVIDENCE

Most of the inductive arguments that you will be called upon to write will rely for their evidence on the reading that you have done as you tried to learn enough about the subject so that you could argue intelligently about it. As you read, you probably made some notes, jotting down the bits of information that tended to support the general claim that you felt inclined to favor. What you were doing was gathering *inductive proof* to support your claim.

Because your reading will prove to be the most frequent source for evidence that you will use to support the claims in your arguments, you probably now realize why we earlier emphasized the importance of learning how to write clear, succinct summaries of the arguments that you read. You must be able to reduce these arguments you encounter to their barest form—the claims and their support—and to render these as summary sentences or paragraphs that will be used as part or even all of the evidence or support for your own arguments.

Sometimes it will serve your purposes best to borrow only *facts* or *statistical data* from your reading sources, using them as inductive support for a claim of your own that is perhaps slightly different from the ones urged by the original authors. On other occasions, you may decide to use your summarized facts or anecdotes as *examples* that point inductively to a general claim that you wish to prove. On still other occasions you may wish to borrow the entire argument as an indication that a renowned authority—one whose opinion deserves to be trusted—has argued for a claim similar to yours.

Regardless of how much or how little you borrow from your reading sources, or for whatever purpose the borrowing is done, you must consider carefully how you will give credit to the original author for the borrowed material. Failure to do so will make you liable to the charge of *plagiarism*—literary theft, representing the work of others as your own. To avoid such a charge, we recommend that you cultivate the habit of working the names of your source authors into your summary statements, the way Jesse Jackson did when he referred to government reports or to columnist William Raspberry.

EXERCISES

1. Read carefully Jason DeParle's "Warning: Sports Stars May Be Hazardous to Your Health," p. 172, paying particular attention to the first 38 paragraphs. What makes this portion an *inductive* argument? Locate the general claim. What is the support? How many separate pieces of support are there? How much support do you feel it takes to make an induction convincing? Is DeParle's induction convincing?
2. Write a concise summary of the first 38 paragraphs of DeParle's argument. Be careful to include the author's name in the summary statement.
3. Examine once again William Buckley's argument, "Let's Return to Regulation of Airlines," p. 150. From what two sources does he draw the supporting data for his argument? Notice how he gives credit to his two sources. What sort of information has Buckley borrowed: facts, examples, analogies, or even whole arguments?

Deduction

In the examples we have analyzed so far, we have not encountered a truly deductive argument. Senator Hollings' argument in favor of reviving the draft does rely on some deductive reasoning, however, and we will point out how he employed that strategy once we have described the elements of a deductive proof.

In this sort of argument, you should remember, the author begins with a *general* principle and proceeds to derive some *particular* principle from it. In most cases it is possible for the author to accomplish this maneuver because the general principle proposed at the outset is nondebatable—something we could not say for the general principles with which Dyer or Eiseley began.

In today's diverse national and world cultures, nondebatable general principles are not so easy to find, and it is perhaps for that reason that such arguments are not used as frequently today as they were in the past. Perhaps you remember your geometry class, where you began with a set of such nondebatable principles: Quantities that are equal to the same quantity are equal to each other, or parallel lines will never meet however far they are extended, or a straight line is the shortest distance between two points. Beginning with such *axioms*—one name for nondebatable principles—you constructed the plane geometry step by step in just the way that Euclid did thousands of years ago. Soon you were demonstrating that side–angle–side was congruent with side–angle–side and all the other convincing theorems, all from that handful of general principles and the proofs that resulted from them. Geometry is a logical system.

What is central in any logical system is a simple device developed by the ancient Greeks and called a *syllogism*. It consists of three steps. The first is the general principle (called a *major premise*) that everyone typically agrees with—for instance, *All fish can swim*. The second is a particular statement (called a *minor premise*) that makes a claim to the effect that something is a member of the general class named in the initial statement: for example, *A trout is a fish*. The third step in the syllogism (called the *conclusion*) is logically inescapable, namely that *A trout can swim*. In other words, if swimming is something nondebatably true about all fish, then it must be true of a particular fish, such as a trout.

While the truths contained in syllogisms are often so immediately obvious that it is difficult to deny them, it is nevertheless difficult for us to reproduce many of these kinds of arguments in our writing nowadays.

In fact, we tend to think of syllogistic or logical reasoning as a bit antiquated or old-fashioned. We are inclined to associate it with the Middle Ages or ancient Greece. We perceive ourselves as citizens of a modern, scientific age, and the reasoning associated with induction—here's the claim or notion and here's the evidence or proof—appeals to us. We don't readily deal in axioms and derived proofs.

If we are patient, however, there is a great deal that we can learn from this sort of reasoning, something that will even allow us to construct better inductive arguments. Let's turn to a truly deductive argument and see how it works. Here is one that you are sure to recognize:

The Declaration of Independence

THOMAS JEFFERSON

When in the course of human events, it becomes necessary 1 for one people to dissolve the political bands which have connected them with another, and to assume among the Powers of the earth, the separate and equal station to which the Laws of Nature and of Nature's God entitle them, a decent respect to the opinions of mankind requires that they should declare the causes which impel them to the separation.

We hold these truths to be self-evident, that all men are 2 created equal, that they are endowed by their Creator with certain unalienable Rights, that among these are Life, Liberty and the pursuit of Happiness. That to secure these rights, Governments are instituted among Men, deriving their just powers from the consent of the governed. That whenever any Form of Government becomes destructive of these ends, it is the Right of the People to alter or to abolish it and to institute new Government, laying its foundation on such principles and organizing its powers in such form, as to them shall seem most likely to effect their Safety and Happiness. Prudence, indeed, will dictate that Governments long established should not be changed for light and transient causes; and accordingly all experience hath shown, that mankind are more disposed to suffer, while evils are sufferable, than to right themselves by abolishing the forms to which they are accustomed. But when a long train of abuses and usurpations pursuing invariably the same Object evinces a design to reduce them under absolute Despotism, it is their right, it is their duty, to throw off such government, and to provide new Guards for their future security. Such has been the patient sufferance of these Colonies; and such is now the necessity which constrains them to alter their former Systems of Government. The history of the present King of Great Britain is a history of repeated injuries and usurpations, all having in direct object the establishment of an absolute Tyranny over these States. To prove this, let Facts be submitted to a candid world.

He has refused his Assent to Laws, the most wholesome and necessary for the public good. 3

He has forbidden his Governors to pass Laws of immediate and pressing importance, unless suspended in their operation till his Assent should be obtained; and when so suspended, he has utterly neglected to attend to them. 4

He has refused to pass other Laws for the accommodations of large districts of people, unless those people would relinquish the right of Representation in the Legislature, a right inestimable to them and formidable to tyrants only. 5

He has called together legislative bodies at places unusual, uncomfortable, and distant from the depository of their Public Records, for the sole purpose of fatiguing them into compliance with his measures. 6

He has dissolved Representative Houses repeatedly, for opposing with manly firmness his invasions on the rights of the people. 7

He has refused for a long time, after such dissolutions, to cause others to be elected; whereby the Legislative Powers, incapable of Annihilation, have returned to the People at large for their exercise, the State remaining in the mean time exposed to all the dangers of invasion from without, and convulsions within. 8

He has endeavoured to prevent the population of these States; for that purpose obstructing the Laws for Naturalization of Foreigners, refusing to pass others to encourage their migrations hither, and raising the conditions of new Appropriations of Lands. 9

He has obstructed the Administration of Justice, by refusing his Assent to Laws for establishing Judiciary Powers. 10

He has made Judges dependent on his Will alone, for the tenure of their offices, and the amount and payment of their salaries. 11

He has erected a multitude of New Offices, and sent hither swarms of Officers to harass our People, and eat out their substance. 12

He has kept among us, in times of peace, Standing Armies without the Consent of our Legislature. 13

He has affected to render the Military independent of and superior to the Civil Power. 14

He has combined with others to subject us to jurisdiction foreign to our constitution, and unacknowledged by our laws; giving his Assent to their acts of pretended Legislation: 15

For quartering large bodies of armed troops among us: 16

For protecting them, by a mock Trial, from Punishment for any murders which they should commit on the Inhabitants of these States: 17

For cutting off our Trade with all parts of the world: 18

For imposing Taxes on us without our Consent: 19

For depriving us in many cases, of the benefits of Trial by Jury: 20

For transporting us beyond Seas to be tried for pretended offences: 21

For abolishing the free System of English Laws in a Neighboring Province, establishing therein an Arbitrary government, and enlarging its boundaries so as to render it at once an example and fit instrument for introducing the same absolute rule into these Colonies: 22

For taking away our Charters, abolishing our most valuable Laws, and altering fundamentally the Forms of our Governments: 23

For suspending our own Legislatures, and declaring themselves invested with Power to legislate for us in all cases whatsoever. 24

He has abdicated Government here, by declaring us out of his Protection and waging War against us. 25

He has plundered our seas, ravaged our Coasts, burnt our towns, and destroyed the Lives of our people. 26

He is at this time transporting large Armies of foreign Mercenaries to compleat the works of death, desolation and tyranny, already begun with circumstances of Cruelty and perfidy scarcely paralleled in the most barbarous ages, and totally unworthy the Head of a civilized nation. 27

He has constrained our fellow Citizens taken Captive on the high Seas to bear Arms against their Country, to become the executioners of their friends and Brethren, or to fall themselves by their Hands. 28

He has excited domestic insurrections amongst us, and has endeavoured to bring on the inhabitants of our frontiers, the merciless Indian Savages, whose known rule of warfare is an undistinguished destruction of all ages, sexes and conditions. 29

In every stage of these Oppressions we have Petitioned for Redress in the most humble terms: Our repeated petitions have 30 been answered only by repeated injury. A Prince, whose character is thus marked by every act which may define a Tyrant, is unfit to be the ruler of a free People.

Nor have we been wanting in attention to our British brethren. We have warned them from time to time of attempts by their legislature to extend an unwarrantable jurisdiction over us. We have reminded them of the circumstances of our emigration and settlement here. We have appealed to their native justice and magnanimity and we have conjured them by the ties of our common kindred to disavow these usurpations, which would inevitably interrupt our connections and correspondence. They too have been deaf to the voice of justice and of consanguinity. We must, therefore acquiesce in the necessity, which denounces our Separation, and hold them, as we hold the rest of mankind, Enemies in War, in Peace, Friends. 31

We, therefore, the Representatives of the United States of America, in General Congress, Assembled, appealing to the Supreme Judge of the world for the rectitude of our intentions, do, in the Name, and by Authority of the good People of these Colonies, solemnly publish and declare, That these United Colonies, are, and of Right ought to be Free and Independent States; that they are Absolved from all Allegiance to the British Crown, and that all political connection between them and the State of Great Britain, is and ought to be totally dissolved; and that as Free and Independent States, they have full power to levy War, conclude Peace, contract Alliances, establish Commerce, and to do all other Acts and Things which Independent States may of right do. And for the support of this Declaration, with a firm reliance on the protection of Divine Providence, we mutually pledge to each other our lives, our fortunes and our sacred Honor. 32

Thomas Jefferson begins his argument with a number of general claims that he hopes his audience will accept. He even says as much when he introduces them in this way: "We hold these truths to be self-evident . . . ." Perhaps the most crucial of Jefferson's self-evident truths is that *when governments become destructive of the rights that they were meant to insure, then it is the right of the citizens to replace such a government* (paragraph 2). This statement, or claim, serves as the argument's *major premise* and is the first step in Jefferson's syllogism.

His next step is to show that *the government of the American colonies has become destructive of the rights it was meant to in-*

sure. This is the second step in Jefferson's syllogism, his *minor premise.* Notice that while Jefferson's major premise was nondebatable, his minor premise was highly debatable; therefore, he had to go to great length to establish *inductively* the truth of it. And this he did by supplying 28 separate pieces of evidence, as facts to be "submitted to a candid world" (paragraphs 3–31).

After enumerating all of these facts, Jefferson feels that he has amply demonstrated the truth of his minor premise and can go on to the incontrovertible third step or *conclusion:* Then *it is the right of the American colonists to replace the government imposed on them by the British crown.* That, of course, is the substance of his final paragraph, which you notice uses the word that normally introduces all deductive conclusions, *therefore.*

Let's now return to Senator Hollings's argument in favor of reviving the draft. Remember that he began by showing that our country's defense was in a pretty sorry state because a volunteer army was increasingly costly to maintain since the number of available men between the ages of 17 and 21 was diminishing; then he inductively demonstrated that the situation was bad and not likely to improve. Hollings next suggested that an equitable draft would be a desirable way to remedy this bad situation, and he argued that claim in a deductive fashion.

In essence, Hollings stated his argument this way: We need an alternative to a volunteer army (such as a drafted army) because our present volunteer army is increasingly expensive. This statement actually contains a syllogism's conclusion (we need an alternative to our present volunteer army) and its minor premise (volunteer armies are increasingly expensive). The major premise, containing the general principle Hollings feels certain his audience will find undebatable, has been left unstated, but we can easily supply it: Increasingly expensive practices should be abandoned.

We can now state the complete syllogism:

(Increasingly expensive practices should be abandoned.)

Our present volunteer army is increasingly expensive.

Therefore, our present volunteer army should be abandoned.

Like Jefferson, Hollings in his major premise has appealed to a general principle, one that he feels his audience will accept intuitively. Also like Jefferson, he has supplied inductive support for his minor premise, showing that increasing expense will inevitably result from our present practice of maintaining a volunteer army. And Hollings' conclusion, like Jefferson's, is undeniably logical—that a volunteer army ought to be abandoned. He must, of course, go on to show that a drafted army is a reasonable alternative.

Having concluded his first deductive proof, Hollings goes on to add two others:

1. We should have a draft to ensure that all citizens will defend their country.
2. We should have a draft to ensure a broader cross section of American citizens in our armed forces.

Now it is probably not quite clear how each of these statements can constitute a deductive proof, one that consists of three statements: a major premise, a minor premise, and a conclusion. In order for all the elements to be present, something extra must be implied. And that is exactly what has happened.

Stated completely, the syllogisms might look something like this:

Ensuring that all citizens will defend their country is something that we need.

A draft will ensure that all citizens will defend their country.

Therefore, a draft is something that we need.

With this sample syllogism in mind, you can likely figure out how the next deductive argument will be spelled out:

A broad cross section of American citizens in our armed forces is something that we need.

A draft will ensure that there is a broad cross section of American citizens in our armed forces.

Therefore, a draft is something that we need.

Those two original statements that contained the deductive proofs are worth looking at one more time:

1. We should have a draft to ensure that all citizens will defend their country.
2. We should have a draft to ensure a broader cross section of American citizens in our armed forces.

These statements are called *enthymemes*. That term is used to describe a syllogism that has one of its premises implied rather than stated overtly. Usually that implied or unspoken premise, as we have seen in the preceding examples, is the major premise, the one that contains the general, undebatable principle to which the audience is expected to give its whole-hearted support.

That is usually the form that most deductive proofs take—an enthymeme consisting of a conclusion and a *because* statement that turns out to be a minor premise. The remaining part of the syllogism, the general claim, or major premise, is implied rather than stated. And that is why most people, especially students in writing classes, have such a difficult time in creating and manipulating syllogisms. It's hard to see the syllogism when only part of it is stated.

It is because of this difficulty that most modern approaches to argumentation have shunned the classical treatment of deductive proofs in favor of other approaches. In the next section we shall examine one such approach that has gained much popularity in recent times.

EXERCISES

1. Have a look at Peter Drucker's essay, "What Employees Need Most," p. 153. It is based on a deductive argument or syllogism. What is that syllogism? If you have trouble formulating that syllogism, you can find our rendering of it in Question 2 under "Questions of Form" on p. 156. Complete the remainder of that question by locating the paragraphs that contain each of the premises of that syllogism.
2. Return to Jack Anderson's argument, "Flag Burning Isn't the Real Issue," p. 144. Once you have familiarized yourself with the overall argument, examine paragraph 9 closely. There is a syllogism contained in it, although Anderson has not stated it in such a way that the premises and conclusion are readily discernible. How would you state the syllogism in its barest form? Here's a hint. The *minor premise* might be stated: A law against flag burning limits our basic freedoms. Now, how would you state the major premise and the conclusion?

The Toulmin Approach

Because the study of classical logic has not been much emphasized in recent times, we do not expect you to feel comfortable in dealing with syllogisms or enthymemes. It has been our experience that when we oblige students to deal with these kinds of things, the results are less than impressive. Here is one such effort:

Some dogs have fuzzy ears.

My dog has fuzzy ears.

Therefore, my dog is some dog.

Of course, there are rules for the construction of syllogisms and logical systems, but this poor attempt violates so many of them that it is hard to know where to begin to assist its perpetrator.

Modern students, we find, respond more eagerly—and with better understanding—to the inductive approach. Its straightforward method of accumulating evidence in support of a general claim constitutes a much more familiar procedure for them—something akin to the scientific method that they encounter in their chemistry and physics classes, where repeated demonstrations convince the observers that certain chemical elements will always bond in predictable ways, or that bodies will fall with predictable accelerations.

Accordingly, you quite likely were convinced by Dr. Dyer's argument from early in Chapter 1 that justice was nonexistent because spiders killed flies and robins killed worms, and so on. The accumulation of evidence in the form of repeated examples urged you to make the inductive leap to his conclusion that justice could not exist in a world where such killings occurred. For us, this sort of reasoning works better than a syllogism.

Very often it has seemed in our classrooms that the coming of the scientific revolution had banished classical logic for good. We and our students had much difficulty fathoming just how those old logicians managed to use their syllogisms to tease the particular out of the general. But at the same time, we also felt that something was missing, that we were giving up something worthwhile in our focus on a strictly scientific method of persuasion.

This is where British philosopher/logician Stephen Toulmin comes in. Toulmin began by noting that classical enthymemes generally consisted of a combination of claim and support—the very stuff with which we began our discussion of the argumentation process back in Chapter 1. You'll recall these arguments:

Justice does not exist because robins eat worms.

Mankind has survived through tenderness because it endures a long, helpless childhood.

Affirmative action is necessary because civil rights laws do not provide compensation for the victims of past discrimination.

Women are good drivers because they are patient.

We need a draft because a volunteer army is extravagantly expensive.

In each of these cases Toulmin would claim that the argument is convincing because the audience is inclined to accept the unstated connecting link between claim and support—that unstated element that will turn the enthymeme into a syllogism, as shown in the combinations that follow.

(In a world where justice exists, robins will not eat worms.)

But robins eat worms.

Therefore, justice does not exist.

(No one can survive a long, helpless childhood without tender treatment.)

Mankind endures a long, helpless childhood.

Therefore, mankind has survived through tenderness.

(Victims should be compensated for their distresses.)

But civil rights laws do not provide compensation for the victims of past discrimination.

Therefore, affirmative action plans, which do provide compensation, are necessary.

(Good drivers have patience.)

Women have patience.

Therefore, women are good drivers.

(Extravagant expenses should be avoided.)

But volunteer armies are extravagantly expensive.

Therefore, we should avoid a volunteer army—and adopt its less expensive alternative, the draft.

Each of the parenthetical statements in the above syllogisms is what we have earlier called a major premise. They are also what Toulmin would call a *warrant*. The warrant is what makes the support for the claim acceptable to the audience.

The enthymemes we have listed above are apparently logically sound, as well as persuasive, and for that reason they can readily be expanded to syllogisms. Toulmin's contribution to the study of argumentation is not so much his modern recasting of the syllogism as it is his blending of the classical and the modern. That blending allows us to observe in the most common of argumentative forms—the claim and support statement—the rudiments of a logical system: pieces that can be connected by a *warrant—a belief that we accept as true, often without proof.*

Look, for instance, at the underlying syllogism of the Declaration of Independence:

> Governments that are destructive of the rights of their citizens should be overthrown.
>
> This government is destructive of the rights of its citizens.
>
> Therefore, this government should be overthrown.

Thomas Jefferson certainly felt that his audience was predisposed to accept his major premise, because he included it in a list of truths that he declared were self-evident. If the prerogative of citizens to overthrow governments that are destructive of their rights is indeed self-evident, as well as inalienable, then Jefferson certainly has a very strong warrant for claiming that this government ought to be overthrown.

Deductive arguments or syllogisms in the classical world had to be valid, had to conform to rules. But in Toulmin's world of the here and now, claims and support may be linked by warrants that appeal to the audience's sense of logic, or of ethics, or of emotions. The *strength of the warrant*—either logically, ethically, or emotionally—will determine just how convincing the argument proves to be. The strength of warrants is the subject of our next chapter.

EXERCISES

1. Glance back at the set of exercises following the discussion of deductive arguments on p. 72. You were asked to construct the syllogism contained in paragraph 9 of Jack Anderson's "Flag Burning Isn't the Real Issue." What did you determine the major premise of that syllogism to be? Does that major premise satisfy the definition we have given for a *warrant*? That is, does it require support, or is it a general claim that most audiences will accept without support? Look also at the syllogism you constructed for Peter Drucker's "What Employees Need Most." Does the major premise of this syllogism qualify as a warrant? Why? Why not?
2. Reread the excerpt from Martin Luther King's "Letter From Birmingham Jail," pp. 60–61. Reduce this paragraph to its claim and support. How would you state the warrant that connects the claim with its supporting evidence?

4

Warrants

Strength of the Warrant

A *warrant*, as we have seen, is an underlying assumption, a belief rooted deeply in the minds of an audience. If we are aware of such a relevant belief, then we have a distinct advantage in supporting the claims of an argument.

If, for example, we can count on our audience's tendency to value blazing fast balls, win–loss records, strikeouts, and earned-run percentages as the measure of great pitching, then we can be sure that we will have a strong argument in favor of Nolan Ryan's greatness as a pitcher when we recount his amazing achievements in each of these categories. If, on the other hand, the audience is not inclined to value these types of achievements, but rather places more stock in fielding, defense against the stolen base, or stinginess with bases on balls, then such an audience is likely to be less impressed with Ryan's accomplishments, and the argument is accordingly weaker.

Consequently, it is important in every argument to assess the attitudes of the audience, just as you would be wise to check the temperature outside before deciding which coat to wear to the movie theater on a night in November. Presumably, that is what Thomas Jefferson did when he composed the Declaration of Independence. He quite correctly gauged the prevailing sentiment among the majority of American colonists, that tyrannical governments ought to be overthrown. And Phyllis McGinley, writing in a lighter vein, examined her probable audience and determined that the overwhelming majority would favor patience as one of the defining characteristics of a good driver. Having made these determinations about their audiences, Jefferson could take the next step and present supporting evidence to show that King George's government in 1776 was tyrannical, and McGinley could go on to demonstrate that women drivers consistently exhibit patience.

The kind of warrant we have just described is one that will work quite well with an audience that is not hostile to your beliefs. A neutral audience—one with no firm convictions about a claim one way or the other—will be frequently swayed by the amassing of factual or statistical support, so long as the underlying warrant does not conflict with some deep-seated conviction.

But what is to be done about a hostile audience? How can a useful warrant be found? Although such a prospect seems impossible, there are ways. Study the following brief argument by Nobel prize-winning novelist John Steinbeck. It is clear from his argument that Steinbeck is offended by the frequent obscenities that he has seen in print during the campus free speech movement of the middle 1960s. It is also clear that he would not likely have gotten very far by rebuking the students at Berkeley or Columbia or Wisconsin for their foul language, telling them that their words were not consistent with decency or decorum. Look at what he does instead.

In a way I hated to leave America last December. Every day 1 was interesting, some of it dangerous, I suppose, but all of it fascinating to me. For instance, the student organizations and picketing and even rioting. It's not so long ago that the biggest and best smash our college students could manage was a panty raid on a girls' dormitory. Serious people despaired of them. Foreign students were politically alive while ours barely managed to swallow goldfish or see how many could get into a telephone booth.

Well, that's all changed, you must admit. A goodly number 2 of our students are raring to go. It's a relief to see. They'll march and picket and tip over automobiles with the best students anywhere. I'd back them against the medieval scholars who tore up the Ile de la Cite in the day of Aucassin. I admire rebellion—any time and against anything. Besides, it passes the time. And it takes energy to study and to riot at the same time.

The Berkeley students who struck a blow for freedom of 3 speech are particularly to be praised. I hope when they get it themselves, they will allow it to others. And I think they should certainly have the right to speak or print four-letter words on the campus as well as off it.

My only reservation about this doesn't come from a censorious impulse, but one of conservation. We don't have many 4 four-letter words of sturdy quality and, when you use them up, there's no place to go. Also, overuse milks all the strength out of them. One of our middle-aged young writers has worn out his stock so completely that a simple English sentence would shock his readers to death.

No, if you crowd a window with diamonds, they become 5 uninteresting. It is the single jewel centered on black velvet, alone and glorious, that jars us into appreciation. Obscenities are too valuable to waste and, if one can combine with another to explode like a star-spangled sky rocket, that is true art and, like all true art, rare and precious.

I may tell you that once long ago, when I was working on a 6 ship, a seaman of Irish extraction dawdled his hand into a winch drum and the steel cable snipped off three of his fingers. For a moment he looked at the wreck which hadn't yet started to bleed and then softly, slowly and sweetly he came up with the greatest curse I have ever heard. It had everything—vulgarity, obscenity, irreverence and sacrilegiousness, all precisely placed in one short staccato burst of prose that peeled the paint off the deck machinery and tattooed itself on the deck engineer's chest. I have cherished this oath ever since, but I wouldn't think of using it. I have never said it aloud, even alone. I am saving it for the time when I need it. But it will have to be an enormous need, a tomwallager of a need, but I am content that when it comes I am equipped for it. Imagine the waste if I had piddled it away on some picayune crisis.

If I am stern about this, it is because I know that overexpo- 7 sure withers the rich bloom of our dear heritage of obscenity.

Since Steinbeck is at odds with his audience (or at least that portion of it that represents the free speech movement), he cannot appeal to a warrant that calls for good manners in speaking, especially the avoidance of shocking obscenities, because it is the right to use just such words that Steinbeck's youthful adversaries are supporting so staunchly. So he looks around for some common ground—something that he and his audience can agree upon. And he finds it in the notion of *conservation*.

In addition to being against the Vietnam War, the radical students of the nineteen-sixties were quite vocal in their support of conservation practices, branding capitalistic and industrial America as a careless and wasteful giant that would, in its pursuit of ever larger profits, soon deplete our rich continent of its natural resources.

Knowing this, Steinbeck can state his warrant with confidence, and he does in the fourth paragraph, where he says: "My only reservation about this doesn't come from a censorious impulse, but one of conservation." The remainder of the argument is quite straightforward: We mustn't waste the power of our obscenities through overuse because they are very limited in number and hence quite precious.

Any educated Greek contemporary of Aristotle could have expanded the enthymeme embedded in Steinbeck's statement into a full-blown syllogism.

Precious things should not be wasted. (major premise)

Obscenities are precious things. (minor premise)

Therefore, obscenities should not be wasted. (conclusion)

Notice, too, how the major premise of this syllogism neatly states the warrant that Steinbeck was at pains to discover. He doesn't need to offer support for it, because he has carefully measured his audience and has determined that it is a premise that they will accept.

The second or minor premise is not quite so obvious, so Steinbeck has to supply some support for it. First, he compares an obscenity to a diamond, commenting that diamonds in great abundance do not dazzle, but a single one, properly displayed, will capture an onlooker. Second, he provides the extended example of the Irish sailor's curse, which he describes as very valuable and very comforting and thus not something to be squandered foolishly. By the time Steinbeck has recounted these examples, the audience can well understand his seemingly curious claim that obscenities are precious, as well as his conclusion that they should not be wasted.

Steinbeck's argument works because it has a strong warrant. And the strength of that warrant depends on three things: its logical appeal, its ethical appeal, and its emotional appeal.

Logical Appeal

A warrant has a logical appeal if it accurately expresses the generalization that is appealed to by the enthymeme. Now, what does that mean? It's what we have been talking about all along. The enthymeme is nothing more than the combination of a claim and its support:

Affirmative action is needed because civil rights laws do not require compensation for past discrimination.

A universal draft is needed because volunteer armies are outrageously expensive.

Obscenities should not be wasted because they are precious.

Women are good drivers because they are patient.

What generalization is appealed to by each of the foregoing claim-plus-support statements (or enthymemes)? Look at these four related statements:

People who have been oppressed should be compensated.

Outrageously expensive things should be avoided.

Precious things should not be wasted.

Good drivers are patient.

Each of these statements is a *warrant*—a justification for making each of the claims contained in the foregoing enthymemes. The logical appeal of each of these warrants can be illustrated and determined by a simple diagram, called by logicians a *Venn diagram:* Take the first term of each warrant above—*oppressed people, outrageously expensive things, precious things, good drivers*—and draw a circle around each as shown in Figure 4.1. Next, draw a larger circle around each of these circles, and label that circle with the

FIGURE 4.1

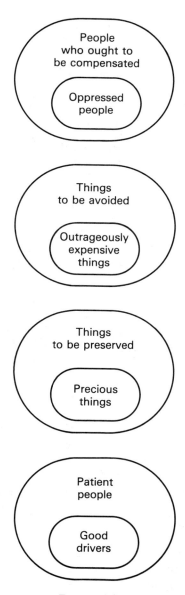

FIGURE 4.2

second term of the warrant—*people who should be compensated, things to be avoided, things to be preserved, patient people* (see Figure 4.2). The test now is to see if the third element, the one that appears in the claim-plus-support statement or enthymeme (but

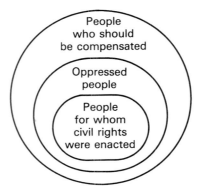

FIGURE 4.3

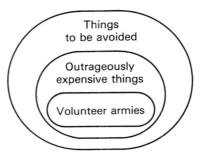

FIGURE 4.4

not in the warrant) can be placed within the innermost circle. If it can, then it must necessarily and logically be a part of the larger circle (see Figure 4.3). People for whom civil rights laws were enacted are among the members of the class of oppressed people; that is, they belong inside the innermost circle. As such, they also belong inside the larger circle of people who should be compensated. Therefore, the logic holds, and the warrant has a strong logical appeal.

The same is true of the next diagram (Figure 4.4). Volunteer armies belong to the class of outrageously expensive things and therefore are unavoidably also members of the class of things to be avoided. While the logic of this warrant is quite compelling, Senator Hollings will have to construct yet another claim-plus-support enthymeme to establish the next part of his argument, namely, that conscripted, or drafted, armies are not outrageously expensive and thus not to be avoided.

Steinbeck's warrant is also logically strong (Figure 4.5). Because

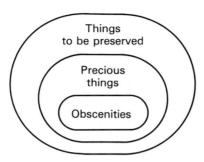

FIGURE 4.5

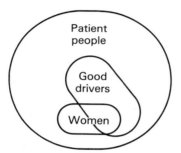

FIGURE 4.6

they belong in the class of precious things, at least according to Steinbeck, obscenities also belong to the larger class of things that ought to be preserved. Now let us examine McGinley's enthymeme and its underlying warrant, arranged as in Figure 4.6. It would be incorrect to include the class of women completely within the circle of good drivers because McGinley's claim is not that all women are good drivers but that they are patient. You can draw the circle representing women in several ways within the outermost circle. Some will intersect the circle of good drivers, and others will not. The logical appeal of McGinley's claim comes from the inverse of the claim that women are patient; that is, that men are not patient. So if we draw the men's circle, it must appear outside the circle of patient people and thus certainly outside the inner circle of good drivers (Figure 4.7).

As Figures 4.6 and 4.7 show, the case for women being good drivers is not as logically compelling as were the three cases represented in the earlier diagrams. Nevertheless, there is certainly logical appeal for the claim that women drive better than men, and that after all was McGinley's contention.

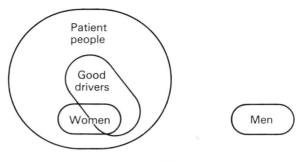

FIGURE **4.7**

Ethical Appeals

McGinley's claim about women drivers not only has logical appeal, but it also has what we shall call *ethical appeal;* that is, it appeals to a sentiment that underlies the beliefs, customs, or practices of a person or society.

The ethical appeal of McGinley's claim rests upon the strength of the warrant that patient people make good drivers, but it goes even deeper—to another warrant that most, if not all, members of our society would subscribe to: As a rule, women are more patient than men.

Similarly, the ethical appeal that lends strength to Jackson's claim about affirmative action is our abiding belief, as a people, that wrongs should be righted—that people who have sustained an injury should be compensated for that damage.

We might go so far as to say that Senator Hollings' claim that volunteer armies should be avoided is supported by the Puritan ethic that places a high value on hard work and paying one's way and which demands that the price of everything ought to be examined.

Steinbeck's claim that obscenities ought to be preserved and used sparingly because they are precious appeals to a similar sense of ethics. It was Steinbeck's special genius that enabled him to discern just that portion of our society's ethical heritage which was still being observed by young radicals of the 1960s. While they had rejected prudery as something puritanical or conservative—labels they would have considered bad—they still believed in the conservative practice of avoiding waste, especially as it applied to limited or endangered natural resources. Steinbeck took advantage of this remaining bias to point out that obscenities were truly precious things that ought to be preserved, particularly because they were in danger of losing their potency and thus their very being.

What is at stake here is the need to examine the values of the audience to determine what sorts of claims will work and which ones won't. Those that match the deeply felt convictions of the audience will succeed more readily than those that do not. The lesson from Steinbeck is just this: Claims that conflict with the underlying beliefs or principles of the audience are likely to be doomed, however logically we frame them, *unless* we discover some way to couch those claims so that they have an ethical appeal as well.

Determining the ethical or cultural convictions of your audience and then fashioning your argument to take advantage of them is just one element of what we mean by ethical appeal. There is yet another—what the ancient Greek rhetoricians called *ethos*. This is the character of the person doing the arguing—you. It is of utmost importance that you establish yourself as someone whose views are worth listening to; in a word, you must be *credible*.

ESTABLISHING CREDIBILITY

Surely you have noticed that public speakers frequently begin a speech or an argument with a joke. While the joke does not necessarily increase their believability in the eyes of the audience, it does tend to make them seem to be the kind of person that the audience will want to believe.

We believe people for two reasons:

1. They are our friends.
2. They are authorities.

For the time being we will deal with the first of these—the appearance of friendship, because it is certainly the case that one does not get to be an authority by telling jokes; nevertheless, it is a *friendly* thing to do.

The point here is simply this: You will make your audience more kindly disposed to your claims if you show that you have a sense of humor. People who keep their sense of humor are less inclined to be threatening, or boring, or overly technical—modes of behavior that tend to repel the average audience.

The ancient rhetoricians also had a name for this tactic; they called it *transfer* and considered it one of the sorts of argumentative flaws they called material fallacies, along with hasty generalizations and false cause. What they would find troublesome about transfer, especially in our modern multimedia society, is that it works, despite its fallacious nature.

Think of any five television commercials that you have seen recently; the chances are pretty good that transfer is involved. For instance, willowy blonds in suggestive dress are often seen in automobile ads; they are desirable, at least to the young male target audience, and that desirability is psychologically "transferred" to the featured automobile.

Similarly, the beer-guzzling rowdies who come to blows over the claims of "Tastes Great!" versus "Less Filling!" are not at all concerned about supporting such claims with certifiable evidence. Their humorous antics are designed for only one purpose—to transfer the amusement and good feeling that you associate with them onto their product: Lite Beer. If you feel good about the fun they seem to be having in their argument over Lite, you might buy a six-pack.

The measure of transfer's success is easily gauged by the frequency of its use. And for that reason it is certainly worth your attention in planning your approach to your audience, whether it be imitating Phyllis McGinley's disarming humor in broaching the subject of women drivers or recognizing the cleverness of John Steinbeck's praising nonconformity in order to stake out a piece of common ground that he could share with his audience of rebellious students. Both were establishing themselves as friendly figures, using time-honored means of establishing their credibility.

Another method of rendering yourself believable, as well as agreeable, is to concede at least some portion of your opponent's argument. As we will note in the next chapter, when we discuss refutation strategies, it is always important to examine views opposing your own, with an eye toward countering them. You are unlikely ever to cause your opponents to discard all of their views and take up all of yours, but if you can bring about at least a partial compromise by giving over some claim that you do not feel is too crucial to your cause, you can score several small victories. First of all, you can draw the opposing sides a bit closer to agreement by narrowing the gap between them. Second, you can win some measure of goodwill from your opponents. Third, you can make yourself appear to be a most agreeable and sensible person in the eyes of the larger, uncommitted audience, toward whom most of your claims are directed.

Phyllis McGinley did not lose anything by admitting that men as a rule were very capable representatives of the human species and that they were, as a rule, quite good at a number of things. That generous concession at the outset of her argument helped both to establish her credibility and to make her male audience less hostile toward her. And Ernest Hollings ingratiated himself with that portion of his audience that might have been hostile to the idea of a draft by quickly conceding that he did not favor a draft like the last one that we had—the unequally administered one that sent thousands of young men from the lower classes to Viet Nam while allowing the more prosperous ones to remain safely stateside in college or in the National Guard or reserves.

You needn't, however, become a jokesmith or give away half your argument to establish yourself as a friendly, nonthreatening figure. But you must always be conscious of the *tone* of your writing. By tone we mean your attitude toward your audience as revealed by your writing. With a turn of a phrase you can reveal yourself either as superior and condescending or as concerned and helpful. Compare the following sentences:

Don't be so stupid as to neglect your audience.
Always keep your audience in mind.

Of the two pieces of almost identical advice, we feel sure that you are more inclined to heed the second one, because it is couched in a more friendly tone. And it's good advice; be a friend to your audience, not an adversary. First, study the audience and determine what its concerns and interests might be; then ensure that your approach— whether it relies on humor, shared concerns, or the like—features subject matter that will be appealing and nonthreatening.

If the tone of your argument establishes you as a friendly figure, then the structure of the argument, including its grammar and spelling, will help to establish you as an *authority*. As John Steinbeck once observed, the wisest philosopher could utter the profoundest of truths with absolutely no effect on his audience if he had neglected to zip up his trousers. Your credibility suffers in exactly the same way with every misspelling and every grammatical blunder.

In the final analysis, however, the authority of your argument quite often will depend on more than good spelling and grammar, on more than the form and the structure of the argument, and on more than the audience's acceptance of you as an authority figure. Quite often, as we have seen, you need to appeal to other authorities. If Lee Iacocca tells you that his company will stand behind its warranty on Chrysler Corporation vehicles, you feel that he, as Chrysler's chairman of the board, is in a position to make such a claim. Similarly, if Charles Schwab tells you that he can save you money on your stock investments, you also feel that he speaks with authority because the brokerage firm that he is representing to you on television bears his name.

In contrast, while you may marvel at the feats of Michael Jordan and Bo Jackson, you are not inclined to believe claims about the athletic shoes associated with their names; indeed, Jordan and Jackson seldom make outright claims, because they know as surely as we do that their amazing feats are mainly the result of their special talents and not the by-product of their equipment. If we are disposed to buy the shoes they endorse, it is because we *transfer* our admiration for Jordan and Jackson onto the shoes and not because we judge them to be authorities in the same way that we do Iaccoca and Schwab.

Thus, when we produce authorities in support of our claims, it is always well to analyze exactly what we are doing. We can gain something by way of transfer simply by name-dropping, hoping that the pleasant feelings of admiration associated with the names of our sources will tend to influence the audience. But such a strategy lacks the credibility of using an authority whose credentials are impeccable, one who is a genuine authority on the subject at hand—not someone who was chosen because his or her name has become a household word.

Emotional Appeals

While we respond to claims that we consider logical, we are also moved to agree with them if they have ethical appeal as well—if they correspond to some deeply felt sentiment that we, as members of a special group, organization, religion, people, or civilization hold to be true—or if they come from a source that we feel we can trust. We are also moved by arguments that lay claim to our emotions.

In his discussion of tragic dramas, the Greek philosopher Aristotle observed that those tragedies were most effective which appealed to our strongest emotions: fear and pity. We can return to Senator Hollings' argument to see how such emotional appeals work.

We have already examined the logical appeal of at least one portion of the senator's argument. Let us look briefly at its ethical appeal as well. When Hollings says, ". . . we need [a military draft] in order to remain true to the ideals that built this country," you can be pretty sure that he is going to make an ethical appeal. But when he points out the enormous expense of maintaining a volunteer army and goes on to show that the "escalating pay and benefits" will lead to "diminishing arms for our troops and lessening our ability to defend ourselves," he is appealing to something else—not to the ethical ideals that built this country but to the *fear* that our country, along with its ideals, could be lost.

In a more modest way, Steinbeck's argument also appeals to fear—fear that our language's few and precious obscenities will be lost or weakened for all time through trivial and excessive use. We may respond to the logical appeal of the enthymeme and to the ethical strength of the warrant that precious things should be protected, but we also are likely to find urgency in the fear that Steinbeck stirs up.

Besides fear, Steinbeck appeals to another emotion—pity. We are moved by the suffering of the maimed Irish sailor, and we judge his response to that suffering—his great and priceless curse—to be justified or warranted. Similarly, we are moved to pity the runner in Jackson's opening illustration, forced to compete with heavy weights on his ankles. And it is to Jackson's credit that he contrived his example so as to appeal to his audience's sense of pity.

Contriving to instill fear or pity in the audience is something that obviously can be done. We can point out dire results or we can hold up sympathetic models. We can also take advantage of the language itself to convey such emotions. By paying attention to the *connotations* (emotional meanings) as well as to the *denotations* (dictionary meanings) of words we can actually tilt the language in our favor. Such a tactic is called *slanting*. Take, for example, the second paragraph of the Declaration of Independence. Jefferson uses several words to describe the behavior of the English crown toward the colonies: *despotism, usurpations, tyranny*. Besides what these words actually mean (their denotations), there is an emotional power or appeal that attaches to them (their connotations) that goes beyond their actual meanings. It is this second aspect of words that has the power to arouse an audience's emotions, and Jefferson was well aware of this impact.

The use of emotion-charged words can be quite effective, as it obviously was in the Declaration of Independence. Quite frequently, however, such a practice can be overdone, as it admittedly was in the 1988 presidential election, where the word *liberal*, the so-called "l-word," was used without regard for its denotation, thereby creating a sense of fear associated with higher taxes, unwise spending, and permissive treatment of criminals. Clearly, the unbridled use of emotionally charged language can give argumentation a bad name. In point of fact, it perhaps already has. Such language practices often are labeled as *rhetoric*, a word that originally meant the effective use of language, particularly in the construction of arguments, but which now is often taken to mean exaggerated, emotion-packed language, usually associated with dishonest or hypocritical politicians or demagogues.

Back to Warrants

We have just seen that the strength of a warrant—that is, the predisposition of the audience to yield to its claim—will be dependent on several factors:

1. Its logical appeal. How does your claim relate to the warrant? Is it a logical part of some pervasive belief that the audience holds?

2. Its ethical appeal. Is the warrant really a part of the audience's system of beliefs—of its culture? Also, how does the audience feel about you? Have you presented yourself as a friendly and credible authority? As the writer, have you given the audience sufficient reason or warrant to be persuaded?

3. Its emotional appeal. Is the audience's warrant based on a fear of dire consequences? Is the audience moved to pity? Has either of these primary emotions been stirred by the slanted use of language?

EXERCISES

1. In earlier exercises you were asked to state the claims contained in certain essays in the Readings section. Return now to four of those essays and, having extracted the claim, determine the nature of the warrant that underlies that claim. To what predisposition or attitude on the part of the audience is the author of each of the following essays appealing?

    a. "Sixty Billion Pounds of Trouble."
    b. "Art and Politics: Self-Righteousness and Silly Yahooism,"
    c. "Frats and Sororities: Greek Rites of Exclusion."
    d. "The Myth of the Student-Athlete."

2. How would you describe the connection between the claim and the warrant in each of the above essays? Try drawing a Venn diagram to illustrate the logical relationship.

3. With what sort of appeal does Gary Turbak begin his essay, "Sixty Billion Pounds of Trouble"? What about the appeal that is implicit in the first paragraph of Brownlee's "The Myth of the Student-Athlete"? Do you detect any slanted or emotionally charged language in their opening paragraphs? What specific words carry an emotional charge?

4. Examine Beck's "Art and Politics: Self-Righteousness and Silly Yahooism," What is the attitude that Beck displays toward the dispute between the Whitney Museum and Congress? What choices of words reveal that attitude? What do those choices of words have to say about Beck's attitude toward her audience? What exactly seems to be

the makeup of that audience? What portion of the reading public has she ruled out as unlikely to be affected by her claim? With what audience will she enjoy the strongest appeal?

5. Who is the chief audience of Lord's "Frats and Sororities"? Upon what evidence would you rely to justify your answer?

5

Refutation

Up to this point we have devoted our attention to composing sound, logical, well-constructed arguments. We have examined claims of fact, value, and policy, and demonstrated how to provide sufficient support for them. In each instance we were arguing *for* a position, a belief, a course of action.

While it is important to know how to argue in support of a claim, it is also important to know how to argue against one. Such counterarguments are what rhetoricians call *refutation* or *rebuttal*. When you refute an opponent's claim, you can attack the support, you can attack the argument's form, or you can attack the warrant. We will examine these three kinds of refutation one at a time. As we do so, keep in mind that these strategies of refutation should also be considered even as you formulate arguments of your own; you should be constantly aware of how your opponent is likely to respond to your claims. If you do that, the result will almost certainly be the strengthening of your own argument, to counter any potential rebuttal. Therefore, as we examine the three refutation strategies, we will also discuss ways in which you can anticipate and neutralize the refutations of your opponents.

Attacking the Support

Remember the way that claims of fact are most often supported. They can be supported inductively by amassing a number of pieces of evidence that tend to support the claim. If the pieces of support are not numerous enough, the argument often fails to be convincing. Such was the case of the foolish mathematician who concluded that all odd numbers were prime (divisible only by themselves or by one) on the basis of his examination of the first odd numbers—1, 3, 5, and 7. If he had examined only the next odd number, 9, he would have noted that it was the product of 3 times 3 and would have seen the error of his ways. His generalization had been made too hastily, on the basis of too little evidence. This is the refutation strategy most frequently employed against claims of fact—an accusation that the opponent has failed to examine all the evidence and has hence made a "hasty generalization." Classical rhetoricians are responsible for that name; furthermore, they contend that the hasty generalization is but one of a large number of "material fallacies," so called because they represent failures of the *material,* or the supporting data necessary to prove a claim. We will examine other material fallacies momentarily, but we have introduced this one first because of its frequent occurrence. (For a concise discussion of all the common sorts of fallacies, see "A Short Guide to Material and Formal Fallacies," in the Appendix.

Perhaps the surest safeguard against hasty generalization is to provide a great deal of evidence, enough to convince your reader that you have examined a very large quantity indeed, so much so that any opponent would find it difficult to present a greater number of opposing examples.

Recall how Martin Luther King contended that African–Americans were justified in their impatient desire for justice and equality. He immediately produced nine pieces of evidence—vivid and poignant examples of injustices and inequities that would certainly have tried the patience of any member of his audience. His audience would have been hard-pressed to produce a greater number of examples to the contrary.

Remember also how Thomas Jefferson contended that George III was a tyrant and then went on to support that claim by producing 28 concrete instances of the king's tyrannical behavior. The sheer number of instances made Jefferson's claim an impressive one because no opponent would be apt to argue that Jefferson had not examined enough instances—that he had reached a *hasty generalization.*

Other inductive strategies for supporting claims of fact, you will recall, involved analogy (or comparison) and causal analysis. The underlying assumption in all analogies is this: If two situations can be shown to be similar in a number of ways, it is likely that they will be similar in an additional one. That additional one, of course, is the one that you seek to prove.

You might, for example, reconsider the argument we posed earlier concerning the location of a McDonald's restaurant. The supposed success of the new operation was based on the similarity it bore to another, already established and successful one: its location near a shopping mall, its flashy revolving sign, and its playground for small customers. An opponent of the project could well appeal to the material fallacy of *false analogy* by demonstrating that, while these similarities do exist, there are also dissimilarities that have not been examined, such as the presence of two other chain fast food restaurants within 100 yards of the proposed site and the presence of a ten-store ethnic food court inside the shopping mall—competitive factors not present at the successful location.

The surest way to guard against the fallacy of false analogy is to draw the comparison very carefully, pointing out as many kinds of similarity as possible while anticipating possible points of dissimilarity. That is what Jesse Jackson did when he likened affirmative action to the compensation given a runner whose ankle weights had been removed part-way through a race. The situations in which black workers found themselves were similar to that of the runner in several ways. They were handicapped by racial prejudice as the runner was handicapped by the weights. The inequities in both cases—the prejudice and the weights—had been recognized and outlawed. And in both cases compensation was justified.

At this point Jackson could have dropped the analogy and argued for the compensation that was due blacks who had suffered discrimination in the job market. And he would have left himself open to the charge of false analogy. Job searches and foot races are, after all, quite unlike, and given no more points of similarity than the ones we have enumerated, the audience might view the analogy as a weak or false one. But Jackson did not stop at that point. Jackson anticipated that most readers would agree that the most logical way of compensating the aggrieved runner would be to have him compete again on another day without the ankle weights. Such a suggestion, while eminently fair in the case of the foot race, would have no counterpart in the job market, where adjustments can be made but where starting all over again is an impossibility. Even to suggest such a prospect would be to court the charge of false analogy.

So Jackson quite cleverly added another point of comparison to his analogy, one that he called "reasonable compensation," which is, after all, what affirmative action purports to be. "If one could devise," Jackson suggests, "some means of compensating the second runner (for example, comparing the runners' times for the last two laps and projecting them over the entire race), a more accurate appraisal of each runner's ability and performance could be made."

By this additional step, Jackson's argument has gained considerable strength, and he has successfully avoided a charge of false analogy.

Causal analysis, another method of support for claims of fact, is frequently subject to charges of fallacy. The most often used fallacy has an impressive Latin name: *Post hoc, ergo propter hoc,* which translates, "After this, therefore because of this." A more common name for this fallacy, and the one that we will use, is *false cause.* This fallacy asserts that just because one event follows another does not mean that the first one caused the second. A normal human reaction to significant events is to seek backward for their cause. But a black cat's crossing your path will have nothing to do with your subsequent auto accident, particularly if you encountered the cat at the beginning of your trip while the accident occurred an hour later and 50 miles away. More likely causes for the accident are sure to be discovered—especially by insurance adjusters.

Similarly, we might also contend that, in addition to making a false analogy, the argument concerning the location of the new McDonald's suffers from false cause as well. The causes advanced for the success of the first McDonald's—location near a mall, attractive sign, and attached playground—all no doubt contributed to the success of the operation. All other things being equal, they could very well have been sufficient cause for the success. But, as we have seen, all other things were not equal; there was another relevant cause that we did not even notice until we examined the site for the new McDonald's and determined that it would encounter stiff competition from two other fast food restaurants and an ethnic food court within the mall— competition that the first location did not experience.

In short, we had not determined the *actual* cause of the first McDonald's success; rather, we had seized upon several possible *false* causes for its success—a tendency that you will do well to guard against.

For a more successful handling of causes in support of a claim, we have only to look once more at Loren Eiseley's argument that tenderness rather than toughness is responsible for humanity's survival. No one is likely to deny the claim that human prominence on the planet is the result of an advanced brain. But a long period of development *after birth* is required in order for that brain capacity to be achieved—a period during which the child is vulnerable and requires the tender protection of parents.

So while brain power is responsible for humanity's survival and rise to power, that added mental capacity was not without its price—a long and relatively helpless growth period—and to overlook that while pointing to mental ability alone is to make a mistake as grave as Eiseley's opponent, who had singled out toughness as the key factor in humanity's ascendency. In reality, as Eiseley has demonstrated, both toughness and increased brain power (traits that humans surely have) were false causes. They were sufficient reasons for survival if all other things had been equal. But as with the

McDonald's locations, all other things were not equal, and these two causes had to bow to the necessary cause that Eiseley convincingly demonstrated—tenderness.

Turning now to claims of value, we must focus upon the usual strategy employed in supporting such claims. We determined that the best way to support any claim of value was to *define* what we meant by value (such as excellence) in the thing or activity being considered, and then to go about showing how the thing or activity meets or exceeds the definition. That is what we did when we claimed that Nolan Ryan was a sensational pitcher. We set up some criteria by which we asserted that good pitching should be judged, and then we measured Ryan's accomplishments against them.

That too is what Phyllis McGinley did when she discussed good drivers; she established three criteria that good drivers must exhibit, and then she demonstrated that women exhibited them more often than men.

Those who wish to refute claims of value frequently point out that not all the facts have been examined—that based on the established criteria, another person or product has a better claim, with accomplishments or characteristics of greater value than those that you have enumerated. This would be an appeal to the fallacy of hasty generalization.

But more often the strategy used in refuting a claim of value is to point to a different material fallacy, that of *special pleading*, often called *card stacking*. We have already alluded to this tactic in connection with the discussion of Nolan Ryan's pitching. The person who grants that by your criteria Ryan is a sensational pitcher will build a case for a different pitcher by alleging that you have called attention to just those traits of a good pitcher that your favorite exhibits, while ignoring those that he lacks. In doing so you were "stacking the cards" in Ryan's favor.

McGinley's argument about women being better drivers than men is also vulnerable to the charge of special pleading; in selecting as important only the traits of practice, caution, and patience, she is ignoring other traits that good drivers ought to have as well, such as quick reflexes and good vision. The person who would most easily and successfully refute her argument would need to focus attention upon those traits she ignores.

Finally, claims of policy, because of their special strategies, are open to several avenues of rebuttal. Remember that in a claim of policy attention must be called to an existing condition—one that is to be acted upon. If it is a bad condition, then the proposed policy would remedy it. If it is a good condition, the proposed policy would preserve it.

First of all, an opponent might well claim that the existing condition has been misjudged—that it is not as good or as bad as it has been represented. In other words, the existing situation has been the victim of special pleading.

Second, the opponent might argue that the course of action recommended will not produce the desired effect—that the thinking involved in predicting the success is based on a false cause, a false analogy, or a hasty generalization.

Let us examine a concrete example, the argument advanced by Senator Hollings for revival of a military draft. Remember that Hollings claimed first of all that the present condition of the U.S. military was deplorable. With a shrinking number of available males of service age, in a few years the cost of attracting volunteers would increase to the point of being prohibitive. To replace the volunteer army with an army of draftees would be not only less expensive, but it would also satisfy other needs, making the army better informed and more broadly based, and thus truly representative of the people it is designed to protect.

To attack Hollings' claim of policy, an opponent would need to attack the senator's evaluation of the current military force in terms of its expense, showing that its costs are not now excessive nor likely to be so in the immediate future. It would also be necessary to determine by what criteria expenses are to be declared prohibitive.

Or, granting Hollings' assessment of the condition of the military, an opponent might argue that the institution of a military draft would not produce the effects Hollings predicts. Rather, it would fail to create a more informed, equitable, and broadly based military at less expense, or, perhaps more likely, it would create other effects that would prove objectionable, such as unemployment problems for the unskilled young men and women who would otherwise have been able to find jobs in the volunteer military.

Attacking the Argument's Form

Another approach to refutation is to attack an argument's form. However, it is difficult to find fault with the form of most arguments. Most arguments consist, as we have seen, of a claim supported by a *because*-statement or perhaps several of them. Usually, the more *because*-statements you can provide, the better your claim will be supported. Accordingly, your argument will be stronger and less vulnerable to refutation.

Nevertheless, at least in studying classical rhetoric, a great deal of attention is devoted to *formal fallacies;* these fallacies are mistakes that can be made in the construction of syllogisms, mistakes that render the syllogism, and thus the argument, invalid. To see how formal fallacies occur, recall that arguments consist of a claim plus at least one *because*-statement for support. This combination usually results in what classical rhetoric calls an enthymeme:

> Obscenities should be preserved because they are precious.
> This government should be overthrown because it is tyrannical.
> Women are good drivers because they are patient.
> A universal draft is needed because volunteer armies are outrageously expensive.

To convert each of these ethymemes into a complete syllogism, it is necessary to supply a general claim, which we have called a warrant, that will show the connection between the claim and its support. The general claim (warrant or major premise) appears below in parentheses.

> (Precious things ought to be preserved.)
>
> Obscenities are precious things.
>
> Therefore, obscenities ought to be preserved.

We have also shown how the relation between the claim and support within the syllogism can be illustrated in a Venn diagram, such as that in Figure 5.1. Because precious things belong to the class of things that ought to be preserved, and because the class of precious things also contains within itself the still smaller class of things we call obscenities, then obscenities must exist within the larger class of things that ought to be preserved. As the diagram shows, the syllogism is correctly formed; it is thus free of formal fallacies and is *valid*.

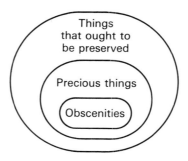

FIGURE 5.1

The same is true of the syllogism contained in the Declaration of Independence:

(Tyrannical governments ought to be overthrown.)

This government is tyrannical.

Therefore, this government ought to be overthrown.

You can draw the Venn diagram for yourself and thereby determine that the syllogism is correctly formed and that the conclusion is therefore valid.

On the other hand, you will recall that the Venn diagram that underlies the enthymeme *Women are good drivers because they are patient* looks like Figure 5.2. While women belong to the larger group of patient people, and while it is also true that good drivers also belong to the larger group of patient people, there is no guarantee that all women belong to the group of good drivers. Some women may be good drivers while others may not. This syllogism is said to be guilty of the formal fallacy of *undistributed middle* and is thus invalid. Without going into a detailed explanation of this fallacy, we can simply state that the syllogism does not succeed because it fails to capture accurately the relationship between the claim and its support: Women are good drivers because they are patient. The only salvation for McGinley's argument lay in the fact that she had excluded all men from the class of patient people, so that they had no chance of belonging to the smaller class of good drivers contained within the larger group of patient people. At least that portion of her argument was formally valid.

Similarly, the ethymeme *A universal draft is needed because volunteer armies are outrageously expensive* can be shown to rest upon an invalid syllogism for at least two reasons. First of all, it

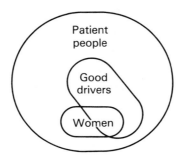

FIGURE 5.2

contains too many terms. Let's see what that means. The syllogism that underlies this claim must look something like this:

> (Outrageously expensive things ought to be avoided.)
>
> Volunteer armies are outrageously expensive.
>
> Therefore, volunteer armies ought to be avoided.

So far, so good. We have a valid syllogism, one that you could test with a Venn diagram. But the syllogism does not mention anything about a universal draft; the universal draft is a term that does not appear in the syllogism. And even if we were to construct another syllogism that includes that term, it would be guilty of the formal fallacy of undistributed middle.

> Outrageously expensive things ought to be avoided.
>
> A universal draft is not outrageously expensive.
>
> Therefore, a universal draft ought not be avoided.

Let's see how that can be illustrated in a Venn diagram (see Figure 5.3). Just because the universal draft does not belong to the class of expensive things, it does not follow that it is also to be excluded from the class of things to be avoided. Indeed, it may be a member of that class. Or it might not. So if Senator Hollings is going to be convincing about the need for a universal draft, he is going to have to rest his case on something besides its relative inexpensiveness, because on that account he is vulnerable to the accusation of arguing fallaciously. To his credit, Hollings does not rest his case on the inexpensiveness of the drafted army; rather he goes on to claim that a drafted army provides a broader, more democratic base—one that is better representative of the people it protects than is the volunteer army, and that claim is valid. Here's how you check it. First, set up the claim, *Drafted armies*

FIGURE 5.3

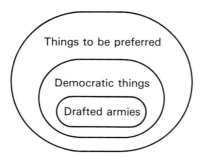

FIGURE 5.4

are to be preferred because they are democratic, as a syllogism. The claim is in reality an enthymeme, so you will need to supply the unstated major premise, shown here in parentheses.

(Democratic things are to be preferred.)

Drafted armies are democratic.

Therefore, drafted armies are to be preferred.

And you could draw a Venn diagram to check that one out (see Figure 5.4).

The conclusion to be drawn from the foregoing discussion is simply this: It's always a good idea to test out each of your claim and support statements by sketching a mental Venn diagram (or a real one if you have a hard time visualizing these things), so that you won't leave yourself open to the kind of refutation that depends on the appeal to formal fallacies.

Attacking the Warrant

We have just seen how the arguments of Phyllis McGinley and Ernest Hollings were at least partially flawed by reason of formal fallacies in the way that they were constructed. Steinbeck's argument about the preciousness of obscenities, on the other hand, issued from a perfectly valid syllogism. It had the added virtue of having a major premise (or warrant) that coincided fairly well with the feelings of the audience toward whom it was directed, namely the radical college students of the nineteen sixties' Free Speech Movement—people who would not likely be swayed by the appeal to clean up their language, but who might find some common ground in an appeal to conservation practices. In other words, Steinbeck's audience would not be likely to challenge his warrant that precious things ought to be preserved.

Although Steinbeck's argument has a sound warrant, such is not the case with Jefferson's. Recall that Jefferson's enthymeme *This government ought to be overthrown because it is a tyranny* rests on the warrant *Tyrannies ought to be overthrown.* The colonists of Jefferson's time certainly found that warrant most agreeable. They found it to be a "self-evident truth," as did Jefferson, so altogether the argument was a very convincing one.

But not every audience would have been so agreeable. Students of Plato will remember that the subject of the dialogue called *Crito* is that the duties of a citizen include the obeying of laws—even those that are unjust or tyrannical. In his prize-winning novels *The Caine Mutiny*, Herman Wouk makes the same case for the much despised Captain Queeg, whose warship's crew mutinied against his crazed and tyrannical command. It was the duty of the *U.S.S. Caine*'s crew, according to the naval lawyer Barney Gruenwald, to support and assist the deranged captain, not to overthrow him.

The insight here is just this: Warrants can be challenged, even those as hallowed as the ones in the Declaration of Independence. Claiming that truths are self-evident doesn't make them so.

If, like Steinbeck, you can find a warrant that is agreeable to your audience, then you will not need to support it. Certainly Jefferson was well enough aware of the prevailing sentiments at the time of the American Revolution that he did not feel compelled to justify the notion that tyrannies ought to be overthrown. But you should be aware that warrants may be challenged.

Stephen Toulmin, too, was aware of this possibility, and he proposed two methods of bolstering or supporting warrants. One method is to supply what he calls *backing*. Backing is nothing more than the kind of support that you are obliged to provide for any claim that you might make: evidence in the way of factual data, statistics, or appeals to authority—arranged either inductively or deductively.

To spend much time and space trying to support a warrant, however, tends to undercut the appeal of that warrant. You are better off to use Steinbeck's strategy and try to find one that will not be rejected or refuted—at least by its intended audience. If the warrant appears weak as a general claim, it is better in the long run to qualify it in some way so that it can be stated succinctly without calling too much attention to its weakness. That is the second of Toulmin's strategies for support: *qualification.*

For instance, Steinbeck could have used that qualification strategy; he would not have sacrificed too much by claiming that *almost all* precious things should be preserved, nor would Jefferson have by admitting that *nearly all* tyrannies should be overthrown. Such qualifications allow you space to maneuver, without providing your opponents room to attack the warrant.

Another and the perhaps most frequent attack upon a warrant is the challenging of its authority. Recall how Jesse Jackson appealed to two authorities: a report by the Equal Employment Opportunity Commission and a column by William Raspberry. The underlying warrant involved here is that these are reliable sources; therefore we can accept their data. However, an audience is under no obligation to accept such sources as reliable.

When you appeal to a source, you are issuing (and depending on) an unspoken warrant: This source is reliable. In effect, the warrant is only as strong as the reputation of the authority. While it is perhaps strategically unwise to spend much time advertising the reputation of each authority whose information or opinions you introduce, it is always wise to remember that such authorities are subject to attack and may therefore need to have their reputations emphasized or even defended.

Another Effective Method of Refutation

There is still another often used method of refutation, but one that does not depend upon attacks against the support, the form of the argument, or the warrant. That is the *reduction to absurdity*. In this approach you pretend to agree with your opponent's claims, but your purpose in doing so quickly becomes apparent as you point out that acceptance of the opponent's claim will lead to some pretty unpleasant consequences, which, of course, your opponent has conveniently overlooked.

Suppose, for example, your opponent argues in favor of animal rights, pointing out that furriers cruelly kill wild animals and that using their pelts for coats is a senseless waste, since other types of clothing provide equal warmth. You might respond by agreeing with these claims but adding that leather shoes and belts should also be outlawed, and perhaps even the eating of meat.

Or suppose your opponent champions the war on drugs, claiming that a significant reduction in the drug traffic will make our city streets safe again for children. You could respond by agreeing that the reduction in drug traffic will be a very good thing indeed—especially for the drug lords, since drugs, like any other commodity, will enjoy a price increase when there is a shortage, and that the crime rate will inevitably rise as pushers and users scramble to get money to pay the higher prices.

In both these cases the opponent's argument has been reduced to an absurdity because of ill effects that had been overlooked.

So how does one prevent having one's argument reduced to an absurdity?

Both arguments we have cited above are victims of the material fallacy *dicto simpliciter*, the unqualified generalization. The killing of animals is wrong. Stopping the drug traffic will promote safety in our cities. These are unqualified generalizations. Remember that Toulmin's logic emphasized the need to qualify one's generalizations.

It should be clear now how the above generalizations might be qualified so as to avoid the reduction to absurdity. If you had to defend such claims, you might argue that killing animals *for their pelts* is wrong and that curtailing the drug traffic will *eventually* lead to safer cities. You would be prepared to concede that slaughtering animals for food, provided that it is done humanely, is not a violation of your principles. And you would also admit that there would be hard times ahead—both for racketeers, as well as many innocent victims—if the war on drugs is to be prosecuted to its ultimate conclusion; you would contend, however, that the price is worth it.

EXERCISES

1. Examine Armstrong's "Let's Keep Christmas Commercial." It is a classic example of refutation, attacking the common complaint that Christmas is overcommercialized. Armstrong appeals to at least two material fallacies in her refutation. Study the list of material fallacies in "A Short Guide to Material and Formal Fallacies" in the Appendix and then determine which she is using to refute her opposition's claim.

2. In her refutation Armstrong finds it necessary to attack a commonly held warrant: Religious things are sacrosanct and should not be cheapened. What strategy does she employ in attacking this warrant?

3. In "The Case Against Man," Asimov must attack the following warrant: Life is precious. How does he go about attacking such a universally held belief?

4. Beck uses a reduction to absurdity refutation in "Art and Politics: Self-Righteousness and Silly Yahooism." In what paragraph does it occur?

6

Putting It All Together

Up to this point we have been discussing the essentials of argumentation: claims and the strategies for supporting and refuting them. This is properly the *middle* of an argument, but it is ordinarily the part you will compose first. After you have framed the basics of your argument, then comes the time for you to work up an introduction for it and to figure out an appropriate conclusion. So let's begin where we ought to—in the middle.

Arranging the Claim and Support

In Chapter 3 we stated our preference for arrangement of claim and support. We believe that it's most advantageous for a writer to begin with a claim and then follow it up with supporting evidence, rather than doing it the other way around: beginning with the evidence and working up to the claim. The latter arrangement is more often suited to oral rather than written presentations.

You will begin your preparation of an argument with a brainstorming session, probing your memory, attempting to determine what you really think about the issue, and which side you will take. Sometimes you will know at the outset which side you will choose; in other cases that initial decision will be more difficult. Your conscience and memory alone may not be enough to help you make that decision. You may need to do some background reading—perhaps quite a bit.

But the time will come to assemble your evidence—the facts, statistics, examples, and comparisons that have guided you to the position you occupy on one side or the other of an issue. Now you must examine the evidence and arrange it in the best order possible.

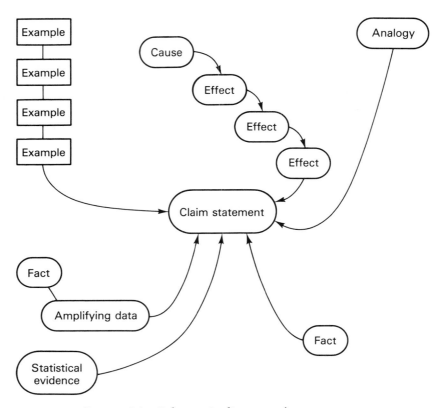

FIGURE 6.1 *Schematic diagram of an argument.*

One device that we have always found useful is the schematic diagram. It appeared in Chapter 3, but it's worth repeating here. Begin by simply stating your claim. Write it down in the middle of a blank page. There—you've begun. Now around that claim, start assembling your supporting evidence. Some pieces of evidence will need additional support; others, perhaps cause–effect sequences, will need to be linked together because they form a connected line of reasoning. Soon your jottings might begin to look something like Figure 6.1.

The First Draft

Once you have assembled the supporting evidence for your claim, you are ready to begin a first draft. Don't bother with an elaborate introduction; just start by stating your claim. Then work your way around your diagram, turning your cryptic jottings into sentences. If you can't think of a good transition between one of your pieces of support and another, forget about it for the time being and press on. A different order may suggest itself later on. Now you are writing, and you need to stick with the central task of translating your initial impressions into sentences.

At this stage fascinating and surprising things start to happen. Often you won't know exactly where you stand with regard to an issue until you are actually engaged in the process of writing down the supporting data. Some evidence you may reject, and other evidence may occur to you as you write. *Just becoming engaged in the writing process is an important method of discovery* every bit as important as the initial step of schematically arranging what you thought you knew. That's why it's important to press on to the completion of that initial effort. You needn't bother with a conclusion, or with matters of tone or credibility. All that can come later—after you've gotten the basic pieces down on paper.

Subsequent Drafts

If you double- or triple-spaced your first draft and left generous margins, you are now ready to begin the process of coaxing your initial ideas into something approximating a final form. The whole procedure may require several drafts, each one addressing a special concern or group of concerns.

Certainly, one thing you'll want to analyze in that first draft is the *order* of presentation. Sometimes the lack of a suitable transition between two key parts (that is, if one did not occur to you right away) is really a clue or suggestion that a better order might be found.

As you ponder the order of your evidence, drawing arrows from one paragraph to an earlier or later one, or cutting and pasting, or moving blocks of writing electronically on a word processor, you'll be tackling the business of transitions as well. Phrases such as *besides that* or *more importantly,* and even enumeration devices such as *first, next,* and *last* will come to mind. You'll take advantage of those wide margins and spaces between the lines to insert transitions, along with amplifying and clarifying information. Sometimes whole paragraphs will grow from these interlinear insertions.

You may, of course, discover during this process that you will need to drop some support that has proved to be less convincing than you judged it to be when you started. Or you may need to search for something to fill a gap that has revealed itself. Often the order of presentation will be dictated by matters of warrants—just what will the attitude of your audience be toward your claim, as well as toward the evidence? You may need to supply *backing* for warrants that your audience may not initially favor. Alternatively, you may wish to restructure your approach to take advantage of an inclination or leaning that you have perceived on the part of your audience. Such things happen as you work with the supporting data, crafting it into its best form.

Once your draft has arrived at that *best form* stage, where all the supporting data has been included and you are reasonably certain that it appears in the most appropriate order, you are ready to attend to beginnings and endings (which we deal with in the final part of this chapter), and you'll need to check for grammatical and mechanical correctness. Such concerns are usually relegated to the last draft, although as you become a more practiced writer, you may attend to such matters almost automatically, along with more important concerns. The crucial point about grammar and mechanics is just this: Do not allow concern for these matters to interfere with the major ones, such as providing adequate support in an effective arrangement.

Using Sources

As we mentioned earlier, the brainstorming session that must precede the composition of any argument must, more often than not, include a good deal of reading. As you read, you will take notes, jotting down the material that you find. Sometimes you will find it useful to copy down brief passages word for word, particularly if the information contained in the passage is especially appropriate or well phrased. But more frequently you will find it useful to summarize what you read. Such summaries will prove to be more useful to you than will directly quoted passages for several good reasons:

1. Summarizing information that you read helps you to understand the material better, forcing you to incorporate the information into your own fund of knowledge.

2. It allows you to impose your own order on the information you are borrowing, adjusting it slightly to serve *your* purpose rather than the purpose of the original author.

3. It allows you to compress a great deal of the original source's information into a brief space, appropriately subordinated to your needs.

We have found that the best place to copy these summaries and briefly quoted passages is on note cards. In addition to the summarized or quoted material, each note card should include the source of the information, that is, the author's name and the work's title, together with the page number on which the borrowed information appeared.

Once you have this information recorded, you will find that it serves much the same purpose as the schematic diagram. You can organize your note cards into related groups that will begin to suggest an order of presentation. Such a practice may not ever completely replace the need for a schematic or outline, but you can derive a great many benefits from shuffling and reorganizing your note cards. They are an invaluable tool in organizing an initial draft. They also are a certain and efficient way to handle the problem of citing your sources.

Citing Sources

If you are a good note taker, you will be careful not to include too much information on a single card. In that way you will end up with a great many bits and pieces of information that you can arrange in a variety of ways. To do otherwise, copying down long passages of directly quoted material or writing overly long summaries of borrowed argument or supporting data, will simply impose too much of the original authors' organization and phrasing on your own presentation, vastly limiting the alternatives that are open to you in stating your case your way.

One reason that most note takers prefer small note cards (either 3 by 5 or 4 by 6 inches) is that the very size limits the amount of material it is possible to include on a single card. If you find yourself needing to use more than one card to complete a quotation or a paraphrase, that is a fairly good sign that the information should be cut or further condensed—or divided into two independent pieces of information, capable of being used in separate locations.

Furthermore, each note card represents a separate borrowed piece of information, each of which must be acknowledged by a *citation*. A citation is simply a prescribed method of indicating that the material has been borrowed. It is a matter both of accuracy—showing the source of your information—and of scholarly honesty—avoiding the charge of *plagiarism*, the academic crime of presenting the ideas of others as though they were your own, just as you wouldn't present something that you had bought as if it were a personally made gift for a friend or relative. Furthermore, as a matter of simple courtesy, you should tell your readers where you found the information that you are using, so that if they want to do some research on the same subject themselves, they can follow your lead.

There are several prescribed methods for citing borrowed information. The one that we use here was developed by the Modern Language Association, an organization of college English and foreign language teachers. It is the prescribed method for citing sources in articles appearing in that association's journal, *PMLA: Publications of the Modern Language Association.* Other journals and periodicals that treat literary topics also use the MLA method of citation. Other organizations specify slightly different citation practices: the American Psychological Association, the Linguistic Society of America, the American Medical Association, and so on. In the course of a college career you may be obliged to use several citation methods. Regardless of their differences in detail, all methods have two things in common:

1. Each provides for a method of citing borrowed information within the text of an article.
2. Each provides a method of recording, at the end of the essay, article, or report, the list of sources from which material was borrowed.

Using the MLA method of citation, we will describe each of these parts of the citation procedure.

CITING SOURCES IN THE TEXT

As we mentioned earlier, borrowed information may take two forms: directly quoted material or summarized material. We will look first at direct quotations.

Directly Quoted Material. Quotations that run less than five lines may be included within a paragraph of the text. Such quotations are almost always introduced by some lead-in like the following: *John Brown recently observed* or *William Green, writing for the local newspaper, stated the case in this way.* The quotations then follow these lead-ins and, of course, are enclosed in quotation marks and begin with a capital letter.

Sometimes it is preferable to tailor or abbreviate the quotation somewhat so that it fits the syntax of the lead-in. You can often save considerable space by doing so. In this case the quotation may not begin with a capital letter (if the first part of it has been deleted). Other omissions usually should be marked by ellipsis dots (three spaced periods . . .); insertions or additions should be placed in brackets.

Long quotations (five lines or more) are indented ten spaces from the left margin and double-spaced. Such quotations must also be introduced by an appropriate lead-in, but they should not be indicated by quotation marks.

Each of these three types of quoted borrowings must be followed by a page number (or numbers) in parentheses, indicating the page(s) on which the borrowed material occurred in its original location. Here are some illustrations of the three techniques. The original source for the quoted material is Peter Drucker's "What Employees Need Most," p. 153.

Short Quotation

According to Peter Drucker, "Ours has become a society of employees" (153).

Long Quotation

Peter Drucker has observed that our world is changing:

Ours has become a society of employees. A hundred years or so ago only one out of every five Americans was employed, i.e., worked for somebody else. Today only one out of every five is not employed but working for himself (153).

Quotation, abbreviated to fit the syntax of the lead-in

Peter Drucker notes that we are now "a society of employees . . . [where] only one out of every five . . . work[s] for himself" (153).

(Note here how the ellipsis marks serve to show where deletions from the original have occurred. The information enclosed in brackets [ ] indicates minor adjustments that have been made to the original.)

If the lead-in to the quotation does not include the author's name, then the name should precede the page number that appears at the quotation's end, as in this example:

One observer has noted, "Ours has become a society of employees" (Drucker, 153).

CITING SUMMARIZED INFORMATION

Summaries of borrowed material are more useful and thus more frequently used than directly quoted borrowings. Here are two examples of ways that the above passage from Drucker might have been summarized and cited:

> Drucker claims that we are increasingly becoming a nation of employees, where only about twenty percent of the people work for themselves (153).

> Today we have become a nation of employees, where, according to one prominent authority, only twenty percent of the people work for themselves (Drucker 153).

(Note that even in summarized material lead-ins are expected, and page citations are a must.)

Occasionally, you may be directed to "suppress documentation." This is an expression used by the editors of newspapers and some magazines. It means to avoid the use of parenthetical page citations, as well as the usual listing at the end of the article of the sources from which you have borrowed. Such is the case in a number of articles that appear in this book; look, for instance, at William Buckley's "Let's Return to Regulation of Airlines," p. 000, in which both quotations and summaries occur without parenthetical page citations. If you are directed to suppress documentation, then it is all the more important that you employ your tags or lead-ins effectively to indicate the sources of your borrowings—as Buckley did. You might even go so far as to elaborate the tag this way:

> As early as 1952, Peter Drucker, writing for *Fortune*, noted that we have turned into "a society of employees."

Such a tactic incorporates into the lead-in a great many of the facts usually documented in the list of works cited at the end of the article.

It is to this listing of works cited that we now turn our attention.

THE LISTING OF WORKS CITED

The listing of works cited in an article, also called "bibliographical entries," appears at the end of a documented article under the heading "Works Cited." There should be one entry for each separate work from which you have borrowed information, and these entries are arranged *alphabetically* according to the last names of their authors. (If the name of the author is not known or is not included with the article, the article is entered in the alphabetical listing according to the first major word in its title.)

Bibliographical entries usually contain the following information:

1. For books: author's name (last name first), title (italicized or underscored), place of publication, publisher, and date of publication.
2. For magazine articles: author's name (last name first), title (in quotation marks), name of magazine (italicized), volume number, date of issue, and the article's inclusive page numbers.
3. For newspaper articles: author's name, if available (last name first), title (in quotation marks), name of the newspaper (italicized), date of issue, and inclusive page numbers.

Here are some typical entries that illustrate these three most frequently occurring types:

Books

WOUK, HERMAN. *Inside Outside.* Boston: Little, Brown, 1985.

The last name comes first so that alphabetical listing may be by last name. The title is italicized (underscored in typescript). The place of publication is separated by a colon from the publishing house, and the date of publication follows a comma. All of this information can be located on the title page of the book. (The date usually appears on the reverse of the title page.)

FINEGAN, EDWARD, and NIKO BISNIER. *Language: Its Structure and Use.* San Diego: Harcourt, 1989.

Here there are two authors. Notice that only the name of the first one appears last name first. The subtitle, *Its Structure and Use,* is separated from the major title, *Language,* by a colon. Only the first place of publication listed on the title page is used in the entry, together with a shortened version of the publishing house, Harcourt Brace Jovanovich, Publishers. The second line is indented five spaces so that the authors' names, used for placing the citations in alphabetical order, can be more easily scanned when a reader is seeking to locate particular citations.

Magazines

MAILER, NORMAN. "Jackie, the Prisoner of Celebrity." *Esquire* December 1983: 185–9.

MOONEY, CAROLYN J. "Higher-Education Conferees Applaud Carnegie Plan to Broaden the Definition of Faculty Scholarship." *The Chronicle of Higher Education* 11 April 1990: A1, A16.

SMITH, MARGUERITE T. "Today's Smartest Ways to Invest for Income." *Money* April 1990: 116–26.

The title of the article is enclosed in quotation marks; the name of the magazine is italicized. The inclusive page numbers follow the colon after the date.

Scholarly Journals

1. Journals with continuous pagination

STOTSKY, SANDRA. "On Learning to Write About Ideas." *College Composition and Communication* 37 (1986): 276–93.

For this kind of article it is important to notice whether the pagination of the issue you are holding begins with page 1 or with some higher number. This one actually begins at page 275. Page 1 occurred at the beginning of Volume 37, two issues earlier. Because the pagination continues throughout the volume, which contains several separate issues, it is not necessary to mention such things as issue number (this is issue number 3) or the month in which this issue appeared (October).

2. Journals that begin each issue with page 1

DEVENY, THOMAS. "Poets and Patrons: Literary Adulation in the Epithalamium of the Spanish Golden Age." *South Atlantic Review* 53.4 (1988): 21–37.

Although this is the fourth issue number in Volume 53, each issue begins with page 1; therefore, the issue number must appear with the volume number in the entry.

Newspapers

FAISON, SETH. "Trade Expert Urges China to Scrap Coastal Strategy." *South China Morning Post* 21 June 1988: 1, 9.

FREEDMAN, ALIX M., and MICHAEL J. McCARTHY. "New Smoke from RJR under Fire." *The Wall Street Journal* 20 Feb. 1990: B1, B9.

We will end this list of example entries here with this warning: We have not attempted to provide you with an exhaustive list of every possible entry. In your search for source materials you will surely encounter books, magazines, and newspapers that will require you to include other types of documentation that we have not illustrated here: names of editors, translators, edition numbers, volume numbers, and the like. We make no apologies for these omissions; rather we encourage you to consult a standard reference grammar or handbook for a more exhaustive list of illustrated entries. You should own such a book, just as you should own a hardbound dictionary; they are a writer's basic tools.

We do not apologize either for limiting our discussion to the MLA style of documentation. Other formats exist, and it will be your task to become familiar with the ones that are required of you. What we have sought to provide you with here is a general idea of the following:

1. the sorts of borrowed information that needs to be cited
2. the use of tags or lead-ins and parenthetical notes for
   a. directly quoted material
   b. summarized borrowings
3. the bibliographical entries in lists of works cited

Furthermore, we realize that one of the reasons for using a book such as this is to save a certain amount of trouble that is involved in library research, locating materials to consult during your brainstorming process. We have provided you with a generous number of readings ranging over many controversial issues, articles that you may read and ponder to sharpen your opinions or to provide you with opinions where you held no deep prior convictions. Furthermore, after the discussion questions which follow each cluster of related essays in the "Varying Voices" readings section, we have provided a short list of additional essays on the same general topic, with their bibliographic information in MLA form.

In the spirit of helping you to save the time and effort of doing library research while you concentrate on the more important skills involved in organizing and executing an argumentative essay, we thus have provided you with enough source materials to support a great many claims that you might wish to make.

That concludes our treatment of how you should construct the middle portion of your arguments. Now let us examine how to make good beginnings and good conclusions.

Background

How many times have you glanced at the "Letters to the Editor" section of your local newspaper's editorial page and seen something like this:

> I don't know where Bill Champion thinks he will get the money to support this latest bit of idiocy, but if he has any intention of raising taxes, then he can start right now hunting for another job next year, because those of us who know better are going to see that he won't misuse any more of our hard-earned money.

Crank letters like this one are written every day by people who are convinced that everyone in the world shares their innermost concerns. They do not, therefore, bother to inform their readers about Bill Champion's identity or exactly what his "latest bit of idiocy" might be. As the letter unfolds, we can begin to deduce that Champion must be a local politician and that the "idiocy" must involve some expenditure of taxpayers' money. Beyond that, the message is limited to Bill Champion (he might understand) and the crank's closest friends—and perhaps not even to them.

To avoid the label of "crank," everyone who argues a point owes the audience a suitable *background.* That is, the audience must be provided with sufficient information, so that they will be able to understand fully the claim that is being made, as well as the support for it. In this case, we, the audience, deserve to know just what Bill Champion's claim of policy is and how he intends to support it. We must also be reminded who Champion is, just in case we are not as informed on local current events as the letter writer. Then, and only then, do we need to learn the crank's reasons for believing the plan to be unworthy of our support.

Considerations like the ones we have just mentioned are what background is all about, and without background information most arguments are doomed, because no audience, however well informed, is likely to be warmly receptive to an argument that begins abruptly with the claim.

Even Ernest Hollings, who begins his argument with his claim, "We need a military draft," immediately retreats, first to define what he means by a draft, more specifically an equitable draft. He then spends three paragraphs sharing some "demographic indicators" with the audience, these being facts that the audience is not likely to know about the shrinking supply of military-aged males. Only *after* providing this background information for assimilation by the reader does Hollings go on to support his claim by emphasizing the huge expenses associated with our current alternative to the draft—our volunteer army.

Similarly, Loren Eiseley begins by sharing a friend's letter, which contained a note of concern over the supposed survival of the tough-minded. This approach allows Eiseley to introduce references to the evolutionists Darwin and Wallace and to reassure the audience that the popular notions of survival of the fittest associated with evolution are poorly understood. Having introduced us to the problem, Eiseley is ready to resolve it.

A good rule of thumb to use in preparing background for your argument is simply to ask yourself, "What information would a reasonably intelligent person need to know in order to understand my claim?" You are certainly not obliged to direct your argument to the most foolish or ignorant members of your audience, but you are better off veering in that direction than in supposing that your audience knows as much as you do about the subject.

Gaining Attention

In addition to providing background information, the introduction to an argument should get its readers' attention. It's always a good idea to remember that in most writing situations your audience is under no obligation to read your argument. You are much more likely to succeed if you can provide a "hook" or "grabber" that will capture the readers' interest, keeping them turning the pages until you've had your say.

Here are a number of attention getters that usually work:

1. Tell a story. (Remember how effective Jackson's story about the race proved to be.)
2. Ask a question. (Should America revive the military draft?)
3. Pose a paradox. (Mankind has survived through tenderness, not toughness.)
4. Make a startling statement. (As an ex-prisoner of war, it hurts me to see our country's flag burned, but I part company with those who want to punish flag burners.)
5. Make lists. (That's what we're doing here.)
6. Use humor. (I can think of only two things that women do better than men: having babies is one; driving is the other.)

Telling a story is a good strategy because all of us are susceptible to stories: we simply like them. Of course, the story should not be so long and detailed that it detracts from the purpose it serves. Jackson's story about the unequal foot race and Eiseley's reference to his friend's concern over his daughter's schooling are about the right length to serve as a hook without getting in the way of the argument. Additionally, each serves in a most effective way to provide background information.

The question, the paradox, and the startling statement are all part of the same strategy: They get your reader to thinking about the claim you are prepared to support. If the reader is uncertain about the answer to the question or perplexed by the paradox or the unexpected statement, then your hook has served its purpose; you have the reader's attention.

Using a list is another especially effective attention getter. Besides providing the reader with a highly organized capsule of the forthcoming argument, it is *visually* effective. The reader's eye is drawn to the list because it is different from other things on the printed page—as are illustrations, charts, or graphs. Once the eye is attracted, the mind is likely to follow, and the audience is "hooked" into reading further.

Finally, humor is useful as a hook for the same reason that the story is: Most of us enjoy a good chuckle. If the humor is directed toward or associated with the claim you are about to make and support, so much the better. All of us have listened to too many after-dinner speakers who begin their addresses by telling the latest joke they have heard, without much regard to how appropriate it is to the subject matter of their speech. While such jokes fail as "hooks" or attention grabbers, they do serve another purpose, and that is why they are an expected part of the after-dinner speech: they help to make the audience more at ease and favorably inclined toward the speaker. They are a first step toward *gaining credibility*, which you have already seen lends *ethos*, or ethical appeal, to your argument.

Conclusions

All good things must end, and so must the arguments that you construct. While there is something to be said for shutting up when you have had your say, it is not good to conclude too abruptly. Conclusions are, as a rule, the place for two sorts of things: summaries and appeals, either to ethics or emotions.

A summary is an excellent way to tie up the scattered ends of an argument, reminding the audience briefly of the ground that has been covered—the claim or claims and their pieces of support. Creating summaries is something that you should be fairly good at by now, having summarized so many arguments—or parts of them—to support your own. It should be a pleasant change to begin a conclusion by summarizing your *own* argument. That, you will recall, is precisely what Loren Eiseley did in his concluding paragraph of "Toughness or Tenderness":

> Man's first normal experience of life involves maternal and paternal care and affection. It continues over the years of childhood. Thus the creature who strives at times to deny the love within himself, to reject the responsibilities to which he owes his own existence, who grows vocal about "tough-mindedness" and "the struggle for existence," is striving to reject his own human heritage. For without the mysteriously increased growth rate of the brain and the correlated willingness of fallible, loving adults to spend years in nursing the helpless offspring they have produced, man would long since have vanished from the earth.

It is all there: the repeated claim that tenderness outweighs toughness because of the extended human childhood needed for increased brainpower, with the resulting need for paternal and maternal care and affection. Eiseley manages to restate his argument with great economy, and that too is important. Like the background statement, the summary should not be so long that it's tedious. Besides, you may wish to follow the summary with an ethical or emotional appeal.

Cicero, the famous Roman orator, insisted that the concluding portion of a speech should be reserved for those kinds of appeal that would earn the speaker the sympathy of the audience. We have already touched upon such appeals—ethical and emotional—as effective means of gaining support for your claims. You may choose to use them in the main body of your argument, or, like Cicero, you may decide to save them for your conclusion.

Certainly Ernest Hollings makes an ethical appeal when he concludes his plea for a draft with these words: "It seems most of us seek painless ways to meet our obligations. Unfortunately, there is no painless way that we can provide for the defense of freedom." It is an ethical appeal because it reminds us of our duties as citizens, our obligation to work for and protect the common good, the *ethos* of our civilization.

If that reminder to our consciences touches our hearts as well, so much the better. Ethics and emotions—*ethos* and *pathos*—are for most of us inextricably entwined; thus it would be quite difficult for us to decide whether Jefferson's concluding appeal in the Declaration of Independence is ethical or emotional: "And for the support of this Declaration, with a firm reliance on the protection of Divine Providence, we mutually pledge to each other our lives, our fortunes and our sacred Honor."

Even Phyllis McGinley's amusing treatment of men and women drivers manages to strike an emotional chord in its conclusion, where she takes a bittersweet glance into the future and imagines an afterlife adventure in which her husband's persistent bad driving habits underscore her claim one last time.

That's about all the advice we have to give you: State your claims, organize your support, cite your sources, and study your audience, measuring the logical, ethical, and emotional appeal your case will produce. You're now prepared to construct some solid arguments. We hope you convince a lot of people.

PART TWO

Reading and Analyzing Arguments

Reading arguments is not completely new to you, of course. Probably, though, you have listened to and otherwise participated in spoken arguments much more often, especially if you like to watch televised talk shows, such as those hosted by Oprah Winfrey and Phil Donahue, or court room dramas, such as *People's Court*. In fact, because so many persuasive situations involve speaking and listening, it might be ideal if we could provide a demonstration videotape, so that we could also help you learn how to listen to and analyze spoken arguments in an immediate, fairly realistic way.

However, we must necessarily limit ourselves to providing samples of written arguments (a few originally presented as speeches), and to putting emphasis on reading and analyzing those written arguments. Most of these samples will be complete essays, although sometimes we will provide shorter pieces, such as single paragraphs or excerpted groups of paragraphs from longer arguments. It should be obvious, by the way, that as you learn to read and analyze written arguments, and to write and revise your own arguments, you will become more proficient in listening carefully and analytically to spoken arguments, as well as in responding to them through spoken or written words.

As for the actual tasks of reading and analyzing written arguments, you know already that we all must make special efforts to understand anything of much complexity, whether it is a concrete object (such as a mechanism or a living organism) or an abstraction (such as a religious belief or a psychological condition—or a written argument). Understanding arguments and the arguing process, whose complexity has already been examined earlier in this book, is therefore generally not a simple or an easy task; doing so will demand mental alertness and persistent effort on your part. Even more of that alertness and effort will be required when you are putting your own arguments in written or spoken form.

Nevertheless, your efforts to understand argumentation, as audience, critic, and creator, will provide significant, even crucial, rewards both to you and to others. Ignoring, standing idly by, or turning your back on human challenges, especially moral ones, can put you in undesirable circumstances, such as those described by the German Lutheran pastor, Martin Niemoeller. Speaking of the Holocaust perpetrated by the Nazis under Adolf Hitler's leadership before and during World War II, Pastor Niemoeller recalled, "They came first for the Communists, and I didn't speak up because I wasn't a Communist. Then they came for the Jews, and I didn't speak up because I wasn't a Jew. Then they came for the Catholics, and I didn't speak up because I was a Protestant. Then they came for me, and by that time there was no one left to speak up." As a result of Pastor Niemoeller's reluctance to get involved in what always seemed to be other people's problems, he was indirectly responsible for the suffering and death of some of those other people, spent four years himself in the Dachau concentration camp, and was indeed fortunate to survive when millions of others perished or were executed. Although none of us expect a return to that hellish time, clearly the human stakes of declining to be involved in controversy, or of being ineffective even when actively involved, can become too high before we realize it.

There are two sorts of suggestions we want to make that will help you to read and to analyze arguments most effectively. While they really work together and often overlap, for instructional purposes you are likely to understand and apply them better if we discuss the two separately. The first sort deal with the physical conditions under which you read any argument, and the second sort focus on mental approaches that will improve your reading.

Physical Aids to Reading Arguments

Some of the suggestions concerning physical aids to reading arguments most effectively are commonsense ones; if you are already successfully reading serious pieces of writing, you are likely already applying some or all of them. But for the benefit of those who are struggling to read difficult selections, and therefore probably aren't using these aids, we are going to review them. We'll start with the most obvious suggestions and move to more subtle or uncommon ones.

1. Get rid of or away from all distractions as much as possible. This suggestion perhaps needs little or no comment, but clearly if you cannot focus on your reading because of distracting sounds, lights, views, smells, living creatures (pets, family members, roommates, friends, and the like), and other interruptions, you will have trouble concentrating on—and thus comprehending—the complex features of many arguments. The real difficulty may be, of course, "getting away from" or "rid of" a particular distraction. If the distraction must remain or if you must stay near it, try to at least reduce the degree of distraction. This may mean working out a schedule of quiet or study times with others who live near you, buying earplugs or even a telephone answering machine, or making various other adjustments. In fact, you may have to use the arguing skills you presently have in order to set up the conditions under which you can best improve those skills.

2. Don't get too comfortable. This is another obvious suggestion. But if you are too relaxed, perhaps lying down on a bed or lounging in an overstuffed chair, the mental effort of following an argument may be overwhelmed and you'll find yourself daydreaming or even asleep, really dreaming. You will be better off at a desk, in a chair that makes you sit up, with good light on what you are reading, and in a room that is cool rather than warm.

3. Read with a pencil or pen in your hand. The only exception to this suggestion is if you are reading an argument in materials that are not your own, such as books or periodicals belonging to a library or another person. Otherwise, you should be actively marking the text, especially in the margins, to indicate key features of the argument, sections that you find confusing or questionable, words that you do not know or understand. It is especially effective to write comments and questions as if you are having a dialogue with the author, for then you are truly engaged or involved with the argument and its subject.

A related hint that some readers find helpful is to let the writing instrument (or your finger) move like a pointer along the line in front of your eyes, leading them through the text; this will tend to keep your attention focused on your reading better, which will improve the efficiency, and therefore the overall speed, with which you complete a piece of reading. You may also find that if you move the pointer at a pace that is a little faster than your normal reading rate, the result will not only be more speed but even better concentration.

4. Have a full-sized dictionary within reach. Dictionaries are the storehouses for meanings of words, of course, and words are the building blocks of all arguments (all writing, for that matter); you must understand the words a writer uses if you are to understand her or his message. Don't stop to look up words as long as you believe you are getting the gist of the writing. However, you will likely find it useful to make a special marginal mark beside troublesome words in your reading, and then go through later and look up the meanings for any words that are still unclear. Neglecting to perform this task may cause you to misunderstand part or all of an argument.

A related hint: Make a single tick mark in your dictionary beside any word you look up; when you open the dictionary to a word that already has two such marks, go ahead and memorize its meaning, for the word clearly is appearing in your reading often enough that you should learn its meaning for efficiency's and understanding's sake.

Mental Aids to Reading Arguments

Clearly the preceding physical suggestions numbered 3 and 4 also have a mental aspect, thereby furnishing a sort of transition to the following suggestions for improving your mental approach to the reading of argumentative samples of writing. As you consider these suggestions, and as you begin to apply them, you may find it helpful to notice how the suggestions influence you to consider more carefully a reading selection's *content* (what it says), as well as its *form* (how it presents its content).

1. Get an overview of the selection *before* you begin reading it. Do this by considering the piece's title (if it has one), since the titles of many works are attempts to put in capsule form the main subject and thesis. For instance, such titles as "In Defense of Voluntary Euthanasia," "Death Penalty's False Promise: An Eye for an Eye," and "The Dangers of Disarming" all not only reveal their basic subjects but even indicate their authors' attitudes toward those subjects; thoughtfully considering such titles, then, can make your job as a reader easier from the start. (All titles are not so helpful, of course; consider what the subjects might be for these, all used for argumentative essays: "Facing Reality," "In the American Grain," and "Sharing the Land and the Legacy.")

Also consider any information provided about the author or authors, or any information that you already have. For instance, if you read newspaper editorial pages regularly, you soon will come to recognize the normal political stance of most syndicated columnists;

thus you will expect Marianne Means to take a liberal position on such questions as abortion and arms control, while both George Will and William F. Buckley typically will take conservative positions. Furthermore, consider the author's real or probable expertise concerning the subject she or he is discussing; for instance, a Nobel prize-winning physicist may be too far out of his realm of knowledge in discussing cures for AIDS, and a great heart surgeon may have little worthwhile to add to a debate on nuclear arms control. Of course, there is a natural human tendency to assume that a person with notable skill or expertise in one realm of activity should be accepted as a knowledgeable authority in another realm; hence, we frequently see media personalities, such as actresses, pop singers, and sports stars, in advertisements where they promote all sorts of consumer products, as if they were experts on fashion, nutrition, or transportation. You will recall, though, that in an argument this is the fallacy of *transfer*.

After considering the title and any author background, look for summaries of the work in such places as the table of contents (for some periodicals and collections of essays), the introduction (for both books and essays), the dust-jacket covers and flaps (for books). If you are reading a book, look at the table of contents and chapter headings in particular, and if reading an essay, flip through it, paying attention to any subheadings or section titles. All of the foregoing can give you a good sense of what you are likely to find in the work itself, especially with regard to its subject, the author's stance on that subject, and the discussion's organization.

2. Pay particular attention to the introductory paragraph or paragraphs of the work, especially when reading essays or single chapters; if the work is a book, give its preface full attention. Do so because it is in these places that authors often explain the purpose and scope of an essay, a chapter, or a book in brief, clear language, no matter how long and complex the work itself may be. Using such clues, try to figure out the author's thesis or main point. It's also a good idea at this time to try writing that thesis down in your own words, which leads to the next suggestion.

3. As you read an argument, pause occasionally to make a concrete record of your reading and understanding of the previous portion. Here you are trying to understand the work better by doing something with it, going beyond merely reading the words. The textual and marginal notes you make (see Physical Suggestion 3) are tied to this suggestion, of course. In particular you may find it useful to mark some or even all transitional words (such as *because, also, but, therefore*) and transitional phrases (such as *on the one hand, not*

only, in conclusion), since these typically are clear signals of steps or phases of the argument. You may also find it useful to number the key parts of the argument in the margins, perhaps using traditional outlining notation (I, IA, IB, II, III, IIIA, IIIB, and so on) as a concrete aid to understanding the argument's structure.

Beyond those notes you will find that creating some written record of your reading on a separate sheet of paper, perhaps also in outline form, will be of great value in comprehending the argument more fully, in being able to analyze its strengths and weaknesses, and in later recalling the basic features of the argument without going to the time and trouble of rereading it.

Your outline may be formal, with the customary groupings using Roman numerals, capital letters, Arabic numerals, and the like, or it may be informal, just a series of phrases and key words, perhaps clustered or webbed in patterns that will help you recall the main points and their means of support. The actual note-taking format is less important than the fact that you have made a permanent record of your reading and your understanding of that particular argument.

4. Stay mentally alert and inquisitive as you read an argument by constantly recalling the kinds of questions journalists ask: *Who? What? When? Where? How? Why?* To read, understand, and analyze arguments you cannot be passive, as we all generally are when we watch television and even as we do much of our reading, especially that of a recreational sort (newspaper sports pages, celebrity gossip columns and magazines, popular novels). Rather, you must have an inquiring mind, of the active, probing sort that a good investigative reporter or a detective needs for success at her or his work. Now let's examine in some detail the use of those six one-word questions (investigators call them "basic interrogatives") that you should keep asking mentally as you read; you need to understand the sorts of information about content and about form that you are likely to gain by asking these six questions.

When you ask "Who?", you are going to be seeking two kinds of information. The first is about the author (as discussed earlier in Mental Suggestion 1): his or her expertise concerning the subject of the argument, biases that she or he holds, and the like. You must also consider the basic audience for whom the argument was originally intended. As you should already realize, writers (and speakers) adapt their language, their styles, their tones, and their supporting examples according to their intended or target audiences. Certainly you would adjust all of these in a dramatically contrasting fashion if you were going to speak on the dangers of drugs to two quite different groups, perhaps today to a first grade class at a nearby elementary school, and tomorrow to a campus group to which you belong. Sometimes the adjustments for a particular audience will be much more subtle, of course, but in any case you should be especially alert for those audience adjustments, since they affect so many aspects of the presentation of the argument.

When you ask "What?", you are focusing on the subject of the argument, figuratively putting it under a strong light for close scrutiny, almost as if you were some sort of research scientist. You want to be aware of every aspect of that subject; here is where your analytical powers really come into play, and where you depend on close, careful reading and other useful resources for better understanding, such as the dictionary. You are trying to ensure that you comprehend as fully as possible both the topic being presented and the author's attitude toward that topic.

When you go on to ask "When?" and "Where?", you will again be considering aspects of audience, for here you want to know the time and place in which this argument was first presented. An argument made in favor of universal military service (the "draft") for young American males changes its basic character when it is made in 1990 rather than in 1862 or 1941 or 1967, and it also changes when its principal audience is intended to be members of the U.S. Congress, or the readers of the *New York Times*, of *Business Week*, or of *Rolling Stone*. Ignoring such changes—or even their possibility—puts you at a disadvantage as a reader.

The foregoing questions relate mainly to the content of the piece of writing. But you must also consider its form. When you ask "How?", you are posing an analytical question about the organization and other rhetorical and logical devices of the argument itself. This is probably the most important question of these six as far as improving your own ability to *write* arguments is concerned, for by asking it you will be trying to determine how the author constructed (in every sense of that word) her or his argument. You will be trying to spot the key elements of success and failure in this piece of writing, hoping to adapt the good and avoid the bad as you craft your own arguments.

As you analyze each argument, you are disassembling it, separating it into its components, just as you might do with any mechanism, such as a bicycle or an automobile. Your intent is to figure out how the argument was put together, or assembled, so that through that analysis you can understand not only how it works as a unified piece of writing, but also how it creates its rhetorical effects, for good or ill, on its audience. Accordingly you will look at the argument's organization, which is analogous to the frame of a bike or a car, and its sentences, which move the argument forward, propelling it just as drive trains and wheels and engines and pedals and chains move other mechanisms. You will even look closely at such smaller parts as transitional devices and even individual words; these are in some ways analogous to a vehicle's paint and chrome trim, which may affect our positive or negative opinion of a vehicle that moves flawlessly.

On the other hand, and just like a car or a bike, if something is faulty or out of tune or badly adjusted, the mechanism will falter or perhaps not even move at all, no matter how flashy or impressive it looks. Thus you will need to determine what argumentative strategies are being used in the reading selection, and whether or not they are being used correctly. You will, for instance, want to determine what claims the writer is making, and how those claims are supported. Which is the writer using, induction or deduction?

As you gain experience in doing this sort of disassembly, learning to spot more quickly any flaws anywhere, you will become not just a better reader but also a better writer. For when you go to create or assemble your own argumentative mechanisms, you will have a much better sense of which parts fit where and how they should be adjusted to run most smoothly. Instead of analysis, you will then be performing even more complicated acts. You will be synthesizing content and form, joining your ideas and their supporting facts with the other pieces of writing (words, phrases, sentences, grammar, punctuation, organization, argumentative techniques, and the like), checking their fit and adjustment (revising and rewriting), performing road tests (reading the argument aloud or to others, or having them read it and react), before you take the argument on a trip to meet the public, which may consist of your instructor, a supervisor, a committee, or some other audience—perhaps thousands of miles away.

When you move on, and reach the last of the investigator's questions, you will ask "Why?" Here you are again considering the author, especially his or her purpose in writing this particular argument. What personal stake might she or he have in this subject? Was she or he paid by some special interest group for writing this argument? Why did he or she choose to publish it in this particular periodical, when it clearly might have appeared elsewhere?

You will also want to consider the argument's warrant, and you must try to determine the sorts of appeals being used: ethical, emotional, or logical. Then you must ask why you or any member of the piece's reading audience should accept the writer's argument. For instance, is there some universal warrant present, to which the writer is appealing? Is the strength of that warrant determined by its logical appeal, or by ethical or emotional considerations?

The answers to questions such as these will help you determine any biases the author may have, and thus will help you decide whether to accept part, all, or none of the writer's argument. You must not become too suspicious of motives, of course, or you will likely lapse into a cynicism that will destroy your ability to trust any other human beings. On the other hand, you certainly cannot read arguments analytically by accepting them at their face value, with your rose-colored glasses in place; then you and your innocence will get steamrolled by the world's realists and hypocrites, who often end up in positions of power and leadership.

Practicing the Suggestions for Reading Arguments

Now the time has come to practice the four physical and four mental suggestions for reading and analyzing arguments. If you haven't already done so, try right now to make all of the physical adjustments that we suggested: get rid of distractions, get somewhat uncomfortable, read with a pencil or pen in your hand, and have a dictionary nearby. Recalling the four mental suggestions, get an overview of the essay that follows before you read it, by considering its title and its author's background, plus any other useful surface information. Then remember to notice in particular the opening paragraphs and also to make some notes in the margin and the text of the essay. Most importantly, you should try to answer the journalist's six questions, giving careful attention to what those help you learn about the essay's content and its form.

The following essay appeared in the August 7, 1989, issue of *Air Force Times*, a civilian-owned weekly newspaper whose principal subscribers and readers are active, reserve, and retired U.S. Air Force commissioned and enlisted personnel. The author, James H. Warner, is a Washington lawyer who as a Marine Corps pilot was a Vietnamese prisoner of war from October 1967 to March 1973.

Freedom—Even for Those Who Burn Flag

JAMES H. WARNER

In March 1973, when we were released from a prisoner of war   1
camp in North Vietnam, we were flown to Clark Air Base in the

Philippines. As I stepped out of the aircraft, I looked up and saw the flag. I caught my breath; then, as tears filled my eyes, I saluted it. I never loved my country more than at that moment.

Although I have received the Silver Star and two Purple Hearts, they were nothing compared with the gratitude I felt then for having been allowed to serve the cause of freedom.

Because the mere sight of the flag meant so much to me after 5½ years as a prisoner, it hurts me to see other Americans willfully desecrate it. But I have been in a communist prison and looked into the pit of hell. I cannot compromise on freedom. It hurts to see the flag burned, but I part company with those who want to punish flag burners.

Early in the imprisonment, the communists told us that we did not have to stay there. If only we would admit we were wrong, we could be released early. If we did not, we would be punished. A handful accepted, most did not. In our minds, early release under those conditions would amount to a betrayal of our comrades, of our country and of our flag.

Because we would not say the words they wanted us to say, they made our lives wretched. Most of us were tortured, and some of my comrades died. I was tortured for most of the summer of 1969. I developed beriberi from malnutrition. I had long bouts of dysentery. I was infested with intestinal parasites. I spent 13 months in solitary confinement. Was our cause worth all of this? Yes, and more.

Rose Wilder Lane, in her magnificent book *The Discovery of Freedom*, said there are two fundamental truths that men must know in order to be free. They must know that all men are brothers, and they must know that all men are born free. Once men accept these two ideas, they never will accept bondage. The power of these ideas explains why it was illegal to teach slaves to read.

One can teach these ideas, even in a communist prison camp. Marxists believe that ideas are merely the product of material conditions; change those material conditions, and one will change the ideas they produce. They tried to "re-educate" us. If we could show them that we would not abandon our belief in fundamental principles, then we could prove the falseness of their doctrine. We could subvert them by teaching them about freedom through our example. We could show them the power of ideas. I did not appreciate this power before I was a prisoner of war.

I remember one interrogation where I was shown a photograph of some Americans protesting the war by burning a flag. "There," the officer said. "People in your country protest against your cause. That proves that you are wrong."

"No," I said. "That proves that I am right. In my country we are

not afraid of freedom, even if it means that people disagree with us."
The officer was on his feet in an instant. He smashed his fist onto
the table and screamed at me to shut up. I was astonished to see
pain, compounded by fear, in his eyes. I have never forgotten the
satisfaction I felt at using his tool against him.

Aneurin Bevan, former official of the British Labor Party, once 10
was asked by Nikita Khrushchev how the British definition of democracy differed from the Soviet view. Bevan responded that if Khrushchev really wanted to know the difference, he should read the
funeral oration of Pericles.

In that speech, recorded in the Second Book of Thucydides' *His-* 11
tory of the Peloponnesian War, Pericles contrasted democratic Athens with totalitarian Sparta. Unlike the Spartans, he said, the Athenians did not fear freedom. Rather, they viewed freedom as the very
source of their strength. As it was for Athens, so it is for America.

We don't need to amend the Constitution in order to punish 12
those who burn our flag. They burn the flag because they hate America and they are afraid of freedom. What better way to hurt them
than with the subversive idea of freedom? Spread freedom; it is the
best weapon we have.

Warner's essay was short enough that you shouldn't have fallen
asleep, and we hope you had no major—or even minor—distractions
while you were reading it. As you look over the essay again, you may
notice that you marked a few words whose meanings weren't made
clear by their contexts, such as *desecrate* in paragraph 2, *beriberi* in
5, *subvert* in 7, plus perhaps a few more. For any puzzling words,
now use your dictionary, remembering to put a tick mark beside
each problem word you look up.

Review the notes you made in the essay's margins, plus any you
made separately. (You may even want to reread the essay and make
more notes or even a summary, often a necessary task for analyzing
and understanding arguments, especially ones that are longer and
more complex than Warner's.) First, let's consider some things you
should have noticed about its content when you tried to get an
overview of the essay. You learned from the title that the general
subject was burning the flag, and that Warner supported freedom for
those who do so. His attitude may have struck you as surprising,
since as a former prisoner of war Warner might be expected to be an
especially fervent patriot. You may recall, too, that during the summer of 1989, the Supreme Court ruled that a Dallas, Texas, man had
the right, under the U.S. Constitution, to burn our country's flag

without punishment, and that the Court's decision provoked strong criticism from President Bush and members of Congress on down to ordinary citizens across our country, with many military veterans and their organizations being particularly outspoken.

Yet here is Warner, who spent 5½ years in a North Vietnamese prison (paragraphs 1, 3) and was decorated for bravery (2), announcing in his essay's title that he supports other citizens' freedom to dishonor the flag that brought tears to his eyes when he first saw it after his release from prison (1). You should also have noticed that Warner is a lawyer, and thus professionally trained to comment on legal questions. Furthermore, he lives and works in our nation's capital, where he should have a heightened sense of government, laws, and patriotism. After all, the executive, legislative, and judicial branches of our government are headquartered there, and monuments to such great leaders as Washington, Jefferson, and Lincoln are prominent features of the city.

What did you notice when you took our suggestion to examine closely the opening paragraphs of this essay? You may have been a little surprised at Warner's organization of his material, the form that he chose for presenting it to us. He goes back in time, to report an episode over sixteen years earlier, and spends his first two paragraphs discussing that experience before announcing his thesis in the last two sentences of paragraph 3. As you analyzed or disassembled his argument further, you should have noticed that twice more (paragraphs 4–5, 8–9) Warner goes back in time, to his prisoner of war experiences. Why do you suppose he goes back so often, and what does his argument gain by his recounting of those earlier times?

As we look at another aspect of his essay, you will recall that earlier in this book much was said about using authorities to provide support for arguments. Certainly Warner, after 5½ years of sickness and torture, including 13 months in solitary confinement, should be an expert on what freedom means, since he was without it so long. Did you notice, though, that he also uses references to others that he considers authorities on freedom? First, he goes so far as to use the label "magnificent" for Rose Wilder Lane's book *The Discovery of Freedom* before he summarizes one of her main points (6); then he uses that point in explaining how it took his prisoner of war experiences to help him learn the real power of ideas, such as freedom. Next Warner describes an episode involving representatives of British democracy and Marxist communism (10). Their discussion, too, turned to freedom, and Aneurin Bevan, the British speaker, used a classical work of history to make his point, that in democratic Athens freedom was thought to create strength rather than to under-mine it (11). Finally Warner compares America to Athens, before wrapping up his argument in the following paragraph. Why does he refer to these other authorities? And what does he expect to gain by comparing today's America to the Athens of over 2000 years ago? These are the sorts of reporter's questions that you need to be con-stantly asking, ones that will lead you to a fuller understanding of and appreciation for a written argument's content and form.

We now need to consider the strongest portion of Warner's argu-ment, paragraphs 8 and 9, where he describes a Communist interro-gating officer's futile attempt to break Warner's commitment to de-mocracy and freedom by showing him a photograph of American antiwar demonstrators burning the flag. Here for the first and only time Warner reports the words spoken in their dialogue, giving the episode a heightened sense of drama and realism, and making this a particularly effective use of narration. Then in four short, emphatic sentences Warner describes his psychological conquest of his captor, when "pain, compounded by fear" invaded the officer's eyes (para-graph 9) and Warner had won their argument about freedom. Warner has wisely organized his material to present his strongest supporting example toward the essay's end, planning there to clinch his point with us readers if he had not already done so.

We will leave this essay after raising two more questions that you also should probably have asked: Why would Warner want his essay published in *Air Force Times*, and why would they want to publish it? Here you must carefully consider the newspaper's audi-ence, just as you should always do, usually as one of your first and most important moves when creating your own arguments.

You are just about ready now to move on to the readings sections of this book. There you will notice that these essays are followed by questions on content and form, much like those we have just asked about Warner's essay on flag burning. You will also find there a variety of suggestions for writing tasks, sometimes directly based on the reading, sometimes on related subjects. You are likely to find it useful to read through those content and form questions, as well as the writing suggestions, *before* you read the essays to which they refer. By doing so, you will get even more of an overview of the essays and will also give yourself additional direction as you read, particularly as you search for answers to the questions. We hope, of course, that you will be trying to apply our four physical and four mental suggestions for improving your reading as you read those essays and any other serious pieces of writing. Most of all, as you read, you should be asking: Who? What? When? Where? How? Why?

Speaking Up: Argumentative Essays
on Various Topics

This first collection of reading selections consists of unrelated example essays that concentrate their arguments on topics of current or continuing interest. The order of the essays in this collection is from least to most difficult; length is a secondary arrangement factor, so that typically the early essays are shorter than the later ones.

Each essay in this section should be considered separately, unless your instructor directs you otherwise, and you should concentrate your energies on these aspects of each essay:

1. Understanding the *content* or subject matter, including the words or vocabulary used and any allusions (references) made to current, historical, or literary persons, places, and events.

2. Understanding the essay's *form*, including the organization and the argumentative and rhetorical strategies used.

3. Special features of *language*, such as use of concrete rather than abstract (and specific rather than general) words and phrases, use of foreign or unusual words and phrases, level of difficulty of diction or word choice.

4. Special features of *tone*, particularly in relation to the essay's apparent intended audience.

5. Special features of *style*, such as sentence and paragraph length, sentence variety and complexity, ease and grace of expression, use of figurative language, and the like.

6. *Other features* of the essay that enhance or detract from the essay's effectiveness as a written argument, such as presence or absence of specific, relevant, and clear examples.

As mentioned earlier in the text, your own writing should automatically and naturally be strengthened by your careful and attentive reading of other writers' arguments, especially when you give thoughtful attention to content and form. The questions that we have placed after each essay are therefore a starting place for analytical thought and constructive discussion, while the writing suggestions there may lead either to classroom discussions or to writing assignments for individuals or groups, as your instructor directs. Examining all of each assigned essay's questions and writing suggestions beforehand is a useful way to get ready to read the essay itself most purposefully, thoroughly, and efficiently.

60 Billion Pounds
of Trouble

GARY TURBAK

On a California beach, a seal flops ashore entangled in a section   1
of nylon fishing net. The plastic has cut into the animal's neck, exposing raw and festering flesh. The seal futilely tries to bite through the tough material. Starving and weary from struggling against its man-made tormenter, the mammal lies down to die.

From the high seas to the Rocky Mountains, plastic is killing   2
wildlife, clogging landfills and disfiguring America's natural beauty. The miracle material of yesteryear has evolved into a significant environmental problem that no one really knows how to solve.

"Plastic consumes precious resources, creates toxic chemicals,   3
does not decompose and is generally not recycled. It's a huge problem," said Brian Lipsett, science adviser for the Citizens Clearinghouse for Hazardous Waste.

First used in 1868 as a substitute for ivory billiard balls, "plas-   4
tic" is now the generic term for thousands of different polymers which are synthesized primarily from petroleum. Now more common than steel, aluminum and copper combined, plastic appears in everything from artificial hearts to Army helmets; it can be as strong or soft, rigid or flimsy, transparent or opaque as scientists want it to be. Above all else, the stuff endures. The plastic you throw in the trash today may still be there 400 years from now.

As litter, plastic is unsightly and deadly. Birds and small animals   5
die after getting stuck in plastic, six-pack beverage rings. Pelicans

accidentally hang themselves with discarded plastic fishing line. Turtles choke on plastic bags or starve when their stomachs become clogged with hard-to-excrete, crumbled plastic. Sea lions poke their heads into plastic rings and have their jaws locked permanently shut. Authorities estimate that plastic refuse annually kills up to 2 million birds and at least 100,000 mammals.

The worst killers of all are plastic drift nets—the strong, two- 6 inch mesh used by commercial fishing fleets. Buoyed at the top, weighted at the bottom and extending for up to 40 miles, the nets become lethal, sea-bound roadblocks that entangle and drown a teeming menagerie of victims. Tens of thousands of seals and a host of sea-going birds, turtles, dolphins and other animals die each year in the nets. When a net is lost or discarded, which happens thousands of times each year, it may travel the seas indefinitely as a silent, phantom killer.

Often, seaborne plastic trash comes ashore in the form of every- 7 thing from AIDS-contaminated medical waste to condoms to disposable diapers. On some beaches, plastic tampon applicators are so ubiquitous they're referred to as "Jersey seashells." In 1987, volunteers cleaned 157 miles of Texas beach and collected more than 200 tons of plastic litter. A one-day scouring of 150 miles of Oregon shoreline yielded 26 tons of plastic.

Who's to blame?   8

"When plastic becomes a nuisance in the marine environment, 9 the problem usually lies with people and the way they use plastic and not with the material itself," said Wayne Pearson, executive director of the Plastics Recycling Foundation, a group of about 50 plastic-packaging companies. Ships dump about 100 million pounds of plastic in the oceans each year, and U.S. Navy vessels contribute four tons per day to that total.

Even when plastic is disposed of properly, it can cause problems. 10 Plastic is the fastest-growing component of a solid waste deluge clogging the nation's landfills, one-third of which are expected to reach capacity in the next five years. Manufacturers produce about 60 billion pounds of plastic annually, and we promptly cast more than one-third of it into the environment. Measured by volume, nearly one-third of the nation's garbage is plastic, and some of it—such as fast-food containers—has a useful lifespan of about two minutes.

"This is really a situation where we have met the enemy and it 11 is us," said Michael Bean, senior attorney with the Environmental Defense Fund. "We all use plastic because it's tremendously convenient. There is no single villain."

Not even the most ardent environmentalist suggests that all 12 plastic be outlawed. The material is simply too useful. Some areas have, however, banned certain kinds of plastic. For example, New York's Suffolk County prohibits plastic grocery bags, and Berkeley, Calif., will soon allow only biodegradable fast-food containers. About 20 states are considering similar measures. In January 1989, the United States and 28 other nations banned the dumping of plastics at sea. The Navy is working to comply by its 1993 target date, but it will take years to clean up what's already there, and enforcement will be difficult.

Another approach is to create plastic that degrades when exposed to sunlight or bacteria. One technique is to mix plastic with cornstarch, which can easily be broken down by microorganisms. Biodegradable plastic garbage bags are available, and 16 states already require that all six-pack rings be degradable. Degradable plastic cannot be used, however, in food containers or long-lived products, and most experts see a limited potential for this solution. 13

Plastic is, however, a good candidate for recycling—at least in theory. Recycled plastic can be turned into new fencing, flower pots, boat docks, patio furniture and other items. Five two-liter plastic soda bottles will yield a ski jacket, and 36 bottles will provide filling for a sleeping bag. "Within five years we'll be recycling half of all plastic beverage containers and in a decade maybe half of all plastic," Pearson predicts. Currently, though, plastic recycling is a problem-plagued infant, and only 1 percent of the material gets a second life. 14

In the end, the best solution may simply be to use less plastic. Although glass, paper and other alternatives are often less convenient, they are available. "The big question," said Bean, "is whether we're ready to pay the outrageous environmental price for a little extra convenience, or whether we'll act responsibly to solve the problems associated with plastic." 15

QUESTIONS OF CONTENT

1. What is plastic made of? When was it first used and for what purpose? Name three plastic items not mentioned by Turbak.
2. What plastic item does Turbak label as the "worst killer" of sea life? Why is it so deadly?
3. What are some of the more repugnant forms of plastic litter that Turbak describes?
4. Who or what is responsible for this inundation of plastic?
5. According to Turbak, why do environmentalists hesitate to argue that all plastic use should be outlawed?

6. What four measures does Turbak mention that are possible ways to reverse this dangerous situation?

QUESTIONS OF FORM

1. In paragraphs 5–7 Turbak makes a claim of fact and supports it inductively. What is that claim? What are the elements of his induction?
2. Turbak quotes two authorities in paragraphs 9 and 11. What is the purpose of their testimony?
3. In paragraph 12, before commencing his policy recommendations, Turbak makes a concession. What is that concession, and what effect does it produce?

SUGGESTIONS FOR WRITING

1. State Turbak's argument as briefly as possible. Try to limit your summary to a single paragraph.
2. What products other than plastic threaten our environment? Think of additional threats to forests, streams, rivers, and oceans; to wild life, both terrestrial and aquatic. Focus on a single harmful product, such as dioxins, nuclear waste, acid rain, carbon dioxide, or chlorofluorocarbons. Then proceed in two steps. Demonstrate that this product or substance indeed poses a threat. You may find it helpful to consult a subject index in your library, such as the *Readers' Guide to Periodical Literature* or, if available, a computer data base, such as *INFOTRAC.* Next state your suggestions for remedying the problem. Be sure to give proper credit to any sources that you use.
3. You (or a group of classmates) operate a factory that manufactures Styrofoam plates, cups, and sandwich cartons. Clearly you do not want fast-food chains to return to paper plates, cups, and wrappers. What sort of case can you build for your products? Examine some recent reports on the specific hazards of Styrofoam before responding. While you will not want to propose that outlets use less Styrofoam, you might want to follow Turbak's lead and champion one of his other recommendations. Do so in a concise, well-supported essay describing your solution(s) to the problem.

Sex Is Not a Spectator Sport

S. I. HAYAKAWA

In current discussions of pornography and obscenity, there is   1
widespread confusion about two matters. First there is sexual behavior and what it means to the participants. Secondly there is the

outside observer of sexual behavior and what it means to him. When a man and a woman make love, enjoying themselves and each other unself-consciously, a rich relationship is reaffirmed and made richer by their lovemaking. However beautiful or sacred that love relationship may be to that man and woman, it would have an entirely different significance to a Peeping Tom, secretly watching the proceedings from outside the window. The sexual behavior is not itself obscene. Obscenity is peculiarly the evaluation of the outside observer. Theoretically the actors may themselves be made the observers. If, for example, unknown to the man and woman, a movie were to be made of their lovemaking, and that movie were to be shown to them later, that lovemaking might take on an entirely different significance. What was performed unself-consciously and spontaneously might be viewed later by the actors themselves with giggling or shame or shock. They might even insist that the film be destroyed—which is entirely different from saying that they would stop making love.

What I am saying is that obscenity and pornography can happen   2
only when sexual events are seen from the outside, from a spectator's point of view. This is the crux of the pornography problem. Pornography is sexual behavior made public through symbolization—by representation in literature, by simulation or enactment in a nightclub act or on stage, by arts such as painting, photography, or the movies. To object to pornographic movies or art is not, as some would have us believe, a result of hang-ups about sex. One may be completely healthy and still object to many of the current representations of sexual acts in the movies and on the stage.

Standards of morality are one thing. Standards of decorum are   3
another. There is nothing immoral about changing one's clothes or evacuating one's bowels. But in our culture people as a rule do not change their clothing in the presence of the other sex, excepting their spouses. Men and women have separate public lavatories, and within them each toilet is in a separate compartment for privacy. Love too needs privacy. Human beings normally make love in private, whether that love is socially sanctioned, as in marriage, or unsanctioned, as in a house of prostitution.

The trouble with sexual intercourse as an object of artistic or   4
literary representation is that its meaning is not apparent in the behavior. Hence serious writers have historically been reticent in their description of sex. In Dante's *Divine Comedy* Francesca tells of her tragic love for Paolo. They were reading an ancient romance and, as they read, their passions suddenly overcame them. What happened? Dante simply has Francesca say, "That day we read no further." The rest is left to the reader's imagination—and the reader cannot help feeling the power of that on-rushing, fatal passion.

Men and women couple with each other for a wide variety of   5
reasons. Sometimes the sexual encounter is the fulfillment of true
love and respect for each other. Sometimes one of the partners is
using sex as an instrument of exploitation or aggression against the
other. Sometimes sex is a commercial transaction, with either party
being the prostitute. Sometimes sex is the expression of neurosis.
Sometimes it is evidence of people getting over their neuroses. However, to the movie camera, as to a Peeping Tom, they are all "doing
the same thing." To concentrate on the mechanics of sex is to ignore
altogether its human significance.

Today movies do not stop at exhibiting copulation. Every kind of   6
aberrant sexual behavior and sadomasochistic perversion is being
shown. The advertisements in the newspaper before me announce
such titles as *Nude Encounter, Too Hot to Handle, Deep Throat, The
Devil in Miss Jones, The Passion Parlor, Hot Kitten,* and *Honeymoon
Suite,* as well as "16 hours of hard-core male stag." The only purpose
of movies such as these, from all I can tell from advertisements and
reviews, is, as D. H. Lawrence expressed it, "to do dirt on sex." Let
the American Civil Liberties Union fight for the right of these movies to be shown. I will not.

QUESTIONS OF CONTENT

1. Hayakawa draws a careful distinction in the opening paragraph. What
distinction does he make and why?
2. Besides lovemaking, Hayakawa alludes to two other human acts that
are customarily accomplished in privacy. What are they, and how are
all three related to what he calls "standards of decorum"?
3. Who are Francesca and Paolo, and what purpose is served in the essay
by Hayakawa's literary allusion to them?
4. Hayakawa does not claim that all sexual unions are an expression of
love. For what other reasons does he suggest that people have sexual
encounters? Why does he bring up these reasons as part of his argument?
5. What kind of organization is the American Civil Liberties Union?
Why and on what basis might the ACLU fight for the right to show
pornographic movies, as Hayakawa implies?

QUESTIONS OF FORM

1. Hayakawa's argument is essentially a claim of value. It consists of
drawing a definition of what is to be valued and showing how some

things correspond to that definition and should, as a consequence, be valued, while others do not correspond to it and should thus not be valued. Where exactly does Hayakawa make that definition?

2. Hayakawa appeals to two authorities. Who are they, and what purpose does each appeal fulfill?

3. In paragraph 5 Hayakawa restates his claim of value in different terms. Where exactly do you find that restatement? Compare it with the earlier claim.

SUGGESTIONS FOR WRITING

1. Summarize Hayakawa's argument in a single well-constructed paragraph.

2. Assume that the psychology department on your campus regularly offers a course entitled "Human Sexuality." It is quite popular among the students because it reportedly features several films that demonstrate techniques of lovemaking. You are scandalized by the use of such films, especially by the whispered comments you have overheard about them. Using Hayakawa's argument as a starting point, write a letter to the campus newspaper objecting to the practice of using such films in the Human Sexuality course.

3. You are a psychology major and you work for the professor who teaches Human Sexuality. Sometimes it is your responsibility to show the films that the student in suggestion 2 objects to. Write a response to that student's probable complaint, defending the practices of the psychology professor. You may also wish to use Hayakawa's argument in defending your position.

Art and Politics: Self-Righteousness and Silly Yahooism

JOAN BECK

"Art should be supported by government and protected from politics."   1

That's the first line in full-page ads placed by the trustees of the   2 Whitney Museum of American Art in recent days in the *New York Times* and *Washington Post* under the headline "Are you going to let politics kill Art?"

It's part of an intensifying nationwide campaign that has in-   3 cluded rallies, letters and protests and is aimed at preventing funding cuts and restrictions on federal appropriations for the National Endowment for the Arts.

What set off the Whitney trustees and other protesters was a   4
chain of silly events that clearly shows why art cannot be supported
by government and still be protected from politics. In the real world,
government money is inseparable from politics.

The flap began with a public furor over two exhibitions partially   5
financed by the NEA. One included photographs by the late Robert
Mapplethorpe that are clearly homoerotic and sadomasochistic. The
other show had the Andres Serrano photograph of a plastic crucifix
submerged in what the artist said was his own urine.

Congress reacted with knee-jerk silliness. The Senate voted to   6
cut NEA grants to the two institutions that organized the exhibitions. The House decided to slash $45,000 out of the NEA's $171
million budget. Congressional conferees will work out the final appropriation agreement in a few days.

In recent weeks, the battle between art and politics has disinte-   7
grated into a fight between self-righteousness and yahooism. Senator
Jesse Helms (R., N.C.) gave Art good reason to stake out a claim on
self-righteousness.

Helms offered an amendment that would forbid use of govern-   8
ment money to produce or disseminate "(1) obscene materials, including but not limited to depictions of sadomasochism, homoeroti-
cism, the exploitation of children or individuals engaged in sex acts;
(2) material which denigrates the objects or beliefs of the adherents
of a particular religion or non-religion; or (3) material which denigrates, debases or reviles a person, group or class of citizens on the
basis of race, creed, sex, handicap, age or national origin."

Helms actually did art an enormous favor.   9

Once the senator had set himself up as a fat and obvious target,   10
the art world no longer needed to defend sadomasochistic photographs or crucifixes dipped in urine as art. It could yell "Censorship!" and attack Congress with the First Amendment. Its self-
righteousness grew until it blossomed into the full-page newspaper
ads.

Of course art should not be censored. Artists should be free to   11
create what they choose (with the minor exceptions the Supreme
Court has allowed to First Amendment freedoms). Galleries and
museums should be free to display whatever art they wish.

But yelling "Art" doesn't give an artist or an exhibitor the right   12
to federal financial support. Refusing to hand over tax dollars for
pornography (however artistic) or crucifixes in urine (no matter how
creative) isn't censorship. And members of Congress have picked up
a lot of signals from constituents that they don't want their tax
dollars paying for what they consider obscene and foolish.

Of course Congress shouldn't be in the business of deciding   13 what is art—or perhaps, what is an ego trip or a publicity gimmick masquerading as Art.

(I wouldn't presume to say what is art and what isn't. But in my profession, you get rather good at recognizing ego trips and publicity gimmicks.) 14

An example that one of Helms' critics uses is the Bible, with its accounts of gang rape, incest, adultery and treacherous murder. Would Helms' amendment, he asks, require Congress to withhold federal funds from colleges whose libraries stock the Bible? 15

There is a simple way out of all this silliness, of course. Congress should just stop funding art and artists. However civilizing, inspiring and uplifting, art doesn't have a convincing claim on the tax dollars of hard-working wage earners, especially when it wraps itself in an esthetic self-righteousness that isolates it from ordinary taxpayers. 16

This need not be a vindictive move. It would simply be the recognition that, as the Whitney ad says, "Art must live free to survive." It would also be an acknowledgment that art and politics will forever be uneasy with each other and that money will always provide a temptation and an excuse for politicians to try to control art. 17

Art is too important to be left to Jesse Helms. Clearly and cleanly separating art and politics would leave the Jesse Helmses no way to impose their taste on art. 18

Art cannot be supported by government and protected from politics. 19

QUESTIONS OF CONTENT

1. What events set off the heated discussion over government funding of art that Beck addresses in this argument?
2. In paragraph 7 Beck asserts, ". . . the battle between art and politics has disintegrated into a fight between self-righteousness and yahooism." Find out the origin and meaning of the term "yahoo," so that you can explain "yahooism" in your own words. Who are the self-righteous in this debate? Who are the yahoos?
3. Why does Beck claim in paragraph 9 that Senator Jesse Helms "actually did art an enormous favor"?
4. Based on the language and examples she uses, what do you think Beck's attitude is toward each of these groups of people: Congress, artists, tax-paying citizens? Whom do you think she expects to read her essay?
5. Look at Beck's concluding paragraph of a single declarative sentence. How is it a tribute or a rebuke to Senator Helms?

QUESTIONS OF FORM

1. Beck's argument is based on a claim of policy. What situation needs to be corrected, and what is the policy that addresses that correction?
2. Beck's argument might be reduced to this claim and support statement: Congress should stop funding art because it isn't qualified to judge what is or is not art. What general warrant tends to make us agree with this claim?
3. What portion of Beck's argument constitutes background information?
4. Look up the definition of *reductio ad absurdum* in "A Short Guide to Material and Formal Fallacies" in the Appendix. How has one of his opponents attempted to use the references to the Bible in paragraph 9 to refute Senator Helms?

SUGGESTIONS FOR WRITING

1. Summarize Beck's argument in a single paragraph.
2. Quite often it is necessary to explain the circumstances surrounding an argument so that the audience will be in a position to take sides. This is particularly true when the subject is one about which general audiences are not likely to be informed. Notice the space that Beck devotes to explaining the issues in this argument before she presents her claim.

   Think about some controversial situation that has arisen recently on your campus. Describe that situation for an audience who will be largely unaware of the case's facts. Then, having made the issues plain, state your claim and support it. As Beck did, use approximately equal amounts of space (1) to explain the situation and (2) to make and support your claim.
3. Put yourself in the position of an artist who has just applied for a federal grant to finance a year's work. You plan to bring art to the nearest inner city area by painting murals on buildings. Your aim is not only to introduce ghetto dwellers to the visual arts but to instill ethnic pride and group solidarity. Write a letter to the editor responding to Beck's column.

Flag Burning Isn't the Real Issue

JACK ANDERSON

Gregory Lee Johnson did something worse than burn the American flag at the Republican Convention in Dallas in 1984. He started   1 a fire under one of the seedier elements of democracy—those who would fight until death to protect their right to tell others what to do.

Sadly, there are enough of those people in the United States to constitute a hefty voting bloc, and now they have their representatives in Congress stuck between that bloc and a hard place. 2

For the record, we never met Gregory Lee Johnson, but we don't like him anyway. He took advantage of the very country that he despises by burning the flag to show his contempt. Then, he dragged the case against him all the way to the Supreme Court, which painfully had to admit that Johnson had a right to burn the flag. 3

Johnson was right and his case was solid, but don't expect us to invite him over to dinner for a spirited debate on freedom of expression. He offended every American who cares deeply about this country. 4

Now Congress has compounded that offense by compromising the right to freedom of expression. Johnson, who doesn't deserve the time it takes to tell him he is a jerk, has sparked a constitutional crisis. 5

Last week, Congress approved the final version of an anti-flag-burning bill and sent it to the president. That bill makes flag-burning a crime, punishable by up to one year in prison. If President Bush doesn't veto the bill, it will be a crime to express one's opinion by putting a match to one's personal property. 6

Where do we go from here? Will it be a crime to tear up a copy of the Bill of Rights? Shall we lock people up for wadding up their "1040-EZ" forms? Shall we arrest them for setting fire to this column? 7

The flag is different, you say. It's a symbol of our freedoms. People die for it. Since Gallup can't take a poll of everyone who has died in the service of their country, that point is up for debate. Soldiers don't die for symbols. At the worst, some soldiers die because they are stuck in a place they don't want to be. At best, some die to protect their country or another country from a hostile takeover by others who would limit their freedom. 8

We don't have to wait for a hostile takeover by outsiders to limit our freedoms. We have Congress and the president and anyone who insists that flag-burning should be against the law. Now we have a law that sets a precedent for eliminating other rights of expression, and all because one American set fire to a flag. 9

The members of Congress who supported the bill did so either through blind patriotism or fear of losing votes. The majority of those who voted against it didn't have the courage to say it was a bad idea. Instead, they said that they opposed a law because a constitutional amendment is what we really need. Why smash the American spirit with a fly swatter when you can use a sledgehammer? 10

President Bush comes from the sledgehammer school of lawmak-   11
ing. He says he doesn't like the bill because it isn't enough. He
wants a constitutional amendment, maybe something that can be
squeezed in right under the Bill of Rights. Bush's shallow presidential campaign was based on exactly the same blather that prompted
the flag-burning bill. Candidate Bush didn't give the country a clue
about how he would stop the drug epidemic or eradicate the deficit
or achieve world peace or house the homeless or feed the hungry.
But, by golly, he promised that your children would say the Pledge of
Allegiance every day whether they wanted to or not.

Gregory Lee Johnson doesn't deserve a law in his honor, much   12
less a constitutional amendment. What he deserves is for everyone
who witnessed his little bit of street theater to tell him exactly what
they thought of it. He expresses himself, we express ourselves and
nobody gets arrested.

QUESTIONS OF CONTENT

1. Anderson asserts in the title of his essay that flag burning is not the
   real issue. What is? Where does he say so?
2. What event caused the controversy over flag burning? What actions
   did Congress and the president take?
3. How does Anderson view the responses of Congress and the President to the flag burning controversy? What is his attitude toward
   Gregory Lee Johnson?
4. At the time Anderson wrote this essay, was flag burning against the
   law? Is it now?

QUESTIONS OF FORM

1. Anderson uses irony a number of times in his presentation. Look up
   irony in the Glossary. Now locate at least three occasions where he
   uses this device, and explain why each instance is ironic.
2. What argumentative tactic is Anderson employing in paragraph 7?
3. Anderson uses an inductive approach to support a claim that he
   makes in paragraph 11. What is the claim, and what are the elements
   of his induction?
4. How would you state Anderson's argument in paragraph 9 in the
   form of a syllogism?
5. Compare Anderson's argument with the one made by James H.
   Warner earlier in the book (p. 129). How are these arguments essentially similar or different?

SUGGESTIONS FOR WRITING

1. Summarize Anderson's argument briefly. Start with his claim and its support.
2. Summarize Anderson's argument and Warner's argument (p. 129). Show how the two arguments tend to reinforce one another.
3. What other activities like flag burning do you find distasteful but do not want to see rendered illegal—for much the same reasons that Anderson cites? In a short essay, defend such an unpopular strategy, using the approach taken by Anderson and Warner.

Does ROTC Belong on College Campuses?

HARRY G. SUMMERS, JR.

As peace appears to be breaking out around the world, "peace activists" like newspaper columnist Colman McCarthy, Jesuits Richard McSoriey and Daniel Berrigan, and others have turned their attention to driving the ROTC program off college campuses. In their fanaticism they are unwittingly undermining one of the most important tenets of American government—civilian control of the military. 1

How to guarantee that the military remains a servant of the people rather than using its weapons to become their master is an age-old problem. As Mao Tse-tung once said, "Political power grows out of the barrel of a gun." But a century before Mao was born, America's Founding Fathers, fresh from their own revolution, wrote specific guarantees into the Constitution to ensure that the American people, through their elected representatives in the Congress, would control the gun. 2

To ensure that no cabal of officers would emerge to usurp civilian control, Congress retained the right to give its advice and consent on the commissioning and promotion of every military officer. Early on, it reserved to itself the appointment of cadets and midshipmen to the Military Academy and the Naval Academy, and later, to the Air Force Academy. 3

Not only did this system make certain that civilians would control the makeup of the officer corps by providing a check on those entering its ranks, it also ensured geographic diversity by having members of the Senate and House nominate cadets and midshipmen from their own states and congressional districts. 4

A further means of maintaining civilian control has been the   5
ROTC program. With roots going back to the Morrill Act of 1862,
which provided for military education at land-grant colleges, the
ROTC was formally established by the National Defense Act of
1916. It is now the primary source of military officers.

In 1988, the last year for which complete figures are available,   6
4,082 of the Army's new lieutenants came from civilian university
ROTC programs, 990 came from West Point, 536 from officer candidate schools and 689 (mainly medical and other professionals) from
direct appointments. ROTC graduates, some 66,000 strong, make up
62.2 percent of all active-duty Army officers.

And they dominate the senior ranks as well. More than half—   7
56.2 percent—of Army generals, including the chairman of the Joint
Chiefs of Staff, Gen. Colin L. Powell, are ROTC graduates.

Ironically, the "peace activists" would do away with ROTC in   8
the name of anti-militarism, even though the program was grounded
in anti-militarism from its inception. ROTC was designed to produce a well-rounded officer corps inculcated with the principles of
freedom, democracy and American values through close contact
with civilian students on an open college campus, and through a
liberal education taught by a primarily civilian academic faculty.
And that's just what has happened.

Anti-militarism and the ROTC go hand in glove. "Americans   9
have a long and proud history of irreverence toward and distrust of
their military," wrote then-Army Chief of Staff Gen. Fred C. Weyand
in 1976. Himself a product of the ROTC program at the University
of California at Berkeley, Weyand knew that true anti-militarism
had served the nation well over the years. Present at the very beginning, it has saved the United States the grief that other countries
have suffered when officers use their troops and guns to bully, coerce
and even overthrow their civilian superiors.

Humorist Art Buchwald gave the commencement address 10   10
years ago when my son graduated from Georgetown University and
from the ROTC program there. Buchwald told of being outside the
White House when President Nixon resigned. The only uniformed
person present was a police officer directing traffic, he said. And he
concluded that when the United States can transfer power under
such circumstances without a single tank in sight or a single bayo-
net being unsheathed, this country has nothing to worry about.

It has nothing to worry about because it can trust its armed   11
forces. And it can trust its armed forces because it can trust its
officer corps. The "peace-activists" would change all that. In the
name of common sense we ought not let them do it.

QUESTIONS OF CONTENT

1. Summers begins his essay by naming some peace activists who are proposing the elimination of ROTC from college campuses. What does he gain by giving their names?
2. What guarantees did the founding fathers establish to ensure that the military would not usurp civilian control of the government?
3. In addition to these controls, what other means of maintaining civilian control does Summers mention?
4. Summers names two very prominent military officers who received their commissions through the ROTC program. Who are they, what important positions did they hold in the military organization, and how does reference to them aid Summers's argument?
5. Why does Summers believe that ROTC creates an antimilitaristic officer corps? Why is that desirable?

QUESTIONS OF FORM

1. In paragraph 9, Summers alludes to the countries that "have suffered when officers use their troops and guns to bully, coerce, and even overthrow their civilian superiors." Why do you suppose he doesn't provide specific examples of such occurrences?
2. Summers argues that ROTC provides us with an antimilitaristic officer corps, which goes a long way toward protecting us from a military overthrow of our government. What is his warrant for such a claim? Where does he state it?
3. Summers uses statistics rather copiously in paragraphs 6 and 7. What claim do these statistics support?
4. What is the purpose of the anecdote contained in paragraph 10? What claim does it tend to support?

SUGGESTIONS FOR WRITING

1. Restate Summers's argument as briefly as you can without sacrificing completeness. Try to limit your summary to a single paragraph.
2. The peace activists call for the elimination of ROTC on antimilitaristic grounds. Summers, on the other hand, defends ROTC by calling it antimilitaristic. Surely the two parties to this argument have something different in mind when they use this term. In a brief essay, discuss the contrasting meanings antimilitaristic must have for Summers and for his opponents.
3. Put yourself in the position of one of the peace activists mentioned in the opening paragraph. What evidence can you produce to support the claim that ROTC should be removed from college campuses? Collect your evidence and present it in a concise essay.

Let's Return to Regulation of Airlines

WILLIAM F. BUCKLEY

I am privy to a spirited exchange between two Very Important   1
People on the subject of the airlines and what they are doing to
passengers as they tighten their oligopolistic vises. Cornell University Professor Alfred Kahn was the spectacular chief of the Civil
Aeronautics Board in the Carter years, and it was he who led the
drive to deregulate. The dramatic question: Will the great deregulator, Fred Kahn, come out in favor of reregulation?

The heat is intense, and nowhere is the flame hotter than from   2
the pen of Donald L. Pevsner, a Miami attorney, travel writer and
entrepreneur, to whom the flying public owes the marvelous relief
we get from overweight-baggage extortion by the airlines, which
used to get away with one-half of 1 percent of the one-way first-class
fare per pound of overweight after 44 pounds. Donald Pevsner was a
friend of deregulation but now contends, in his heated epistles designed to win over the soul of Fred Kahn, that what has come out of
it all is an overwhelming and arrogant duopoly controlling the major
airline hubs—and in some cases, a monopoly.

In the old days, Pevsner reminds us, back when air fares were   3
regulated on the grounds that air routes were natural monopolies or
duopolies, the guiding criteria were as follows: Airlines could charge
a fare sufficient to give them a 12 percent profit on their operations,
assuming that the average flight was 55 percent sold.

What, by that standard, is now happening? Pevsner rolls up his   4
sleeves.

The current airline industry load factor (i.e., the percentage of   5
filled seats) is between 65 percent and 70 percent. And the bellwether price of a ticket (economy class, non-super saver) is greatly
inflated. Pevsner gives the example of New York City to Cleveland
and compares the increase in traveler cost with the increase in cost
to a consumer of a new Cadillac.

Between 1964 and 1989, the cost of the Cadillac went from   6
about $6,600 to $26,000. The cost of a one-way, economy, non-discounted ticket on an airline went from $28.61 to $225. The Cadillac had gone up four times (keeping pace, roughly, with the path of
inflation), while the air fare had gone up eight times. With the dramatic attrition of post-regulation, fare-competing airlines, the result
has been a higher load factor and correspondingly higher profits.

Now the particular victims of the airlines' policies, Pevsner   7
says—and here he is not contradicted by Kahn—are the coach-class
passengers who cannot take advantage of the increasingly constrain-

ing low-fare requirements: You now often have to buy your ticket two weeks ahead, not one week ahead; you have to spend Saturday night at your point of destination; etc. These bellwether charges are imposed on at least 20 percent of all airline passengers, the people who have to pay the full fare.

It is correctly observed by Kahn that the majority who fall in this   8 classification are passengers whose way is being paid by their employers. That is all very well, says Pevsner, but it doesn't release, say, American Airlines from the charge of gouging merely because it is established that IBM is paying for that gouge—which is passed on to IBM clients and to all taxpayers via the Internal Revenue Service. Besides, there are many exceptions: Americans who need suddenly to go to a sickbed or a funeral, or who need to go and come back before the next weekend and cannot therefore plan ahead and buy into the lower fare relief system.

Kahn, in advocating deregulation back in the '70s, admitted that   9 he did not think that a travel route with an airline dominating more than 70 percent of passenger traffic should be free from regulation.

Pounce! Pevsner insists that two airlines, on a single route, in   10 fact do not compete: Their fares are almost invariably identical, like cigarette prices. He then takes the major American cities and demonstrates that in all but one hub market to and from New York City, two carriers control 85 percent or better of all the traffic, permitting effective duopolistic control of the route. In some cases—e.g., if you want to fly to New York—you have no option at all [other] than to deal with monopolies (US Air from Charlotte and Dayton, Northwest from Memphis, American from Nashville, TWA from St. Louis, Delta from Salt Lake City have 100 percent of the business).

Why don't competitors come in? Pevsner laughs, though he   11 finds this hard to do under the circumstances. You can't get domestic capital, you can't get foreign money, you can't get airport landing slots or gates, you get rooked by the computer reservation networks, you can't buy modern planes without crippling delays—you name it.

Pevsner concludes his letter to (his old friend) Kahn: "If you and   12 I do not come to the rescue, Fred, just who will?"

QUESTIONS OF CONTENT

1. Buckley informs the reader that his essay will consist of a summary of two points of view. Who are the authors of these competing positions, and where does Buckley introduce them?

2. What does Buckley mean by the word *duopoly* that he first uses in paragraph 2? What does he mean by *deregulation?* Why did deregulation take place?
3. Before fare deregulation, what formula did the government prescribe for airline fares? Did fares increase or decrease after deregulation?
4. What restrictions on airline competition does Pevsner name? Why do you suppose airlines serving the same routes don't compete for a larger share of the passenger market by offering lower fares?

QUESTIONS OF FORM

1. Although he is reporting the positions of two authorities, Buckley himself takes a position, aligning himself with one writer against the other. Where does he make it clear which party he supports? How does he do this?
2. In paragraph 6 Buckley uses a comparison. What is its purpose; that is, what claim does this tactic support? He makes another in paragraph 10. What is the purpose this time?
3. The structure of a usual claim of policy involves a statement of a situation in need of remedy, followed by the suggested remedy. Locate these parts in Buckley's presentation.
4. Kahn, according to Buckley, makes a concession in paragraph 9. What use does Pevsner make of that concession? How could you state the reasoning in the form of a syllogism?

SUGGESTIONS FOR WRITING

1. Without calling attention to the sources of Buckley's information, state as straightforwardly as you can the essential claim of policy that Buckley is making in this essay. Limit yourself to no more than two paragraphs.
2. Examine your own campus scene. Can you think of some situation that has, as a result of a policy change, produced an undesirable effect (a tuition increase, changes in dorm visitation privileges, new parking restrictions, the hiring of a new food services manager, revision of degree requirements)? Follow Buckley's strategy. State the crucial change, list the undesirable results, and then call for a return to the earlier, better times.
3. Can you defend the practices of airline fare deregulation? Is there a universal warrant to which you might appeal in order to get your audience to view such deregulation in a more favorable light? Isn't the notion of free enterprise and competition at the very heart of American business and the capitalist system? How might you use this notion to support the position favoring deregulation of airline fares? Frame this argument in an essay of no more than five paragraphs.

What Employees Need Most

PETER DRUCKER

Most of you . . . will be employees all your working life, working 1
for somebody else and for a pay check. And so will most, if not all, of
the thousands of other young Americans . . . in all the other schools
and colleges across the country.

Ours has become a society of employees. A hundred years or so 2
ago only one out of every five Americans at work was employed, i.e.,
worked for somebody else. Today only one out of five is not employed
but working for himself. And where fifty years ago "being employed"
meant working as a factory laborer or as a farmhand, the employee of
today is increasingly a middle-class person with a substantial formal
education, holding a professional or management job requiring intellectual and technical skills. Indeed, two things have characterized
American society during these last fifty years: the middle and upper
classes have become employees; and middle-class and upper-class
employees have been the fastest-growing groups in our working
population—growing so fast that the industrial worker, that oldest
child of the Industrial Revolution, has been losing in numerical importance despite the expansion of industrial production.

This is one of the most profound social changes any country has 3
ever undergone. It is, however, a perhaps even greater change for the
individual young person about to start. Whatever he does, in all
likelihood he will do it as an employee; wherever he aims, he will
have to try to reach it through being an employee.

Yet you will find little if anything written on what it is to be an 4
employee. You can find a great deal of very dubious advice on how to
get a job or how to get a promotion. You can also find a good deal on
work in a chosen field, whether it be metallurgy or salesmanship,
the machinist's trade or bookkeeping. Every one of these trades requires different skills, sets different standards, and requires a different preparation. Yet they all have employeeship in common. And
increasingly, especially in the large business or in government, employeeship is more important to success than the special professional knowledge or skill. Certainly more people fail because they
do not know the requirements of being an employee than because
they do not adequately possess the skills of their trade; the higher
you climb the ladder, the more you get into administrative or executive work, the greater the emphasis on ability to work within the
organization rather than on technical competence or professional
knowledge.

Being an employee is thus the one common characteristic of 5 most careers today. The special profession or skill is visible and clearly defined; and a well-laid-out sequence of courses, degrees, and jobs leads into it. But being an employee is the foundation. And it is much more difficult to prepare for it. Yet there is no recorded information on the art of being an employee.

The first question we might ask is: what can you learn in college   6
that will help you in being an employee? The schools teach a great many things of value to the future accountant, the future doctor, or the future electrician. Do they also teach anything of value to the future employee? The answer is: "Yes—they teach the one thing that it is perhaps most valuable for the future employee to know. But very few students bother to learn it."

This one basic skill is the ability to organize and express ideas in   7
writing and in speaking.

As an employee you work with and through other people. This   8
means that your success as an employee—and I am talking of much more here than getting promoted—will depend on your ability to communicate with people and to present your own thoughts and ideas to them so they will both understand what you are driving at and be persuaded. The letter, the report or memorandum, the ten-minute spoken "presentation" to a committee are basic tools of the employee.

Of course . . . if you work on a machine your ability to express   9
yourself will be of little importance. But as soon as you move one step up from the bottom, your effectiveness depends on your ability to reach others through the spoken or the written word. And the further away your job is from manual work, the larger the organization of which you are an employee, the more important it will be that you know how to convey your thoughts in writing or speaking. In the very large organization, whether it is the government, the large business corporation, or the military, this ability to express oneself is perhaps the most important of all the skills a [person] can possess.

Of course, skill in expression is not enough by itself. You must   10
have something to say in the first place. The popular picture of the engineer, for instance, is that of a man who works with a slide rule, T square, and compass. And engineering students reflect this picture in their attitude toward the written word as something quite irrelevant to their jobs. But the effectiveness of the engineer—and with it his usefulness—depends as much on his ability to make other people understand his work as it does on the quality of the work itself.

Expressing one's thoughts is one skill that the school can really   11
teach, especially to people born without natural writing or speaking talent. Many other skills can be learned later—in this country there

are literally thousands of places that offer training to adult people at work. But the foundations for skill in expression have to be laid early: an interest in and an ear for language; experience in organizing ideas and data, in brushing aside the irrelevant, in wedding outward form and inner content into one structure; and above all, the habit of verbal expression. If you do not lay these foundations during your school years, you may never have an opportunity again.

If you were to ask me what strictly vocational courses there are   12
in the typical college curriculum, my answer—now that the good old habit of the "theme a day" has virtually disappeared—would be: the writing of poetry and the writing of short stories. Not that I expect many of you to become poets or short-story writers—far from it. But these two courses offer the easiest way to obtain some skill in expression. They force one to be economical with language. They force one to organize thought. They demand of one that he give meaning to every word. They train the ear for language, its meaning, its precision, its overtones—and its pitfalls. Above all they force one to write.

I know very well that the typical employer does not understand   13
this as yet, and that he may look with suspicion on a young college graduate who has majored, let us say, in short-story writing. But the same employer will complain—and with good reason—that the young [people] whom he hires when they get out of college do not know how to write a simple report, do not know how to tell a simple story, and are in fact virtually illiterate. And he will conclude—rightly—that the young [people] are not really effective, and certainly not employees who are likely to go very far.

QUESTIONS OF CONTENT

1. Drucker claims that during the past century our country has undergone a most profound social change. What is the nature of that change?
2. What, according to Drucker, is the present ratio of employees to employers? What was the ratio a century ago? Why has this change occurred, and will it affect you?
3. In paragraph 6 Drucker asks the following question: "What can you learn in college that will help you in being an employee?" What answer does he supply?
4. Name three occupations in which writing and speaking ability are crucial to success. How important are these abilities in your likely vocation?

5. What courses found in most college curricula does Drucker suggest for students who wish to improve their communication skills?

QUESTIONS OF FORM

1. In the opening paragraph, Drucker makes a claim. What is that claim, and how does he support it?
2. Drucker's essay begins with a syllogism that we might state in this way:

   All employees must be able to communicate effectively.

   You will be an employee.

   Therefore, you must be able to communicate effectively.

   Where does Drucker state the major premise of this syllogism? Where does he state the minor premise?
3. If we think of Drucker's major premise, as stated in question 2, as a warrant, then we see also that it is not one that Drucker expects his audience to accept without some support or *backing*. What kind of backing does he supply?
4. Examine paragraph 3, specifically its last sentence. It contains several instances of sexist diction: that is, use of the masculine pronoun to refer to both men and women—a practice that many modern readers find confusing and even offensive. How might you rewrite that sentence to clearly include both sexes?

SUGGESTIONS FOR WRITING

1. Summarize Drucker's argument in a paper that does not exceed three paragraphs. When you make your summary, do not take over Drucker's argument as though it is your own; be careful to mention him as the source of your information.
2. Using the same argumentative strategy employed by Drucker in this essay, create your own argument advocating another essential skill or attitude that all employees should strive to develop. Alternatively, you might argue for a skill that a specific profession would find indispensable, for example, a teacher, coach, restaurant manager, computer scientist, or lawyer. Argue for the development of this skill and, as Drucker does, recommend a course of action that will enable the reader to achieve the skill.
3. You are applying for a job. Write a letter arguing that the communications skills you have developed through both formal and informal education make you an ideal candidate. To complete this assignment, you will also need to furnish a brief description of the job for which you are applying.

What's Wrong with Black English

RACHEL L. JONES

William Labov, a noted linguist, once said about the use of black   1
English, "It is the goal of most black Americans to acquire full
control of the standard language without giving up their own culture." He also suggested that there are certain advantages to having
two ways to express one's feelings. I wonder if the good doctor might
also consider the goals of those black Americans who have full control of standard English but who are every now and then troubled by
that colorful, grammar-to-the-winds patois that is black English.
Case in point—me.

I'm a 21-year-old black born to a family that would probably be   2
considered lower-middle class—which in my mind is a polite way of
describing a condition only slightly better than poverty. Let's just
say we rarely if ever did the winter-vacation thing in the Caribbean.
I've often had to defend my humble beginnings to a most unlikely
group of people for an even less likely reason. Because of the way I
talk, some of my black peers look at me sideways and ask, "Why do
you talk like you're white?"

The first time it happened to me I was nine years old. Cornered   3
in the school bathroom by the class bully and her sidekick, I was
offered the opportunity to swallow a few of my teeth unless I satisfactorily explained why I always got good grades, why I talked "proper"
or "white." I had no ready answer for her, save the fact that my
mother had from the time I was old enough to talk stressed the
importance of reading and learning, or that L. Frank Baum and Ray
Bradbury were my closest companions. I read all my older brothers'
and sisters' literature textbooks more faithfully then they did, and
even lightweights like the Bobbsey Twins and Trixie Belden were
allowed into my bookish inner circle. I don't remember exactly what
I told those girls, but I somehow talked my way out of a beating.

I was reminded once again of my "white pipes" problem while   4
apartment hunting in Evanston, Illinois, last winter. I doggedly
made out lists of available places and called all around. I would
immediately be invited over—and immediately turned down. The
thinly concealed looks of shock when the front door opened clued
me in, along with the flustered instances of "just getting off the
phone with the girl who was ahead of you and she wants the rooms."
When I finally found a place to live, my roommate stirred up old
memories when she remarked a few months later, "You know, I was

surprised when I first saw you. You sounded white over the phone." Tell me another one, sister.

I should've asked her a question I've wanted an answer to for years: how does one "talk white"? The silly side of me pictures a rabid white foam spewing forth when I speak. I don't use Valley Girl jargon, so that's not what's meant in my case. Actually, I've pretty much deduced what people mean when they say that to me, and the implications are really frightening.

It means that I'm articulate and well-versed. It means that I can talk as freely about John Steinbeck as I can about Rick James. It means that "ain't" and "he be" are not staples of my vocabulary and are only used around family and friends. (It is almost Jekyll and Hydeish the way I can slip out of academic abstractions into a long, lean, double-negative-filled dialogue, but I've come to terms with that aspect of my personality.) As a child, I found it hard to believe that's what people meant by "talking proper"; that would've meant that good grades and standard English were equated with white skin, and that went against everything I'd ever been taught. Running into the same type of mentality as an adult has confirmed the depressing reality that for many blacks, standard English is not only unfamiliar, it is socially unacceptable.

James Baldwin once defended black English by saying it had added "vitality to the language," and even went so far as to label it a language in its own right, saying, "Language [i.e., black English] is a political instrument" and a "vivid and crucial key to identity." But did Malcolm X urge blacks to take power in this country "any way y'all can"? Did Martin Luther King, Jr. say to blacks, "I has been to the mountaintop, and I done seed the Promised Land"? Toni Morrison, Alice Walker and James Baldwin did not achieve their eloquence, grace and stature by using only black English in their writing. Andrew Young, Tom Bradley and Barbara Jordan did not acquire political power by saying, "Y'all crazy if you ain't gon vote for me." They all have full command of standard English, and I don't think that knowledge takes away from their blackness or commitment to black people.

I know from experience that it's important for black people, stripped of culture and heritage, to have something they can point to and say, "This is ours, *we* can comprehend it, *we* alone can speak it with a soulful flourish." I'd be lying if I said that the rhythms of my people caught up in "some serious rap" don't sound natural and right to me sometimes. But how heartwarming is it for those same brothers when they hit the pavement searching for employment? Studies have proven that the use of ethnic dialects decreases power in the marketplace. "I be" is acceptable on the corner, but not with the boss.

Am I letting capitalistic, European-oriented thinking fog the is-   9
sue? Am I selling out blacks to an ideal of assimilating, being as much like whites as possible? I have not formed a personal political ideology, but I do know this: it hurts me to hear black children use black English, knowing that they will be at yet another disadvantage in an educational system already full of stumbling blocks. It hurts me to sit in lecture halls and hear fellow black students complain that the professor "be tripping dem out using big words dey can't understand." And what hurts most is to be stripped of my own blackness simply because I know my way around the English language.

I would have to disagree with Labov in one respect. My goal is   10
not so much to acquire full control of both standard and black English, but to one day see more black people less dependent on a dialect that excludes them from full participation in the world we live in. I don't think I talk white; I think I talk right.

QUESTIONS OF CONTENT

1. What is the attitude of Jones toward black English? How does her attitude compare with James Baldwin's? With William Labov's?
2. Growing up as she did in a lower middle-class family, how does Jones account for her command of standard English?
3. How does she define standard English or "talking white"?
4. What advantage does Jones see for blacks who do have a command of standard English?

QUESTIONS OF FORM

1. Claims of value, such as Jones's, typically consist of a definition of the thing to be valued. Then there is a measurement of other items that are less valued against that definition (or set of criteria). Where and how does Jones actually do this?
2. For whom is this argument intended? Is its audience most likely to be blacks or whites? What response could be expected from each of these groups?
3. Where does Jones use her references to authorities like William Labov, James Baldwin, Malcolm X, Martin Luther King, Jr., and others in support of her claim?

4. In paragraph 9, Jones begins by asking two rhetorical questions. What do you think the answers might be? How effective was that strategy?

SUGGESTIONS FOR WRITING

1. Summarize Jones's position as fairly and as accurately as you can.
2. You are a black American, and you have experienced many of the doubts and travails that Jones describes. But you are convinced that apartments are frequently unavailable to black persons (as Jones describes in paragraph 4) because of their race and not because they speak a nonstandard dialect. You even suspect that prejudiced white people exaggerate the supposed backwardness of black English as an excuse for behaving the way they do. Write a brief refutation of Jones's position by calling attention to these speculations, as well as to any other sentiments that you might feel.
3. You are a young teacher, assigned to an inner city high school. Many of the school's black students are quite vocal in their disdain for the English that they are expected to use in the classroom and in their writing assignments. They claim that standard English is the language of the white shopkeeper, the landlord, the politician—and yes, even the teacher, white or black. Its one purpose is to keep them down. How do you respond to this argument? Write an essay addressed to these students, suitable for publication in a high school newspaper.

The Myth of the Student-Athlete

SHANNON BROWNLEE

College sport is being undermined by its own mythology. The entire enterprise is founded on the whimsical notion of the amateur, the scholar-athlete who studies and trains hard and is rewarded for his efforts, not with money but with sporting values and, above all, an education. But this implicit bargain has today become a mockery, and the cause is an overriding need—both psychological and economic—to win. 1

Consider the economics: The teams competing in Pasadena's Rose Bowl this week will each walk away with $6 million. Bowl games alone were worth more than $55 million last season, and basketball powers will rake in a $1 billion bonanza over seven years 2

starting in 1991 for granting CBS the privilege of broadcasting college games.

That's big business—a business sustained by the dreams of ath-   3
letes, a disproportionate number of whom are black. Few of those
dreams come true. Fewer than 30 percent of football and basketball
players graduate, a rate far lower than for all students, and only a
tiny fraction make it to the pros. While a handful of exemplary
programs can claim to graduate nearly 100 percent—Notre Dame,
Duke and Penn State, for example—too many follow the lead of
Memphis State, which graduated six out of 58 basketball players
between 1973 and 1983.

These broken bargains can be traced to the peculiar economics of   4
college sports. Despite the enormous sums of money involved, athletics are not a profitable enterprise for most colleges. Only about 45
athletic departments operate in the black each year. And only a few of
those—notably Penn State, Notre Dame and Miami—do so consistently, because college sports as they're staged today, and football in
particular, are very expensive businesses. Says John Slaughter, former
chancellor of the University of Maryland, who is now president of
Occidental College, "Winning is the thing that ensures the income.
Football and basketball have to make money, and they have to win to
make money, and that's how the cycle becomes so vicious."

The cycle has become vicious indeed. Last year, 21 universities   5
were penalized by the National Collegiate Athletic Association
(NCAA) for infractions ranging from falsifying entrance exams to
wooing recruits with cash to paying players, while an additional 28
were under NCAA investigation. Such ethical lapses belie the myth
that college sports provide a moral education, and the effect is clear
in the behavior of athletes. Since 1987, more than 250 college athletes have been arrested for violent crimes ranging from fistfights to
attempted murder.

Why do universities tolerate a business that is exploitative and   6
violent—and loses money on top of it all? First, and most obviously,
a lot of people—from coaches to recruiters to concessionaires—
make their living off it. And some make a very good living; college
coaches earn as much as $1 million a year in salary and endorsement
fees. But more to the point, big-time college sports satisfy a psychological need. As Robert Atwell, president of the American Council
on Education, notes, "It's the nature of this highly competitive society of ours that loves winners and hates losers. College sports feed
the insatiable appetite of the American male to be a couch potato
and watch all this stuff."

Corruption and violence are nothing new in college athletics,   7 but the money has increased the pressure on recruiters to pay more attention to athletic prowess than to character. Last January, the University of Oklahoma's athletic dorm was the scene of a gang rape. The same month, one teammate shot another over a cassette tape, and quarterback Charles Thompson sold cocaine to an FBI agent. Four Sooners are now in prison, and the NCAA has put the team on three years' probationary exclusion from TV appearances and postseason play for "major violations" including drug use and payments to players.

Oklahoma has plenty of company in its misery. Just last month, two more universities, Maryland and North Carolina State, joined the ranks of those being punished, and while NCAA Executive Director Richard Schultz insists that "99 percent of everything that is going on in intercollegiate athletics today is exceptionally positive," the truth is that 10 to 20 percent of Division I athletic programs are in trouble with the NCAA's enforcement office at any given time.   8

There are signs that educators have reached their limit. A *U.S. News* poll conducted last summer revealed that nearly 86 percent of college presidents now believe the pressures for success on the playing fields interfere with the primary educational mission of America's schools. Their frustration is evident in the words of Gordon Gee, president of the University of Colorado, who says, "We've got to deprofessionalize college athletics and return to the Greek notion of amateur competition."   9

But those days never existed, not in Olympia, and certainly not on the college gridiron, and it is the perpetuation of that myth that has college sports so conflicted. From its beginnings shortly after the Civil War, football has been soiled by violence and commercialism, as teams made use of older, tougher "tramp" players, students in name only. After numerous deaths on the gridiron, President Teddy Roosevelt ordered colleges in 1905 to take control of their student-run teams.   10

In doing so, administrators found that football was profitable. Yale's nationally ranked team, for example, had amassed a reserve of $100,000 (about $2 million today). Professional sport was considered degrading for institutions of higher learning, but money and football were so intimately entwined that the colleges could not possibly disentangle the two without killing the sport altogether. Instead, the universities created the illusion of amateurism by forming the NCAA to "retain a clear line of demarcation between college athletics and professional sports."   11

While college athletes are technically amateurs—their scholarships cover tuition, fees, books, room and board—their sweat is the fuel that runs an enormous machine. In 1988, Division I-A football   12 generated $500 million in gate, TV and licensing revenues and untold amounts from corporate sponsors and boosters. Ironically, this income rarely shows up on university ledgers. At many big-time schools, athletic departments are run as separate corporations—financially shaky corporations. The University of Michigan, for example, one of the largest athletic departments in the country, operates 21 sports on a $21.3 million budget. Last year, the Wolverines were $2.6 million in the hole.

The explanation is simple: To make money, a school has to   13
spend it. At the University of Colorado, all of the modest $4.5 million that football earns is churned right back into football, a practice that paid off this season, when the perennially mediocre Buffaloes won a trip to the Orange Bowl with their 11–0 record. Of the $4.1 million CU will take home from its Orange Bowl appearance this week, $3.1 million will be distributed evenly among the eight schools in the Big Eight Conference, including Oklahoma State and Oklahoma, both on NCAA probation. Ten days of carnival in Miami gobbled up the rest.

Boosters, athletic directors, presidents and coaches like to claim   14
that a winning program translates into something they call "the intangibles," prestige and donations for a school. "How many people know we have a Nobel Prize winner this year?" asks Jon Burianek, Colorado's associate athletic director. "Not many compared with the number who know this football team's Cinderella story."

Maybe so, but the fact is a high-profile team benefits the athletic   15
department, not the university. James Frey, a sociologist at the University of Nevada at Las Vegas, citing 12 different studies conducted over the past 50 years, concludes, "There's no relation between a winning record and donations that come into the university for academic programs."

As critics see it, the most hypocritical justification offered for   16
football's excesses is that the game builds character. The values that truly can be gained from sports—an appreciation for hard work, sportsmanship, the joy of playing—have been distorted by the desperate need to win. Boosterism is the perfect example. As Rick Telander, author of *The Hundred Yard Lie,* points out, "The Bull Gators, the booster club of the University of Florida, is giving money to win—not to build character but to beat the living daylights out of Florida State. That's got nothing to do with education."

To be sure, not all athletes object to the system. Some view   17
college as a mere formality standing between them and lucrative professional contracts. Colleges serve as farm teams for the National Football League and National Basketball Association, which have struck a cozy deal with the NCAA by agreeing not to take an athlete

before his college eligibility is up. Deion "Neon" Sanders, a defensive back of electrifying physical talents who signed a $4.4-million four-year contract last April with the Atlanta Falcons, graced few classrooms with his presence during his senior year at Florida State. Asked whether he wanted to be in college, Sanders told Telander, "No, but I have to be."

But for every athlete who makes it to the big time there are   18 hundreds more who neglect their studies in the mistaken belief that they too can cash in on their physical skills for a shot at a sweeter life. In reality, the road to the pros, where salaries in the NFL average $256,000 and in the NBA $650,000, is long and narrow. More than 17,600 young men play Division I-A basketball and football, and each year only 150 of them will reach the big leagues; even fewer will last more than a year or so. Yet according to a recent NCAA Presidents Commission study of athletes, more than 23 percent of college athletes (and 44 percent of the blacks) believe they are headed for the pros. "There's nothing wrong with having those dreams," says Thomas Tutko, a sports psychologist at San Jose State University. "It's when you sacrifice everything else that the problem occurs."

The blame for the dismal state of college athletics must be   19 shared—with the media for worshiping athletes and with the high schools for failing at basic education. "Colleges and universities are receiving products of an inferior educational system," says Richard Lapchick, director of the Center for the Study of Sport in Society at Northeastern University. "They didn't create the attitudes of the players, the high schools did." And increasingly, the sins of the colleges are being visited upon the lower schools. In many parts of the country, high-school coaches recruit elementary-school students. Last year, high-school games began appearing on television.

Arthur Ashe, the only black male tennis player ever to win at   20 Wimbledon, believes that black athletes suffer most acutely from the worship of sports. Only 4 percent of Division I college students are black, yet they represent 56 percent of basketball players and 37 percent of football players—in part, says Ashe, because "the screening of black athletes in black communities starts very early. It is cold-blooded; and by the time a young black boy is 13, we know if he's a good athlete or not, and junior-high coaches have already started recruiting him."

Even those who come to college hoping to exchange their physi-   21 cal skills for a degree often discover the promise of an education is an illusion. And no wonder. The NCAA Presidents Commission study found that football and basketball players devote, on average, 30 hours a week to their sport, 16 more hours than they spend in class. Detroit Lions running back Barry Sanders, last year's Heisman

Trophy winner, quit school early to turn pro, saying that college athletes spend so much time on sports they "might as well get paid for it."

College presidents will have a chance to act on their concerns at 22 the annual NCAA meeting next week, where they will discuss shortening the basketball season and spring football practice. There will also be further debate over Proposition 42, the NCAA's plan to refuse scholarships to students who score below 700 on the standardized college-entrance exams. Critics charge that Prop 42 discriminates against black athletes, while others maintain that such measures will eventually force high schools to prepare their athletes academically. Already, seven states have adopted a "no pass, no play" rule. NCAA members are likely to endorse a plan devised by Senator Bill Bradley (D-N.J.) to make graduation rates public.

All of which amounts to modest tinkering. More effective would 23 be to marry the number of athletic scholarships the NCAA will allow to a school's graduation rate and to divorce monetary incentives from winning by bringing athletic departments back under the president's control. Better yet, require winning teams to share TV and bowl receipts with all Division I schools, an idea not likely to be greeted enthusiastically. "When I brought this up," says the Council on Education's Atwell, "[Georgetown basketball coach] John Thompson blasted me. He said, 'Am I the only capitalist in the room? Georgetown money belongs to Georgetown.' "

Some proponents of reform would go so far as to pay college 24 players, thus ending the hypocrisy of the amateur student-athlete. Certainly, the NFL and NBA ought to be contributing to the training of their future recruits, if not by starting farm teams then by aiding college programs. But more than anything, coaches, athletic directors, college presidents and the NCAA must acknowledge—as polls reveal the general public already has—that college basketball and football are careering out of control. "[Football] has become a business, carried on too often by professionals, bringing in vast gate receipts, demoralizing student ethics and confusing the ideals of sport, manliness and decency." These words were delivered at the University of Wisconsin by historian Frederick Jackson Turner. The year was 1906.

QUESTIONS OF CONTENT

1. According to Brownlee, what is the main cause behind the myth of the student-athlete, and what are the two elements of that cause?

2. While college sports, especially football and basketball, are big business, only about how many university athletic departments actually make a profit each year?
3. Why is Arthur Ashe a noteworthy commentator on black athletes, who make up a disproportion of college basketball and football players?
4. Beginning with its title, this essay focuses on the contrasts between the myths and the realities of college sports. Besides the student-athlete myth, what other myths does Brownlee describe?
5. At least how far back in American history has college football been a national problem? How, if at all, are current problems different?

QUESTIONS OF FORM

1. This essay is founded on a claim, stated in paragraph 1; put that claim into a single declarative statement. Is this a claim of fact, value, or policy?
2. Which cause of the excessive concern with winning does Brownlee analyze more completely, the psychological or the economic? Why do you suppose this is so?
3. Brownlee often uses financial statistics, especially dollar amounts, to support one line of argument, that economic considerations play a major role in college sports. In how many of the essay's 24 paragraphs do financial data appear, and what effect does that amount of use have on the force of Brownlee's argument?
4. What are some of the proposed reforms (claims of policy) for college sports?
5. How does Brownlee refute the commonly held warrant that winning college athletic programs result in increased financial support for academic programs?

SUGGESTIONS FOR WRITING

1. Compose a letter to a friend in high school who is trying to decide whether or not to accept an athletic scholarship at an NCAA Division I college in order to finance his or her education; use Brownlee's essay in arguing for or against acceptance.
2. Consider the basketball or football program at a college in your region of the United States, and show that the situation of its players either confirms or refutes Brownlee's argument.
3. Assume that you are the president of your college or a nearby one that plays intercollegiate basketball. A wealthy graduate has just offered your college a gift of a half million dollars, the only restriction being that his son, a moderately talented senior basketball player who has not yet lettered, be allowed to play at least ten minutes of

every home game. Write a letter responding to this offer; be prepared to explain the reasoning behind your letter's contents.

Let's Keep Christmas Commercial

GRACE APRIL OURSLER ARMSTRONG

Every year right after Halloween, the world becomes Christmas-conscious—and people begin deploring. If only we could have a *real* Christmas, they say. The good old kind. Quiet, inexpensive, simple, devout. If only we could retrieve the holy day from the hands of vulgar moneygrubbers, they say. They say, with earnest horror, that the price tag has become the liturgical symbol of the season.

As a Christian, I do find facets of the Christmas season ridiculous, offensive or disturbing, but I believe most complaints about the commercialization of Christmas are unconsciously hypocritical nonsense. I'm afraid that often the complainers are kidding themselves, striking spiritual poses. I'm not ashamed to admit that if I had to spend Christmas somewhere far from the crowd and the vulgar trappings, I'd hate it. I love the lights, the exquisite ones in *boutiques*, the joyful ones in village centers, even the awkward ones strung on drugstores and filling stations. I love the Santa Clauses, including those on street corners, the intricately animated windows, the hot bewilderment of the bargain basement, the sequins of the dime store. Cut off from the whole wild confusion, I'd not be holier. I'd be forlorn. So, I suspect, would most of us.

What's supposed to be wrong with a commercialized Christmas?

For one thing, it's usually said that Christmas has become the time of parties where people drink and eat too much. ("Turning Yuletide into fooltide"—that exact phrase was used to describe the holiday in Merrie Olde England, so those who yearn for the "good old Christmas" should carefully define their terms.) Oddly enough, it seems to me that often the people who most loudly criticize this holiday partying are those folks who acquire Christmas hangovers and indigestion. And they deplore it as if no one ever had to avoid hangovers, indigestion or exhaustion at any other time of the year.

They say that commercialization has made the buying of Christmas presents a rat race. God knows, most of the gifts we peddle to each other have nothing to do with the infant of Bethlehem. For my part, I enjoy gawking in the catalogues at the new luxuries for people who have everything. My imagination romps over items for my private Ostentatious Wastefulness list: silver-plated golf clubs, hundred-dollar dresses for little girls to spill ice cream on. Dime and department stores are crammed with gifts no wise man would bring anyone. Things like stuffed dinosaurs twelve feet high and replicas of the *Pietà* that glow in the dark.

With rare exceptions it is foolishly pompous to get scandalized 6 and accuse manufacturers, advertisers and vendors of desecrating Christmas by trying to sell what you or I may think is silly junk. Obviously some people like it and buy it, and that's their business. It's said to be the fault of the commercializers that parents buy overpriced, unnecessary toys for children. And that's a fancy alibi. If you don't like what's being hawked this Christmas, you don't have to buy it. And if you're a sucker, your problem isn't seasonal.

Christians began giving presents to each other to celebrate Jesus' 7 birthday in imitation of the Wise Men who came to Bethlehem. The basic idea was and is to bring joy, to honor God in others, and to give in His name with love for all. But in our social structure, with or without the blessings of the Internal Revenue Service, Christmas presents serve many purposes. Gift givers are, in practice, often diplomats, almoners, egoists, or investors. A shiny box with gold ribbon may be a guilt assuager, a bribe, a bid for attention, or merely payment for services past or future. And what is in the box must look rightly lavish, conveying subliminal impact while not costing too much. That kind of petty ugliness we all know about. And we know that often, too, gift givers play Santa Claus against their will, badgered by cozy reminders in the parking lot about how the boys wish you Season's Greetings, or by collections taken up in offices, clubs, Sunday schools, Scouts and third grades.

But are extortion, begging, status seeking and advantage taking so 8 unusual among us that they occur only once a year? Isn't it more realistic to admit that whatever is sleazy about Christmas isn't seasonal?

After all, the instinct and art of commercialization are neither 9 good nor bad. People normally, naturally, make a living from every kind of want, aspiration and occasion. We exploit births, weddings, deaths, first communions, bar mitzvahs, the wish to smell nice, the craving for amusement, and the basic desires for housing, clothes, love and food. Is anything more commercialized than food? But no one complains when millions cash in on our need to eat.

Do we assume that eating is so earthy and undignified that com- 10 mercialization upgrades it, while celebrating Christmas should be so totally ethereal a process that it shouldn't be treated in a human way? If so, we are both pretentious and mistaken. We are creatures who both eat and worship, and God doesn't want us as split personalities. When Christ once raised a little girl from death, the next thing He did was to tell her mother to feed her.

Simony is a sin, the sin of trying to buy or sell what is sacred.   11
But this is not simony or sin, this peddling of manger sets, this
pitchman heralding the season. No one can buy or sell Christmas.
No one can steal it from us, or ruin it for us, except ourselves. If we
become self-seeking, materialistic, harried and ill-willed in this
Christmas melee, that's our problem, not the fault of the world in
which we live.

Some people are dismayed today in a different way, because they   12
honestly fear Christmas is being de-Christianized, made nonsectar-
ian. They are upset when someone who does not share their faith
sets up a tree and exchanges gifts and wishes them "Season's Greetings" instead of naming the holy day. They resent the spelling
"Xmas." Others fret over the way Santa Claus and snowmen crowd
out the shepherds. Put Christ back into Christmas, these offended
people cry.

As far as I know, Christ never left it. He could never be cut out of   13
Christmas, except in the privacy of individual hearts. I don't care if
some people designate Xmas as the Time for Eggnog, or Toys. Let
them call it the Time to Buy New Appliances, the Time to Use the
Phone, or the Time for New Loans. The antics of the rest of the
world can't change Christmas. Why on earth should we expect everyone to share our special joy our way?

Actually, what bothers most people who decry the vulgar Ameri-   14
can Christmas is a matter of taste, not of morals or of religious
commitment. Taste is a very personal matter, relative, changing and
worldly; we're all a rather tacky lot anyway, religious or not. Some
Christians like those new stark liturgical Christmas cards, and some
dote on luminous plastic crèches, and I hate both, and the Lord
doesn't care a bit. Maybe you can't stand Rudolf, are bored with the
same old carols, and cringe at Santa in a helicopter. But don't blame
your discomfort on commercialization and become righteous and
indignant. After all, if your taste is better than that of most other
people, you're probably proud of it, and you should be willing to
suffer the consequences in kindly forbearance.

I believe the root of complaints about commercialized Christ-   15
mas is that we're falling into the dangerous habit of thinking that
religion is somehow coarsened by contact with real people. I suspect
that unconsciously we're embarrassed at the prospect of trying to
live with God here and now. At times we modern Christians seem to
have a neurotic refusal to embrace reality in the name of the Lord
who was the supreme realist, and maker of the real.

It's always easier, if you're not doing very well religiously, to   16
insist that the secularizing world prevents you from devotion.
Christmas is meant to be lived in the noisy arena of the shopping

day countdown, amid aluminum trees, neckties and counterfeit French perfume. If all the meditation I get around to is listening to Scrooge and Tiny Tim, or begging heaven for patience to applaud a school pageant, I'm a fool to blame anyone but myself. Census time in Bethlehem was distracting too.

I know a man who confides that he learns more about patience 17 and love of his neighbor in post-office lines than anywhere else. More than one mother has learned that Christmas shopping on a tight budget can be a lesson in mortification, humility, willpower and joy. There's grist for meditation in the reflection of tree lights in a sloshy puddle. Families have their own customs, their private windows on glory. And families that are honest and relaxed find that the commercially generated atmosphere of goodwill hinders them not at all in their celebration. God works in wondrous ways still, even among assemble-it-yourself toys.

Christmas is a parable of the whole Christian venture. The Chris- 18 tian's attitude toward it, his willingness to make it relevant repeatedly in his own time and space, is a symptom of his whole encounter with God. The first Christmas happened, so Christians believe, because God lovingly plunged Himself into human nature to transform it. He is not honored by men and women who want to disown other people's human nature in His name.

Let's not make the mealy-mouthed error of complaining that 19 paganism threatens Christmas today. Christmas has already absorbed and recharged the vestiges of Druid feasts, Norse gods and sun worship. Christmas took the world as it was and built on it, and it's still doing just that.

To those who fear that Christmas is prostituted by the almighty 20 dollar, I suggest that it's remarkable and beautiful that Christmas is publicly touted at all. Nor do I make that suggestion, as some might suspect, in a tone of meek appeasement to groups that object to Christmas celebrations in public schools, or crèches in town squares. Realistically, I know that in our society what is important to people and concerns them deeply, whether it's cancer or get-rich-quick schemes, patriotism or religion, is talked about and exploited.

If Christmas becomes for some people primarily a subject for 21 commercials, at least God is getting equal time with toothpaste. If people didn't care about Him, He wouldn't even get that.

In good taste or bad, by your standards or mine, the fact of 22 Christ, the good news of the meeting of heaven and earth, the tidings of love and peace for human nature, are announced everywhere. It is still true that he who has ears to hear will hear.

QUESTIONS OF CONTENT

1. In paragraphs 4–8, according to Armstrong, people who deplore the commercialization of Christmas usually claim that the real meaning of Christmas has been undermined by three kinds of human activity. What human activities are these?
2. Armstrong suggests in paragraph 14 that the source of much criticism of America's commercialization of Christmas is that it offends our sense of good taste. She disagrees with this claim and suggests that it is not really commercialism that we find distasteful but something else. That something else is pivotal to her argument; what is it?
3. In order for her argument to succeed, Armstrong must demonstrate two things: her religious background and her knowledge of Christian traditions surrounding Christmas. Where in her essay does she demonstrate these things?
4. What does Armstrong mean when she says in paragraph 18 that Christmas is a parable of the whole Christian venture?
5. Why does Armstrong consider the commercialization of Christmas a hopeful rather than a dreadful thing?

QUESTIONS OF FORM

1. Paragraph 2 contains both a *concession* and a *claim.* Identify each.
2. Armstrong calls attention to the material fallacy of *false cause* in refuting the claim that the commercialization of Christmas tempts people to buy overpriced, unnecessary junk. She says that such a claim is a fancy alibi—that if people are suckers, their problem isn't seasonal; the real cause of their problem is human nature and not Christmas and its attendant commercialism. She appeals to the same fallacy in paragraphs 7 and 8. Explain how that appeal is made.
3. *Special pleading* is the fallacy of examining only part of the evidence (the part that suits one's purposes) while ignoring or minimizing other evidence. In paragraph 9 Armstrong accuses her opponents of this kind of pleading. How exactly does she do this? Where is she guilty of the same fallacy?
4. In arguing for the commercialization of Christmas, Armstrong finds it necessary to attack a warrant that is practically unopposed in the Christian world: Religious things are precious and should not be cheapened. In order to prevail, she must call attention to a warrant whose appeal is even stronger. What warrant is that?

SUGGESTIONS FOR WRITING

1. In a concise essay, state the basic elements of Armstrong's position.
2. Think about your own campus culture. What are some claims that

you take for granted, that you've heard repeated over and over? Consider these:

The humanities are useless for career seekers.
Athletics are overemphasized.
The drinking age should be lowered.
Residence hall life is too restrictive.
The cafeteria food is awful.

Now take your cues from Armstrong and attempt to refute one of these often accepted claims—or another college-related one of your own devising. Consider Armstrong's use of the material fallacies of false cause and special pleading and try to show that your opponents have been victimized by them.

3. Choose another unpopular stand and defend it as Armstrong does in "Let's Keep Christmas Commercial." First, determine the warrant that makes the claim unpopular. Then attack that warrant either by (a) showing that it has insufficient support or backing or by (b) locating another and stronger warrant, one supportive of your claim, that your opponents can share.

4. Now try something really difficult. Refute Armstrong's argument from either a Christian or a non-Christian point of view. Examine the evidence that she presents, and demonstrate that she has misrepresented the situation. Consider such questions as these as you prepare to write: Suppose you are a non-Christian—does her argument have the same force for you? How much of it is dependent on Christian ideals and doctrine?

Warning: Sports Stars May Be Hazardous to Your Health

JASON DE PARLE

In case you missed it, the 1989 press guide to the Women's International Tennis Association is an impressive volume. Its glossy pages bear tribute to what the guide immodestly calls "one of the greatest success stories of the modern sports world"—how women's tennis stepped from obscurity into the limelight of the Virginia Slims circuit, where in 1989 players competed for more than $17 million in prize money. Just twenty years earlier, the nation's best women tennis players languished before small crowds on high school courts. Now, the guide says, with their own massage therapists and "state-of-the-art forecasting system," they've become "synonymous with style."

They're synonymous with wealth, too: Chris Evert's $8.6 mil- 2
lion in lifetime earnings placed her a distant second to Martina
Navratilova's $14 million. But most of all, they're synonymous with
fine physical form. Sprinkled throughout the media guide are photos
of athletes in peak physical condition: Manuela Maleeva bends "low
for a forehand volley," "Hana Mandlikova intently awaits a return,"
"Gabriela Sabatini puts to use her 'smashing' backhand."

Those of us less physically gifted than Hana Mandlikova can't 3
help but envy the strength in her legs, power in her arms, and stam-
ina in her lungs as she pauses, racket poised, before exploding into
her backhand. It's precisely the rareness of these qualities that
brings us to admire her so, and to pause a moment when looking at
her picture. Because as Mandlikova intently awaits a return, she
does so in front of a big sign that says "Virginia Slims"—a product
not known for promoting the powers of heart and lung that lie at the
center of her trade. In fact, throughout the guide—not to mention
the nation's sports pages and television broadcasts—we find these
stars showcasing their enviable talents in front of cigarette ads. The
bold corporate logo of the Virginia Slims series emphasizes the bond:
a woman, sassy and sleek, holds a racket in one hand and a cigarette
in the other.

This is odd. Tennis champions, after all, are models of health, 4
particularly the health of heart and lungs, where endurance is essential. And cigarette smoking, as the Surgeon General has reminded
us, "is the chief avoidable cause of death in our society"—death,
more precisely, from heart and lung disease.

The fit athletes of the Virginia Slims circuit who swat balls in 5
front of cigarette ads, in a tournament named for a cigarette brand,
pocketing large sums from a cigarette company's largesse, are but a
small subset of the great marriage of sports and tobacco. A large and
growing number of sports now lend their athletes' credibility as fine
physical specimens to the tobacco companies, whose products, by
the Surgeon General's estimate, kill about 1,000 people a day.

Cigarette manufacturers exploit sporting events in a variety of 6
ways, ranging from such old-fashioned strategies as stadium advertising to the underwriting of sports, such as Winston Series Drag Racing or Marlboro Cup horseracing. When the pitchmen of Philip Morris say, "You've come a long way baby," they could very well be
congratulating themselves; their success in co-opting the nation's
health elite to promote a product that leads to an array of fatal
diseases is extraordinary.

But they couldn't have done it alone. For starters, they needed 7
the cooperation of the athletes, and, with a few praiseworthy exceptions, they've gotten it. When Billie Jean King set out 20 years ago to

find a sponsor for women's tennis, she may have needed Philip Morris as much as it needed her. But these days, she and the other stars of women's tennis have actually had to fight off other corporate sponsors who would welcome the chance to take over. The tobacco companies have also needed the help of sports journalists, and, again, they've gotten it. The daily papers have been silent. The big magazines, like *Sports Illustrated,* are thick with tobacco ads and thin on tobacco critics. And the networks have been perfectly happy to show an infield decked with Marlboro banners, race cars painted with Marlboro signs, officials wearing Marlboro logos—while pretending that cigarette ads are still banned from the air.

The marriage of cigarettes and sports has at least three insidious   8
consequences. The first, and perhaps most troubling, is that it obscures the connection of cigarettes and disease, subliminally and perhaps even consciously. Quick: speak the words "Virginia Slims" and what do you see? (A) Chris Evert, or (B) the cancer ward? If you answered (A)—and most people do—then Philip Morris has you right where it wants you. (The recognition of this power is why the soccer star Pele won't pose near cigarette signs.) The second troubling fact about cigarettes' tryst with sport is that it allows them to penetrate the youth market. Cigarette spokesmen self-righteously insist they have no such goal. But tobacco companies desperately need teen smokers for the simple reason that few people start smoking once they are adults; and there's scarcely anyone more glamorous to a teenager than a star athlete. The third reason why cigarettes' infiltration of athletics is bad is that is circumvents the ban on television ads. Previously, cigarette companies had to hire actors to play athletes in their commercials, but now they've got the real thing.

Emphysema Slims

For those keeping moral score, cigarettes' involvement with aero-   9
bic sports, like tennis and soccer, is probably the most indefensible, since the respiratory fitness those sports require and represent is precisely what cigarettes deprive people of. That is, race car drivers can smoke and drive, but soccer stars certainly can't smoke and sprint. That doesn't mean race car drivers are welcome to promote cigarettes, of course. Their ties to tobacco endanger the public health by continuing to make cigarettes seem glamorous to kids, and by keeping the cigarette signs on T.V.

For leads on many of the following items, I am indebted to Dr.   10
Alan Blum, a Baylor physician whose anti-smoking research and

protests (like the staging of an "Emphysema Slims") makes him the Don King of the anti-smoking world:

Soccer: Besides the world's most enviable lungs, soccer offers   11
cigarettes two other advantages: wild overseas popularity at a time when American tobacco companies are stepping up their Third World trade, and a growing popularity among American youth.

Camel cigarettes, manufactured by R.J. Reynolds, was one of   12
four major sponsors of the 1986 World Cup in Mexico City. Among the privileges it received in return was the chance to post four seven-meter Camel signs next to the field, where the world-wide television audience of 650 million for the final game alone could see them.

Earlier in the decade, RJR even tried to field its own World Cup   13
club. In sponsoring the 1983 "Winston Team America Series," it compiled an all-star team and held a 30-game series against the pros in major stadiums across the country. During half-time, fans joined a contest to kick a ball through the letter "o" in a Winston sign.

Baseball: Cigarette companies have billboard ads in 22 of the 24   14
Major League ballparks in the United States, typically in spots that enhance broadcast coverage. The camera near the visiting team dug-out at Shea Stadium, for instance, which is used to capture men leading off first base, frames the player with the Marlboro sign in left-center. At Fenway Park in Boston, a sign for the Jimmy Fund for cancer research, a favorite Red Sox charity, hangs above the right field bleacher. So does a Marlboro sign.

Skiing: For about eight years, Loew's sponsored the Newport Ski   15
Weekend, which offered half-price lift tickets in exchange for ciga-rette boxes. Philip Morris invites skiers at a number of Western resorts to take the "Marlboro Challenge," a plunge down a timed race course festooned with Marlboro flags.

In the 1983–84 season, RJR's brand, Export A, became the official   16
sponsor of the Canadian Ski Association, which oversees the coun-try's major competitions. The company's original contract called for "the exclusive right . . . to identify itself or its products (including name, logo, and colours) on: flags, poles, course markers, scoreboards, award presentations, start banners . . . all buildings, podiums, back-drops. . . ." To be sure no one missed the point, the contract added: "The Association shall use its best efforts to have the events telecast on national network television."

But the Canadian skiers rebelled, with some refusing to accept   17
league trophies. The contract was modified following the protest, and the controversy led finally to a ban on all tobacco advertising in Canada. Ken Read, who represented Canada twice in Olympic skiing and is now a broadcaster, was among the leaders of the protest. "I think it's inappropriate for a cigarette to sponsor any sporting

event—period," he said. "It's incompatible with the objective of sport—to promote a healthy lifestyle."

I asked Read what he thought about the cigarette companies' 18 argument that they're only promoting brand loyalty and, therefore, not encouraging kids to smoke. "That's absolute garbage," he said. "When you're using sports as a tool, you're influencing youth."

Horse racing: Rather than take over an existing horse race, in 19 1973 Philip Morris simply went out and created one from scratch: the nationally-televised Marlboro Cup, which it sponsored until 1987.

In an interview with *The Daily Racing Form*, Ellen Merlo, direc- 20 tor of marketing promotions at Philip Morris, explained the event's appeal: "First, it has created enormous visibility for Marlboro. There are newspaper stories leading up to and following the race that mention the Marlboro name frequently, and this is excellent exposure. Secondly, the image of horse racing and the imagery of the Marlboro Man campaign seem to have reinforced each other. The man on the horse theme is central to both, and we feel it has worked well as a partnership."

Autoracing: Since 1971, RJR has been the chief sponsor of 21 NASCAR's premier circuit, the $18 million, 29-race Winston Cup Series. This is a sport that has other problems besides cigarette sponsorship, of course—such as encouraging 16-year-olds to play Richard Petty on the interstate. As they do, the word "Winston" may quickly come to mind: one of the races is called the Winston 500; another is simply known as The Winston. The driver who accumulates the most points during the season wins the $1 million Winston Cup. The driver who wins three of the top four races wins a bonus called, accurately, the Winston Million—you get the idea.

"We're in the cigarette business. We're *not* in the sports busi- 22 ness. We *use* sports as an avenue for advertising our products . . . ," said Wayne Robertson, an RJR executive, in a trade journal. "We can go into an area where we're marketing an event, measure sales during the event and measure sales after the event, and see an increase in sales."

If this list seems lengthy, don't forget it omits the Vantage Golf 23 Scoreboard, Salem Pro-Sail races, Lucky Strike bowling, the Winston Rodeo, Benson & Hedges on Ice, and any number of other cigarette-sponsored sports. It also omits Camille Duvall, champion water skier and cover girl for an issue of *Philip Morris Magazine*, where the company that insists its interest in athletes has nothing to do with glamour, describes her as "gorgeous—swimsuit issue, pack-it-in-Paulina, no-exaggeration, gorgeous."

Those who think that tobacco's conquest of sport is complete, 24 however, can take heart—according to the *Chicago Sun-Times*, Philip Morris recently lost the $12,000 sponsorship of the U.S. boomerang team to an anti-smoking group called Doctors Ought to Care, which is run by Alan Blum. Philip Morris "promised us all kinds of publicity," the team captain, Eric Shouffer, told the newspaper. "If we'd wear big Philip Morris logos on our chest, they told us we'd be on 'Good Morning America' and so on."

It wasn't just conscience that governed the team's decision,   25
Shouffer said, but practical considerations, too: One member is an asthmatic "who falls over dead when he gets near smokers."

Hacking Hags

Whether or not the figure of 1,000 deaths a day presents tobacco   26
companies with a moral challenge, it certainly presents them with an economic one: how to replace the thousands of people their products kill each week. To some extent, cigarette companies have been losing the war. In 1965, 40 percent of American adults smoked; by 1987, this figure had dropped off to 29 percent. But while cigarette consumption is declining, it's declining least among blacks, women, high school drop-outs, blue-collar workers, and other groups whose members tend to lead more difficult lives. The more marginal one's status in society, the more likely one is to smoke.

Since 1971, when the ban on televised cigarette ads took effect,   27
the cigarette companies' efforts to reach their target audiences have grown more complicated. The story of the ad ban is an interesting one in itself, and perhaps its most salient moral is that, despite the immense wealth and power of the tobacco companies, there is, in fact, much that one person can do. In this case, the person was John Banzhaf, a 26-year-old law school graduate. Noting the saturation of TV with cigarette ads, he sent off a three-page letter to the Federal Communications Commission, arguing that the Fairness Doctrine required broadcasters to give anti-smoking groups their say. To nearly everyone's surprise, the FCC agreed, announcing in 1967 that henceforth broadcasters should air one anti-smoking spot for every three or four cigarette commercials.

Anti-smoking groups took to the air with an inordinate amount   28
of creativity. Though television viewers were still being blitzed with ads that showed happy smokers in vigorous poses, now they received other visions too: a Marlboro-like man, bursting boldly through the saloon doors, only to collapse in a fit of coughs; a wrinkled hag on a respirator, cigarette in hand, asking, "Aren't I sexy?" Though still outnumbered, these hacking, wincing images of death

began to register: cigarette consumption declined in each of the next four years. The cigarette companies weren't just losing the battle; through the Fairness Doctrine they were subsidizing the other side's artillery. In 1970, they went to Congress to say they wanted out.

The withdrawal wasn't as easy as it might seem, however. If one 29 company withdrew its ads, it ceded an advantage to its competitors: if all withdrew at once, they were subject to antitrust reprisals for collusion. What they needed was an order: ban us, they asked. Perhaps the constituency least pleased by this prospect was the broadcasters, who were then banking about $250 million a year in tobacco ad revenues. Though Congress finally passed the ban over the broadcasters' objections, the TV executives, to whom the term "conscience-stricken" could not fairly be applied, did win a soothing concession: the ban didn't take effect until midnight on January 1, 1971—after the commercial-thick bowl games were aired.

Cigarette strategists now had to contend with a more compli- 30 cated world. They still needed to saturate the culture with the idea that smoking leads to happiness, but television, their most powerful weapon, seemed off limits. *Seemed* is the operative word here. By channeling some of that $250 million ad budget into sports sponsorship, cigarette companies were right back on the air. Consider the timing: Virginia Slims, born 1971; Winston Cup racing, born 1971; Marlboro Cup horse racing, born 1973. Sports sponsorship has become such an spectacular success that by now all kinds of corporations want in—the John Hancock Bowl, the Mazda Gator Bowl. "We have a waiting list for inside billboards," says Jane Allen, who works in the marketing department of the Charlotte Motor Speedway. "Everybody in the business knows it's because of TV coverage."

Of course, cigarette companies couldn't co-opt athletics if athlet- 31 ics wasn't willing to be co-opted. For the most part, that willingness consists not of active promotion but of silence, which is just as necessary to the cigarette salesmen's success. Imagine how many baseball fans, teenage and adult, would get the message if Darryl Strawberry held a press conference to denounce the indecency the Marlboro sign lends to the Shea Stadium outfield. Or better yet, trotted out with a paint brush to cover it up. What could the Mets management do? Bench him?

While Strawberry's probably valuable enough to get away with it 32 on his own, lots of lesser players aren't. Alone, that is. But imagine if the entire Mets roster signed a petition, refusing to play the 1990 season under the Marlboro banner—refusing to donate their authority as athletes, T.V. stars, and teen idols to the nation's number one health hazard. Look northward, New York Mets! The Canadian skiers told RJR to drop dead—you can, too!

What the athletes need is a little leadership, and one place where 33
you might hope to find it is the office of Dr. Bobby Brown, the
American League president, former New York Yankee, and *cardiolo-
gist*. In 1985, Alan Blum, the anti-smoking activist, wrote to Brown
and suggested he do something to remove cigarette ads from stadiums. Brown wrote back a nothing-I-can-do letter ("legally permitted," "forced to recognize an individual's rights") promising se-
renely that, "This is an ongoing problem, however, that we will
continue to address."

I called Brown recently to see how the progress was coming. 34
Major League Baseball, after all, forbids athletes from smoking in
uniform—why can't it forbid them from playing in front of cigarette
billboards? Isn't the purpose of the uniform ban to keep baseball
players from promoting cigarettes? Brown couldn't have been more
disingenuous: he said he didn't know the reason athletes were forbidden to smoke in uniform, just that it was on the books and he didn't
feel compelled to change it.

As for billboards, Brown agreed that "anytime you have advertis- 35
ing, the tobacco companies think you have a chance of increasing
sales—that's why they're doing it." To remove them, however,
would be "unrealistic," since tobacco companies could still adver-
tise elsewhere, such as in subways. Maybe even Brown didn't want
to hear himself offer this explanation, however, because he began to
sound annoyed. "Who are you, sir?" he asked. "Who funds you?"
When I suggested that subways might not pack the prestige of Major
League Baseball, and, anyway, someone needed to take the first step,
he got angrier. "It's *unrealistic* for tobacco ads to be removed from
baseball parks," he said. Then he hung up.

Most athletes can probably claim to have given the issue little 36
thought (some too convincingly). Brown at least can claim that he's
not actively soliciting the billboards, just shrugging his shoulders
while others do. But I'd like to know what people like Billie Jean
King, Chris Evert, and Martina Navratilova—athletes who have
thought it over, and pledged the cigarette companies their fidelity—
can claim, but they aren't returning phone calls on the issue.

"I believe in free enterprise," King said in 1983, on one of the few 37
times she's been publicly quizzed on her tobacco ties (significantly,
it wasn't a journalist but an anti-smoking activist who asked the
question). King went on to say that "Personally, I hate cigarette
smoking. I hate cigarettes. Ninety-five percent of the girls do"—as
though this excuses her prominent role in their promotion over the
past two decades, as though this justifies her taking the court against
Bobby Riggs in 1973 dressed in Virginia Slims colors, with Virginia
Slims sequins on her chest. What she's saying is this: Let someone

else get lung cancer; it won't be me; and I'll get rich and famous in the process.

In the two decades that King's been selling Philip Morris her image of vigor—she not only played Riggs, remember, she beat him—lung cancer has overtaken breast cancer as a leading cause of women's death. And what are King & Co. doing about it now? Continuing to coo about how "loyal" Philip Morris has been while rebuffing a bid by Proctor & Gamble in 1988 to take over the women's tour.

'A Loophole'

Just as it takes a certain physiological culture for cancer to conquer a lung, it takes a certain journalistic one for tobacco to conquer sports. And sports journalists, for the most part, have provided it. The major components of this culture are indifference ("I just report the news; I don't make it") and rationalization ("It's a legal product; people can make their own choices")—with a generous sprinkling of publisher's greed, in the form of cigarette ads. Relish for a moment the thought of a Sam Donaldson of sport trailing Chris Evert and you get a sense of how vulnerable athletes would be to a determined inquiry: "Ms. Evert, lung cancer has just surpassed breast cancer as a killer of women; why do you display your athletic talents in front of that Virginia Slims banner? Don't you care about the welfare of women? Does money mean that much to you?"

And it's not as though sports journalists can't see what's going on. As Lydia Stephans, programming manager for ABC Sports, said, "I'm sure that's why Virginia Slims put up that money—so they could get that recognition, the association with sports and health. Otherwise why would they want to pump millions of dollars into sports? They can't do it by putting a commercial on the T.V. They used to show people sailing around smoking cigarettes. So now they do it through sports. . . . On their behalf, I think it's clever. They've found a loophole."

As for the dailies, no one who has walked past the sports desk of an average American newspaper is likely to confuse it for a breeding ground of social reform. The idea that they have a moral obligation to speak out against tobacco's role in sport is likely to strike many sportswriters as about as compelling as their obligation to champion educational reform in Zambia. For lots of them, it's just not on the radar.

"We haven't done the piece you're doing. It's a legitimate story. I'm glad you're doing it," said Leonard Shapiro, sports editor at *The*

38

39

40

41

42

Washington Post, who was more thoughtful about the topic than most of the journalists I spoke to. "Maybe it's become such an ingrained part of our culture, it's something we don't even notice."

What are the sports editors' options? One strategy might just be 43 to rename the event. When Ellen Merlo of Philip Morris brags about "the newspaper stories leading up to and following the race that mention the Marlboro name frequently," sportswriters could decide that henceforth the "Marlboro Cup" will just become "The Cup." (Newspapers routinely make such judgments about proper editorial content, screening out, say, obscenity.) Failing that, how about a big "Surgeon General's Warning: Smoking Causes Lung Cancer, Heart Disease, Emphysema, and May Complicate Pregnancy" slapped on the photos of the tourney?

The sportswriter who, by chance, does develop a Donaldson com- 44 plex on the issue isn't likely to find great encouragement from above. For one, a number of newspapers have actually allied themselves as co-sponsors of cigarette-backed sporting events. *The Houston Chronicle, The Houston Post, The Boston Herald,* and the *Los Angeles Times* have all joined Philip Morris as backers of Virginia Slims events, while the *Atlanta Journal* joins RJR in financing the Atlanta Journal 500.

Ad Men

More to the point is a basic fact of American journalism: Publish- 45 ers like the income from cigarette ads, and few are likely to regard an anti-tobacco crusade as a boon to business. Not many will respond as forthrightly as Mark Hoop, publisher of the *Twin Cities Reader,* who flatly fired the reporter whose preview of the Kool Jazz Festival pointed out that Duke Ellington had died of lung cancer. (When later asked by ABC News if he'd really said, "If we have to fly to Louisville, Kentucky, and crawl on bended knees and beg the cigarette company not to take their ads out of our newspaper, we'll do that," Hoop said, "True.") But those with a subtler touch will still find a way to communicate that inordinate crusading on the issue does not enhance journalists' career advancement.

While actual cigarette advertising in many papers is modest, it's 46 not so modest that publishers are anxious to lose it. (A recent 12-page advertising supplement for Marlboro Grand Prix racing in *The New York Times Magazine* cost close to $300,000, according to the *Times's* advertising department.) And the conglomerate nature of cigarette ownership may mean that other ad revenues are also at stake: RJR's holdings include Nabisco, Del Monte, and Kentucky

Fried Chicken, while Philip Morris controls those of Seven-Up, the Miller Brewing Company, and General Foods, makers of Jello, Maxwell House, Tang, Oscar Mayer, and so forth. Let no one mistake the point—the cigarette companies haven't been shy about exercising this clout. After the advertising firm Saatchi & Saatchi produced a recent anti-smoking commercial for Northwest Airlines, RJR pulled its *$70 million* Nabisco account.

The media's own conglomerate status means it has more than   47
one flank exposed. Denunciations of RJR in *The Washington Post* could mean fewer ads for Camels, Oreos, and Smirnoff in *Newsweek*, just as an attack on Virginia Slims in *The New York Times* could lead to the end of the $900,000 of tobacco ads that appeared last year in its wholly-owned *Tennis* magazine. Obviously, both the *Post* and *Times* have had unkind words for tobacco; but neither can claim to have provided the kind of unforgiving coverage that tobacco has earned with a product that *every two years* kills more Americans than have died in all the wars of this century.

And that's just the daily press. For a sense of how cigarette   48
revenues have shaped the attitudes of the magazine world, consider the views of George Gross, executive vice president of the Magazine Publishers of America. He recently went before Congress to warn that restrictions on cigarette advertising could lead to a surge in smoking, since "the prominent health warnings now carried in all magazine tobacco advertising will not be seen by millions of readers." Now there's an original argument.

Meanwhile, a 1986 study by the University of Michigan School   49
of Public Health found that no other category of magazines— fashion, politics, general-interest, and so forth—relies more heavily on tobacco ads than do sports magazines. On the average, tobacco provided 11.3 percent of the sports journals' income, down slightly from 14.0 in 1976—but up impressively from pre-ad ban days of 1966, when it was only 2.1 percent. *Sports Illustrated*, the industry giant, weighed in at 11.3 percent—or $27 million.

The Dangers of Milk

What kinds of inhibitions might such revenues induce? It's cer-   50
tainly fair to say that *Sports Illustrated*, itself part of a larger Time, Inc. empire full of cigarette ads, hasn't brought an exceptionally skeptical view to the issue of tobacco and sports. "It's a fringe thing," says Peter Carry, the magazine's executive editor. In 1977, the magazine did find space for "Chaws," a nine-page celebration of chewing tobacco by an array of baseball stars. Sample? "I'll stick a

chaw in my mouth and everything seems to get a little brighter," said pitcher Rick Reuschel.

Meanwhile, one could suggest that *Sports Illustrated* has been less than zealous in publishing alternative points of view. Ask Greg Connolly, a Massachusetts dentist hired by Major League baseball to help athletes quit chewing tobacco. In 1986, Connolly says he contacted the magazine and offered to write a piece about the program. He said that two different editors, including baseball editor Steve Wulf, warned him that higher-ups might find a possible "conflict of interest" with advertisers, but Wulf told him to try it nonetheless. Connolly turned it in, but the piece never ran.

So what—maybe Connolly can't write. But that wasn't the explanation that Wulf gave Howard Wolinsky, a *Chicago Sun-Times* medical writer, when Wolinsky asked what happened. Wolinsky says Wulf told him, "based on common sense, magazines do not like to upset their advertisers by publishing stories that are negative on an advertised product." When I called Wulf he confirmed that he had warned Connolly about possible conflicts of interest, and he acknowledged the conversation with Wolinsky. He said he was speaking to Wolinsky about magazines in general, not *Sports Illustrated*, which he said "does not let its advertisers dictate its editorial content." His fears about the possible conflict of interest, he said, "turned out not to be the case. The sole reason it didn't run was for editorial purposes."

Judging from another *Sports Illustrated* article, the magazine seems to think that tobacco isn't just a "fringe" issue in sports but also in health. In 1983, the magazine ran a 10-page article deploring the sad state of "fitness" in America, explaining how poor diet and a lack of exercise contribute to heart disease and general ill health. The article doesn't exactly ignore tobacco. Cigarettes show up twice. First the magazine argues, "The problem is not only too little exercise—the culprits in the case of children include TV and, recently, video games—but too many cigarettes, too many calories and a diet far too rich in salt and saturated fats. . . ." Next, it advises "'lifestyle' changes, such as cutting out cigarettes. . . . *Just as important* is the need to 'engineer' more activity into daily life. Use stairs instead of elevators. Leave your car at the far end of the parking lot. . . ." (Emphasis added.)

With the messy little business of cigarettes put behind, the magazine turned a tarter tongue toward a real social blight: sweetened water. The Los Angeles public pools were offering free admission "to children producing wrappers from Kool-Aid packages," the authors said. "Of course, the appropriateness of such an association with Kool-Aid, a product not ordinarily thought of as promoting fitness,

might be questioned." Imagine how heartless those Kool-Aid ped-
dlers are! Of all the things to push on kids! The writers went on to
document another crass exercise of corporate power, blasting the
National Dairy Council for "disseminating educational material on
nutrition that pointedly neglects to suggest that readers might want
to restrict their intake of eggs, whole milk, butter." Why the dairy
council even gave those milk pamphlets to kids! Rascals! Have they
no shame?

The same issue that emphasized the dangers of elevators and   55
eggs more than Marlboros, Camels, or Winstons happened to have
ten pages of cigarette advertising. Among the ads was a two-page
spread from the Tobacco Institute, which asked "Is cigarette advertising a major reason why kids smoke?" and answered, "No." When I
asked Jerry Kirshenbaum, the fitness article's co-author, how the
ethics of that ad compared to the Dairy Council's plug for milk, he
said, "I really don't think I want to discuss this any further."

Interestingly, *Sports Illustrated* did run a very hard-hitting arti-   56
cle last year on beer's effect on sports, which shows the magazine
hasn't just simply tuned out on moral issues. Beer's involvement in
sport, through sponsorship and advertising, led the magazine "to
wonder just what kind of cultural hypocrisy is going on when
Americans relentlessly insist on immersing sport—our most wholesome, most admired, even (sometimes) most heroic institution—in
a sea of intoxicating drink." *SI* suggested that this was "cynical,
ironic, immoral, hypocritical. . . ." The magazine's beer-ad revenues in 1988 were $6.3 million—significant, but far short of to-
bacco's $35 million. And perhaps equally significant, beer compa-
nies don't feel as imperilled, and hence, as vindictive, as cigarette
makers do.

Carry, the executive editor and a former smoker, said that quit-   57
ting was one of the hardest things he'd ever done. But as far as
tobacco's involvement with sports, "I would say on the level of the
world's evils, I would say it ranks pretty low."

While it would certainly help if *Sports Illustrated* saved its   58
righteous indignation for Kools instead of Kool Aid, the tobacco
companies have friends in even higher places—television. It was
the broadcasters, remember, who did their level best to keep cigarette commercials on the air. These days, televised tennis and autoracing don't sell cigarette ads but do sell equally lucrative car ads
and truck ads and beer ads instead.

The small group of network executives who control the nation's   59
sports programming have unique power where tobacco and athletics
are concerned. If the heads of CBS, ABC, and NBC simply turned on

the TV, saw the whirl of Marlboro cars, flags, and banners, and said, "Hey, that's a cigarette ad—don't show it," the game would be over. Without the magnifying effects of broadcast coverage, tobacco's 20-year outbreak of sports fever would meet its antibiotic. (To protect themselves from losing a competitive advantage to some less scrupulous, upstart station, the networks could seek a ruling from the FCC, pointing out tobacco's circumvention of the law. And, of course, the FCC needn't be shy; it could always instigate an investigation itself.) A few "sports" might go under, at least in their present forms. Then again, if the Winston Cup can't exist without Winston, then isn't it more cigarette ad than sport, after all?

QUESTIONS OF CONTENT

1. What are some examples of "the marriage of sports and tobacco" (paragraph 8)?
2. What three groups have generally cooperated with the tobacco companies to make the "marriage" so successful?
3. What are three bad results of the "marriage"?
4. What legislation which went into effect in 1971 caused tobacco companies to become major sponsors of sports events?
5. What kind of cancer has displaced breast cancer as the leading cause of female cancer-related deaths in the last twenty years? What brand of cigarettes for women was introduced in 1971? What sort of connection do you see between these two facts?
6. What country created a "divorce" of tobacco and sports that eventually led to a total ban on tobacco advertising? Why do you suppose De Parle refers to that experience?

QUESTIONS OF FORM

1. How has De Parle created emphasis via contrast in the opening paragraphs of his essay?
2. What makes his argument inductive?
3. How do the data De Parle cites from a 1986 University of Michigan study of magazines give additional support to his claim of a "marriage" between sports and tobacco?
4. What warrant regarding the connection between tobacco and health underlies De Parle's entire essay?
5. What claim is De Parle supporting when he quotes the Canadian Ken Read in paragraphs 17–18?

SUGGESTIONS FOR WRITING

1. De Parle sarcastically calls George Gross's rationalization for opposing new restriction on cigarette ads in magazines and newspapers "an original argument." It is, in fact, an example of an unwitting *reduction to absurdity* on Gross's part. In an essay of no more than 550 words, explain the absurdity of Gross's statement, quoted in paragraph 48.
2. Write a letter to a sports star who participates in tobacco company-sponsored events, using information from De Parle's essay to persuade her or him to boycott such events.
3. Try revising this basic essay, using *breweries* (also major sponsors of sporting events) in place of tobacco companies, but making a similar argument. As an alternative, write an essay criticizing wealthy athletes who take large fees for endorsing name-brand athletic clothing, shoes, and other expensive products, thereby pushing a consumerist viewpoint on the general public, but especially on children and teenagers all across our country.

The Warming of the World

CARL SAGAN

When humans first evolved—in the savannahs of East Africa a few million years ago—our numbers were few and our powers feeble. We knew almost nothing about controlling our environment—even clothing had yet to be invented. We were creatures of the climate, utterly dependent upon it.

A few degrees hotter or colder on average, and our ancestors were in trouble. The toll taken much later by the ice ages, in which average land temperatures dropped some 8°C (centigrade, or Celsius), must have been horrific. And yet, it is exactly such climatic change that pushed our ancestors to develop tools and technology, science and civilization. Certainly, skills in hunting, skinning, tanning, building shelters and refurbishing caves must owe much to the terrors of the deep ice age.

Today, we live in a balmy epoch, 10,000 years after the last major glaciation. In this climatic spring, our species has flourished; we now cover the entire planet and are altering the very appearance of our world. Lately—within the last century or so—humans have acquired, in more ways than one, the ability to make major changes in that climate upon which we are so dependent. The Nuclear Winter findings are one dramatic indication that we can change the climate—in this case, in the spasm of nuclear war. But I wish here to describe a different kind of climatic danger, this one slower, more subtle and arising from intentions that are wholly benign.

It is warm down here on Earth because the Sun shines. If the Sun were somehow turned off, the Earth would rapidly cool. The oceans would freeze, eventually the atmosphere itself would condense out and our planet would be covered everywhere by snowbanks of solid oxygen and nitrogen 10 meters (about 30 feet) high. Only the tiny trickle of heat from the Earth's interior and the faint starlight would save our world from a temperature of absolute zero.

We know how bright the Sun is; we know how far from it we are; and we know what fraction of the sunlight reaching the Earth is reflected back to space (about 30 percent). So we can calculate— with a simple mathematical equation—what the average temperature of the Earth should be. But when we do the calculation, we find that the Earth's temperature should be about 20°C below the freezing point of water, in stark contradiction to our everyday experience. What have we done wrong?

As in many such cases in science, what we've done wrong is to forget something—in this case, the atmosphere. Every object in the universe radiates some kind of light to space; the colder the object, the longer the wavelength of radiation it emits. The Earth—much colder than the Sun—radiates to space mainly in the infrared part of the spectrum, not the visible. Were the Sun turned off, the Earth would soon be indetectable in ordinary visible light, though it would be brilliantly illuminated in infrared light.

When sunlight strikes the Earth, part is reflected back into the sky; much of the rest is absorbed by the ground and heats it—the darker the ground, the greater the heating. The ground radiates back upward in the infrared. Thus, for an airless Earth, the temperature would be set solely by a balance between the incoming sunlight absorbed by the surface and the infrared radiation that the surface emits back to space.

When you put air on a planet, the situation changes. The Earth's atmosphere is, generally, still transparent to visible light. That's why we can see each other when we talk, glimpse distant mountains and view the stars.

But in the infrared, all that is different. While the oxygen and nitrogen in the air are transparent in both the infrared and the visible, minor constituents such as water vapor (H_2O) and carbon dioxide (CO_2) tend to be much more opaque in the infrared. It would be useless for us to have eyes that could see at a wavelength, say, of 15 microns in the infrared, because the air is murky black there.

Accordingly, if you add air to a world, you heat it: The surface now has difficulty when it tries to radiate back to space in the infrared. The atmosphere tends to absorb the infrared radiation, keeping heat near the surface and providing an infrared blanket for the world. There is very little CO_2 in the Earth's atmosphere—only 0.03 percent. But that small amount is enough to make the Earth's atmosphere opaque in important regions of the infrared spectrum. CO_2 and H_2O are the reason the global temperature is not well below freezing. We owe our comfort—indeed, our very existence—to the fact that these gases are present and are much more transparent in the visible than in the infrared. Our lives depend on a delicate balance of invisible gases. Too much blanket, or too little, and we're in trouble.

This property of many gases to absorb strongly in the infrared   11
but not in the visible, and thereby to heat their surroundings, is called the "greenhouse effect." A florist's greenhouse keeps its planty inhabitants warm. The phrase "greenhouse effect" is widely used and has an instructive ring to it, reminding us that we live in a planetary-scale greenhouse and recalling the admonition about living in glass houses and throwing stones. But, in fact, florists' greenhouses do not keep warm by the greenhouse effect; they work mainly by inhibiting the movement of air inside, another matter altogether.

We need look only as far as the nearest planet to see an example   12
of an atmospheric greenhouse effect gone wild. Venus has in its atmosphere an enormous quantity of carbon dioxide (roughly as much as is buried as carbonates in all the rocks of the Earth's crust). There is an atmosphere of CO_2 on Venus 90 times thicker than the atmosphere of the Earth and containing some 200,000 times more CO_2 than in our air. With water vapor and other minor atmospheric constituents, this is enough to make a greenhouse effect that keeps the surface of Venus around 470°C (900°F)—enough to melt tin or lead.

When humans burn wood or "fossil fuels" (coal, oil, natural gas,   13
etc.), they put carbon dioxide into the air. One carbon atom (C) combines with a molecule of oxygen (O_2) to produce CO_2. The development of agriculture, the conversion of dense forest to comparatively sparsely vegetated farms, has moved carbon atoms from plants on the ground to carbon dioxide in the air. About half of this new CO_2 is removed by plants or by the layering down of carbonates in the oceans. On human time-scales, these changes are irreversible: Once the CO_2 is in the atmosphere, human technology is helpless to remove it. So the overall amount of CO_2 in the air has been growing—at least since the industrial revolution. If no other factors

operate, and if enough CO_2 is put into the atmosphere, eventually the average surface temperature will increase perceptibly.

There are other greenhouse gases that are increasingly abundant   14
in the Earth's atmosphere—halocarbons, such as the Freon used in refrigerator cooling systems; or nitrous oxide (N_2O), produced by automobile exhausts and nitrogenous fertilizers; or methane (CH_4), produced partly in the intestines of cows and other ruminants.

But let's for the moment concentrate on carbon dioxide: How   15
long, at the present rates of burning wood and fossil fuels, before the global climate becomes significantly warmer? And what would the consequences be?

It is relatively simple to calculate the immediate warming from   16
a given increase in the CO_2 abundance, and all competent calculations seem to be in good agreement. More difficult to estimate are (1) the rate at which carbon dioxide will continue to be put into the atmosphere (it depends on population growth rates, economic styles, alternative energy sources and the like) and (2) feedbacks—ways in which a slight warming might produce other, more drastic, effects.

The recent increase in atmospheric CO_2 is well documented.   17
Over the last century, this CO_2 buildup should have resulted in a few tenths of a degree of global warming, and there is some evidence that such a warming has occurred.

The National Academy of Sciences estimates that the present   18
atmospheric abundance of CO_2 is likely to double by the year 2065, although experts at the academy predict a one-in-20 chance that it will double before 2035—when an infant born today becomes 50 years old. Such a doubling would warm the air near the surface of the Earth by 2°C or 3°C—maybe by as much as 4°C. These are average temperature values; there would naturally be considerable local variation. High latitudes would be warmed much more, although a baked Alaska will be some time coming.

There would be precipitation changes. The annual discharge of   19
rivers would be altered. Some scientists believe that central North America—including much of the area that is now the breadbasket of the world—would be parched in summer if the global temperature increases by a few degrees. There would be some mitigating effects; for example, where plant growth is not otherwise limited, more CO_2 should aid photosynthesis and make more luxuriant growth (of weeds as well as crops). If the present CO_2 injection into the atmosphere continued over a few centuries, the warming would be greater than from all other causes over the last 100,000 years.

As the climate warms, glacial ice melts. Over the last 100 years,   20
the level of the world's oceans has risen by 15 centimeters (6 inches).

A global warming of 3°C or 4°C over the next century is likely to bring a further rise in the average sea level of about 70 centimeters (28 inches). An increase of this magnitude could produce major damage to ports all over the world and induce fundamental changes in the patterns of land development. A serious speculation is that greenhouse temperature increases of 3°C or 4°C could, in addition, trigger the disintegration of the West Antarctic Ice Sheet, with huge quantities of polar ice falling into the ocean. This would raise sea level by some 6 meters (20 feet) over a period of centuries, with the eventual inundation of all coastal cities on the planet.

There are many other possibilities that are poorly understood, 21 including the release of other greenhouse gases (for example, methane from peat bogs) accelerated by the warming climate. The circulation of the oceans might be an important aspect of the problem. The scientific community is attempting to make an environmental-impact statement for the entire planet on the consequences of continued burning of fossil fuels. Despite the uncertainties, a kind of consensus is in: Over the next century or more, with projected rates of burning of coal, oil and gas, there is trouble ahead.

The problem is difficult for at least three different reasons: 22

(1) We do not yet fully understand how severe the greenhouse 23 consequences will be.

(2) Although the effects are not yet strikingly noticeable in every- 24 day life, to deal with the problem, the present generation might have to make sacrifices for the next.

(3) The problem cannot be solved except on an international 25 scale: The atmosphere is ignorant of national boundaries. South African carbon dioxide warms Taiwan, and Soviet coal-burning practices affect productivity in America. The largest coal resources in the world are found in the Soviet Union, the United States and China, in that order. What incentives are there for a nation such as China, with vast coal reserves and a commitment to rapid economic development, to hold back on the burning of fossil fuels because the result might, decades later, be a parched American sunbelt or still more ghastly starvation in sub-Saharan Africa? Would countries that might benefit from a warmer climate be as vigorous in restraining the burning of fossil fuels as nations likely to suffer greatly?

Fortunately, we have a little time. A great deal can be done in 26 decades. Some argue that government subsidies lower the price of fossil fuels, inviting waste; more efficient usage, besides its economic advantage, could greatly ameliorate the CO_2 greenhouse problem. Parts of the solution might involve alternative energy sources, where appropriate: solar power, for example, or safer nuclear fission reactors, which, whatever their other dangers, produce no greenhouse gases of importance. Conceivably, the long-awaited advent of commercial nuclear fusion power might happen before the middle of the next century.

However, any technological solution to the looming greenhouse   27
problem must be worldwide. It would not be sufficient for the United States or the Soviet Union, say, to develop safe and commercially feasible fusion power plants: That technology would have to be diffused worldwide, on terms of cost and reliability that would be more attractive to developing nations than a reliance on fossil fuel reserves or imports. A serious, very high-level look at patterns of U.S. and world energy development in light of the greenhouse problem seems overdue.

During the last few million years, human technology, spurred in   28
part by climatic change, has made our species a force to be reckoned with on a planetary scale. We now find, to our astonishment, that we pose a danger to ourselves. The present world order is, unfortunately, not designed to deal with global-scale dangers. Nations tend to be concerned about themselves, not about the planet; they tend to have short-term rather than long-term objectives. In problems such as the increasing greenhouse effect, one nation or region might benefit while another suffers. In other global environmental issues, such as nuclear war, all nations lose. The problems are connected: Constructive international efforts to understand and resolve one will benefit the others.

Further study and better public understanding are needed, of   29
course. But what is essential is a global consciousness—a view that transcends our exclusive identification with the generational and political groupings into which, by accident, we have been born. The solution to these problems requires a perspective that embraces the planet and the future. We are all in this greenhouse together.

QUESTIONS OF CONTENT

1. Scientists calculate that the temperature of the earth—given its distance from the sun and the sun's heat—should be $-20°C$. Why, according to Sagan, is the earth warmer than that predicted temperature, and how is that related to his essay's thesis?
2. What is the "greenhouse effect"? What elements or conditions contribute to it?
3. What nearby celestial neighbor furnishes an example of the greenhouse effect gone wild? What are its surface temperatures?
4. Scientists calculate that the CO_2 in our atmosphere will double by

2065, perhaps as early as 2035. According to Sagan, what effects will that produce?

5. To overcome the impending problems posed by the greenhouse effect, what does Sagan recommend besides further study and better public understanding?

QUESTIONS OF FORM

1. Sagan's argument is an example of a claim of fact supported inductively through cause and effect analysis. What claim of fact is Sagan supporting?
2. Sagan begins expositorily, explaining how the earth is warmed and the effect that the atmosphere has on that warming. At what point does he shift into an argumentative stance?
3. If atmospheric CO_2 doubles by the middle of the next century, Sagan poses some immediate consequences, as well as some remote ones. Where does he state these?
4. What sort of appeal is Sagan making in paragraphs 26–29?

SUGGESTIONS FOR WRITING

1. Summarize Sagan's essay in no more than three paragraphs.
2. For an interesting rebuttal of Sagan's argument, read Robert J. Bidinotto's "What Is the Truth about Global Warming?" in the February 1990 issue of *Reader's Digest*. Now add Bidinotto's rebuttal to the summary you've just written. What is the best way to proceed? Should you just add a summary of Bidinotto's arguments at the end? Or should you insert it rebuttal by rebuttal?
3. Think about several troublesome issues that plague your campus: drug use, student parking, anti-intellectual student culture, careerism, AIDS. Take Sagan's approach and examine first the causes of this condition; then turn your attention to the effects that you can predict, both short term and long term, if this condition continues unchecked.
4. Now widen your scope beyond your campus. Examine your hometown. What are some conditions that prevail there that are apt to prove troublesome, if not disastrous, if they are not changed or redirected? How did these conditions arise, and what do you predict the results to be if they continue unchanged? Again, follow Sagan's pattern, of exposition turning into argument.
5. Propose a policy that will address either of the dire conditions you have presented in suggestion 3 or 4 above. Demonstrate that your recommended policy will produce desirable results.

Cultural Literacy
and the Schools

E. D. HIRSCH, JR.

Let me begin with a picture of what I mean by true literacy. It is 1
good to start with our national educational goals, because unless we
can agree upon our goals, we cannot deal forthrightly with the political and ideological issues that public education must always entail.
Let me depict our educational goal as a social one, using the unforget-
table vision of Martin Luther King, Jr. in his speech "I Have a Dream."
Those of you who heard that speech or teach it will know what I am
thinking. King had a vision in which the children of former slave
owners sit down at the table of equality with the children of former
slaves, a vision of an America where men and women deal with each
other as equals and judge each other on their character rather than
their origins. King had a dream of a classless society. To help us share
his dream, he quoted from our most traditional texts, from Jefferson,
the Bible, and patriotic and religious songs. We all know those traditional passages and songs. King reminded us that his dream has been
shared and cherished by all Americans of good will.

The dream of Thomas Jefferson and Martin Luther King, Jr. car- 2
ries a very specific educational implication in the modern world: No
modern society can think of becoming a classless society except on
the basis of universal literacy. Never mind for the moment the various utilitarian and humanistic arguments in favor of literacy. I am
considering now an even more basic principle that sponsored our
Jeffersonian system of public education in the first place. It is the
principle that people in a democracy can be left free to think and
decide things for themselves because they can all communicate
with each other. Universal communication is the canvas for King's
vision as well as Jefferson's. And universal communication is possible in our modern world only on the basis of universal literacy.
Americans must be able to talk to each other not just in person or by
telephone but across time and space through reading and writing.
We can add to that traditional democratic imperative to literacy the
well-known economic imperative that has been brought by the technological age. Today, only someone who reads well can adjust to
changes in technology and the job market or can participate in our
cultural and political life. From these very elementary considerations, it is obvious that genuine literacy must be a paramount and
minimal goal of a high school education.

But what, more specifically, does that goal mean for the curricu-   3
lum? That depends on what we mean by literacy. I would define
literacy in this way: To be truly literate, a high school graduate
must be able to grasp the meaning of written materials in any field
or subject, provided that those materials are addressed to a general
reader. High school graduates should be able to read serious newspapers, for instance. Remember what Jefferson said about reading
newspapers:

> Were it left to me to decide whether we should have a government
> without newspapers, or newspapers without a government, I should
> not hesitate a moment to prefer the latter. But I should mean that
> every man should receive those papers and be capable of reading
> them.

That last comment of Jefferson's is often omitted. But it is the cru-   4
cial one. Every American should be able to read serious books, newspapers, and articles addressed to the general reader. And our high
school graduates should also be able to convey information in writing to a general readership. Universal literacy means that every citizen must be able to give as well as receive written information.

Literacy in this fundamental sense requires not just technical   5
proficiency but also "cultural literacy." What I mean by this term
may become clear in a provisional way as I describe a recent experience.

A few years ago, I was conducting some experiments at the   6
University of Virginia to measure the effectiveness of a piece of
writing when it is read by ordinary audiences. We were measuring
the actual effects of writing rather than mere opinions of its quality.
Our readers in the experiment (who were mainly university students) performed just as we expected them to as long as we kept the
topics simple and familiar. Then, one memorable day we transferred
our experiments from the university to a community college, and
my complacency about adult literacy was forever shattered. This
community college was located in Richmond, Virginia, and the
irony of the location will appear in a moment. Our first experiments
went well, because we began by giving the students a paper to read
on the topic of friendship. When reading about friendship, these
young men and women showed themselves to be, on the average,
just as literate as university students. The evidence showed that,
based on the usual criteria of speed and accurate recall, the community college and university groups were equally skilled readers. But
that evidence changed with the next piece of writing we asked them

to read. It was a comparison of the characters of Ulysses S. Grant and Robert E. Lee, and the students' performance on that task was, to be blunt, illiterate. Our results showed that Grant and Lee were simply not familiar names to these young adults in the capital of the Confederacy. The students' speed and recall declined because they had to continually backtrack through the unfamiliar material to test out different hypotheses about what was meant or referred to.

Shortly after that disorienting experience, I discovered that Professor Richard Anderson of the Center for Reading Research at the University of Illinois and other researchers in psycholinguistics had reached firm conclusions about the importance of background knowledge in reading. For instance, in one experiment, Anderson and his colleagues discovered that an otherwise literate audience in India could not properly read a simple text about an American wedding. But, by the same token, an otherwise literate audience in America could not properly read a simple text about an Indian wedding. Why not? Structurally speaking, the texts were similar and the audiences were similar. It wasn't a matter of vocabulary or phonics or word recognition; it was a matter of cultural literacy. Anderson and others showed that to read a text with understanding one needs to have the background knowledge that the author has tacitly assumed the reader to have. This tacit knowledge is fundamental to literacy.

What these experiments demonstrate is that the idea that reading is a general, transferable skill unrelated to subject matter is essentially wrong, containing only the following grain of truth. Reading is a general skill only with regard to its rather elementary aspects, those involving phonics, parsing strategies, guessing strategies, eye habits, and so on. While these elementary skills are important, normally endowed students, once they acquire the rudiments, need not be continually drilled in them. Such skills are always being used, and every reading task will automatically exercise, improve, and automate them. With that single elementary exception, then, the usual picture of reading as a general skill is wrong. Reading skill varies from task to task, because reading skill depends on specific background knowledge.

To illustrate the dependency of literacy on cultural literacy, I shall quote a recent snippet from *The Washington Post:*

> A federal appeals panel today upheld an order barring foreclosure on a Missouri farm, saying that U.S. Agriculture Secretary John R. Block has reneged on his responsibilities to some debt-ridden farmers. The appeals panel directed the USDA to create a system of processing loan deferments and of publicizing them as it said Congress had

intended. The panel said that it is the responsibility of the agriculture secretary to carry out this intent "not as a private banker, but as a public broker."

Imagine that item being read by persons who have been trained   10
to read but are as culturally illiterate as were my community college students. They might possibly know words like foreclosure, but they would surely not understand the text as a whole. Who gave the order that the federal panel upheld? What is a federal appeals panel? Even if culturally illiterate readers bothered to look up individual words, they would not have much idea of the reality being referred to. Nor, in reading other texts, would they understand references to such things as, say, the equal protection clause or Robert E. Lee, no matter how well they could read a text on friendship. But a truly literate American does understand references to the equal protection of the laws and Robert E. Lee and newspaper reports like the one I just quoted. As a practical matter, newspaper reporters and writers of books cannot possibly provide detailed background information on every occasion. Think, if they did, how much added information would be needed even in the short item that I quoted from *The Washington Post*. Every sentence would need a dozen sentences of explanation! And each of those sentences would need a dozen more.

Writers work with an idea of what their audiences can be ex-   11
pected to know. They assume, they must assume, a "common reader" who knows the things that are known by other literate persons in the culture.

When I say that these writers must assume such background   12
knowledge, I am affirming a fact about language use that sociolinguists and psycholinguists have known for twenty years: The explicit words of a text are just the tip of the iceberg in a linguistic transaction. In order to understand even the surface of a text, a reader must have the sort of background knowledge that was assumed, for example, in *The Washington Post* report that I quoted.

To understand that paragraph, literate readers would know in   13
the backs of their minds that the American legal system allows a judgment at a lower level to be reversed at a higher level. They would know that a judge can tell the executive branch what it can or cannot do to farmers and other citizens, and they would know a lot more that is relevant. But none of their knowledge would have to be highly detailed. They wouldn't need to know, for instance, whether an appeals panel is the final level before the Supreme Court. In general, readers need to share a cloudy but still accurate sense of the *realities* that are being referred to in a piece of writing. This allows them to make the necessary associations.

Besides this topic-determined knowledge, the reader needs to   14
know less explicit and less topic-defined matters, such as culturally
shared attitudes, values, conventions, and connotations that the
writer assumes the reader to have. The writer cannot start from
ground zero, even in a children's reader designed for the first grade.
The subtlety and complexity of written communication is directly
dependent upon a shared background.

To an ill-informed adult who is unaware of what literate persons   15
are expected to know, the assumption by writers that their readers
possess cultural literacy could be regarded as a conspiracy of the
literate against the illiterate for the purpose of keeping them out of
the club. Although newspaper reporters, writers of books, and the
framers of the verbal SAT necessarily make assumptions about the
things literate persons know, no one ever announces what that body
of information is. So, although we Americans object to pronouncements about what we all should know, there is a body of information
that literate people *do* know. And this creates a kind of silent, *de
facto* dictating from on high about the things adults should know in
order to be truly literate.

Our silence about the explicit contents of cultural literacy leads   16
to the following result, observable in the sociology of the verbal SAT.
This exam is chiefly a vocabulary test, which, except for its omission
of proper names and other concrete information, constitutes a test of
cultural literacy. Hence, when young people from deprived backgrounds ask how they can acquire the abilities tested on the verbal
SAT, they are told, quite correctly under present circumstances, that
the only way to acquire that knowledge is through wide reading in
many domains over many years. This is advice that deprived students
already in high school are not in a position to take. Thus there remains a strong correlation between the verbal SAT score and socioeconomic status. Students from middle-class and upper-middle-class
backgrounds get their knowledge for the verbal SAT not just from
reading, but through the pores, from talk at home and social chitchat.

What follows from this situation goes to the heart of the school   17
curriculum. It means nothing less than that the whole conceptual
basis of the curriculum as inculcating skills independently of specific content has been wrong—and not just a little wrong, but fundamentally so. The influence of this mistaken educational formalism
upon our policies has been, in my opinion, a chief cause of our
educational failures in the domain of literacy.

The skills orientation to education has assumed that the particu-   18
lar contents of the curriculum can be arbitrary. Any good content

will develop the skill of reading. But, on the contrary, the information that is taken for granted between literate people is not arbitrary. Although quite fuzzy at the edges, this information is known to be central by every truly literate person in our culture. I stress *our* literate culture, because the information shared by literate Americans is different from the information shared by literate Germans or Russians. Literacy in every nation depends on a specifically national literate culture.

Of course, no literate national culture makes absolute sense. 19 Although Shakespeare might be better than Racine in absolute terms, we don't tell the French that they should abandon Racine for Shakespeare. For purposes of national education in America or France, neither Shakespeare nor Racine could be replaced in their respective cultures as necessary background knowledge for literacy and communication. Although we may admire our traditional culture for its own sake, it is mainly for these instrumental reasons (that is, to achieve true literacy and widescale communication) that our central traditional materials must continue to be taught and learned.

If our high school graduates are to be literate, our school curricu- 20 lum must ensure, at a minimum, that students acquire those facts of cultural literacy that are requisite to true literacy. To accomplish this, the school curriculum needs significant improvement, particularly in grades K through ten. By *improvement*, I do not suggest that it must be completely overhauled. And I do not say that we need what is usually meant by the term "core curriculum." The proposal to introduce a substantial core curriculum in literature whereby every child reads *Silas Marner, Julius Caesar,* and *A Tale of Two Cities* is, I think, lacking in appropriate subtlety. A core of shared information must indeed be learned. But the means by which it is conveyed may vary a good deal. The destination is one, but the routes are many. No educational reform can succeed if it fails to keep students and teachers motivated and interested. Different pupils require different materials, and so do different teachers. For that reason alone, we need to keep diversity and local judgment at the heart of the curriculum. But we also need to be sure that our students get the ABCs of knowledge in the earlier grades. How, then, can we keep a desirable flexibility in the curriculum and also ensure that our students get the core knowledge they need in order to become literate Americans?

In broaching a solution to this problem, let me make a distinc- 21 tion between two kinds of knowledge taught in school. The two kinds are both necessary, but they are quite distinct. I call them "extensive" and "intensive" knowledge. I'll describe extensive knowledge first. It tends to be broad, but superficial. It is often learned by rote. It is mainly enumerative. It consists of atomic facts and categories. It does not put things together. It's the kind of knowledge possessed by the Major General in Gilbert and Sullivan's *Pirates of Penzance:*

> I am the very model of a modern Major General,
> I've information vegetable, animal, and mineral,
> I know the kings of England, and I quote the fights historical,
> From Marathon to Waterloo in order categorical;
> I'm very well acquainted too with matters mathematical,
> I understand equations, both the simple and quadratical,
> About binomial theorem I'm teeming with a lot o' news—
> With many cheerful facts about the square of the hypotenuse.

This was comic because these cheerful facts were *all* the Major   22
General knew, and they offered him no help in military strategy. Everybody in his audience also knew those same facts, which were part of the intellectual baggage that every schoolboy acquired in nineteenth-century Britain. It was clear to Gilbert and Sullivan's audience that this knowledge was just a lot of isolated, schoolboy facts that the Major General couldn't put together in any useful way.

Understanding how to put things together is the contribution of   23
intensive study. Suppose that instead of just being able to list the fights historical, the Major General wanted to learn something about war and strategy. To gain that knowledge, he would have to study at least a battle or two in some detail. Yet it might not greatly matter which battle he studied carefully. It could be the battle of Austerlitz, or the battle of Waterloo. But in order to gain a coherent idea of nineteenth-century warfare, General Stanley would have needed to study specific examples of warfare. Therefore, any new fact about it that he encountered could be grafted upon or accommodated to the model-idea that he had gained from, say, the battle of Austerlitz. To generalize from this illustration, if we want to make isolated facts fit together in some coherent way, we must acquire models of how they do so from detailed, intensive study and experience.

The school curriculum should foster this intensive learning as   24
much as possible. Indeed, it should be the chief substance of the school curriculum, particularly in the later grades. At the same time, intensive study is also the most flexible part of the school curriculum. For building mental models, it doesn't greatly matter whether the Shakespeare play read in ninth grade is *Macbeth* or *Julius Caesar:* What does matter is whether our idea of Shakespeare

is formed on an actual, concrete experience of a Shakespearian play. Such intensive learning is necessary, because the mental model we get from the detailed study of an example lets us connect our atomic facts together and build a coherent picture of reality. On the other hand, since the chief function of intensive study is to get examples for such models, our choice of examples can vary with circumstances and should depend on students' knowledge and interest. That is why a lock-step core curriculum is both unnecessary and undesirable for the intensive part of the curriculum. On the other hand, there is a limit to the flexibility of the intensive curriculum. A play by Neil Simon or George Chapman is no effective substitute for a play by Shakespeare.

Although we must gain intensive knowledge to make coherent   25
sense out of facts, we must also gain a store of particular, widely shared background facts in order to make sense of what we read. This extensive part of the curriculum, the part that is crucial to shared knowledge and literacy, has been neglected.

The best time to get this extensive background information is   26
before tenth grade, and the earlier the better. In early grades, children are fascinated by straightforward information. Our official modern distaste for old-fashioned memorization and rote learning seems more pious than realistic. Young children are eager to master the materials essential for adult life, and if they believe in the materials they will proudly soak them up like sponges and never forget them. There is a tremendous weight of human tradition across many cultures to support this view. At about age thirteen, young Catholics get confirmed, having memorized the materials they must know in adult life. At the same age, young Jews get bar mitzvahed. At around the same age, young tribal boys and girls must show that they have mastered the rites of passage into the tribe.

There are good reasons why these universal traditions of early   27
acculturation should have come into being. They correspond to something that seems almost biological in its appropriateness and necessity. Human beings function in the world only by becoming members of a culture. The human species survives through social and cultural organizations, not through instinct. Young children have an urge to become acculturated into the adult world by learning the facts of the tribe long before they can make sense out of them.

But in neglecting the extensive part of the school curriculum, we   28
have forsaken the responsibility that rests with the adult members of any tribe. For many decades, we have followed educational theories and ideologies that have now turned out to be inadequate. We have

forgotten the acculturative responsibilities of the earlier grades. In a larger historical perspective, we can see that we lost touch with our earlier educational traditions, and, as a consequence, whole generations of schoolchildren lost touch with earlier traditions of our national culture. But those decades did not and could not signal a permanent change in American education, because the failure to include schoolchildren in our literate traditions is in conflict with some of the root purposes of national education.

A lot of us are beginning to recognize our earlier mistakes. That   29
is one of the meanings of the current educational reform movement. We are beginning to see that educational formalism—the idea that we can teach reading and writing as formal skills only—is not sound and has not worked. We have also seen the superficiality of believing that a literate nation can abandon its traditions and remake its literate culture from scratch according to some new ideology. That is a mistake not in moral terms, but in practical terms. When the national languages were fixed in the eighteenth century, some of the cultural baggage that went with each language also became fixed. The two elements, language and cultural baggage, cannot be disentangled. If one believes in literacy, one must also believe in *cultural literacy*.

A great deal is at stake in understanding and acting on these   30
truths as soon as possible. For most children, the opportunity of acquiring cultural literacy, once lost in the early grades, is lost for good. That is most likely to be true with children of parents who have not themselves mastered the literate national culture. To deprive these children of cultural literacy in the early grades is to deprive most of them forever. By contrast, children from literate families may get at home what the schools have failed to provide. It is the neediest, therefore, who suffer most from our failure to live up to our educational responsibility to teach the traditional extensive curriculum.

What are the specific contents of that extensive curriculum? Let   31
me be quite specific about goals, even if not about the contents of each grade level. I said that the extensive curriculum consists of broad, often superficial information that is taken for granted in writings directed to a mature general reader. Let me now list some of that information under appropriate categories. American readers are assumed to know vaguely who the following pre-1865 people were (I give just the briefest beginning of an alphabetical list, stopping with H.): John Adams, Benedict Arnold, Daniel Boone, John Brown, Aaron Burr, John C. Calhoun, Henry Clay, James Fenimore Cooper, Lord Cornwallis, Davy Crockett, Emily Dickinson, Stephen A. Douglas,

Frederick Douglass, Jonathan Edwards, Ralph Waldo Emerson, Benjamin Franklin, Robert Fulton, Ulysses S. Grant, Alexander Hamilton, and Nathaniel Hawthorne. Most of us know rather little about most of these names, but that little is of crucial importance because it enables writers to assume a foundation from which they can treat in detail whatever they wish to focus upon.

Here is another alphabetical list: Antarctic Ocean, Arctic Ocean, 32 Atlantic Ocean, Baltic Sea, Black Sea, Caribbean Sea, Gulf of Mexico, North Sea, Pacific Ocean, Red Sea. It has a companion list: Alps, Appalachians, Himalayas, Rocky Mountains, Mt. Everest, Mt. Vesuvius, the Matterhorn. Because writers mention these things without explanation, readers need to have them as part of their intellectual baggage.

Another category is the large realm of allusion that belongs to 33 our literary and mythic heritage. These traditional myths enable writers to say complex things compactly and to use the emotive and ironic values of allusion. Here is a sampling of such taken-for-granted materials from the literature that one often gets in childhood: Adam and Eve, Cain and Abel, Noah and the Flood, David and Goliath, the 23rd Psalm, Humpty Dumpty, Jack Sprat, Jack and Jill, Little Jack Horner, Cinderella, Jack and the Beanstalk, Mary Had a Little Lamb, The Night Before Christmas, Peter Pan, Pinocchio, The Princess and the Pea.

Here are some patriotic songs that are generally known: The 34 Battle Hymn of the Republic; Columbia, the Gem of the Ocean; My Country, 'Tis of Thee; America the Beautiful; The Star-Spangled Banner; This Land Is Your Land; Yankee Doodle.

At random I will add (alphabetically) such personages as Achilles, Adonis, Aeneas, Agamemnon, Antigone, and Apollo. Not to 35 mention Robin Hood, Paul Bunyan, Satan, Sleeping Beauty, Sodom and Gomorrah, the Ten Commandments, and Tweedledum and Tweedledee.

Obviously you don't expect me to give the whole list of cultural 36 literacy here. But perhaps it would surprise you to learn that I could do so if I had the time and you had the patience. In fact, such a list was compiled, after much consultation, by a historian, a natural scientist, and myself. It represents background knowledge that people need to have by the time they graduate from high school. Although the list is 131 pages long, it could be cut down by about a third for the pre-tenth-grade age group. Perhaps its most important feature is its limited character. It represents a specific, finite body of superficial knowledge, which, if taught to youngsters in the context of a good *intensive* curriculum, would enable them to understand serious materials directed to a general reader.

Any such list is of course open to objections like the following: 37
Why aren't there more women on the list? Why isn't there more
representation of Chicano culture? Doesn't your list simply certify
and perpetuate the existing WASP, establishment culture? Must this
status quo, traditional material be the only method of achieving
universal literacy? Won't this return to traditional materials make
our culture even more static, dull and monolithic than it already is?

My reply is that the various movements that have been resisting   38
such cultural dominance have been working reasonably effectively
and will continue to do so. Also, as Catherine Stimpson, the well-
known feminist literary critic and former editor of the feminist journal *Signs*, recently observed, we must distinguish between people
who are actively trying to change our literate culture and those who
are trying to make a useful dictionary of its current structure. Unless
the two functions are kept separate, the dictionary makers like me,
who are trying to make a serviceable list, will lose their credibility
and usefulness.

Stimpson's shrewd observation describes a situation that teach-   39
ers always find themselves in. Although we are citizens who want to
work for social and political ends, such as a more pluralistic culture,
we are also professionals whose personal politics must stop at the
classroom door. In our roles as teachers, we have an obligation to be
descriptive lexicographers, to tell our students what they currently
need in order to be literate. If we disapprove of the current literate
culture and want to change some of its elements, we should pursue
outside the classroom the sort of cultural politics that Catherine
Stimpson pursues. But until we succeed in changing the literate
culture, we must not misinform our students by pretending that its
contents are just what we wish them to be. Of course, we also have
an obligation to explain to our students why it is, for example, that a
pre-1865 list of Americans whom a culturally literate person might
be expected to know of would not include many blacks. The content
of a society's cultural literacy bears witness to its sins as well as its
successes.

I mentioned feminism as an example of cultural change because   40
it has succeeded in altering our collective usages. It has made us self-
conscious about gender words and gender attitudes. Similarly, the
civil rights movement succeeded in changing our usages in such
ways as effectively removing the word "nigger" from the English
language—a beneficent change, indeed! This kind of change goes on
all the time, for both good and ill. As a result, the content of cultural
literacy is always changing, as is obvious to everyone in the case of
such words as *DNA* and *software*.

What may not be obvious is that the *central* content of cultural   41
literacy has not changed very much in the last hundred years. What
changes is at the periphery, not at the center. These days, writers can
assume their readers know who Gerald Ford is, but thirty years from
now they probably won't make that assumption. On the other hand,
thirty years from now writers will continue to assume that George
Washington could not tell a lie and that Scrooge hated Christmas. Of
course, no single item of cultural literacy has any importance by
itself. But the bulk of such items, taken together, are as important as
anything we teach.

In the technological age, Washington and the Cherry Tree, and   42
Scrooge and Christmas, the fights historical, the oceans geographi-
cal, the beings animalculous, and all the other shared materials of
literate culture have become more, not less, important. The more
we become computerized, the more we need not just shared scientific knowledge but also shared fairy tales, Greek myths, historical
images, and so on. Let me explain this paradox. The more special-
ized and technical our civilization becomes, the harder it is for non-
specialists to participate in the decisions that deeply affect their
lives. The growing power of the technological class will create, according to experts, more and more distance between the rest of us
and the ruling cadre of technicians who control the systems. The
technicians with their arcane specialties will not be able to communicate with us, nor we with them. This contradicts the basic principles of democracy and must not be allowed to happen.

The only antidote to this problem of specialization was put for-   43
ward many centuries ago by Cicero. He said that each of us should
be trained to communicate our special knowledge to the rest of our
society in the language of ordinary people. That this Ciceronian
ideal *can* be achieved is proven by those literate scientists who are
able to write for a general literate public. But such a literate culture
can only be achieved if all of us, including technicians, share enough
traditional background material to enable complex communication
to occur.

In conclusion, I want to stress again that the only skills that train   44
for life are those knowledge-based activities that continue specifically to be used in life. Reading and writing, of course, continue to be
used. Everyone knows they are absolutely central to productive membership in our society and to the ability to acquire new knowledge-
based skills when needed. Reading and writing at the high levels
required for such future flexibility are skills that are based on a large,
complex system of world knowledge that I have called cultural literacy. Imparting this knowledge to our students, through the study of

the humanities and the sciences, is the chief responsibility of our educational system.

Our schools have not imparted these essential facts and words, because in recent times we have not been willing as a nation to decide what the essential facts and words are. Despite our national virtues of diversity and pluralism, our failure to decide upon the core content of cultural literacy has created a positive barrier to adult literacy in this country, and thus to full citizenship and full acculturation into our society. We Americans need to be decisive and explicit about the background information that a citizen should know in order to be literate in the 1980s. Access to this democratic literate culture is not only a proper goal of our curriculum but is also the only possible way of realizing the dream of Jefferson and King.

45

QUESTIONS OF CONTENT

1. How does Hirsch define true literacy?
2. What did Hirsch's experiment involving readers from the University of Virginia and a Richmond community college reveal about the nature of reading skill?
3. Journalists direct their articles toward a "common reader." How does Hirsch define this common reader, and how is this common reader crucial to his notion of cultural literacy? Who seems to be the intended audience for his own essay?
4. Why does Hirsch believe that there is a high correlation between SAT verbal scores and socioeconomic status, and how is that relationship important to his argument?
5. What does Hirsch mean when he says, ". . . the whole conceptual basis of the curriculum as inculcating skills independently of specific content has been wrong . . . ," and how does he use that point in his essay?
6. What are some examples of the kinds of extensive knowledge that go to make up what Hirsch calls cultural literacy? How does he feel these things should be taught?
7. How is Hirsch's notion of the *central* content of cultural literacy related to what writers of today, such as yourself, assume about their readers, and what writers in the future (as close as 30 years) are likely to assume about their audiences?

QUESTIONS OF FORM

1. Hirsch is making a claim of policy. What situation does he intend his policy to remedy? How would you state his claim in its barest form?

2. How does Hirsch use a quotation from *The Washington Post* to explain the connection between literacy and *cultural* literacy?
3. What purpose is served in Hirsch's argument by his comparison of "extensive" and "intensive" knowledge?
4. Hirsch does not even begin to formulate his claim until around paragraph 25. Why has he waited so long to do this? What was he doing before that?
5. How does Hirsch defend himself against the potential claim in paragraph 37 that what he calls cultural literacy tends to perpetuate White Anglo-Saxon Protestant culture? What use does he make of the pronouncements of feminist writer Catherine Stimpson?

SUGGESTIONS FOR WRITING

1. Can you reduce the whole of Hirsch's argument to a single paragraph? Give it a try. Then expand that summary to a longer paper, perhaps of five or so paragraphs, inserting examples that you were forced to neglect in your more abbreviated version.
2. Consider your own primary and secondary education. Can you name any significant learning problem other than the one that Hirsch describes in his essay? Describe that problem, and then formulate your own claim of policy, recommending as Hirsch does a specific course of action that will resolve the problem.
3. You are a spokesperson for the American Civil Liberties Union. You are approached by a group such as the Black Students Union or National Organization of Women, who claim that the reform movement in education Hirsch is describing has created a conservative bias in favor of perpetuating WASP (White Anglo-Saxon Protestant) culture. You have seen how Hirsch responded to this criticism, but you have not seen the actual charges. How would you formulate an argument for one such group? What examples might you use to support your claim? Make your case in a paper of about five paragraphs.

Frats and Sororities: The Greek Rites of Exclusion

M. G. LORD

My interest in fraternities began innocently, on a balmy night last fall, when a friend and I attempted to drive across the campus of the University of Michigan at Ann Arbor, where, after ten years as a journalist in New York City, I was back in school on a fellowship. We were heading to a movie that people said had great special effects. I couldn't say. Due to the special effects on the street, we never made it to the theater.

Hundreds of white women swarmed along Hill Street—our route and the university's fraternity row. They huddled in packs, hugging and squealing and sometimes singing, defiantly stopping traffic. The crowd reeked of money: pearl necklaces and the effects of orthodontia were everywhere in evidence. According to statistics on sorority membership at Michigan, there must have been a few blacks and Asians present, but I didn't see any. Just four blocks of blond people—Kewpie doll faces, retroussé noses—a living Leni Riefenstahl tableau.

I've since learned that what I witnessed was part of "Rush," the process by which fraternities and sororities select new members, but I had no words for it at the time. My companion, an associate professor of anthropology, was not at a similar loss. She called their strange rites "codified white exclusionary ritual."

About one in four of Michigan's undergraduates participates in this "white exclusionary ritual" each fall, according to Jo Rumsey, the assistant director of housing information. This year 779 new members were inducted into fraternities, almost twice the number that joined in 1975. "We lost 30 to 40 percent of the fraternities in the late sixties and early seventies," Rumsey said, "but since 1975, at least nine chapters—including three which are predominantly Jewish—have come back. They're certainly a strong influence on undergraduate life."

Michigan is not alone in its Greek revival. From the late 1960s to the early 1970s at the University of California, Berkeley, the number of women rushing sororities had dwindled to about 150 per year; now it's five times that. On campuses where chartered sororities never existed—Yale, Princeton, the University of Chicago—new chapters have been "colonized," an interesting choice of verb by a group almost entirely of white Protestants. Even at Amherst College, where fraternities were abolished in 1984, they continue to thrive unofficially off campus. In the past ten years, fraternity membership has doubled—even though the full-time undergraduate population has increased only by 20 percent, from 5 million to 6 million. And undergraduate sorority membership has grown by about 30 percent, from 180,000 in 1975 to 240,000 in 1985.

If any one thing is emblematic of the difference between the class of '87 and the class of '77, I think it's the resurgence of these organizations. During the 1960s and 1970s, students sought alternative social activities that promoted integration and discouraged racism and sexism—activities that many of today's college students consider comical. "We don't have to pay attention to that stuff," an undergraduate quipped only half-facetiously. "Back then they were all on drugs."

Not only have fraternities been resurrected, they've also been cosmetically retouched. Crude proscriptions against blacks and Jews are out. Occasional black members are in, showcased to counter charges of racism. But nothing, in fact, has changed.   7

These clubs are "racist and anti-Semitic by way of pure deletion," explains Wendy Martin, a recent Michigan graduate who rushed a sorority her senior year as fieldwork for an anthropology course. "It's not so much 'us' and 'them'; they're not even articulated as another. If they don't rush your sorority, they simply don't exist."   8

And when a few organizations at Michigan ostensibly made a play for minority membership, it backfired. "First I see a Tri-Delt with a sweatshirt on and she never speaks to me, then they send flyers around saying they want their sorority to be more 'diverse.' I think it's a bunch of bullshit," says Mary Walker, a black junior at Michigan. "I can't see joining a white organization if they don't make an effort to get to know me in class. It's hypocritical. It's tokenism. They're just trying to look good."   9

Add alcohol to the system (which members regularly do) and the tacit racism becomes overt. At the University of Pennsylvania, "Black students regularly report that they are subjected to verbal racial abuse when they walk down Locust Walk," the university's fraternity row, says Jaqui Wade, director of the Afro-American studies program. "It becomes worse on Thursday or Friday or Saturday nights when they're having their parties." And at Michigan this spring three members of Alpha Tau Omega, a predominantly white Christian fraternity, stole a mock jail cell built on campus to publicize the plight of Soviet Jews. Their excuse? "We did so while drunk, without malicious intent."   10

Ironically, racism was very much a concern at Michigan last winter. Two incidents—the distribution of a racist leaflet in a dormitory and the broadcast of racist jokes by one of the campus radio stations—attracted national media attention. Some students took advantage of the publicity to criticize the low number of minority students on campus and the lower number of minority faculty members.   11

At no point, however, was the racist behavior of the Greek system challenged. This struck me as odd—particularly since at least one of the incidents, the radio broadcast, seeemed almost innocuous when compared with the jarring ritual I'd witnessed on the street the previous fall. Although the contents of the broadcast were repugnant   12 and inappropriate, they were no more revolting than what Manhattan disc jockey Howard Stern—on whom the student host's program was modeled—airs regularly in the undergraduate's hometown. For what the young disc jockey apologetically termed "ninety seconds of bad judgment," he was blasted by *The New York Times, Newsweek* and National Public Radio. Yet when 5,000 undergraduates participate in the monthlong white exclusionary rites of Rush, it isn't considered a problem. When I suggested to Michigan president Harold Shapiro that it may be, he responded, "The fraternities are all integrated now."

Violence against women, another component of fraternity life, is   13
more difficult behavior to ignore. Once again the distinction involves language: was the victim "willing" or "raped"? And, as in the case of racially motivated vandalism, alcohol blurs the distinction.

According to Bernice R. Sandler, director of the Association of   14
American Colleges' Project on the Status and Education of Women and co-author, with Julie Kuhn Ehrhart, of *Campus Gang Rape: Party Games?* at least fifty documented gang rapes have occurred in fraternities in the past two or three years. "Fraternity members have a word for gang rape: they call it 'pulling train,'" says Sandler. "Charts of how many beers it took to seduce various sorority women are common in fraternity houses." And if a woman actually does press charges against a fraternity, "their excuse is, 'She asked for it'—even if she was unconscious."

Often women are reluctant to report rapes because they fear   15
they'll be stigmatized, which is what usually happens, Sandler says. "Fraternity brothers harass them, say they deserved it because they'd been drinking. Well, that's like saying because there's money in your purse you deserve to be robbed." And, adds Sandler, to protect someone accused, "Brothers will remain silent or even lie."

In a paper published last April, Mary Koss, a psychologist at Kent   16
State University, concluded that 15 percent of all college women (a startling one in seven) had had a forced-sex experience that met the legal definition of "completed rape." According to Koss's data, one-on-one acquaintance rape is not restricted to fraternities but, she told me, "We found that a significant predictor of a male's sexual aggression was the extent to which he involved himself in a peer group that sexually objectified women, that discussed women in sexual terms, that created a climate of 'scoring.'"

"Studies have shown that men who join fraternities have a   17
much greater need to dominate than those who don't," says Andrew Merton, associate professor of English at the University of New Hampshire, who has written about fraternities and rape since 1979. "I think these men are scared of women, scared of dealing with them

in any way approaching a basis of equality. They see women only in a sexual context, in a context where men are rule-makers. And there's a tremendous pressure to drink in fraternities. Drinking allows the guys to act upon the sexual stereotypes in their heads and then say, 'Oh, it wasn't really my fault. I didn't know what I was doing.' "

He adds, "If the fraternities constituted a state of the union, it   18
would be a very small one, with about half the population of Vermont. If, in a state that size, fifty confirmed gang rapes took place within two or three years, impartial observers might begin to wonder about the place."

Of course, not all fraternity members swashbuckle their way   19
through college, raping and pillaging. But any group that sets itself up as elite, discriminates on the basis of race, religion and gender, posts lewd and degrading charts relating to the opposite sex and conspires to protect members from the consequences of criminal activities performed while drunk seems less likely than other campus clubs to promote sympathy between individuals of different race, religion and sex.

"As a black person, I begin to worry whenever groups—partic-   20
ularly groups of whites—permit themselves a kind of thuggish behavior as a group that they'd never dare to think about as individuals," says James Snead, an assistant professor of English at Yale. "When these kids were growing up, white male America was seen as a country on its way to wimpdom. It was possible to infer that everyone was picking on the white male and that he had no recourse—except to band together and revert to a more primitive kind of behavior."

Jaqui Wade concurs: "These white males who have been social-   21
ized to believe that the world was theirs—and they didn't have to compete with black men and women and white women—now feel the tensions of that competition. They're very, very threatened and they're acting out."

Four years ago, the Michigan chapter of Sigma Alpha Mu, a   22
predominantly Jewish fraternity, held a "jungle party" at which three members painted their bodies black, wore tribal paint and rings through their noses. After *The Michigan Daily,* the campus newspaper, ran photographs of the event, blacks protested. The group's president claimed to be stunned. "It is difficult to know how minorities feel about certain practices," he said. "There is a lack of knowledge in general as to what those sensitivities are."

Historically, Jews and blacks have responded to white Protestant   23
exclusion by forming their own support groups. In addition to three predominantly Jewish fraternities in the National Interfraternity

Conference, and two predominantly Jewish sororities in the National Panhellenic Conference, there is also a black Greek system, the National Pan-Hellenic Council, made up of eight black men's and women's organizations. The oldest black fraternity, Alpha Phi Alpha, was founded at Cornell University in 1906, and its members have included Thurgood Marshall, Martin Luther King, Jr., and Andrew Young. Although membership is selective and confers status, black Greek organizations are different from their white counterparts. They rush at different times, and on white campuses they are havens from white exclusion. They also preserve minority culture and prevent dilution of minority identity. In the late 1960s and early 1970s, when white Greek membership plummeted, black Greek membership remained about the same as it is now.

One reason colleges tolerate fraternities is that they can't afford   24
not to. "The reason fraternities don't get abolished in smaller schools is that the trustees are generally terrified of offending the alumni and cutting off large, essential contributions," said G. Armour Craig, acting president of Amherst in 1984, the year fraternities were abolished there. Another is the fiction that if Jews and blacks are allowed to form their own organizations, white exclusiveness is acceptable—the old "separate but equal" refrain.

This leads to packs socializing with packs rather than individuals   25
with individuals. At Michigan, members of Alpha Phi Alpha complain that when they play a "friendly" game of basketball with a white fraternity, it is often anything but. "If the game is close, a white referee will call it their way," says Marcus Webster, former president of Alpha Phi Alpha. "But when we play other black fraternities, the referees let us beat each other up. They don't call anything."

Fraternities are not the same on every campus. For example, half   26
the members of the Yale chapter of the Kappa Kappa Gamma sorority are either Jewish, Hispanic, Asian, American Indian or black. In the Yale environment, the group could almost be described as anti-elitist—the response of public-school girls who couldn't find a place in other organizations. Some members, however, received a rude shock when they stayed on vacation at a Kappa house at the University of California, Los Angeles. "It was another world," said Jennifer Maxwell, a founding member of the Yale chapter. "An immense house with Kappa things everywhere—Kappa jewelry, Kappa clothes, everything. It was supposedly one of the most selective groups. . . . Everyone was gorgeous and had blonde hair." She paused, "I would never have been accepted into a group like that." Would anyone in the Yale chapter? "Probably not."

Yet establishing a chapter at Yale—like having a token black—   27
is a public relations coup for the sorority. Like eighteenth-century

European empire builders, fraternities must "colonize" to survive. "Most of the interest in them is generated from the outside," said Lloyd Suttle, associate dean of administrative and student affairs at Yale. "We don't give them a room to meet in. They put an ad in the newspaper and rent a room at the Holiday Inn."

And the students clearly want what the organizations have to 28 offer. "It's a cold cruel world out there and you need friends," says Jon Baruch, a member of Alpha Epsilon Pi at Michigan. "A fraternity provides instant friendship." It also provides scholarships, low-interest loans and lodging when one travels. Members talk incessantly about networking with alumni. They point out that twenty-one Presidents, including Ronald Reagan, were in fraternities, not to mention fifty-two current members of the Senate and 33 percent of the House of Representatives. They talk about the time they volunteer to social service and the money they raise for charity. They make fraternities sound like a force for good.

But they're not telling the whole story, which is more along the 29 lines of the following open letter from the grand president of Kappa Alpha Theta (the oldest women's fraternity) to her sisters:

> We still have alumnae who are reluctant to recommend anyone other than the traditional white, Anglo-Saxon Protestant. And this is their right: The purpose of the recommendation system is to give alumnae the opportunity to highlight personal friends and the daughters of friends, not to provide a "ticket" for everyone. . . . Last year, one of our chapters pledged the first black woman on a campus with traditionally "all-white" sorority membership. This year, another Theta chapter on an all-white Greek campus affiliated the first black woman. Both chapters are to be congratulated for not being afraid to take risks. And there were risks. Why? Because there were people who warned the chapters that if they pledged these women, they would not receive recommendations or pledges in the future. And some men's fraternities told the chapters they would not continue to "party" with Thetas at these two schools.

The use of the word "ticket" should dispel any lingering doubts 30 about the practice of "white exclusionary ritual" among fraternal organizations. According to *Webster's Third New International Dictionary*, the word means "a certificate or token of a right . . . as of admission" or "a means to something desirable." It's an unusually vulgar and explicit word—a word that a member would not be likely to use with outsiders; a word that smacks of the 1950s, of a world in which even tokenism is a "risk."

"This is elite ritual practice, not redneck ritual practice," ex- 31 plains Susan Harding, the associate professor of anthropology at the

University of Michigan with whom I first glimpsed the rites of Rush. "It's tacky to be verbally racist but perfectly acceptable to discriminate through your behavior, through your choices. Elite racism is implicit, acted-out, behaved—not expressed in language. And fraternities are a training ground for that kind of elite racial practice."

I'm not advocating the abolition of fraternities. It doesn't work— 32 they spring up unofficially off campus. Nor am I sneering at the impulse to join selective organizations. I remember what it was like to be an adolescent—insecure and character deficient—and although I didn't solicit invitations to belong, I didn't refuse them either. Ironically, though, the secret society I joined at Yale turned out to be exclusionary only in number. Some clever members in the 1960s revamped the organization so that it was half black and Hispanic— and thus could never revert to its original, all-male, all-white status. It was the only fully racially integrated environment I'd ever experienced—considerably richer, I discovered, than being sequestered with Xeroxes of myself. But many kids with my character deficiencies, which I suspect is the majority, won't have the chance to make that discovery. They'll join fraternities instead.

Fraternities invest white bread with cachet. It's an impressive 33 sleight of hand. "They work on your soul," explains Clayton Eshleman, National Book Award-winning poet and translator, who pledged Phi Delta Theta at the University of Indiana in the 1950s. "There were motifs of Greek mythology in the rituals and lots of Greek words in the bylaws. It was a way to give a kind of old, fake European feel to a dull, safe Hoosier life."

QUESTIONS OF CONTENT

1. On what university campus did Lord make his initial observations about fraternities and sororities? What other campuses does he use for examples? How useful are the added examples?
2. Although his major thesis seems to be the racism that is inherent in many Greek organizations, Lord pauses (paragraphs 13–19) to discuss another troublesome issue. What is it?
3. What are some of the reasons that Lord suggests for this rise of racism among fraternities and sororities?
4. Are black fraternities and sororities immune to these problems? How are they like white Greek organizations? How do they differ?
5. Based on Lord's essay, what seem to be some of the risks involved for Greek organizations that attempt to overcome racist trends and extend their membership to members of other races?

QUESTIONS OF FORM

1. Lord is making a complicated claim of fact, but before doing so he provides what sorts of supporting evidence? Which sort seems more convincing to you, and why?
2. How does he expand on his first claim of fact, regarding racism and anti-Semitism, made in paragraph 7?
3. How has Lord used comparison and contrast to make a claim of policy late in his essay? Why might he have delayed so long?
4. The conclusion of Lord's essay is flat and anticlimactic, especially in comparison with the detailed anecdotal support he has consistently used. How might he have ended more forcefully?

SUGGESTIONS FOR WRITING

1. Summarize Lord's attitudes toward Greek organizations. Prepare your summary for a general audience consisting of young adults, some college trained, some not.
2. Now make the same summary, but this time address an audience of fraternity or sorority members.
3. Assume that you are a new pledge of a white Christian fraternity or sorority, somewhat disturbed by Lord's essay. Draw upon your personal experience to do one of the following:
   a. Refute Lord's claims of racism and sexism by pointing out that such abuses do not exist on your campus.
   b. Support Lord's position by pointing out similar disturbing situations that you have personally witnessed and then call for corrective measures.
4. Our society has many exclusionary organizations, of course, other than Greek-letter ones. Recall those you have belonged to or encountered, perhaps in high school or in college, and then write a letter to Mr. Lord, suggesting that he consider reporting on one whose faults you describe in enough detail so that he might be encouraged to investigate it. If possible, use one or more means of support that he employed. (Your instructor may want you to try this in groups rather than alone.)

The Case Against Man

ISAAC ASIMOV

The first mistake is to think of mankind as a thing in itself. It   1
isn't. It is part of an intricate web of life. And we can't think even of

life as a thing in itself. It isn't. It is part of the intricate structure of a planet bathed by energy from the Sun.

The Earth, in the nearly 5 billion years since it assumed approximately its present form, has undergone a vast evolution. When it first came into being, it very likely lacked what we would today call an ocean and an atmosphere. These were formed by the gradual outward movement of material as the solid interior settled together.

Nor were ocean, atmosphere, and solid crust independent of each other after formation. There is interaction always: evaporation, condensation, solution, weathering. Far within the solid crust there are slow, continuing changes, too, of which hot springs, volcanoes, and earthquakes are the more noticeable manifestations here on the surface.

Between 2 billion and 3 billion years ago, portions of the surface water, bathed by the energetic radiation from the Sun, developed complicated compounds in organization sufficiently versatile to qualify as what we call "life." Life forms have become more complex and more various ever since.

But the life forms are as much part of the structure of the Earth as any inanimate portion is. It is all an inseparable part of a whole. If any animal is isolated totally from other forms of life, then death by starvation will surely follow. If isolated from water, death by dehydration will follow even faster. If isolated from air, whether free or dissolved in water, death by asphyxiation will follow still faster. If isolated from the Sun, animals will survive for a time, but plants would die, and if all plants died, all animals would starve.

It works in reverse, too, for the inanimate portion of Earth is shaped and molded by life. The nature of the atmosphere has been changed by plant activity (which adds to the air the free oxygen it could not otherwise retain). The soil is turned by earthworms, while enormous ocean reefs are formed by coral.

The entire planet, plus solar energy, is one enormous intricately interrelated system. The entire planet is a life form made up of nonliving portions and a large variety of living portions (as our own body is made up of nonliving crystals in bones and nonliving water in blood, as well as of a large variety of living portions).

In fact, we can pursue the analogy. A man is composed of 50 trillion cells of a variety of types, all interrelated and interdependent. Loss of some of those cells, such as those making up an entire leg, will seriously handicap all the rest of the organism: serious damage to a relatively few cells in an organ, such as the heart or kidneys, may end by killing all 50 trillion.

In the same way, on a planetary scale, the chopping down of an entire forest may not threaten Earth's life in general, but it will produce serious changes in the life forms of the region and even in the nature of the water runoff and, therefore, in the details of geological structure. A serious decline in the bee population will affect the numbers of those plants that depend on bees for fertilization, then the numbers of those animals that depend on those particular bee-fertilized plants, and so on.

Or consider cell growth. Cells in those organs that suffer con-   10
stant wear and tear—as in the skin or in the intestinal lining—grow and multiply all life long. Other cells, not so exposed, as in nerve and muscle, do not multiply at all in the adult, under any circumstances. Still other organs, ordinarily quiescent, as liver and bone, stand ready to grow if that is necessary to replace damage. When the proper repairs are made, growth stops.

In a much looser and more flexible way, the same is true of the   11
"planet organism" (which we study in the science called ecology). If cougars grow too numerous, the deer they live on are decimated, and some of the cougars die of starvation, so that their "proper number" is restored. If too many cougars die, then the deer multiply with particular rapidity, and cougars multiply quickly in turn, till the additional predators bring down the number of deer again. Barring interference from outside, the eaters and the eaten retain their proper numbers, and both are the better for it. (If the cougars are all killed off, deer would multiply to the point where they destroy the plants they live off, and more would then die of starvation than would have died of cougars.)

The neat economy of growth within an organism such as a human   12
being is sometimes—for what reason, we know not—disrupted, and a group of cells begins growing without limit. This is the dread disease of cancer, and unless that growing group of cells is somehow stopped, the wild growth will throw all the body structure out of true and end by killing the organism itself.

In ecology, the same would happen if, for some reason, one par-   13
ticular type of organism began to multiply without limit, killing its competitors and increasing its own food supply at the expense of that of others. That, too, could end only in the destruction of the larger system—most or all of life and even of certain aspects of the inanimate environment.

And this is exactly what is happening at this moment. For thou-   14
sands of years, the single species Homo sapiens, to which you and I have the dubious honor of belonging, has been increasing in numbers. In the past couple of centuries, the rate of increase has itself increased explosively.

At the time of Julius Caesar, when Earth's human population is   15
estimated to have been 150 million, that population was increasing

at a rate such that it would double in 1,000 years if that rate remained steady. Today, with Earth's population estimated at about 4,000 million (26 times what it was in Caesar's time), it is increasing at a rate which, if steady, will cause it to double in 35 years.

The present rate of increase of Earth's swarming human population qualifies Homo sapiens as an ecological cancer, which will destroy the ecology just as surely as any ordinary cancer would destroy an organism. 16

The cure? Just what it is for any cancer. The cancerous growth must somehow be stopped. 17

Of course, it will be. If we do nothing at all, the growth will stop, as a cancerous growth in a man will stop if nothing is done. The man dies and the cancer dies with him. And, analogously, the ecology will die and man will die with it. 18

How can the human population explosion be stopped? By raising the deathrate, or by lowering the birthrate. There are no other alternatives. The deathrate will rise spontaneously and finally catastrophically, if we do nothing—and that within a few decades. To make the birthrate fall, somehow (almost *any* how, in fact), is surely preferable, and that is therefore the first order of mankind's business today. 19

Failing this, mankind would stand at the bar of abstract justice (for there may be no posterity to judge) as the mass murderer of life generally, his own included, and mass disrupter of the intricate planetary development that made life in its present glory possible in the first place. 20

Am I too pessimistic? Can we allow the present rate of population increase to continue indefinitely, or at least for a good long time? Can we count on science to develop methods for cleaning up as we pollute, for replacing wasted resources with substitutes, for finding new food, new materials, more and better life for our waxing numbers? 21

Impossible! If the numbers continue to wax at the present rate. 22

Let us begin with a few estimates (admittedly not precise, but in the rough neighborhood of the truth). 23

The total mass of living objects on Earth is perhaps 20 trillion tons. There is usually a balance between eaters and eaten that is about 1 to 10 in favor of the eaten. There would therefore be about 10 times as much plant life (the eaten) as animal life (the eaters) on Earth. There is, in other words, just a little under 2 trillion tons of animal life on Earth. 24

But this is all the animal life that can exist, given the present quantity of plant life. If more animal life is somehow produced, it will strip down the plant life, reduce the food supply, and then enough animals will starve to restore the balance. If one species of 25 animal life increases in mass, it can only be because other species correspondingly decrease. For every additional pound of human flesh on Earth, a pound of some other form of flesh must disappear.

The total mass of humanity now on Earth may be estimated at   26 about 200 million tons, or one ten-thousandth the mass of all animal life. If mankind increases in numbers ten thousandfold, then Homo sapiens will be, perforce, the *only* animal species alive on Earth. It will be a world without elephants or lions, without cats or dogs, without fish or lobsters, without worms or bugs. What's more, to support the mass of human life, all the plant world must be put to service. Only plants edible to man must remain, and only those plants most concentratedly edible and with minimum waste.

At the present moment, the average density of population of the   27 Earth's land surface is about 73 people per square mile. Increase that ten thousandfold and the average density will become 730,000 people per square mile, or more than seven times the density of the workday population of Manhattan. Even if we assume that mankind will somehow spread itself into vast cities floating on the ocean surface (or resting on the ocean floor), the average density of human life at the time when the last nonhuman animal must be killed would be 310,000 people per square mile over all the world, land and sea alike, or a little better than three times the density of modern Manhattan at noon.

We have the vision, then, of high-rise apartments, higher and   28 more thickly spaced than in Manhattan at present, spreading all over the world, across all the mountains, across the Sahara Desert, across Antarctica, across all the oceans; all with their load of humanity and with no other form of animal life beside. And on the roof of all those buildings are the algae farms, with little plant cells exposed to the Sun so that they might grow rapidly and, without waste, form protein for all the mighty population of 35 trillion human beings.

Is that tolerable? Even if science produced all the energy and   29 materials mankind could want, kept them all fed with algae, all educated, all amused—is the planetary high-rise tolerable?

And if it were, can we double the population further in 35 more   30 years? And then double it again in another 35 years? Where will the food come from? What will persuade the algae to multiply faster than the light energy they absorb makes possible? What will speed up the Sun to add the energy to make it possible? And if vast supplies of fusion energy are added to supplement the Sun, how will we get rid of the equally vast supplies of heat that will be produced? And after the icecaps are melted and the oceans boiled into steam, what?

Can we bleed off the mass of humanity to other worlds? Right   31 now, the number of human beings on Earth is increasing by 80 million per year, and each year that number goes up by 1 and a fraction percent. Can we really suppose that we can send 80 million people per year to the Moon, Mars, and elsewhere, and engineer those worlds to support those people? And even so, merely remain in the same place ourselves?

No! Not the most optimistic visionary in the world could honestly convince himself that space travel is the solution to our population problem, if the present rate of increase is sustained. 32

But when will this planetary high-rise culture come about? How long will it take to increase Earth's population to that impossible point at the present doubling rate of once every 35 years? If it will take 1 million years or even 100,000, then, for goodness sake, let's not worry just yet. 33

Well, we don't have that kind of time. We will reach that dead end in no more than 460 years. 34

At the rate we are going, without birth control, then even if science serves us in an absolutely ideal way, we will reach the planetary high-rise with no animals but man, with no plants but algae, with no room for even one more person, by A.D. 2430. 35

And if science serves us in less than an ideal way (as it certainly will), the end will come sooner, much sooner, and mankind will start fading long, long before he is forced to construct that building that will cover all the Earth's surface. 36

So if birth control *must* come by A.D. 2430 at the very latest, even in an ideal world of advancing science, let it come *now*, in heaven's name, while there are still oak trees in the world and daisies and tigers and butterflies, and while there is still open land and space, and before the cancer called man proves fatal to life and the planet. 37

QUESTIONS OF CONTENT

1. Asimov says that it is incorrect to think of mankind as a thing in itself. What does he propose instead?
2. Asimov claims that our entire planet, together with one outside ingredient, represents an enormous, intricate, interrelated system. What is that outside ingredient, and what role does it play in the system?
3. In paragraph 11, Asimov introduces an example involving deer and cougars. What is the point of this example?
4. According to Asimov, one life form on our planet is outgrowing its food supply. What life form is that?

5. Asimov likens mankind to a dread disease. What disease is that, and how exactly does mankind's behavior suggest such a comparison?
6. Mankind will become extinct, according to Asimov, unless one or the other of two alternatives occurs. What are these alternatives?
7. At its present rate of growth, how long will it be before mankind will reach a point beyond which it cannot continue to grow?

QUESTIONS OF FORM

1. In paragraph 19 Asimov presents his audience with his major claim: The population explosion must be stopped. Why has he waited so long to make this claim? What has he been doing prior to this?
2. Asimov draws an analogy between our planet and the human body. What is his purpose in doing this?
3. Asimov's argument may be classified as a claim of policy. We have seen that such claims consist of two parts: a description of an existing situation and a suggested course of action to remedy that situation (or to maintain it). Where exactly does Asimov attend to these two parts?
4. Of the two alternatives presented in paragraph 19, Asimov clearly prefers one. How does he go about supporting it?
5. In constructing his argument Asimov apparently must argue against one of the most honored of warrants: Human life is precious. How does he manage to overcome that handicap?

SUGGESTIONS FOR WRITING

1. Summarize Asimov's argument in a paper of no more than three paragraphs.
2. Think about mankind's present situation. Surely overpopulation is not the only thing that threatens human existence. Choose another threat to humanity and then proceed after Asimov's fashion to construct an analogy to assist the audience in understanding the gravity of the situation.
3. In his final argument in favor of his recommended policy, Asimov uses what rhetoric calls an *alternative syllogism*. It works like this:

> A is either B or C. (Helga is either German or Italian.)
>
> A is not C. (Helga is not Italian.)
>
> Therefore, A is B. (Therefore, Helga is German.)

Trace the operation of this syllogism in Asimov's essay; then examine the situation that you wrote about for suggestion 2 above. Try to use Asimov's strategy in supporting your policy recommendation. Try to reduce the alternatives to two, and then demonstrate as Asimov did that one of the alternatives is prefereable by showing the negative effects produced by the other course of action.

Taking Sides: Differing Arguments on Important Issues

This readings section provides a series of pairs of essays, each pair focused on the same basic subject. While both essays are on the same subject, each author has a different perspective on that subject and argues for his or her own ideas regarding it. Sometimes the two authors are at opposing poles, but just as often their ideas are closer, comparing more than they contrast. Therefore you should watch not just for places where the ideas of the two essays differ, but also where they share some common ground. By reading the related essays in pairs, you should be able to improve your ability to notice both small and large differences in opinions and arguments, and therefore you should learn how to increase the subtlety and the effectiveness of your own arguments.

As in the previous section, we have furnished questions of form and of content, as well as suggestions for writing; these appear after the second essay of each pair. Again, we encourage you to look over the questions and writing suggestions *before* reading the two essays, and to refer to them as needed *while* you read, so that you'll comprehend more fully the essays' subject matter and their argumentative strategies.

Compulsory National Service for Young Americans

National Service in Return for College Assistance

DAVID MCCURDY

As students in Tiananmen Square were willingly paying the 1
supreme sacrifice to bring democracy to China, we were engaged in a
strenuous debate about whether our own youths should continue to
receive the opportunities of democracy without offering something
in return. That debate continues.

The controversy centers on the proposed Citizenship and Na- 2
tional Service Act, which was introduced by Sen. Sam Nunn of
Georgia and myself. The act would require students seeking federal
college assistance to spend one or two years of national service in
the military or in communities as civilian workers.

The proposal is based on the premise that our young people must 3
move beyond the narcissism of the Reagan years and the lingering
aftereffects of Vietnam, which led many to ask what their country
could do for them.

Defenders of the current student assistance programs refuse to 4
acknowledge that these programs are not creating educational opportunities for those who need them most. They complain that making
students earn their benefits is cruel, and that national service will
discriminate against the poor and excuse the affluent.

But under the present system, college enrollment among stu- 5
dents from minority and blue collar families has dropped 10 percent
in the last decade. According to the American Council on Education,
only about 30 percent of our black youths are enrolled in college, and
middle-class students who are fortunate enough to receive loans are
strapped with huge, long-term debts.

The details of the Citizenship and National Service bill are, in- 6
deed, complicated and many of them are yet to be ironed out. But we
are certainly willing to work with critics to establish a solid demonstration program to measure the cost and effects of this program.

We will not, however, abandon the basic principle of national 7
service that rests at the heart of the democratic philosophy. As

Walter Lippmann said at a class reunion at Harvard, 49 years ago: "For every hope that you entertain, you have a task that you must perform. For every good that you wish to preserve, you will have to sacrifice your comfort and ease. There is nothing for nothing any longer."

Confusing Student Aid and Patriotism

WILLIAM D. FORD

Public service by Americans of all ages, but particularly young people, should be encouraged and rewarded as a highly desirable national goal. As President Bush said in his inaugural address: "We must bring in the generations, harnessing the unused talent of the elderly and the unfocused energy of the young. . . ." 1

A number of thoughtful bills on the subject have been introduced by Reps. Matthew G. Martinez and Leon E. Panetta of California, Rep. Constance A. Morella and Sen. Barbara A. Mikulski of Maryland, Sen. Christopher J. Dodd of Connecticut, and Sen. Claiborne Pell of Rhode Island. 2

However, the bill that has received the most attention, the Citizenship and National Service Act introduced by Sen. Sam Nunn of Georgia and Rep. Dave McCurdy of Oklahoma, raises the most troublesome questions. Under the Nunn–McCurdy bill, in return for one or two years of work at subsistence wages in either civilian or military service, young volunteers would earn "national-service vouchers" worth $10,000 to $12,000 per year of service. The vouchers could be used for college, job training, or housing. Graduates of this Citizens Corps might also be given preference in college admission or federal employment. State and local governments would develop projects and place the participants. Retirees paid a modest hourly wage would handle supervision and administration. 3

The existing student financial-aid programs would be largely phased out, in part to pay for this new program and in part because of the sponsors' philosophy that current student-aid "entitlements" should be "converted into benefits earned through service." 4

Let me leave to others the implications of this proposal for our nation's military manpower needs and its relationship to existing service-related education-benefit programs. (It should be noted, however, that the statement of Congressman McCurdy, a senior member 5 of the House Armed Services Committee, upon introducing the bill, at least raises the suspicion that he sees the proposal as a way to raid the budget of the Education Department to meet military-manpower objectives. ("The defense budget cannot withstand the increases in already high levels of compensation that would be necessary to attract sufficient numbers of qualified youth into military service," he said.)

6 The Nunn–McCurdy bill represents a misunderstanding of current student-aid programs, outdated ideas about the national labor market and participation in postsecondary education, a narrow view of public service and patriotism, and an oversimplified approach to the delivery of public services.

7 The current student-aid programs are not "entitlements." Only lenders who make guaranteed loans are "entitled" to subsidy payments and reimbursements for defaults if they perform up to legislative standards. Students apply for federal aid, and the amount they receive depends on the availability of funds and the discretion of lenders and postsecondary institutions. No students are "entitled" to any aid, and most students receive less than their demonstrated need.

8 Replacing the current student-aid programs with "national-student vouchers" cannot be justified on the ground that the current programs are "not working." It is true that in the last decade the student-aid programs have not grown as fast as college costs, that the purchasing power of Pell grants has shrunk by about 50 per cent, and that there has been a dramatic shift from grants to loans. However, these are the consequences of the programs' being starved for funds during the Reagan years, not of flaws in the programs' design.

9 In addition, it is hard to see how this erosion in student aid will be alleviated by the Nunn–McCurdy bill. The measure envisions about 700,000 young volunteers in the program each year. Federal student-aid programs serve about two million first-year students annually. Thus, the Nunn-McCurdy bill would serve fewer than half as many students aspiring to postsecondary education as the current student-aid programs serve. The measure is expected to cost $5-billion a year more than the student-aid programs it would replace (largely because its vouchers are not linked to the costs of a particular educational program and are not tied to a student's financial need, in contrast to the student-aid programs).

10 According to one estimate, it would cost the federal government about $50-billion a year under the Nunn–McCurdy bill to serve the same number of people now receiving federal student aid, which costs $9-billion annually. Under the Nunn–McCurdy bill a volunteer would earn $20,000 to $24,000 in postsecondary-education benefits

and perhaps have access to limited student loans. Under current student-aid programs, a student can receive, based on need, up to $99,300 in federal assistance for an undergraduate education, of which $43,000 may be in non-repayable grants. In short, the Nunn-McCurdy bill would serve fewer students, cost more, and in some cases provide less aid per student.

There are other problems with the proposal. The existing 11 student-aid programs already serve those who are not college-bound, so a new program that supports both college attendance and job training is unnecessary. In fact, roughly one-third to one-half of federal student aid supports students in postsecondary occupational courses of every description. Indeed, far from being "regressive" because they are limited to the college-bound, the current student-aid programs are more progressive than the Nunn–McCurdy bill. The existing programs serve non-high-school graduates who have the ability to benefit from postsecondary education, while the Nunn–McCurdy program would be limited to high-school graduates.

The Nunn–McCurdy bill is based on the false premise that access to education beyond high school should be a privilege for the few who have "earned" it as a reward for their public service. The reality is that we need to "give" as much education as we can to as many students as are willing to take it.

By the mid-1990's it is predicted that 75 per cent of all jobs will 13 require some postsecondary education, mostly technical. Between 1989 and 2000, more than 80 per cent of the new entrants to the labor force will be women, members of minority groups, immigrants, and people with disabilities. Of the children who entered elementary school in the fall of 1986, 25 per cent were from impoverished families, 14 per cent were children of unmarried parents, 15 per cent were physically or mentally handicapped, 15 per cent were immigrants who spoke a language other than English, 40 per cent will live in a broken home before they reach 18, and 10 per cent have poorly educated, even illiterate, parents.

Thus, we need larger numbers of more highly skilled and educated workers, and we presently have in the education pipeline more people who present more difficult challenges to educators. Policies that aggressively seek to keep more people in school longer serve the national interest. Policies, such as the Nunn–McCurdy bill, that would delay postsecondary education and erect new barriers to access do not serve the national interest.

What would be, in effect, a mandatory two-year waiting period 15 between high school and postsecondary education for low-income people would undoubtedly discourage many from continuing their education. When the national investment in student aid persuades or permits a student to continue his or her education, that student is serving the nation by becoming a more productive worker, a more informed citizen, and a more prosperous taxpayer who will repay many times over in increased taxes the student aid received.

The Nunn–McCurdy bill is based on the outdated premise that periods of full-time service followed by periods of full-time study or training will accommodate the needs of students pursuing an education beyond high school. It is estimated that 40 per cent of today's undergraduates are older than 25 and that 60 per cent of all college students are attending part time. Many of those attending part time have jobs and family responsibilities. It obviously makes no sense to tell a 24-year-old mother of two who wants to study part time while holding a job and receiving student aid that she has to take a subsistence-wage job for a year or two in order to receive federal aid. Yet such a student is much more the rule than the exception.   16

The Nunn–McCurdy bill is narrow-minded in its view of public service and patriotism. Rather than calling on the altruism and generosity of all Americans, it holds the educational aspirations of the poor hostage to public service, while excusing the affluent. For a low-income student who wants to continue education beyond high school, there would be nothing "voluntary" about the Nunn–McCurdy bill. Rather than defining patriotism and public service as the obligation and civic duty we all have because we live in a free, peaceful, and prosperous land, the bill defines them narrowly as obligations in return for specific benefits such as student aid. Recipients of student aid owe no more to America than do all Americans.   17

Finally, the Nunn–McCurdy bill envisions making a significant contribution toward solving some of our nation's most pressing problems—illiteracy, inadequate health care, homelessness, environmental degradation, crime, insufficient care for children and the elderly—with an approach reminiscent of Stalinist industrialization in the 1930's: Throw legions of untrained and inexperienced young amateurs at the problem. Perhaps the authors of the bill should talk to our trained and experienced teachers, law-enforcement officers, social workers, health professionals, and conservationists to see how "helpful" they feel the "volunteers" would be.   18

Congress should create new opportunities and incentives for public service without dismantling our commitment to equal educational opportunity. While the Nunn–McCurdy bill does not hit the mark, I am confident that the 101st Congress will develop legislation to meet the need to encourage more public service.   19

QUESTIONS OF CONTENT

1. What are the provisions of the proposed Citizenship and National Service Act? Who introduced this legislation?
2. Read carefully paragraph 4 of McCurdy's essay. It is a summary of what he believes to be his opponents' views. How closely does that summary resemble William Ford's position?
3. Why does McCurdy think that present financial assistance programs for students are not working satisfactorily?
4. In paragraph 5 of his essay Ford suggests that one effect of the Citizenship and National Service Act would be to raid the federal education budget to meet military objectives. Why does he make this claim, and what provisions of the act seem to bear out his contention?
5. How does Ford excuse the apparent shortcomings of current student aid programs?
6. What provision does the Nunn–McCurdy bill have for assisting non-high-school graduates?

QUESTIONS OF FORM

1. What is McCurdy's claim? What warrant supports that claim? Where does he state it?
2. In paragraph 10, Ford claims that the Nunn–McCurdy bill would "serve fewer students, cost more, and in some cases provide less aid per student than current student assistance practices." What sort of evidence does he provide to support these claims, and how effective is that evidence?
3. In paragraph 12 Ford states that the Nunn–McCurdy bill is based on a "false premise," namely, that college education is a privilege that must be earned as a reward for public service. Does McCurdy make such a claim?
4. Ford offers a wealth of statistical data in paragraph 13. What is its apparent purpose?
5. In paragraph 17 Ford attacks the warrant used by McCurdy. How exactly does he do that?

SUGGESTIONS FOR WRITING

1. Write an objective summary of each of the two stated positions. Be careful not to favor one side or the other. Limit your presentation to no more than five paragraphs.
2. Prepare a brief address to a student society whose members are almost all recipients of some amount of federal assistance. They are concerned about possible passage of the Nunn–McCurdy bill and

have asked you to explain it to them. You are a spokesperson for the campus administration, supportive of the status quo; you want to see student benefits remain as they are. Establish your credibility by explaining to your audience both sides of the issue, but throw your support behind Ford's position.

3. You are a new member of Representative McCurdy's staff, chosen to speak to a student group at a college in Oklahoma. This group is made up of students receiving federal financial assistance. They fear the passage of the Nunn–McCurdy bill, and you sense their hostility. What will you say to ease tensions? How can you establish your credibility? Can you appeal to their sense of what is right? Can you appeal to any shared emotion that will make the audience hear you more favorably? Having done these things, now state your case in support of the bill.

WOMEN IN COMBAT

Military Takes Equality Too Far

EDWARD SIMS

The United States is, in its form of government, the ideal for the 1
world's countless millions. Everyone is presumed equal, enjoys
equal rights under the law and there is great public and political
pressure to suppress any idea that there are sexual, racial or other
differences.

But differences exist, in sex, race and in other fields. 2

One that politicians are currently refusing to address—it would 3
lose them votes—but that should be faced is the non-selective feminization of U.S. military services.

A recent book on this subject is disturbing reading. It's titled 4
Weak Link by Brian Mitchell (Regnery Gateway). This serious study
shows that Americans are playing with fire, or worse, by playing
politics with the military services.

The commanders of all the services have in recent years been 5
under intense political pressure to introduce what's called career
equality between the sexes. At the service academies physical training is now conducted on a double standard, one for males and one for
females—much easier requirements.

This inevitably lowers the physical standard average in each 6
service. Feminists have gone so far as to demand the elimination of
some physical training activities because women were not doing
well—and they have been eliminated.

War, of course, is not the place for social engineering and ab- 7
stract ideology. If war comes, the nation's military will be handicapped. If more politically inspired feminization of the military continues, national security will be even more dangerously jeopardized.

In many military jobs physical strength is highly important, 8
decisive as to effectiveness. Yet an Army study in 1982 showed that
while 64 percent of all men had the strength to perform heavy jobs,
only 3 percent of the women did.

But because of political pressure on the services, women have 9
been and are being assigned to jobs they can't perform. One example

is found in the Army, which assigns women to artillery supply jobs when they can't lift the shells.

In the Air Force there are women incapable of carrying their own 10 tool kits serving as aircraft mechanics. In the Navy, where 84 percent of the jobs are considered very heavy, a majority of women are unable to close watertight doors! Etc.

Pregnancy is another growing concern in all the services—and 11 could be crippling in wartime. Most of the service mothers, unfortunately, are single. What happens to them when an emergency rises?

Do they abandon their children and concentrate on their duty? 12 That's asking too much. In the only test, in Korea, in the mid 1970s, when U.S. forces went to full alert, some women brought their children to their posts, others simply headed for the rear to get their children evacuated, abandoning their posts.

The "everyone must be treated the same" propaganda of the day, 13 plus the pressure from politicians, has turned the military services and academies into social experiments. Recently a girl was selected as commandant of cadets at West Point.

That pleased the idealists. But she is exempt from combat, by 14 law, and it's peculiar, to say the least, to idealistically promote females to be the leaders of military services in which they're barred from military combat—the purpose of the service!

U.S. military services have more females—about 20 percent 15 already—than any other in the world. The pressure is on to get more into more jobs, even into combat infantry jobs!

In many countries, the military is limited to males. In time of 16 war, that could be a critical factor. It's time for the service chiefs to take a firm stand (and for politicians to stop pressuring them) against non-selective feminization of the military services, before it's too late.

Women in Combat? Give It a Try and See If It Works

MARIANNE MEANS

Next to the overblown specter of unisex toilets, it was the vision 1 of women as potential cannon fodder that did in the Equal Rights Amendment.

Yet there they were on the spot in Panama, female soldiers conducting themselves with dignity and honor in real live combat. They 2 were only supposed to capture some dogs, but they killed a few of the enemy and got shot at in return.

Manuel Noriega's thugs didn't politely ask "Male or female?" before firing. Nor were the guns aimed by females any less business-like than those fired by men.

Does this mean Congress may discover it's time to get real?

It would take some doing. Few things terrify politicians more than the prospect of being accused of sending beautiful young women—possible loving mothers, all—off to do battle, even to protect vital American interests.

The image of woman as fragile flower dies hard. Even after years of equal rights agitation, little boys are still supposed to play with soldiers while little girls content themselves with tea sets and dolls. Men are born to be warriors; women to be desk-bound bureaucrats.

Even after the military brass a decade ago finally got serious about training women and coping with the problems of a dual-sex army, nobody in power wanted to be blamed for females returning home in body bags. They were not deterred in this sentiment by the fact parents also cry inconsolably when males return in body bags.

Ratification of the late, lamented ERA would have let Congress off the hook, constitutionally ending sex discrimination in the military as elsewhere. But without that pressure Congress has refused to eliminate the old restrictions that keep women from military jobs considered the most dangerous. Laws forbid women in the Navy, Marines and Air Force from serving in combat; the Army is allowed to perpetuate that policy through its own regulations.

This arrangement is inherently artificial in a world of high-technology weapons where there are few distinctions between what's a safe job and what's not. The illusion was stripped away with the invasion of Panama, in which about 600 women were involved. To be on the scene was to be within range of a bullet.

Congress is going to hold hearings soon into this question. Rep. Patricia Schroeder, D-Colo., and others plan to introduce legislation to open up all jobs in the armed forces to women, initially on an experimental basis. But emotions still run high against it.

Senate Armed Services Chairman Sam Nunn, the Democrats' chief spear carrier on matters military, says that despite Panama he continues to favor the ban.

"The burden is on those who advocate it be changed," he said ominously, citing physical differences and "overall morale of the force."

As a practical matter, access to combat jobs is important because they are the prestigious stepping stones for promotion into the highest ranks. Nearly half of all military jobs are closed to women, who make up about 11 percent of the armed forces. By overprotecting women, the military holds them back, condemning them to inferior roles.

And more is at stake than individual female careers. Women in general cannot expect to enjoy the full opportunities of society if they do not fully participate in its responsibilities.   14

In peacetime, the question of whether women should fight alongside men has not been a burning issue. But the Panama invasion is a reminder that the purpose of the military is to prepare the troops for a war that everyone hopes won't come. That means all the troops, not just some of them.   15

All recruits of both sexes join of their own choice, knowing that their basic mission—no matter how rarely called upon—is fighting. It is a responsibility they must share equally.   16

Way back in 1978, Secretary of Transportation Brock Adams, speaking in his capacity as head of the Coast Guard, urged that the ban on women in combat be lifted. A civilian and a liberal Democrat at that, Adams was dismissed as a troublemaker.   17

Military women have been quietly pushing into more and more job categories as their numbers grow. At least one female loading supervisor flew on six missions aboard an Air Force transport during the invasion of Grenada. But more visible women such as pilots were not allowed near Grenada until the Marines were in firm control of the island.   18

Yet women in uniform are still primarily curiosities.   19

Much of Capitol Hill regards them as distractions for the men. The idea is that males in battle would be too upset about seeing a wounded female to give their all to fighting the enemy. This oddly assumes that seeing a wounded male is not similarly upsetting.   20

A variation on this theme has male soldiers so tender-hearted they would spend their time protecting female colleagues rather than plotting the enemy's destruction. This harkens back to chivalry, an ancient practice presumed to be popular in the army though long ignored in the civilian world. Has anyone seen a young man give up his seat on a crowded bus to a woman lately?   21

There is also the familiar canard that women will cry and panic in battle. Its credibility depends upon a refusal to admit that all humans, including men, sometimes cry—with a special dispensation for Ronald Reagan, whose sentimental weeping was an art form.   22

Nunn or no Nunn, this stuff is baloney. Women who are physically weak or unwilling to fight don't voluntarily sign up for the military. Those that do are professionals. They should be given the chance to prove it.   23

QUESTIONS OF CONTENT

1. One of Sims's reasons for opposing women being allowed in combat is that women are often physically incapable of performing strenuous tasks. Where does Means address this issue? How effectively?
2. Why does Sims object to a woman being chosen as commandant of cadets at West Point? What do you suppose Means's reaction would be to Sims's objection?
3. Means claims that ratification of the ERA would have "taken Congress off the hook," in regard to the combat status of women in the armed forces. What is the ERA, and how would it have resolved the issue for Congress?
4. What are Means's chief reasons for favoring combat roles for women? What are Sims's chief reasons for opposing such a move?
5. What happened during the U.S. invasion of Panama in December 1989 to bring this issue into focus? How accurately has Means described the episode?
6. In paragraphs 11 and 12 of his essay, Sims addresses the issue of pregnancy and child care among women in the military. What does Means have to say on this subject?

QUESTIONS OF FORM

1. Both Sims and Means appeal to authorities. What authorities does each use and for what purpose?
2. Both Sims and Means cite statistics. What is the effect of their use? Do you notice any significant discrepancy in their statistics?
3. In his third paragraph, Sims refers to "the non-selective feminization of the U.S. military services." What does Sims mean by this term? Why doesn't he simply say that he is opposed to women training for combat roles?
4. How does Sims support his claim that nonselective feminization of the U.S. military is a poor policy?
5. Why does the U.S. Congress, according to Means, find it so difficult to face up to combat roles for women? She suggests that there is a *warrant* to which many of them must subscribe. What is that warrant, and where does she state it?
6. Means employs the same argumentative strategy in paragraphs 7, 20, and 22 of her essay. How would you describe that strategy?
7. Senator Sam Nunn says, "The burden is on those who advocate [that the armed forces' policy on women in combat] be changed." What specifically does he mean by the term *burden?*
8. Both authors depend to some extent on emotional appeals, especially using word choice to criticize; find examples of such uses in both essays, and be prepared to comment on their effectiveness.
9. What word choices made by Sims might women find offensive or

insulting? How might a male career military officer react to specific words or examples chosen by Means?

SUGGESTIONS FOR WRITING

1. Summarize these two arguments in a paper of up to three pages. Do not take sides, but state clearly the major claims made and supported by both Sims and Means. Be especially careful to associate the names of the authors with their arguments.
2. Take sides with either Sims or Means and point out the superiority of one's claims over the other's by showing that support for those claims is more compelling or that the reasoning is more logical. You may find it convenient to summarize the substance of both arguments in a brief background statement before going on to take sides. Or you may wish to pattern your strategy after that used by George Will in his essay "The Case Against Drug Legalization" (p. 320) in which he compares two opposing arguments, taking sides with one over the other.
3. Assume that you have a seventeen-year-old niece who can meet all of the admission requirements for one of the U.S. service academies and has indicated her desire to apply to one of them, with the intent of making a career in one of the armed forces. Write a letter to her in which you encourage her or discourage her; support your position by references to the writing of either Sims or Means—or of both authors. (Your instructor may require that you do additional research, for instance regarding the woman who was commandant of cadets at West Point in 1989–90.)

The Pros and Cons of Recycling

The Garbage Glut Is Everyone's Business

EDITORS OF *USA TODAY*

Garbage just won't go away. 1

And we can't ignore it anymore. 2

There are fewer and fewer places to dump it. 3

The "pooh pooh choo choo"—5,000 tons of sewage sludge—is 4
chugging its way back to Baltimore after a month-long trip, first to
Donaldsonville, La., where residents turned up their noses, then to
Moss Point, Miss., where the welcome mat also was yanked.

Five train cars of rotting refuse from Philadelphia heading for 5
Brazil, Ind., met the same fate last month. A court order turned it
around and sent it back home.

And in Los Angeles, trash trucks hustle from one dump to an- 6
other, trying to find one that hasn't taken in its daily quota. Unless
something is done by 1992, the city will be turning out 6,000 tons of
garbage a day with no place to put it.

Across the USA, city and county officials are longing for the 7
good old days, when the mountains of garbage produced by conspicu-
ous consumption were whisked away, never to be whiffed again.

But garbage that used to be dumped, burned, then buried is now 8
burying us.

Landfills, where most trash winds up, are disappearing at an 9
alarming rate. The Environmental Protection Agency expects that
2,000 of them will disappear within four years.

What's worse, landfills have not proved to be the busy little bio- 10
degraders that people expected. They've actually preserved hot dogs
and carrots for 15 years; 20-year-old newspapers can still be read.

What can be done? Plenty. 11

▶ We can produce less trash. 12

More firms are finding ways to reduce packaging waste. And the 13
federal government has set a goal of reducing garbage production by
25% by 1992.

▶ We can convert more trash to energy. 14

Tazewell County, Ill., hopes to turn methane gas at its landfill   15
into electricity for 2,400 homes. More communities need to seek
ways to convert waste to power.

▶ And we can recycle more of our trash.   16

Thirty states are implementing laws to separate trash for recy-   17
cling; 10 have mandatory separation.

The recycling idea is catching on. Two-thirds in a recent poll   18
said they had recycled some garbage.

Minnesota dairy farmers are finding that shredded newspapers   19
make great cow bedding. School cafeterias and fastfood restaurants
earn money by recycling plastic foam products. New Yorkers return
three-quarters of their bottles and cans for deposits each year, keeping 100 million tons of trash out of landfills.

Such efforts show that individuals can make a huge difference.   20
But the writer across the page [Harry Schwartz] thinks the price is
too high. He'd rather pay someone else to do his sorting.

The price might be steeper than he thinks. In Woodbury, N.J.,   21
he'd pay a fine of up to $500 a day for not sorting his trash. In
Hamburg, N.Y., he would forfeit trash pickup.

The price is steep because the consequences are dire. We can be   22
buried in our own refuse if we don't act soon. Ignoring garbage won't
make it go away. Dealing with it will.

It's a dirty job, but everybody has to do it.   23

The Garbage Glut Is None of My Business

HARRY SCHWARTZ

At my age, I don't have the time, the energy or the desire to   1
become a trash man.

All those proposals to have me spend my time sorting trash,   2
putting paper in one pile, glass in another, etc., leave me cold.

I pay taxes to have my trash collected, and I expect those who   3
spend my taxes will do their job rather than attempt to draft me into
the ranks of their workers. I was drafted in World War II, and that
was enough.

If there is a need to have trash sorted, then let the authorities do   4
it. The people who collect my trash can go through it to segregate
whatever they want to. If that requires more trash collectors and
therefore more taxes, I'll be glad to pay up.

But the idea of trashing my life and making me part of the collection system has as much appeal as joining East Germany's Communist Party.

What is so special about trash that makes the environmentalists so frenzied about getting all of us involved in the problem?

Nobody ever asked me to teach my kids when they were going to grade school. Nobody suggests I should personally deliver my letters to my correspondents. And no good liberal wants me to get a gun so I can defend my home against burglars and similar lowlifes.

So why do I have to get involved in trash?

If the situation is so desperate that it makes sense to talk seriously about conscripting millions of Americans, then why not move to cut the volume of trash?

Most of my trash, for example, consists of newspapers. Every Sunday morning, I get about 15 pounds of newspaper deposited at my front door, and that's just two newspapers. Most of those pages are devoted to advertisements for things I have no interest in buying. So why not simply order that no newspaper, daily or Sunday, be allowed to print more than four pages a day? Then I could easily get by on one can of trash a week, not four or five, as now.

But, of course, there are similar golden opportunities in other fields. Think of all the elaborate Christmas wrappings that are going to end up in the trash piles this next month or so. A single law banning all elaborate or special wrapping for packages could do a great deal to diminish the volume of trash and, thus, ease the supposed trash crisis.

I can already hear the counterarguments: My proposals would be acts of dictatorship and would violate the freedom of the press. Horrors, my opponents will say.

But it is precisely the press which is backing the move to draft me to become a trash man.

When the press stops urging a dictatorial move against me and my free time, I'll be glad to stop urging the most obvious way to cut the current trash mountain.

Turnabout is fair play, I say.

QUESTIONS OF CONTENT

1. Why, according to the *USA Today* editors, is the need for recycling so urgent?

2. What methods of dealing with the garbage glut do the editors recommend?

3. What have some local governments done to encourage recycling?

4. How does Harry Schwartz feel about the need for recycling? With what part of the editors' argument does he take exception?

5. What does Schwartz say makes up the major part of the garbage in his household? How does he propose to reduce it?

QUESTIONS OF FORM

1. As do most claims of policy, the claim made by the editors of *USA Today* begins with a claim of fact before making the recommendation of policy. Where exactly do each of these parts of the argument occur?

2. How do the editors support their initial claim of fact?

3. How many recommendations of policy do the editors provide? How do they support each of them?

4. What aspect of the editor's argument does Harry Schwartz attack: the support, the form, or the warrant?

5. What is Schwartz doing in paragraph 7? How is this an example of *reduction to absurdity* (see "A Short Guide to Material and Formal Fallacies" in the Appendix)? How might you counter or refute Schwartz here?

6. Schwartz's argument is based on two somewhat questionable claims: (1) that cooperation with recycling activities will turn him into a "trash man" and (2) that 75–80 percent of domestic trash is newspapers. How might you exploit the weakness of these claims in a rebuttal? How might you strengthen them to avoid rebuttal?

SUGGESTIONS FOR WRITING

1. Try to summarize these two positions without taking sides. Once you have done that, rewrite your summary to favor one side over the other.

2. Make a few inquiries at your school's cafeteria, classroom or office buildings and dormitories. What happens to the garbage produced on these sites? What better use might you recommend? Write a paper recommending such a policy. If some recycling is being done, determine who is doing it and make that a part of your argument. (Acknowledging the recycling already being done can serve as a concession to gain the goodwill of those you are encouraging to do more.) Grapple with the problem of who should become involved in the recycling efforts: the school, the students, the garbage collectors.

3. Besides recycling, the editors of *USA Today* recommend two other approaches: reducing the amount of garbage produced and converting

garbage into energy. Examine the garbage facts about your school as you were asked to do in suggestion 2. Do you find any opportunities for garbage reduction or energy production? If so, write a brief argument recommending such procedures. Begin with a claim of fact which demonstrates that a garbage glut exists on your campus, and then make recommendations for reducing the amount of garbage and/or converting a portion of it into energy.

4. Write a letter to Mr. Schwartz, from one U.S. citizen to another, either supporting or criticizing his stance on recycling, trying to have more objectivity and depth in your statement than he does in his. (Does he speak for all of us, for instance, when he offers to pay more taxes to avoid sorting his trash?)

The Usefulness of Studying a Second Language

We Need a Nationwide Effort to Encourage, Enhance, and Expand Our Students' Proficiency in Languages

DANIEL SHANAHAN

In 1904, at a hearing on the mistreatment of immigrant laborers, the president of the Reading Railroad told a Congressional committee: "These workers don't suffer—they don't even speak English."

Working conditions in the United States have come a long way since then, but the attitude in this country toward people who do not speak English hasn't changed very much. While few of us would support the contention that non-English speakers somehow have no right to equal protection under the law, it has become more acceptable in recent years to oppose such things as bilingual education and bilingual ballots that attempt to address problems faced by speakers of languages other than English.

The issue is a relatively simple one, but it has a complex social and historical background. Before the revival of ethnic pride in the 1960's and 70's, most immigrants who came to this country tried to "launder" much of their cultural past, and their native languages were among the first things to go. For them, learning English was an act of faith in the new land they had adopted. Although the price was steeper than many of them realized at the time, most were willing, even happy, to pay it.

But in the 1960's, the civil-rights movement forced a reassessment of what was "American," and many once-acceptable means of distinguishing among groups were seen as undemocratic, to be ferreted out and eliminated wherever they were found. It is unfortunate that during that period the issue of language (largely as it applied to Hispanic Americans) became fused with the issue of civil rights.

As a result, bilingual issues were overwhelmed by emotional baggage, first the liberal guilt of the 60's and 70's and then the conservative reaction of the Reagan era. Lost in the shuffle was a much more vital issue, and one which pivots not on questions of deprivation of civil rights, but on America's ability to remain a viable actor in the increasingly global environment by becoming more competent linguistically.

The "official language" propositions that have been passed in 17 states in recent years—three in last fall's elections—are clear signs that the electorate does not understand the true effect of the language issue on the national interest. Most such propositions pass because of fear and resentment on the part of the majority language group. While the campaign advertisements run by supporters of the proposals do not overtly express resentment over money spent to serve those who do not speak English, the sentiments expressed by voters who support the initiatives often can be summed up in some variation of the statement: "My parents had to learn English when they came to this country. . . ." 6

Resentment is, of course, a more or less unacceptable basis for policy analysis, so supporters' justifications of English-only initiatives usually play on fears: of social disunity, of economic hardship, of the cost of cultural plurality. Canada is most frequently cited as an example of the way cultural plurality, maintained through linguistic plurality, can lead to social instability. Putting aside for the moment the fact that Canada not only survived Quebec's "quiet revolution" but also profited from it, as the economic boom in Quebec is now demonstrating, such analysis of the language issue ignores the extent to which the entire world is rapidly becoming a stage on which the players must speak more than one language to survive and compete economically. 7

The Japanese have led the way in learning second—and third—languages to further their economic competitiveness. It can be argued that the difficulty of their own language made it unlikely that foreigners would learn it and forced them to learn the languages of others, but it can just as easily be argued that this apparent liability simply led them to see the handwriting on the wall more quickly than others, and it thus becomes a competitive advantage. 8

Europeans have always been proficient in other languages, largely because of the high concentration of different languages in their relatively small geographic space. Being multilingual is helping them establish an economic union that looms as a powerful force in the already crowded and competitive global marketplace. 9

Even in developing countries, where one might expect lack of education to limit multilingualism, many people speak a regional dialect at home and the language of the dominant cultural group in 10 the workplace: some also speak the European language of the colonial period as well. Against this international backdrop, the spectacle of Americans passing laws to limit the languages used in their country can only be seen as self-destructive.

Of course, there must be a standard language in a country, if only   11
for the purpose of efficiency, but the language is designated by practice, not by law. In the United States, the standard language is and always has been English. The question should not be whether we should spend money to make it possible for immigrants to use their native languages in official situations, nor should it be whether we encourage others, children especially, to maintain a language other than English. Quite clearly, the question ought to be whether we should undertake a nationwide effort to encourage, enhance, and expand multilingual proficiency among native speakers of English, as well as among non-natives.

The answer to that question must be a resounding and unequivo-   12
cal Yes.

It is nothing less than criminal for a country so admittedly lan-   13
guage poor and so strapped for competitive advantages in the international marketplace to be adopting myopic and regressive language laws that reinforce the naive monolingual bias that threatens to isolate and weaken it. Yet it is also understandable that Americans want clarity and perhaps a degree of reassurance in our increasingly volatile and shifting ethnic and linguistic environment.

A compromise addressing both sides of the issue must be found,   14
and I believe it will not be as hard to come by as some people might imagine.

Let Congress pass a law designating English the "standard" lan-   15
guage of the United States, but let the measure also include the appropriation of sufficient money to insure that 20 years from now all Americans graduating from high school will be proficient in a second language.

Let a high-school diploma and college admission be denied to   16
anyone without a sufficient level of proficiency. And let proficiency in a second language—at the level of a native speaker—be required for graduation from college and entry into civil-service and private-sector white-collar employment. In other words, let us put our money where our mouths are. The price tag for instituting such requirements—including the cost of training the needed teachers over five years—would be less than the budget for the Strategic Defense Initiative for two fiscal years. Moreover, the benefits would

be far greater. For only with such determined policies can we hope to calm fears about language plurality and insure that we do not become a culture of monolingual dinosaurs.

We have 29 years, nearly triple the time President Kennedy allowed when he committed us to reaching the moon. By comparison, the expenditures required to create a linguistically proficient nation would be insignificant. The benefits, not only in economic terms but also in terms of enhancing our understanding of other cultures and of ourselves, would be beyond measure. The costs, should we fail to act decisively, could eventually prove to be catastrophic.   17

Importance of Studying
Languages Questioned

WALTER ULRICH

I have always been puzzled by the arguments of those like Daniel Shanahan who argue that everybody should be expected to learn a foreign language.   1

While I agree that it is important to learn about other cultures, this could better be accomplished by requiring classes on the history, government, environment, and traditions of other countries. The learning of another language provides only indirect knowledge of a minute part of a single country's culture; the time spent in learning one language would be much better spent developing a broad understanding of a variety of cultures—an understanding that does not require an in-depth knowledge of specific languages.   2

The economic benefits of language study are also overclaimed. Overlooking the problem of deciding in high school or college which language a student will need to know 10 or 20 years later (knowing how to speak German will not help you if you are dealing with a Japanese client), a more serious question is why *all* students should be required to develop this skill. After all, just because we need doctors does not mean that every student should go to medical school; similarly, just because an understanding of languages is important in business does not mean that we all should know a language.   3

Our time and money would be best spent concentrating on developing the expertise of a limited number of language experts instead of diffusing our efforts on students who will never need or use the knowledge.   4

QUESTIONS OF CONTENT

1. How does Shanahan feel about the proposition that English should be adopted as the official standard language of the United States?
2. How does Shanahan feel about bilingual education, that is, the educational policy prescribing that immigrants to the United States may start learning their school subjects in their native language while they also are learning English?
3. Why does Shanahan think that Japanese and Europeans have an advantage over Americans in the business world?
4. How many years does Shanahan propose that the United States be given to develop his policy of requiring all high school graduates to be proficient in a second language? Why does he think that is a proper amount of time?
5. Instead of developing a second language proficiency, what does Ulrich propose as an alternative?
6. Why does Ulrich think that learning a second language is usually wasted effort?

QUESTIONS OF FORM

1. Shanahan does not actually state his claim of policy until paragraph 11. What was he doing before that?
2. What bad state of affairs does Shanahan's claim of policy seek to remedy? Where does he outline that state of affairs?
3. Where does Shanahan present the good effects that his policy might be expected to produce?
4. What part of Shanahan's argument does Ulrich attack: the support, the form of the argument, or the warrant?
5. What counterproposal does Ulrich offer to Shanahan? How convincing is his counterproposal?

SUGGESTIONS FOR WRITING

1. Summarize the positions taken by Shanahan and Ulrich. Be especially careful to remain neutral in your presentation.
2. Summarize the positions of Shanahan and Ulrich, but side with one against the other. Read over the William F. Buckley essay "Let's Return to Regulation of the Airlines" (p. 150) or George Will's "The Case against Drug Legalization" (p. 320) for examples of the use of this sort of summarizing-while-taking-sides technique.
3. What middle course can you suggest that might be acceptable to both Shanahan and Ulrich? Examine possible compromises and present your best solution. Use a summary of the Shanahan and Ulrich positions as an introduction to your own notions.

THE VALUE OF A LIBERAL
ARTS EDUCATION

The Practicality of the
Liberal Arts Major

DEBRA SIKES and BARBARA MURRAY

Current trends indicate that by the year 2000 the average person   1
will change careers at least twice during a lifetime. How does the
entering college student prepare for career mobility which has never
before been necessary? Our fathers decided what they wanted to do
in life, which was very often what their fathers had done—went to
college or apprenticed themselves, and pursued the same career until retirement. Our mothers assumed one of the nurturing roles in
society, if they assumed a role outside of the home at all. Things
have certainly changed. No longer is life so simple.

Adaptability and lifelong learning are now the cornerstones of   2
success. What direction does a person take to prepare for a lifetime
of change? The one degree which provides training which never
becomes obsolete is the liberal arts degree; it teaches you how to
think. It also teaches you how to read, write and speak intelligently,
get along with others, and conceptualize problems. For the first time
in several decades, the liberal arts degree is coming to the forefront
of the employment field.

Growing ranks of corporate executives are lamenting that col-   3
lege students are specializing too much and too early. What corporate America really needs, according to chief executive officers of
major corporations, is students soundly grounded in the liberal
arts—English, especially—who then can pick up more specific business or technical skills on the job. Few students, however, seem to
be listening to this message. Today's best selling courses offer evidence that students want to take courses that provide direct job
related skills rather than the most basic survival skills in the workplace: communication and thinking skills. They want courses they
can parlay into jobs—and high paying ones at that. Certainly, we can
understand this mentality when we consider trends indicating that
this generation will be the first who will not be able to do better
economically than their parents. They don't want to leave anything

to chance. Historically, the liberal arts degree was good insurance for a poverty level existence. Students are looking to history to provide some answers it simply cannot give. They would do well to examine the present.

One of the big problems in the liberal arts community is that we 4
do not market what we have to offer. Students very often fail to see the practicality of studying Shakespeare as preparation for a career in the business community. Perhaps some of us have locked ourselves in the ivory tower a little too long extolling the virtues of a liberal education as preparation for citizenship and life only to the neglect of it as preparation for career or careers. Education for education's sake is noble but impractical to today's college student who is facing a competitive and rapidly changing job market. They want and deserve to know how their courses will help them to get a job. We as educators owe them some answers; we must be accountable not only for learning but also for providing information regarding the transferability of classroom skills into the workplace.

In an attempt to provide answers, we conducted a research proj- 5
ect in the Dallas metroplex last year, assuming the role of the liberal arts graduate seeking employment in the fields of government, banking, business, and industry. Using informational interviewing as our method of job hunting and obtaining data, we conducted twenty-five interviews with a diversity of executive officers, ranging from personnel directors to the chairman of the board of an exclusive department store and the state governor. We wished to validate, through practical and current research, that not only does the liberal arts degree provide the best preparation for a lifetime of change, but it also provides a plethora of employment opportunities. We do not claim our research to be all encompassing, but we do feel its practicality was rewarding. We gathered data as to how the liberal arts major should present himself on paper and in person, where her best chances for employment are, and what he can do to augment the liberal arts degree. We were able to draw several conclusions as to how the liberal arts community could better prepare students for professional mobility.

The Liberal Arts Degree Is Marketable

Ninety percent of those interviewed responded they would hire 6
a liberal arts major for an entry level position which could lead to the executive suite if the position itself were not executive level. The chairman of the board of a major department store in Dallas responded to the question, "For what position would you hire a

liberal arts graduate?" with a direct, "Any position in the company." When asked if a buyer wouldn't need to have special skills, he replied, "Taste is acquired or learned, and the liberal arts major could certainly learn this skill on the job." This interview is typical of the responses.

Skills Acquired with a Liberal Arts Background Are Most Desired by Employers

We were not at all surprised to learn that the skills cited as the   7
most desirable in an employee are those skills acquired from a liberal arts background. The cited skills are listed below in order of importance.

1. Oral communication
2. Written communication
3. Interpersonal
4. Analytical thinking
5. Critical thinking
6. Leadership

Although these skills are not solely acquired through the mastery of an academic discipline, the discipline serves as a vehicle for developing or refining these skills.

Liberal Arts Majors Can Enhance Their Credentials

Adaptability and lifelong learning are the cornerstones of suc-   8
cess in today's complex and rapidly changing society. No longer can the person who is steeped in one academic discipline, but knows nothing about anything else, meet today's demands. Based on the data we accumulated, our recommendations for the liberal arts major are the following:

1. A basic knowledge of accounting
2. Computer literacy
3. Second major in a business field
4. Multiple minors
5. Advanced degree in another field

The key here is adaptability and diversity. Contrary to what most people believe, the higher a skill level an individual can claim, the more marketable he is. About those individuals who complain that they are "overeducated" we can only assume that they are marketing themselves on the wrong level. "Overeducation" is a term whose time will not come in the foreseeable future. The problem many individuals will face is a narrowness of education rather than "overeducation."

Unlike Aristotle, who is believed to have known everything there 9 was to know at the time he lived, it is impossible for us to deal with the voluminous amounts of information which are produced daily. The lifelong learning which we have alluded to will not always be acquired through the traditional sixteen-week college course. We in the community college need to provide a smorgasbord of opportunities for individuals who wish to increase their mobility and options.

The time has come to rethink what education really is and how 10 it relates to the functions of society. Perhaps what a liberal education does for an individual, which is more important than anything else, is to prepare him for more learning. The liberal arts background equips one with thinking skills; and those, coupled with the desire to learn, are the best preparation for career and life that any of us can possess.

The Liberal Arts Religion

CAROLINE BIRD

The academic dean of a famous old college lowered her voice, 1 glanced apprehensively around her office, and confessed: "I just wish I had the guts to tell parents that when you get out of this place you aren't prepared to *do anything.*"

Actually, it did not take much guts. The "best" colleges are the 2 liberal arts schools which are the most "academic"—they don't teach students anything useful in particular. Even after they have to face the world, alumni expect no more. In a study intended to probe what graduates seven years out of college thought their colleges should have given them, the Carnegie Commission found overwhelming preference for "liberal" over "vocational" goals.[1]

What does anyone mean by "a liberal education"? People shift 3 their ground when they try to explain what it is and why it is so important. It's hard to tell whether they're talking about *subjects* that can be studied in school, such as philosophy and literature; a *process* of learning or thinking; or a *personal transformation* ("college opened my eyes"); or a *value system* to which the wise and honest can repair.

The *subject matter* of the liberal arts used to be the classics. If 4 not the ancients, then newer books on history, sociology, economics, science, and other products of the minds of men. As we near the twenty-first century, however, most educators have given up the attempt to pass on the "great tradition of Western man" in a four-year core curriculum. It's not *what* you study, they say, it's *how* you study it.

"A liberal education is an experience that is philosophical in the broadest sense," David Truman, dean of Columbia and later president of Mount Holyoke, has said. "The particular subjects do not so much contain this quality as provide jointly a possible means of approaching it. The liberal arts, then, include those subjects that can most readily be taught so as to produce an understanding of the modes of thought, the grounds of knowledge, and their interrelations, established and to be discovered."

In plainer language alumni say, "College taught me how to think for myself." If you ask people what they mean by thinking and how college teaches it, they recoil from the implication that the kind of thinking they mean is a specific skill, such as the art of rhetoric, but start talking about a "whole new way of looking at the world"—a personal transformation.

Personal transformation, not only in how one's mind works but in how one views the world and oneself, is the most cherished expectation—and sometimes it is achieved. "College changed me inside," one alumnus told us. Some wax poetic. "The liberal arts education aspires to expand the imaginative space and time in which a person lives." Others talk about the "broadening" that occurs when a young woman from a Midwest farming town encounters adults who don't regret the fact that MacArthur was not elected President, or when the son of a city plumber learns that the police are not always right and that some people on welfare aren't cheating. Discoveries like this are valuable, alumni say, because they force students to "formulate the values and goals of my life," as the Carnegie Commission puts it.

And this turns out to be the hidden agenda of a liberal arts education. A value system, a standard, a set of ideals to keep you pointed in the right direction, even if you can't get there. "Like Christianity, the liberal arts are seldom practiced and would probably be hated by the majority of the populace if they were," said one defender.

The analogy is apt. The fact is, of course, that the liberal arts are a religion in every sense of that term. When people talk about them, their language becomes elevated, metaphorical, extravagant, theoretical, and reverent.

In answering a black student who charged the Kirkland College curriculum with "irrelevance," President Samuel F. Babbit remonstrated that her liberal arts education aimed to expose her "to the values, the successes, the failures of great minds, great men and women engaged in every conceivable endeavor through the study of history and literature and art and the other disciplines that man has formed in order to understand where he has been and how to order his world."

"The purpose of the liberal arts is not to teach businessmen   11
business," Alfred Whitney Griswold, former president of Yale, told an alumni gathering. Rather, he went on, it is to "awaken and develop the intellectual and spiritual powers in the individual before he enters upon his chosen career, so that he may bring to that career the greatest possible assets of intelligence, resourcefulness, judgment, and character."

These thickets of verbal foliage are embarrassing to the more   12
sensitive spokesmen for higher education. John T. Retalliata, president of the Illinois Institute of Technology, told an audience of parents in 1973, "I suppose a generalized goal is to have your sons and daughters, somehow, become 'educated' and, with that education, become well-employed and happy." Clark Kerr, notable as the embattled president of the University of California during the 1960s, told a 1972 television audience that "generally, the studies show that people who've been to college, oh, enjoy life more, they have more varied interests, they participate more in community activities." On another occasion, he told Alan Pifer, president of the Carnegie Corporation, that "with all that has happened in the world of knowledge in recent years, it is really impossible for people in higher education to come to agreement on what constitutes a liberal education."

Intellectuals have trouble describing the benefits of a liberal   13
education because the liberal arts are a religion, the established religion of the ruling class. The exalted language, the universal setting, the ultimate value, the inability to define, the appeal to personal witness, the indirectness, the aphorisms—these are all the familiar modes of religious discourse.

As with religion, no proof is required, only faith. You don't have   14
to prove the existence of God. You don't have to understand the Virgin Birth. You don't have to prove that Camus is better than Jacqueline Susann. Camus is sacred, so Camus is better and so are the people who dig him. If you don't dig Camus, the trouble is not with Camus, but with you.

Faith in personal salvation by the liberal arts is professed in a   15
creed intoned on ceremonial occasions such as commencements. It is blasphemy to take the promises literally, and if you don't

understand what the words mean, you are only admitting your lack of grace.

Take, for instance, the goal of college most fervently sought by 16 the alumni queried by the Carnegie Commission, "development of my abilities to think and express myself." Only the captious dare to ask, "What do you mean by your ability to think?" If you inquire, it very quickly develops that those who value this objective aren't talking about what the Swiss educator Jean Piaget, the semanticist Noam Chomsky, or the Harvard psychologist Jerome Bruner mean when they talk about "thinking."[2] The kind of "thinking" the cognitive psychologists are talking about has to be acquired long before you are old enough to go to college, and if Piaget is right, most of it has to be learned before a child is old enough to go to school. What the alumni and employers expect college to teach is the habit of logical analysis and the conventions of rhetoric that make it possible to resolve differences of view on human affairs by debate and discussion. Colleges with very small classes try to give their students practice in the art of dialogue, but the students who speak up in class are usually the ones who have already learned how at the dinner table at home and in bull sessions with friends.

If the liberal arts are a religious faith, the professors are its 17 priests. Professors are not accountable to the laity they serve. They themselves define the boundaries of their authority and choose their own successors. Their authority is unassailable, because by definition they know best. As such, they are invulnerable to lay criticism. One of the educators with whom I talked dismissed the doubts of students out of hand. "I am not convinced that eighteen-year-olds can or should be expected to know what college will ultimately do for them."

The professors disclaim arbitrary personal power. They go by 18 rules. They contend that right is not what they think but what the sacred scriptures or the ecclesiastical courts decree. Professors say that truth is what comes out when you subject data to a process called the scientific method, and it is this process, rather than its product, that is written in the stars. But the process itself, this very scientific method, is also a product of the mind of man, and it may not be the only process the mind of man can devise. Other processes may produce other kinds of truth. No one, for instance, would suggest that the visions of William Blake could be "disproved" by the scientific method.

Colleges govern themselves by their own rules and sometimes 19 confront civil authority. Only during the 1960s, when the students were out of control, did college administrators admit the right of the local police to "invade" the campus. And, like the church, American colleges have used their credibility to exercise political, economic, and social power in an irresponsible way. Along with access to heaven, they don't mind controlling access to the good things of this world. So long as the diploma is a credential for good jobs, giving or withholding it determines the fare of students here on earth. The colleges do not claim that they are preparing candidates for executive work, for instance, but they do not renounce their role as gatekeeper of the best jobs. As one professor told us, "We can't help it that the big companies like to hire our graduates."

To be blunt, the colleges have been as willing as the church to   20
grab the power the faithful thrust upon them. Through their power to issue the diploma, they decide the fate of individuals. Through their power to determine who shall be admitted to college, they select as "naturally better" those who manipulate abstract symbols and unwittingly consign to the damnation of dead-end, second-class role those whose intelligence is manual, visual, or artistic. The power we allow them to have makes our society more vulnerable to words and abstractions than it would otherwise be, and it is not necessary to have a settled opinion on whether this is good or bad to recognize the danger of subjecting young people during their formative years to control by authorities who are pursuing objectives that leave most of the population cold. We think they are benign, therefore we accept their rule over our young. Imagine the outcry at the very idea of turning our surplus young people over to the military for safekeeping!

Americans have always been sensitive to the attempts of their   21
armed forces to use military competence as a basis for exercising political power. But we do not distrust the same kind of bid when it comes from the professoriate. Through their control of research, they decide what frontiers of knowledge shall be pushed back. Through their interpretation of the scientific method, if not the sacred writings of "the great Western tradition," they decide what shall be accepted as good, or true, or even beautiful.

But just as technical progress threatened the various monopolies   22
of the church at the end of the Middle Ages, so the information explosion today threatens the monopoly of college over knowledge.

Of all the forms in which ideas are disseminated, the college   23
professor lecturing his class is the slowest and the most expensive. The culturally deprived for whom college is supposedly so broadening are in the best position to see this. "I can read a book just as good as the man can talk," a black woman student told us. "Nine chances out of ten that's all you get—a professor who's just reading out of the book."

A better college experience would, no doubt, have provided more   24 stimulation than students encountered in the overloaded colleges of the 1960s. But this begs the issue.

Today you don't have to go to college to read the great books.   25
You don't have to go to college to learn about the great ideas of Western man. If you want to learn about Milton, or Camus, or even Margaret Mead, you can find them. In paperbacks. In the public library. In museum talks. In the public lectures most colleges offer for free. In adult education courses given by local high schools. People don't storm these sources because they aren't interested, and there's no particular reason why they should be. Forcing people to "learn" about them by all sorts of social and economic carrots and sticks implies that those who have had contact with "high culture" are somehow better than other people.

And if you do want to learn, it isn't always necessary to go to the   26
original source. I say this knowing that I am stamping myself as an academic heretic. But the culture consumer should be able to decide for himself exactly why, when, how much, and in what form he would like to partake of Daniel Defoe's *Robinson Crusoe*, or Milton's *Areopagitica*, or Simone de Beauvoir's *The Second Sex*. When I was in high school during the 1920s, the whole English class took a month to read *Ivanhoe*, Sir Walter Scott's novel about the crusades. In 1969 my eight-year-old son zipped through a Classic Comic version in fifteen minutes, and I don't think the original warranted the extra time it would have taken him. If you are not interested in the development of the English novel, *Robinson Crusoe* can be an exasperating, slow-moving yarn, significant only because the name has become a symbol of lone adventure and one of the passwords recognized by all men who consider themselves educated. Milton's *Areopagitica* is another password, important for what it says and when it was said. There's a benefit in knowing about these works, but the benefit to any particular person at a particular time may not justify the cost of taking them raw. For many people, and many purposes, it makes more sense to read a summary, an abstract, or even listen to a television critic.

The problem is no longer how to provide access to the broadening   27
ideas of the great cultural tradition, not even how to liberate young people so that they can adopt a different life-style than the one in which they were reared. The problem is the other way around: how to choose among the many courses of action proposed to us, how to edit the stimulations that pour into our eyes and ears every waking hour. A college experience that piles option on option and stimulation on stimulation merely adds to the contemporary nightmare. Increasingly, overloaded undergraduates give up the attempt to reason and flirt, half seriously, with the occult, which leaves vexing decisions to fate.

In order to deal with options, you need values. When Morris   28
Keeton and Conrad Hilberry attempted to define a liberal education
in their book *Struggle and Promise: A Future for Colleges*, they
found that one of the recurrent themes was that it provides "an
integrated view of the world which can serve as an inner guide,"[3]
and more than four-fifths of the alumni queried by the Carnegie
Commission said they expected that their college should have
"helped me to formulate values and goals of my life." The formation
of values may not be the first goal mentioned in discussions of a
liberal education, but it tends to be the final ground on which hard-
pressed defenders take their stand.

How does a student acquire a standard of values? The liberally   29
educated are forbidden, by their own creed, from any procedure so
simple as telling students what is right and good. In theory a student
is taught how to decide for himself, but in practice it doesn't work
quite that way. All but the wayward and the saints take their values
of the good, the true, and the beautiful from the people around them.
When we speak of students acquiring "values" in college, we often
mean that they will acquire the values—and sometimes we mean
only the tastes—of their professors.

The values of professors may well be "higher" than many stu-   30
dents can expect to encounter elsewhere, but often those values
aren't relevant to the situations in which students find themselves
in college or later. Too many academics systematically overvalue
symbols and abstractions. Historians will recall that it was a professor of history, President Woodrow Wilson, who sent American soldiers abroad to "make the world safe for democracy."

In addition to a distressing confusion of symbol and thing, profes-   31
sors are sometimes painfully ignorant of many essential facts of life.
A lot of them know very little about the economic structure of the
United States, and their notions of what goes on inside major corporations are based on books written forty years ago about conditions
prevailing fifty years ago. And they may also be partially responsible
for some of the "alienation" of the young because they have encouraged the belief that transactions of power and money are to be
avoided as a dirty business.

In so doing, of course, they are intuitively defending the legiti-   32
macy of their own power. A poor boy who wanted to make good in
the Middle Ages had to become a priest and at least profess to see the
world in spiritual terms. A poor boy who wants to make good in
twentieth-century America has to get a liberal education and at least
profess to see the world in intellectual terms.

The academic elite are the self-proclaimed guardians of what's   33
right. Who's to tell them when they are wrong? Academics pride

themselves on introducing students to a free marketplace of ideas, but they are the ones who make the rules, and the rules themselves can perpetuate dangerous distortions of reality. Not so long ago, for instance, no painter who drew pubic hair on a nude figure could expect to be taken seriously as an artist. It would have been vulgar to see it. The oversight is amusing now, but it was not trivial. Victorian prudery was hard to combat because it was a convention of the "best people." It's easy to laugh, but harder to be sure that we are not overlooking some other facts of life today.

A liberal arts education does, of course, transmit standards of value, and those in charge assume, almost as self-confidently as that great Victorian, Matthew Arnold, that "the best that has been known and thought in the world" is what they say it is. Intellectual leaders today worry about sounding snobbish, but they are just as sure as the great eighteenth-century English essayist Richard Steele that "it is the great aim of education to raise ourselves above the vulgar." And those who have been so educated are happy to accept the distinction. At Harvard commencements there is an audible sigh of emotion when the president, as he has done for 300 years, welcomes the new graduates into "the fellowship of educated men." (Since 1970, it has been "the fellowship of educated men and women.") 34

NOTES

1. "When alumni were forced to choose between a general education and a career-oriented education, they overwhelmingly endorsed the idea of a general education," Joe L. Spaeth and Andrew M. Greeley reported in *Recent Alumni and Higher Education*, a Carnegie Commission study published by McGraw-Hill, New York, in 1970. The study queried 40,000 graduates of the class of 1961 in 135 colleges in 1961, 1962, 1963, 1964, and 1968.

2. For a quick introduction to the slippery concepts involved in thinking about thinking, see the section "The Elements and Vehicles of Thought," pp. 188–237, in Berelson & Steiner, *Human Behavior, An Inventory of Scientific Findings*, Harcourt Brace, New York, 1964.

3. A dogged attempt to cope with the verbal foliage surrounding definitions of a liberal education appears in Morris Keeton and Conrad Hilberry's *Struggle and Promise: A Future for Colleges*, McGraw-Hill, New York, 1969, p. 260. They identify several common elements including cultivation of the intellect; encouragement of "independent judgment" or "critical thought"; liberating the individual so that he can see the world in perspectives other than his own; evoking an integrated view of the world which can serve as an inner guide; equipping the individual to serve his society.

QUESTIONS OF CONTENT

1. What two things do Sikes and Murray declare to be the cornerstones of success in the modern era? Why do they feel that a liberal arts education provides these things?
2. Sikes and Murray conducted a series of interviews in the Dallas area. What hypothesis was their interview designed to test? How well did it, in fact, confirm or disprove their hypothesis?
3. According to Sikes and Murray, what skills are most valued by employers?
4. Caroline Bird cites a Carnegie Commission report. What does the report conclude? What is her reaction to its findings?
5. Bird mentions several attempts to define a liberal education. What are they? How does she define it?
6. According to Bird, what modern technology threatens the university's monopoly on knowledge? Why is that so?
7. Why does Bird object to college professors being the arbiters of taste and values?

QUESTIONS OF FORM

1. What sorts of evidence do Sikes and Murray provide to support their contention that a liberal education is both practical and marketable?
2. Why is the definition of a liberal education so important to both sides of this debate?
3. Reread content question 3 above. Why were the answers to this question so easy to locate? What attention-getting devices do the authors employ in this section of their argument?
4. As the title of her essay suggests, Bird makes an extended analogy between the study of the liberal arts and the profession of a religious faith. What common elements does she point out? What claim is the analogy meant to support?
5. To what authorities does Bird appeal? Each of her appeals to authority is meant to support what elements of her arguments?

SUGGESTIONS FOR WRITING

1. Here is a topic sentence for a brief essay that you can complete by summarizing succinctly the opposing views of the two articles presented in this section: Not everyone currently agrees that the time-honored liberal arts college curriculum is the best educational path to pursue.
2. Assume that you are a humanities major finishing your junior year— a little too late to be thinking about a major alteration in your educa-

tional plans. You have not settled on exactly what you intend to do after graduation. You have ruled out teaching; law school remains a possibility, but only after you have worked full time for a couple of years to pay off your educational loans. You generally accept Sikes and Murray's views on the value of the degree that is now within your reach, and you are confident that your communication skills will be marketable. How might you respond to Bird's article, which was published in your campus newspaper? Write a letter to the editor defending your degree choice, drawing as needed upon the essay by Murray and Sikes.

3. Unlike the student in suggestion 2, you are about to graduate with a degree from one of the following professional schools on your campus: nursing, business, or engineering. What is your response to the appearance of the Bird article in the student newspaper? Would you feel inclined to attack it? Or would you support it against the criticisms of students like the one described above? Write your own letter to the editor.

SEXISM

Facing up to Sexism

MICHAEL W. HIRSCHORN

When French playwright Jean Genet wrote *The Balcony* he 1
noted that the best way to portray true good in the world was to
force his audiences to confront true evil. Fake judges, generals, and
bishops parade through a whorehouse, living out their petty hypocri-
sies and in the process exposing the so-called justice of the establishment as so many lies.

Genet was convinced of the immorality of the system, so he had 2
no doubt that his audiences would react in disgust as the wanton
decadence and hypocrisy of the establishment figures before them
on the stage

That point was apparently lost on those here at *The Crimson* 3
who thought that refusing to publish a *Playboy* recruitment ad was
the best way to attack immorality.

Some will argue that refusing to publish an advertisement is 4
censorship. They are clearly wrong, for a newspaper must have control over its own pages, and it's certainly within *The Crimson's*
prerogative, both legally and ethically, to refuse space to whomever
it chooses.

Some will argue that refusing to publish an advertisement in- 5
fringes on free speech. Not really, for advertising is not free speech,
and, in any case, the *Playboy* ad is not an opinion. As one editor
noted at Sunday's in-house discussion of the ad issue, one must be
able to disagree with an opinion, and the counter-argument to the
Playboy solicitation is "No, a *Playboy* photographer will *not* be at
the Somerville Holiday Inn this week."

Yet, free speech is not a substanceless concept that we mouth 6
whenever we want to prove that, yes, we really are democrats with a
small "d." Free speech is the last defense of the just, for it is always
the less popular, less acceptable opinion that gets quashed when
freedom of expression is restricted.

This truism is not relevant to *Playboy*, for the magazine, thanks 7
in part to news coverage generated by *The Crimson's* dispute and by

259

prominent coverage on page one of this newspaper, is having "free speech" a-plenty. The argument is relevant to those who voted not to publish the advertisement, because they failed to see their own self-interest. Put simply, they did not have enough faith in our community to believe that female students would be as repulsed by the concept of posing nude for *Playboy* (and by the magazine itself) as women at *The Crimson* were.

If, in fact, more than a handful of women do decide to pose for   8
Playboy, then there are some problems in this society whose roots lie far deeper than *The Crimson* or *Playboy* and which would make *The Crimson's* little gesture seem trivial indeed. Does *The Crimson* really believe it can or should protect society from itself?

If anything, I believe Harvard women are turned off by the ad and   9
will react strongly against the magazine and all it may stand for. Like Genet, I believe that moral goals are achieved by getting everything out in the open and allowing the people to see and react against evil.

Martin Luther King understood this dynamic when he trooped,   10
cameras rolling, into the most reactionary, racist neighborhoods in Chicago and revealed the evil of racism as it had never been seen before. Were it not for King, those neighborhoods would have continued their ways and the nation would never have been forced to face the ugliness of its people. As a result of the efforts of King and others, the social consensus was changed.

And yet, the majority at *The Crimson* believed they were further-   11
ing a noble cause by quashing the *Playboy* ad. People who read about *The Crimson's* decision around the country—everything that happens at Harvard goes national—will get a good chuckle, as will the editors of *Playboy*, who will once again be able to make the fallacious argument that they are persisting despite the oppression of a bunch of Harvard prudes.

Meanwhile, those who argued to pull the ad, satisfied with their   12
victory, have not bothered to take their case to the rest of the Harvard population. Ironically, now that *The Crimson's* pages are pure, no one seems terribly worried about convincing women who might want to pose that what they're doing runs counter to everything for which women at Harvard and elsewhere have been fighting for decades.

Moral crusaders should never be ashamed of the truth, because   13
the truth will always work in their favor. The fight to rid society of pornography is a noble one, but it will only be won when and if enough Americans are forced to confront their own sexism.

That cause was not furthered by the actions of the majority, for   14
they took the spotlight off *Playboy* and the women of Harvard and

turned it on *The Crimson.* The editors are to be congratulated on their victory, but they must realize it was only a Pyrrhic one.

Taking a Stand
Against Sexism

KRISTIN A. GOSS

The Crimson's decision not to run *Playboy*'s advertisement re-   1
cruiting Harvard women for its October "Women of the Ivy League" issue was both the very most and the very least the newspaper could do to fight the institutionalized exploitation of women.

Those who claim the staff endeavored to "censor" *Playboy,* or to   2
protect Harvard women from themselves, miss the point of the majority's intentions, just as they did seven years ago when *The Crimson* rejected the same ad.

The questions is clearly not one of hiding information or of   3
paternalism, but of refusing to support, either tacitly or overtly, a publication whose *raison d'être* is the objectification of women and the exploitation of womankind. It is a question of integrity.

Playboy editors must not expect us—a group of undergraduates   4
who are ourselves either morally repulsed by the pornography racket or in the very least respectful of such feelings of collective degradation in our peers—to aid and abet their objectionable cause.

They should also not expect us to keep silent, as they attempt to   5
make sex objects out of our classmates by offering five times as much money to those who take their clothes off as to those who remain clothed. This is not sexuality; it is sexism.

Those who say *The Crimson* singlehandedly stifled *Playboy*'s   6
message have no argument. *Playboy* could have spent the same amount of money that running an ad in *The Crimson* would cost to make somewhere in the neighborhood of 10,000 photocopied posters, which would have effectively reached every undergraduate, professor and administrator on this campus, and then some. It could have run an advertisement on WHRB. It did run one in the *Independent* and in the *Boston Herald.*

The Crimson's rejection of the ad clearly did not compromise   7
Playboy's rights to freedom of expression. The newspaper has not as an institution prevented *Playboy* photographer David Chan from coming to campus.

Nor has it implied that Harvard women cannot decide for   8

themselves whether to pose before him; they can and will make a proper, reasoned decision in either case.

Nor has *The Crimson* censored *Playboy;* the newspaper is in fact   9
on record as supporting pornography's First Amendment right to exist.

The newspaper staff has used its editorial discretion to state that   10
its toleration of pornography—by default, because the alternative would be worse—does not preclude protest. It has expressed the view held by many of its editors that while *Playboy* and other forms of institutionalized sexism may be "socially acceptable," they should not be so.

Social acceptability is a function of which group controls society   11
and to what extent minority voices can influence the spectrum of opinion. Just as racist ads of 50 years ago were socially acceptable to a white-dominated society, so are sexist ads today threatening to females who, despite the women's liberation movement, still have a long way to go to gain equality.

Any woman who has walked down the street and been verbally   12
harassed, and any woman who has feared rape while walking alone in her own neighborhood at night—I might add there is not one female who has not—knows that fighting the image of woman-as-object, woman-as-silenced victim, woman-as-sex-organ remains among her most urgent tasks.

Sexism is most dangerous when it's subtle, when it is so deeply   13
embedded in a culture that it becomes socially acceptable, as *Playboy* has. And so, you speak out, you yell, you rant and you rave when you recognize this subtle destruction. There is no other way to jar society out of its passive acceptance of the objectification of women, even though in this society it happens to be legal.

In not running the ad, *The Crimson* has taken that initiative.   14
Seven years from now, when *Playboy* again decides to try its luck with a whole new batch of Ivy League women, we can only hope all Ivy League newspapers will decide not to extend their helping hands. It is both the most and the least they can do.

QUESTIONS OF CONTENT

1. Why does Hirschorn believe that *The Crimson* was wrong in denying ad space to *Playboy?*
2. Who are Jean Genet and Martin Luther King? Why does Hirschorn use them as examples?
3. What reasons does Goss give for refusing to run the *Playboy* ad?

4. In paragraphs 1 and 10 Goss claims that sexism is "institutionalized." What does she mean by that?

QUESTIONS OF FORM

1. Hirschorn begins by making two concessions. What are they, and what did he hope to gain by making them?
2. How do the examples drawn from Genet and King tend to bolster Hirschorn's argument?
3. In paragraph 11 Goss refers to the racist ads that appeared in newspapers fifty years ago. In doing so she is using an analogy. How exactly does that analogy work?
4. The majority of *The Crimson*'s staff, according to Goss, chose not to support *Playboy*'s sexism, despite the paper's support of "pornography's First Amendment right to exist." How does she justify that apparent contradiction? Why do you suppose she even mentions it?

SUGGESTIONS FOR WRITING

1. Briefly summarize the positions taken by Hirschorn and Goss.
2. The *Playboy* photographer has just arrived on your campus. How do you feel about his presence there? Examine your values and write a letter to your campus paper stating your attitude toward the pictorial article that will probably appear after his visit.
3. You are the editor of the campus paper, and, like Goss, you must respond to *Playboy*'s request for ad space. What will your response be? Write an editorial justifying that response.

THE DEATH PENALTY

The Deterrent Effect
of the Death Penalty

ERNEST VAN DEN HAAG

Crime is going to be with us as long as there is any social order 1
articulated by laws. There is no point making laws that prohibit
some action or other (e.g., murder or theft) unless there is some
temptation to commit it. And however harsh the threats of the law,
they will not restrain some people, whether because they discount
the risk of punishment or because they are exposed to extraordinary
temptation. They may hope for an immense profit; or be passion-
ately angry or vindictive; or be in such misery that they feel they
have nothing to lose. Thus, I repeat, the problem every society must
attempt to solve (in part by means of punishment) is not eliminating
crime but controlling it.

That threats will not deter everybody all the time must be ex- 2
pected. And it must also be expected that persons committed to
criminal activity—career criminals—are not likely to be restrained
by threats; nor are persons strongly under the influence of drugs or
intoxicated by their own passions. However, if threats are not likely
to deter habitual offenders, they are likely to help deter people from
becoming habitual offenders.

People are not deterred by exactly calculating the size of the 3
threat and the actual risk of suffering punishment against the likely
benefit of the crime they consider committing. Few people calculate
at all. Rather, the effect of threats is to lead most people to ignore
criminal opportunities most of the time. One just does not consider
them—any more than the ordinary person sitting down for lunch
starts calculating whether he could have Beluga caviar and cham-
pagne instead of his usual hamburger and beer. He is not accustomed
to caviar, and one reason he is not accustomed to it is that it costs
too much. He does not have to calculate every time to know as
much. Similarly, he is not accustomed to breaking the law, and one
reason is that it costs too much. He does not need to calculate.

It is quite a different matter if one asks, not: "Do threats deter?" 4

but rather: "How much does one threat deter compared to another?" Does the most severe threat deter significantly more? Does the added deterrence warrant the added severity? Thus, no one pondering the death penalty will contend that it does not deter. The question is: Does it deter more than alternative penalties proposed, such as life imprisonment or any lengthy term of imprisonment?

In the past many attempts were made to determine whether the death penalty deters the crimes for which it was threatened—capital crimes—more than other penalties, usually life imprisonment, mitigated by parole (and amounting therefore to something like ten years in prison in most cases). Most of these attempts led to ambiguous results, often rendered more ambiguous by faulty procedures and research methods. Frequently, contiguous states—one with and the other without the death penalty—were compared. Or states were compared before and after abolition. Usually these comparisons were based on the legal availability or unavailability of the death penalty rather than on the presence or absence of executions and on their frequency. But what matters is whether the death penalty is practiced, not whether theoretically it is available. Finally, nobody would assert that the death penalty—or any crime-control measure—is the only determinant of the frequency of the crime. The number of murders certainly depends as well on the proportion of young males in the population, on income distribution, on education, on the proportion of various races in the population, on local cultural traditions, on the legal definition of murder, and on other such factors.

Comparisons must take all of these matters into account if they are to evaluate the effect threatened penalties may have in deterring crimes. In contiguous states, influential factors other than the death penalty may differ; they may even differ in the same state before and after abolition. Hence, differences (or equalities) in capital crime frequencies cannot simply be ascribed to the presence or absence of the death penalty. Moreover, one does not know how soon a change in penalties will make a difference, if it ever does, or whether prospective murderers will know that the death penalty has been abolished in Maine and kept in Vermont. They certainly will know whether or not there is a death penalty in the United States. But in contiguous states? Or within a short time after abolition or reinstatement?

Theoretically, experiments to avoid all these difficulties are possible. But they face formidable obstacles in practice. If, for instance, the death penalty were threatened for murders committed on Monday, Wednesday, and Friday, and life imprisonment for murders committed on Tuesday, Thursday, and Saturday, we would soon see which days murderers prefer, i.e., how much the death penalty deters on Monday, Wednesday, and Friday over and above life imprisonment threatened for murders committed on the other days. If we find no difference, the abolitionist thesis that the death penalty adds no deterrence over and above the threat of life imprisonment would be confirmed.

In the absence of such experiments, none of the available studies   8
seems conclusive. Recently such studies have acquired considerable mathematical sophistication, and some of the more sophisticated studies have concluded, contrary to what used to be accepted scholarly opinion, that the death penalty can be shown to deter over and above life imprisonment. Thus, Isaac Ehrlich, in a study published in the *American Economic Review* (June 1975), concluded that, over the period 1933–1969, "an additional execution per year . . . may have resulted on the average in 7 or 8 fewer murders."

Other studies published since Ehrlich's contend that his results   9
are due to the techniques and periods he selected, and that different techniques and periods yield different results. Despite a great deal of research on all sides, one cannot say that the statistical evidence is conclusive. Nobody has claimed to have *disproved* that the death penalty may deter more than life imprisonment. But one cannot claim, either, that it has been proved statistically in a conclusive manner that the death penalty does deter more than alternative penalties. This lack of proof does not amount to disproof. However, abolitionists insist that there ought to be proof positive.

Unfortunately, there is little proof of the sort sought by those   10
who oppose the death penalty for the deterrent effect of any sort of punishment. Nobody has statistically shown that 4 years in prison deter more than 2, or 20 more than 10. We assume as much. But I know of no statistical proof. One may wonder why such proof is demanded for the death penalty but not for any other. To be sure, death is more serious a punishment than any other. But 10 years in prison are not exactly trivial either. . . .

If it is difficult, perhaps impossible, to prove statistically—and   11
just as hard to disprove—that the death penalty deters more from capital crimes than available alternative punishments do (such as life imprisonment), why do so many people believe so firmly that the death penalty is a more effective deterrent?

Some are persuaded by irrelevant arguments. They insist that   12
the death penalty at least makes sure that the person who suffered it will not commit other crimes. True. Yet this confuses incapacitation with a specific way to bring it about: death. Death is the surest way to bring about the most total incapacitation, and it is irrevocable. But does incapacitation need to be that total? And is irrevocability necessarily an advantage? Obviously it makes correcting mistakes

and rehabilitation impossible. What is the advantage of execution, then, over alternative ways of achieving the desired incapacitation?

More important, the argument for incapacitation confuses the   13 elimination of one murderer (or of any number of murderers) with a reduction in the homicide rate. But the elimination of any specific number of actual or even of potential murderers—and there is some doubt that the actual murderers of the past are the most likely future (potential) murderers—will not affect the homicide rate, except through deterrence. There are enough potential murderers around to replace all those incapacitated. Deterrence may prevent the potential from becoming actual murderers. But incapacitation of some or all actual murderers is not likely to have much effect by itself. Let us then return to the question: Does capital punishment deter more than life imprisonment?

Science, logic, or statistics often have been unable to prove what   14 common sense tells us to be true. Thus, the Greek philosopher Zeno some 2,000 years ago found that he could not show that motion is possible; indeed, his famous paradoxes appear to show that motion is impossible. Though nobody believed them to be true, nobody succeeded in showing the fallacy of these paradoxes until the rise of mathematical logic less than a hundred years ago. But meanwhile, the world did not stand still. Indeed, nobody argued that motion should stop because it had not been shown to be logically possible. There is no more reason to abolish the death penalty than there was to abolish motion simply because the death penalty has not been, and perhaps cannot be, shown statistically to be a deterrent over and above other penalties. Indeed, there are two quite satisfactory, if nonstatistical, indications of the marginal deterrent effect of the death penalty.

In the first place, our experience shows that the greater the threat-   15 ened penalty, the more it deters. Ceteris paribus, the threat of 50 lashes, deters more than the threat of 5; a $1,000 fine deters more than a $10 fine; 10 years in prison deter more than 1 year in prison—just as, conversely, the promise of a $1,000 reward is a greater incentive than the promise of a $10 reward, etc. There may be diminishing returns. Once a reward exceeds, say, $1 million, the additional attraction may diminish. Once a punishment exceeds, say, 10 years in prison (net of parole), there may be little additional deterrence in threatening additional years. We know hardly anything about diminishing returns of penalties. It would still seem likely, however, that the threat of life in prison deters more than any other term of imprisonment.

The threat of death may deter still more. For it is a mistake to   16 regard the death penalty as though it were of the same kind as other penalties. If it is not, then diminishing returns are unlikely to apply. And death differs significantly, in kind, from any other penalty. Life in prison is still life, however unpleasant. In contrast, the death penalty does not just threaten to make life unpleasant—it threatens to take life altogether. This difference is perceived by those affected. We find that when they have the choice between life in prison and execution, 99 percent of all prisoners under sentence of death prefer life in prison. By means of appeals, pleas for commutation, indeed by all means at their disposal, they indicate that they prefer life in prison to execution.

From this unquestioned fact a reasonable conclusion can be   17
drawn in favor of the superior deterrent effect of the death penalty. Those who have the choice in practice, those whose choice has actual and immediate effects on their life and death, fear death more than they fear life in prison or any other available penalty. If they do, it follows that the threat of the death penalty, all other things equal, is likely to deter more than the threat of life in prison. One is most deterred by what one fears most. From which it follows that whatever statistics fail, or do not fail, to show, the death penalty is likely to be more deterrent than any other.

Suppose now one is not fully convinced of the superior deterrent   18
effect of the death penalty. I believe I can show that even if one is genuinely uncertain as to whether the death penalty adds to deterrence, one should still favor it, from a purely deterrent viewpoint. For if we are not sure, we must choose either to (1) trade the certain death, by execution, of a convicted murderer for the probable survival of an indefinite number of murder victims whose future murder is less likely (whose survival is more likely)—if the convicted murderer's execution deters prospective murderers, as it might, or to (2) trade the certain survival of the convicted murderer for the probable loss of the lives of future murder victims more likely to be murdered because the convicted murderer's nonexecution might not deter prospective murderers, who could have been deterred by executing the convicted murderer.

To restate the matter: If we were quite ignorant about the mar-   19
ginal deterrent effects of execution, we would have to choose—like it, or not—between the certainty of the convicted murder's death by execution and the likelihood of the survival of future victims of other murderers on the one hand, and on the other his certain survival and the likelihood of the death of new victims. I'd rather execute a man convicted of having murdered others than to put the lives of innocents at risk. I find it hard to understand the opposite choice.

Rolling the Dice to Decide Who Dies

VIVIAN BERGER

Since 1984, when the Court of Appeals held unconstitutional 1
the last vestige of the death penalty in New York State, New York
has been one of fewer than a third of the states in this country that
do not provide for capital punishment. In each of the past few years,
however, our Legislature has passed bills reauthorizing death as the
sanction for certain types of murder. Governor Cuomo, a committed
opponent of capital punishment as was Governor Carey before him,
has consistently vetoed these efforts. But sooner or later the governor will relinquish office. Surely, therefore, a time will come when
the state acquires as chief executive someone who either supports
execution or declines to counter the lawmakers' wishes. Then New
Yorkers, acting through their elected officials, will have to regard the
death penalty as more than a mere symbolic gesture—a banner to
wave in the war against crime.

Because that point may be in the offing, the New York Bar, 2
whose collective opinion should weigh heavily in the final decision
whether we remain an abolitionist state, must begin to think seriously about the issues. I, like our governor, fervently oppose capital
punishment; and I do so based on considerable experience with how
it operates, not just with the rhetoric that surrounds it. I hope to
persuade those of you who have no opinion on the subject and perhaps even some who currently favor reviving the death sentence in
New York that such a course has nothing to commend it. To the
contrary, reinstatement would amount to a giant step backward in
this state's historical march toward a decent and efficient system of
justice.

To plunge yourself right into the reality of capital punishment, 3
imagine that you are sitting on a jury in Georgia or Florida or some
other death-penalty state in the following cases. Your awesome task
is to determine whether the defendant should receive life imprisonment or death. Even if you could in fact never sentence a person to
die, you must try to envision that possibility—for the prosecution
would have struck you for cause unless you had indicated on voir-
dire that you would consider the option of death. Here are the five
cases in cameo:

> #1. A 19-year-old man, John, and his companion stole a young 4
> woman's purse on the street, pushed her to the ground, and

jumped into their nearby car. A taxi driver, observing the theft, sought to block their getaway with his cab. The defendant, John, shot and killed him. It was his first violent offense.

#2. A 19-year-old man, Joe, tried to grab the purse of a 54-year-old woman in a shopping center parking lot. She resisted and began screaming. They struggled for the purse and Joe shot her once in the side, killing her. He had prior misdemeanor convictions for shoplifting and simple battery as well as a felony conviction for theft.

#3. A 21-year-old man, Robert, drove up to an all-night self-service station and filled his tank. He was paying for the gas with a "hot" credit card when the attendant, a college student, became suspicious that the card was stolen. Robert then shot the attendant once, killing him instantly, in order to avoid being arrested for the credit-card theft. Robert had previous convictions for an unarmed juvenile robbery and the burglary of a store.

#4. A 20-year-old man, Nickie, who was under the influence of drugs, broke into a neighbor's apartment and bludgeoned her and her 8-year-old daughter to death with a hammer. He said later that he had done it because he liked to see blood. Nickie had past convictions for robbery and attempted aggravated rape.

#5. A 26-year-old man, Stephen, together with a 17-year-old friend, burglarized the home of an elderly widow for whom the friend had done yard work. They were planning to rob her. The woman ended by being raped, beaten, and strangled as well as robbed. The defendant, Stephen, admitted that the two of them had raped and robbed her. He insisted, however (and no witness supported or contradicted his story) that only the friend had killed the victim and that he, Stephen, had tried in vain to stop the murder. He had previously committed an unarmed "date rape."

Ask yourself which, if any, of these men you would have sentenced to life in prison and which to death. Next, try to guess how the actual jurors decided these cases. In fact, #1, John, the purse-snatcher who shot the cabbie, received life. #2, Joe, the other purse-snatcher who shot the 54-year-old woman, was sentenced to die. #3, Robert, the credit-card thief who shot the attendant at the gas service station, got death as well; he is one of my clients. #4, Nickie, the hammer-bludgeoner who liked to see blood, got life imprisonment. Finally, #5, Stephen, who robbed and raped and may (or may not) have strangled the widow, was sentenced to death; he is also my client.

Whether or not you called any of the cases correctly, you might want to ask yourself: "Did the divergent results make sense?" If there was a pattern, I must say it eludes me. But for the moment, taking some liberties with the facts and treating my examples as hypothetical instead of the true accounts which they are, I want the reader to consider the possibility that jurors in a couple of the cases that ended in death might likelier have opted for life imprisonment if they had received some more information. For example, suppose the sentencing jurors had heard that Joe had been the incredibly abused child of a violent alcoholic father and a battered, helpless, incompetent mother? That the father had made a game of placing Joe and his siblings in a tight circle and throwing heavy objects like glass ashtrays into the air for the pleasure of seeing who would be hit? That Joe had at last run away from home at the age of 12, camped for some months in a Dempsey dumpster, and then been taken in by a man who sheltered him in return for homosexual favors? That during his one, too-brief experience in foster care when he was nine, Joe responded with great affection and excellent behavior to the love and attention of his foster mother? Or, to take another example, suppose the jury had known that Stephen had an IQ in the high 50's or low 60's? That confronted once with a power mower that wasn't running, Stephen put water from a hose inside it because he had seen others fill the machine but never realized that not *any* type of liquid would do?

Of course, no one knows how real jurors would have reacted to the scenarios I described. But experts in capital defense work agree that no matter how appalling the crime, twelve not unduly sentimental jurors may well decide to spare a defendant when shown that he is a human being with some explanation if not excuse for his horrible acts. Yet while the jurors routinely hear the worst things about the defendant, including usually his criminal record, what is shocking is that in so many cases they hear *nothing* else about him that might be deemed relevant to sentence. (Why this occurs, and what it means for the operation of capital punishment, I will explore further shortly.) What they *do* necessarily learn is the race of both defendant and victim. If I had recounted some more examples of the type I asked you to judge as a juror and told you the race of the persons involved, or at least the victim's, you might have begun to detect a pattern that did not emerge from the *pertinent* data. To this topic, too, I will soon return. But what I hope I have done thus far is to give the reader a "slice of death." At the very least, by relating these sadly prosaic stories, I wanted to scotch the notion which so

10

11

many people have that death is reserved for special cases: the serial killers, the depraved torturers, the Mafia hit men. In New York we deal with the Joes and Stephens each week by the hundreds.

A bit of history sheds some light on how Capital Punishment   12 U.S.A. acquired its present salient features. The watershed came when the United States Supreme Court handed down the landmark *Furman v. Georgia* in 1972. *Furman* invalidated all existing death sentence statutes as violative of the Eighth Amendment's ban on cruel and unusual punishment and thus depopulated state death rows of their 629 occupants. Although there was no majority opinion and only Justices Brennan and Marshall would have held execution to be intrinsically cruel and unusual, Justice Stewart captured the essence of the centrist justices' view—that the death penalty *as actually applied* was unconstitutionally arbitrary—in his famous analogy between the imposition of a capital sentence and the freakishness of a strike of lightning. Being "struck" by a capital sentence was cruel and unusual in the same way as being hit by a lightning bolt: the event was utterly capricious and random.

But worse, if possible, than death sentences that are entirely arbi-   13 trary in the sense that a strike of lightning is freakish are those imposed on invidious grounds: where the lightning rod is race, religion, gender, or class. As Justice Douglas trenchantly remarked: "The Leopolds and Loebs are given prison terms, not sentenced to death." Blacks, however, were disproportionately sentenced to die, especially for the rape of white females. Indeed, the abolitionist campaign, which culminated in the *Furman* decision, had its genesis in the effort to eliminate capital punishment for rape. So perhaps, historically, the death penalty was really less "unusual" than "cruel": an invisible hand, and clearly a white one, was sorting out whites from blacks and thereby creating a pattern of results that many decent people abhorred.

Probably the justices hoped and believed that after *Furman* the   14 death penalty in the United States would remain dead; if so, they were wrong. Many legislatures simply determined to try until they got it right. And in 1976, in *Gregg v. Georgia* and its four companion cases, a majority of the Court upheld the post-Furman capital punishment statutes of Georgia, Florida, and Texas against a challenge to their facial validity, while simultaneously nullifying the revised laws of two other states. Those states had sought to resolve the randomness problem identified in *Furman* by ensuring that lightning would strike *all* persons convicted of murder in the first degree, rather than just a hapless few. In rejecting this tack, the Court noted that mandatory death sentence laws did not really resolve the problem but instead "simply papered [it] over" since juries responded by refusing to convict certain arbitrarily chosen defendants of first-degree murder.

More importantly, though, the justices ratified the so-called   15
guided discretion statutes at issue in three of the five cases. The
Court specifically approved some features of the new statutes which
it expected would reduce the capriciousness of capital punishment
and at the same time further the goal of individualization in sentencing. Thus, to take Georgia's law as a sample, the *Gregg* majority
endorsed its provision for separate trials on guilt and penalty and
automatic appellate review of sentences of death. The bifurcated
trial innovation permitted the admission of evidence relevant only
to sentence (for instance, the defendant's prior convictions) in a way
that would not prejudice the jury in deciding guilt or innocence. The
Court also emphasized that, at the penalty trial, not only did the
state have to prove some aggravating circumstances beyond the fact
of the murder itself (for example, torture or a previous record of
criminal violence) but also defendants had the opportunity to offer
evidence in mitigation—brave-conduct medals, or thrown ashtrays
and waterlogged mowers.

It is basically under these post-*Gregg* schemes that Capital Pun-   16
ishment U.S.A. has been operating for over a decade. Until recently,
however, only a handful of executions occurred every year. But in
the mid-80s, in the wake of four adverse Supreme Court decisions—
after a period in which the Court had overturned the capital sentence in 14 out of 15 cases, the engine of death acquired new steam.
In 1984 alone, there were 21 executions (almost twice as many as in
all of the years following *Gregg*); 1985 and 1986 saw 18 apiece, and
the body count continues to grow. Thus, *Furman II* is hardly on the
horizon now. That being so, if our next governor permits the enactment of capital statutes, the Court will surely not "veto" them:
members of the Bar should understand that New York will have not
dead-letter laws but dying defendants.

Why should New Yorkers oppose this result? Some believe that   17
capital punishment inherently violates human dignity. But because
many disagree with that view and my expertise is only lawyering,
not moral philosophy, I leave it to others to debate the ultimate
ethical issues. I take my stand with an eminent colleague, Professor
Charles L. Black, Jr. Like me, refusing to resolve the basic clash of
values, he reminds us wisely that there is "no abstract capital punishment." Asked how he would feel about the death penalty if only
its administration were perfected, the professor replies: "What
would you do if an amoeba were taught to play the piano?" In other
words, it's a silly question; capital punishment *is* as it *does*. Therefore, the often high-flown rhetoric bandied about by the pros and

antis assumes, in my view, second place to the homely facts that make the American "legal system not good enough to choose people to die." I end with a few of the reasons why, which I hope that those who support or are open to reviving the death sentence in New York take deeply to heart.

Consider, first, the arbitrariness of the death penalty—how, in 18 the real world, capital punishment must be forever married to caprice. From the initial decision to charge through the determination of sentence, the criminal justice system in general is rife with unreviewable discretion. The capital setting provides all of the same opportunities (and several more) for virtually unconstrained choice: the players roll the dice in a game where the stakes consist of life or death. Non-exhaustively, the prosecutor must decide such things as whether to charge capital murder instead of a lesser degree of homicide; whether to plea bargain with the accused or, in a multi-defendant case, whether to grant one of the defendants immunity or some other concession in return for cooperating with the state; and whether, if the defendant is convicted of a potentially capital charge, to move the case to the penalty phase and attempt to obtain a verdict of death. Many of those choices and especially the likelihood of plea bargaining will be dramatically affected by factors that have little or nothing to do with the nature of the crime or the strength of the evidence. These factors include geography (district attorneys have different policies on capital punishment, not to speak of varying amounts of dollars to spend on costly capital litigation); political concerns like the proximity of an election; the perceived acumen and aggressiveness of defense counsel; and the desires of the victim's family.

Other players than the prosecutor occupy key roles, too, of 19 course. These include the judge and jury and, depending on local practice, the governor, administrative board, or both, who may be requested to grant clemency. Jurors, it is worth noting, not only possess the completely unreviewable discretion to acquit or compromise on lesser charges; they are also asked, in penalty trials, to determine such intrinsically fuzzy questions as "Will the defendant kill again?" or "Was this murder especially heinous, atrocious, or cruel?" or "Do the aggravating circumstances outweigh the proof in mitigation?" The latter inquiry forces jurors to try to assess how, for instance, the fact that the murder occurred during the course of a robbery and was committed to eliminate a witness should be balanced against the facts that the defendant was high on crack, is a first offender, and has a wife and three children who love him. Could *you* meaningfully weigh such factors?

Consider, second, that these sources of arbitrariness are exacer- 20 bated by extreme variations in the performance of defense counsel. Ineffective assistance of counsel completely permeates the penalty phase of capital trials in the post-*Gregg* era. With regard to cases like Stephen's and Joe's and the others with which I began this piece, I pointed out how often the jury hears nothing personal about the defendant even when substantial mitigating proof is readily available, yet I did not explain this phenomenon. The explanation is simply that many defense attorneys do little or nothing by way of investigation geared to sentencing issues and hence do not themselves learn what they should be spreading before the jury. Why do attorneys drop the ball at the penalty phase with such depressing regularity? Some lack the knowledge, experience, or will to assume the role demanded of them in the unique capital setting. Lawyers find it easier to hunt for what one whom I know called "eyeball witnesses" than to construct a psychodrama about a protagonist who is frequently hostile, uncommunicative, beset with mental or emotional problems, or all of the above—especially when to do so involves searching out potential witnesses (family, friends, neighbors, teachers) who, like the client, usually hail from a different racial or socioeconomic milieu from counsel. Others curtail their investigations on account of shockingly low compensation. Still others "throw in the towel" once the verdict of guilt is in. Whatever the causes of these derelictions, most or all can be expected both to cross jurisdictional lines and to continue into the future.

Consider, finally, the last but hardly the least point in my brief   21 against the death penalty—racial discrimination in sentencing. In its modern guise, racial bias focuses primarily on the race of the *victim*, not the defendant. Sophisticated studies by social scientists have demonstrated that murderers of whites are much likelier to be sentenced to death than murderers of blacks. In Georgia, for instance, Professor David Baldus's prizewinning study revealed that, after one accounted for dozens of variables that might legitimately affect punishment, the killer of a white stood a *4.3 times* greater chance of receiving death than did a person who killed a black! The reason for these results is clear and as firmly rooted in our history as prejudice against the black defendant: white society places a premium upon white life. New Yorkers inclined to discount such division on grounds of race as a regional Southern phenomenon need only recall the tensions evoked by the Howard Beach and Goetz trials to see how very wrong they are. In any event, capital punishment only magnifies inequalities of race that persist in the criminal justice system and in American society generally.

Last term, the Supreme Court rejected a challenge, grounded on   22 the damning Baldus statistics, to the death penalty as applied in

Georgia. Assuming the validity of the study, the Court nonetheless held 5–4 in *McCleskey v. Kemp* that unless a capital defendant could prove that some specific actor or actors purposely discriminated in his case, thereby causing his sentence of death, neither the Eighth Amendment nor Equal Protection was offended. I hope, however, that New Yorkers will be offended by, and wary of, the prospect of even risking racially tainted sentencing where a person's life is at stake.

There *is* no good reason to take that risk. The death penalty has not been shown to deter murder. Administering it with even the minimum amount of decency will further increase the logjams in our crowded courts and will likely cost more in the end than the alternative of long-term imprisonment. At worst, some innocent men and women will be executed as time goes by. At best, the guilty we choose to kill will be morally indistinguishable from the rest whose lives we opt to spare. New York cannot—in any sense of the word—afford to resurrect such a bankrupt system. Thoughtful citizens should be proud that our last two governors have resisted the siren call of capital "justice." The Bar, therefore, should strongly support the principled and pragmatic stance of opposition to capital punishment.

23

QUESTIONS OF CONTENT

1. Van den Haag suggests in paragraph 5 a number of factors that determine the frequency of murders. What are these factors?
2. Van den Haag makes a distinction between the death penalty as *deterrent* and as *incapacitation.* How are these two different?
3. What effect does he believe the use of the death penalty will have on the crime rate? Why?
4. What is Berger's chief objection to the death penalty?
5. What does Berger mean in paragraph 17 when she says "capital punishment *is* as it *does*"?
6. In what area does Berger feel that defense counsels are generally ineffective in capital cases? Why?
7. What does Berger feel is the single most important determining factor in the administration of the death penalty in murder cases?

QUESTIONS OF FORM

1. In paragraph 14 Van den Haag admits that science, logic, and statistics are incapable of proving that capital punishment acts as a deter-

rent (what the earlier portion of his essay had examined). To what line of reasoning does he finally resort? How does that argument work?

2. Both Van den Haag and Berger use examples to illustrate their claims. How do these examples differ?

3. What does Berger's argument gain by having its readers imagine themselves as jury members on five cases in a death-penalty state?

4. Why does Berger withhold certain information from the examples that she provides (paragraphs 4–8)? What sort of information is she withholding? What sort of effect does that information have when she later divulges it?

5. Notice that Berger often refers to various legal authorities and to actual court cases in her essay, while Van den Haag does not. What difference, if any, does that make in the effectiveness of either argument?

SUGGESTIONS FOR WRITING

1. Summarize these two positions in a concise essay. Keep your stance as neutral as possible.

2. You are Vivian Berger, and you have just read the following statement by William Buckley:

> The business about the poor and the black suffering excessively from capital punishment is no argument against capital punishment. It is an argument against the *administration* of justice, not against the penalty. Any punishment can be unfairly or unjustly applied. Go ahead and reform the process by which capital punishment is inflicted, if you wish; but don't confuse maladministration with the merits of capital punishment.

How do you respond? Compose a letter to Buckley's magazine, *National Review*, stating your response.

3. You are convinced, like Van den Haag, that the death penalty is necessary, given the increasing crime rate in our society. Prepare a presentation, suitable for delivery at a campus forum, that supports Van den Haag's position. Here are two additional sources that you might like to use. Mention each by name as you introduce any borrowed ideas or words.

BERNS, WALTER. "For Capital Punishment." In *For Capital Punishment: Crime and Morality of the Death Penalty*. New York: Basic Books, 1979.

MENCKEN, H. L. "The Death Penalty." In *A Mencken Chrestomathy*. New York: Alfred A. Knopf, 1954.

Animal Rights

The Case for Animal Rights

TOM REGAN

I regard myself as an advocate of animal rights—as a part of the animal rights movement. That movement, as I conceive it, is committed to a number of goals, including:

- the total abolition of the use of animals in science;
- the total dissolution of commercial animal agriculture;
- the total elimination of commercial and sport hunting and trapping.

There are, I know, people who profess to believe in animal rights but do not avow these goals. Factory farming, they say, is wrong—it violates animals' rights—but traditional animal agriculture is all right. Toxicity tests of cosmetics on animals violates their rights, but important medical research—cancer research, for example—does not. The clubbing of baby seals is abhorrent, but not the harvesting of adult seals. I used to think I understood this reasoning. Not any more. You don't change unjust institutions by tidying them up.

What's wrong—fundamentally wrong—with the way animals are treated isn't the details that vary from case to case. It's the whole system. The forlornness of the veal calf is pathetic, heart-wrenching; the pulsing pain of the chimp with electrodes planted deep in her brain is repulsive; the slow, tortuous death of the racoon caught in the leg-hold trap is agonizing. But what is wrong isn't the pain, isn't the suffering, isn't the deprivation. These compound what's wrong. Sometimes—often—they make it much, much worse. But they are not the fundamental wrong.

The fundamental wrong is the system that allows us to view animals as our resources, here for us—to be eaten, or surgically manipulated, or exploited for sport or money. Once we accept this view of animals—as our resources—the rest is as predictable as it is regrettable. Why worry about their loneliness, their pain, their death? Since animals exist for us, to benefit us in one way or another, what harms them really doesn't matter—or matters only if it starts to bother us, makes us feel a trifle uneasy when we eat our veal escalope, for example. So, yes, let us get veal calves out of solitary confinement, give them more space, a little straw, a few companions. But let us keep our veal escalope.

But a little straw, more space and a few companions won't   4 eliminate—won't even touch—the basic wrong that attaches to our viewing and treating these animals as our resources. A veal calf killed to be eaten after living in close confinement is viewed and treated in this way; but so, too, is another who is raised (as they say) "more humanely." To right the wrong of our treatment of farm animals requires more than making rearing methods "more humane"; it requires the total dissolution of commercial animal agriculture.

How we do this, whether we do it or, as in the case of animals in   5 science, whether and how we abolish their use—these are to a large extent political questions. People must change their beliefs before they change their habits. Enough people, especially those elected to public office, must believe in change—must want it—before we will have laws that protect the rights of animals. This process of change is very complicated, very demanding, very exhausting, calling for the efforts of many hands in education, publicity, political organization and activity, down to the licking of envelopes and stamps. As a trained and practicing philosopher, the sort of contribution I can make is limited but, I like to think, important. The currency of philosophy is ideas—their meaning and rational foundation—not the nuts and bolts of the legislative process, say, or the mechanics of community organization. That's what I have been exploring over the past ten years or so in my essays and talks and, most recently in my book, *The Case for Animal Rights.* I believe the major conclusions I reach in the book are true because they are supported by the weight of the best arguments. I believe the idea of animal rights has reason, not just emotion, on its side.

In the space I have at my disposal here I can only sketch, in the   6 barest outline, some of the main features of the book. Its main themes—and we should not be surprised by this—involve asking and answering deep, foundational moral questions about what morality is, how it should be understood and what is the best moral theory, all considered. I hope I can convey something of the shape I think this theory takes. The attempt to do this will be (to use a word a friendly critic once used to described my work) cerebral, perhaps too cerebral. But this is misleading. My feelings about how animals are sometimes treated run just as deep and just as strong as those of my more volatile compatriots. Philosophers do—to use the jargon of the day—have a right side to their brains. If it's the left side we contribute (or mainly should), that's because what talents we have reside there.

How to proceed? We begin by asking how the moral status of animals has been understood by thinkers who deny that animals have rights. Then we test the mettle of their ideas by seeing how well they stand up under the heat of fair criticism. If we start our thinking in this way, we soon find that some people believe that we have no duties directly to animals, that we owe nothing to them, that we can do nothing that wrongs them. Rather, we can do wrong acts that involve animals, and so we have duties regarding them, though none to them. Such views may be called indirect duty views. By way of illustration: suppose your neighbor kicks your dog. Then your neighbor has done something wrong. But not to your dog. The wrong that has been done is a wrong to you. After all, it is wrong to upset people, and your neighbor's kicking your dog upsets you. So you are the one who is wronged, not your dog. Or again: by kicking your dog your neighbor damages your property. And since it is wrong to damage another person's property, your neighbor has done something wrong—to you, of course, not to your dog. Your neighbor no more wrongs your dog than your car would be wronged if the windshield were smashed. Your neighbor's duties involving your dog are indirect duties to you. More generally, all of our duties regarding animals are indirect duties to one another—to humanity. 7

How could someone try to justify such a view? Someone might say that your dog doesn't feel anything and so isn't hurt by your neighbor's kick, doesn't care about the pain since none is felt, is as unaware of anything as is your windshield. Someone might say this, but no rational person will, since, among other considerations, such a view will commit anyone who holds it to the position that no human being feels pain either—that human beings also don't care about what happens to them. A second possibility is that though both humans and your dog are hurt when kicked, it is only human pain that matters. But, again, no rational person can believe this. Pain is pain wherever it occurs. If your neighbor's causing you pain is wrong because of the pain that is caused, we cannot rationally ignore or dismiss the moral relevance of the pain that your dog feels. 8

Philosophers who hold indirect duty views—and many still do—have come to understand that they must avoid the two defects just noted: that is, both the view that animals don't feel anything as well as the idea that only human pain can be morally relevant. Among such thinkers the sort of view now favored is one or other form of what is called *contractarianism.* 9

Here, very crudely, is the root idea: morality consists of a set of 10 rules that individuals voluntarily agree to abide by, as we do when we sign a contract (hence the name contractarianism). Those who understand and accept the terms of the contract are covered directly; they have rights created and recognized by, and protected in, the contract. And these contractors can also have protection spelled out for others who, though they lack the ability to understand morality and so cannot sign the contract themselves, are loved or cherished by those who can. Thus young children, for example, are unable to sign contracts and lack rights. But they are protected by the contract none the less because of the sentimental interests of others, most notably their parents. So we have, then, duties involving these children, duties regarding them, but no duties to them. Our duties in their case are indirect duties to other human beings, usually their parents.

As for animals, since they cannot understand contracts, they obviously cannot sign; and since they cannot sign, they have no rights. Like children, however, some animals are the objects of the sentimental interest of others. You, for example, love your dog or cat. So those animals that enough people care about (companion animals, whales, baby seals, the American bald eagle), though they lack rights themselves, will be protected because of the sentimental interests of people. I have, then, according to contractarianism, no duty directly to your dog or any other animal, not even the duty not to cause them pain or suffering; my duty not to hurt them is a duty I have to those people who care about what happens to them. As for other animals, where no or little sentimental interest is present—in the case of farm animals, for example, or laboratory rats—what duties we have grow weaker and weaker, perhaps to vanishing point. The pain and death they endure, though real, are not wrong if no one cares about them. 11

When it comes to the moral status of animals, contractarianism could be a hard view to refute if it were an adequate theoretical approach to the moral status of human beings. It is not adequate in this latter respect, however, which makes the question of its adequacy in the former case, regarding animals, utterly moot. For consider: morality, according to the (crude) contractarian position before us, consists of rules that people agree to abide by. What people? Well, enough to make a difference—enough, that is, *collectively* to have the power to enforce the rules that are drawn up in the contract. This is very well and good for the signatories but not so good for anyone who is not asked to sign. And there is nothing in contractarianism of the sort we are discussing that guarantees or requires that everyone will have a chance to participate equally in framing the rules of morality. The result is that this approach to 12 ethics could sanction the most blatant forms of social, economic, moral and political injustice, ranging from a repressive caste system to systematic racial or sexual discrimination. Might, according to this theory, does make right. Let those who are the victims of injustice suffer as they will. It matters not so long as no one else—no contractor, or too few of them—cares about it. Such a theory takes one's moral breath away . . . as if, for example, there would be nothing wrong with apartheid in South Africa if few white South Africans were upset by it. A theory with so little to recommend it at the level of the ethics of our treatment of our fellow humans cannot have anything more to recommend it when it comes to the ethics of how we treat our fellow animals.

The version of contractarianism just examined is, as I have   13
noted, a crude variety, and in fairness to those of a contractarian persuasion it must be noted that much more refined, subtle and ingenious varieties are possible. For example, John Rawls, in his *A Theory of Justice,* sets forth a version of contractarianism that forces contractors to ignore the accidental features of being a human being—for example, whether one is white or black, male or female, a genius or of modest intellect. Only by ignoring such features, Rawls believes, can we ensure that the principles of justice that contractors would agree upon are not based on bias or prejudice. Despite the improvement a view such as Rawls's represents over the cruder forms of contractarianism, it remains deficient: it systematically denies that we have direct duties to those human beings who do not have a sense of justice—young children, for instance, and many mentally retarded humans. And yet it seems reasonably certain that, were we to torture a young child or a retarded elder, we would be doing something that wronged him or her, not something that would be wrong if (and only if) other humans with a sense of justice were upset. And since this is true in the case of these humans, we cannot rationally deny the same in the case of animals.

Indirect duty views, then, including the best among them, fail to   14
command our rational assent. Whatever ethical theory we should accept rationally, therefore, it must at least recognize that we have some duties directly to animals, just as we have some duties directly to each other. The next two theories I'll sketch attempt to meet this requirement.

The first I call the cruelty-kindness view. Simply stated, this   15
says that we have a direct duty to be kind to animals and a direct duty not to be cruel to them. Despite the familiar, reassuring ring of these ideas, I do not believe that this view offers an adequate theory. To make this clearer, consider kindness. A kind person acts from a certain kind of motive—compassion or concern, for example. And

that is a virtue. But there is no guarantee that a kind act is a right act. If I am a generous racist, for example, I will be inclined to act kindly towards members of my own race, favoring their interests above those of others. My kindness would be real and, so far as it goes, good. But I trust it is too obvious to require argument that my kind acts may not be above moral reproach—may, in fact, be positively wrong because rooted in injustice. So kindness, notwithstanding its status as a virtue to be encouraged, simply will not carry the weight of a theory of right action.

Cruelty fares no better. People or their acts are cruel if they display either a lack of sympathy for or, worse, the presence of enjoyment in another's suffering. Cruelty in all its guises is a bad thing, a tragic human failing. But just as a person's being motivated by kindness does not guarantee that he or she does what is right, so the absence of cruelty does not ensure that he or she avoids doing what is wrong. Many people who perform abortions, for example, are not cruel, sadistic people. But that fact alone does not settle the terribly difficult question of the morality of abortion. The case is no different when we examine the ethics of our treatment of animals. So, yes, let us be for kindness and against cruelty. But let us not suppose that being for the one and against the other answers questions about moral right and wrong.

Some people think that the theory we are looking for is utilitarianism. A utilitarian accepts two moral principles. The first is that of equality: everyone's interests count, and similar interests must be counted as having similar weight or importance. White or black, American or Iranian, human or animal—everyone's pain or frustration matters, and matters just as much as the equivalent pain or frustration of anyone else. The second principle a utilitarian accepts is that of utility: do the act that will bring about the best balance between satisfaction and frustration for everyone affected by the outcome.

As a utilitarian, then, here is how I am to approach the task of deciding what I morally ought to do: I must ask who will be affected if I choose to do one thing rather than another, how much each individual will be affected, and where the best results are most likely to lie—which option, in other words, is most likely to bring about the best results, the best balance between satisfaction and frustration. That option, whatever it may be, is the one I ought to choose. That is where my moral duty lies.

The great appeal of utilitarianism rests with its uncompromising egalitarianism: everyone's interests count and count as much as the like interests of everyone else. The kind of odious discrimination that some forms of contractarianism can justify—discrimination based on race or sex, for example—seems disallowed in principle by utilitarianism, as is speciesism, systematic discrimination based on species membership.

The equality we find in utilitarianism, however, is not the sort [20] an advocate of animal or human rights should have in mind. Utilitarianism has no room for the equal moral rights of different individuals because it has no room for their equal inherent value or worth. What has value for the utilitarian is the satisfaction of an individual's interests, not the individual whose interests they are. A universe in which you satisfy your desire for water, food and warmth is, other things being equal, better than a universe in which these desires are frustrated. And the same is true in the case of an animal with similar desires. But neither you nor the animal have any value in your own right. Only your feelings do.

Here is an analogy to help make the philosophical point clearer: [21] a cup contains different liquids, sometimes sweet, sometimes bitter, sometimes a mix of the two. What has value are the liquids: the sweeter the better, the bitterer the worse. The cup, the container, has no value. It is what goes into it, not what they go into, that has value. For the utilitarian you and I are like the cup; we have no value as individuals and thus no equal value. What has value is what goes into us, what we serve as receptacles for; our feelings of satisfaction have positive value, our feelings of frustration negative value.

Serious problems arise for utilitarianism when we remind our- [22] selves that it enjoins us to bring about the best consequences. What does this mean? It doesn't mean the best consequences for me alone, or for my family or friends, or any other person taken individually. No, what we must do is, roughly, as follows: we must add up (somehow!) the separate satisfactions and frustrations of everyone likely to be affected by our choice, the satisfactions in one column, the frustrations in the other. We must total each column for each of the options before us. That is what it means to say the theory is aggregative. And then we must choose that option which is most likely to bring about the best balance of totaled satisfactions over totaled frustrations. Whatever act would lead to this outcome is the one we ought morally to perform—it is where our moral duty lies. And that act quite clearly might not be the same one that would bring about the best results for me personally, or for my family or friends, or for a lab animal. The best aggregated consequences for everyone concerned are not necessarily the best for each individual.

That utilitarianism is an aggregative theory—different individu- [23] als' satisfactions or frustrations are added, or summed, or totaled—is the key objection to this theory. My Aunt Bea is old, inactive, a cranky, sour person, though not physically ill. She prefers to go on living. She is also rather rich. I could make a fortune if I could get my hands on her money, money she intends to give me in any event, after she dies, but which she refuses to give me now. In order to avoid a huge tax bite, I plan to donate a handsome sum of my profits to a local children's hospital. Many, many children will benefit from my generosity, and much joy will be brought to their parents, relatives and friends. If I don't get the money rather soon, all these ambitions will come to naught. The once-in-a-lifetime opportunity to make a real killing will be gone. Why, then, not kill my Aunt Bea? Oh, of course I *might* get caught. But I'm no fool and, besides, her doctor can be counted on to co-operate (he has an eye for the same investment and I happen to know a good deal about his shady past). The deed can be done . . . professionally, shall we say. There is very little chance of getting caught. And as for my conscience being guilt-ridden, I am a resourceful sort of fellow and will take more than sufficient comfort—as I lie on the beach at Acapulco—in contemplating the joy and health I have brought to so many others.

Suppose Aunt Bea is killed and the rest of the story comes out as 24 told. Would I have done anything wrong? Anything immoral? One would have thought that I had. Not according to utilitarianism. Since what I have done has brought about the best balance between totaled satisfaction and frustration for all those affected by the outcome, my action is not wrong. Indeed, in killing Aunt Bea the physician and I did what duty required.

This same kind of argument can be repeated in all sorts of cases, 25 illustrating, time after time, how the utilitarian's position leads to results that impartial people find morally callous. It is wrong to kill my Aunt Bea in the name of bringing about the best results for others. A good end does not justify an evil means. Any adequate moral theory will have to explain why this is so. Utilitarianism fails in this respect and so cannot be the theory we seek.

What to do? Where to begin anew? The place to begin, I think, is 26 with the utilitarian's view of the value of the individual—or, rather, lack of value. In its place, suppose we consider that you and I, for example, do have value as individuals—what we'll call *inherent* value. To say we have such value is to say that we are something more than, something different from, mere receptacles. Moreover, to ensure that we do not pave the way for such injustices as slavery or sexual discrimination, we must believe that all who have inherent value have it equally, regardless of their sex, race, religion, birthplace and so on. Similarly to be discarded as irrelevant are one's talents or skills, intelligence and wealth, personality or pathology, whether one is loved and admired or despised and loathed. The genius and the retarded child, the prince and the pauper, the brain surgeon and the fruit vendor, Mother Teresa and the most unscrupulous used-car salesman—all have inherent value, all possess it equally, and all have an equal right to be treated with respect, to be treated in ways that do not reduce them to the status of things, as if they existed as resources for others. My value as an individual is independent of my usefulness to you. Yours is not dependent on your usefulness to me. For either of us to treat the other in ways that fail to show respect for the other's independent value is to act immorally, to violate the individual's rights.

Some of the rational virtues of this view—what I call the rights   27
view—should be evident. Unlike (crude) contractarianism, for example, the rights view *in principle* denies the moral tolerability of any and all forms of racial, sexual or social discrimination; and unlike utilitarianism, this view *in principle* denies that we can justify good results by using evil means that violate an individual's rights—denies, for example, that it could be moral to kill my Aunt Bea to harvest beneficial consequences for others. That would be to sanction the disrespectful treatment of the individual in the name of the social good, something the rights view will not—categorically will not—ever allow.

The rights view, I believe, is rationally the most satisfactory   28
moral theory. It surpasses all other theories in the degree to which it illuminates and explains the foundation of our duties to one another—the domain of human morality. On this score it has the best reasons, the best arguments, on its side. Of course, if it were possible to show that only human beings are included within its scope, then a person like myself, who believes in animals rights, would be obliged to look elsewhere.

But attempts to limit its scope to humans only can be shown to   29
be rationally defective. Animals, it is true, lack many of the abilities humans possess. They can't read, do higher mathematics, build a bookcase or make *baba ghanoush*.[1] Neither can many human beings, however, and yet we don't (and shouldn't) say that they (these humans) therefore have less inherent value, less of a right to be treated with respect, than do others. It is the *similarities* between those human beings who most clearly, most non-controversially have such value (the people reading this, for example), not our differences, that matter most. And the really crucial, the basic similarity is simply this: we are each of us the experiencing subject of a life, a conscious creature having an individual welfare that has importance to us whatever our usefulness to others. We want and prefer things,

---

1. A Middle Eastern eggplant-sesame oil dip.

believe and feel things, recall and expect things. And all these dimensions of our life, including our pleasure and pain, our enjoyment and suffering, our satisfaction and frustration, our continued existence or our untimely death—all make a difference to the quality of our life as lived, as experienced, by us as individuals. As the same is true of those animals that concern us (the ones that are eaten and trapped, for example), they too must be viewed as the experiencing subjects of a life, with inherent value of their own.

Some there are who resist the idea that animals have inherent value. "Only humans have such value," they profess. How might this narrow view be defended? Shall we say that only humans have the requisite intelligence, or autonomy, or reason? But there are many, many humans who fail to meet these standards and yet are reasonably viewed as having value above and beyond their usefulness to others. Shall we claim that only humans belong to the right species, the species *Homo sapiens?* But this is blatant speciesism. Will it be said, then, that all—and only—humans have immortal souls? Then our opponents have their work cut out for them. I am myself not ill-disposed to the proposition that there are immortal souls. Personally, I profoundly hope I have one. But I would not want to rest my position on a controversial ethical issue on the even more controversial question about who or what has an immortal soul. That is to dig one's hole deeper, not to climb out. Rationally, it is better to resolve moral issues without making more controversial assumptions than are needed. The question of who has inherent value is such a question, one that is resolved more rationally without the introduction of the idea of immortal souls than by its use.

Well, perhaps some will say that animals have some inherent value, only less than we have. Once again, however, attempts to defend this view can be shown to lack rational justification. What could be the basis of our having more inherent value than animals? Their lack of reason, or autonomy, or intellect? Only if we are willing to make the same judgment in the case of humans who are similarly deficient. But it is not true that such humans—the retarded child, for example, or the mentally deranged—have less inherent value than you or I. Neither, then, can we rationally sustain the view that animals like them in being the experiencing subjects of a life have less inherent value. *All* who have inherent value have it *equally*, whether they be human animals or not.

Inherent value, then, belongs equally to those who are the experiencing subjects of a life. Whether it belongs to others—to rocks and rivers, trees and glaciers, for example—we do not know and may never know. But neither do we need to know, if we are to make the case for animal rights. We do not need to know, for example, how many people are eligible to vote in the next presidential election before we can know whether I am. Similarly, we do not need to know how many individuals have inherent value before we can know that some do. When it comes to the case for animal rights, then, what we need to know is whether the animals that, in our culture, are routinely eaten, hunted and used in our laboratories, for example, are like us in being subjects of a life. And we do know this. We do know that many—literally, billions and billions—of these animals are the subjects of a life in the sense explained and so have inherent value if we do. And since, in order to arrive at the best theory of our duties to one another, we must recognize our equal inherent value as individuals, reason—not sentiment, not emotion—reason compels us to recognize the equal inherent value of these animals and, with this, their equal right to be treated with respect.

That, very roughly, is the shape and feel of the case for animal   33
rights. Most of the details of the supporting argument are missing. They are to be found in the book to which I alluded earlier. Here, the details go begging, and I must, in closing, limit myself to four final points.

The first is how the theory that underlies the case for animal   34
rights shows that the animal rights movement is a part of, not antagonistic to, the human rights movement. The theory that rationally grounds the rights of animals also grounds the rights of humans. Thus those involved in the animal rights movement are partners in the struggle to secure respect for human rights—the rights of women, for example, or minorities, or workers. The animal rights movement is cut from the same moral cloth as these.

Second, having set out the broad outlines of the rights view, I can   35
now say why its implications for farming and science, among other fields, are both clear and uncompromising. In the case of the use of animals in science, the rights view is categorically abolitionist. Lab animals are not our tasters; we are not their kings. Because these animals are treated routinely, systematically as if their value were reducible to their usefulness to others, they are routinely, systematically treated with a lack of respect, and thus are their rights routinely, systematically violated. This is just as true when they are used in trivial, duplicative, unnecessary or unwise research as it is when they are used in studies that hold out real promise of human benefits. We can't justify harming or killing a human being (my Aunt Bea, for example) just for these sorts of reason. Neither can we do so even in the case of so lowly a creature as a laboratory rat. It is not just refinement or reduction that is called for, not just larger, cleaner cages, not just more generous use of anaesthetic or the elimination of multiple surgery, not just tidying up the system. It is com-

plete replacement. The best we can do when it comes to using animals in science is—not to use them. That is where our duty lies, according to the rights view.

As for commercial animal agriculture, the rights view takes a   36
similar abolitionist position. The fundamental moral wrong here is not that animals are kept in stressful close confinement or in isolation, or that their pain and suffering, their needs and preferences are ignored or discounted. All these *are* wrong, of course, but they are not the fundamental wrong. They are symptoms and effects of the deeper, systematic wrong that allows these animals to be viewed and treated as lacking independent value, as resources for us—as, indeed, a renewable resource. Giving farm animals more space, more natural environments, more companions does not right the fundamental wrong, any more than giving lab animals more anaesthesia or bigger, cleaner cages would right the fundamental wrong in their case. Nothing less than the total dissolution of commercial animal agriculture will do this, just as, for similar reasons I won't develop at length here, morality requires nothing less than the total elimination of hunting and trapping for commercial and sporting ends. The rights view's implications, then, as I have said, are clear and uncompromising.

My last two points are about philosophy, my profession. It is,   37
most obviously, no substitute for political action. The words I have written here and in other places by themselves don't change a thing. It is what we do with the thoughts that the words express—our acts, our deeds—that changes things. All that philosophy can do, and all I have attempted, is to offer a vision of what our deeds should aim at. And the why. But not the how.

Finally, I am reminded of my thoughtful critic, the one I men-   38
tioned earlier, who chastised me for being too cerebral. Well, cerebral I have been: indirect duty views, utilitarianism, contractarianism—hardly the stuff deep passions are made of. I am also reminded, however, of the image another friend once set before me—the image of the ballerina as expressive of disciplined passion. Long hours of sweat and toil, of loneliness and practice, of doubt and fatigue: those are the discipline of her craft. But the passion is there too, the fierce drive to excel, to speak through her body, to do it right, to pierce our minds. That is the image of philosophy I would leave with you, not "too cerebral" but *disciplined passion.* Of the discipline enough has been seen. As for the passion: there are times, and these not infrequent, when tears come to my eyes when I see, or read, or hear of the wretched plight of animals in the hands of humans. Their pain, their suffering, their loneliness, their innocence, their death. Anger. Rage. Pity. Sorrow. Disgust. The whole creation groans under the weight of the evil we humans visit upon these mute, powerless creatures. It is

our hearts, not just our heads, that call for an end to it all, that demand of us that we overcome, for them, the habits and forces behind their systematic oppression. All great movements, it is written, go through three stages: ridicule, discussion, adoption. It is the realization of this third stage, adoption, that requires both our passion and our discipline, our hearts and our heads. The fate of animals is in our hands. God grant we are equal to the task.

The "Animal Rights" War on Medicine

JOHN G. HUBBELL

In the predawn hours of July 4, 1989, members of the Animal Liberation Front (ALF), an "animal rights" organization, broke into a laboratory at Texas Tech University in Lubbock. Their target: Prof. John Orem, a leading expert on sleep-disordered breathing.

The invaders vandalized Orem's equipment, breaking recorders, oscilloscopes and other instruments valued at some $70,000. They also stole five cats, halting his work in progress—work that could lead to an understanding of disorders such as Sudden Infant Death Syndrome (SIDS), or crib death, which kills over 5000 infants every year.

An organization known as People for the Ethical Treatment of Animals (PETA), which routinely issues press releases on ALF activities, quoted ALF claims that biomedical scientists are "animal-Nazis" and that Orem "abuses, mutilates and kills animals as part of the federal grant gravy train."

That was only the beginning of the campaign. A month later, on August 18, animal-rights activists held statewide demonstrations against Orem, picketing federal buildings in several Texas cities. The result: a flood of hate mail to the scientist and angry letters to the National Institutes of Health (NIH), which had awarded Orem more than $800,000 in grants. Finally PETA, quoting 16 "experts," filed a formal complaint with the NIH which called Orem's work "cruel" and without "scientific significance." The public had no way of knowing that none of the 16 had any expertise in sleep-disordered breathing or had ever been in Orem's lab.

NIH dispatched a team of authorities in physiology, neuroscience and pulmonary and veterinary medicine who, on September 18, reported back. Not only did they find the charges against Orem to be unfounded, but they judged him an exemplary researcher and his work "important and of the highest scientific quality."

PETA first intruded on the public consciousness in 1981, during   6
a notorious episode in Silver Spring, Md. That May, a personable college student named Alex Pacheco went to research psychologist Edward Taub for a job. Taub was studying monkeys under an NIH grant, searching for ways to help stroke victims regain use of paralyzed limbs. Pacheco said he was interested in gaining laboratory experience. Taub offered him a position as a volunteer, which Pacheco accepted.

Late that summer, Taub took a vacation, leaving his lab in the   7
care of his assistants. As he was about to return to work on September 11, an assistant called. Police, armed with a search warrant, were confiscating the monkeys: there was also a crowd of reporters on hand.

To his amazement, Taub was charged with 119 counts of cruelty   8
to animals—most based on information provided to the police by Alex Pacheco, who, it turned out, was one of PETA's founders.

After five years in the courts, Taub was finally cleared of all   9
charges. Yet the animal-rights movement never ceased vilifying him, producing hate mail and death threats. Amid the controversy the NIH suspended and later terminated Taub's grant (essentially for not buying new cages, altering the ventilation system or providing regular visits by a veterinarian). Thorough investigations by the American Physiological Society and the Society for Neuroscience determined that, in the words of the latter, the NIH decision was "incommensurate with the deficiencies cited." Yet a program that could have benefited many of the 2.5 million Americans now living with the debilitating consequences of stroke came to a screeching halt.

Wiped out financially, Taub lost his laboratory, though the work   10
of this gifted researcher had already helped rewrite accepted beliefs about the nervous system.

Dramatic Progress. The animal-rights movement has its roots in   11
Europe, where anti-vivisectionists have held the biomedical research community under siege for years. In 1875, Britain's Sir George Duckett of the Society for the Abolition of Vivisection declared: "Vivisection is monstrous. Medical science has little to learn, and nothing can be gained by repetition of experiments on living animals."

This sentiment is endlessly parroted by contemporary "activ-   12
ists." It is patently false. Since Duckett's time, animal research has

led to vaccines against diphtheria, polio, measles, mumps, whooping cough, rubella. It has meant eradication of smallpox, effective treatment for diabetes and control of infection with powerful antibiotics.

The cardiac pacemaker, microsurgery to reattach severed limbs, and heart, kidney, lung, liver and other transplants are all possible because of animal research. In the early 1960s, the cure rate for acute lymphocytic leukemia in a child was four percent. Today, because of animal research, the cure rate exceeds 70 percent. Since the turn of the century, animal research has helped increase our life-span by nearly 28 years. And now animal research is leading to dramatic progress against AIDS and Alzheimer's disease.   13

Animals themselves have benefited. We are now able to extend and improve the lives of our pets and farm animals through cataract surgery, open-heart surgery and cardiac pacemakers, and can immunize them against rabies, distemper, anthrax, tetanus and feline leukemia. Animal research is an unqualified success story.   14

We should see even more spectacular medical breakthroughs in the coming decades. But not if today's animal-rights movement has its way.   15

Anti-Human Absurdities. In the United States, the movement is spearheaded by PETA, whose leadership insists that animals are the moral equivalent of human beings. Any differentiation between people and animals constitutes "speciesism," as unethical as racism. Says PETA co-founder and director Ingrid Newkirk, "There really is no rational reason for saying a human being has special rights. . . . A rat is a pig is a dog is a boy." She compares the killing of chickens with the Nazi Holocaust. "Six million people died in concentration camps," she told the *Washington Post*, "but six billion broiler chickens will die this year in slaughterhouses."   16

Newkirk has been quoted as saying that meat-eating is "primitive, barbaric, arrogant," that humans have "grown like a cancer. We're the biggest blight on the face of the earth," and that if her father had a heart attack, "it would give me no solace at all to know his treatment was first tried on a dog."   17

The movement insists that animal research is irrelevant, that researchers simply refuse to move on to modern techniques. "The movement's big buzzword is 'alternatives,' meaning animals can now be replaced by computers and tissue cultures," says Bessie Borwein, associate dean for research-medicine at the University of Western Ontario. "That is nonsense. You cannot study kidney transplantation or diarrhea or high blood pressure on a computer screen."   18

"A tissue culture cannot replicate a complex organ," echoes Frederick Goodwin, head of the U.S. Alcohol, Drug Abuse and Mental Health Administration (ADAMHA).   19

What do the nation's 570,000 physicians feel about animal re-   20
search? A 1988 American Medical Association survey found that 97
percent of doctors support it, despite the animal-rights movement's
propaganda to the contrary.

"Without animal research, medical science would come to a total   21
standstill," says Dr. Lewis Thomas, best-selling author and scholar-
in-residence at New York's Cornell University Medical College.

"As a human being and physician, I cannot conceive of telling   22
parents their sick child will die because we cannot use all the tools
at our disposal," says pioneering heart surgeon Dr. Michael E.
DeBakey of Houston's Baylor College of Medicine. "How will they
feel about a society that legislates the rights of animals above those
of humans?"

"The power of today's medical practice is based on research—   23
and that includes crucial research involving animals," adds Dr.
Louis W. Sullivan, Secretary of the U.S. Department of Health and
Human Services.

Radical Infiltration. How then have the animal-rights activists   24
achieved respectability? By exploiting the public's rightful concern
for humane treatment of animals. ADAMHA's Goodwin explains:
"They have gradually taken over highly respectable humane societies by using classic radical techniques: packing memberships and
steering committees and electing directors. They have insidiously
gained control of one group after another."

The average supporter has no idea that societies which tradition-   25
ally promoted better treatment for animals, taught pet care, built
shelters and cared for strays are now dedicated to ending the most
effective kind of medical research. For example, the Humane Society
of the United States (HSUS) insists it is not anti-vivisectionist; yet it
has persistently stated that animal research is often unnecessary. It
published an editorial by animal-rights proponent Tom Regan endorsing civil disobedience for the cause. Says Frederick A. King,
director of the Yerkes Regional Primate Center of Emory University,
"HSUS flies a false flag. It is part of the same group that has attempted to do severe damage to research."

PETA's chairman, Alex Pacheco, says that it is best to be "strategi-   26
cally assertive" in seeking reforms while never losing sight of the
ultimate goal: "total abolition" of "animal exploitation." This strategy has worked. It has taken the research community about ten years
to realize that it is not dealing with moderates. It is dealing with
organizations like ALF, which since 1988 has been on the FBI's list of
domestic terrorist organizations. And with Trans-Species Unlimited,
which trumpets: "The liberation of animal life can only be achieved
through the radical transformation of human consciousness and the

overthrow of the existing power structures in which human and animal abuse are entrenched."

Consider some of the movement's "liberation activities":   27

• In the early hours of April 3, 1989, hooded animal-rights activ-   28
ists broke into four buildings at the University of Arizona at Tucson.
They smashed expensive equipment, spray-painted messages such
as "Scum" and "Nazis" and stole 1231 animals. They set fire to two
of the four buildings.

ALF took credit for the destruction, the cost of which amoun-   29
ted to more than $200,000. Fifteen projects were disrupted. One
example: 30 of 1160 mice taken by ALF were infected with Crypto-
sporidium, a parasite that can cause severe intestinal disease in
humans. The project's aim was to develop an effective disinfectant
for Cryptosporidium-contaminated water. Now, not only is the
work halted but researchers warn that, with less than expert handling, the stolen mice could spread cryptosporidiosis, which remains untreatable.

• On October 26, 1986, an ALF contingent broke into two facili-   30
ties at the University of Oregon at Eugene. The equipment the intruders smashed and soaked with red paint included a $10,000 mi-
croscope, an electrocardiogram machine, an X-ray machine, an
incubator and a sterilizer. At least 150 research animals were taken.
As a result, more than a dozen projects were seriously delayed, including research by neuroscientist Barbara Gordon-Lickey on visual
defects in newborns. An ALF statement called the neuroscientist a
"butcher" and claimed that the animals had found new homes
through "an intricate underground railroad network, much like the
one used to transport fugitive slaves to the free states of the North in
the last century."

Police caught up with one of the thieves: Roger Troen, 56, of   31
Portland, Ore., a member of PETA. He was tried and convicted.
PETA denied complicity, but Ingrid Newkirk said that PETA would
pay Troen's legal expenses, including an appeal of his conviction.
PETA then alleged to the NIH that the university was guilty of 12
counts of noncompliance with Public Health Service policy on humane care and use of laboratory animals.

Following a lengthy investigation, investigators found all PETA's   32
charges groundless. "To the contrary," their report to the NIH stated,
"evidence suggests a firm commitment to the appropriate care and
use of laboratory animals."

But animal-rights extremists continued their campaign against   33
Gordon-Lickey. They posted placards urging students not to take her
courses because she tortured animals. As Nobel Laureate Dr. David
H. Hugel of Harvard University, a pioneer in Gordon-Lickey's field,

says, "Their tactics are clear. Work to increase the costs of research, and stop its progress with red tape and lawsuits."

• Dr. Herbert Pardes, president of the American Psychiatric Association, arrived in New York City in 1984 to take over as chairman of psychiatry at Columbia University. His office was in the New York State Psychiatric Institute, part of the Columbia Presbyterian Medical Center complex. Soon after, he noticed that people were handing out leaflets challenging the value of animal research. They picketed Dr. Pardes's home and sent him envelopes containing human feces.   34

Another Columbia scientist received a phone call on December 1, 1988, from someone who said, "We know where you live. How much insurance do you have?" A few mornings later, he found a pool of red paint in front of his house. On January 4, 1989, a guest cottage at his country home burned down.   35

Devastating Results. How effective has the animal-rights movement been? Very. Although recent polls reveal that more than 70 percent of Americans support animal research, about the same number believe the lie that medical researchers torture their animals.   36

According to ADAMHA's Frederick Goodwin, the movement has at its disposal at least $50 million annually, millions of which it dedicates to stopping biomedical research. It has been especially successful in pressuring state legislatures, as well as Congress, which in turn has pressured the federal health establishment. As a result, new regulations are demoralizing many scientists and driving up the cost of research. (For fiscal 1990, an estimated $1.5 billion—approximately 20 percent of the entire federal biomedical-research budget—may be needed to cover the costs of proposed regulation changes and increased security.)   37

At Stanford University, a costly security system has had to be installed and 24-hour guards hired to protect the animal-research facilities. As a consequence of the April 1989 raid at the University of Arizona at Tucson, the school must now spend $10,000 per week on security, money that otherwise could have been used for biomedical research.   38

Threats of violence to researchers and their families are having an effect as well. "It's hard to measure," says Charles R. McCarthy, director of the Office for Protection from Research Risks at the NIH. "But all of a sudden there is a hole in the kind of research being done."   39

In the past two years, for instance, there has been a 50- to 60-percent drop in the number of reports published by scientists using primates to study drug abuse. Reports on the use of primates to learn about severe depression have ended altogether.   40

And what of our future researchers? Between 1977 and 1987 41
there was a 28-percent drop in the number of college students graduating with degrees in biomedical science, and the growing influence
of the animal-rights movement may add to that decline.

Stop the Fanatics. How are we to ensure that the animal-rights 42
movement does not put an end to progress in medical research?

1. Don't swallow whole what the movement says about horrors 43
in our biomedical-research laboratories. With rare exceptions, experimental animals are treated humanely. Biomedical researchers know
that an animal in distress is simply not a good research subject.
Researchers are embarked on an effort to alleviate misery, not cause
it.

2. There are many humane societies that are truly concerned 44
with animal welfare and oppose the animal-rights movement. They
deserve your support. But before you contribute, make sure the society has not been taken over by animal-rights extremists. If you are
not sure, contact iiFAR (incurably ill For Animal Research), P.O. Box
1873, Bridgeview, Ill. 60455. This organization is one of medical
research's most effective allies.

3. Oppose legislation at local, state and federal levels that is 45
designed to hamper biomedical research or price it out of business.
Your representatives in government are lobbied by the animal-rights
movement all the time. Let them know how *you* feel.

4. Support HR 3270, the "Farm Animal and Research Animal 46
Facilities Protection Act of 1989," introduced by Rep. Charles
Stenholm (D., Texas). This bill would make the kinds of break-ins
and vandalism ALF has been perpetrating a federal offense subject to
a maximum of three years in prison and/or a fine of up to $10,000.
Also support HR 3349, the "Health Facilities Protection and Primate
Center Rehabilitation Act of 1989," introduced by Rep. Henry A.
Waxman (D., Calif.). This bill makes criminal assaults on federally
funded facilities a federal offense.

If we want to defeat the killer diseases that still confront us— 47
AIDS, Alzheimer's, cancer, heart disease and many others, the misguided fanatics of the animal-rights movement must be stopped.

QUESTIONS OF CONTENT

1. To what forms of animal rights is Tom Regan committed?
2. What does he see as wrong about treating animals as resources?
3. What theories of animal rights does Regan examine and reject before

proposing his own? What name does he associate with the position that he endorses?

4. What activities of the Animal Liberation Front (ALF) and People for the Ethical Treatment of Animals (PETA) does Hubbell mention, and how is this list of illustrations useful in supporting his argument?

5. If, in order to reduce animal suffering, animal subjects are no longer to be used in laboratory experiments, what does Hubbell believe the result will be? What life-threatening diseases does he mention that have been brought under control through animal research?

6. How does Hubbell feel about compromise positions, such as substituting other things for animals in medical experiments, e.g., computer models or tissue cultures?

7. Compare Hubbell's attitude toward ALF and PETA with his attitude toward HSUS (Humane Societies of the United States). Does he feel that the latter pose a threat to animal research?

QUESTIONS OF FORM

1. Regan's argument is a claim of value. He examines three positions on animal rights and finds each inferior to the position that he favors. How does he define that position, and what ingredient that it possesses is missing in the others?

2. Regan explicitly rejects the contractarian position. What is that position, and how do the attitudes we have toward children and the mentally impaired figure into our acceptance or rejection of this position?

3. Hubbell uses an inductive strategy to support the claims of his argument. What claims does he make, and what sort of inductive support does he present to support those claims?

4. Hubbell concludes with a list of suggestions, turning his argument away from facts toward policy. In your judgment, which of Hubbel's concerns is of greater importance in this argument: his vilification of animal rights activists or his policy recommendations? Can the former not exist without the latter? Justify your response.

5. Examine paragraphs 12, 20, and 36 in Hubbell's essay. You will find there some examples of "slanting," or "colored diction." How, for example would the effect differ if you were to substitute the word *claim* for *lie* in the last sentence of paragraph 36? Or *repeated* for *parroted* in paragraph 12? How about substituting *claims* for *propaganda* in paragraph 20? Can you locate other instances of such slanting in Hubbell's essay? How about Regan's?

SUGGESTIONS FOR WRITING

1. You have been asked to state the position of People for the Ethical Treatment of Animals (PETA) at a meeting of the local humane

society. The members are genuinely sensitive and intelligent people who are divided in their attitudes toward the use of animals in medical testing, vegetarianism, and the use of animals in sporting events like hunting or rodeos. Using Regan's essay as your chief source, summarize PETA's position as completely and as fairly as you can.

2. A student group on your campus has registered loud and repeated concern over the use of rats in psychology experiments. You are employed in the psychology laboratory as a work/study student. Your duties are mostly janitorial, but the closing of the lab or any reduction in use of lab rats would likely stop this source of income, crucial to your meeting your educational expenses. Write a letter to the campus newspaper in which you use Hubbell's article as your basis for justifying the continued operation of the lab and for refuting the objections of the group that wishes to shut it down.

3. Assume that you are a member of the Humane Society, but that you enjoy Big Macs and you wear leather belts and shoes. However, you do not especially like fur coats, and you generally feel that animals in the wild and in zoos should be treated humanely. You have not thought much about research animals. You cringe when you read about the torture of rabbits in experiments to develop cosmetics, but at the same time you favor the testing of drugs and surgical procedures on animals before they are used on humans. Can you reconcile these views? Write a paper in which you present a compromise position that you justify.

Evolution Versus Creationism

Evolution as Fact and Theory

STEPHEN JAY GOULD

Kirtley Mather, who died last year at age eighty-nine, was a 1
pillar of both science and the Christian religion in America and one
of my dearest friends. The difference of half a century in our ages
evaporated before our common interests. The most curious thing we
shared was a battle we each fought at the same age. For Kirtley had
gone to Tennessee with Clarence Darrow to testify for evolution at
the Scopes trial of 1925. When I think that we are enmeshed again in
the same struggle for one of the best documented, most compelling
and exciting concepts in all of science, I don't know whether to
laugh or cry.

According to idealized principles of scientific discourse, the 2
arousal of dormant issues should reflect fresh data that give renewed life to abandoned notions. Those outside the current debate
may therefore be excused for suspecting that creationists have
come up with something new, or that evolutionists have generated
some serious internal trouble. But nothing has changed; the creationists have not a single new fact or argument. Darrow and Bryan
were at least more entertaining than we lesser antagonists today.
The rise of creationism is politics, pure and simple; it represents
one issue (and by no means the major concern) of the resurgent
evangelical right. Arguments that seemed kooky just a decade ago
have reentered the mainstream.

Creationism Is Not Science

The basic attack of the creationists falls apart on two general 3
counts before we even reach the supposed factual details of their
complaints against evolution. First, they play upon a vernacular misunderstanding of the word "theory" to convey the false impression
that we evolutionists are covering up the rotten core of our edifice.
Second, they misuse a popular philosophy of science to argue that
they are behaving scientifically in attacking evolution. Yet the same

299

philosophy demonstrates that their own belief is not science, and that "scientific creationism" is therefore meaningless and self-contradictory, a superb example of what Orwell called "newspeak."

In the American vernacular, "theory" often means "imperfect   4
fact"—part of a hierarchy of confidence running downhill from fact to theory to hypothesis to guess. Thus the power of the creationist argument: Evolution is "only" a theory, and intense debate now rages about many aspects of the theory. If evolution is less than a fact, and scientists can't even make up their minds about the theory, then what confidence can we have in it? Indeed, President Reagan echoed this argument before an evangelical group in Dallas when he said (in what I devoutly hope was campaign rhetoric): "Well, it is a theory. It is a scientific theory only, and it has in recent years been challenged in the world of science—that is, not believed in the scientific community to be as infallible as it once was."

Well, evolution *is* a theory. It is also a fact. And facts and theories   5
are different things, not rungs in a hierarchy of increasing certainty. Facts are the world's data. Theories are structures of ideas that explain and interpret facts. Facts do not go away when scientists debate rival theories to explain them. Einstein's theory of gravitation replaced Newton's, but apples did not suspend themselves in midair pending the outcome. And human beings evolved from apelike ancestors whether they did so by Darwin's proposed mechanisms or by some other, yet to be discovered.

Moreover, "fact" does not mean "absolute certainty." The final   6
proofs of logic and mathematics flow deductively from stated premises and achieve certainty only because they are *not* about the empirical world. Evolutionists make no claim for perpetual truth, though creationists often do (and then attack us for a style of argument that they themselves favor). In science, "fact" can only mean "confirmed to such a degree that it would be perverse to withhold provisional assent." I suppose that apples might start to rise tomorrow, but the possibility does not merit equal time in physics classrooms.

Evolutionists have been clear about this distinction between   7
fact and theory from the very beginning, if only because we have always acknowledged how far we are from completely understanding the mechanisms (theory) by which evolution (fact) occurred. Darwin continually emphasized the difference between his two great and separate accomplishments: establishing the fact of evolution, and proposing a theory—natural selection—to explain the mechanism of evolution. He wrote in *The Descent of Man:* "I had two distinct objects in view; firstly, to show that species had not been separately created, and secondly, that natural selection had been the chief agent of change. . . . Hence if I have erred in . . .

having exaggerated its [natural selection's] power. . . . I have at least, as I hope, done good service in aiding to overthrow the dogma of separate creations."

Thus Darwin acknowledged the provisional nature of natural   8
selection while affirming the fact of evolution. The fruitful theoretical debate that Darwin initiated has never ceased. From the 1940s through the 1960s, Darwin's own theory of natural selection did achieve a temporary hegemony that it never enjoyed in his lifetime. But renewed debate characterizes our decade, and, while no biologist questions the importance of natural selection, many now doubt its ubiquity. In particular, many evolutionists argue that substantial amounts of genetic change may not be subject to natural selection and may spread through populations at random. Others are challenging Darwin's linking of natural selection with gradual, imperceptible change through all intermediary degrees; they are arguing that most evolutionary events may occur far more rapidly than Darwin envisioned.

Scientists regard debates on fundamental issues of theory as a   9
sign of intellectual health and a source of excitement. Science is—and how else can I say it?—most fun when it plays with interesting ideas, examines their implications, and recognizes that old information may be explained in surprisingly new ways. Evolutionary theory is now enjoying this uncommon vigor. Yet amidst all this turmoil no biologist has been led to doubt the fact that evolution occurred; we are debating *how* it happened. We are all trying to explain the same thing: the tree of evolutionary descent linking all organisms by ties of genealogy. Creationists pervert and caricature this debate by conveniently neglecting the common conviction that underlies it, and by falsely suggesting that we now doubt the very phenomenon we are struggling to understand.

Using another invalid argument, creationists claim that "the   10
dogma of separate creations," as Darwin characterized it a century ago, is a scientific theory meriting equal time with evolution in high school biology curricula. But a prevailing viewpoint among philosophers of science belies this creationist argument. Philosopher Karl Popper has argued for decades that the primary criterion of science is the falsifiability of its theories. We can never prove absolutely, but we can falsify. A set of ideas that cannot, in principle, be falsified is not science.

The entire creationist argument involves little more than a   11
rhetorical attempt to falsify evolution by presenting supposed contradictions among its supporters. Their brand of creationism, they claim, is "scientific" because it follows the Popperian model in trying to demolish evolution. Yet Popper's argument must apply in

both directions. One does not become a scientist by the simple act of trying to falsify another scientific system; one has to present an alternative system that also meets Popper's criterion—it too must be falsifiable in principle.

"Scientific creationism" is a self-contradictory, nonsense phrase   12 precisely because it cannot be falsified. I can envision observations and experiments that would disprove any evolutionary theory I know, but I cannot imagine what potential data could leave creationists to abandon their beliefs. Unbeatable systems are dogma, not science. Lest I seem harsh or rhetorical, I quote creationism's leading intellectual, Duane Gish, Ph.D., from his recent (1978) book *Evolution! The Fossils Say No!* "By creation we mean the bringing into being by a supernatural Creator of the basic kinds of plants and animals by the process of sudden, or fiat, creation. We do not know how the Creator created, what processes He used, *for He used processes which are not now operating anywhere in the natural universe* [Gish's italics]. This is why we refer to creation as special creation. We cannot discover by scientific investigations anything about the creative processes used by the Creator." Pray tell, Dr. Gish, in the light of your last sentence, what then is "scientific" creationism?

The Fact of Evolution

Our confidence that evolution occurred centers upon three general arguments. First, we have abundant, direct, observational evidence of evolution in action, from both the field and the laboratory. It ranges from countless experiments on change in nearly everything about fruit flies subjected to artificial selection in the laboratory to the famous British moths that turned black when industrial soot darkened the trees upon which they rest. (The moths gain protection from sharp-sighted bird predators by blending into the background.) Creationists do not deny these observations; how could they? Creationists have tightened their act. They now argue that God only created "basic kinds," and allowed for limited evolutionary meandering within them. Thus toy poodles and Great Danes come from the dog kind and moths can change color, but nature cannot convert a dog to a cat or a monkey to a man.

The second and third arguments for evolution—the case for major   14 changes—do not involve direct observation of evolution in action. They rest upon inference, but are no less secure for that reason. Major evolutionary change requires too much time for direct observation on the scale of recorded human history. All historical sciences rest upon inference, and evolution is no different from geology, cosmology, or human history in this respect. In principle, we cannot observe processes that operated in the past. We must infer them from results that still survive: living and fossil organisms for evolution, documents and artifacts for human history, strata and topography for geology.

The second argument—that the imperfection of nature reveals 15 evolution—strikes many people as ironic, for they feel that evolution should be most elegantly displayed in the nearly perfect adaptation expressed by some organisms—the chamber of a gull's wing, or butterflies that cannot be seen in ground litter because they mimic leaves so precisely. But perfection could be imposed by a wise creator or evolved by natural selection. Perfection covers the tracks of past history. And past history—the evidence of descent—is our mark of evolution.

Evolution lies exposed in the *imperfections* that record a history 16 of descent. Why should a rat run, a bat fly, a porpoise swim, and I type this essay with structures built of the same bones unless we all inherited them from a common ancestor? An engineer, starting from scratch, could design better limbs in each case. Why should all the large native mammals of Australia be marsupials, unless they descended from a common ancestor isolated on this island continent? Marsupials are not "better," or ideally suited for Australia; many have been wiped out by placental mammals imported by man from other continents. This principle of imperfection extends to all historical sciences. When we recognize the etymology of September, October, November, and December (seventh, eighth, ninth, and tenth, from the Latin), we know that two additional items (January and February) must have been added to an original calendar of ten months.

The third argument is more direct: Transitions are often found in 17 the fossil record. Preserved transitions are not common—and should not be, according to our understanding of evolution (see next section)—but they are not entirely wanting, as creationists often claim. The lower jaw of reptiles contains several bones, that of mammals only one. The nonmammalian jawbones are reduced, step by step, in mammalian ancestors until they become tiny nubbins located at the back of the jaw. The "hammer" and "anvil" bones of the mammalian ear are descendants of these nubbins. How could such a transition be accomplished? the creationists ask. Surely a bone is either entirely in the jaw or in the ear. Yet paleontologists have discovered two transitional lineages or therapsids (the so-called mammal-like reptiles) with a double jaw joint—one composed of the old quadrate and articular bones (soon to become the hammer and anvil), the other of the squamosal and dentary bones (as in modern mammals). For that matter, what better transitional form could we desire than the oldest human, *Australopithecus afarensis*, with its apelike palate, its human upright stance, and a cranial capacity larger than any ape's of the same body size but a full 1,000 cubic centimeters below ours? If God made each of the half dozen human species discovered in ancient rocks, why did he create in an unbroken temporal sequence of progressively more modern features—increasing cranial capacity, reduced face and teeth, larger body size? Did he create to mimic evolution and test our faith thereby?

An Example of Creationist Argument

Faced with these facts of evolution and the philosophical bankruptcy of their own position, creationists rely upon distortion and innuendo to buttress their rhetorical claim. If I sound sharp or bitter, indeed I am—for I have become a major target of these practices.   18

I count myself among the evolutionists who argue for a jerky, or episodic, rather than a smoothly gradual, pace of change. In 1972 my colleague Niles Eldredge and I developed the theory of punctuated equilibrium [*Discover*, October]. We argued that two outstanding facts of the fossil record—geologically "sudden" origin of new species and failure to change thereafter (stasis)—reflect the predictions of evolutionary theory, not the imperfections of the fossil record. In most theories, small isolated populations are the source of new species, and the process of speciation takes thousands or tens of thousands of years. This amount of time, so long when measured against our lives, is a geological microsecond. It represents much less than 1 percent of the average life span for a fossil invertebrate species—more than 10 million years. Large, widespread, and well-established species, on the other hand, are not expected to change very much. We believe that the inertia of large populations explains the stasis of most fossil species over millions of years.   19

We proposed the theory of punctuated equilibrium largely to provide a different explanation for pervasive trends in the fossil record. Trends, we argued, cannot be attributed to gradual transformation within lineages, but must arise from the differential success of certain kinds of species. A trend, we argued, is more like climbing a flight of stairs (punctuations and stasis) than rolling up an inclined plane.   20

Since we proposed punctuated equilibria to explain trends, it is infuriating to be quoted again and again by creationists—whether   21 through design or stupidity, I do not know—as admitting that the fossil record includes no transitional forms. Transitional forms are generally lacking at the species level, but are abundant between larger groups. The evolution from reptiles to mammals, as mentioned earlier, is well documented. Yet a pamphlet entitled "Harvard Scientists Agree Evolution Is a Hoax" states: "The facts of punctuated equilibrium which Gould and Eldredge . . . are forcing Darwinists to swallow fit the picture that Bryan insisted on, and which God has revealed to us in the Bible."

Continuing the distortion, several creationists have equated the   22
theory of punctuated equilibrium with a caricature of the beliefs of Richard Goldschmidt, a great early geneticist. Goldschmidt argued, in a famous book published in 1940, that new groups can arise all at once through major mutations. He referred to these suddenly transformed creatures as "hopeful monsters." (I am attracted to some aspects of the noncaricatured version, but Goldschmidt's theory still has nothing to do with punctuated equilibrium.) Creationist Luther Sunderland talks of the "punctuated equilibrium hopeful monster theory" and tells his hopeful readers that "it amounts to tacit admission that antievolutionists are correct in asserting there is no fossil evidence supporting the theory that all life is connected to a common ancestor." Duane Gish writes, "According to Goldschmidt, and now apparently according to Gould, a reptile laid an egg from which the first bird, feathers and all, was produced." Any evolutionist who believed such nonsense would rightly be laughed off the intellectual stage; yet the only theory that could ever envision such a scenario for the evolution of birds is creationism—God acts in the egg.

Conclusion

I am both angry at and amused by the creationists; but mostly I   23
am deeply sad. Sad for many reasons. Sad because so many people who respond to creationist appeals are troubled for the right reason, but venting their anger at the wrong target. It is true that scientists have often been dogmatic and elitist. It is true that we have often allowed the white-coated, advertising image to represent us—"Scientists say that Brand X cures bunions ten times faster than . . . ." We have not fought it adequately because we derive benefits from appearing as a new priesthood. It is also true that faceless bureaucratic state power intrudes more and more into our lives and removes choices that should belong to individuals and communities. I can understand that requiring that evolution be taught in the schools might be seen as one

more insult on all these grounds. But the culprit is not, and cannot be, evolution or any other fact of the natural world. Identify and fight your legitimate enemies by all means, but we are not among them.

I am sad because the practical result of this brouhaha will not be   24
expanded coverage to include creationism (that would also make me sad), but the reduction or excision of evolution from high school curricula. Evolution is one of the half dozen "great ideas" developed by science. It speaks to the profound issues of genealogy that fascinate all of us—the "roots" phenomenon writ large. Where did we come from? Where did life arise? How did it develop? How are organisms related? It forces us to think, ponder, and wonder. Shall we deprive millions of this knowledge and once again teach biology as a set of dull and unconnected facts, without the thread that weaves diverse material into a supple unity?

But most of all I am saddened by a trend I am just beginning to   25
discern among my colleagues. I sense that some now wish to mute the healthy debate about theory that has brought new life to evolutionary ideology. It provides grist for creationist mills, they say, even if only by distortion. Perhaps we should lie low and rally round the flag of strict Darwinism, at least for the moment—a kind of old-time religion on our part.

But we should borrow another metaphor and recognize that we   26
too have to tread a straight and narrow path, surrounded by roads to perdition. For if we ever begin to suppress our search to understand nature, to quench our own intellectual excitement in a misguided effort to present a united front where it does not and should not exist, then we are truly lost.

A Reply to Gould

DUANE T. GISH

In his essay "Evolution as Fact and Theory" [May 1981], Stephen   1
Jay Gould states that creationists claim creation is a scientific theory. This is a false accusation. Creationists have repeatedly stated that neither creation nor evolution is a scientific theory (and each is equally religious). Gould in fact quotes from my book, *Evolution? The Fossils Say No!*, in which I state that both concepts of origins fail the criteria of a scientific theory.

Gould uses the argument of Sir Karl Popper that the primary   2
criterion of a scientific theory is its potential falsifiability, and then uses this sword to strike down creation as a scientific theory. Fine.

Gould surely realizes, however, that this is a two-edged sword. Sir Karl has used it to strike down evolution as a scientific theory, stating that Darwinism is not a testable scientific theory, but a metaphysical research program (*Unended Quest*, 1976).

Another criterion that must apply to a scientific theory is the ability to repeatedly observe the events, processes, or properties used to support the theory. There were obviously no human witnesses to the origin of the universe, the origin of life, or in fact to the origin of a single living thing, and even if evolution were occurring today, the process would require far in excess of all recorded history to produce sufficient change to document evolution. Evolution has not and cannot be observed any more than creation.   3

Gould states, "Theories are structures of ideas that explain and interpret facts." Certainly, creation and evolution can both be used as theories in that sense. Furthermore, one or the other must be true, since ultimately they are the only two alternatives we have to explain origins.   4

Gould charges creationists with dogma. Please note, however, Gould's own dogmatism. His use of the term "fact of evolution" appears throughout his paper. Furthermore, Gould seems to have a strange view of the relationship of fact and theory. He says, "Facts do not go away when scientists debate rival theories to explain them. Einstein's theory of gravitation replaced Newton's, but apples did not suspend themselves in midair pending the outcome. And human beings evolved from apelike ancestors whether they did so by Darwin's proposed mechanism or by some other, yet to be discovered." Well, evolutionists believe indeed that both apes and hydrogen evolved into people (the latter just took longer), but neither has ever been observed. All of us, however, have seen apples fall off trees.   5

Gould's "fact of evolution" immediately deteriorates into "three general arguments," two of which quickly deteriorate further into mere inferences. Gould's only direct observational evidence for evolution (his first argument) is experiments on fruit flies and observations on peppered moths in Britain. Neither, of course, offers evidence for evolution, for from beginning to end fruit flies remain fruit flies and peppered moths remain peppered moths. The task of the evolutionist is to answer the question how moths came to be moths, tigers came to be tigers, and people came to be people. In fact, this type of evidence is what Gould himself has sought in recent years to discredit as an explanation for the origin of higher categories.   6

Gould's second argument is an inference based on *imperfections*. He mentions homologous structures as evidence for evolution from a common ancestor. Gould should know first that many, if not most, homologous structures are not even possessed by the assumed   7 common ancestor and secondly that the actual evidence (particularly that from genetics) is so contradictory to what is predicted by evolution that Sir Gavin de Beer titled his Oxford biology reader (1971) on that subject *Homology, an Unsolved Problem.* Sir Gavin, along with S. C. Harland, felt compelled to suggest that organs, such as the eye, remain unchanged while the genes governing these structures become wholly altered during the evolutionary process! The whole Darwinian edifice collapses if that is true.

Gould's third argument is based on inferences drawn from the fossil record. The fossil record, with its "explosive appearance" (the term often used by geologists) of the highly complex creatures found in Cambrian rocks, for which no ancestors have been found, and the systematic absence of transitional forms between all higher categories of plants and animals, has proven an embarrassment to evolutionists ever since Darwin. Gould's argument, however, is that "transitions are often found in the fossil record." That is surprising indeed, since he seems intent in other publications to convey just the opposite opinion.

For example, in his 1977 *Natural History* essay "The Return of Hopeful Monsters," after recounting the derision meted out to Richard Goldschmidt for his hopeful-monster mechanism of evolution, Gould says, "I do, however, predict that during the next decade Goldschmidt will be largely vindicated in the world of evolutionary biology." Why? Among others, "The fossil record with its abrupt transitions offers no support for gradual change." A bit later: "All paleontologists know that the fossil record contains precious little in the way of intermediate forms; transitions between major groups are characteristically abrupt." Many similar statements by Gould and others could be cited.

Finally, Gould assails Sunderland and me for linking him to a hopeful-monster mechanism whereby a reptile laid an egg and a bird was hatched. He says an evolutionist who believed such nonsense would rightly be laughed off the intellectual stage. Let's see, then, what Goldschmidt really did say. In *The Material Basis of Evolution*, Goldschmidt says, "I need only quote Schindewolf (1936), the most progressive investigator known to me. He shows by examples from fossil material that the major evolutionary advances must have taken place in single large steps. . . . He shows that the many missing links in the paleontological record are sought for in vain because they have never existed: 'The first bird hatched from a reptilian egg.' " By Gould's own testimony, then, Goldschmidt, Gould's hero of the next decade, should be laughed off the intellectual stage.

Along with thousands of other creation scientists, in view of a wealth of evidence from thermodynamics, probability relationships, biology, molecular biology, paleontology, and cosmology, I have become convinced that evolution theory is scientifically untenable and that the concept of direct, special creation is a far more credible explanation.

QUESTIONS OF CONTENT

1. Gould accuses his opponents of misuing the word *theory*. What does he mean by this word? What do his opponents mean? What major political figure seems to have adopted the creationists' definition of the word?
2. How can evolution be both theory and fact, as Gould claims? How does it differ from natural selection?
3. Gould says that scientific creationism is nonsense because it cannot be falsified. What does he mean by that?
4. Gould offers three arguments that support evolution. What are they?
5. Gish denies that creationism is a scientific theory and denies also that evolution is. How does he do this?
6. What is Gould doing in his final paragraph? How is that related to Gish's claim in his opening paragraph that evolution is religious?
7. In paragraphs 8–9, Gish seems to have caught Gould in a contradiction. What is that contradiction? How accurately is it stated?

QUESTIONS OF FORM

1. Gould charges that creationism "falls apart on two general counts," that creationist arguments exhibit two kinds of fallacies. Consult "A Short Guide to Material and Formal Fallacies" in the Appendix and try to determine which fallacies are present in the faulty reasoning that Gould describes.
2. Gould makes three arguments for evolution by natural selection. Reduce each to its barest essentials. What is the *because*-statement for each?
3. Gould charges that creationists cannot produce such arguments as those mentioned in question 2 to support their claims; instead, they resort to "distortion and innuendo." He offers two examples of what he means by that in paragraphs 19–22. Compare these examples of Gould's with the arguments that Gish produces in his essay. How accurately has Gould described a creationist argument? Where, if at all, does Gish offer any claims for creationism that are structured like Gould's arguments for evolution?
4. How does each writer attempt to establish credibility with the portion of his audience that might be hostile?

SUGGESTIONS FOR WRITING

1. Present a summary of each of the two arguments that would be suitable for inclusion in a printed program to be distributed at a forum featuring both Gould and Gish as principal speakers.
2. You are the editor of the campus newspaper, and you have just received a letter from an irate parent, accusing the college of being godless and misguided for teaching evolution in its biology classes. Write a response to this letter in which you employ some of Gould's arguments. You plan to run your response as an editorial alongside the parent's letter. Be most careful in your response to maintain objectivity; you do not want to offend this person.
3. You have just read the exchange of letters between the antievolutionist parent and the editor of the school paper, as described in suggestion 2. You feel that the editor's reply deserves an appropriate creationist response, and you intend to use Gish's article as the basis for that response. Compose that letter, using as many of Gish's arguments as you can. You may, of course, offer additional arguments in defense of your position.

Varying Voices: Multiple Viewpoints on Crucial Questions

This readings section is also arranged differently from its predecessors, for it provides multiple essays on four different topics: the American drug problem, sex roles, euthanasia, and gun control. Typically, the four or five essays examine or present different viewpoints, so that you will get a reasonably varied view of the subject. (You will notice that the essays on gun control are an exception; while quite different in their approaches, they share essentially the same viewpoint.)

Once more we have provided questions that will direct your attention to the content and form of each essay, and that will also help you make useful comparisons and contrasts among the essays in that particular group; these questions and the related writing suggestions appear after all of that group's essays. The suggestions for writing usually will require you (unless your instructor directs otherwise) to compose your own papers or essays by drawing material from several or all of the essays in that group. Furthermore, we have provided citations for additional essays you may want to read for your research. Certainly, as before, you will find it helpful to read the questions and writing suggestions for each group of essays before you read the essays themselves.

How Can America Win
Its War on Drugs?

Why We're Losing
the War on Drugs

RACHEL FLICK

American radar in the Bahamas spotted a suspicious-looking small plane heading north. U.S. Customs and a Drug Enforcement Administration (DEA) interdiction force called Op Bat gave chase. The plane dropped a bundle that looked as if it might contain drugs into the sea, then flew on. Customs and Op Bat could not agree who should stay with the drugs and who should follow the plane. While they argued, the pilot slipped away, and a passing boat scooped up the bundle and escaped.

• New York City narcotics officers seized Santiago Martinez after he handed a buyer a heroin-filled packet from the 23 he had stashed inside his sweat shirt. The arrest was Martinez's sixth. This time, the assistant district attorney recommended a year. Martinez got 60 days. Within ten months of his release, he had been arrested on drug charges four more times.

• After he was incarcerated, Miami-based cocaine smuggler Max Mermelstein arranged delivery of a 550-kilo load of cocaine he had left in a warehouse. He simply used a prison pay phone to do it. That's how easy it is for convicted dealers to maintain their outside business.

If you get the sense from such incidents that we're accomplishing little in the so-called war on drugs, you're right. We're spending billions of dollars, yet squandering much of it in confusion, weakness, rivalry and mismanagement.

"What war on drugs?" asks Rep. Charles Rangel (D., N.Y.), chairman of the House Select Committee on Narcotics Abuse and Control. Former federal prosecutor Richard Gregorie of Florida's Southern District says he felt "a lot like the grunts in Vietnam—we are not being allowed to win."

The Bush Administration has unveiled its long-awaited strategy, calling for a get-tough attitude at every level of government—from federal agencies to the town hall. But if we are to win the drug war, we must take a hard look at why we have been losing. It's time to fix the five failings that have bedeviled our efforts. We must:

1. Stop letting criminals' rights come first. Last year drug-   7
dealing gangs controlled the Rockwell Gardens public-housing development in Chicago. They shook down terrorized tenants, held
shoot-outs on the sidewalks and ran a wide-open drug market. Then,
in September 1988, the Chicago Housing Authority launched "Operation Clean Sweep," which sought to stanch the drug flow by
"keeping out people who don't belong." Visitors had to show identification, with only residents being admitted from midnight to 9 a.m.

After the sweep of just one building, the project's crime rate   8
dropped 32 percent. Tenants were ecstatic. Yet the American Civil
Liberties Union (ACLU) sued, claiming the operation violated tenants' civil liberties. Both the curfew and the ID rule had to be
abandoned.

Ultimately, the drug war is fought not in Congress or the White   9
House, but in America's streets, schoolyards, offices, factories and
housing projects. Yet, too often, when authorities on these battle-
grounds try to get tough, they are accused of violating civil rights
and liberties. These challenges, backed by decades of imaginative
rulings from federal courts, mean that even when local authorities
want to, they frequently cannot do their jobs.

Across America, police are handicapped by the "exclusionary   10
rule," which bars critical evidence if officers even inadvertently violate search-and-seizure guidelines. When search warrants are obtained, defendants can still beat the rap.

Detroit police last fall searched a small film-development booth   11
and discovered three pounds of cocaine, $34,000 in currency, 11 guns
and a silencer. They promptly arrested the booth operator. The police had obtained the search warrant by citing extensive evidence as
to why they expected to find exactly what they did. However, a
second judge declared the evidence inadequate and the search a violation of the operator's rights. He walked.

Juveniles have even more rights. In New York, the courts have   12
ruled that juvenile offenders have the right to a trial within 90 days.
If the prosecution is not ready by then, the case is dismissed—even
if the delay is caused by the defendant himself.

Civil liberties should not overrule practical action against drugs,   13
especially for minors, who need authority. Rep. Kweisi Mfume (D.,
Md.)—told by police, parents and teachers that beepers are the
"devices of choice" for drug-dealing youths—has proposed curbing
their sale to people under 21. The ACLU has threatened to sue if
Mfume's bill passes. In drug-plagued Washington, D.C., where homicide has taken 27 children this year, the city council twice voted

for a temporary curfew on youths under 17. The ACLU sued, and the curfew was struck down.

Says Detroit's U.S. Attorney Stephen Markman: "The idea that   14
the Constitution is somehow hostile to the war on crime is a misreading of the Constitution." We have to free our elected officials to exercise their legitimate authority to protect those they represent.

2. Build more prisons. When the *National Law Journal* asked   15
prosecutors nationwide to name their No. 1 problem in fighting drugs, the answer was: "Limited prison space."

One reason is that in the 1970s federal courts began applying the   16
Constitution's ban on "cruel and unusual punishment" to prison conditions like cell size, food service, medical care, recreational facilities, staffing and supplies. These court-enforced standards have since drastically reduced the number of usable beds. Thirty-five state prison systems and uncounted local jails are under court order to reduce crowding.

To comply with such orders, massive numbers of prisoners are   17
released. Typical, says Philadelphia District Attorney Ronald D. Castille, is the man arrested by local police in October 1987 for robbery and aggravated assault. Released on bail, he was arrested a month later for cocaine possession "with intent to deliver" and again granted bail. Ignoring trial dates, he evaded police until May 1988, when he was arrested again on cocaine-peddling charges. Because of jail overcrowding he was let go as soon as he was booked, without posting bail. Three more times in the next year, he was arrested for selling cocaine and freed because of jail overcrowding. Not until his seventh arrest, last June, was he finally imprisoned.

Prisons are expensive to build and run. By 1988 the average cost   18
nationwide to build a prison "bed" was $70,000. Maintaining a prisoner in that bed for one year runs as high as $25,000.

We will have to spend whatever it takes. The federal govern-   19
ment, whose prison system is now 60 percent over capacity, is trying. Ten new federal prisons are under construction; several old ones are being expanded. This year President Bush has asked for $1.5 billion to build another 24,000 cells.

Still, new prisons take up to three years to build. In the mean-   20
time, one inexpensive alternative supported by the Administration is "boot camps." Often set up on military bases due for closing, they emulate state programs where young offenders receive "shock incarceration."

At Mississippi's Regimented Inmate Discipline Program, for in-   21
stance, first-time felons awake at 5 a.m., clean their barracks, do exercises and raise the American flag. Their day is divided between

classroom education and Parris Island-style drilling. The boot camp is cheap, safe and effective at reducing recidivism.

3. Fight drugs at the source. The coca fields of Peru's Upper   22
Huallaga Valley are the source of half the cocaine smuggled into the United States. The crops are contained, visible and accessible. Since 1987, the United States and Peru have jointly tested herbicides for use against this crop. Yet this spring, after leftist guerrillas, allied with drug interests, murdered scores of local police, Peruvian President Alan García curtailed the program.

Most illegal drugs consumed in the United States are produced   23
abroad, many in identifiable areas by known people. But because the international drug fight is dangerous and diplomatically complicated, some officials here and abroad are reluctant to get involved.

Nowhere was this more striking than in the aftermath of Operation Blast Furnace in 1986, carried out in the Chapare region of   24
Bolivia, where one-fourth of the world's coca was then grown. The Bolivian government asked U.S. troops and helicopters to help in a search-and-destroy mission against cocaine production.

While Blast Furnace lasted, "we literally shut down the coca   25
market in Bolivia," says Thomas Kelly, deputy administrator at the DEA. Nevertheless, the operation will probably not be repeated. Why? Because the use of American troops sparked accusations that the United States had violated Bolivia's sovereignty. "I don't think another Latin American government is going to invite us to carry out law-enforcement activities that are their proper, sovereign responsibility," says a State Department official.

Problems of sovereignty are reasons to plan our attack with care,   26
not to refuse to act. Rather than second-guess operations like Blast Furnace, we should find "ways to do this again which would not destabilize" the region, says former Assistant Secretary of State Elliott Abrams. We should not shrink from using U.S. personnel, who are sometimes the most effective drug soldiers. As soon as our soldiers departed, Bolivia's war on drugs faltered.

Most of all, we need a real plan for places like the Upper   27
Huallaga. Any policy that does not include specific plans for attacking specific crops is a cop-out, not a strategy.

4. Decide who's in charge. Last April 3, U.S. Customs Service   28
agents in Mendocino County, California, were poised to nab a ship packed with ten tons of Colombian marijuana. An informant on shore was talking to the ship by radio, helping to lure the vessel to a drop-off site. But a Coast Guard unit, unaware of the operation, overheard the radio messages and cut in. The ship fled, and the bust was blown.

Federally supported drug treatment is equally confused. A Con-   29
gressional investigation discovered that the states never spent $777
million in the federal funds earmarked for drug education, treatment
and rehabilitation. Uncle Sam's rules for using the money were too
specific to be practical for the states.

With 58 federal agencies and departments involved, the drug   30
fight has become a swamp of rivalry, misdirection, duplication and
waste. Last year, a new law finally called for one man to coordinate
federal drug policy. President Bush appointed former Education Secretary William J. Bennett to be the so-called Drug Czar.

But the Bush Administration has been slow to support its new   31
czar. For instance, in June, while Bennett was still writing the Administration's policy on drug testing, Constance B. Newman, the
President's choice to head the Office of Personnel Management,
stated her own position. She declared at her Senate confirmation
hearing that she wants to limit employee drug testing and was confirmed in part on that basis. Newman had not consulted Bennett.

If the drug czar is to exert the control his title implies, he will   32
need more backing from Bush in situations like that one. He will
also need less interference from Congress, where at least 70 committees and subcommittees oversee the drug fight. A single body in each
house should be responsible. We can't win the war on drugs with
every soldier acting like a general.

5. Put the blame where it belongs. People start taking drugs   33
for a range of reasons. But the hard truth is that each individual is
responsible for his own actions—both for starting drugs and for
quitting them. Our drug policies have not acknowledged this. "We
view addiction as chronic, like arthritis or diabetes, more than as
a problem that can be cured," says Dr. Charles R. Schuster, director of the National Institute on Drug Abuse. One result of this
outlook is that, in some cases, addiction is now considered a "handicap" under the U.S. law that protects the handicapped against
job discrimination.

The way to hold individuals responsible is to make them pay a   34
price. Currently, that price is not steep. Bob Schirn, a Los Angeles
County prosecutor, says, "It's very rare that a person who has a
history only of drug possession will go to prison." In New York City,
most of those convicted of possessing drugs are sentenced at best to
"time served"—the day or two spent awaiting arraignment. Wayne
County, Michigan, Assistant Prosecutor Richard Padzieski says, "I
can't say that a lot of people in Detroit fear the drug laws."

Last March, on the other hand, Phoenix, Ariz., launched a get-   35
tough program—called "Do Drugs. Do Time."—with lessons for the
entire nation. "We don't just take their dope and write a report,"

says Lt. John Buchanan of the county's drug unit. "They go to jail, and that door slams."

The cars of those who bought or consumed drugs in them are   36
confiscated. First offenders are offered a choice between a trial or about a year of treatment, at their own expense (as much as $2000). The treatment includes compulsory drug tests.

Ben Wallace (not his real name) was a drug abuser for 12 years,   37
shattering two marriages and ruining himself financially. But his arrest in Phoenix ended his addiction; he did not want to go to prison. "It was either 'You end it, or you go,' " he says. "I ended it."

William Bennett believes the real reason for the drug epidemic is   38
that the 1960s and '70s are not yet behind us. In those troubled decades, Bennett says, our most influential institutions were "giving permission, even encouragement, to use drugs. Our basic institutions have still not recovered."

Bennett is right. A recent drug-use survey reveals that our waver-   39
ing commitment to drug enforcement has, inevitably, produced uneven and disappointing results. The strongest among us are beginning to respond to the war on drugs, but the most troubled—the young and unemployed—remain increasingly prone to the ravages of hard-core addiction.

We must never forget that the enemy we are fighting is not a   40
chemical or a country or a social condition. Rather, it is each and every individual who sells, consumes or condones an illegal drug. The billions of tax dollars we spend to cope with the human wreckage left by drugs are being stolen from our pockets by every unpunished drug kingpin, every strutting street dealer and every "upright" citizen covertly snorting cocaine.

We are a nation mugged. We need the guts, the resolve and the   41
righteous anger to act against the assailant. This commitment will have to come from all of us—our President, Congress, states, courts, cities and each and every American. Without it, no czar, no program and no amount of money will help.

We've Lost the War on Drugs, So Let's Call It Off

MIKE ROYKO

Poor William Bennett, the nation's chief drug warrior. He's   1
outgunned, outnumbered, underfinanced and overwhelmed. In other words, he can't win.

The other side—those who use drugs, sell drugs and profit from   2
drugs—has become too big and powerful.

As we've just seen in Colombia, one of the world's biggest drug   3
suppliers, if a presidential candidate displeases the drug kings, they
just kill him.

Sure, the Colombian authorities are putting on a big show, round-   4
ing up the usual suspects and all that. But for what? The judges there
are afraid that if they send any of the biggies to jail, they'll be murdered, too. Which they will.

And as we've just seen in this country, if the price is right,   5
almost anyone can be corrupted. One of the top federal agents in the
famous "French Connection" case was just nailed for being part of a
big drug deal. Once he was a hero chasing the bad guys. Now he's
one of the bad guys.

There really isn't any "drug war" because the war has long been   6
lost for a number of reasons.

Reason one: popular demand. Many Americans choose to use   7
drugs. Some are back-alley crackheads who will eventually die. Others are outwardly respectable coke sniffers who will slowly screw up
their lives. And still others are pot smokers who won't hurt themselves anymore than the guy who has two or three martinis after
work. Drugs are used at every level of society, from the ghetto to the
penthouse.

Reason two: the profits are staggering. The street pusher makes   8
big money. His supplier makes bigger bucks. The smugglers make
even more. The foreign suppliers make billions. Entire governments
are corrupted or intimidated. Law enforcement people, from the pa-
trol cop up to and beyond judges, are bought off. And when bribe
money doesn't talk, automatic weapons do.

Reason three: There just aren't enough cops to make a tiny dent   9
in the drug industry. Chicago has about 3 million people, give or take
a few hundred thousand illegal aliens.

That gives us one cop for every 265 people. But not really. At any   10
given moment, some are on vacation, some on sick leave, some
shuffling papers. And they're working three shifts and on weekends.
So realistically, we probably don't have one working cop for every
1,500 people.

And they're busy with other chores, chasing speeders and drun-   11
ken drivers, breaking up family fights or tavern brawls, looking for
muggers, porch climbers, rapists, flashers, killers and people who
don't buy their auto stickers.

There are 135 cops assigned to full-time narcotics duty. That's   12
one for every 22,222 Chicagoans. So if every dealer AND cokehead
did his or her selling and sniffing on a street corner in broad daylight,

the local narcs couldn't keep up with them. And if they did—well, that leads us to the next problem.

Reason four: Where would we put them? The local jails, the 13 state prisons, the federal prisons—just about every slammer in the country is overcrowded. Build more, you say? We are, and the taxpayers are already screaming that they pay too much. Hire more cops? That costs money. Build rehab centers? Drug detention camps? More money. We want it both ways—solve the problem, but don't send the bill to me.

Reason five: The local authorities say they can't cope with the 14 drug industry, that the flow has to be stopped at the borders or at the sources. The problem is that there are thousands of ways and thousands of places to bring drugs in. And there aren't enough border patrols, Coast Guard boats and planes, federal narcs or anything else to stop the flow. And we're not going to send troops into Colombia, Peru, Mexico or any of the other big exporting nations to shoot it out with the armies of the drug cartels. Those governments don't want us there. Even if they did, we'd have to become a permanent occupying military force, which is impossible. And once we left, they'd be back in business. Meanwhile, our importers would find other sources.

So what is the solution? Well, Bennett can keep making speeches 15 and pleading for more federal bucks, while knowing he won't get them. And we can keep telling our children to "just say no," while a certain percentage of them will be saying yes.

Or we can say: Let's call off the war and make the best of the 16 peace. We can view drugs the way we view liquor. If you want it, and are of legal age and have the price, you can have booze. If you want to become a lush, that's a problem for you, your liver and your family. Liquor can be a terrible curse for some people but for most it isn't. And at least we don't have gangs blasting each other and innocent bystanders for territorial rights. Plus, we collect a tax on every sip.

Yes, I'm saying that we might as well legalize the junk. Put taxes 17 on it, license the distributors, establish age limits and treat it like hooch. If someone wants to sniff away their nose or addle their brain, so be it.

They're doing it now, anyway, and at least we'd be rid of the gun 18 battles, the corruption, and the wasted money and effort trying to save the brains and noses of those who don't want them saved.

It is this society's position that if you choose to be a falling down 19 drunken bum and wind up in the gutter, that is your right.

So if you want to sniff or snort or puff your way into the gutter, 20 that should be your right, too.

Look at it this way: It's a lot easier to sweep up gutters than to 21 fight a hopeless war.

The Case Against Drug Legalization

GEORGE WILL

The dynamics of public opinion lag behind events, so the drug   1
crisis probably peaked before anxiety did. And now, when drug use is
decreasing, calls for surrender—legalization—are increasing.

Alcohol does much more damage—illness, accidents, violence,   2
lost productivity, premature death—than cocaine and heroin combined. Yet many advocates of drug legalization favor (this is econo-
mist Milton Friedman's formulation) treating drugs "exactly the
same way you treat alcohol."

Alcohol is much less addictive than heroin or cocaine and, be-   3
sides, has long been a pervasive, rooted social phenomenon in a way
that cocaine need not become. Surely it is perverse to argue for
decriminalizing one drug on the ground that it currently does less
damage than a drug that is legal.

Friedman argues that criminalization is "not working," that it   4
costs society more than legalization would and that government has
no right to interfere with free choices that do not interfere with the
free choices of others. Thus Friedman is logically committed to un-
leashing existing drugs—and as many "designer drugs" as perverse
chemists concoct in the future.

What of Friedman's bald assertion that the fight against drugs is   5
"not working"? Drug use is declining from peaks reached in this
decade. The number of heroin addicts is approximately the same as
it was in 1972 when defeatists warned of exponential growth—an
"epidemic"—and when Friedman urged legalization.

Containment of drugs is indeed costly. So has been containment   6
of communism—costly, but a bargain. If drugs are legalized, asks
James Q. Wilson, "in what proportion of auto fatalities would the
state police report that the driver was nodding off on heroin or recklessly driving on a coke high? In what proportion of spouse-assault
and child-abuse cases would the local police report that crack was
involved? In what proportion of industrial accidents would safety
investigators report that the forklift or drill-press operator was in a
drug-induced stupor or frenzy?"

Legalizers urge: Tax drug sales and use the billions to provide   7
"treatment on demand." But Wilson argues that "demand" for treatment often is a result of judicial coercion, and society could not
compel treatment for consumption of a legal commodity. Wilson
makes these and other decisive points in a dazzling essay in the
February 1990 issue of *Commentary.*

Wilson proves that Friedman, the high priest of market capital-   8
ism, is talking rot about markets and price mechanisms. If Friedman
had been heeded in 1972 the price of heroin would have fallen 95
percent. Friedman concedes only that lower drug prices "might"
increase demand. But then again, he thinks demand for cheap legal
drugs might not increase because drugs would lose the appeal of
being "forbidden fruit."

Friedman really thinks that appeal, and pushers, create demand.   9
But as Wilson says, friends, not pushers, recruit addicts. Pushers
dislike dealing with non-addicts because they might be undercover
policemen.

Wilson says that most veterans who acquired a habit in the drug   10
bazaar of Saigon kicked it when they came home. At home, the
criminal law made continuing the habit involve risking one's personal and professional lives and one's bodily safety by "making an
illegal contact with a disreputable dealer in a threatening neighborhood" to buy a possibly contaminated drug. Does Friedman think
demand would not rise if the people making and selling aspirins
were making and selling heroin and cocaine?

Legalization would cause drug prices to crash; then taxation   11
would raise them. How far? Government, calculating rates of consumption at various tax levels, would decide the "right amount" of
addiction. If government priced drugs above what criminals could
profitably sell them for, there would be two markets, and there
would be no laws suppressing demand by stigmatizing use.

Legalizers say young people would be excluded from the free   12
market for drugs. Oh? And today no young people obtain cigarettes
or alcohol.

When asked about advertising legal drugs, Friedman flinches. He   13
favors prohibiting advertising of drugs in newspapers or on television because people must see such advertising "whether they chose
to see it or not." What rubbish. Friedman is caught. Advertising
exists to inform and influence choices. If drug use is a private choice
concerning which society should be permissive, drug sellers should
be free to compete for market shares.

Friedman's monomaniacal worship of "free choice"—even re-   14
garding addictive substances—is less a philosophy than a fetish. It
demonstrates the intellectual poverty of libertarianism, the anti-
political and anti-social doctrine of severe individualism.

As Wilson says in the core of his essay, no society is a mere   15
aggregation of independently formed individuals. Society, without
which human character is inconceivable and by which character is
formed, depends on a certain level of dignity, responsibility and

empathy. Determining that level is difficult, "but if crack and heroin use do not fall below it, what does?"

This also does: Today, interest in legalization is increasing as   16
drug abuse becomes increasingly concentrated among poor minorities. That is proof that many privileged people are failing to measure up to minimal standards of responsibility and empathy.

Legalization Holds No Answer
to Drugs

MARIANNE MEANS

Since President Bush outlined his modest skirmish against   1
drugs, an astonishing phenomenon has been taking root among intellectuals of both the right and left.

Increasingly, respected voices are raised to advocate the legaliza-   2
tion of drugs, arguing that the violence accompanying the spread of crack, crank, cocaine and other substances is due mostly to corruption spawned by the huge profits of peddling a product that is against the law. The notion is that if selling drugs were legal, crime would go down, drugs would lose some of their allure and the government could both regulate and tax the stuff.

Proponents point to Prohibition, a nationwide ban on alcoholic   3
beverages a half century ago that made Al Capone's gang rich and created criminals of millions of otherwise law-abiding citizens who were stubbornly devoted to their nightly toddy. Totally unenforceable, it was repealed by popular demand. Gin went from the bathtub to the store shelves and consumption of liquor soared by 350 percent.

No national public official has yet bought the spurious reasoning   4
for legalization; it remains a distinctly minority view. But the administration underestimates the smooth simplicity of the argument and the rapidity with which it is becoming a subject of serious public and private debate.

Legalization appeals to those who despair that drug abuse can   5
ever be controlled; ironically, the president fueled this pessimism with a drug strategy so financially limited that its goal is only a 50 percent reduction in the use of drugs over the next 10 years.

It also appeals to those who disagree with the administration's   6
insistence that social users of marijuana are as guilty as crack ad-

dicts. Middle-class casual users do not want to admit they are doing anything wrong.

This is a frightening trend. It is a cruel hoax to suggest that the   7
problem with drugs is their illegality rather than their addictive nature and their disastrous chemical impact upon both mind and body.

Comparisons between alcohol abuse and serious drug addiction   8
are dangerously misleading. The former can create health and social problems but the latter is virtually guaranteed to do so and do it in a terrifying way that is likely to injure others.

Crack and crank are relatively new drugs for which we have no   9
long-term health statistics. It would be playing with fire to approve of something about which we know so little. Thus far, there is no proven treatment.

There are few reliable, current figures reflecting the full scope of   10
the present drug epidemic, in part because it has hit hardest among the poor, for whom it is only one of many problems.

But 85 percent of those who drink alcohol rarely become intoxi-   11
cated and 90 percent never become addicted. The opposite is true of cocaine and crack. Surveys indicate 70 percent of users who experi-ment with cocaine become addicted. Heroin and crack, which can hook victims after only one or two uses, are worse.

A new study shows that 51 percent of high school students who   12
drank liquor reported they had experienced "very high" levels of intoxication whereas 75 percent of whose who used cocaine reported being similarly bombed.

Too much liquor may lead to accidents and abusive behavior but   13
it does not regularly trigger violence, paranoia and insanity to the extent that crack and cocaine do. Shootings and beatings among crack users are not entirely due to criminals fighting over profits. A simple family quarrel can set off murder and mayhem. The presi-dent's Office of National Drug Control Policy describes a typical reaction as "quick resort to violence on minimal provocation."

Hospital emergencies for overdoses, injuries and other problems   14
due to crack went up 121 percent between 1985 and 1987. Intensive care for babies born with AIDS or crack addictions passed on by their mothers runs to $2.5 billion a year and is mounting. Intravenous drug use is now the single largest source of new HIV-AIDS virus infections; about one-half of all AIDS deaths are drug-related.

Legalization would make drugs cheaper and more readily avail-   15
able, easily tripling their usage just as alcohol consumption shot up after Prohibition. In fact, there would be nothing financial, moral or legally punitive to stop their spread.

This would be a social disaster. Capitulating to drugs would be   16
appallingly dangerous. With ever-expanding usage, none of us would
be safe from the consequences of highway, airplane and job accidents
and random street violence. Yet without criminal sanctions prevention would be impossible; we have enough difficulty trying to prevent such problems now.

We would be recklessly jeopardizing our future. It would become   17
morally difficult to teach youngsters to avoid drugs. If society endorsed addictive drugs as insufficiently harmful to be sold over the
counter, how would children be motivated to stay away? Would
taxpayers bother to pay for treatment and education centers?

The Food and Drug Administration forbids the marketing of   18
foodstuffs that tests indicate can cause cancer in rats. History would
have nothing good to say about a society that found drugs a lesser
threat.

The way to fight drug crime is not to make it legal. The way to   19
fight it is to fight it.

QUESTIONS OF CONTENT

1. Rachel Flick gives five reasons why the United States is losing its war
   on drugs. What are they? Which ones seem the most and least convincing, and why?
2. Mike Royko lists five reasons why he believes the war on drugs has
   already been lost. What are they? Which of them do you judge to be
   the most and least convincing, and why? How many of his reasons
   does he share with Flick, and which writer seems to make the
   stronger case for the shared reasons?
3. In his article arguing against drug legalization, George Will cites two
   authorities: Milton Friedman and John Q. Wilson. What positions do
   each of these authorities take in the debate?
4. Marianne Means mentions that proponents of drug legalization often point to the repeal of Prohibition as an argument for their position. What was Prohibition, and how does what happened before
   and after its repeal tend to support the views of those favoring drug
   legalization? How might an opponent of legalization, such as Means
   or Will, refute the historical reference to our country's experience
   with Prohibition?
5. The American Civil Liberties Union (ACLU) comes under serious
   attack in Rachel Flick's article. What charge does she make against
   this organization? From what you can infer by reading George Will's
   article, would Milton Friedman agree or disagree with Flick's indict-
   ment of the ACLU?

QUESTIONS OF FORM

1. In the five main divisions of Rachel Flick's essay, she advocates five courses of action that the United States must undertake in order to win its war on drugs. Each of these divisions thus contains a claim of policy. First, show how in each of the five instances the supporting examples illustrate (1) the dire situation that must be corrected and (2) the good effects that adoption of her policy would produce. Then discuss how convincingly each of the five is presented.

2. Royko's argument is divided into two parts: the first fourteen paragraphs and the last eight. How would you describe Royko's argumentative strategies in each of these major divisions?

3. In paragraph 4 of his essay, George Will provides us with a capsule summary of the three parts of Milton Friedman's argument, a tactic that classical rhetoric calls a *partition*. Pick out the three parts, and then determine which of Will's paragraphs that follow are devoted to each of the issues that he sets forth in that partition.

4. Marianne Means argues forcefully that there is no justifiable analogy between using alcohol and using drugs. Explain her refutation of this analogy.

5. Examine Flick's and Royko's essays, and then those of Will and Means, to ascertain what argumentative techniques they share and also how they differ. Which depend on reference to authority, for instance, or on the use of statistics? If one essay seems clearly more convincing than its counterpart, try to determine why that is so.

SUGGESTIONS FOR WRITING

1. Study carefully George Will's "The Case Against Drug Legalization." It is essentially a summary of two essays: one by Milton Friedman, the other by John Q. Wilson. Now do the same for the essays by Mike Royko and Marianne Means, which take opposing views on the legalization of drugs. Now write your own essay following Will's lead; he took the side of Wilson against Friedman. You take the side of Royko against Means—or vice versa.

2. Using material that you have drawn from each of the four essays in this section, construct your own argument containing at least three claims of policy—courses of action that you advocate for the government that will correct the currently bad drug situation and produce good results. Use appropriate documentation practices in crediting your authorities. You may find it useful beforehand to review (or even to read for the first time) the section called "Using Sources" in Chapter 6, Putting It All Together.

3. In addition to the four essays in this section, examine those listed below, as well as others if directed to do so by your instructor, and then prepare a well-documented paper supporting or rejecting the

case for drug legalization. Again, you may find it worthwhile to refer to Chapter 6 before proceeding.

ADDITIONAL REFERENCES

FRIEDMAN, MILTON. *"Prohibition and Drugs."* Newsweek 79 (1 May 1972), 104.

GESSNER, ELIZABETH, *et al.* "We Already Know the Folly of Decriminalization of Drugs." *The New York Times,* 20 Oct. 1989, A14.

"An Open Letter to William Bennett." *The Wall Street Journal,* 7 September 1989, A16.

WILSON, JAMES Q. "Against the Legalization of Drugs." *Commentary* 8.2 (1990): 21–28.

ARE SEX ROLES REALLY CHANGEABLE?

Paid Homemaking: An Idea
in Search of a Policy

WILLIAM J. BYRON, S.J.

Parents in the U.S. have no economic incentive to care for their   1
children at home. If that strikes no one as strange, it is only because
our nation takes it for granted that economic incentives belong in
the marketplace and other motives explain behavior at home. So,
full-time care for a "priceless" child by that child's natural parent in
a supportive home environment is unrewarded economically.

Those who know the price of everything and the value of noth-   2
ing are, as Oscar Wilde said so well, cynics. What can be said of a
nation that regards its children as priceless, but attaches no economic value to child-care by the person best qualified to provide it?
Shortsighted will do for the moment. Further reflection might
prompt us to label as both unwise and dangerous the absence of
national support for parents who want to be full-time homemakers.

The issue is complicated. Children are our nation's greatest trea-   3
sure, our most precious resource. In the vast majority of cases, children develop best in a stable family unit, in an environment of
love—of parents for each other and of both for the child. Moreover,
children need to experience parental love expressed in the form of
presence. An attentive, affirming presence seems to work best.

Yet, we know that parents are often left without partners. We   4
also know that economic necessity frequently drives both parents
into the labor market. Sometimes, a desire to give full stretch to
one's talents encourages mothers for whom employment is not an
economic necessity to step into the job market. (Our cultural pre-
sumption that fathers can enjoy that same full stretch only in employment other than homemaking remains unchallenged, even unexamined.) Then there are those mothers who go to work only for
the sake of their offspring, to supplement the family income so that
the youngsters can have more—more material things, more and better education, more developmental opportunities, but less parental
presence. Presence (or absence, depending on your point of view) is

the coin in which the parent-child relationship pays the price for two-paycheck marriages, or for one-parent households where the parent is employed outside the home.

Should homemakers be paid for their services? Not housekeep-   5
ers, babysitters, or day-care providers, but homemakers—parents who choose to devote full time to the task of rearing children.

On Nov. 24, 1983, the Vatican published a "Charter on the   6
Rights of the Family." It is the product of worldwide consultation and a formal process of reflection and research that began in 1980. The charter speaks principally to governments. Article 10 declares:

> Families have a right to social and economic order in which the organization of work permits the members to live together and does not hinder the unity, well-being, health and the stability of the family, while offering also the possibility of wholesome recreation.
>
> a) Remuneration for work must be sufficient for establishing and maintaining a family with dignity, either through a suitable salary, called a "family wage," or through other social measures such as family allowances or the remuneration of the work in the home of one of the parents; it should be such that mothers will not be obliged to work outside the home to the detriment of family life and especially of the education of the children.
>
> b) The work of the mother in the home must be recognized and respected because of its value for the family and for society.

Those "other social measures" lie, for the most part, undesigned   7
and hidden in the imaginations of academics and social theorists. Government should be encouraging their development. Although the Vatican statement targets no specific purse from which home-makers' pay could be drawn, the only likely source is government. Neil Gilbert, in *Capitalism and the Welfare State* (Yale University Press, 1983), proposes that the full-time homemaker receive a "social credit" for each year spent at home with children who are under 17 years of age. According to this plan, accumulated credits would either pay for higher education or entitle the homemaker to preferred hiring status in the Civil Service once the youngsters are raised and the parent is ready to enter or reenter the labor market. Gilbert specifies the Federal government as the provider of this benefit which, like a veteran's benefit, would compensate the home-maker for time spent out of the workforce, but in service to the nation.

In Gilbert's scheme, each unit of social credit (one child per year   8
of full-time care) could be exchanged for either "(a) tuition for four units of undergraduate academic training, (b) tuition for three units

of technical school training, (c) tuition for two units of graduate education, or (d) an award of one-fourth of a preference point on federal civil service examinations." The parent is the implied beneficiary of the tuition grant in this G.I. Bill-type scenario. The policy would surely be more attractive and effective if an option to designate the homemaker's child as the educational beneficiary were made explicit.

The social credit idea bars no parent, male or female, from opting for paid employment or professional activity outside the home. It doesn't even discourage outside work. It simply provides an incentive to parents who might prefer homemaking to labor market activity. It also answers the need of those parents who bring home the second paycheck just "to put the kids through college." Under this plan, they would stay home, accumulate the social credits, and eventually redeem them in tuition payments.   9

When the legislative imagination takes up this idea, as I hope will be the case before long, some constraints will have to be set. The first would be an appropriate family income limit above which neither parent would be eligible. Those who do qualify could, if the policy so directs, be required to treat as taxable income the cash value of the credits exchanged for tuition. By keeping the benefit tax-free, however, legislators would preserve for the beneficiary freedom of choice between independent and state-supported higher education. Spending the credits for tuition at the higher priced independent colleges would mean a higher cash value and thus more taxable income. It is better to keep the benefit tax-free.   10

It is conceivable that the eligible person who decides to be a full-time homemaking parent would soon become economically active at home. "Worksteading" is the new word for this. With the arrival of the "information economy" and the installation of computers and word processors in the home, the probability of more at-home paid employment rises sharply. Protection for the integrity of the social credit program could come from the Internal Revenue Service and would have to be written into the law. It would be easy to come up with an IRS device that would decertify from social credit eligibility the homemaker who reports earnings above a relatively low limit specified in the law. Again, the economic incentive. In this case, the threatened loss of the credit would serve as encouragement to hold firm on the homemaking commitment in the face of attractive remunerative at-home business opportunities.   11

The credits would, of course, be nontransferable from family to family. Some might argue for a limit on the number of credits one homemaker could earn (Gilbert suggests a three-child maximum),   12 but sensitivity to parental freedom with respect to family size would be an important consideration in any public policy relating to the family.

The program would be more flexible, and thus more practical   13
and attractive, if parents could alternate on the full-time home-maker responsibility. In effect, the parents would commit themselves, as a couple, to the provision of one full-time homemaker's services each year from the birth of a child until that child reaches his or her 17th birthday. This would open up the possibility for a mother (more often than not, the mother will be the parent with full-time homemaking responsibilities) to work outside the home. There would be no loss of credit so long as the father personally provides the child care. It is worth noting that a shared responsibility for earning social credits through homemaking could promote cooperation over career competition between spouses in the modern marriage.

The value of the credit would best be expressed as a percentage   14
of the cost of higher education—100% of the cost of tuition, fees, and books, regardless of the college chosen. The inclusion of other expenses that complete the so-called "cost of attending" (room and board, transportation, spending money) would be a matter of legislative choice. The point of specifying the percentage, rather than an absolute sum, is to relieve the parent of anxiety concerning the erosion of the credit by inflation and the consequent inability—17 years later—to convert the credits into payment for tuition, fees, and books. It seems to me that one year's credit should be worth one-17th of the price, at the point of consumption, of tuition, fees, and books. The total cost of tuition, fees, and books ("costs of education," as distinguished from "cost of attendance") would be completely covered in those cases where a child received full-time parental home care for the first 17 years of life.

The proposal is clearly intended to reinforce the nuclear family   15
unit by rewarding a parent for remaining at home. As a policy idea, it will go nowhere unless there is widespread conviction that society needs the services of full-time homemakers.

Such persons need not be confined to quarters all day long. They   16
would be free to be with their youngsters in a variety of at-home and out-of-home ways and at times not possible for the busy parent burdened with a work schedule. The homemaker's schedule would focus on the child. It would promote parental presence—to the child. When one considers how such time might be spent, expressions like "creative leisure" and "shared learning" come to mind, as do thoughts of joint participation in arts, crafts, games, museum visits, sightseeing

"voyages of discovery," and similar engagements. School plays and athletic contests would attract more spectators. The schools themselves would be able to draw on a larger supply of volunteer service. As the nation deplores the condition of its schools, it should notice the promise this policy holds for the promotion of life of the mind *at home,* a development which would be nothing but good for the schools.

This policy proposal is open to the criticism that it envisions a   17
middle-class program that would be unavailable to the working poor who, credits or not, could not afford not to work. The criticism is quite fair. This proposal would not meet the needs of those who absolutely have to work. They demonstrate the power of economic incentives; many—by no means all—would prefer to be homemakers. To meet their needs (and to assist others who are less pressed for funds, but most anxious to combine careers and parental responsibilities), it is important to consider for inclusion in a national family policy measures that would encourage flexible work schedules, make day-care facilities more widely available, and make child-care expenses more readily deductible.

In addition, Gilbert deals with an issue that will certainly be   18
raised by many voices in this policy debate:

> For women who want a balanced family life and a full-time career, a family credit scheme would open a successive route along which both are possible. Because this route encompasses a 25-to-30-year period of employment, it may close off a few career options which require early training and many years of preparation. There must be some price for enjoying the choice of two callings in life. This is a different path from the continuous paid career line that men typically follow. It may be better.

I have tested the social credit idea in the op-ed forum and in   19
conversations with friends. The strongest negative reaction chided me for trying to "bribe" people into child-care, "to shoehorn women back into the kitchen and/or the nursery."

On the other hand, the mother of two disabled sons applauded   20
the idea: "The need for social reform to strengthen the family is so great that one would imagine that America as a nation and as a culture depends on the policy you advocate. It is indeed puzzling how an issue that is so fundamental—and so simply obvious—could have been overlooked for so long." The policy, by the way, might well allow for extra credits for homemakers serving handicapped children.

Endorsement of the idea also came from a middle-aged male who   21
described himself as a "well traveled parent who longs for more time
in the home."

A public affairs director in a Federal agency offered a reflective   22
comment which touches upon the crucial question of who will
guide the formation of values in one's children:

> As a career woman who has been on both sides of the fence (I stayed
> home until the children were 10 and 14 and then joined the work
> force 10 years ago), I think your plan has merit. It seems to me that I
> have been extremely lucky—I was able to start a career later in life
> because of extremely hard work and fortunate circumstances. Not
> everyone is so positioned. I would not have wanted someone else
> "raising" my children and giving them different views on morality
> and philosophy from my own. Each parent wants to pass on his
> basic beliefs to his children, and it is impossible for young women
> today to do that if they see their child for one or two hectic hours a
> day.

R. Sargent Shriver, Democratic candidate for Vice President in   23
1972, called my attention to a speech he gave on "The Family"
during that campaign. He repeated the maxim: What is good for
families is good for nations; what hurts families, hurts nations. He
further remarked that "the institution that has served human beings
best and disappointed them least is the family."

A retired obstetrician, himself a father of eight, found the pro-   24
posal to be "on target." In his medical practice, he said, he "was
always well aware of the importance of a mother or parent in a home
at all times with growing children; there can be no substitute."

Recently, I talked with a 36-year-old man whose educational   25
credentials include a doctorate and a law degree. He has worked as a
college professor, as well as a lawyer. His *curriculum vitae* notes his
full-time service as a "homemaker" for the past three years. His
wife, also a lawyer, has been in the labor market while he cares for
two young children at home. Another child was expected soon. With
the birth of their third child, the lawyer-mother planned to remain
at home as the professor-lawyer-father returned to paid employment
in the market economy. This is easy enough for well-educated professionals, but it only happens when parents regard it as important that
their children have the full-time attention of one or the other
throughout childhood.

Less well-educated parents are no less concerned about child   26
development, just less able, for economic reasons, to consider full-
time homemaking as a real option. If the option were available, it

would be just that—an option, not an enforced condition. People would be free to take it or leave it, as their values and preferences direct.

We have no such option in the U.S. today because of the presence 27
of economic pressure and the absence of a national family policy. The social credit idea addresses a policy vacuum. It surely deserves some discussion and debate.

Needed: A Policy for Children When Parents Go to Work

MAXINE PHILLIPS

Opponents of day care still call for women to return to home and 1
hearth, but the battle is really over. Now the question is: Will day care continue to be inadequately funded and poorly regulated, or will public policy begin to put into place a system that rightly treats children as our most valuable national resource?

More than 50% of the mothers of young children are in the work 2
force before their child's first birthday. An estimated 9.5 million pre-schoolers have mothers who work outside the home. Most women, like most men, are working to put food on the table. Many are the sole support of their families. They are economically unable to stay at home, although many would prefer to do so.

Decent child care is now an issue that cuts across political and 3
class lines. But this reality has not yet caught up with public policy. Conservative Sen. Orrin G. Hatch (R-Utah) is sponsoring a bill that would authorize $325 million in child-care costs for poor children. Liberal Sen. Christopher J. Dodd (D-Conn.) has just introduced a $2.5 billion bill for better child care, a far-reaching piece of legislation backed by 20 other senators and more than 100 members of the House. The Dodd measure would be a big improvement over current legislation, carrying provisions for information and referral, for standards and for monitoring that would have an impact on all children. But because eligible families could not earn more than 115% of a state's median income, the greatest impact would be on children of the working poor.

As long as public policy treats day care as a service for the poor, 4
it will be vulnerable to . . . [having its] funds [cut] . . . .

Thus at one end of the spectrum we have far too few publicly 5
funded day-care slots limited to poverty-level families. At the other

are high-quality nonprofit centers available to the well-to-do. For the vast majority, in what *Business Week* calls the "the day-care crisis of the middle-class," there is a crazy quilt of arrangements with neighbors, relatives and poorly staffed centers.

A barrage of negative day-care information assaults the working   6
mother, claiming that her children will not bond properly with her, will suffer emotionally and intellectually and will be exposed to deadly diseases.

True, many women rightly feel uncomfortable about leaving chil-   7
dren in many situations available. Day-care workers' salaries are in the lowest 10%. Shoddy licensing statutes often allow one person to care for as many as six or eight infants. Unlicensed centers abound because working parents cannot pay the fees for the better ones. About 500,000 children are in scandalously unfit profit-making centers, which spend 45% less per child than federally funded nonprofit centers.

The average day-care cost is $60 per week—often as much as   8
30% of a working mother's salary. Quality day care costs about three times as much in urban situations, clearly beyond the reach of most families.

My family was among the lucky ones. When our daughter was 9   9
months old we enrolled her in a wonderful place where she has consistent, well-trained, loving caretakers, play equipment we could never afford at home and the intellectual stimulation that comes from being with other children overseen by concerned adults. Two years later, her verbal ability and social skills confirm the choice we made. I sometimes worry that her days at home are not as rich as her days at the center.

Yet this kind of care, considered a societal responsibility in such   10
countries as France or Sweden, is available here only to the lucky or the privileged few.

Today, when most Americans will need child care at some time   11
in their lives, day care should be a service universally available regardless of income. Then, as with public schools, parents can choose whether or not to use it.

This is what a national child-care policy would look like: 12

It would start with a family-leave law. If we seriously believe,   13
as do most parents and other experts, that children should be with their parents in the early months when bonding is so important, why does society make it economically impossible? Unlike Canada, Italy, Sweden and many other nations, the United States has no national system of parental leave. Many women must return to work within a week or two of giving birth or risk losing their jobs.

Yet a proposal in Congress this year to allow 16 weeks of unpaid parental leave met such resistance from the business community that it is almost dead.

Second, good policy would include neighborhood nonprofit day-   14
care facilities open to everyone. These places would have parents involved, on the board and in the center. They would accommodate a variety of work schedules, with extra staff available for deployment to the homes of sick children whose parents could not make other arrangements.

Initial costs would be high (conservative estimates start at $30   15
billion) but must be measured against the lost tax revenues from people who would work—or work more productively—if reliable day care were available, not to mention the societal costs of children poorly cared for early in life.

Third, it would include after-school care for older children.   16
Latch-key youngsters are a concern for all working parents; their lack of supervision poses a danger to them and to society.

These are the building blocks of a national system but the foun-   17
dation must be a true commitment to the family unit.

This means prenatal care, nutrition, health care for both adults   18
and children, decent welfare benefits to allow parents to feed, shelter and clothe their children—plus assurances that both mothers and fathers can find work at wages that allow them to live decent family lives. These programs are expensive but no more so than programs already in place to pick up the wreckage caused by their absence. As long as America approaches child care in piecemeal fashion—as part of a welfare package or as a service only for children at poverty levels—we perpetuate the belief that this is an individual problem. We no longer believe that about education. In the current reality, why do we continue to believe it about child care?

Are these proposals utopian? No. Large parts are in place in   19
every Western industrial society but our own.

We look most frequently to the public schools and Social Security   20
as examples of entitlement accepted by the general society but I find added inspiration from a courageous group of parents who have already led the way in sensitizing the nation's conscience. Parents of developmentally disabled children, faced with a lifetime of caring for their youngsters and fears of what will happen after the parents die, organized to campaign for special funds and services. The results— including mandated education for all handicapped children—are far from perfect but demonstrate how parents can help society accept responsibility for some children. Now parents must help society accept responsibility for all of them.

Mother Love

NANCY FRIDAY

We are raised to believe that mother love is different from other   1
kinds of love. It is not open to error, doubt, or the ambivalence of
ordinary affections. This is an illusion.

Mothers may love their children, but they sometimes do not like   2
them. The same woman who may be willing to put her body between her child and a runaway truck will often resent the day-by-
day sacrifice the child unknowingly demands of her time, sexuality,
and self-development.

A woman without a daughter may try to explore life's infinite   3
possibilities. Her own mother left out so much. But when a daughter
is born, fears she thought she had conquered long ago are re-aroused.
Now there is another person, not simply dependent on her, but *like*
her. The mother's progress into a larger sexuality is halted. Ground
gained that she could have held alone is abandoned. She retreats and
entrenches herself in the cramped female stance of security and
defense. The position is fondly hailed as mother protector. It is the
position of fear. She may be only half alive but she is safe, and so is
her daughter. She now defines herself not as a woman but primarily
as a mother. Sex is left out, hidden from the girl who must never
think of her mother in danger: in sex. It is only with the greatest
effort that the girl will be able to think of herself that way.

When women's lives were more predictable, we could more eas-   4
ily afford this enigmatic picture of womanhood. When we had no
alternative but to repeat our mother's life, our mistakes and disap-
pointments were pretty much confined to her space, her margin of
error and unhappiness. I do believe our grandmothers, even our
mothers, were happier; not knowing as much as we do and not
having our options, there was less to be unhappy about. A woman
might give up her sexuality, hate being a housewife, not like children, but if every woman was doing it, how could she articulate her
frustration? She could feel it certainly, but you can't want what you
don't know about. Television, for instance, gave them no sense of
thwarted expectations. Today women's lives are changing at a rate
and by a necessity we couldn't control if we wanted to; we need all
the energy that suppression consumes. If we are going to fill more
than women's traditional role, we can't afford the exhaustion that
goes with constant emotional denial. There are pressures on women
other than the "maternal instinct." They are the new economic and
social demands. Even if we decide to lead our mothers' lives, the fact

is that our daughter may not. We may continue, through denial and repression, to keep alive the idealization of motherhood for another generation, but where will that leave her?

If women are going to be lawyers as well as mothers, they must differentiate between the two, and then differentiate once again about their sexuality. That is the third—and *not* mutually exclusive—option. As the world changes, and women's place in it, mothers must consciously present this choice to their daughters. A woman may incorporate all three choices within herself—and even more—but at any given moment she must be able to say to herself and her daughter, "I chose to have you because I wanted to be a mother. I chose to work—to have a career, to be in politics, to play the piano—because that gives me a different feeling of value about myself, a value that is not greater nor lesser than motherhood, only different. Whether you choose to work or not, to be a mother or not, it will have nothing to do with your sexuality. Sexuality is the third option—as meaningful as either of the other two."

The truth is that the woman and the mother are often at war with one another—in the same body. Like so many women since the world began, my mother could not believe in this opposition of the two desires. Tradition, society, her parents, religion itself told her that there was no conflict; that motherhood was the logical and natural end product of sex. Instead of believing what every woman's body tells every woman's mind, that sexuality and eroticism are a fundamentally different and opposite drive to motherhood, my mother accepted the lie. She took as her act of faith the proposition that if she were a real woman, she would be a good mother and I would grow up the same. If I repeated her path and pattern of motherhood, it would justify and place the final stamp of value on what she had done. It would say her attitude, behavior, and deepest feelings were not split, but were in fact in harmony, a woman in unison with nature.

Some women do make this choice gladly. They may be the majority, but my mother was not one of them. As I am not—her daughter in this too. Even in a good marriage, many women resent the matronly, nonsexual role their children force them to play. My mother didn't even have a good marriage; she was a young widow.

Frightened as she was, as much in need of my father as my sister and I were of her, mother had no choice but to pretend that my sister and I were the most important part of her life; that neither fear, youth and inexperience, loss, loneliness or her own needs could shake the unqualified and invincible love she felt for us. My mother had no body of woman-to-woman honesty and shared experience to use in her fight against the folk wisdom that said just being a woman carried all the inherent wisdom needed to be a mother—that it was either "natural" to her, or she was a failure as a woman.

In all the years we lived together, it is a shame we never talked 9 honestly about our feelings. What neither of us knew then was that I could have stood honesty, no matter how frightening. Her angers, disillusionments, fears of failure, rage—emotions I seldom saw—I could have come to terms with them if she had been able to speak to me. I would have grown used to the idea that while mother loved me, at times other emotions impaired that love, and developed trust that in time her love for me would always return. Instead, I was left trying to believe in some perfect love she said she had for me, but in which I could not believe. I did not understand why I couldn't feel it no matter what her words said. I grew to believe that love itself, from her or anybody else, was a will-o'-the-wisp, coming or going for reasons I could not control. Never knowing when or why I was loved, I grew afraid to depend on it.

The older I get, the more of my mother I see in myself. The more 10 opposite my life and my thinking grow from hers, the more of her I hear in my voice, see in my facial expression, feel in the emotional reactions I have come to recognize as my own. It is almost as if in extending myself, the circle closes in to completion. She was my first and most lasting model. To say her image is not still a touchstone in my life—and mine in hers—would be another lie. I am tired of lies. They have stood in the way of my understanding myself all my life. I have always known that what my husband loves most in me is that I have my own life. I have always felt that I had partially deceived him in this; I am very clever at pretense. My work, my marriage, and my new relationships with other women are beginning to make his assumptions about me true—that I am an independent, separate individual. They have allowed me to respect myself, and admire my own sex. What still stands between me and the person I would like to be is this illusion of perfect love between my mother and me. It is a lie I can no longer afford.

The Androgynous Man

NOEL PERRIN

The summer I was 16, I took a train from New York to Steam- 1 boat Springs, Colo., where I was going to be assistant horse wrangler at a camp. The trip took three days, and since I was much too shy to talk to strangers, I had quite a lot of time for reading. I read all of

Gone With the Wind. I read all of the interesting articles in a couple of magazines I had, and then I went back and read all the dull stuff. I also took all the quizzes, a thing of which magazines were even fuller then than now.

The one that held my undivided attention was called "How Masculine/Feminine Are You?" It consisted of a large number of inkblots. The reader was supposed to decide which of four objects each blot most resembled. The choices might be a cloud, a steam-engine, a caterpillar, and a sofa. 2

When I finished the test, I was shocked to find that I was barely masculine at all. On a scale of 1 to 10, I was about 1.2. Me, the horse wrangler? (And not just wrangler, either. That summer, I had to skin a couple of horses that died—the camp owner wanted the hides.) 3

The results of that test were so terrifying to me that for the first time in my life I did a piece of original analysis. Having unlimited time on the train, I looked at the "masculine" answers over and over, trying to find what it was that distinguished real men from people like me—and eventually I discovered two very simple patterns. It was "masculine" to think the blots looked like man-made objects, and "feminine" to think they looked like natural objects. It was masculine to think they looked like things capable of causing harm, and feminine to think of innocent things. 4

Even at 16, I had the sense to see that the compilers of the test were using rather limited criteria—maleness and femaleness are both more complicated than that—and I breathed a huge sigh of relief. I wasn't necessarily a wimp, after all. 5

That the test did reveal something other than the superficiality of its makers I realized only many years later. What it revealed was that there is a large class of men and women both, to which I belong, who are essentially androgynous. That doesn't mean we're gay, or low in the appropriate hormones, or uncomfortable performing the jobs traditionally assigned our sexes. (A few years after that summer, I was leading troops in combat and, unfashionable as it now is to admit this, having a very good time. War is exciting. What a pity the 20th century went and spoiled it with high-tech weapons.) 6

What it does mean to be spiritually androgynous is a kind of freedom. Men who are all-male, or he-man, or 100% red-blooded Americans, have a little biological set that causes them to be attracted to physical power, and probably also to dominance. Maybe even to watching football. I don't say this to criticize them. Completely masculine men are quite often wonderful people: good husbands, good (though sometimes overwhelming) fathers, good members of society. Furthermore, they are often so unself-consciously at ease in the world that other men seek to imitate them. They just 7 aren't as free as androgynes. They pretty nearly have to be what they are; we have a range of choices open.

The sad part is that many of us never discover that. Men who are   8
not 100% red-blooded Americans—say those who are only 75% red-blooded—often fail to notice their freedom. They are too busy trying to copy the he-men ever to realize that men, like women, come in a wide variety of acceptable types. Why this frantic imitation? My answer is mere speculation, but not casual. I have speculated on this for a long time.

Partly they're just envious of the he-man's unconscious ease.   9
Mostly they're terrified of finding that there may be something wrong with them deep down, some weakness at the heart. To avoid discovering that, they spend their lives acting out the role that the he-man naturally lives. Sad.

One thing that men owe to the women's movement is that this   10
kind of failure is less common than it used to be. In releasing themselves from the single ideal of the dependent woman, women have more or less incidentally released a lot of men from the single ideal of the dominant male. The one mistake the feminists have made, I think, is in supposing that all men need this release, or that the world would be a better place if all men achieved it. It wouldn't. It would just be duller.

So far I have been pretty vague about just what the freedom of   11
the androgynous man is. Obviously it varies with the case. In the case I know best, my own, I can be quite specific. It has freed me most as a parent. I am, among other things, a fairly good natural mother. I like the nurturing role. It makes me feel good to see a child eat—and it turns me to mush to see a 4-year-old holding a glass with both small hands, in order to drink. I even enjoyed sewing patches on the knees of my daughter Amy's Dr. Dentons when she was at the crawling stage. All that pleasure I would have lost if I had made myself stick to the notion of the paternal role that I started with.

Or take a smaller and rather ridiculous example. I feel free to   12
kiss cats. Until recently it never occurred to me that I would want to, though my daughters have been doing it all their lives. But my elder daughter is now 22, and in London. Of course, I get to look after her cat while she is gone. He's a big, handsome farm cat named Petrushka, very unsentimental, though used from kittenhood to being kissed on the top of the head by Elizabeth. I've gotten very fond of him (he's the adventurous kind of cat who likes to climb hills with you), and one night I simply felt like kissing him on the top of the head, and did. Why did no one tell me sooner how silky cat fur is?

Then there's my relation to cars. I am completely unembar-   13 rassed by my inability to diagnose even minor problems in whatever object I happen to be driving, and don't have to make some insider's remark to mechanics to try to establish that I, too, am a "Man With His Machine."

The same ease extends to household maintenance. I do it, of 14 course. Service people are expensive. But for the last decade my house has functioned better than it used to because I have had the aid of a volume called "Home Repairs Any Woman Can Do," which is pitched just right for people at my technical level. As a youth, I'd as soon have touched such a book as I would have become a transvestite. Even though common sense says there is really nothing sexual whatsoever about fixing sinks.

Or take public emotion. All my life I have easily been moved by 15 certain kinds of voices. The actress Siobhan McKenna's, to take a notable case. Give her an emotional scene in a play, and within ten words my eyes are full of tears. In boyhood, my great dread was that someone might notice. I struggled manfully, you might say, to suppress this weakness. Now, of course, I don't see it as a weakness at all, but a kind of fulfillment. I even suspect that the true he-men feel the same way, or one kind of them does, at least, and it's only the poor imitators who have to struggle to repress themselves.

Let me come back to the inkblots, with their assumption that 16 masculine equates with machinery and science, and feminine with art and nature. I have no idea whether the right pronoun for God is He, She, or It. But this I'm pretty sure of. If God could somehow be induced to take that test, God would not come out macho and not feminismo, either, but right in the middle. Fellow androgynes, it's a nice thought.

Motherhood: Who Needs It?

BETTY ROLLIN

Motherhood is in trouble, and it ought to be. A rude question is 1 long overdue: Who needs it? The answer used to be (1) society and (2) women. But now, with the impending horrors of overpopulation, society desperately *doesn't* need it. And women don't need it either. Thanks to the Motherhood Myth—the idea that having babies is something that all normal women instinctively want and need and will enjoy doing—they just *think* they do.

The notion that the maternal wish and the activity of mother- 2 ing are instinctive or biologically predestined is baloney. Try asking most sociologists, psychologists, psychoanalysts, biologists—many of whom are mothers—about motherhood being instinctive: it's like asking department store presidents if their Santa Clauses are real. "Motherhood—instinctive?" shouts distinguished sociologist/author Dr. Jessie Bernard. "Biological destiny? Forget biology! If it were biology, people would die from not doing it."

"Women don't need to be mothers any more than they need spaghetti," says Dr. Richard Rabkin, a New York psychiatrist. "But if you're in a world where everyone is eating spaghetti, thinking they need it and want it, you will think so too. Romance has really contaminated science. So-called instincts have to do with stimulation. They are not things that well up inside of you."

"When a woman says with feeling that she craved her baby from within, she is putting into biological language what is psychological," says University of Michigan psychoanalyst and motherhood-researcher Dr. Frederick Wyatt. "There are no instincts," says Dr. William Goode, president-elect of the American Sociological Association. "There are reflexes, like eye-blinking, and drives, like sex. There is no innate drive for children. Otherwise, the enormous cultural pressures that there are to reproduce wouldn't exist. There are no cultural pressures to sell you on getting your hand out of the fire."

There are, to be sure, biologists and others who go on about biological destiny, that is, the innate or instinctive goal of motherhood. (At the turn of the century, even good old capitalism was explained by a theorist as "the *instinct* of acquisitiveness.") And many psychoanalysts will hold the Freudian view that women feel so rotten about not having a penis that they are necessarily propelled into the child-wish to replace the missing organ. Psychoanalysts also make much of the psychological need to repeat what one's parent of the same sex has done. Since every woman has a mother, it is considered normal to wish to imitate one's mother by being a mother.

There is, surely, a wish to pass on love if one has received it, but to insist women must pass it on in the same way is like insisting that every man whose father is a gardener has to be a gardener. One dissenting psychoanalyst says, simply, "There is a wish to comply with one's biology, yes, but we needn't and sometimes we shouldn't." (Interestingly, the woman who has been the greatest contributor to child therapy and who has probably given more to children than anyone alive is Dr. Anna Freud, Freud's magnificent daughter, who is not a mother.)

Anyway, what an expert cast of hundreds is telling us is, simply, that biological *possibility* and desire are not the same as biological *need*. Women have childbearing equipment. To choose not to use the equipment is no more blocking what is instinctive than it is for a man who, muscles or no, chooses not to be a weight lifter.

So much for the wish. What about the "instinctive" *activity* of mothering? One animal study shows that when a young member of a species is put in a cage, say, with an older member of the same species, the latter will act in a protective, "maternal" way. But that goes for both males and females who have been "mothered" themselves. And studies indicate that a human baby will also respond to whoever is around playing mother—even if it's father. Margaret Mead and many others frequently point out that mothering can be a fine occupation, if you want it, for either sex. Another experiment with monkeys who were brought up without mothers found them lacking in maternal behavior toward their own offspring. A similar study showed that monkeys brought up without other monkeys of the opposite sex had no interest in mating—all of which suggests that both mothering and mating behavior are learned, not instinctual. And, to turn the cart (or the baby carriage) around, baby ducks who lovingly follow their mothers seemed, in the mother's absence, to just as lovingly follow wooden ducks or even vacuum cleaners.

If motherhood isn't instinctive, when and why, then, was the Motherhood Myth born? Until recently, the entire question of maternal motivation was academic. Sex, like it or not, meant babies. Not that there haven't always been a lot of interesting contraceptive tries. But until the creation of the diaphragm in the 1880's, the birth of babies was largely unavoidable. And, generally speaking, nobody really seemed to mind. For one thing, people tend to be sort of good sports about what seems to be inevitable. For another, in the past, the population needed beefing up. Mortality rates were high, and agricultural cultures, particularly, have always needed children to help out. So because it "just happened" and because it was needed, motherhood was assumed to be innate.

Originally, it was the word of God that got the ball rolling with "Be fruitful and multiply," a practical suggestion, since the only people around then were Adam and Eve. But in no time, supermoralists like St. Augustine changed the tone of the message: "Intercourse, even with one's legitimate wife, is unlawful and wicked where the conception of the offspring is prevented," he, we assume, thundered. And the Roman Catholic position was thus cemented. So then and now, procreation took on a curious value among people who viewed (and view) the pleasures of sex as sinful. One could partake in the sinful pleasure, but feel vindicated by the ensuing birth. Motherhood cleaned up sex. Also, it cleaned up women, who have always been considered somewhat evil, because of Eve's transgression (". . . but the woman was deceived and became a transgressor. Yet woman will be saved through bearing children . . .," I Timothy, 2:14–15), and somewhat dirty because of menstruation.

And so, based on need, inevitability, and pragmatic fantasy—the   11
Myth *worked*, from society's point of view—the Myth grew like corn in Kansas. And society reinforced it with both laws and propaganda—laws that made woman a chattel, denied her education and personal mobility, and madonna propaganda that she was beautiful and wonderful doing it and it was all beautiful and wonderful to do. (One rarely sees a madonna washing dishes.)

In fact, the Myth persisted—breaking some kind of record for   12
long-lasting fallacies—until something like yesterday. For as the truth about the Myth trickled in—as women's rights increased, as women gradually got the message that it was certainly possible for them to do most things that men did, that they live longer, that their brains were not tinier—then, finally, when the really big news rolled in, that they could choose whether or not to be mothers—what happened? The Motherhood Myth soared higher than ever. As Betty Friedan made oh-so-clear in *The Feminine Mystique*, the '40's and '50's produced a group of ladies who not only had babies as if they were going out of style (maybe they were) but, as never before, they turned motherhood into a cult. First, they wallowed in the aesthetics of it all—natural childbirth and nursing became maternal musts. Like heavy-bellied ostriches, they grounded their heads in the sands of motherhood, only coming up for air to say how utterly happy and fulfilled they were. But, as Mrs. Friedan says only too plainly, they weren't. The Myth galloped on, moreover, long after making babies had turned from practical asset to liability for both individual parents and society. With the average cost of a middle-class child figured conservatively at $30,000 (not including college), any parent knows that the only people who benefit economically from children are manufacturers of consumer goods. Hence all those gooey motherhood commercials. And the Myth gathered momentum long after sheer numbers, while not yet extinguishing us, have made us intensely uncomfortable. Almost all of our societal problems, from minor discomforts like traffic to major ones like hunger, the population people keep reminding us, have to do with there being too many people. And who suffers most? The kids who have been so mindlessly brought into the world, that's who. They are the ones who have to cope with all of the difficult and dehumanizing conditions brought on by overpopulation. They are the ones who have to cope with the psychological nausea of feeling unneeded by society. That's not the only reason for drugs, but, surely, it's a leading contender.

Unfortunately, the population curbers are tripped up by a roman-   13
tic, stubborn, ideological hurdle. How can birth-control programs

really be effective as long as the concept of glorious motherhood remains unchanged? (Even poor old Planned Parenthood has to euphemize—why not Planned Unparenthood?) Particularly among the poor, motherhood is one of the few inherently positive institutions that are accessible. As Berkeley demographer Judith Blake points out, "Poverty-oriented birth control programs do not make sense as a welfare measure . . . as long as existing pronatalist policies . . . encourage mating, pregnancy, and the care, support, and rearing of children." Or, she might have added, as long as the less-than-idyllic child-rearing part of motherhood remains "in small print."

Sure, motherhood gets dumped on sometimes: Philip Wylie's   14
Momism got going in the '40's and Philip Roth's *Portnoy's Complaint* did its best to turn rancid the chicken-soup concept of Jewish motherhood. But these are viewed as the sour cries of a black humorist here, a malcontent there. Everyone shudders, laughs, but it's like the mouse and the elephant joke. Still, the Myth persists. Last April, a Brooklyn woman was indicted on charges of manslaughter and negligent homicide—eleven children died in a fire in a building she owned and criminally neglected—"But," sputtered her lawyer, "my client, Mrs. Breslow, is a mother, a grandmother, and a great-grandmother!"

Most remarkably, the Motherhood Myth persists in the face of   15
the most overwhelming maternal unhappiness and incompetence. If reproduction were merely superfluous and expensive, if the experience were as rich and rewarding as the cliché would have us believe, if it were a predominantly joyous trip for everyone riding—mother, father, child—then the going everybody-should-have-two-children plan would suffice. Certainly, there are a lot of joyous mothers, and their children and (sometimes, not necessarily) their husbands reflect their joy. But a lot of evidence suggests that for more women than anyone wants to admit, motherhood can be miserable. ("If it weren't," says one psychiatrist wryly, "the world wouldn't be in the mess it's in.")

There is a remarkable statistical finding from a recent study of Dr.   16
Bernard's, comparing the mental illness and unhappiness of married mothers and single women. The latter group, it turned out, was both markedly less sick and overtly more happy. Of course, it's not easy to measure slippery attitudes like happiness. "Many women have achieved a kind of reconciliation—a conformity," says Dr. Bernard,

> that they interpret as happiness. Since feminine happiness is supposed to lie in devoting one's life to one's husband and children, they do that; so *ipso facto*, they assume they are happy. And for many women, untrained for independence and "processed" for

motherhood, they find their state far preferable to the alternatives, which don't really exist.

Also, unhappy mothers are often loath to admit it. For one thing, if in society's view not to be a mother is to be a freak, not to be a *blissful* mother is to be a witch. Besides, unlike a disappointing marriage, disappointing motherhood cannot be terminated by divorce. Of course, none of that stops such a woman from expressing her dissatisfaction in a variety of ways. Again, it is not only she who suffers but her husband and children as well. Enter the harridan housewife, the carping shrew. The realities of motherhood can turn women into terrible people. And, judging from the 50,000 cases of child abuse in the U.S. each year, some are worse than terrible.

In some cases, the unpleasing realities of motherhood begin even   17
before the beginning. In *Her Infinite Variety*, Morton Hunt describes young married women pregnant for the first time as "very likely to be frightened and depressed, masking these feelings in order not to be considered contemptible. The arrival of pregnancy interrupts a pleasant dream of motherhood and awakens them to the realization that they have too little money, or not enough space, or unresolved marital problems. . . ."

The following are random quotes from interviews with some   18
mothers in Ann Arbor, Mich., who described themselves as reasonably happy. They all had positive things to say about their children, although when asked about the best moment of their day, they *all* confessed it was when the children were in bed. Here is the rest:

> Suddenly I had to devote myself to the child totally. I was under the illusion that the baby was going to fit into my life, and I found that I had to switch my life and my schedule to fit *him*. You think, "I'm in love, I'll get married, and we'll have a baby." First there's two, then three, it's simple and romantic. You don't even think about the work. . . .

> You never get away from the responsibility. Even when you leave the children with a sitter, you are not out from under the pressure of the responsibility. . . .

> I hate ironing their pants and doing their underwear, and they never put their clothes in the laundry basket. . . . As they get older, they make less demands on our time because they're in school, but the demands are greater in forming their values. . . . Best moment of the day is when all the children are in bed. . . . The worst time of the day is 4 P.M., when you have to get dinner started, the kids are tired, hungry and crabby—everybody wants to talk to you about *their* day . . . your day is only half over.

Once a mother, the responsibility and concern for my children became so encompassing. . . . It took me a great deal of will to keep up other parts of my personality. . . . To me, motherhood gets harder as they get older because you have less control. . . . In an abstract sense, I'd have several. . . . In the nonabstract, I would not have any. . . .

I had anticipated that the baby would sleep and eat, sleep and eat. Instead, the experience was overwhelming. I really had not thought particularly about what motherhood would mean in a realistic sense. I want to do *other* things, like to become involved in things that are worthwhile—I don't mean women's clubs—but I don't have the physical energy to go out in the evenings. I feel like I'm missing something . . . the experience of being somewhere with people and having them talking about something—something that's going on in the world.

Every grownup person expects to pay a price for his pleasures, but 19 seldom is the price as vast as the one endured "however happily" by most mothers. We have mentioned the literal cost factor. But what does that mean? For middle-class American women, it means a life style with severe and usually unimagined limitations; i.e., life in the suburbs, because who can afford three bedrooms in the city? And what do suburbs mean? For women, suburbs mean other women and children and leftover peanut-butter sandwiches and car pools and seldom-seen husbands. Even the Feminine Mystiqueniks—the housewives who finally admitted that their lives behind brooms (OK, electric brooms) were driving them crazy—were loath to trace their predicament to their children. But it is simply a fact that a childless married woman has no child-work and little housework. She can live in a city, or, if she still chooses the suburbs or the country, she can leave on the commuter train with her husband if she wants to. Even the most ardent job-seeking mother will find little in the way of great opportunities in Scarsdale. Besides, by the time she wakes up, she usually lacks both the preparation for the outside world and the self-confidence to get it. You will say there are plenty of city-dwelling working mothers. But most of those women do additional-funds-for-the-family kind of work, not the interesting career kind that takes plugging during childbearing years.

Nor is it a bed of petunias for the mother who does make it 20 professionally. Says writer-critic Marya Mannes:

If the creative woman has children, she must pay for this indulgence with a long burden of guilt, for her life will be split three ways between them and her husband and her work. . . . No woman with any heart can compose a paragraph when her child is in trouble. . . . The creative woman has no wife to protect her from intrusion. A man at his desk in a room with closed door is a man at work. A woman at a desk in any room is available.

Speaking of jobs, do remember that mothering, salary or not, is a   21
job. Even those who can afford nurses to handle the nitty-gritty still
need to put out emotionally. "Well-cared-for" neurotic rich kids are
not exactly unknown in our society. One of the more absurd aspects
of the Myth is the underlying assumption that, since most women
are biologically equipped to bear children, they are psychologically,
mentally, emotionally, and technically equipped (or interested) to
rear them. Never mind happiness. To assume that such an exacting,
consuming, and important task is something almost all women are
equipped to do is far more dangerous and ridiculous than assuming
that everyone with vocal chords should seek a career in the opera.

A major expectation of the Myth is that children make a not-so-   22
hot marriage hotter, or a hot marriage, hotter still. Yet almost every
available study indicates that childless marriages are far happier.
One of the biggest, of 850 couples, was conducted by Dr. Harold
Feldman of Cornell University, who states his finding in no uncertain terms: "Those couples with children had a significantly lower
level of marital satisfaction than did those without children." Some
of the reasons are obvious. Even the most adorable children make for
additional demands, complications, and hardships in the lives of
even the most loving parents. If a woman feels disappointed and
trapped in her mother role, it is bound to affect her marriage in any
number of ways: she may take out her frustrations directly on her
husband, or she may count on him too heavily for what she feels she
is missing in her daily life.

". . . You begin to grow away from your husband," says one of   23
the Michigan ladies. "He's working on his career and you're working
on your family. But you both must gear your lives to the children.
You do things the children enjoy, more than things you might enjoy." More subtle and possibly more serious is what motherhood
may do to a woman's sexuality. Often when the stork flies in, sexuality flies out. Both in the emotional minds of some women *and* in the
minds of their husbands, when a woman becomes a mother, she
stops being a woman. It's not only that motherhood may destroy her
physical attractiveness, but its madonna concept may destroy her
feelings of sexuality.

And what of the payoff? Usually, even the most self-sacrificing   24
of maternal self-sacrificers expects a little something back. Gratified
parents are not unknown to the Western world, but there are proba-

bly at least just as many who feel, to put it crudely, shortchanged. The experiment mentioned earlier—where the baby ducks followed vacuum cleaners instead of their mothers—indicates that what passes for love from baby to mother is merely a rudimentary kind of object attachment. Without necessarily feeling like a Hoover, a lot of women become disheartened because babies and children are not only not interesting to talk to (not everyone thrills at the wonders of da-da-ma-ma talk) but they are generally not empathetic, considerate people. Even the nicest children are not capable of empathy, surely a major ingredient of love, until they are much older. Sometimes they're never capable of it. Dr. Wyatt says that often, in later years particularly, when most of the "returns" are in, it is the "good mother" who suffers most of all. It is then she must face a reality: The child—the appendage with her genes—is not an appendage, but a separate person. What's more, he or she may be a separate person who doesn't even like her—or whom she doesn't really like.

So if the music is lousy, how come everyone's dancing? Because   25 the motherhood minuet is taught freely from birth, and whether or not she has rhythm or likes the music, every woman is expected to do it. Indeed, she *wants* to do it. Little girls start learning what to want—and what to be—when they are still in their cribs. Dr. Miriam Keiffer, a young social psychologist at Bensalem, the Experimental College of Fordham University, points to studies showing that

> at six months of age, mothers are already treating their baby girls and boys quite differently. For instance, mothers have been found to touch, comfort, and talk to their females more. If these differences can be found at such an early stage, it's not surprising that the end product is as different as it is. What is surprising is that men and women are, in so many ways, similar.

Some people point to the way little girls play with dolls as proof of their innate motherliness. But remember, little girls are *given* dolls. When Margaret Mead presented some dolls to New Guinea children, it was the boys, not the girls, who wanted to play with them, which they did by crooning lullabies and rocking them in the most maternal fashion.

By the time they reach adolescence, most girls, unconsciously or   26 not, have learned enough about role definition to qualify for a master's degree. In general, the lesson has been that no matter what kind of career thoughts one may entertain, one must, first and foremost, be a wife and mother. A girl's mother is usually her first teacher. As Dr. Goode says, "A woman is not only taught by society to have a child; she is taught to have a child who will have a child." A woman who has hung her life on the Motherhood Myth will almost always reinforce her young married daughter's early training by pushing for grandchildren. Prospective grandmothers are not the only ones. Husbands, too, can be effective sellers. After all, they have the Fatherhood Myth to cope with. A married man is *supposed* to have children. Often, particularly among Latins, children are a sign of potency. They help him assure the world—and himself—that he is the big man he is supposed to be. Plus, children give him both immortality (whatever that means) and possibly the chance to become more in his lifetime through the accomplishments of his children, particularly his son. (Sometimes it's important, however, for the son to do better, but not *too* much better.)

Friends, too, can be counted on as myth-pushers. Naturally one   27
wants to do what one's friends do. One study, by the way, found a correlation between a woman's fertility and that of her three closest friends. The negative sell comes into play here, too. We have seen what the concept of non-mother means (cold, selfish, unwomanly, abnormal). In practice, particularly in the suburbs, it can mean, simply, exclusion—both from child-centered activities (that is, most activities) and child-centered conversations (that is, most conversations). It can also mean being the butt of a lot of unfunny jokes. ("Whaddya waiting for? An immaculate conception? Ha ha.") Worst of all, it can mean being an object of pity.

In case she's escaped all those pressures (that is, if she was   28
brought up in a cave), a young married woman often wants a baby just so that she'll (1) have something to do (motherhood is better than clerk/typist, which is often the only kind of job she can get, since little more has been expected of her and, besides, her boss also expects her to leave and be a mother); (2) have something to hug and possess, to be needed by and have power over; and (3) have something to *be*—e.g., a baby's mother. Motherhood affords an instant identity. First, through wifehood, you are somebody's wife; then you are somebody's mother. Both give not only identity and activity, but status and stardom of a kind. During pregnancy, a woman can look forward to the kind of attention and pampering she may not ever have gotten or may never otherwise get. Some women consider birth the biggest accomplishment of their lives, which may be interpreted as saying not much for the rest of their lives. As Dr. Goode says, "It's like the gambler who may know the roulette wheel is crooked, but it's the only game in town." Also, with motherhood, the feeling of accomplishment is immediate. It is really much faster and easier to make a baby than paint a painting, or write a book, or get to the point of accomplishment in a job. It is also easier in a way to shift focus from self-development to child development—particularly since, for women, self-development is considered selfish. Even un-

wed mothers may achieve a feeling of this kind. (As we have seen, little thought is given to the aftermath.) And, again, since so many women are underdeveloped as people, they feel that, besides children, they have little else to give—to themselves, their husbands, to their world.

You may ask why then, when the realities do start pouring in, does a woman want to have a second, third, even fourth child? OK, (1) just because reality is pouring in doesn't mean she wants to *face* it. A new baby can help bring back some of the old illusions. Says psychoanalyst Dr. Natalie Shainess, "She may view each successive child as a knight in armor that will rescue her from being a 'bad unhappy mother.' " (2) Next on the horror list of having no children, is having one. It suffices to say that only children are not only OK, they even have a high rate of exceptionality. (3) Both parents usually want at least one child of each sex. The husband, for reasons discussed earlier, probably wants a son. (4) The more children one has, the more of an excuse one has not to develop in any other way.

What's the point? A world without children? Of course not. Nothing could be worse or more unlikely. No matter what anyone says in *Look* or anywhere else, motherhood isn't about to go out like a blown bulb, and who says it should? Only the Myth must go out, and now it seems to be dimming.

The younger-generation females who have been reared on the Myth have not rejected it totally, but at least they recognize it can be more loving to children not to have them. And at least they speak of adopting children instead of bearing them. Moreover, since the new nonbreeders are "less hung-up" on ownership, they seem to recognize that if you dig loving children, you don't necessarily have to own one. The end of the Motherhood Myth might make available more loving women (and men!) for those children who already exist.

When motherhood is no longer culturally compulsory, there will, certainly, be less of it. Women are now beginning to think and do more about development of self, of their individual resources. Far from being selfish, such development is probably our only hope. That means more alternatives for women. And more alternatives means more selective, better, happier, motherhood—and childhood and husbandhood (or manhood) and peoplehood. It is not a question of whether or not children are sweet and marvelous to have and rear; the question is, even if that's so, whether or not one wants to pay the price for it. It doesn't make sense any more to pretend that women need babies, when what they really need is themselves. If God were still speaking to us in a voice we could hear, even He would probably say, "Be fruitful. Don't multiply."

QUESTIONS OF CONTENT

1. What incentive does Byron's proposal offer a parent who engages in homemaking? Who will pay for this plan?
2. What precaution does Byron offer that will ensure the equitability of the plan?
3. What is Phillips' strongest objection to government support for child care as it now stands?
4. Phillips likens her child care proposal to what other two entitlement programs sponsored by the government?
5. Friday believes something has happened in women's lives, making not just mother love but other aspects of women's lives more complicated; what has changed, and how have women's lives changed as a result?
6. Women, according to Friday, have three options. What are they, and how are they related to the modern problem of mother love?
7. What is androgyny? According to Perrin, what benefits does it confer on those who realize that they have it? Are those who never realize it any the worse for their failure?
8. What is ironic (in unexpected contrast) about Perrin's relationship with cats, cars, home repairs, and public emotion?
9. Does Rollin think that motherhood is instinctive? Why? Why not?
10. What alternative to motherhood does Rollin offer?

QUESTIONS OF FORM

1. Byron's essay is a claim of policy. Locate the two typical components of such claims: that is, the claim of fact and then the suggested policy. Now do the same for the Phillips essay. What similarities and/or differences do you see in the approaches of these two authors?
2. What kind of claim does Friday make in her essay? How does she support her claim? How could she have made the support more objective?
3. State Perrin's thesis about androgyny in terms of a claim of policy. Then, state it in terms of a claim of value. Which seems to you the more accurate description of what Perrin is doing?
4. Rollin asserts that, as a rule, childless marriages prove to be happier than those with children. What evidence does she produce in support of her claim?
5. To argue against motherhood is a very difficult thing to do because of the prevailing warrant that favors the institution of motherhood. How does Rollin attempt to overcome this handicap?
6. All of the essays in this section have emotional appeals; which ones seem to depend most heavily on such appeals? What sorts of material fallacies, if any, do you notice in those more emotion-based essays?

SUGGESTIONS FOR WRITING

1. After you have carefully reread the Byron and Phillips articles, try to decide which scenario you prefer for your future. How do you want the government to dedicate your tax dollars: on incentives to keep child care in the home or on improved child care outside the home? Weigh the alternatives carefully and then compose a letter to your congressman urging support for your proposal.

2. You are a young woman, engaged to be married. Your parents are quite pleased with your spousal choice and have more than once expressed that satisfaction to you. They have also confided to you their eagerness to become grandparents. However, you and your fiance have discussed having children and have decided to wait. You wish to pursue a career, and depending on the rewards that could very well materialize, you may even decide to opt against motherhood. Explain your feelings to your parents in a letter. Use as many of the insights from this series of essays as you wish, but refer specifically to each source that you use, following the suggestions in Chapter 6's section entitled "Using Sources." Remember, though, it's still a letter, so stop short of using formal citations.

3. You are a young husband and father who has stayed at home for the past three years to care for your infant daughter while your wife has pursued a career in advertising for the television industry. She is now pregnant with your second child and after some negotiating has reached an agreement with her employer that will allow her to remain at home to care for the children after the second child is born, while continuing to do research and produce advertising copy on a part-time basis.

   You wish to return to the business scene as a marketing analyst, a profession you had followed for three years after graduation from college until an untimely transfer and your wife's pregnancy caused you to resign and assume your homemaking role. You are preparing your job resumé and feel obliged to explain your three-year lapse in employment. What do you say in your letter to your prospective employer? Write that letter and justify your past three years, presenting that experience as an asset, rather than a drawback. After all, you enjoyed the experience, and you may even choose, at some future time, to return to it. Mention such sources as you see fit, but give them appropriate credit when you do.

4. Examine the following brief bibliography. The articles contained in it may prove useful to you in preparing your responses to suggestions 2 and 3, since they furnish several additional dimensions of the issue of changing sex roles not addressed in the articles included in this section. To acquire some practice in working with documentation, write a paper in which you present a consistent picture of shifting sex roles, drawing material from at least three articles. Your instructor may want you to use one or more of the articles printed in this section, with the others coming from the following list, or from

your own library research, as she or he directs. Use the citation methods described in "Citing Your Sources" in Chapter 6.

Additional References

DeGregoria, Barbara. "Women Must Challenge the Limits and Expand Options in Sex Role Development." *Education* 109 (Winter 1988): 160–64.

Friedan, Betty. "Where Do We Go From Here? Next Step for Today's Working Women—and Men." *Working Woman* Nov. 1986: 153–55.

Jackson, Linda A., *et al.* "Gender, Gender Role, and Physical Appearance." *The Journal of Psychology* 121 (1987): 51–56.

"The Short Life of the Androgynous Person." *Christianity Today* 2 October 1987: 35.

Walker, Alexis J., and Linda Thompson. "Gender in Families: Women and Men in Marriage, Work, and Parenthood." *Journal of Marriage and the Family* 51 (1989): 845–71.

WHO SHOULD CONTROL THE RIGHT TO DIE?

Euthanasia Is Sometimes Justified

LOWELL O. ERDAHL

Doctors, families, and patients themselves now face many 1
choices that were not available to previous generations. The use of
"artificial" life-support systems inevitably leads to situations that
require choices concerning the rightness or wrongness of "pulling
the plug" and raises as never before the issue of mercy killing or
euthanasia, which literally means "good death."

These changes, however, did not create the problem. . . . The 2
possibility of deliberately ending the life of a suffering person has
always been present. We note that in at least two ways medical
advances make consideration of mercy killing less pressing than in
times past. One is that many formerly devastating illnesses and
conditions of distressing disability can now be cured, corrected, or
managed so that meaningful life is now possible. The other is that
painkilling drugs eliminate much of the intense suffering formerly
experienced by millions. The prospect of such suffering moved Ma-
hatma Gandhi, who lived with great reverence for life and opposition to violence, to contemplate the possibility of being required by
love and sacred duty to take the life of his own child as the only
means of relieving the anguish of incurable rabies. We thank God
that the comforts of modern medicine now offer alternatives for the
relief of such suffering.

Difficult Cases

On the other hand, the ability to maintain biological functions 3
that would have otherwise ceased has brought the question of euthanasia into sharper focus. The difficult cases are not those in which
brain death has already occurred. When the brain is dead, the person
has died. There is, therefore, no justification for maintaining the
biological functions, except temporarily in order to preserve organs
for transplant. The agonizing cases are those in which the person

remains alive but with little, if any, prospect of healing and meaningful life.

The pro-life perspective—which grants that there are tragic exceptional circumstances when the taking of life is justifiable, but which opposes all forms of institutionalized and established killing—also applies to mercy killing. That is, passive or even active euthanasia may sometimes be justifiable in a specific situation, but it is wrong when institutionalized in accepted practice, as, for example, under Hitler in the Nazi era. . . .

Although passive euthanasia is widely accepted, there are strong emotional and legal barriers to active euthanasia. Doctors are permitted to refrain from treatments that would prolong their patients' lives, but are not allowed to administer drugs to kill them. Is such a distinction between passive and active euthanasia always morally justifiable? Are there circumstances in which it is right to practice active euthanasia?

Although it is tempting to take an absolute stand against active euthanasia, the recognition of tragic, exceptional circumstances makes it impossible for me to do so. Just as there are situations in which it may be justifiable to kill the unborn, the enemy warrior, or the criminal intent on murder, there may be also circumstances in which active euthanasia is more compassionate than passive. Is it, for example, more kind to cause death by dehydration and starvation than it is to kill the patient by lethal injection? In both cases the motive and effect are exactly the same; only the method is different. Is it possible that in some cases the sin of omission (permitting death by dehydration and starvation) may be greater than the sin of commission (causing death by lethal injection)?

Emotionally it is obviously much easier for the family and doctor to permit the patient to die than to deliberately kill the patient. But is there a similar logical and moral difference? Raising such a question reminds us of the extent to which emotion, rather than logical or moral considerations, often prevails in life and death decisions. Many people, for example, are appalled at the thought of deliberately killing their 95-year-old grandmother who has been in a coma for months and for whom there is no prospect of meaningful life; but at the same time they are advocates of abortion on demand. Is it not, however, more moral to deliberately act to end life's final suffering than to foreclose the possibility of life fulfillment at its beginning? The point of this observation is not to affirm active euthanasia (to me it is more of an argument against easy abortion), but to underscore the emotional rather than ethical basis of many of our decisions.

Risking the Slippery Slope

While granting that it may be morally justifiable in exceptional   8
circumstances, I see great danger in the cultural and legal acceptance
of active euthanasia. Taking this step places our feet on a slippery
slope on which we can quickly slide into easy and irreverent mercy
killing for unjustifiable reasons and then on into the institutionalized and established practice of euthanasia for economic and social
purposes, as practiced by Hitler. If laws are changed to permit active euthanasia in rare, justifiable circumstances, it will require
extreme vigilance to prevent these exceptions from becoming standard practice.

It is reported that the average age of nursing-home residents is   9
now 83 and rising. Medical costs continue to escalate, in spite of efforts to contain them. Some speak of the responsibility of the elderly
to die in order to ease the burden on the younger generation. These
signs of our times tell of increasing pressure for public acceptance of
active as well as passive euthanasia. They are small steps down a road
that could lead to provisions for the permitted, and possibly even
required, elimination not only of the suffering, senile, and elderly, but
also of others of all ages who have been determined to be nonproductive members of society. Therefore, even though there may be exceptional circumstances in which active euthanasia is justified, I believe
that it is wiser public policy to continue to prohibit it altogether
rather than risk the temptations and tendencies of this slippery slope.

In summary, passive euthanasia may be justifiable (1) when it is   10
determined that the patient is irreversibly comatose, (2) when the
treatment prolongs imminent and inevitable death, and (3) when the
treatment itself is so traumatic that it is inhumane to administer it.
In addition to these criteria, active euthanasia should never be permitted or even considered unless it is clearly inhumane to let an
illness run its course and there are no other means of ending meaningless suffering. . . .

The pro-life alternatives to euthanasia include everything possi-   11
ble to provide compassionate and often costly care of the ill, infirm,
and elderly. The true test of a society's faithfulness to the pro-life
perspective is not only in its opposition to killing but also in its
willingness to make adequate provision for those who are suffering
and nonproductive. As costs of care increase, individuals in specific
circumstances and society as a whole will be strongly tempted to
sell out both compassion and responsible reverence for life in exchange for economic considerations. If the day comes when euthanasia is established as an economic policy, we will have ceased to be

either fully moral or fully human. It is imperative that we oppose every step toward irresponsible euthanasia and also affirm the reordering of the priorities and expenditures of our personal and corporate life in order to provide the compassionate care every human being deserves. If we are not vigilant in opposition to unjustifiable euthanasia, we may one day be haunted by horrors more antiseptic, but no less terrifying, than Hitler's "final solution."

Last Rights

MICHAEL G. MAUDLIN

Two tragedies. In 1983 Nancy Cruzan, then aged 26, smashed   1
her car and was left severely brain damaged. Although not hooked up to any life-sustaining machinery, she is now fed through a tube connected to her stomach. In 1985 Larry McAfee broke his neck in a motorcycle accident. Today he is a quadraplegic confined to a wheelchair and a portable ventilator.

The courts have been asked to help both of them die.   2

Joe and Joyce Cruzan, Nancy's parents, won their initial court   3
case in Missouri where they sought legal authority to withhold food and fluid from their daughter. The state successfully appealed the decision to the state supreme court. Missouri State Supreme Court Judge Edward Robertson wrote in his decision that this was not a case where the court was asked "to let someone die," but "to allow the medical profession to make Nancy die by starvation and dehydration." Now the family has appealed, and for the first time the Supreme Court will hear a euthanasia case.

McAfee acted on his own behalf, asking the Georgia court for   4
three things: first, that his respirator be supplied with a timed turn-off switch; second, that he be provided with a sedative; and third, that he be guaranteed no one will turn the respirator back on after he turns it off. (He has turned off his respirator in the past, but changed his mind and asked that it be turned back on.) The court has agreed to be McAfee's accomplice.

Both situations are tragic, but tragic circumstances should not   5
be an excuse for ending life. Life is a gift from God, created by him and redeemed by his Son's death. God has made it clear that as stewards we are not to kill what is his and that we must protect the weak among us (Exod. 20:13; Matt. 25:31–46).

Both of these cases reveal a principle that violates God's trust. In   6
Nancy Beth Cruzan v. *Robert Harmon*, the lower court accepted

"quality of life" as a basis for deciding who should live. By arguing that death is in Nancy's best interest, they are saying her present life is not worth living. We agree with the many organizations representing the retarded, the handicapped, and the aged who worry that this decision may lead to the "mercy killing" of those who some people feel lead lives that are not worth living.

The same thinking is behind the McAfee case. McAfee has been 7 shuffled across the country from nursing home to intensive care unit to nursing home without ever being provided the proper care and support that would enable him to live a functional and independent life. As Paul Longmore said in the *Atlanta Constitution*, instead of providing financial help and service, "all the 'able-bodied' people connected with the case have been quick to support Mr. McAfee in his testimony that he longer gets any enjoyment out of life." Thus the court not only grants him the freedom to commit suicide, it has also agreed to give assistance.

The "right to die" lobby is a growing force in this country, but it 8 is a mere extension of the thinking that is behind proabortion groups. For many people, life is a disposable commodity, thrown out when inconvenient or costly—whether that life is a "fetus," a grandparent, or even their own. Also, it is assumed that life or death is a decision we have every right to make.

For the same reasons that Christians oppose abortion, we must 9 be just as diligent in fighting euthanasia. With the utmost energy we must urge and pray that the Supreme Court will not repeat the horror that has been *Roe* v. *Wade*. And just as the maturing prolife movement discovered that it cannot protest abortion without being willing to help those mothers who choose life, so too we must be willing to show that we prize all life by providing the money and services to help the Larry McAfees among us.

In Defense of Voluntary Euthanasia

SIDNEY HOOK

A few short years ago, I lay at the point of death. A congestive 1 heart failure was treated for diagnostic purposes by an angiogram that triggered a stroke. Violent and painful hiccups, uninterrupted for several days and nights, prevented the ingestion of food. My left side and one of my vocal cords became paralyzed. Some form of pleurisy set in, and I felt I was drowning in a sea of slime. At one point, my heart stopped beating; just as I lost consciousness, it was thumped back into action again. In one of my lucid intervals during those days of agony, I asked my physician to discontinue all life-supporting services or show me how to do it. He refused and predicted that someday I would appreciate the unwisdom of my request.

A month later, I was discharged from the hospital. In six months, I   2
regained the use of my limbs, and although my voice still lacks its old resonance and carrying power I no longer croak like a frog. There remain some minor disabilities and I am restricted to a rigorous, low sodium diet. I have resumed my writing and research.

My experience can be and has been cited as an argument against   3
honoring requests of stricken patients to be gently eased out of their pain and life. I cannot agree. There are two main reasons. As an octogenarian, there is a reasonable likelihood that I may suffer another "cardiovascular accident" or worse. I may not even be in a position to ask for the surcease of pain. It seems to me that I have already paid my dues to death—indeed, although time has softened my memories they are vivid enough to justify my saying that I suffered enough to warrant dying several times over. Why run the risk of more?

Secondly, I dread imposing on my family and friends another   4
grim round of misery similar to the one my first attack occasioned.

My wife and children endured enough for one lifetime. I know   5
that for them the long days and nights of waiting, the disruption of their professional duties and their own familial responsibilities counted for nothing in their anxiety for me. In their joy at my recovery they have been forgotten. Nonetheless, to visit another prolonged spell of helpless suffering on them as my life ebbs away, or even worse, if I linger on into a comatose senility, seems altogether gratuitous.

But what, it may be asked, of the joy and satisfaction of living, of   6
basking in the sunshine, listening to music, watching one's grandchildren growing into adolescence, following the news about the fate of freedom in a troubled world, playing with ideas, writing one's testament of wisdom and folly for posterity? Is not all that one endured, together with the risk of its recurrence, an acceptable price for the multiple satisfactions that are still open even to a person of advanced years?

Apparently those who cling to life no matter what, think so. I do   7
not.

The zest and intensity of these experiences are no longer what   8
they used to be. I am not vain enough to delude myself that I can in the few remaining years make an important discovery useful for mankind or can lead a social movement or do anything that will be historically eventful, no less event-making. My autobiography, which describes a record of intellectual and political experiences of some historical value, already much too long, could be posthumously published. I have had my fill of joys and sorrows and am not greedy for more life. I

have always thought that a test of whether one had found happiness in one's life is whether one would be willing to relive it—whether, if it were possible, one would accept the opportunity to be born again.

Having lived a full and relatively happy life, I would cheerfully 9
accept the chance to be reborn, but certainly not to be reborn again as an infirm octogenarian. To some extent, my views reflect what I have seen happen to the aged and stricken who have been so unfortunate as to survive crippling paralysis. They suffer, and impose suffering on others, unable even to make a request that their torment be ended.

I am mindful too of the burdens placed upon the community, 10
with its rapidly diminishing resources, to provide the adequate and costly services necessary to sustain the lives of those whose days and nights are spent on mattress graves of pain. A better use could be made of these resources to increase the opportunities and qualities of life for the young. I am not denying the moral obligation the community has to look after its disabled and aged. There are times, however, when an individual may find it pointless to insist on the fulfillment of a legal and moral right.

What is required is no great revolution in morals but an enlarge- 11
ment of imagination and an intelligent evaluation of alternative uses of community resources.

Long ago, Seneca observed that "the wise man will live as long 12
as he ought, not as long as he can." One can envisage hypothetical circumstances in which one has a duty to prolong one's life despite its costs for the sake of others, but such circumstances are far removed from the ordinary prospects we are considering. If wisdom is rooted in knowledge of the alternatives of choice, it must be reliably informed of the state one is in and its likely outcome. Scientific medicine is not infallible, but it is the best we have. Should a rational person be willing to endure acute suffering merely on the chance that a miraculous cure might presently be at hand? Each one should be permitted to make his own choice—especially when no one else is harmed by it.

The responsibility for the decision, whether deemed wise or 13
foolish, must be with the chooser.

Can't We Put My Mother to Sleep?

ALAN L. OTTEN

When I was a boy, my family had a beloved bulldog. Eventually 1
he became very old—blind, incontinent, wheezing heavily, barely

able to eat or walk. We took him to the vet and, as the euphemism then had it, the vet "put Jerry to sleep."

Every few days now, I go to visit my 90-year-old mother in a   2
nearby nursing home, more to salve my own conscience probably than to do her any meaningful service. For her, in fact, there is little I can do. She lies on her side in bed, legs drawn rigidly into a fetal position, blinks at me uncomprehendingly as I prattle on about family doings, and rarely utters a sound except a shriek of pain when the attendants turn her from one side to the other in their constant battle to heal her horrible bedsores. She must be hand-fed, and her incontinency requires a urethral catheter.

Why do we treat our aged and loved animals better than we treat   3
our aged and loved human beings? Shouldn't a humane, caring society—as ours is supposed to be—begin to consider ways to put my long-suffering mother, and the steadily growing number of miserable others like her, peacefully to sleep?

Empty Lives

My mother is far from a unique case now, and as our society   4
continues to age, there'll be more and more like her—very old people, enduring barren year after barren year, with chronic diseases that unfortunately do not kill but merely irrevocably waste the body and destroy the mind.

Doctors, nursing homes and hospitals work to keep these old   5
people alive with tube feeding, nutritional supplements, antibiotics at the first sign of infection. For what? Are we really doing these people any favor by fighting so hard to prolong their lives?

I am not talking about physically impaired old people who may   6
still be mentally alert, or those whose minds are, as the young people say, out to lunch but who are still comparatively fit physically. I am talking about the many thousands of old men and women disastrously and hopelessly crippled both in mind and body. Does it really make sense to keep extending lives that are so empty of even an occasional moment of recognition or joy—unable to know a loved grandchild, savor a long-favorite food, carry on even the simplest conversation?

As the Rev. John Paris, a Jesuit priest who teaches ethics at Holy   7
Cross College, says: "In our determination to prolong life at any cost, we have forgotten that dying is part of the process of living. These people's bodies are telling them there really is no purpose in going on, and yet we make them go on."

Hard-Won Progress

Of late, there seems to be a growing though reluctant recognition that a mentally competent person who is terminally ill or in extreme pain should be able to refuse respirators or other life-lengthening measures. Even more reluctantly, some states are accepting the next of kin's right to make such a decision for a terminally ill but mentally incompetent patient.

Yet this hard-won progress doesn't help the growing numbers like my mother. Heart and lungs are working, whatever is wrong with spine and limbs and mind. There is no respirator to be unplugged. No doctor can pronounce her a terminal case. The only sure prognosis is constant pain and misery as long as she lives.

Over and over, healthy middle-aged people today voice their dread of ending their days in this vegetative state. Over and over, ailing old men and women wail, "Why is God punishing me this way? Why can't I die?"

The Patient's Best Interest

Euthanasia has tended to be a dirty word in this country, but isn't it time to respond to these *cris de coeur?* American medicine is supposed to operate in the best interest of the patient; prolonging a life of incurable wretchedness turns that standard upside down.

The euthanasia slope is, of course, slippery, but that doesn't make descent impossible. We just must walk extra carefully.

Doctors and medical ethicists surely should be able to work out the best possible techniques for making so sensitive a decision, hedging them around with special safeguards. Many hospitals use ethics committees to set guidelines for withdrawing life-support systems from the terminally ill. Couldn't these committees similarly set rules for deciding when and how to withdraw life from elderly men and women whose minds and bodies are tragically wrecked beyond repair?

Many doctors say they would be prepared, at a minimum, to let nature take its course as these people deteriorate—foregoing the tube feeding, antibiotics and other delaying mechanisms. That would at least bring natural death a little sooner. And actually, several doctors tell me, this approach is already being used more often than society realizes.

A further step would be to withhold food and water; debate over   15
the wisdom and ethics of this is already under way among lawyers,
doctors and ethicists. The New Jersey Supreme Court, in a recent
trailblazing decision, held that food and water could be withdrawn
to hasten a dying person's end if that was clearly what the person
wished or would have wished.

Interestingly, when I told several doctors and ethicists about my   16
mother, they all offered the same suggestion: Take her home, keep
her comfortable, moisten her lips and bathe off her body from time
to time, but nothing more. In essence, just hold her hand and help
her through the dying.

Quick and Humane

But why must it be done this slow, hard way? Why not a pill,   17
injection or other quick and more humane method, once the doctors' committee or other decision-making panel has agreed there's
no point in making the elderly persons suffer any longer?

Clearly, opposition to this entire proposal will be intense. In   18
the recent Baby Doe controversy, the administration and Congress
rushed to mandate the continuation of life, however dismal, and presumably the same response awaits the first case of Old Lady Doe.

Yet the public may be readier to move than many leaders think.   19
Opinion polls show overwhelming—and steadily rising—support
for the idea of allowing terminally ill patients to die quickly. A
recent Harris Poll, for example, found 85% now, as against 62% in
1973, endorsing a terminally ill patient's right to tell the doctor to
stop trying to extend life, and 61% now (as against only 37% in
1973) favoring the patient's right to ask the doctor actually to "put
him out of his misery."

True, these questions involve the terminally ill, yet the remark-   20
ably high percentages can't help but indicate substantial, though
admittedly smaller, support for similar treatment of the hopelessly
vegetative.

The Quality of Life

"We need to educate people to the idea that the quality of life is   21
more important than mere length of life," argues University of Virginia ethicist Joseph Fletcher. "Our cultural tradition holds that life
has absolute value, but that's really not good enough any more.
Sometimes, no life may be better."

I'm sure that if my mother could think and speak, she would agree.   22

QUESTIONS OF CONTENT

1. According to Erdahl's opening paragraph, what are two phrases that serve as synonyms for the term *euthanasia?* Which term does he seem to prefer, and why do you suppose he does so?
2. How does Erdahl differentiate between "passive" and "active" euthanasia? How are these related to "institutionalized" euthanasia, and why does he oppose that form?
3. According to Maudlin's description, what are the main differences between the physical and mental conditions of Nancy Cruzan and Larry McAfee?
4. What role do the courts have in the fates of Cruzan and McAfee?
5. To what extent did Sidney Hook recover from the critical illness that had nearly killed him?
6. According to Hook, who or what else suffers when a critically ill person continues to live?
7. How is the title of Otten's essay related to his argument?
8. According to Otten, to what degree did American opinions regarding euthanasia change between 1973 and 1985? What reason does he give, or what do you surmise as a reason, for this shift?

QUESTIONS OF FORM

1. Where does Erdahl refer to the use of euthanasia by Hitler and what does his argument gain by those repeated references to the World War II Holocaust?
2. What is the "slippery slope" danger mentioned in paragraphs 8–9 of "Euthanasia Is Sometimes Justified" and in paragraphs 6–7 of "Last Rights"? How are the two related?
3. What warrant is behind the references to God and the Old and New Testament passages in Maudlin's paragraphs 5–6? Since the Bible sometimes contradicts itself, and not everyone in our culture is either a Jew or a Christian, how useful is reference to it as an authority in an argument?
4. What force is added to Hook's argument by having him relate his personal experience of critical illness, as opposed to having such an illness described by a narrator removed from direct involvement, as in Maudlin's essay describing the circumstances of Cruzan and McAfee?

5. What is the analogy used by Alan Otten to support his claim, what are the points of similarity, and how appropriate is it?
6. In which paragraphs does Otten refer to his mother's condition and what desirable attribute does his essay gain by that repetition?
7. Although Otten's essay has considerable emotional force because of his descriptions of his mother's suffering, he also often uses *rhetorical questions* to strengthen his case; where does he do so, and what, if anything, does his essay gain by those uses?

SUGGESTIONS FOR WRITING

1. Using real examples from your experience or from those near you (family, friends, co-workers, and the like), write a well-supported essay agreeing with or refuting the Roman philosopher Seneca's assertion, as quoted in Hook's essay, that "the wise man will live as long as he ought, not as long as he can" (paragraph 12).
2. Both Erdahl and Maudlin connect the ethical problems of active euthanasia to those of abortion; in a well-reasoned letter to either author, agree or disagree with their contention that a relationship exists.
3. In paragraph 18 of his essay, Otten refers to the "recent [that is, *circa* 1985] Baby Doe controversy." Use your library research skills to find out the facts of that national controversy over euthanasia, starting with the article by Nat Hentoff listed in the bibliography below, and present them in a concise written summary.
4. You have been deeply moved by reading about the accident which left Nancy Cruzan in "Last Rights" severely brain-damaged and therefore a "human vegetable," unable to communicate. Write a statement addressed "To Whom It May Concern" or to a specific person or persons, in which you argue convincingly for how you want to be treated under similar circumstances. Your instructor may want you to cite some of the articles in this section, or some of those listed below, or others you locate in a library, following the advice offered in the "Using Sources" section of Chapter 6.

Additional References

CALLAHAN, DANIEL. "Euthanasia and Health-Care: Mortal Questions." *Current* Nov. 1988: 11–19.

GIANELLI, DIANE M. "Would Aiding in Dying Make MDs Hired Killers?" *American Medical News* 16 Feb. 1990: 3–4.

GIBBS, NANCY. "Love and Let Die." *Time* 19 March 1990: 62–70.

HENTOFF, NAT. "The Awful Privacy of Baby Doe." *The Atlantic* Jan. 1985: 54–60.

KASS, LEON R. "Death with Dignity and the Sanctity of Life." *Commentary* March 1990: 33–43.

MALCOLM, ANDREW H. "The Ultimate Decision." *The New York Times Magazine* 3 Dec. 1989: 38.

REICHEL, WILLIAM, and ARTHUR J. DYCK. "Euthanasia: A Contemporary Moral Quandary." *The Lancet* 2 Dec. 1989: 1321–23.

ROSENBLATT, ROGER. "The Quality of Mercy Killing." *Time* 26 Aug. 1985: 74.

Remember to give appropriate credit not only for quotations that you borrow but also for ideas and numerical data.

WHAT SHOULD BE DONE ABOUT GUN CONTROL?

Shooting Down Gun Myths

ROBERT J. SPITZER

The media event that began on Dec. 22, 1984, when subway 1
rider Bernhard Hugo Goetz responded to a demand for $5 from four
youths with bullets from a .38-caliber revolver serves as a recent
reminder that what historian Richard Hofstadter once labeled the
"gun culture" is still tightly woven into the fabric of the American
psyche. Much has been written about the political and criminologi-
cal consequences of gun control, including the proliferation of weapons (especially cheap handguns), the effectiveness or ineffectiveness
of various gun control measures and the almost staggering influence
of the National Rifle Association in preventing stricter gun laws.

Yet there has been surprisingly little public examination of the 2
central constitutional question pertaining to guns—namely, the
meaning of the Second Amendment: "A well regulated militia being
necessary to the security of a free state, the right of the people to
keep and bear arms shall not be infringed." The oft-repeated cry of
gun control opponents extolling the so-called individual "right to
keep and bear arms" has been accepted by most of the public (a 1978
survey reported that 88 percent of Americans believe they have an
individual right to bear arms) in large part because it has often and
stridently been repeated. A simple examination of how the courts
have interpreted the Second Amendment shows, however, that
those who think the Constitution gives them a right to tote a gun
have not got a leg to stand on.

The Second Amendment admittedly has not received as much of 3
the Supreme Court's attention over the years as have other Bill of
Rights issues, like free speech, free press and the right to counsel.
But four cases provide the basis for understanding the Supreme
Court's thinking on the matter over the last century.

The first Supreme Court ruling on the Second Amendment oc- 4
curred in a case called *U.S.* v. *Cruikshank* (1876). Speaking for the
Court, Chief Justice Morrison R. Waite said the right "of bearing

arms for a lawful purpose is not a right granted by the Constitution, nor is it in any manner dependent upon that instrument for its existence." The Cruikshank case established two principles: First, the Second Amendment does not afford an individual right to bear arms (as distinct from an individual's participation in a collective body or militia); second, the Second Amendment is not legally "incorporated"—that is, does not apply to the states through the due process and equal protection clauses of the 14th Amendment. The concept of "incorporation" is highly important in understanding the scope of the Second Amendment and the Bill of Rights as a whole. The process of incorporation has been the means by which the courts have extended constitutional protections to individuals in non-Federal cases. In 1876, none of the Bill of Rights had been incorporated; today, however, most of the constitutional protections we take for granted, like protection from unreasonable searches and seizures and the rights of free assembly and free exercise of religion, protect us because the Supreme Court "incorporated" them. The Court has never, however, "incorporated" the Second Amendment.

The second important court case was *Presser* v. *Illinois* (1886). In   5
that case, the Court reaffirmed *Cruikshank,* and stated that the Second Amendment does not apply to the states (is not "incorporated") and affirmed that though the states have the right to form militias, they are also free to regulate the circumstances under which citizens bear arms, within the parameters of state constitutions.

In an 1894 case, *Miller* v. *Texas,* the Supreme Court upheld the   6
right of states to regulate arms and said again that the Second Amendment did not apply to the states. The fourth and most important case came in 1939. *U.S.* v. *Miller* involved a challenge to Federal gun regulations stemming from the National Firearms Act of 1934. Speaking for a unanimous Court, Justice James C. McReynolds affirmed the right of the Federal Government to regulate firearms (in particular, transport and possession) and stated unambiguously that citizens possess a constitutional right to bear arms only in connection with service in a militia. Justice McReynolds also cited the Cruikshank and Presser cases as precedent, affirming the principles articulated in those cases.

The continued pertinence of the Miller case is indicated by two   7
other recent Supreme Court cases. In a 1972 case, *Adams* v. *Williams,* Justices William O. Douglas and Thurgood Marshall issued a joint dissent in which they cited Miller and affirmed their view that the state could regulate firearms as it saw fit. The case itself, however, did not deal with the Second Amendment. In 1980, Justice Harry A. Blackman commented in a footnote to his majority opinion

(*Lewis* v. *U.S.*) that the Miller case represented the Court's thinking on gun control.

One final case warrants mention, though it was not reviewed by   8
the Supreme Court. On June 8, 1981, the village of Morton Grove, Ill., enacted an ordinance that banned the possession of handguns, except for police, prison officials, the military, collectors and others needing guns for their work. Residents who owned guns could keep and use them in licensed gun clubs, however. The ordinance was challenged by the National Rifle Association and their sympathizers. Both the Federal District Court and the Federal Court of Appeals rejected the arguments of the ordinance opponents. Both Federal courts said that the Second Amendment did not apply to the states, that there was no individual right to bear arms, that the Morton Grove ordinance was a reasonable exercise of authority and that the right to bear arms applies only to the maintenance of a well regulated militia (as was said in *Miller*).

The case of *Quilici* v. *Village of Morton Grove* was appealed to   9
the Supreme Court, but it declined to hear the case, leaving the lower Federal court ruling as the operative interpretation.

This recitation of cases demonstrates the Court's long recogni-   10
tion of the right of the Government to regulate the ownership and use of firearms as it sees fit. The fact that sweeping national regulations have not been enacted is not due to a lack of constitutional authority, but rather to the political clout of gun control opponents and a gun "mythology" perpetuated in large part by gun enthusiasts.

Even if we examine the intentions of the founding fathers, it is   11
clear that their considerations in authorizing the Second Amendment lay with national defense. The citizen militia was considered the military force least threatening to democratic values and institutions. They feared the baneful consequences of a regular standing army, as European and earlier American history were replete with examples of tyrannies extended by such armies. Despite these fears, the founding fathers were also well aware of the military limitations of an army composed of part-time soldiers, and provision was made in the Constitution (Article I, Section 8) for both a militia and a standing army. The role of the citizen militia was formally supplanted in 1916 by the National Defense Act, which recognized the National Guard as the militia. And, of course, early fears of a standing army that would overthrow American democratic institutions never materialized.

Thus, the Second Amendment protects a "right to keep and bear   12
arms" only for service in a "well regulated militia" that has not been called up since the beginning of the 19th century. As Bill of Rights

scholar Irving Brant observed, the Second Amendment "comes to life chiefly on the parade floats of rifle associations and in the propaganda of mail-order houses selling pistols to teen-age gangsters."

Many have applauded the actions of Bernhard Goetz as legitimate self-defense, or as justifiable vigilantism. But even if we accept the propriety of his actions, how do we disentangle his "right" to carry and use a gun from the less ambiguous case of James Alan Kearbey, a 14-year-old junior high school student who, on Jan. 21, entered his Goddard, Kan., school with an M-1 rifle and a .357 magnum pistol (popularized in Clint Eastwood's film *Dirty Harry*). Kearbey shot and killed the school principal and wounded three others. Goddard English teacher Darlene Criss ironically described the town as "the safest place in America."   13

The Goetz case and the Kearbey case both argue for Government to exercise its right to regulate the possession and use of firearms. But as the merits of gun control are debated, it is time that we once and for all excised erroneous references to an individual, constitutionally based "right" to bear arms.   14

The NRA Is Right

JOSH SUGARMANN

One tenet of the National Rifle Association's faith has always been that handgun controls do little to stop criminals from obtaining handguns. For once, the NRA is right and America's leading handgun control organization is wrong. Criminals don't buy handguns in gun stores. That's why they're criminals. But it isn't criminals who are killing most of the 20,000 to 22,000 people who die from handguns each year. We are.   1

This is an ugly truth for a country that thinks of handgun violence as a "crime" issue and believes that it's somehow possible to separate "good" handguns (those in our hands for self-defense) from "bad" handguns (those in the hands of criminals).   2

Contrary to popular perception, the most prevalent form of handgun death in America isn't murder but suicide. Of the handgun deaths that occur each year, approximately 12,000 are suicides. An additional 1,000 fatalities are accidents. And of the 9,000 handgun deaths classified as murders, most are not caused by predatory strangers. Handgun violence is usually the result of people being angry, drunk,   3 careless, or depressed—who just happen to have a handgun around. In all, fewer than 10 percent of handgun deaths are felony-related.

Though handgun availability is not a crime issue, it does represent a major public health threat. Handguns are the number one weapon for both murder and suicide and are second only to auto accidents as the leading cause of death due to injury. Of course there are other ways of committing suicide or crimes of passion. But no means is more lethal, effective, or handy. That's why the NRA is ultimately wrong. As several public health organizations have noted, the best way to curb a public health problem is through prevention— in this case, the banning of all handguns from civilian hands.

The Enemy Is Us

For most who attempt suicide, the will to die lasts only briefly. Only one out of every ten people attempting suicide is going to kill himself no matter what. The success or failure of an attempt depends primarily on the lethality of the means. Pills, razor blades, and gas aren't guaranteed killers, and they take time. Handguns, however, lend themselves well to spontaneity. Consider that although women try to kill themselves four times as often as men, men succeed three to four times as often. For one reason: women use pills or less lethal means; men use handguns. This balance is shifting, however, as more women own or have access to handguns. Between 1970 and 1978 the suicide rate for young women rose 50 percent, primarily due to increased use of handguns.

Of course, there is no way to lock society's cupboard and prevent every distraught soul from injuring him or herself. Still, there are ways we can promote public safety without becoming a nation of nannies. England, for instance, curbed suicide by replacing its most common means of committing suicide—coal stove gas—with less toxic natural gas. Fifteen years after the switch, studies found that suicide rates had dropped and remained low, even though the number of suicide *attempts* had increased. "High suicide rates seem to occur where highly lethal suicidal methods are not only available, but also where they are culturally acceptable," writes Dr. Robert Markush of the University of Alabama, who has studied the use of handguns in suicide.

Most murders aren't crime-related, but are the result of arguments between friends and among families. In 1985, 59 percent of all murders were committed by people known to the victim. Only 15 percent were committed by strangers, and only 18 percent were the result of felonious activity. As the FBI admits every year in its *Uni-*

form Crime Reports, "murder is a societal problem over which law enforcement has little or no control." The FBI doesn't publish separate statistics on who's killing whom with handguns, but it is assumed that what is true of all murders is true of handgun murders.

Controlling the Vector

Recognizing that eliminating a disease requires prevention, not   8
treatment, health professionals have been in the forefront of those calling for a national ban on handguns. In 1981, the Surgeon General's Select Panel for the Promotion of Child Health traced the "epidemic of deaths and injuries among children and youth" to handguns, and called for "nothing short of a total ban." It is estimated that on average, one child dies from handgun wounds each day. Between 1961 and 1981, according to the American Association of Suicidology, the suicide rate for 15- to 24-year-olds increased 150 percent. The report linked the rise in murders and suicides among the young to the increased use of firearms—primarily handguns. In a 1985 report, the Surgeon General's Workshop on Violence and Public Health recommended "a complete and universal ban on the sale, manufacture, importation, and possession of handguns (except for authorized police and military personnel)."

Not surprisingly, the American Public Health Association, the   9
American Association of Suicidology, and the American Psychiatric Association are three of the 31 national organizations that are members of National Coalition to Ban Handguns (NCBH).

Comparing the relationship between handguns and violence to   10
mosquitos and malaria, Stephen P. Teret, co-director of the Johns Hopkins Injury Prevention Center says, "As public health professionals, if we are faced with a disease that is carried by some type of vehicle/vector like a mosquito, our initial response would be to control the vector. There's no reason why if the vehicle/vector is a handgun, we should not be interested in controlling the handgun."

The NRA refers to handgun suicides, accidental killings, and   11
murders by acquaintances as "the price of freedom." It believes that handguns right enough wrongs, stop enough crimes, and kill enough criminals to justify these deaths. But even the NRA has admitted that there is no "adequate measure that more lives are saved by arms in good hands than are lost by arms in evil hands." Again, the NRA is right.

A 1985 NCBH study found that a handgun is 118 times more   12
likely to be used in a suicide, murder, or fatal accident than to kill a criminal. Between 1981 and 1983, nearly 69,000 Americans lost

their lives to handguns. During that same period there were only 583 justifiable homicides reported to the FBI, in which someone used a handgun to kill a stranger—a burglar, rapist, or other criminal. In 1982, 19 states reported to the FBI that not once did a private citizen use a handgun to kill a criminal. Five states reported that more than 130 citizens were murdered with handguns for each time a handgun was justifiably used to kill a criminal. In no state did the number of self-defense homicides approach the murder toll. Last year, a study published in the *New England Journal of Medicine* analyzing gun use in the home over a six-year period in the Seattle, Washington, area found that for every time a firearm was used to kill an intruder in self-defense, 198 lives ended in murders, suicides, or accidents. Handguns were used in more than 70 percent of those deaths.

Although handguns are rarely used to kill criminals, an obvious   13 question remains: How often are they used merely to wound or scare away intruders? No reliable statistics are available, but most police officials agree that in a criminal confrontation on the street, the handgun-toting civilian is far more likely to be killed or lose his handgun to a criminal than successfully use the weapon in self-defense. "Beyond any doubt, thousands more lives are lost every year because of the proliferation of handguns than are saved," says Joseph McNamara, chief of police of San Jose, who has also been police chief in Kansas City, a beat cop in Harlem, and is the author of a book on defense against violent crime. Moreover, most burglaries occur when homes are vacant, so the handgun in the drawer is no deterrent. (It would also probably be the first item stolen.)

Faced with facts like these, anti-control advocates often turn to   14 the argument of last resort: the Second Amendment. But the historic 1981 Morton Grove, Illinois, ban on handgun sale and possession exploded that rationale. In 1983, the U.S. Supreme Court let stand a lower court ruling that stated, "Because the possession of handguns is not part of the right to keep and bear arms, [the Morton Grove ordinance] does not violate the Second Amendment."

Criminal Equivocation

Unfortunately, powerful as the NRA is, it has received addi-   15 tional help from the leading handgun control group. Handgun Control Inc. (HC) has helped the handgun lobby by setting up the perfect strawman for the NRA to shoot down. "Keep handguns out of the wrong hands," HCI says. "By making it more difficult for criminals, drug addicts, etc., to get handguns and by ensuring that law-abiding citizens know how to maintain their handguns, we can reduce handgun violence," it promises. Like those in the NRA, HCI chairman Nelson T. "Pete" Shields "firmly believe(s) in the right of law-abiding citizens to possess handguns . . . for legitimate purposes."

In its attempt to paint handgun violence solely as a crime issue, HCI goes so far as to sometimes ignore the weapon's non-crime death tally. In its most recent poster comparing the handgun murder toll in the U.S. with that of nations with strict handgun laws, HCI states: "In 1983, handguns killed 35 people in Japan, 8 in Great Britain, 27 in Switzerland, 6 in Canada, 7 in Sweden, 10 in Australia, and 9,014 in the United States." Handguns *killed* a lot more than that in the United States. About 13,000 suicides and accidents more.   16

HCI endorses a ban only on short-barrelled handguns (the preferred weapon of criminals). It advocates mandatory safety training, a waiting period during which a background check can be run on a purchaser, and a license to carry a handgun, with mandatory sentencing for violators. It also endorses mandatory sentencing for the use of a handgun in a crime. According to HCI communications director Barbara Lautman, together these measures would "attack pretty much the heart of the problem."   17

HCI appears to have arrived at its crime focus by taking polls. In his 1981 book, *Guns Don't Die—People Do*, Shields points out that the majority of Americans don't favor a ban on handguns. "What they do want, however, is a set of strict laws to control the easy access to handguns by the criminal and the violence prone—*as long as those controls don't jeopardize the perceived right of law-abiding citizens to buy and own handguns for self defense* [italics his]." Shields admits "this is not based on any naive hope that criminals will obey such laws. Rather, it is based on the willingness of the rest of us to be responsible and accountable citizens, and the knowledge that to the degree we are, we make it more difficult for the criminal to get a handgun." This wasn't always HCI's stand. Founded in 1974 as the National Council to Control Handguns, HCI originally called a ban on private handgun possession the "most effective" solution to reducing violent crime rapidly and was at one time a member of NCBH. Michael Beard, president of NCBH, maintains the HCI's focus on crime "started with a public relations concern. Some people in the movement felt Americans were worried about crime, and that was one way to approach the problem. That's the problem when you use public opinion polls to tell you what your position's going to be. And I think a lot of the handgun control movement has looked at whatever's hot at the time and tried to latch onto that, rather than sticking to the basic message that there is a relationship between the availability of handguns and the handgun violence in our society. . . .   18

Ultimately, nothing short of taking the product off the market is really going to have an effect on the problem."

HCI's cops and robbers emphasis has been endlessly frustrating   19
to many in the anti-handgun movement. HCI would offer handgun control as a solution to crime, and the NRA would effectively rebut their arguments with the commonsensical observation that criminals are not likely to obey such laws. I can't help but think that HCI's refusal to abandon the crime argument has harmed the long-term progress of the movement.

Saturated Dresser Drawers

In a nation with 40 million handguns—where anyone who   20
wants one can get one—it's time to face a chilling fact. We're way past the point where registration, licensing, safety training, waiting periods, or mandatory sentencing are going to have much effect. Each of these measures may save some lives or help catch a few criminals, but none—by itself or taken together—will stop the vast majority of handgun suicides or murders. A "controlled" handgun kills just as effectively as an "uncontrolled" one.

Most control recommendations merely perpetuate the myth   21
that with proper care a handgun can be as safe a tool as any other. Nothing could be further from the truth. A handgun is not a blender.

Those advocating a step-by-step process insist that a ban would   22
be too radical and therefore unacceptable to Congress and the public. A hardcore 40 percent of the American public has always endorsed banning handguns. Many will also undoubtedly argue that any control measure—no matter how ill-conceived or ineffective—would be a good first step. But after more than a decade, the other foot hasn't followed.

In other areas of firearms control there has been increasing recog-   23
nition that bans are the most effective solution. The only two federal measures passed since the Gun Control Act of 1968 have been bans. In each case, the reasoning was simple: the harm done by these objects outweighed any possible benefit they brought to society. In 1986, Congress banned certain types of armor-piercing "cop-killer" bullets. There was also a silver lining to last year's NRA-McClure-Volkmer handgun "decontrol" bill, which weakened the already lax Gun Control Act of 1968, making it legal, for instance, for people to transport unloaded, "not readily accessible" handguns interstate. A last-minute amendment added by pro-control forces banned the future production and sale of machine guns for civilian use.

Unfortunately, no law has addressed the major public health   24 problem. Few suicides, accidental killings, or acquaintance murders are the result of cop-killer bullets or machine guns.

Outlawing handguns would in no way be a panacea. Even if handgun production stopped tomorrow, millions would remain in the dresser drawers of America's bedrooms—and many of them would probably stay there. Contrary to NRA fantasies, black-booted fascists would not be kicking down doors searching for handguns. Moreover, the absolute last segment of society to be affected by any measure would be criminals. The black market that has fed off the legal sale of handguns would continue for a long while. But by ending new handgun production, the availability of illegal handguns can only decrease. 25

Of course, someone who truly wants to kill himself can find another way. A handgun ban would not affect millions of rifles and shotguns. But experience shows that no weapon provides the combination of lethality and convenience that a handgun does. Handguns represent only 30 percent of all the guns out there but are responsible for 90 percent of firearms misuse. Most people who commit suicide with a firearm use a handgun. At minimum, a handgun ban would prevent the escalation of killings in segments of society that have not yet been saturated by handgun manufacturers. Further increases in suicides among women, for example, might be curtailed. 26

But the final solution lies in changing the way handguns and handgun violence are viewed by society. Public health campaigns have changed the way Americans look at cigarette smoking and drunk driving and can do the same for handguns. 27

For the past 12 years, many in the handgun control movement have confined their debate to what the public supposedly wants and expects to hear—not to reality. The handgun must be seen for what it is, not what we'd like it to be. 28

The N.R.A. in a Hunter's Sights

ROBERT HUGHES

Like George Bush and thousands of other people, I am a Small White Hunter. Which means that, two or three times a year, one scrambles into one's brush pants and jacket, pulls on a pair of snake boots and goes ambling off on a sedate horse with friends and dogs in pursuit of quail in a pine forest in southern Georgia. Or spends cold predawn hours in a punt on Long Island Sound, or a damp blind on a 1

California marsh, waiting for the gray light to spread and the ducks to come arrowing in.

I have done this at intervals most of my life, ever since I was 2 eleven years old in Australia and my father first issued me a single-shot .22 and two bullets and told me to bring back one rabbit. I hope to keep doing it as long as I can walk and see.

I don't shoot deer anymore; the idea of large-game trophy hunt- 3 ing repels me. But I have never thought there was anything wrong with killing as much small game in one day as I and a few friends could eat in the evening—no more than that and always within the limits. On a good day I can break 24 targets out of 25 at trapshooting, and 22 or so at skeet, which is O.K. for an art critic.

In short, I am supposed—if you believe the advertisements of 4 the National Rifle Association—to be exactly the kind of person whose rights the N.R.A. claims to want to protect. Why, then, have I never joined the N.R.A.? And why do I think of this once omnipotent though now embattled lobby as the sportsman's embarrassment and not his ally?

The answer, in part, goes back to the famous Second Amend- 5 ment of the American Constitution, which the N.R.A. keeps brandishing like Holy Writ. "A well-regulated militia, being necessary to the security of a free State," it reads, "the right of the people to keep and bear arms shall not be infringed."

The part the N.R.A. quotes is always the second half. The first 6 half is less convenient because it undermines the lobby's propaganda for universal weaponry.

The Founding Fathers, in their wisdom—and more pointedly, 7 their experience—distrusted standing armies. They associated British ones with tyranny and lacked the money and manpower to create their own. Without a citizen's militia, the Revolution would have failed. Does the Constitution let you have the second half of the Second Amendment, the right to keep and bear arms, without the first part, the intended use of those arms in the exercises and, when necessary, the campaigns of a citizens' militia to which the gun owner belongs—as in Switzerland today? That is still very much a subject for legal debate.

The constitutional framers no more had in mind the socially 8 psychotic prospect of every Tom, Dick and Harriet with a barnful of MAC-10s, Saturday night specials and AK-47s than, in writing the First Amendment, they had in mind the protection of child-porn video, which did not exist in the 18th century either. Nowhere does the Constitution say the right to bear arms means the right to bear any or all arms. *Which* arms is the real issue. At present, firepower has outstripped the law's power to contain it within rational limits.

Where the N.R.A. has always revealed its nature as a paranoid   9
lobby, a political anachronism, is in its rigid ideological belief that
any restriction on the private ownership of *any* kind of hand-held
gun leads inexorably to *total* abolition of *all* gun ownership—that, if
today the U.S. Government takes the Kalashnikov from the hands of
the maniac on the school playground, it will be coming for my
Winchester pump tomorrow. There is no evidence for this absurd
belief, but it remains an article of faith. And it does so because the
faith is bad faith: the stand the N.R.A. takes is only nominally on
behalf of recreational hunters. The people it really serves are gun
manufacturers and gun importers, whose sole interest is to sell as
many deadly weapons of as many kinds to as many Americans as
possible. The N.R.A. never saw a weapon it didn't love. When American police officers raised their voices against the sale of "cop-killer"
bullets—Teflon-coated projectiles whose sole purpose is to penetrate body armor—the N.R.A. mounted a campaign to make people
believe this ban would infringe on the rights of deer hunters, as
though the woods of America were full of whitetails in Kevlar vests.
Now that the pressure is on to restrict public ownership of semiautomatic assault weapons, we hear the same threadbare rhetoric about
the rights of hunters. No serious hunter goes after deer with an Uzi
or an AK-47; those weapons are not made for picking off an animal
in the woods but for blowing people to chopped meat at close-to-
medium range, and anyone who needs a banana clip with 30 shells
in it to hit a buck should not be hunting at all. These guns have only
two uses: you can take them down to the local range and spend a lot
of money blasting off 500 rounds an afternoon at silhouette targets
of the Ayatullah, or you can use them to off your rivals and create
lots of police widows. It depends on what kind of guy you are. But
the N.R.A. doesn't care—underneath its dumb incantatory slogans
("Guns don't kill people; people kill people"), it is defending both
guys. It helps ensure that cops are outgunned right across America.
It preaches hunters' rights in order to defend the distribution of
weapons in what is, in effect, a drug-based civil war.

But we who love hunting have much more to fear from the   10
backlash of public opinion caused by the N.R.A.'s pig-headedness
than we do from the Government. Sensible hunters see the need to
follow the example of other civilized countries. All fireable guns
should be licensed; delays and stringent checks should be built into
their purchase, right across the board; and some types, including
machine guns and semiautomatic assault weapons, should not be
available to the civilian public at all. It is time, in this respect, that
America enter the 20th century, since it is only a few years away
from the 21st.

The Right to Bear Arms

WARREN E. BURGER

Our metropolitan centers, and some suburban communities of America, are setting new records for homicides by handguns. Many of our large centers have up to 10 times the murder rate of all of Western Europe. In 1988, there were 9000 handgun murders in America. Last year, Washington, D.C., alone had more than 400 homicides—setting a new record for our capital.

The Constitution of the United States, in its Second Amendment, guarantees a "right of the people to keep and bear arms." However, the meaning of this clause cannot be understood except by looking to the purpose, the setting and the objectives of the draftsmen. The first 10 amendments—the Bill of Rights—were not drafted at Philadelphia in 1787; that document came two years later than the Constitution. Most of the states already had bills of rights, but the Constitution might not have been ratified in 1788 if the states had not had assurances that a national Bill of Rights would soon be added.

People of that day were apprehensive about the new "monster" national government presented to them, and this helps explain the language and purpose of the Second Amendment. A few lines after the First Amendment's guarantees—against "establishment of religion," "free exercise" of religion, free speech and free press—came a guarantee that grew out of the deep-seated fear of a "national" or "standing" army. The same First Congress that approved the right to keep and bear arms also limited the national army to 840 men; Congress in the Second Amendment then provided:

> "A well regulated Militia, being necessary to the security of a free State, the right of the people to keep and bear Arms, shall not be infringed."

In the 1789 debate in Congress on James Madison's proposed Bill of Rights, Elbridge Gerry argued that a state militia was necessary:

> "to prevent the establishment of a standing army, the bane of liberty . . . Whenever governments mean to invade the rights and liberties of the people, they always attempt to destroy the militia in order to raise an army upon their ruins."

We see that the need for a state militia was the predicate of the "right" guaranteed; in short, it was declared "necessary" in order to have a state military force to protect the security of the state. That Second Amendment clause must be read as though the word "because" was the opening word of the guarantee. Today, of course, the "state militia" serves a very different purpose. A huge national defense establishment has taken over the role of the militia of 200 years ago.

Some have exploited these ancient concerns, blurring sporting 6
guns—rifles, shotguns and even machine pistols—with all firearms, including what are now called "Saturday night specials." There is, of course, a great difference between sporting guns and handguns. Some regulation of handguns has long been accepted as imperative; laws relating to "concealed weapons" are common. That we may be "over-regulated" in some areas of life has never held us back from more regulation of automobiles, airplanes, motorboats and "concealed weapons."

Let's look at the history. 7

First, many of the 3.5 million people living in the 13 original 8
Colonies depended on wild game for food, and a good many of them required firearms for their defense from marauding Indians—and later from the French and English. Underlying all these needs was an important concept that each able-bodied man in each of the 13 independent states had to help or defend his state.

The early opposition to the idea of national or standing armies was 9
maintained under the Articles of Confederation; that confederation had no standing army and wanted none. The state militia—essentially a part-time citizen army, as in Switzerland today—was the only kind of "army" they wanted. From the time of the Declaration of Independence through the victory at Yorktown in 1781, George Washington, as the commander-in-chief of these volunteer-militia armies, had to depend upon the states to send those volunteers.

When a company of New Jersey militia volunteers reported for 10
duty to Washington at Valley Forge, the men initially declined to take an oath to "the United States," maintaining, "Our country is New Jersey." Massachusetts Bay men, Virginians and others felt the same way. To the American of the 18th century, his state was his country, and his freedom was defended by his militia.

The victory at Yorktown—and the ratification of the Bill of 11
Rights a decade later—did not change people's attitudes about a national army. They had lived for years under the notion that each state would maintain its own military establishment, and the seaboard states had their own navies as well. These people, and their fathers and grandfathers before them, remembered how monarchs had used standing armies to oppress their ancestors in Europe. Americans wanted no part of this. A state militia, like a rifle and

powder horn, was as much a part of life as the automobile is today; pistols were largely for officers, aristocrats—and dueling.

Against this background, it was not surprising that the provision concerning firearms emerged in very simple terms with the significant predicate—basing the right on the *necessity* for a "well regulated militia," a state army.   12

In the two centuries since then—with two world wars and some lesser ones—it has become clear, sadly, that we have no choice but to maintain a standing national army while still maintaining a "militia" by way of the National Guard, which can be swiftly integrated into the national defense forces.   13

Americans also have a right to defend their homes, and we need not challenge that. Nor does anyone seriously question that the Constitution protects the right of hunters to own and keep sporting guns for hunting game any more than anyone would challenge the right to own and keep fishing rods and other equipment for fishing— or to own automobiles. To "keep and bear arms" for hunting today is essentially a recreational activity and not an imperative of survival, as it was 200 years ago; "Saturday night specials" and machine guns are not recreational weapons and surely are as much in need of regulation as motor vehicles.   14

Americans should ask themselves a few questions. The Constitution does not mention automobiles or motorboats, but the right to keep and own an automobile is beyond question; equally beyond question is the power of the state to regulate the purchase or the transfer of such a vehicle and the right to license the vehicle and the driver with reasonable standards. In some places, even a bicycle must be registered, as must some household dogs.   15

If we are to stop this mindless homicidal carnage, is it unreasonable:

1) to provide that, to acquire a firearm, an application be made reciting age, residence, employment and any prior criminal convictions?   16

2) to require that this application lie on the table for 10 days (absent a showing for urgent need) before the license would be issued?

3) that the transfer of a firearm be made essentially as with that of a motor vehicle?

4) to have a "ballistic fingerprint" of the firearm made by the manufacturer and filed with the license record so that, if a bullet is found in a victim's body, law enforcement might be helped in finding the culprit?

These are the kind of questions the American people must answer if we are to preserve the "domestic tranquility" promised in the Constitution.   17

QUESTIONS OF CONTENT

1. Spitzer examines four Supreme Court rulings on the regulation of firearms in the United States. What do these rulings tend to prove?
2. Why does Spitzer claim that our founding fathers preferred a militia to a standing army?
3. Despite Sugarman's admission that handgun controls would not keep such weapons away from criminals, why does he persist in claiming that such controls would reduce the annual number of deaths caused by handguns?
4. Why does Robert Hughes claim that the NRA quotes only the second half of the Second Amendment to the U.S. Constitution? What is there in the first half that the NRA finds convenient to neglect?
5. Warren Burger insists that the main purpose of the Second Amendment was not to ensure the right to bear arms but some other, more fundamental right. What is that right?

QUESTIONS OF FORM

1. Would you characterize the method of argumentation used by Spitzer as induction or deduction? What sort of evidence does he offer in support of his claim?
2. In the title of his essay Sugarman states that the NRA is right, and he repeatedly makes that assertion as he develops his argument. How many times in all does Sugarman make that statement? And yet the thrust of his argument is clearly against the NRA. What name is usually associated with this sort of tactic? How effective do you find it to be in this essay?
3. Sugarman suggests an analogy between the control of handguns and the prevention of disease. How exactly does that analogy work?
4. In "A Short Guide to Material and Formal Fallacies," look up *slippery slope*. How does this fallacy apply to the argument that Hughes imputes to the NRA?
5. Warren Burger makes an apt comparison when he likens the government's right to register and regulate firearms to its right to register and regulate other things. Which other things does he mention?
6. Burger shifts from refutation to a claim of policy at the conclusion of his argument. What proposal does he make?

SUGGESTIONS FOR WRITING

1. Summarize the major thesis of each of these gun control arguments in a well-organized paper. Try to arrange the argument summaries according to some scale of importance that you can justify.
2. Pick at least two of the strongest gun control arguments that you have examined in this section and include references to them in a

letter that you intend to send to your congressman, who has long been a supporter of the gun lobby. In your letter be sure to give credit for the arguments that you borrow, following the guidelines in Chapter 6's section entitled "Using Sources."

3. You have been a hunter all your life, and you are more than a little offended by the selection of articles in this section, which you immediately recognized as being all on one side of the gun control controversy. You would like to mount a rebuttal, but there is little in these articles that can assist you very much. Here is a brief bibliography that should provide you with some help:

CASSIDAY, J. WARREN. "The Case for Firearms." *Time* 29 Jan. 1990: 22.

"Gun Control Gets Readers Fired Up." *US News and World Report* 31 March 1986: 74.

HODGKINS, ALLEN R. "Right to Bear Arms Underlies All Our Liberties." *The New York Times* 22 Dec. 1989: 22.

KATES, DON B. "Why Gun Control Won't Work." *Commonweal* 13 March 1981: 136–38.

LOFTIN, COLIN, *et al.* "Mandatory Sentencing and Firearms Violence." *Law and Society Review* 17 (1983): 287–318.

Be sure to give appropriate credit for your borrowed ideas and words.

Selected Classic Arguments

This final section of sample essays consists of arguments from distant as well as fairly recent history; some are perhaps already familiar, while undoubtedly others will be new to you. All have been reprinted often enough over the years that they may be considered "classics"; that is, they have survived the so-called "test of time." Certainly they demonstrate effective or even unique means of arguing for thought-provoking ideas, so that you should find each essay worth the effort spent to understand it.

However, you may indeed find yourself struggling somewhat to comprehend these essays, for at least three reasons. First, a couple of them, those by Plato and Machiavelli, were not only written quite long ago but also appeared originally in languages other than English, and thus they have been translated, from Greek and Italian respectively. Sometimes subtleties of thought and expressions fade under those circumstances, although we think these are accurate and accessible translations.

A more important difficulty may arise because the English language of several of the other essays is from earlier eras and in England's version of English, not America's; thus you may find yourself straining somewhat now and then to interpret those essays' older or different forms of English expression.

Finally, all of these classic essays deal with relatively complex or sophisticated ideas and were composed not only for intelligent audiences but often for ones more highly educated than you are right now. However, at this point in this text and in your English course, you certainly should have had much contact with complex ideas, and indeed you are probably not only intelligent but are also moving briskly toward becoming well educated. Thus we are confident that you can handle the challenges these selections present.

Even so, we have decided to offer you a little extra help with these classic essays, in the form of short introductions to each author and the particular selection from his or her work. Also, as we did with the first group of reading selections, we have again provided you with questions of content and of form at the end of each essay, plus some suggestions for related writing (subject to modification by your instructor); review of all of these, along with reading each work's introduction, will make your study of any of these classical arguments easier and more rewarding.

The Duty of a Citizen

PLATO

A citizen of the city-state of Athens, Plato (429–347 B.C.) was one of three great philosophers of classical Greece. The second was Aristotle, who studied with Plato in his Academy, founded in 387 B.C. Plato himself had studied with the other great Greek philosopher, Socrates (469–399 B.C.), whose teachings and life are preserved in such works of Plato as The Republic *and the* Apology, Crito, *and* Phaedo. *These last three works describe the trial, imprisonment, and death of Socrates. The selection that follows is excerpted from the* Crito *and, like almost all of Plato's work, consists of a dialogue between Socrates and someone else. Unjustly condemned to death by a jury of Athenian citizens, and now in prison, Socrates has been conversing with Crito, a prosperous friend and follower.*

soc. Let us consider the matter together, and do you either refute me if you can, and I will be convinced; or else cease, my dear friend, from repeating to me that I ought to escape against the wishes of the Athenians: for I highly value your attempts to persuade me to do so, but I may not be persuaded against my own better judgment. And now please to consider my first position, and try how you can best answer me. 1

cr. I will. 2

soc. Are we to say that we are never intentionally to do wrong, or that in one way we ought and in another we ought not to do wrong, or is doing wrong always evil and dishonourable, as I was just 3 now saying, and as has been already acknowledged by us? Are all our former admissions which were made within a few days to be thrown away? And have we, at our age, been earnestly discoursing with one another all our life long only to discover that we are no better than children? Or, in spite of the opinion of the many, and in spite of consequences whether better or worse, shall we insist on the truth of what was then said, that injustice is always an evil and dishonour to him who acts unjustly? Shall we say so or not?

CR. Yes.   4

SOC. Then we must do no wrong?   5

CR. Certainly not.   6

SOC. Nor when injured injure in return, as the many imagine;   7
for we must injure no one at all?

CR. Clearly not.   8

SOC. Again, Crito, may we do evil?   9

CR. Surely not, Socrates.   10

SOC. And what of doing evil in return for evil, which is the   11
morality of the many—is that just or not?

CR. Not just.   12

SOC. For doing evil to another is the same as injuring him?   13

CR. Very true.   14

SOC. Then we ought not to retaliate or render evil for evil to any   15
one, whatever evil we may have suffered from him. But I would have you consider, Crito, whether you really mean what you are saying. For this opinion has never been held, and never will be held, by any considerable number of persons; and those who are agreed and those who are not agreed upon this point have no common ground, and can only despise one another when they see how widely they differ. Tell me, then, whether you agree with and assent to my first principle, that neither injury nor retaliation nor warding off evil by evil is ever right. And shall that be the premise of our argument? Or do you decline and dissent from this? For so I have ever thought, and continue to think; but, if you are of another opinion, let me hear what you have to say. If, however, you remain of the same mind as formerly, I will proceed to the next step.

CR. You may proceed, for I have not changed my mind.   16

SOC. Then I will go on to the next point, which may be put in   17
the form of a question:—Ought a man to do what he admits to be right, or ought he to betray the right?

CR. He ought to do what he thinks right.   18

SOC. But if this is true, what is the application? In leaving the   19
prison against the will of the Athenians, do I wrong any? Or rather do I not wrong those whom I ought least to wrong? Do I not desert

the principles which were acknowledged by us to be just—what do you say?

CR. I cannot tell, Socrates; for I do not know.   20

SOC. Then consider the matter in this way:—Imagine that I am   21
about to play truant (you may call the proceeding by any name which you like), and the laws and the government come and interrogate me: 'Tell us, Socrates,' they say, 'what are you about? are you not going by an act of yours to overturn us—the laws, and the whole state, as far as in you lies? Do you imagine that a state can subsist and not be overthrown, in which the decisions of law have no power, but are set aside and trampled upon by individuals? What will be our answer, Crito, to these and the like words? Any one, and especially a rhetorician, will have a good deal to say on behalf of the law which requires a sentence to be carried out. He will argue that this law should not be set aside; and shall we reply, 'Yes; but the state has injured us and given an unjust sentence.' Suppose I say that?

CR. Very good, Socrates.   22

SOC. 'And was that our agreement with you?' the law would   23
answer; 'or were you to abide by the sentence of the state?' And if I were to express my astonishment at their words, the law would probably add: 'Answer, Socrates, instead of opening your eyes—you are in the habit of asking and answering questions. Tell us,—What complaint have you to make against us which justifies you in attempting to destroy us and the state? In the first place did we not bring you into existence? Your father married your mother by our aid and begat you. Say whether you have any objection to urge against those of us who regulate marriage?' None, I should reply. 'Or against those of us who after birth regulate the nurture and education of children, in which you also were trained? Were not the laws, which have the charge of education, right in commanding your father to train you in music and gymnastic?' Right, I should reply. 'Well then, since you were brought into the world and nurtured and educated by us, can you deny in the first place that you are our child and slave, as your fathers were before you? And if this is true you are not on equal terms with us; nor can you think that you have a right to do to us what we are doing to you. Would you have any right to strike or revile or do any other evil to your father or your master, if you had one, because you have been struck or reviled by him, or received some other evil at his hands?—you would not say this? And because we think right to destroy you, do you think that you have any right to destroy us in return, and your country as far as in you lies? Will you, O professor of true virtue, pretend that you are justified in this? Has a philosopher like you failed to discover that our country is more to be valued and higher and holier far than mother or father or

any ancestor, and more to be regarded in the eyes of the gods and of men of understanding? also to be soothed, and gently and reverently entreated when angry, even more than a father, and either to be persuaded, or if not persuaded, to be obeyed? And when we are punished by her, whether with imprisonment or stripes, the punishment is to be endured in silence; and if she leads us to wounds or death in battle, thither we follow as is right; neither may any one yield or retreat or leave his rank, but whether in battle or in a court of law, or in any other place, he must do what his city and his country order him; or he must change their view of what is just; and if he may do no violence to his father or mother, much less may he do violence to his country.' What answer shall we make to this, Crito? Do the laws speak truly, or do they not?

CR. I think that they do. 24

SOC. Then the laws will say, 'Consider, Socrates, if we are speaking truly that in your present attempt you are going to do us an injury. For, having brought you into the world, and nurtured and educated you, and given you and every other citizen a share in every good which we had to give, we further proclaim to any Athenian by the liberty which we allow him, that if he does not like us when he has become of age and has seen the ways of the city, and made our acquaintance, he may go where he pleases and take his goods with him. None of us laws will forbid him or interfere with him. Any one who does not like us and the city, and who wants to emigrate to a colony or to any other city, may go where he likes, retaining his property. But he who has experience of the manner in which we order justice and administer the state, and still remains, has entered into an implied contract that he will do as we command him. And he who disobeys us is, as we maintain, thrice wrong; first, because in disobeying us he is disobeying his parents; secondly, because we are the authors of his education; thirdly, because he has made an agreement with us that he will duly obey our commands; and he neither obeys them nor convinces us that our commands are unjust; and we do not rudely impose them, but give him the alternative of obeying or convincing us;—that is what we offer, and he does neither. 25

'These are the sort of accusations to which, as we were saying, you, Socrates, will be exposed if you accomplish your intentions; you, above all other Athenians.' Suppose now I ask, why I rather than anybody else? They will justly retort upon me that I above all other men have acknowledged the agreement. 'There is clear proof,' they will say, 'Socrates, that we and the city were not displeasing to you. Of all Athenians you have been the most constant resident in the city, which, as you never leave, you may be supposed to love. For you never went out of the city either to see the games, except once when you 26 went to the Isthmus, or to any other place unless when you were on military service; nor did you travel as other men do. Nor had you any curiosity to know other states or their laws: your affections did not go beyond us and our state; we were your special favourites, and you acquiesced in our government of you; and here in this city you begat your children, which is a proof of your satisfaction. Moreover, you might in the course of the trial, if you had liked, have fixed the penalty at banishment; the state which refuses to let you go now would have let you go then. But you pretended that you preferred death to exile, and that you were not unwilling to die. And now you have forgotten these fine sentiments, and pay no respect to us the laws, of whom you are the destroyer; and are doing what only a miserable slave would do, running away and turning your back upon the compacts and agreements which you made as a citizen. And first of all answer this very question: Are we right in saying that you agreed to be governed according to us in deed, and not in word only? Is that true or not?' How shall we answer, Crito? Must we not assent?

CR. We cannot help it, Socrates.   27

SOC. Then will they not say: 'You, Socrates, are breaking the   28
covenants and agreements which you made with us at your leisure, not in any haste or under any compulsion or deception, but after you have had seventy years to think of them, during which time you were at liberty to leave the city, if we were not to your mind, or if our covenants appeared to you to be unfair. You had your choice, and might have gone either to Lacedaemon or Crete, both which states are often praised by you for their good government, or to some other Hellenic or foreign state. Whereas you, above all other Athenians, seemed to be so fond of the state, or, in other words, of us her laws (and who would care about a state which has no laws?), that you never stirred out of her; the halt, the blind, the maimed were not more stationary in her than you were. And now you run away and forsake your agreements. Not so, Socrates, if you will take our advice; do not make yourself ridiculous by escaping out of the city.

'For just consider, if you transgress and err in this sort of way,   29
what good will you do either to yourself or to your friends? That your friends will be driven into exile and deprived of citizenship, or will lose their property, is tolerably certain; and you yourself, if you fly to one of the neighboring cities, as, for example, Thebes or Megara, both of which are well governed, will come to them as an enemy, Socrates, and their government will be against you, and all patriotic citizens will cast an evil eye upon you as a subverter of the laws, and you will confirm in the minds of the judges the justice of their own condemnation of you. For he who is a corrupter of the laws is more than likely to be a corrupter of the young and foolish portion of mankind. Will you then flee from well-ordered cities and

virtuous men? And is existence worth having on these terms? Or will you go to them without shame, and talk to them, Socrates? And what will you say to them? What you say here about virtue and justice and institutions and laws being the best things among men? Would that be decent of you? Surely not. But if you go away from well-governed states to Crito's friends in Thessaly, where there is great disorder and licence, they will be charmed to hear the tale of your escape from prison, set off with ludicrous particulars of the manner in which you were wrapped in a goatskin or some other disguise, and metamorphosed as the manner is of runaways; but will there be no one to remind you that in your old age you are not ashamed to violate the most sacred laws from a miserable desire of a little more life? Perhaps not, if you keep them in a good temper; but if they are out of temper you will hear many degrading things; you will live, but how?—as the flatterer of all men, and the servant of all men; and doing what?—eating and drinking in Thessaly, having gone abroad in order that you may get a dinner. And where will be your fine sentiments about justice and virtue? Say that you wish to live for the sake of your children—you want to bring them up and educate them—will you take them into Thessaly and deprive them of Athenian citizenship? Is this the benefit which you will confer upon them? Or are you under the impression that they will be better cared for and educated here if you are still alive, although absent from them; for your friends will take care of them? Do you fancy that if you are an inhabitant of Thessaly they will take care of them, and if you are an inhabitant of the other world that they will not take care of them? Nay; but if you who call themselves friends are good for anything, they will—to be sure they will.

'Listen, then, Socrates, to us who have brought you up. Think not of life and children first, and of justice afterwards, but of justice first, that you may be justified before the princes of the world below. For neither will you nor any that belong to you be happier or holier or juster in this life, or happier in another, if you do as Crito bids. Now you depart in innocence, a sufferer and not a doer of evil; a victim, not of the laws but of men. But if you go forth, returning evil for evil, and injury for injury, breaking the covenants and agreements which you have made with us, and wronging those whom you ought least of all to wrong, that is to say, yourself, your friends, your country, and us, we shall be angry with you while you live, and our brethren, the laws of the world below, will receive you as an enemy; for they will know that you have done your best to destroy us. Listen, then, to us and not to Crito.'

This, dear Crito, is the voice which I seem to hear murmuring in my ears, like the sound of the flute in the ears of the mystic; that voice, I say, is humming in my ears, and prevents me from hearing any other. And I know that anything more which you may say will be vain. Yet speak, if you have anything to say.

cr. I have nothing to say, Socrates.   32

soc. Leave me then, Crito, to fulfil the will of God, and to   33
follow whither he leads.

QUESTIONS OF CONTENT

1. What does Crito propose that Socrates do to avoid death? How is Socrates' situation analogous to that of American males subject to the draft during the Vietnam War? What were their options, besides entering the military and possibly being crippled for life or even dying because of their wounds?
2. What reasons does Socrates give for rejecting Crito's proposal? Which reason seems best to you, and why?
3. Why do you suppose Socrates feels so strongly about remaining loyal to the Athenian laws when they have been unjustly used to condemn him to death?
4. Socrates' conclusion in paragraph 30 seems to depend on a warrant stemming from a belief in an afterlife, where each person will again be judged; what does his argument lose in force if someone does not hold such a belief?

QUESTIONS OF FORM

1. What, if anything, does Plato gain by presenting this argument in dialectic (conversational) form?
2. The argument of Socrates is deductive, though not easy to pick out. What warrant serves as the major premise of his basic syllogism? What sorts of backing or support does he provide?
3. Note Socrates' use in paragraphs 28–29 of comparison and contrast between various city-states of his time; what does he probably hope to accomplish by that comparative approach, and how effective is it?
4. A special feature of the Socratic dialogue is the persistent use of the *rhetorical question* (see the Glossary of Useful Terms in the Appendix), where agreement by the audience is either expected or urged, thus advancing the argument. Where do you find Socrates using this device most effectively to elicit agreement from Crito?

SUGGESTIONS FOR WRITING

1. Write a concise summary of the argument of Socrates.
2. Imagine yourself, like Crito, trying to help save the life of a friend

wrongly condemned to die; write out a brief argument for an alternative modern means to safety.

3. Trade papers written for suggestion 2 with a classmate and pretend you are that person's friend, and also someone who feels as strongly about his or her home area as Socrates did; try writing a refutation of your classmate's suggestion.

4. Compare Socrates' ideas in paragraphs 24–26 with those expressed by Jefferson in paragraph 2 of the Declaration of Independence. Clearly Socrates and Jefferson are at odds here. With whom are you inclined to agree? May a nation's citizens rise against their government as Jefferson claims, or may they not, as Socrates claims? Make your case in an essay, providing suitable support for your opinion.

The Morals of a Prince

NICCOLO MACHIAVELLI
Translated by M. K. Marriott

A native of Florence, Italy, Niccolò Machiavelli (1469–1527) had a diverse career, typical for a Renaissance humanist such as himself. He served Florence (then a republic) and also the great Medici family as a political emissary, and sometimes as a commercial or a military one, traveling widely and observing acutely. Although also a dramatist, novelist, and historian, Machiavelli won lasting fame as the author of The Prince *(written 1513, published 1532), a political treatise on the art of governing. The fame of this small guidebook for new leaders grows from its later chapters, 15–26, which describe the personal attributes of a successful ruler. Although presenting an ideal of leadership, it is realistically grounded in Machiavelli's own direct experience of power politics. As a consequence, "Machiavellian" has become a negative term, one associated with lack of scruples, even wickedness, for* The Prince *reflects its author's pessimism about human nature and openly advises rulers to use hypocrisy and other amoral means to achieve worthwhile ends. The essay reprinted here comprises Chapters 15–18 of* The Prince.

Concerning Things for Which Men, and Especially Princes, Are Praised or Blamed

It remains now to see what ought to be the rules of conduct for a   1
prince towards subject and friends. And as I know that many have

written on this point, I expect I shall be considered presumptuous in mentioning it again, especially as in discussing it I shall depart from the methods of other people. But, it being my intention to write a thing which shall be useful to him who apprehends it, it appears to me more appropriate to follow up the real truth of a matter than the imagination of it; for many have pictured republics and principalities which in fact have never been known or seen, because how one lives is so far distant from how one ought to live, that he who neglects what is done for what ought to be done, sooner effects his ruin than his preservation; for a man who wishes to act entirely up to his professions of virtue soon meets with what destroys him among so much that is evil.

Hence it is necessary for a prince wishing to hold his own to know how to do wrong, and to make use of it or not according to necessity. Therefore, putting on one side imaginary things concerning a prince, and discussing those which are real, I say that all men when they are spoken of, and chiefly princes for being more highly placed, are remarkable for some of those qualities which bring them either blame or praise; and thus it is that one is reputed liberal, another miserly . . . ; one is reputed generous, one rapacious; one cruel, one compassionate; one faithless, another faithful; one effeminate and cowardly, another bold and brave; one affable, another haughty; one lascivious, another chaste; one sincere, another cunning; one hard, another easy; one grave, another frivolous; one religious, another unbelieving, and the like. And I know that every one will confess that it would be most praiseworthy in a prince to exhibit all the above qualities that are considered good; but because they can neither be entirely possessed nor observed, for human conditions do not permit it, it is necessary for him to be sufficiently prudent that he may know how to avoid the reproach of those vices which would lose him his state; and also to keep himself, if it be possible, from those which would not lose him it; but this not being possible, he may with less hesitation abandon himself to them. And again, he need not make himself uneasy at incurring a reproach for those vices without which the state can only be saved with difficulty, for if everything is considered carefully, it will be found that something which looks like virtue, if followed, would be his ruin; whilst something else, which looks like vice, yet followed brings him security and prosperity.

Concerning Liberality and Meanness

Commencing then with the first of the above-named characteristics, I say that it would be well to be reputed liberal. Nevertheless, liberality exercised in a way that does not bring you the reputation for it, injures you; for if one exercises it honestly and as it should be exercised, it may not become known, and you will not avoid the reproach of its opposite. Therefore, anyone wishing to maintain among men the name of liberal is obliged to avoid no attribute of magnificence; so that a prince thus inclined will consume in such acts all his property, and will be compelled in the end, if he wish to maintain the name of liberal, to unduly weigh down his people, and tax them, and do everything he can to get money. This will soon make him odious to his subjects, and becoming poor he will be little valued by anyone; thus, with his liberality, having offended many and rewarded few, he is affected by the very first trouble and imperilled by whatever may be the first danger; recognising this himself, and wishing to draw back from it, he runs at once into the reproach of being miserly.

Therefore, a prince, not being able to exercise this virtue of liberality in such a way that it is recognised, except to his cost, if he is wise he ought not to fear the reputation of being mean, for in time he will come to be more considered than if liberal, seeing that with his economy his revenues are enough, that he can defend himself against all attacks, and is able to engage in enterprises without burdening his people; thus it comes to pass that he exercises liberality towards all from whom he does not take, who are numberless, and meanness towards those to whom he does not give, who are few.

We have not seen great things done in our time except by those who have been considered mean; the rest have failed. Pope Julius the Second was assisted in reaching the papacy by a reputation for liberality, yet he did not strive afterwards to keep it up, when he made war on the King of France; and he made many wars without imposing any extraordinary tax on his subjects, for he supplied his additional expenses out of his long thriftiness. The present King of Spain would not have undertaken or conquered in so many enterprises if he had been reputed liberal. A prince, therefore, provided that he has not to rob his subjects, that he can defend himself, that he does not become poor and abject, that he is not forced to become rapacious, ought to hold of little account a reputation for being mean, for it is one of those vices which will enable him to govern.

And if anyone should say: Cæsar obtained empire by liberality, and many others have reached the highest positions by having been liberal, and by being considered so, I answer: Either you are a prince in fact, or in a way to become one. In the first case this liberality is dangerous, in the second it is very necessary to be considered liberal; and Cæsar was one of those who wished to become pre-eminent in Rome; but if he had survived after becoming so, and had not moderated his expenses, he would have destroyed his government. And if anyone should reply: Many have been princes, and have done great things with armies, who have been considered very liberal, I reply: Either a prince spends that which is his own or his subjects' or else that of others. In the first case he ought to be sparing, in the second he ought not to neglect any opportunity for liberality. And to the prince who goes forth with his army, supporting it by pillage, sack, and extortion, handling that which belongs to others, this liberality is necessary, otherwise he would not be followed by soldiers. And of that which is neither yours nor your subjects' you can be a ready giver, as were Cyrus, Cæsar, and Alexander; because it does not take away your reputation if you squander that of others, but adds to it; it is only squandering your own that injures you.

And there is nothing wastes so rapidly as liberality, for even whilst you exercise it you lose the power to do so, and so become either poor or despised, or else, in avoiding poverty, rapacious and hated. And a prince should guard himself, above all things, against being despised and hated; and liberality leads you to both. Therefore it is wiser to have a reputation for meanness which brings reproach without hatred, than to be compelled through seeking a reputation for liberality to incur a name for rapacity which begets reproach with hatred.

7

Concerning Cruelty and Clemency, and Whether It Is Better to Be Loved Than Feared

Coming now to the other qualities mentioned above, I say that every prince ought to desire to be considered clement and not cruel. Nevertheless he ought to take care not to misuse this clemency. Cesare Borgia was considered cruel; notwithstanding, his cruelty reconciled the Romagna, unified it, and restored it to peace and loyalty. And if this be rightly considered, he will be seen to have been much more merciful than the Florentine people, who, to avoid a reputation for cruelty, permitted Pistoia to be destroyed. Therefore a prince, so long as he keeps his subjects united and loyal, ought not to mind the reproach of cruelty; because with a few examples he will be more merciful than those who, through too much mercy, allow disorders to arise, from which follow murder or robbery; for these are wont to injure the whole people, whilst those executions which originate with a prince offend the individual only.

8

And of all princes, it is impossible for the new prince to avoid the imputation of cruelty, owing to new states being full of dangers. Hence Virgil, through the mouth of Dido, excuses the inhumanity of her reign owing to its being new, saying:

9

"Res dura, et regni novitas me talia cogunt
Moliri, et late fines custode tueri."*

Nevertheless he ought to be slow to believe and to act, nor should he himself show fear, but proceed in a temperate manner with prudence and humanity, so that too much confidence may not make him incautious and too much distrust render him intolerable.

Upon this a question arises: whether it be better to be loved than   10
feared or feared than loved? It may be answered that one should wish to be both, but, because it is difficult to unite them in one person, it is much safer to be feared than loved, when, of the two, either must be dispensed with. Because this is to be asserted in general of men, that they are ungrateful, fickle, false, cowards, covetous, and as long as you succeed they are yours entirely; they will offer you their blood, property, life, and children, as is said above, when the need is far distant; but when it approaches they turn against you. And that prince who, relying entirely on their promises, has neglected other precautions, is ruined; because friendships that are obtained by payments, and not by greatness or nobility of mind, may indeed be earned, but they are not secured, and in time of need cannot be relied upon; and men have less scruple in offending one who is beloved than one who is feared, for love is preserved by the link of obligation which, owing to the baseness of men, is broken at every opportunity for their advantage; but fear preserves you by a dread of punishment which never fails.

Nevertheless a prince ought to inspire fear in such a way that, if   11
he does not win love, he avoids hatred; because he can endure very well being feared whilst he is not hated, which will always be as long as he abstains from the property of his citizens and subjects and from their women. But when it is necessary for him to proceed against the life of someone, he must do it on proper justification and for manifest cause, but above all things he must keep his hands off the property of others, because men more quickly forget the death of their father than the loss of their patrimony. Besides, pretexts for taking away the property are never wanting; for he who has once begun to live by robbery will always find pretexts for seizing what belongs to others; but reasons for taking life, on the contrary, are more difficult to find and sooner lapse. But when a prince is with his army, and has under control a multitude of soldiers, then it is quite necessary for him to disregard the reputation of cruelty, for without it he would never hold his army united or disposed to its duties.

----

*Translation: "Hard times and the newness of my realm oblige me to do these things and to look to the keeping of my borders."

Among the wonderful deeds of Hannibal this one is enumerated: 12
that having led an enormous army, composed of many various races
of men, to fight in foreign lands, no dissensions arose either among
them or against the prince, whether in his bad or in his good fortune.
This arose from nothing else than his inhuman cruelty, which, with
his boundless valour, made him revered and terrible in the sight of
his soldiers, but without that cruelty, his other virtues were not
sufficient to produce this effect. And short-sighted writers admire
his deeds from one point of view and from another condemn the
principal cause of them. That it is true his other virtues would not
have been sufficient for him may be proved by the case of Scipio,
that most excellent man, not only of his own times but within the
memory of man, against whom, nevertheless, his army rebelled in
Spain; this arose from nothing but his too great forbearance, which
gave his soldiers more licence than is consistent with military discipline. For this he was upbraided in the Senate by Fabius Maximus,
and called the corruptor of the Roman soldiery. The Locrians were
laid waste by a legate of Scipio, yet they were not avenged by him,
nor was the insolence of the legate punished, owing entirely to his
easy nature. Insomuch that some one in the Senate, wishing to excuse him, said there were many men who knew much better how
not to err than to correct the errors of others. This disposition, if he
had been continued in the command, would have destroyed in time
the fame and glory of Scipio; but, he being under the control of the
Senate, this injurious characteristic not only concealed itself, but
contributed to his glory.

Returning to the question of being feared or loved, I come to the 13
conclusion that, men loving according to their own will and fearing
according to that of the prince, a wise prince should establish himself on that which is in his own control and not in that of others; he
must endeavour only to avoid hatred, as is noted.

Concerning the Way in Which Princes Should Keep Faith

Everyone admits how praiseworthy it is in a prince to keep faith, 14
and to live with integrity and not with craft. Nevertheless our experience has been that those princes who have done great things have
held good faith of little account, and have known how to circumvent
the intellect of men by craft, and in the end have overcome those
who have relied on their word. You must know there are two ways of
contesting, the one by the law, the other by force; the first method is
proper to men, the second to beasts; but because the first is frequently not sufficient, it is necessary to have recourse to the second.

Therefore it is necessary for a prince to understand how to avail himself of the beast and the man. This has been figuratively taught to princes by ancient writers, who describe how Achilles and many other princes of old were given to the Centaur Chiron to nurse, who brought them up in his discipline; which means solely that, as they had for a teacher one who was half beast and half man, so it is necessary for a prince to know how to make use of both natures, and that one without the other is not durable. A prince, therefore, being compelled knowingly to adopt the beast, ought to choose the fox and the lion; because the lion cannot defend himself against snares and the fox cannot defend himself against wolves. Therefore, it is necessary to be a fox to discover the snares and a lion to terrify the wolves. Those who rely simply on the lion do not understand what they are about. Therefore a wise lord cannot, nor ought he to, keep faith when such observance may be turned against him, and when the reasons that caused him to pledge it exist no longer. If men were entirely good this precept would not hold, but because they are bad, and will not keep faith with you, you too are not bound to observe it with them. Nor will there ever be wanting to a prince legitimate reasons to excuse this non-observance. Of this endless modern examples could be given, showing how many treaties and engagements have been made void and of no effect through the faithlessness of princes; and he who has known best how to employ the fox has succeeded best.

But it is necessary to know well how to disguise this characteristic, and to be a great pretender and dissembler; and men are so simple, and so subject to present necessities, that he who seeks to deceive will always find some one who will allow himself to be deceived. One recent example I cannot pass over in silence. Alexander the Sixth did nothing else but deceive men, nor ever thought of doing otherwise, and he always found victims; for there never was a man who had greater power in asserting, or who with greater oaths would affirm a thing, yet would observe it less; nevertheless his deceits always succeeded according to his wishes, because he well understood this side of mankind.

Therefore it is unnecessary for a prince to have all the good qualities I have enumerated, but it is very necessary to appear to have them. And I shall dare to say this also, that to have them and always to observe them is injurious, and that to appear to have them is useful; to appear merciful, faithful, humane, religious, upright, and to be so, but with a mind so framed that should you require not to be so, you may be able and know how to change to the opposite.

And you have to understand this, that a prince, especially a new one, cannot observe all those things for which men are esteemed, being often forced, in order to maintain the state, to act contrary to fidelity, friendship, humanity, and religion. Therefore it is necessary for him to have a mind ready to turn itself accordingly as the winds and variations of fortune force it, yet, as I have said above, not to diverge from the good if he can avoid doing so, but, if compelled, then to know how to set about it.

For this reason a prince ought to take care that he never lets 18
anything slip from his lips that is not replete with the above-named five qualities, that he may appear to him who sees and hears him altogether merciful, faithful, humane, upright, and religious. There is nothing more necessary to appear to have than this last quality, inasmuch as men judge generally more by the eye than by the hand, because it belongs to everybody to see you, to few to come in touch with you. Every one sees what you appear to be, few really know what you are, and those few dare not oppose themselves to the opinion of the many, who have the majesty of the state to defend them; and in the actions of all men, and especially of princes, which it is not prudent to challenge, one judges by the result.

For that reason, let a prince have the credit of conquering and 19
holding his state, the means will always be considered honest, and he will be praised by everybody; because the vulgar are always taken by what a thing seems to be and by what comes of it; and in the world there are only the vulgar, for the few find a place there only when the many have no ground to rest on.

One prince of the present time, whom it is not well to name, 20
never preaches anything else but peace and good faith, and to both he is most hostile, and either, if he had kept it, would have deprived him of reputation and kingdom many a time.

QUESTIONS OF CONTENT

1. In his work Machiavelli blends pragmatism about princely behavior with cynicism about the conduct of the general public, so that he often argues in support of hypocrisy, for seeming rather than being; where do you see this tendency?
2. Machiavelli repeatedly examines alternative behaviors a prince or leader might choose; where does he do so, and how appropriate today is his advice in each place?
3. Machiavelli insists in paragraph 11 that one of the worst actions of a leader is confiscating property, for "men more quickly forget the death of their father than the loss of their patrimony [inheritance

from one's father]." Assuming this was once an accurate assessment of human psychology, and also good advice, how useful is Machiavelli's advice now, and why?

4. In paragraph 18, Machiavelli suggests why hypocritical behavior is so desirable when he describes how people judge. How does he say they judge? Do you agree that his claim is an accurate reflection of many people? Why, or why not? Even if what he says is true, is this an acceptable excuse for hypocrisy?

QUESTIONS OF FORM

1. This essay is organized by comparison/contrast; what two things are being compared, and what is gained by this approach?
2. What warrant having to do with the effectiveness of a ruler seems to lie behind this whole essay?
3. Although you may not recognize many of his allusions or references to political figures of his own and earlier times, you should recognize the sort of appeal which Machiavelli employs so often. What sort is it, and why is it so useful for this particular subject?
4. In this essay's most famous section (paragraph 14), Machiavelli uses *analogy* to argue for particular kinds of princely behavior; how appropriate and useful are his comparisons of a prince to a fox and a lion?

SUGGESTIONS FOR WRITING

1. Write a summary of one of the four sections of Machiavelli's essay.
2. Write a letter to a newly-elected or appointed leader, attempting to convince her or him to read and to heed (or to avoid) the advice in one of this essay's four sections.
3. Attack or defend one of these statements by Machiavelli, remembering to provide specific support for your point of view:
    a. " ... a man [or woman] who wishes to act entirely up to his [her] professions of virtue soon meets with what destroys him [her] among so much that is evil." (Paragraph 1)
    b. " ... if one exercises it [liberality] honestly and as it should be exercised, it may not become known, and you will not avoid the reproach of its opposite." (Paragraph 3)
    c. " ... friendships that are obtained by payments, and not by greatness or nobility of mind, may indeed be earned, but they are not secured, and in time of need cannot be relied upon. ...." (Paragraph 10)
    d. "Everyone sees what you appear to be, [but] few really know what you are. ..." (Paragraph 18)

A Modest Proposal

JONATHAN SWIFT

An English clergyman born in Ireland, Jonathan Swift (1667–1745)
is best known as the author of Gulliver's Travels *(1726), certainly*
one of the foremost satirical works in English or any other lan-
guage. A writer of political tracts, poems, and essays, Swift's satiri-
cal power is obvious in his ironic masterpiece, "A Modest Pro-
posal" (1729). Careful readers can detect, behind his mask of calm
reason and matter-of-fact language, Swift's genuine concern for
the plight of the Irish poor, who were suffering mass starvation in
the 1720s under oppressive British rule.

It is a melancholy object to those who walk through this great 1
town [Dublin], or travel in the country, when they see the streets,
the roads, and cabin-doors, crowded with beggars of the female sex,
followed by three, four, or six children, all in rags, and importuning
every passenger for an alms. These mothers, instead of being able to
work for their honest livelihood, are forced to employ all their time
in strolling to beg sustenance for their helpless infants; who, as they
grow up, either turn thieves for want of work, or leave their dear
native country to fight for the Pretender in Spain, or sell themselves
to the Barbadoes.

I think it is agreed by all parties, that this prodigious number of 2
children in the arms, or on the backs, or at the heels of their mothers, and frequently of their fathers, is, in the present deplorable state
of the kingdom, a very great additional grievance; and, therefore,
whoever could find out a fair, cheap, and easy method of making
these children sound, useful members of the commonwealth, would
deserve so well of the public, as to have his statue set up for a
preserver of the nation.

But my intention is very far from being confined to provide only 3
for the children of professed beggars; it is of a much greater extent,
and shall take in the whole number of infants at a certain age, who
are born of parents in effect as little able to support them, as those
who demand our charity in the streets.

As to my own part, having turned my thoughts for many years 4
upon this important subject, and maturely weighed the several
schemes of our projectors, I have always found them grossly mistaken in their computation. It is true, a child, just dropped from its

dam, may be supported by her milk for a solar year, with little other nourishment; at most, not above the value of two shillings, which the mother may certainly get, or the value in scraps, by her lawful occupation of begging; and it is exactly at one year old that I proposed to provide for them in such a manner, as, instead of being a charge upon their parents, or the parish, or wanting food and raiment for the rest of their lives, they shall, on the contrary, contribute to the feeding and partly to the clothing, of many thousands.

There is likewise another great advantage in my scheme, that it will prevent those voluntary abortions, and that horrid practice of women murdering their bastard children, alas, too frequent among us! sacrificing the poor innocent babes, I doubt more to avoid the expense than the shame, which would move tears and pity in the most savage and inhuman breast.

The number of souls in this kingdom being usually reckoned one million and a half, of these I calculate there may be about two hundred thousand couple whose wives are breeders; from which number I subtract thirty thousand couple, who are able to maintain their own children (although I apprehend there cannot be so many, under the present distresses of the kingdom); but this being granted, there will remain a hundred and seventy thousand breeders. I again subtract fifty thousand, for those women who miscarry, or whose children die by accident or disease within the year. There only remain a hundred and twenty thousand children of poor parents annually born. The question therefore is, How this number shall be reared and provided for? which, as I have already said, under the present situation of affairs, is utterly impossible by all the methods hitherto proposed. For we can neither employ them in handicraft, or agriculture; we neither build houses (I mean in the country,) nor cultivate land: they can very seldom pick up a livelihood by stealing, till they arrive at six years old, except where they are of towardly parts; although I confess they learn the rudiments much earlier; during which time they can, however, be properly looked upon only as probationers; as I have been informed by a principal gentleman in the county of Cavan, who protested to me, that he never knew above one or two instances under the age of six, even in a part of the kingdom so renowned for the quickest proficiency in that art.

I am assured by our merchants, that a boy or a girl before twelve years old is no saleable commodity; and even when they come to this age they will not yield above three pounds, or three pounds and a half-a-crown at most, on the exchange; which cannot turn to account either to the parents or kingdom, the charge of nutriment and rags having been at least four times that value.

I shall now, therefore, humbly propose my own thoughts, which [8] I hope will not be liable to the least objection.

I have been assured by a very knowing American of my acquain- [9] tance in London, that a young healthy child, well nursed, is, at a year old, a most delicious, nourishing, and wholesome food, whether stewed, roasted, baked, or boiled; and I make no doubt that it will equally serve in a fricassee or a ragout.

I do therefore humbly offer it to public consideration, that of the [10] hundred and twenty thousand children already computed, twenty thousand may be reserved for breed; whereof only one-fourth part to be males; which is more than we allow to sheep, black-cattle, or swine; and my reason is, that these children are seldom the fruits of marriage, a circumstance not much regarded by our savages, therefore one male will be sufficient to serve four females. That the remaining hundred thousand may, at a year old, be offered in sale to the persons of quality and fortune through the kingdom; always advising the mother to let them suck plentifully in the last month, so as to render them plump and fat for a good table. A child will make two dishes at an entertainment for friends; and when the family dines alone, the fore or hind quarter will make a reasonable dish, and, seasoned with a little pepper or salt, will be very good boiled on the fourth day, especially in winter.

I have reckoned, upon a medium, that a child just born will [11] weigh twelve pounds, and in a solar year, if tolerably nursed, will increase to twenty-eight pounds.

I grant this food will be somewhat dear, and therefore very [12] proper for landlords, who, as they have already devoured most of the parents, seem to have the best title to the children.

Infants' flesh will be in season throughout the year, but more [13] plentifully in March, and a little before and after: for we are told by a grave author, an eminent French physician, that fish being a prolific diet, there are more children born in Roman Catholic countries about nine months after Lent, than at any other season; therefore, reckoning a year after Lent, the markets will be more glutted than usual, because the number of Popish infants is at least three to one in this kingdom; and therefore it will have one other collateral advantage, by lessening the number of Papists among us.

I have already computed the charge of nursing a beggar's child (in [14] which list I reckon all cottagers, labourers, and four-fifths of the farmers) to be about two shillings per annum, rags included; and I believe no gentleman would repine to give ten shillings for the carcass of a good fat child, which, as I have said, will make four dishes of excellent nutritive meat, when he has only some particular friend, or his own family, to dine with him. Thus the squire will learn to be a good landlord, and grow popular among his tenants; the mother will have eight shillings net profit, and be fit for work till she produces another child.

Those who are more thrifty (as I must confess the times require) may flay the carcass; the skin of which, artificially dressed, will make admirable gloves for ladies, and summer-boots for fine gentlemen. 15

As to our city of Dublin, shambles [slaughter houses] may be appointed for this purpose in the most convenient parts of it, and butchers, we may be assured, will not be wanting; although I rather recommend buying the children alive, then dressing them hot from the knife, as we do roasting pigs. 16

A very worthy person, a true lover of his country, and whose virtues I highly esteem, was lately pleased, in discoursing on this matter, to offer a refinement upon my scheme. He said, that many gentlemen of this kingdom, having of late destroyed their deer, he conceived that the want of venison might be well supplied by the bodies of young lads and maidens, not exceeding fourteen years of age, nor under twelve; so great a number of both sexes in every country being now ready to starve for want of work and service; and these to be disposed of by their parents, if alive, or otherwise by their nearest relations. But, with due deference to so excellent a friend, and so deserving a patriot, I cannot be altogether in his sentiments; for as to the males, my American acquaintance assured me, from frequent experience, that their flesh was generally tough and lean, like that of our schoolboys, by continual exercise, and their taste disagreeable; and to fatten them would not answer the charge. Then as to the females, it would, I think, with humble submission, be a loss to the public, because they soon would become breeders themselves: and besides, it is not improbable that some scrupulous people might be apt to censure such a practice (although indeed very unjustly), as a little bordering upon cruelty; which, I confess, has always been with me the strongest objection against any project, how well soever intended. 17

But in order to justify my friend, he confessed that this expedient was put into his head by the famous Psalmanazar, a native of the island Formosa, who came from thence to London above twenty years ago; and in conversation told my friend, that in his country, when any young person happened to be put to death, the executioner sold the carcass to persons of quality as a prime dainty; and that in his time the body of a plump girl of fifteen, who was crucified for an attempt to poison the emperor, was sold to his imperial majesty's prime minister of state, and other great mandarins of the court, in 18 joints from the gibbet, at four hundred crowns. Neither indeed can I deny, that, if the same use were made of several plump young girls in this town, who, without one single groat to their fortunes, cannot stir abroad without a chair, and appear at playhouse and assemblies in foreign fineries which they never will pay for, the kingdom would not be the worse.

Some persons of a desponding spirit are in great concern about 19 that vast number of poor people, who are aged, diseased, or maimed; and I have been desired to employ my thoughts, what course may be taken to ease the nation of so grievous an encumbrance. But I am not in the least pain upon that matter, because it is very well known, that they are every day dying, and rotting, by cold and famine, and filth and vermin, as fast as can be reasonably expected. And as to the young labourers, they are now in almost as hopeful a condition: they cannot get work, and consequently pine away for want of nourishment, to a degree, that if at any time they are accidentally hired to common labour, they have not strength to perform it; and thus the country and themselves are happily delivered from the evils to come.

I have too long digressed, and therefore shall return to my sub- 20 ject. I think the advantages by the proposal which I have made are obvious and many, as well as of the highest importance.

For first, as I have already observed, it would greatly lessen the 21 number of Papists, with whom we are yearly over-run, being the principal breeders of the nation, as well as our most dangerous enemies; and who stay at home on purpose to deliver the kingdom to the Pretender, hoping to take their advantage by the absence of so many good Protestants, who have chosen rather to leave their country than stay at home and pay tithes against their conscience to an Episcopal curate.

Secondly, The poorer tenants will have something valuable of 22 their own, which by law may be made liable to distress, and help to pay their landlord's rent; their corn and cattle being already seized, and money a thing unknown.

Thirdly, Whereas the maintenance of a hundred thousand chil- 23 dren, from two years old and upward, cannot be computed at less than ten shillings a piece per annum, the nation's stock will be thereby increased fifty thousand pounds per annum, beside the profit of a new dish introduced to the tables of all gentlemen of fortune in the kingdom, who have any refinement in taste. And the money will circulate among ourselves, the goods being entirely of our own growth and manufacture.

Fourthly, The constant breeders, beside the gain of eight shil- 24 lings sterling per annum by the sale of their children, will be rid of the charge of maintaining them after the first year.

Fifthly, This food would likewise bring great custom to taverns; where the vintners will certainly be so prudent as to procure the best receipts for dressing it to perfection, and, consequently, have their houses frequented by all the fine gentlemen, who justly value themselves upon their knowledge in good eating; and a skilful cook, who understands how to oblige his guests, will contrive to make it as expensive as they please.   25

Sixthly, This would be a great inducement to marriage, which all wise nations have either encouraged by rewards, or enforced by laws and penalties. It would increase the care and tenderness of mothers toward their children, when they were sure of a settlement for life to the poor babes, provided in some sort by the public, to their annual profit or expense. We should see an honest emulation among the married women, which of them could bring the fattest child to the market. Men would become as fond of their wives during the time of their pregnancy as they are now of their mares in foal, their cows in calf, their sows when they are ready to farrow; nor offer to beat or kick them (as is too frequent a practice) for fear of a miscarriage.   26

Many other advantages might be enumerated. For instance, the addition of some thousand carcasses in our exportation of barrelled beef; the propagation of swine's flesh, and improvement in the art of making good bacon, so much wanted among us by the great destruction of pigs, too frequent at our table; which are no way comparable in taste or magnificence to a well-grown, fat, yearling child, which, roasted whole, will make a considerable figure at a lord mayor's feast, or any other public entertainment. But this, and many others, I omit, being studious of brevity.   27

Supposing that one thousand families in this city would be constant customers for infants' flesh, beside others who might have it at merry-meetings, particularly at weddings and christenings, I compute that Dublin would take off annually about twenty thousand carcasses; and the rest of the kingdom (where probably they will be sold somewhat cheaper) the remaining eighty thousand.   28

I can think of no one objection, that will possibly be raised against this proposal, unless it should be urged, that the number of people will be thereby much lessened in the kingdom. This I freely own, and it was indeed one principal design in offering it to the world. I desire the reader will observe, that I calculate my remedy for this one individual kingdom of Ireland, and for no other that ever was, is, or I think ever can be, upon earth. Therefore let no man talk to me of other expedients: of taxing our absentees at five shillings a   29 pound: of using neither clothes, nor household furniture except what is our own growth and manufacture: of utterly rejecting the materials and instruments that promote foreign luxury: of curing the expensiveness of pride, vanity, idleness, and gaming in our women: of introducing a vein of parsimony, prudence, and temperance: of learning to love our country, in the want of which we differ even from Laplanders, and the inhabitants of Topinamboo: of quitting our animosities and factions, nor acting any longer like the Jews, who were murdering one another at the very moment their city was taken: of being a little cautious not to sell our country and conscience for nothing: of teaching landlords to have at least one degree of mercy toward their tenants: lastly, of putting a spirit of honesty, industry, and skill into our shopkeepers; who, if a resolution could now be taken to buy only our native goods, would immediately unite to cheat and exact upon us in the price, the measure, and the goodness, nor could ever yet be brought to make one fair proposal of just dealing, though often and earnestly invited to it.

Therefore I repeat, let no man talk to me of these and the like   30
expedients, till he has at least some glimpse of hope, that there will be ever some hearty and sincere attempt to put them in practice.

But, as to myself, having been wearied out for many years with   31
offering vain, idle, visionary thoughts, and at length utterly despairing of success, I fortunately fell upon this proposal; which, as it is wholly new, so it has something solid and real, of no expense and little trouble, full in our own power, and whereby we can incur no danger in disobliging England. For this kind of commodity will not bear exportation, the flesh being of too tender a consistence to admit a long continuance in salt, although perhaps I could name a country, which would be glad to eat up our whole nation without it.

After all, I am not so violently bent upon my own opinions as to   32
reject any offer proposed by wise men, which shall be found equally innocent, cheap, easy, and effectual. But before something of that kind shall be advanced in contradiction to my scheme, and offering a better, I desire the author, or authors, will be pleased maturely to consider two points. First as things now stand, how they will be able to find food and raiment for a hundred thousand useless mouths and backs. And, secondly, there being a round million of creatures in human figure throughout this kingdom, whose whole subsistence put into a common stock would leave them in debt two millions of pounds sterling, adding those who are beggars by profession, to the bulk of farmers, cottagers, and labourers, with the wives and children who are beggars in effect; I desire those politicians who dislike my overture, and may perhaps be so bold as to attempt an answer, that they will first ask the parents of these mortals, whether they

would not at this day think it a great happiness to have been sold for food at a year old, in the manner I prescribe, and thereby have avoided such a perpetual scene of misfortunes, as they have since gone through, by the oppression of landlords, the impossibility of paying rent without money or trade, the want of common sustenance, with neither house nor clothes to cover them from the inclemencies of the weather, and the most inevitable prospect of entailing the like, or greater miseries, upon their breed for ever.

I profess, in the sincerity of my heart, that I have not the least 33 personal interest in endeavouring to promote this necessary work, having no other motive than the public good of my country, by advancing our trade, providing for infants, relieving the poor, and giving some pleasure to the rich. I have no children by which I can propose to get a single penny; the youngest being nine years old, and my wife past child-bearing.

QUESTIONS OF CONTENT

1. This satirical essay uses understatement as its principal ironic device to focus attention on the desperate poverty of many Irish people in the 1720s. Who might be among Swift's intended audience for this essay, and how can you tell?
2. What is the particular problem Swift sees, and how does he propose to solve it?
3. What benefits of his proposal does Swift point out?
4. Why do you suppose Swift, who never married, included facts about a fictitious family in his final paragraph?

QUESTIONS OF FORM

1. Swift has obviously made a claim of policy, but it is pretty clearly an outrageous and exaggerated proposal, and thus is not modest at all. Why might he have chosen this ironic approach?
2. How is his entire argument at the same time both serious and an example of one kind of material fallacy?
3. Swift's tone of calm reason masks the murderous reality of his proposal; where are there particularly effective instances of this artfully ironic language?
4. Note how often Swift provides specific calculations or statistics; what does his essay gain by this practice? Similarly, what does he gain by carefully enumerating the probable benefits of his proposal in paragraphs 21–27?

SUGGESTIONS FOR WRITING

1. Examine carefully the six advantages of Swift's proposal that he describes in paragraphs 21–26, and then write a logical refutation of one of those, making clear why you find fault with it.
2. Using a tone of calm reason similar to Swift's, compose your own outrageous satirical proposal for curing some current social malady.
3. Now, in the form of a straightforward claim of policy, write your denunciation and proposed solution of the same problem satirized in suggestion 2, citing first the claim of fact (the deplorable situation), followed by the proposed solution. Which of these efforts seems to you to be the more effective approach—or the one most worth pursuing?

An Argument Against Payment of Salaries to Executive Officers of the Federal Government

BENJAMIN FRANKLIN

A native of Boston, Benjamin Franklin (1706–1790) moved as a teenager to Philadelphia, where he eventually became a leading citizen by living the sensible precepts he outlined in the many editions of Poor Richard's Almanack, *which he compiled and published. By his fortieth year, his writing, printing, and publishing ventures had made him wealthy enough to retire from business, but his active mind and bodily vigor impelled him into other arenas, including science and technology (where he was constantly experimenting and inventing) and public service. He was one of the signers of the Declaration of Independence, the first American ambassador to France, and a delegate to the new republic's Constitutional Convention, where he made the following speech on June 2, 1787.*

Sir, it is with reluctance that I rise to express a disapprobation of   1
any one article of the plan, for which we are so much obliged to the honorable gentleman who laid it before us. From its first reading, I have borne a good will to it, and, in general, wished it success. In this particular of salaries to the executive branch, I happen to differ; and, as my opinion may appear new and chimerical, it is only from a persuasion that it is right, and from a sense of duty, that I hazard it. The Committee will judge of my reasons when they have heard them, and their judgment may possibly change mine. I think I see

inconveniences in the appointment of salaries; I see none in refusing them, but on the contrary great advantages.

Sir, there are two passions which have a powerful influence in the affairs of men. These are *ambition* and *avarice:* the love of power and the love of money. Separately, each of these has great force in prompting men to action; but when united in view of the same object, they have in many minds the most violent effects. Place before the eyes of such men a post of *honor,* that shall at the same time be a place of *profit,* and they will move heaven and earth to obtain it. The vast number of such places it is that renders the British government so tempestuous. The struggles for them are the true source of all those factions which are perpetually dividing the nation, distracting its councils, hurrying it sometimes into fruitless and mischievous wars, and often compelling a submission to dishonorable terms of peace.

And of what kind are the men that will strive for this profitable pre-eminence, through all the bustle of cabal, the heat of contention, the infinite mutual abuse of parties, tearing to pieces the best of characters? It will not be the wise and moderate, the lovers of peace and good order, the men fittest for the trust. It will be the bold and violent, the men of strong passions and indefatigable activity in their selfish pursuits. These will thrust themselves into your government, and be your rulers. And these, too, will be mistaken in the expected happiness of their situation; for their vanquished competitors, of the same spirit, and from the same motives, will perpetually be endeavoring to distress their administration, thwart their measures, and render them odious to the people.

Besides these evils, sir, though we may set out in the beginning with moderate salaries, we shall find that such will not be of long continuance. Reasons will never be wanting for proposed augmentations, and there will always be a party for giving more to the rulers, that the rulers may be able in return to give more to them. Hence, as all history informs us, there has been in every state and kingdom a constant kind of warfare between the governing and the governed; the one striving to obtain more for its support, and the other to pay less. And this alone has occasioned great convulsions, actual civil wars, ending either in dethroning of the princes or enslaving of the people.

Generally, indeed, the ruling power carries its point, and we see the revenues of princes constantly increasing, and we see that they are never satisfied, but always in want of more. The more the people are discontented with the oppression of taxes, the greater need the prince has of money to distribute among his partisans, and pay the troops that are to suppress all resistance and enable him to plunder at pleasure. There is scarce a king in a hundred, who would not, if he could, follow the example of Pharaoh—get first all the people's money, then all their lands, and then make them and their children servants forever.

It will be said that we do not propose to establish kings. I know it. But there is a natural inclination in mankind to kingly government. It sometimes relieves them from aristocratic domination. They had rather have one tyrant than five hundred. It gives more of the appearance of equality among citizens; and that they like. I am apprehensive, therefore—perhaps too apprehensive—that the government of these states may in future times end in a monarchy. But this catastrophe, I think, may be long delayed, if in our proposed system we do not sow the seeds of contention, faction, and tumult, by making our posts of honor places of profit. If we do, I fear that, though we employ at first a number and not a single person, the number will in time be set aside; it will only nourish the foetus of a king (as the honorable gentleman from Virginia very aptly expressed it), and a king will the sooner be set over us.

It may be imagined by some that this is an utopian idea, and that we can never find men to serve us in the executive department, without paying them well for their services. I conceive this to be a mistake. Some existing facts present themselves to me, which incline me to a contrary opinion. The High Sheriff of a county in England is an honorable office, but it is not a profitable one. It is rather expensive, and therefore not sought for. But yet it is executed, and well executed, and usually by some of the principal gentlemen of the country. In France, the office of Counsellor, or member of their judiciary parliaments, is more honorable. It is therefore purchased at a high price; there are indeed fees on the law proceedings, which are divided among them, but these fees do not amount to more than three per cent on the sum paid for the place. Therefore, as legal interest is there at five per cent, they in fact pay two per cent for being allowed to do the judiciary business of the nation, which is at the same time entirely exempt from the burden of paying them any salaries for their services. I do not, however, mean to recommend this as an eligible mode for our judiciary department. I only bring the instance to show that the pleasure of doing good and serving their country, and the respect such conduct entitles them to, are sufficient motives with some minds to give up a great portion of their time to the public, without the mean inducement of pecuniary satisfaction.

Another instance is that of a respectable society, who have made the experiment, and practiced it with success, now more than a hundred years. I mean the Quakers. It is an established rule with

6

7

8

them that they are not to go to law, but in their controversies they must apply to their monthly, quarterly, and yearly meetings. Committees of these sit with patience to hear the parties, and spend much time in composing their differences. In doing this, they are supported by a sense of duty and the respect paid to usefulness. It is honorable to be so employed, but it was never made profitable by salaries, fees, or perquisites. And indeed, in all cases of public service, the less the profit the greater the honor.

To bring the matter nearer home, have we not seen the greatest   9 and most important of our offices, that of General of our Armies, executed for eight years together, without the smallest salary, by a patriot whom I will not now offend by any other praise; and this, through fatigues and distresses, in common with the other brave men, his military friends and companions, and the constant anxieties peculiar to his station? And shall we doubt finding three or four men in all the United States, with public spirit enough to bear sitting in peaceful council, for perhaps an equal term, merely to preside over our civil concerns, and see that our laws are duly executed? Sir, I have a better opinion of our country. I think we shall never be without a sufficient number of wise and good men to undertake, and execute well and faithfully, the office in question.

Sir, the saving of the salaries, that may at first be proposed, is not   10 an object with me. The subsequent mischiefs of proposing them are what I apprehend. And therefore it is that I move the amendment. If it is not seconded or accepted, I must be contented with the satisfaction of having delivered my opinion frankly, and done my duty.

QUESTIONS OF CONTENT

1. When Franklin says he wants to avoid paying salaries to three or four persons in the executive branch of our government, whom does he probably mean? Who would be the equivalent persons at the state and the city or county levels?
2. What government does Franklin indicate is already flawed because it has posts whose holders receive both power and money? Why is this probably a useful point to bring up with his fellow delegates to the Constitutional Convention?
3. Why, for his audience, are Franklin's references in paragraphs 5–6 to princes and kings, and also to the Egyptian Pharoah, particularly apt?
4. The delegates to the Constitutional Convention did not accept Franklin's amendment. What, if anything, has happened since that time to make American citizens wish that the vote had been in favor of his

idea? What, on the other hand, are some practical limitations to Franklin's proposal, both in terms of the current size and complexity of our government and of the strength of patriotic impulses in our time, especially when weighed against personal financial situations?

QUESTIONS OF FORM

1. Originally a speech, Franklin's argument has a rather formal tone and is clearly organized to present his claim of policy in a straightforward fashion. How does he use cause–effect analysis to urge his point, beginning in paragraph 2?
2. Why, given America's recent history at the time of this speech, did Franklin apparently feel in paragraph 4 that he did not need to provide specific examples in support of his discussion of the "warfare between the governing and the governed" and the results of that warfare?
3. Particularly considering his audience, which of the four analogies he uses in paragraphs 7–9 do you think are the most appropriate ones to choose in supporting his claim of value, that his idea is not a Utopian one? Why does he probably save the example of General Washington for last?
4. Notice that Franklin, like Swift in "A Modest Proposal," at the end of his essay also denies one obvious reason for making his propsal. Why might that be placed so late?

SUGGESTIONS FOR WRITING

1. Arguments similar to Franklin's are heard across our country every time the U.S. Congress or a state legislature proposes to raise its salary. Using Franklin's essay as your inspiration and starting place, compose a hypothetical letter to the editor of a local paper in which you argue for or against increasing the salary of an office holder who represents you.
2. Franklin is a man of varied experience, able to see both the bad and good in humans. Take one of Franklin's statements regarding human behavior and write an essay in which you demonstrate that his assertion is either correct or incorrect; try using an analogy or a current example, as he did, in support of your case.
3. Consider some of the scandals in American politics—Watergate, Iran–Contra, the savings and loan bailout, as well as local or state ones that you may know about. Could any of these have been lessened or avoided if Franklin's proposal had been adopted for all levels of government? Write an essay in which you illustrate the truth or falsity of such a claim in reference to one such scandal involving an elected executive leader.

Declaration of Sentiments

ELIZABETH CADY STANTON

One of the earliest and most able proponents of women's rights in America was Elizabeth Cady Stanton (1815–1902). Married to the abolitionist leader Henry B. Stanton and the mother of five children, she still found time to join Susan B. Anthony in founding the National Women's Suffrage Group and to serve as its president, to write extensively for magazines of her era, and to help write the History of Woman Suffrage *(1881–1886). In 1848 Mrs. Stanton was a leader in organizing the first women's rights convention in America. The convention, with her guidance, used* The Declaration of Independence *as a model in creating its own declaration, reprinted here.*

When, in the course of human events, it becomes necessary for one portion of the family of man to assume among the people of the earth a position different from that which they have hitherto occupied, but one to which the laws of nature and of nature's God entitle them, a decent respect to the opinions of mankind requires that they should declare the causes that impel them to such a course.

We hold these truths to be self-evident: that all men and women are created equal; that they are endowed by their Creator with certain inalienable rights; that among these are life, liberty, and the pursuit of happiness; that to secure these rights governments are instituted, deriving their just powers from the consent of the governed. Whenever any form of government becomes destructive of these ends, it is the right of those who suffer from it to refuse allegiance to it, and to insist upon the institution of a new government, laying its foundation on such principles, and organizing its powers in such form, as to them shall seem most likely to effect their safety and happiness. Prudence, indeed, will dictate that governments long established should not be changed for light and transient causes; and accordingly all experience hath shown that mankind are more disposed to suffer, while evils are sufferable, than to right themselves by abolishing the forms to which they were accustomed. But when a long train of abuses and usurpations, pursuing invariably the same object, evinces a design to reduce them under absolute despotism, it is their duty to throw off such government, and to provide new guards for their future security. Such has been the patient sufferance of the women under this government, and such is now the necessity which constrains them to demand the equal station to which they are entitled.

The history of mankind is a history of repeated injuries and usurpations on the part of man toward woman, having in direct object the establishment of an absolute tyranny over her. To prove this, let facts be submitted to a candid world. 3

He has never permitted her to exercise her inalienable right to the elective franchise. 4

He has compelled her to submit to laws, in the formation of which she had no voice. 5

He has withheld from her rights which are given to the most ignorant and degraded men—both natives and foreigners. 6

Having deprived her of this first right of a citizen, the elective franchise, thereby leaving her without representation in the halls of legislation, he has oppressed her on all sides. 7

He has made her, if married, in the eye of the law, civilly dead. 8

He has taken from her all right in property, even to the wages she earns. 9

He has made her, morally, an irresponsible being, as she can commit many crimes with impunity, provided they be done in the presence of her husband. In the covenant of marriage, she is compelled to promise obedience to her husband, he becoming, to all intents and purposes, her master—the law giving him power to deprive her of her liberty, and to administer chastisement. 10

He has so framed the laws of divorce, as to what shall be the proper causes, and in case of separation, to whom the guardianship of the children shall be given, as to be wholly regardless of the happiness of women—the law, in all cases, going upon a false supposition of the supremacy of man, and giving all power into his hands. 11

After depriving her of all rights as a married woman, if single, and the owner of property, he has taxed her to support a government which recognizes her only when her property can be made profitable to it. 12

He has monopolized nearly all the profitable employments, and from those she is permitted to follow, she receives but a scanty remuneration. He closes against her all the avenues to wealth and distinction which he considers most honorable to himself. As a teacher of theology, medicine, or law, she is not known. 13

He has denied her the facilities for obtaining a thorough education, all colleges being closed against her. 14

He allows her in Church, as well as State, but a subordinate position, claiming Apostolic authority for her exclusion from the ministry, and, with some exceptions, from any public participation in the affairs of the Church. 15

He has created a false public sentiment by giving to the world a different code of morals for men and women, by which moral delin- 16 quencies which exclude women from society are not only tolerated, but deemed of little account in man.

He has usurped the prerogative of Jehovah himself, claiming it as   17
his right to assign for her a sphere of action, when that belongs to her conscience and to her God.

He has endeavored, in every way that he could, to destroy her   18
confidence in her own powers, to lessen her self-respect, and to make her willing to lead a dependent and abject life.

Now, in view of this entire disenfranchisement of one-half the   19
people of this country, their social and religious degradation—in view of the unjust laws above mentioned, and because women do feel themselves aggrieved, oppressed, and fraudulently deprived of their most sacred rights, we insist that they have immediate admission to all the rights and privileges which belong to them as citizens of the United States.

In entering upon the great work before us, we anticipate no   20
small amount of misconception, misrepresentation, and ridicule; but we shall use every instrumentality within our power to effect our object. We shall employ agents, circulate tracts, petition the State and National legislatures, and endeavor to enlist the pulpit and the press in our behalf. We hope this Convention will be followed by a series of Conventions embracing every part of the country.

QUESTIONS OF CONTENT

1. Thomas Jefferson's villain in 1776 was King George III of England, but who is Mrs. Stanton's? Who is her probable audience?
2. Which one of the "repeated injuries and usurpations" listed in paragraphs 4–18 seems the worst to you? Which ones, if any, still take place?
3. In paragraph 20 Stanton and her peers make clear their intent to make their grievances widely known. What difficulties did they apparently face, as made implicit in the list of "injuries and usurpations" and explicit in this concluding paragraph?

QUESTIONS OF FORM

1. Compare Stanton's Declaration with Jefferson's, reprinted earlier in this book. Where are they identical in content? In form? What basis can you see for any important changes in content or in form?
2. Why do you think Stanton chose the denial of the right to vote as the

first grievance to list? Which other grievance might also have been a good choice to head up the list?
3. Select three examples of words or phrases with emotional appeal, and be prepared to explain their appeal; then pick out at least one word or phrase that you think could be changed for the better, and be prepared to justify your recommendation.
4. Stanton is making a claim of policy, but she has not provided information on any benefits that would result from the changes she desires. What might be some of the benefits and why do you suppose she didn't name any?

SUGGESTIONS FOR WRITING

1. Write a letter to Mrs. Stanton as if she were still able to receive it, and describe the current state of one of the grievances she originally listed.
2. Assume you are an adult American male in 1848, the editor of the local newspaper in an area similar to the one where you now live; write a brief editorial in which you explain why you are agreeing to or refusing Mrs. Stanton's request to reprint her "Declaration of Sentiments" in your newspaper.

Ain't I a Woman?

SOJOURNER TRUTH

Born a slave in New York State, Sojourner Truth (1797–1883), escaped to freedom in 1827 and eventually became a fiery speaker (she was illiterate) on behalf of Christian, racial, and women's causes. Originally called Isabella Van Wagener, in 1843 Truth gave herself the symbolic names by which she is now known, and she began to travel and speak widely, focusing especially on abolitionist causes in the decade before the Civil War. After the war, under the influence of Elizabeth Cady Stanton, she turned her oratorical powers more fully to the cause of women's rights; but she had begun that crusade much earlier, as can be seen in her most famous speech, first given in 1851 and presented below in essay form. "Ain't I a Woman?" has been adapted here from the version that first appeared in The History of Woman Suffrage *(1881–1886), edited by Mrs. Stanton and others.*

Well, children, where there is such a racket there must be something out of kilter. I think that between the Negroes of the South and   1 the women of the North, all talking about rights, the white men will be in a fix pretty soon. But what's all this here talking about?

That man yonder says that women need to be helped into car-   2
riages, and lifted over ditches, and to have the best place every-where. But nobody ever helps me into carriages, or over ditches, or gives me any best place! And ain't I a woman? Look at me! Look at my arm! I have ploughed and planted, and gathered into barns, and no man could head me! And ain't I a woman? I could work as much and eat as much as a man—when I could get it—and bear the lash as well! And ain't I a woman? I have borne thirteen children, and seen most of them sold off to slavery, and when I cried out with my mother's grief, none but Jesus heard me! And ain't I a woman?

Then they talk about this thing in the head. What's this that   3
they call it? ["Intellect," someone in the crowd whispers.] That's it, honey. What's that got to do with women's rights or with Negro's rights? If my cup won't hold but a pint, and yours holds a quart, wouldn't you be mean not even to let me have my little half-measure full?

Then that little man in black there, he says women can't have as   4
much rights as men, because Christ wasn't a woman! Where did your Christ come from? Where did your Christ come from? From God—and a *woman!* Man had nothing to do with Him.

If the first woman God ever made was strong enough to turn the   5
world upside down all alone, then these women together ought to be able to turn it back, and to get it right side up again! And now that they are asking to do it, men better let them!

I'm obliged to you for hearing me, and now old Sojourner ain't   6
got nothing more to say.

QUESTIONS OF CONTENT

1. How can you tell this work was first presented as a speech? What in the speech suggests Truth's amount of formal education?
2. Where do you see evidence of Truth's age? Of her religion? Of her background as a slave? As a mother?
3. Paragraphs 2, 3, and 4 focus on different aspects of an individual human; what are those three aspects?
4. What does the "little man in black" represent? Who is the woman that turned the world upside down by herself? How is she related to whatever the little man in black represents?

QUESTIONS OF FORM

1. Probably the most important features of Truth's speech are her constant use of rhetorical questions and her use of repetition. How do those work in tandem to give her message extra force?
2. This brief speech is clearly organized, with an introduction, a conclusion, and four paragraphs that form the work's main body. How are the four central paragraphs linked by subject? What claims does she make in each? What is the special connection between paragraphs 4 and 5?
3. How is comparison used to support Truth's claims in each of the four body paragraphs?
4. Only in paragraph 2 does Truth use examples to support her claim; why do you suppose that might be so, and how effective are they?
5. Truth makes appeals to pity in two of her body paragraphs. What are those appeals and how effective are they in advancing her argument?

SUGGESTIONS FOR WRITING

1. Although this speech by Truth is focused on equal rights for women, it also touches on the question of equal rights for black Americans. Try rewriting her work to focus on equal rights for some group other than women, using essentially her same organization and approach. As an alternative, try modernizing her examples in paragraph 2 for any group, including women.
2. Presumably there are descendants of Truth all across America. Write a letter to one of them, describing your honest reaction to his or her ancestor's speech; be specific about what you see as its strengths and/ or weaknesses.
3. Assume you are either of the two men that Truth points to in paragraphs 2 and 4, and write a concise refutation of her charge against you.

Crime and Criminals

CLARENCE DARROW

Considered the most brilliant criminal lawyer of his day, Clarence Darrow (1857–1938) is probably most famous for the so-called Monkey Trial in Dayton, Tennessee. There he defended John Scopes against a charge of teaching evolution in the local high school. Though Scopes was found guilty and fined, objective onlookers agree that Darrow had actually outdone William Jennings

Bryan, an equally famous lawyer, orator, and politician. Darrow's numerous publications include two books: Crime: Its Cause and Treatment *(1922) and* The Story of My Life *(1932). However, the essay below was originally presented in 1902 as a speech to the inmates of the Cook County Jail in Chicago.*

If I looked at jails and crimes and prisoners in the way the ordinary person does, I should not speak on this subject to you. The reason I talk to you on the question of crime, its cause and cure, is because I really do not in the least believe in crime. There is no such thing as a crime as the word is generally understood. I do not believe there is any sort of distinction between the real moral condition of the people in and out of jail. One is just as good as the other. The people here can no more help being here than the people outside can avoid being outside. I do not believe that people are in jail because they deserve to be. They are in jail simply because they can not avoid it on account of circumstances which are entirely beyond their control and for which they are in no way responsible.

I suppose a great many people on the outside would say I was doing you harm if they should hear what I say to you this afternoon, but you can not be hurt a great deal anyway, so it will not matter. Good people outside would say that I was really teaching you things that were calculated to injure society, but it's worthwhile now and then to hear something different from what you ordinarily get from preachers and the like. These will tell you that you should be good and then you get rich and be happy. Of course we know that people do not get rich by being good, and that is the reason why so many of you people try to get rich some other way, only you do not understand how to do it quite as well as the fellow outside.

There are people who think that everything in this world is an accident. But really there is no such thing as an accident. A great many folk admit that many of the people in jail ought not to be there, and many who are outside ought to be in. I think none of them ought to be here. There ought to be no jails, and if it were not for the fact that the people on the outside are so grasping and heartless in their dealings with the people on the inside, there would be no such institution as jails.

I do not want you to believe that I think all you people here are angels. I do not think that. You are people of all kinds, all of you doing the best you can, and that is evidently not very well—you are people of all kinds and conditions and under all circumstances. In one sense everybody is equally good and equally bad. We all do the best we can under the circumstances. But as to the exact things for which you are sent here, some of you are guilty and did the particular act because you needed the money. Some of you did it because you are in the habit of doing it, and some of you because you are born to it, and it comes as natural as it does, for instance, for me to be good.

Most of you probably have nothing against me, and most of you   5
would treat me the same as any other person would; probably better than some of the people on the outside would treat me, because you think I believe in you and they know I do not believe in them. While you would not have the least thing against me in the world you might pick my pockets. I do not think all of you would, but I think some of you would. You would not have anything against me, but that's your profession, a few of you. Some of the rest of you, if my doors were unlocked, might come in if you saw anything you wanted—not out of any malice to me, but because that is your trade. There is no doubt there are quite a number of people in this jail who would pick my pockets. And still I know this, that when I get outside pretty nearly everybody picks my pocket. There may be some of you who would hold up a man on the street, if you did not happen to have something else to do, and needed the money; but when I want to light my house or my office the gas company holds me up. They charge me one dollar for something that is worth twenty-five cents, and still all these people are good people; they are pillars of society and support the churches, and they are respectable.

When I ride on the streetcars, I am held up—I pay five cents for a   6
ride that is worth two-and-a-half cents, simply because a body of men have bribed the city council and legislature, so that all the rest of us have to pay tribute to them.

If I do not want to fall into the clutches of the gas trust and   7
choose to burn oil instead of gas, then good Mr. Rockefeller holds me up, and he uses a certain portion of his money to build universities and support churches which are engaged in telling us how to be good.

Some of you are here for obtaining property under false   8
pretenses—yet I pick up a great Sunday paper and read the advertisements of a merchant prince—"Shirtwaists for 39¢, marked down from $3."

When I read the advertisements in the paper I see they are all   9
lies. When I want to get out and find a place to stand anywhere on the face of the earth, I find that it has all been taken up long ago before I came here, and before you came here, and somebody says, "Get off, swim into the lake, fly into the air; go anywhere, but get off." That is because these people have the police and they have the jails and the judges and the lawyers and the soldiers and all the rest

of them to take care of the earth and drive everybody off that comes in their way.

A great many people will tell you that all this is true, but that it 10 does not excuse you. These facts do not excuse some fellow who reaches into my pocket and takes out a five-dollar bill; the fact that the gas company bribes the members of the legislature from year to year, and fixes the law, so that all you people are compelled to be "fleeced" whenever you deal with them; the fact that the streetcar companies and the gas companies have control of the streets and the fact that the landlords own all the earth, they say, has nothing to do with you.

Let us see whether there is any connection between the crimes 11 of the respectable classes and your presence in jail. Many of you people are in jail because you have really committed burglary. Many of you, because you have stolen something: in the meaning of the law, you have taken some other person's property. Some of you have entered a store and carried off a pair of shoes because you did not have the price. Possibly some of you have committed murder. I can not tell what all of you did. There are a great many people here who have done some of these things who really do not know themselves why they did them. I think I know why you did them—every one of you; you did these things because you were bound to do them. It looked to you at the time as if you had a chance to do them or not, as you saw fit, but still after all you had no choice. There may be people here who had some money in their pockets and who still went out and got some more money in a way society forbids. Now you may not yourselves see exactly why it was you did this thing, but if you look at the question deeply enough and carefully enough you would see that there were circumstances that drove you to do exactly the thing which you did. You could not help it any more than we outside can help taking the positions that we take. The reformers who tell you to be good and you will be happy, and the people on the outside who have property to protect—they think that the only way to do it is by building jails and locking you up in cells on weekdays and praying for you Sundays.

I think that all of this has nothing whatever to do with right 12 conduct. I think it is very easily seen what has to do with right conduct. Some so-called criminals—and I will use this word because it is handy, it means nothing to me—I speak of the criminals who get caught as distinguished from the criminals who catch them— some of these so-called criminals are in jail for first offenses, but nine-tenths of you are in jail because you did not have a good lawyer and of course you did not have a good lawyer because you did not have enough money to pay a good lawyer. There is no very great danger of a rich man going to jail.

Some of you may be here for the first time. If we would open the doors and let you out, and leave the laws as they are today, some of you would be back tomorrow. This is about as good a place as you can get anyway. There are many people here who are so in the habit of coming that they would not know where else to go. There are people who are born with the tendency to break into jail every chance they get, and they can not avoid it. You can not figure out your life and see why it was, but still there is a reason for it, and if we were all wise and knew all the facts we could figure it out.   13

In the first place, there are a good many more people who go to jail in the winter time than in the summer. Why is this? Is it because people are more wicked in winter? No, it is because the coal trust begins to get in its grip in the winter. A few gentlemen take possession of the coal, and unless the people will pay $7 or $8 a ton for something that is worth $3, they will have to freeze. Then there is nothing to do but to break into jail, and so there are many more in jail in the winter than in summer. It costs more for gas in the winter because the nights are longer, and people go to jail to save gas bills. The jails are electric-lighted. You may not know it, but these economic laws are working all the time, whether we know it or do not know it.   14

There are more people who go to jail in hard times than in good times—few people comparatively go to jail except when they are hard up. They go to jail because they have no other place to go. They may not know why, but it is true all the same. People are not more wicked in hard times. That is not the reason. The fact is true all over the world that in hard times more people go to jail than in good times, and in winter more people go to jail than in summer. Of course it is pretty hard times for people who go to jail at any time. The people who go to jail are almost always poor people—people who have no other place to live first and last. When times are hard then you find large numbers of people who go to jail who would not otherwise be in jail.   15

Long ago, Mr. Buckle, who was a great philosopher and historian, collected facts and he showed that the number of people who are arrested increased just as the price of food increased. When they put up the price of gas ten cents a thousand I do not know who will go to jail, but I do know that a certain number of people will go. When the meat combine raises the price of beef I do not know who is going to jail, but I know that a large number of people are bound to go. Whenever the Standard Oil Company raises the price of oil, I know that a certain number of girls who are seamstresses, and who   16 work night after night long hours for somebody else, will be compelled to go out on the streets and ply another trade, and I know that Mr. Rockefeller and his associates are responsible and not the poor girls in the jails.

First and last, people are sent to jail because they are poor. Sometimes, as I say, you may not need money at the particular time, but you wish to have thrifty forehanded habits, and do not always wait until you are in absolute want. Some of you people are perhaps plying the trade, the profession, which is called burglary. No man in his right senses will go into a strange house in the dead of night and prowl around with a dark lantern through unfamiliar rooms and take chances of his life if he has plenty of good things of the world in his own home. You would not take any such chances as that. If a man had clothes in his clothes-press and beefsteak in his pantry, and money in the bank, he would not navigate around nights in houses where he knows nothing about the premises whatever. It always requires experience and education for this profession, and people who fit themselves for it are no more to blame than I am for being a lawyer. A man would not hold up another man on the street if he had plenty of money in his own pocket. He might do it if he had one dollar or two dollars, but he wouldn't if he had as much money as Mr. Rockefeller has. Mr. Rockefeller has a great deal better holdup game than that.

The more that is taken from the poor by the rich, who have the chance to take it, the more poor people there are who are compelled to resort to these means for a livelihood. They may not understand it, they may not think so at once, but after all they are driven into that line of employment.

There is a bill before the Legislature of this State to punish kidnaping children with death. We have wise members of the Legislature. They know the gas trust when they see it and they always see it—they can furnish light enough to be seen, and this Legislature thinks it is going to stop kidnaping children by making a law punishing kidnapers of children with death. I don't believe in kidnaping children, but the Legislature is all wrong. Kidnaping children is not a crime, it is a profession. It has been developed with the times. It has been developed with our modern industrial conditions. There are many ways of making money—many new ways that our ancestors knew nothing about. Our ancestors knew nothing about a billion-dollar trust; and here comes some poor fellow who has no other trade and he discovers the profession of kidnaping children.

This crime is born, not because people are bad; people don't kidnap other people's children because they want the children or because they are devilish, but because they see a chance to get some money out of it. You cannot cure this crime by passing a law punishing by death kidnapers of children. There is only one way to cure it. There is one way to cure all the offenses, and that is to give the people a chance to live. There is no other way, and there never was any other way since the world began, and the world is so blind and stupid that it will not see. If every man and woman and child in the world had a chance to make a decent, fair, honest living, there would be no jails, and no lawyers and no courts. There might be some persons here or there with some peculiar formation of their brain, like Rockefeller, who would do these things simply to be doing them; but they would be very, very few, and those should be sent to a hospital and treated, and not sent to jail; and they would entirely disappear in the second generation, or at least in the third generation.

I am not talking pure theory. I will just give you two or three illustrations.   21

The English people once punished criminals by sending them   22
away. They would load them on a ship and export them to Australia. England was owned by lords and nobles and rich people. They owned the whole earth over there, and the other people had to stay in the streets. They could not get a decent living. They used to take their criminals and send them to Australia—I mean the class of criminals who got caught. When these criminals got over there, and nobody else had come, they had the whole continent to run over, and so they could raise sheep and furnish their own meat, which is easier than stealing it; these criminals then became decent, respectable people because they had a chance to live. They did not commit any crimes. They were just like the English people who sent them there, only better. And in the second generation the descendants of those criminals were as good and respectable a class of people as there were on the face of the earth, and then they began building churches and jails themselves.

A portion of this country was settled in the same way, landing   23
prisoners down on the southern coast; but when they got here and had a whole continent to run over and plenty of chances to make a living, they became respectable citizens, making their own living just like any other citizen in the world; but finally these descendants of the English aristocracy, who sent the people over to Australia, found out they were getting rich, and so they went over to get possession of the earth as they always do, and they organized land syndicates and got control of the land and ores, and then they had just as many criminals in Australia as they did in England. It was not because the world had grown bad; it was because the earth had been taken away from the people.

Some of you people have lived in the country. It's prettier than it   24 is here. And if you have ever lived on a farm you understand that if you put a lot of cattle in a field, when the pasture is short they will jump over the fence; but put them in a good field where there is plenty of pasture, and they will be law-abiding cattle to the end of time. The human animal is just like the rest of the animals, only a little more so. The same thing that governs in the one governs in the other.

Everybody makes his living along the lines of least resistance. A wise man who comes into a country early sees a great undeveloped land. For instance, our rich men twenty-five years ago saw that Chicago was small and knew a lot of people would come here and settle, and they readily saw that if they had all the land around here it would be worth a good deal, so they grabbed the land. You cannot be a landlord because somebody has got it all. You must find some other calling. In England and Ireland and Scotland less than 5 percent own all the land there is, and the people are bound to stay there on any kind of terms the landlords give. They must live the best they can, so they develop all these various professions—burglary, picking pockets and the like.   25

Again, people find all sorts of ways of getting rich. These are diseases like everything else. You look at people getting rich, organizing trusts, and making a million dollars, and somebody gets the disease and he starts out. He catches it just as a man catches the mumps or the measles; he is not to blame, it is in the air. You will find men speculating beyond their means, because the mania of money-getting is taking possession of them. It is simply a disease; nothing more, nothing less. You can not avoid catching it; but the fellows who have control of the earth have the advantage of you. See what the law is; when these men get control of things, they make the laws. They do not make the laws to protect anybody; courts are not instruments of justice; when your case gets into court it will make little difference whether you are guilty or innocent; but it's better if you have a smart lawyer. And you can not have a smart lawyer unless you have money. First and last it's a question of money. Those men who own the earth make the laws to protect what they have. They fix up a sort of fence or pen around what they have, and they fix the law so the fellow on the outside can not get in. The laws are really organized for the protection of the men who rule the world. They were never organized or enforced to do justice. We have no system for doing justice, not the slightest in the world.   26

Let me illustrate: Take the poorest person in this room. If the community had provided a system of doing justice the poorest person in this room would have as good a lawyer as the richest, would he not? When you went into court you would have just as long a   27 trial, and just as fair a trial as the richest person in Chicago. Your case would not be tried in fifteen or twenty minutes, whereas it would take fifteen days to get through with a rich man's case.

Then if you were rich and were beaten, your case would be taken   28
to the Appellate Court. A poor man can not take his case to the Appellate Court; he has not the price; and then to the Supreme Court, and if he were beaten there he might perhaps go to the United States Supreme Court. And he might die of old age before he got into jail. If you are poor, it's a quick job. You are almost known to be guilty, else you would not be there. Why would any one be in the criminal court if he were not guilty? He would not be there if he could be anywhere else. The officials have no time to look after all these cases. The people who are on the outside, who are running banks and building churches and making jails, they have no time to examine six hundred or seven hundred prisoners each year to see whether they are guilty or innocent. If the courts were organized to promote justice the people would elect somebody to defend all these criminals, somebody as smart as the prosecutor—and give him as many detectives and as many assistants to help, and pay as much money to defend you as to prosecute you. We have a very able man for State's Attorney, and he has many assistants, detectives and policemen without end, and judges to hear the cases—everything handy.

Most of all our criminal code consists in offenses against prop-   29
erty. People are sent to jail because they have committed a crime against property. It is of very little consequence whether one hundred people more or less go to jail who ought not to go—you must protect property, because in this world property is of more importance than anything else.

How is it done? These people who have property fix it so they   30
can protect what they have. When somebody commits a crime it does not follow that he has done something that is morally wrong. The man on the outside who has committed no crime may have done something. For instance: to take all the coal in the United States and raise the price two dollars or three dollars when there is no need of it, and thus kill thousands of babies and send thousands of people to the poorhouse and tens of thousands to jail, as is done every year in the United States—this is a greater crime than all the people in our jails ever committed, but the law does not punish it. Why? Because the fellows who control the earth make the laws. If you and I had the making of the laws, the first thing we would do would be to punish the fellow who gets control of the earth. Nature put this coal in the ground for me as well

as for them, and nature made the prairies up here to raise wheat for me as well as for them, and then the great railroad companies came along and fenced it up.

Most of all, the crimes for which we are punished are property crimes. There are a few personal crimes, like murder—but they are very few. The crimes committed are mostly those against property. If this punishment is right the criminals must have a lot of property. How much money is there in this crowd? And yet you are all here for crimes against property. The people up and down the Lake Shore have not committed crimes, still they have so much property they don't know what to do with it. It is perfectly plain why those people have not committed crimes against property; they make the laws and therefore do not need to break them. And in order for you to get some property you are obliged to break the rules of the game. I don't know but what some of you may have had a very nice chance to get rich by carrying the hod for one dollar a day, twelve hours. Instead of taking that nice, easy profession, you are burglar. If you had been given a chance to be a banker you would rather follow that. Some of you may have had a chance to work as a switchman on a railroad where you know, according to statistics, that you can not live and keep all your limbs more than seven years, and you can get fifty dollars or seventy-five dollars a month for taking your lives in your hands, and instead of taking that lucrative position you choose to be a sneak thief, or something like that. Some of you made that sort of choice. I don't know which I would take if I was reduced to this choice. I have an easier choice.

I will guarantee to take from this jail, or any jail in the world, five hundred men who have been the worst criminals and lawbreakers who ever got into jail, and I will go down to our lowest streets and take five hundred of the most abandoned prostitutes, and go out somewhere where there is plenty of land, and will give them a chance to make a living, and they will be as good as the average in the community.

There is a remedy for the sort of condition we see here. The world never finds it out, or when it does find out it does not enforce it. You may pass a law punishing every person with death for burglary, and it will make no difference. Men will commit it just the same. In England there was a time when one hundred offenses were punishable with death, and it made no difference. The English people strangely found out that so fast as they repealed the severe penalties and so fast as they did away with punishing men by death, crime decreased instead of increased; that the smaller the penalty the fewer the crimes.

Hanging men in our county jails does not prevent murder. It 34
makes murderers.

And this has been the history of the world. It's easy to see how to 35
do away with what we call crime. It is not so easy to do it. I will tell
you how to do it. It can be done by giving the people a chance to live—
by destroying special privileges. So long as big criminals can get the
coal fields, so long as the big criminals have control of the city council
and get the public streets for streetcars and gas rights, this is bound to
send thousands of poor people to jail. So long as men are allowed to
monopolize all the earth, and compel others to live on such terms as
these men see fit to make, then you are bound to get into jail.

The only way in the world to abolish crime and criminals is to 36
abolish the big ones and the little ones together. Make fair conditions of life. Give men a chance to live. Abolish the right of private
ownership of land, abolish monopoly, make the world partners in
production, partners in the good things of life. Nobody would steal if
he could get something of his own some easier way. Nobody will
commit burglary when he has a house full. No girl will go out on the
streets when she has a comfortable place at home. The man who
owns a sweatshop or a department store may not be to blame himself for the condition of his girls, but when he pays them five dollars,
three dollars, and two dollars a week, I wonder where he thinks they
will get the rest of their money to live. The only way to cure these
conditions is by equality. There should be no jails. They do not
accomplish what they pretend to accomplish. If you would wipe
them out there would be no more criminals than now. They terror-
ize nobody. They are a blot upon any civilization, and a jail is an
evidence of the lack of charity of the people on the outside who
make the jails and fill them with the victims of their greed.

QUESTIONS OF CONTENT

1. According to Darrow, what is the basic cause for the existence of
   prisons and prisoners? Do you agree, or not?
2. Why does Darrow believe more people go to jail in winter than in any
   other season, and in hard economic times rather than good? How
   convincing are his explanations for the causes?
3. Several of Darrow's examples show their age; which ones do so?
   What might you put in their places? Which examples are still appropriate, indicating that the problem seen by Darrow still exists?
4. How does Darrow use the early history of Australia in his argument?
5. What is the relationship between property and crime, according to
   Darrow?

6. How does Darrow propose to solve the problem of crime? How well do you think his solution might have worked in his time? In ours?

QUESTIONS OF FORM

1. Who was Darrow's original audience? What influence does that audience have on the examples he uses?
2. What is Darrow's apparent *tone?* Why do you suppose he adopted it? How does he achieve it?
3. Darrow's argument is essentially an extended claim of policy; where and how does he use comparisons and cause–effect analyses to illustrate the situation his policy would correct?
4. Darrow states in paragraph 20 that there would be no criminals if everyone were given the chance to make a decent living; how does he support this proposition?
5. How effective is the analogy he provides in paragraph 24?
6. Where in his argument does Darrrow announce his solution to the problem of crime and criminals? How wise was he to place it there?

SUGGESTIONS FOR WRITING

1. Summarize Darrow's basic argument.
2. Take one of Darrow's supporting examples and rewrite it for a modern audience of law-abiding citizens rather than jailed criminals.
3. Attack or defend one of these assertions by Darrow:
   a. "When I read the advertisements in the papers I see they are all lies." (Paragraph 9)
   b. "There is no very great danger of a rich man going to jail." (Paragraph 12)
   c. "First and last, people are sent to jail because they are poor." (Paragraph 17)
   d. "Everybody makes his living along the lines of least resistance." (Paragraph 25)
   e. "Nobody will commit burglary when he has a house full." (Paragraph 36)

The Indispensable Opposition

WALTER LIPPMANN

A prolific journalist and political commentator, Walter Lippmann (1889–1974) published over 4000 newspaper columns and 20 books in a distinguished career that stretched from World War I to the Vietnam War. An acute critic and accomplished prose stylist, his writing and reasoning powers are fully apparent in the essay below, which first appeared in the August 1939 issue of The Atlantic Monthly.

Were they pressed hard enough, most men would probably confess that political freedom—that is to say, the right to speak freely and to act in opposition—is a noble ideal rather than a practical necessity. As the case for freedom is generally put today, the argument lends itself to this feeling. It is made to appear that, whereas each man claims his freedom as a matter of right, the freedom he accords to other men is a matter of toleration. Thus, the defense of freedom of opinion tends to rest not on its substantial, beneficial, and indispensable consequences, but on a somewhat eccentric, a rather vaguely benevolent, attachment to an abstraction.   1

It is all very well to say with Voltaire, "I wholly disapprove of what you say, but will defend to the death your right to say it," but as a matter of fact most men will not defend to the death the rights of other men: if they disapprove sufficiently what other men say, they will somehow suppress those men if they can.   2

So, if this is the best that can be said for liberty of opinion, that a man must tolerate his opponents because everyone has a "right" to say what he pleases, then we shall find that liberty of opinion is a luxury, safe only in pleasant times when men can be tolerant because they are not deeply and vitally concerned.   3

Yet actually, as a matter of historic fact, there is a much stronger foundation for the great constitutional right of freedom of speech, and as a matter of practical human experience there is a much more compelling reason for cultivating the habits of free men. We take, it seems to me, a naïvely self-righteous view when we argue as if the right of our opponents to speak were something that we protect because we are magnanimous, noble, and unselfish. The compelling reason why, if liberty of opinion did not exist, we should have to invent it, why it will eventually have to be restored in all civilized countries where it is now suppressed, is that we must protect the right of our opponents to speak because we must hear what they have to say.   4

We miss the whole point when we imagine that we tolerate the freedom of our political opponents as we tolerate a howling baby next door, as we put up with the blasts from our neighbor's radio because we are too peaceable to heave a brick through the window. If this were all there is to freedom of opinion, that we are too   5 goodnatured or too timid to do anything about our opponents and our critics except to let them talk, it would be difficult to say whether we are tolerant because we are magnanimous or because we are lazy, because we have strong principles or because we lack serious convictions, whether we have the hospitality of an inquiring mind or the indifference of an empty mind. And so, if we truly wish to understand why freedom is necessary in a civilized society, we must begin by realizing that, because freedom of discussion improves our own opinions, the liberties of other men are our own vital necessity.

We are much closer to the essence of the matter, not when we quote Voltaire, but when we go to the doctor and pay him to ask us the most embarrassing questions and to prescribe the most disagreeable diet. When we pay the doctor to exercise complete freedom of speech about the cause and cure of our stomachache, we do not look upon ourselves as tolerant and magnanimous, and worthy to be admired by ourselves. We have enough common sense to know that if we threaten to put the doctor in jail because we do not like the diagnosis and the prescription it will be unpleasant for the doctor, to be sure, but equally unpleasant for our own stomachache. That is why even the most ferocious dictator would rather be treated by a doctor who was free to think and speak the truth than by his own Minister of Propaganda. For there is a point, the point at which things really matter, where the freedom of others is no longer a question of their right but of our own need.

The point at which we recognize this need is much higher in some men than in others. The totalitarian rulers think they do not need the freedom of an opposition: they exile, imprison, or shoot their opponents. We have concluded on the basis of practical experience, which goes back to Magna Carta and beyond, that we need the opposition. We pay the opposition salaries out of the public treasury.

In so far as the usual apology for freedom of speech ignores this experience, it becomes abstract and eccentric rather than concrete and human. The emphasis is generally put on the right to speak, as if all that mattered were that the doctor should be free to go out into the park and explain to the vacant air why I have a stomachache. Surely that is a miserable caricature of the great civic right which men have bled and died for. What really matters is that the doctor should tell me what ails me, and that I should listen to him; that if I do not like what he says I should be free to call in another doctor; and that then the first doctor should have to listen to the second doctor; and that out of all the speaking and listening, the give-and-take of opinions, the truth should be arrived at.

This is the creative principle of freedom of speech, not that it is a   9
system for the tolerating of error, but that it is a system for finding
the truth. It may not produce the truth, or the whole truth all the
time, or often, or in some cases ever. But if the truth can be found,
there is no other system which will normally and habitually find so
much truth. Until we have thoroughly understood this principle, we
shall not know why we must value our liberty, or how we can
protect and develop it.

Let us apply this principle to the system of public speech in a   10
totalitarian state. We may, without any serious falsification, picture a
condition of affairs in which the mass of the people are being addressed through one broadcasting system by one man and his chosen
subordinates. The orators speak. The audience listens but cannot and
dare not speak back. It is a system of one-way communication; the
opinions of the rulers are broadcast outwardly to the mass of the
people. But nothing comes back to the rulers from the people except
the cheers; nothing returns in the way of knowledge of forgotten
facts, hidden feelings, neglected truths, and practical suggestions.

But even a dictator cannot govern by his own one-way inspira-   11
tion alone. In practice, therefore, the totalitarian rulers get back the
reports of the secret police and of their party henchmen down among
the crowd. If these reports are competent, the rulers may manage to
remain in touch with public sentiment. Yet that is not enough to
know what the audience feels. The rulers have also to make great
decisions that have enormous consequences, and here their system
provides virtually no help from the give-and-take of opinion in the
nation. So they must either rely on their own intuition, which cannot be permanently and continually inspired, or, if they are intelligent despots, encourage their trusted advisers and their technicians
to speak and debate freely in their presence.

On the walls of the houses of Italian peasants one may see in-   12
scribed in large letters the legend, "Mussolini is always right." But if
that legend is taken seriously by Italian ambassadors, by the Italian
General Staff, and by the Ministry of Finance, then all one can say is
heaven help Mussolini, heaven help Italy, and the new Emperor of
Ethiopia.

For at some point, even in a totalitarian state, it is indispensable   13
that there should exist the freedom of opinion which causes opposing opinions to be debated. As time goes on, that is less and less easy
under a despotism; critical discussion disappears as the internal opposition is liquidated in favor of men who think and feel alike. That
is why the early successes of despots, of Napoleon I and of Napoleon
III, have usually been followed by an irreparable mistake. For in
listening only to his yes men—the others being in exile or in concen-

tration camps, or terrified—the despot shuts himself off from the truth that no man can dispense with.

We know all this well enough when we contemplate the dictator- 14 ships. But when we try to picture our own system, by way of contrast, what picture do we have in our minds? It is, is it not, that anyone may stand up on his own soapbox and say anything he pleases, like the individuals in Kipling's poem who sit each in his separate star and draw the Thing as they see it for the God of Things as they are. Kipling, perhaps, could do this, since he was a poet. But the ordinary mortal isolated on his separate star will have an hallucination, and a citizenry declaiming from separate soapboxes will poison the air with hot and nonsensical confusion.

If the democratic alternative to the totalitarian one-way broad- 15 casts is a row of separate soapboxes, then I submit that the alternative is unworkable, is unreasonable, and is humanly unattractive. It is above all a false alternative. It is not true that liberty has developed among civilized men when anyone is free to set up a soapbox, is free to hire a hall where he may expound his opinions to those who are willing to listen. On the contrary, freedom of speech is established to achieve its essential purpose only when different opinions are expounded in the same hall to the same audience.

For, while the right to talk may be the beginning of freedom, the 16 necessity of listening is what makes the right important. Even in Russia and Germany a man may still stand in an open field and speak his mind. What matters is not the utterance of opinions. What matters is the confrontation of opinions in debate. No man can care profoundly that every fool should say what he likes. Nothing has been accomplished if the wisest man proclaims his wisdom in the middle of the Sahara Desert. This is the shadow. We have the substance of liberty when the fool is compelled to listen to the wise man and learn; when the wise man is compelled to take account of the fool, and to instruct him; when the wise man can increase his wisdom by hearing the judgment of his peers.

That is why civilized men must cherish liberty—as a means of 17 promoting the discovery of truth. So we must not fix our whole attention on the right of anyone to hire his own hall, to rent his own broadcasting station, to distribute his own pamphlets. These rights are incidental; and though they must be preserved, they can be preserved only by regarding them as incidental, as auxiliary to the substance of liberty that must be cherished and cultivated.

Freedom of speech is best conceived, therefore, by having in 18 mind the picture of a place like the American Congress, an assembly where opposing views are represented, where ideas are not merely uttered but debated, or the British Parliament, where men who are free to speak are also compelled to answer. We may picture the true condition of freedom as existing in a place like a court of law, where witnesses testify and are cross-examined, where the lawyer argues against the opposing lawyer before the same judge and in the presence of one jury. We may picture freedom as existing in a forum where the speaker must respond to questions; in a gathering of scientists where the data, the hypothesis, and the conclusion are submitted to men competent to judge them; in a reputable newspaper which not only will publish the opinions of those who disagree but will re-examine its own opinion in the light of what they say.

Thus the essence of freedom of opinion is not in mere toleration   19
as such, but in the debate which toleration provides: it is not in the venting of opinion, but in the confrontation of opinion. That this is the practical substance can readily be understood when we remember how differently we feel and act about the censorship and regulation of opinion purveyed by different media of communication. We find then that, in so far as the medium makes difficult the confrontation of opinion in debate, we are driven towards censorship and regulation.

There is, for example, the whispering campaign, the circulation   20
of anonymous rumors by men who cannot be compelled to prove what they say. They put the utmost strain on our tolerance, and there are few who do not rejoice when the anonymous slanderer is caught, exposed, and punished. At a higher level there is the moving picture, a most powerful medium for conveying ideas, but a medium which does not permit debate. A moving picture cannot be answered effectively by another moving picture; in all free countries there is some censorship of the movies, and there would be more if the producers did not recognize their limitations by avoiding political controversy. There is then the radio. Here debate is difficult: it is not easy to make sure that the speaker is being answered in the presence of the same audience. Inevitably, there is some regulation of the radio.

When we reach the newspaper press, the opportunity for debate   21
is so considerable that discontent cannot grow to the point where under normal conditions there is any disposition to regulate the press. But when newspapers abuse their power by injuring people who have no means of replying, a disposition to regulate the press appears. When we arrive at Congress we find that, because the membership of the House is so large, full debate is impracticable. So there are restrictive rules. On the other hand, in the Senate, where the conditions of full debate exist, there is almost absolute freedom of speech.

This shows us that the preservation and development of freedom   22 of opinion are not only a matter of adhering to abstract legal rights, but also, and very urgently, a matter of organizing and arranging sufficient debate. Once we have a firm hold on the central principle, there are many practical conclusions to be drawn. We then realize that the defense of freedom of opinion consists primarily in perfecting the opportunity for an adequate give-and-take of opinion; it consists also in regulating the freedom of those revolutionists who cannot or will not permit or maintain debate when it does not suit their purposes.

We must insist that free oratory is only the beginning of free   23
speech; it is not the end, but a means to an end. The end is to find the truth. The practical justification of civil liberty is not that self-expression is one of the rights of man. It is that the examination of opinion is one of the necessities of man. For experience tells us that it is only when freedom of opinion becomes the compulsion to debate that the seed which our fathers planted has produced its fruit. When that is understood, freedom will be cherished not because it is a vent for our opinions but because it is the surest method of correcting them.

The unexamined life, said Socrates, is unfit to be lived by man.   24
This is the virtue of liberty, and the ground on which we may best justify our belief in it, that it tolerates error in order to serve the truth. When men are brought face to face with their opponents, forced to listen and learn and mend their ideas, they cease to be children and savages and begin to live like civilized men. Then only is freedom a reality, when men may voice their opinions because they must examine their opinions.

The only reason for dwelling on all this is that if we are to   25
preserve democracy we must understand its principles. And the principle which distinguishes it from all other forms of government is that in a democracy the opposition not only is tolerated as constitutional but must be maintained because it is in fact indispensable.

The democratic system cannot be operated without effective   26
opposition. For, in making the great experiment of governing people by consent rather than by coercion, it is not sufficient that the party in power should have a majority. It is just as necessary that the party in power should never outrage the minority. That means that it must listen to the minority and be moved by the criticisms of the minority. That means that its measures must take account of the minority's objections, and that in administering measures it must remember that the minority may become the majority.

The opposition is indispensable. A good statesman, like any   27
other sensible human being, always learns more from his opponents than from his fervent supporters. For his supporters will push him to

disaster unless his opponents show him where the dangers are. So if he is wise he will often pray to be delivered from his friends, because they will ruin him. But, though it hurts, he ought also to pray never to be left without opponents; for they keep him on the path of reason and good sense.

The national unity of a free people depends upon a sufficiently 28 even balance of political power to make it impracticable for the administration to be arbitrary and for the opposition to be revolutionary and irreconcilable. Where that balance no longer exists, democracy perishes. For unless all the citizens of a state are forced by circumstances to compromise, unless they feel that they can affect policy but that no one can wholly dominate it, unless by habit and necessity they have to give and take, freedom cannot be maintained.

QUESTIONS OF CONTENT

1. Lippmann begins his argument by describing the usual rationale for the political right of freedom of speech; what is that rationale?
2. Lippmann says freedom of speech is not a noble ideal but a practical necessity; for whom is it a necessity, the speaker or the listener? Why is that so?
3. As he describes it, what does freedom of speech help us find or reach? Why is reaching or finding that worthwhile?
4. What sorts of places or circumstances does Lippmann think best represent freedom of speech in the sense he most values? Which house of the U. S. Congress best represents that preferred kind of freedom of speech?
5. Read paragraphs 23–28 carefully; what do you think Lippmann's opinion would be regarding those who burn the American flag? Would he probably condemn or would he defend their right to do so?

QUESTIONS OF FORM

1. Lippmann presents both a claim of value and a claim of policy in his argument; how might you concisely state each one?
2. Notice Lippmann's several uses of analogy. Why is his use of the analogy of a doctor in paragraphs 6–9 particularly effective in explaining what he means by real freedom of speech?
3. Where and how does Lippmann use comparisons other than analogy to support his claim?
4. What seems to be the warrant that is behind Lippman's argument, and where is it expressed most obviously?

SUGGESTIONS FOR WRITING

1. Find out the basic facts of the backgrounds of Voltaire and Socrates, and after presenting that information in an orderly fashion, also explain why they are appropriate authorities for Lippmann to allude to in a discussion of the right of freedom of speech.
2. Look again at paragraph 18. Besides the places or circumstances listed by Lippmann, what others are likely forums for freedom of speech in the best sense of that right? In an organized paper, explain why a forum he lists, or one you name, is especially valuable as a place where the truth can be sought and debated.
3. Examine some of the recent political or business scandals in America in light of Lippmann's claims about the value of the opposition. Do the facts of such debacles as Watergate, Iran–Contra, or the savings and loan bailout bear out or do they refute Lippmann's contentions? Write an essay in which you deal with the appropriateness of his argument with regard to one of these events or to another recent one that you know about. (Your instructor may ask you to do limited library research in order to make sure that your essay is well supported with accurate facts regarding the scandal you choose.)

How to Mark a Book

MORTIMER J. ADLER

A longtime (1930–1952) professor of philosophy at the University of Chicago, Mortimer J. Adler (1902–) was then for decades associated with the Great Books of the Western World series of Encyclopaedia Britannica. *Over thirty books have his name on them, as author, coauthor, or editor. The essay below is an important section of Dr. Adler's best-known work,* How to Read a Book: The Art of Getting a Liberal Education *(1940; revised edition 1972).*

You know you have to read "between the lines" to get the most   1
out of anything. I want to persuade you to do something equally important in the course of your reading. I want to persuade you to "write between the lines." Unless you do, you are not likely to do the most efficient kind of reading.

I contend, quite bluntly, that marking up a book is not an act of   2
mutilation but of love.

You shouldn't mark up a book which isn't yours. Librarians (or   3
your friends) who lend you books expect you to keep them clean, and you should. If you decide that I am right about the usefulness of

marking books, you will have to buy them. Most of the world's great books are available today, in reprint editions, at less than a dollar.

There are two ways in which one can own a book. The first is the property right you establish by paying for it, just as you pay for clothes and furniture. But this act of purchase is only the prelude to possession. Full ownership comes only when you have made it a part of yourself, and the best way to make yourself a part of it is by writing in it. An illustration may make the point clear. You buy a beefsteak and transfer it from the butcher's ice-box to your own. But you do not own the beefsteak in the most important sense until you consume it and get it into your bloodstream. I am arguing that books, too, must be absorbed in your bloodstream to do you any good.

Confusion about what it means to *own* a book leads people to a false reverence for paper, binding, and type—a respect for the physical thing—the craft of the printer rather than the genius of the author. They forget that it is possible for a man to acquire the idea, to possess the beauty, which a great book contains, without staking his claim by pasting his bookplate inside the cover. Having a fine library doesn't prove that its owner has a mind enriched by books; it proves nothing more than that he, his father, or his wife, was rich enough to buy them.

There are three kinds of book owners. The first has all the standard sets and best-sellers—unread, untouched. (This deluded individual owns woodpulp and ink, not books.) The second has a great many books—a few of them read through, most of them dipped into, but all of them as clean and shiny as the day they were bought. (This person would probably like to make books his own, but is restrained by a false respect for their physical appearance.) The third has a few books or many—every one of them dog-eared and dilapidated, shaken and loosened by continual use, marked and scribbled in from front to back. (This man owns books.)

Is it false respect, you may ask, to preserve intact and unblemished a beautifully printed book, an elegantly bound edition? Of course not. I'd no more scribble all over the first edition of *Paradise Lost* than I'd give my baby a set of crayons and an original Rembrandt! I wouldn't mark up a painting or a statue. Its soul, so to speak, is inseparable from its body. And the beauty of a rare edition or of a richly manufactured volume is like that of a painting or a statue.

But the soul of a book *can* be separated from its body. A book is more like the score of a piece of music than it is like a painting. No great musician confuses a symphony with the printed sheets of music. Arturo Toscanini reveres Brahms, but Toscanini's score of the C-minor Symphony is so thoroughly marked up that no one but the maestro himself can read it. The reason why a great conductor makes notations on his musical scores—marks them up again and again each time he returns to study them—is the reason why you should mark up your books. If your respect for magnificent binding or typography gets in the way, buy yourself a cheap edition and pay your respects to the author.

Why is marking up a book indispensable to reading it? First, it keeps you awake. (And I don't mean merely conscious; I mean wide awake.) In the second place, reading, if it is active, is thinking, and thinking tends to express itself in words, spoken or written. The marked book is usually the thought-through book. Finally, writing helps you remember the thoughts you had, or the thoughts the author expressed. Let me develop these three points.   9

If reading is to accomplish anything more than passing time, it must be active. You can't let your eyes glide across the lines of a book and come up with an understanding of what you have read. Now an ordinary piece of light fiction, like say, *Gone with the Wind*, doesn't require the most active kind of reading. The books you read for pleasure can be read in a state of relaxation, and nothing is lost. But a great book, rich in ideas and beauty, a book that raises and tries to answer great fundamental questions, demands the most active reading of which you are capable. You don't absorb the ideas of John Dewey the way you absorb the crooning of Mr. Vallee. You have to reach for them. That you cannot do while you're asleep.   10

If, when you've finished reading a book, the pages are filled with your notes, you know that you read actively. The most famous *active* reader of great books I know is President Hutchins, of the University of Chicago. He also has the hardest schedule of business activities of any man I know. He invariably reads with a pencil, and sometimes, when he picks up a book and pencil in the evening, he finds himself, instead of making intelligent notes, drawing what he calls "caviar factories" on the margins. When that happens, he puts the book down. He knows he's too tired to read, and he's just wasting time.   11

But, you may ask, why is writing necessary? Well, the physical act of writing, with your own hand, brings words and sentences more sharply before your mind and preserves them better in your memory. To set down your reaction to important words and sentences you have read, and the questions they have raised in your mind, is to preserve those reactions and sharpen those questions.   12

Even if you wrote on a scratch pad, and threw the paper away when you had finished writing, your grasp of the book would be surer. But you don't have to throw the paper away. The margins (top and bottom, as well as side), the end-papers, the very space between   13 the lines, are all available. They aren't sacred. And, best of all, your marks and notes become an integral part of the book and stay there forever. You can pick up the book the following week or year, and there are all your points of agreement, disagreement, doubt, and inquiry. It's like resuming an interrupted conversation with the advantage of being able to pick up where you left off.

And that is exactly what reading a book should be: a conversa-   14
tion between you and the author. Presumably he knows more about the subject than you do; naturally, you'll have the proper humility as you approach him. But don't let anybody tell you that a reader is supposed to be solely on the receiving end. Understanding is a two-way operation; learning doesn't consist in being an empty receptacle. The learner has to question himself and question the teacher. He even has to argue with the teacher, once he understands what the teacher is saying. And marking a book is literally an expression of your differences, or agreements of opinion, with the author.

There are all kinds of devices for marking a book intelligently   15
and fruitfully. Here's the way I do it:

1. *Underlining:* Of major points, of important or forceful state-   16
   ments.
2. *Vertical lines at the margin:* To emphasize a statement al-   17
   ready underlined.
3. *Star, asterisk, or other doo-dad at the margin:* To be used   18
   sparingly, to emphasize the ten or twenty most important statements in the book. (You may want to fold the bottom corner of each page on which you use such marks. It won't hurt the sturdy paper on which most modern books are printed, and you will be able to take the book off the shelf at any time and, by opening it at the folded-corner page, refresh your recollection of the book.)
4. *Numbers in the margin:* To indicate the sequence of points   19
   the author makes in developing a single argument.
5. *Numbers of other pages in the margin:* To indicate where else   20
   in the book the author made points relevant to the point marked; to tie up the ideas in a book, which, though they may be separated by many pages, belong together.
6. *Circling of key words or phrases.*   21
7. *Writing in the margin, or at the top or bottom of the page, for*   22
   the sake of: Recording questions (and perhaps answers) which a passage raised in your mind; reducing a complicated discussion to a simple statement; recording the sequence of major points right through the book. I use the end-papers at the back of the book to make a personal index of the author's points in the order of their appearance.

The front end-papers are, to me, the most important. Some peo-　23
ple reserve them for a fancy bookplate. I reserve them for fancy
thinking. After I have finished reading the book and making my
personal index on the back endpapers, I turn to the front and try to
outline the book, not page by page, or point by point (I've already
done that at the back), but as an integrated structure, with a basic
unity and an order of parts. This outline is, to me, the measure of my
understanding of the work.

If you're a die-hard anti-book-marker, you may object that the　24
margins, the space between the lines, and the end-papers don't give
you room enough. All right. How about using a scratch-pad slightly
smaller than the page-size of the book—so that the edges of the
sheets won't protrude? Make your index, outlines, and even your
notes on the pad, and then insert these sheets permanently inside
the front and back covers of the book.

Or, you may say that this business of marking books is going to　25
slow up your reading. It probably will. That's one of the reasons for
doing it. Most of us have been taken in by the notion that speed of
reading is a measure of our intelligence. There is no such thing as the
right speed for intelligent reading. Some things should be read quickly
and effortlessly, and some should be read slowly and even laboriously.
The sign of intelligence in reading is the ability to read different
things differently according to their worth. In the case of good books,
the point is not to see how many of them you can get through, but
rather how many can get through you—how many you can make
your own. A few friends are better than a thousand acquaintances. If
this be your aim, as it should be, you will not be impatient if it takes
more time and effort to read a great book than it does a newspaper.

You may have one final objection to marking books. You can't　26
lend them to your friends because nobody else can read them without being distracted by your notes. Furthermore, you won't want to
lend them because a marked copy is a kind of intellectual diary, and
lending it is almost like giving your mind away.

If your friend wishes to read your *Plutarch's Lives,* "Shake-　27
speare," or *The Federalist Papers,* tell him, gently but firmly, to buy
a copy. You will lend him your car or your coat—but your books are
as much a part of you as your head or your heart.

QUESTIONS OF CONTENT

1. Why does Adler think it is fine to mark up a book of your own?
2. How many kinds of book owners are there? Which kind does Adler
   clearly think is best? What is your opinion?

3. What are three useful results of marking in a book when reading it? Which do you think matters most?
4. How can writing in a book result in a "conversation" with its author, as Adler claims? Why is such a conversation useful?
5. Beginning with paragraph 16, Adler describes how he marks a book; which one of his techniques seems most useful to you, and why?

QUESTIONS OF FORM

1. Which of his examples or allusions indicate that Adler wrote this essay over fifty years ago? What changes would you make to update the essay?
2. How does the classification and comparison/contrast of book owners in paragraph 6 advance Adler's argument?
3. Adler uses analogies in paragraphs 4 and 8; what does he compare and how successful are these analogies in clarifying and supporting his points?
4. Adler's essay is clearly a claim of policy; how would you summarize his claim, and what warrant related to reading books lies behind his claim?
5. Adler makes two concessions, where he admits to two drawbacks of marking up a book when reading it; what are they and how appropriate is his placement of them in his essay?

SUGGESTIONS FOR WRITING

1. Write an essay in which you discuss the value of Adler's advice for a student in a subject or course other than English.
2. Choose one of the other essays in this Classic Arguments section and show, using specific references to that essay, how it "demands the most active reading of which you are capable" (paragraph 10).
3. Choose some type of reading material that does not need to be marked, in your opinion, and write a well-supported persuasive essay demonstrating why it doesn't.

Letter from Birmingham Jail

MARTIN LUTHER KING, JR.

An ordained Baptist minister who received a Ph.D. in theology from Boston University, the Reverend Martin Luther King, Jr., (1929–1968) was the foremost leader of the civil rights movement of the 1960s. But Dr. King's efforts to secure civil liberties and fair treatment for black Americans actually began in the 1950s, first in organizing a boycott of public buses with segregated seating in Montgomery, Alabama, and then as the director and one of the founders of the Southern Christian Leadership Conference. Jailed repeatedly for his civil rights efforts, Dr. King wrote this essay in 1963, in response to criticism of his work in Birmingham, Alabama, by local white clergy. An advocate of nonviolence, he is following in the path of Thoreau and Gandhi when he argues here for civil disobedience as a reasonable means, under the circumstances, for advancing the cause of integration. The next year he was awarded the Nobel Peace Prize for his work. Ironically, four years later, violence, in the form of an assassin's bullet, cut short Dr. King's efforts on behalf of equality and justice.

April 16, 1963

My Dear Fellow Clergymen:

While confined here in the Birmingham city jail, I came across your 1 recent statement calling my present activities "unwise and untimely." Seldom do I pause to answer criticism of my work and ideas. If I sought to answer all the criticisms that cross my desk, my secretaries would have little time for anything other than such correspondence in the course of the day, and I would have no time for constructive work. But since I feel that you are men of genuine good will and that your criticisms are sincerely set forth, I want to try to answer your statement in what I hope will be patient and reasonable terms.

I think I should indicate why I am here in Birmingham, since 2 you have been influenced by the view which argues against "outsiders coming in." I have the honor of serving as president of the Southern Christian Leadership Conference, an organization operating in every southern state, with headquarters in Atlanta, Georgia. We have some eighty-five affiliated organizations across the South, and one of them is the Alabama Christian Movement for Human Rights. Frequently we share staff, educational and financial resources with our affiliates. Several months ago the affiliate here in Birmingham asked us to be on call to engage in a nonviolent direct-action program if such were deemed necessary. We readily consented, and when the hour came we lived up to our promise. So I, along with several members of my staff, am here because I was invited here. I am here because I have organizational ties here.

But more basically, I am in Birmingham because injustice is 3 here. Just as the prophets of the eighth century B.C. left their villages and carried their "thus saith the Lord" far beyond the boundaries of their home towns, and just as the Apostle Paul left his village of Tarsus and carried the gospel of Jesus Christ to the far corners of the Greco-Roman world, so am I compelled to carry the gospel of freedom beyond my own home town. Like Paul, I must constantly respond to the Macedonian call for aid.

Moreover, I am cognizant of the interrelatedness of all communi-   4
ties and states. I cannot sit idly by in Atlanta and not be concerned about what happens in Birmingham. Injustice anywhere is a threat to justice everywhere. We are caught in an inescapable network of mutuality, tied in a single garment of destiny. Whatever affects one directly, affects all indirectly. Never again can we afford to live with the narrow, provincial "outside agitator" idea. Anyone who lives inside the United States can never be considered an outsider anywhere within its bounds.

You deplore the demonstrations taking place in Birmingham.   5
But your statement, I am sorry to say, fails to express a similar concern for the conditions that brought about the demonstrations. I am sure that none of you would want to rest content with the superficial kind of social analysis that deals merely with effects and does not grapple with underlying causes. It is unfortunate that demonstrations are taking place in Birmingham, but it is even more unfortunate that the city's white power structure left the Negro community with no alternative.

In any nonviolent campaign there are four basic steps: collection   6
of the facts to determine whether injustices exist; negotiation; self-purification; and direct action. We have gone through all these steps in Birmingham. There can be no gainsaying the fact that racial injustice engulfs this community. Birmingham is probably the most thoroughly segregated city in the United States. Its ugly record of brutality is widely known. Negroes have experienced grossly unjust treatment in the courts. There have been more unsolved bombings of Negro homes and churches in Birmingham than in any other city in the nation. These are the hard, brutal facts of the case. On the basis of these conditions, Negro leaders sought to negotiate with the city fathers. But the latter consistently refused to engage in good-faith negotiation.

Then, last September, came the opportunity to talk with leaders   7
of Birmingham's economic community. In the course of the negotiations, certain promises were made by the merchants—for example, to remove the stores' humiliating racial signs. On the basis of these promises, the Reverend Fred Shuttlesworth and the leaders of the Alabama Christian Movement for Human Rights agreed to a morato-

rium on all demonstrations. As the weeks and months went by, we realized that we were the victims of a broken promise. A few signs, briefly removed, returned; the others remained.

As in so many past experiences, our hopes had been blasted, and the shadow of deep disappointment settled upon us. We had no alternative except to prepare for direct action, whereby we would present our very bodies as a means of laying our case before the conscience of the local and the national community. Mindful of the difficulties involved, we decided to undertake a process of self-purification. We began a series of workshops on nonviolence, and we repeatedly asked ourselves: "Are you able to accept blows without retaliating?" "Are you able to endure the ordeal of jail?" We decided to schedule our direct-action program for the Easter season, realizing that except for Christmas, this is the main shopping period of the year. Knowing that a strong economic-withdrawal program would be the by-product of direct action, we felt that this would be the best time to bring pressure to bear on the merchants for the needed change. 8

Then it occurred to us that Birmingham's mayoral election was coming up in March, and we speedily decided to postpone action until after election day. When we discovered that the Commissioner of Public Safety, Eugene "Bull" Connor, had piled up enough votes to be in the run-off, we decided again to postpone action until the day after the run-off so that the demonstrations could not be used to cloud the issues. Like many others, we waited to see Mr. Connor defeated, and to this end we endured postponement after postponement. Having aided in this community need, we felt that our direct-action program could be delayed no longer. 9

You may well ask: "Why direct action? Why sit-ins, marches and so forth? Isn't negotiation a better path?" You are quite right in calling for negotiation. Indeed, this is the very purpose of direct action. Nonviolent direct action seeks to create such a crisis and foster such a tension that a community which has constantly re-fused to negotiate is forced to confront the issue. It seeks so to dramatize the issue that it can no longer be ignored. My citing the creation of tension as part of the work of the nonviolent-resister may sound rather shocking. But I must confess that I am not afraid of the word "tension." I have earnestly opposed violent tension, but there is a type of constructive, nonviolent tension which is necessary for growth. Just as Socrates felt that it was necessary to create a tension in the mind so that individuals could arise from the bondage of myths and half-truths to the unfettered realm of creative analysis and objective appraisal, so must we see the need for nonviolent gadflies to create the kind of tension in society that will help men 10 rise from the dark depths of prejudice and racism to the majestic heights of understanding and brotherhood.

The purpose of our direct-action program is to create a situation 11 so crisis-packed that it will inevitably open the door to negotiation. I therefore concur with you in your call for negotiation. Too long has our beloved Southland been bogged down in a tragic effort to live in monologue rather than dialogue.

One of the basic points in your statement is that the action that I 12 and my associates have taken in Birmingham is untimely. Some have asked: "Why didn't you give the new city administration time to act?" The only answer that I can give to this query is that the new Birmingham administration must be prodded about as much as the outgoing one, before it will act. We are sadly mistaken if we feel that the election of Albert Boutwell as mayor will bring the millennium to Birmingham. While Mr. Boutwell is a much more gentle person than Mr. Connor, they are both segregationists, dedicated to maintenance of the status quo. I have hope that Mr. Boutwell will be reasonable enough to see the futility of massive resistance to desegregation. But he will not see this without pressure from devotees of civil rights. My friends, I must say to you that we have not made a single gain in civil rights without determined legal and nonviolent pressure. Lamentably, it is an historical fact that privileged groups seldom give up their privileges voluntarily. Individuals may see the moral light and voluntarily give up their unjust posture; but, as Reinhold Niebuhr has reminded us, groups tend to be more immoral than individuals.

We know through painful experience that freedom is never vol- 13 untarily given by the oppressor; it must be demanded by the oppressed. Frankly, I have yet to engage in a direct-action campaign that was "well timed" in the view of those who have not suffered unduly from the disease of segregation. For years now I have heard the word "Wait!" It rings in the ear of every Negro with piercing familiarity. This "Wait" has almost always meant "Never." We must come to see, with one of our distinguished jurists, that "justice too long delayed is justice denied."

We have waited for more than 340 years for our constitutional 14 and God-given rights. The nations of Asia and Africa are moving with jetlike speed toward gaining political independence, but we still creep at horse-and-buggy pace toward gaining a cup of coffee at a lunch counter. Perhaps it is easy for those who have never felt the stinging darts of segregation to say, "Wait." But when you have seen vicious mobs lynch your mothers and fathers at will and drown your sisters and brothers at whim; when you have seen hate-filled policemen curse, kick and even kill your black brothers and sisters; when you see the vast majority of your twenty million Negro brothers smothering in an airtight cage of poverty in the midst of an affluent society; when you suddenly find your tongue twisted and your speech stammering as you seek to explain to your six-year-old daughter why she can't go to the public amusement park that has just been advertised on television, and see tears welling up in her eyes when she is told that Funtown is closed to colored children, and see ominous clouds of inferiority beginning to form in her little mental sky, and see her beginning to distort her personality by developing an unconscious bitterness toward white people; when you have to concoct an answer for a five-year-old son who is asking: "Daddy, why do white people treat colored people so mean?"; when you take a cross-country drive and find it necessary to sleep night after night in the uncomfortable corners of your automobile because no motel will accept you; when you are humiliated day in and day out by nagging signs reading "white" and "colored"; when your first name becomes "nigger," your middle name becomes "boy" (however old you are) and your last name becomes "John," and your wife and mother are never given the respected title "Mrs."; when you are harried by day and haunted by night by the fact that you are a Negro, living constantly at tiptoe stance, never quite knowing what to expect next, and are plagued with inner fears and outer resentments; when you are forever fighting a degenerating sense of "nobodiness"—then you will understand why we find it difficult to wait. There comes a time when the cup of endurance runs over, and men are no longer willing to be plunged into the abyss of despair. I hope, sirs, you can understand our legitimate and unavoidable impatience.

You express a great deal of anxiety over our willingness to break 15
laws. This is certainly a legitimate concern. Since we so diligently urged people to obey the Supreme Court's decision of 1954 outlawing segregation in the public schools, at first glance it may seem rather paradoxical for us consciously to break laws. One may well ask: "How can you advocate breaking some laws and obeying others?" The answer lies in the fact that there are two types of laws: just and unjust. I would be the first to advocate obeying just laws. One has not only a legal but a moral responsibility to obey just laws. Conversely, one has a moral responsibility to disobey unjust laws. I would agree with St. Augustine that "an unjust law is no law at all."

Now, what is the difference between the two? How does one 16
determine whether a law is just or unjust? A just law is a man-made code that squares with the moral law or the law of God. An unjust law is a code that is out of harmony with the moral law. To put it in the terms of St. Thomas Aquinas: An unjust law is a human law that is not rooted in eternal law and natural law. Any law that uplifts

human personality is just. Any law that degrades human personality is unjust. All segregation statutes are unjust because segregation distorts the soul and damages the personality. It gives the segregator a false sense of superiority and the segregated a false sense of inferiority. Segregation, to use the terminology of the Jewish philosopher Martin Buber, substitutes an "I-it" relationship for an "I-thou" relationship and ends up relegating persons to the status of things. Hence segregation is not only politically, economically and sociologically unsound, it is morally wrong and sinful. Paul Tillich has said that sin is separation. Is not segregation an existential expression of man's tragic separation, his awful estrangement, his terrible sinfulness? Thus it is that I can urge men to obey the 1954 decision of the Supreme Court, for it is morally right; and I can urge them to disobey segregation ordinances, for they are morally wrong.

Let us consider a more concrete example of just and unjust laws.   17
An unjust law is a code that a numerical or power majority group compels a minority group to obey but does not make binding on itself. This is *difference* made legal. By the same token, a just law is a code that a majority compels a minority to follow and that it is willing to follow itself. This is *sameness* made legal.

Let me give another explanation. A law is unjust if it is inflicted   18
on a minority that, as a result of being denied the right to vote, had no part in enacting or devising the law. Who can say that the legislature of Alabama which set up that state's segregation laws was democratically elected? Throughout Alabama all sorts of devious methods are used to prevent Negroes from becoming registered voters, and there are some counties in which, even though Negroes constitute a majority of the population, not a single Negro is registered. Can any law enacted under such circumstances be considered democratically structured?

Sometimes a law is just on its face and unjust in its application.   19
For instance, I have been arrested on a charge of parading without a permit. Now, there is nothing wrong in having an ordinance which requires a permit for a parade. But such an ordinance becomes unjust when it is used to maintain segregation and to deny citizens the First-Amendment privilege of peaceful assembly and protest.

I hope you are able to see the distinction I am trying to point out.   20
In no sense do I advocate evading or defying the law, as would the rabid segregationist. That would lead to anarchy. One who breaks an unjust law must do so openly, lovingly, and with a willingness to accept the penalty. I submit that an individual who breaks a law that conscience tells him is unjust, and who willingly accepts the penalty of imprisonment in order to arouse the conscience of the com-

munity over its injustice, is in reality expressing the highest respect for law.

Of course, there is nothing new about this kind of civil disobedi- 21 ence. It was evidenced sublimely in the refusal to Shadrach, Meshach and Abednego to obey the laws of Nebuchadnezzar, on the ground that a higher moral law was at stake. It was practiced superbly by the early Christians, who were willing to face hungry lions and the excruciating pain of chopping blocks rather than submit to certain unjust laws of the Roman Empire. To a degree, academic freedom is a reality today because Socrates practiced civil disobedience. In our own nation, the Boston Tea Party represented a massive act of civil disobedience.

We should never forget that everything Adolf Hitler did in Ger- 22 many was "legal" and everything that Hungarian freedom fighters did in Hungary was "illegal." It was "illegal" to aid and comfort a Jew in Hitler's Germany. Even so, I am sure that, had I lived in Germany at the time, I would have aided and comforted my Jewish brothers. If today I lived in a Communist country where certain principles dear to the Christian faith are suppressed, I would openly advocate disobeying that country's antireligious laws.

I must make two honest confessions to you, my Christian and 23 Jewish brothers. I must confess that over the past few years I have been gravely disappointed with the white moderate. I have reached the regrettable conclusion that the Negro's great stumbling block in his stride toward freedom is not the White Citizen's Counciler or the Ku Klux Klanner, but the white moderate, who is more devoted to "order" than to justice; who prefers a negative peace which is the absence of tension to a positive peace which is the presence of justice; who constantly says: "I agree with you in the goal you seek, but I cannot agree with your methods of direct action"; who paternalistically believes he can set the timetable for another man's freedom; who lives by a mythical concept of time and who constantly advises the Negro to wait for a "more convenient season." Shallow understanding from people of good will is more frustrating than absolute misunderstanding from people of ill will. Lukewarm acceptance is much more bewildering than outright rejection.

I had hoped that the white moderate would understand that law 24 and order exist for the purpose of establishing justice and that when they fail in this purpose they become the dangerously structured dams that block the flow of social progress. I had hoped that the white moderate would understand that the present tension in the South is a necessary phase of the transition from an obnoxious negative peace, in which the Negro passively accepted his unjust plight, to a substantive and positive peace, in which all men will respect the dignity and worth of human personality. Actually, we who engage in nonviolent direct action are not the creators of tension. We merely bring to the surface the hidden tension that is already alive. We bring it out in the open, where it can be seen and dealt with. Like a boil that can never be cured so long as it is covered up but must be opened with all its ugliness to the natural medicines of air and light, injustice must be exposed, with all the tension its exposure creates, to the light of human conscience and the air of national opinion before it can be cured.

In your statement you assert that our actions, even though peace-   25 ful, must be condemned because they precipitate violence. But is this a logical assertion? Isn't this like condemning a robbed man because his possession of money precipitated the evil act of robbery? Isn't this like condemning Socrates because his unswerving commitment to truth and his philosophical inquiries precipitated the act by the misguided populace in which they made him drink hemlock? Isn't this like condemning Jesus because his unique God-consciousness and never-ceasing devotion to God's will precipitated the evil act of crucifixion? We must come to see that, as the federal courts have consistently affirmed, it is wrong to urge an individual to cease his efforts to gain his basic constitutional rights because the quest may precipitate violence. Society must protect the robbed and punish the robber.

I had also hoped that the white moderate would reject the myth   26 concerning time in relation to the struggle for freedom. I have just received a letter from a white brother in Texas. He writes: "All Christians know that the colored people will receive equal rights eventually, but it is possible that you are in too great a religious hurry. It has taken Christianity almost two thousand years to accomplish what it has. The teachings of Christ take time to come to earth." Such an attitude stems from a tragic misconception of time, from the strangely irrational notion that there is something in the very flow of time that will inevitably cure all ills. Actually, time itself is neutral; it can be used either destructively or constructively. More and more I feel that the people of ill will have used time much more effectively than have the people of good will. We will have to repent in this generation not merely for the hateful words and actions of the bad people but for the appalling silence of the good people. Human progress never rolls in on wheels of inevitability; it comes through the tireless efforts of men willing to be co-workers with God, and without this hard work, time itself becomes an ally of the forces of social stagnation. We must use time creatively, in the knowledge that the time is always ripe to do right. Now is the time to make real the promise of democracy and transform our pending national elegy into a creative psalm of brotherhood. Now is the time to lift our national policy from the quicksand of racial injustice to the solid rock of human dignity.

You speak of our activity in Birmingham as extreme. At first I 27 was rather disappointed that fellow clergymen would see my nonviolent efforts as those of an extremist. I began thinking about the fact that I stand in the middle of two opposing forces in the Negro community. One is a force of complacency, made up in part of Negroes who, as a result of long years of oppression, are so drained of self-respect and a sense of "somebodiness" that they have adjusted to segregation; and in part of a few middle-class Negroes who, because of a degree of academic and economic security and because in some ways they profit by segregation, have become insensitive to the problems of the masses. The other force is one of bitterness and hatred, and it comes perilously close to advocating violence. It is expressed in the various black nationalist groups that are springing up across the nation, the largest and best-known being Elijah Muhammad's Muslim movement. Nourished by the Negro's frustration over the continued existence of racial discrimination, this movement is made up of people who have lost faith in America, who have absolutely repudiated Christianity, and who have concluded that the white man is an incorrigible "devil."

I have tried to stand between these two forces, saying that we 28 need emulate neither the "do-nothingism" of the complacent nor the hatred and despair of the black nationalist. For there is the more excellent way of love and nonviolent protest. I am grateful to God that, through the influence of the Negro church, the way of nonviolence became an integral part of our struggle.

If this philosophy had not emerged, by now many streets of the 29 South would, I am convinced, be flowing with blood. And I am further convinced that if our white brothers dismiss as "rabble-rousers" and "outside agitators" those of us who employ nonviolent direct action, and if they refuse to support our nonviolent efforts, millions of Negroes will, out of frustration and despair, seek solace and security in black-nationalist ideologies—a development that would inevitably lead to a frightening racial nightmare.

Oppressed people cannot remain oppressed forever. The yearn- 30 ing for freedom eventually manifests itself, and that is what has happened to the American Negro. Something within has reminded him of his birthright of freedom, and something without has reminded him that it can be gained. Consciously or unconsciously, he has been caught up by the *Zeitgeist*, and with his black brothers of Africa and his brown and yellow brothers of Asia, South America and the Caribbean, the United States Negro is moving with a sense of great urgency toward the promised land of racial justice. If one recognizes this vital urge that has engulfed the Negro community, one should readily understand why public demonstrations are taking place. The Negro has many pent-up resentments and latent frustrations, and he must release them. So let him march; let him make prayer pilgrimages to the city hall; let him go on freedom rides—and try to understand why he must do so. If his repressed emotions are not released in nonviolent ways, they will seek expression through violence; this is not a threat but a fact of history. So I have not said to my people: "Get rid of your discontent." Rather, I have tried to say that this normal and healthy discontent can be channeled into the creative outlet of nonviolent direct action. And now this approach is being termed extremist.

But though I was initially disappointed at being categorized as an   31 extremist, as I continued to think about the matter I gradually gained a measure of satisfaction from the label. Was not Jesus an extremist for love: "Love your enemies, bless them that curse you, do good to them that hate you, and pray for them which despitefully use you, and persecute you." Was not Amos an extremist for justice: "Let justice roll down like waters and righteousness like an everflowing stream." Was not Paul an extremist for the Christian gospel: "I bear in my body the marks of the Lord Jesus." Was not Martin Luther an extremist: "Here I stand; I cannot do otherwise, so help me God." And John Bunyan: "I will stay in jail to the end of my days before I make a butchery of my conscience." And Abraham Lincoln: "This nation cannot survive half slave and half free." And Thomas Jefferson: "We hold these truths to be self-evident, that all men are created equal . . . ." So the question is not whether we will be extremists, but what kind of extremists we will be. Will we be extremists for hate or for love? Will we be extremists for the preservation of injustice or for the extension of justice? In that dramatic scene on Calvary's hill three men were crucified. We must never forget that all three were crucified for the same crime—the crime of extremism. Two were extremists for immorality, and thus fell below their environment. The other, Jesus Christ, was an extremist for love, truth and goodness, and thereby rose above his environment. Perhaps the South, the nation and the world are in dire need of creative extremists.

I had hoped that the white moderate would see this need. Perhaps   32 I was too optimistic; perhaps I expected too much. I suppose I should have realized that few members of the oppressor race can understand the deep groans and passionate yearnings of the oppressed race, and still fewer have the vision to see that injustice must be rooted out by strong, persistent and determined action. I am thankful, however, that some of our white brothers in the South have grasped the meaning of this social revolution and committed themselves to it. They are still all too few in quantity, but they are big in quality. Some—such as Ralph McGill, Lillian Smith, Harry Golden, James McBride Dabbs, Ann Braden and Sarah Patton Boyle—have written about our struggle in eloquent and prophetic terms. Others have marched with us down nameless streets of the South. They have languished in filthy, roach-infested jails, suffering the abuse and brutality of policemen who view them as "dirty nigger-lovers." Unlike so many of their moderate brothers and sisters, they have recognized the urgency of the moment and sensed the need for powerful "action" antidotes to combat the disease of segregation.

Let me take note of my other major disappointment. I have been 33 so greatly disappointed with the white church and its leadership. Of course, there are some notable exceptions. I am not unmindful of the fact that each of you has taken some significant stands on this issue. I commend you, Reverend Stallings, for your Christian stand on this past Sunday, in welcoming Negroes to your worship service on a nonsegregated basis. I commend the Catholic leaders of this state for integrating Spring Hill College several years ago.

But despite these notable exceptions, I must honestly reiterate 34 that I have been disappointed with the church. I do not say this as one of those negative critics who can always find something wrong with the church. I say this as a minister of the gospel, who loves the church; who was nurtured in its bosom; who has been sustained by its spiritual blessings and who will remain true to it as long as the cord of life shall lengthen.

When I was suddenly catapulted into the leadership of the bus 35 protest in Montgomery, Alabama, a few years ago, I felt we would be supported by the white church. I felt that the white ministers, priests and rabbis of the South would be among our strongest allies. Instead, some have been outright opponents, refusing to understand the freedom movement and misrepresenting its leaders; all too many others have been more cautious than courageous and have remained silent behind the anesthetizing security of stained-glass windows.

In spite of my shattered dreams, I came to Birmingham with the 36 hope that the white religious leadership of this community would see the justice of our cause and, with deep moral concern, would serve as the channel through which our just grievances could reach the power structure. I had hoped that each of you would understand. But again I have been disappointed.

I have heard numerous southern religious leaders admonish 37 their worshipers to comply with a desegregation decision because it is the law, but I have longed to hear white ministers declare: "Follow this decree because integration is morally right and because the Negro is your brother." In the midst of blatant injustices inflicted upon the Negro, I have watched white churchmen stand on the sideline and mouth pious irrelevancies and sanctimonious trivialities. In the midst of a mighty struggle to rid our nation of racial and economic injustice, I have heard many ministers say: "Those are social issues, with which the gospel has no real concern." And I have watched many churches commit themselves to a completely otherworldly religion which makes a strange, un-Biblical distinction between body and soul, between the sacred and the secular.

I have traveled the length and breadth of Alabama, Mississippi   38
and all the other southern states. On sweltering summer days and crisp autumn mornings I have looked at the South's beautiful churches with their lofty spires pointing heavenward. I have beheld the impressive outlines of her massive religious-education buildings. Over and over I have found myself asking: "What kind of people worship here? Who is their God? Where were their voices when the lips of Governor Barnett dripped with words of interposition and nullification? Where were they when Governor Wallace gave a clarion call for defiance and hatred? Where were their voices of support when bruised and weary Negro men and women decided to rise from the dark dungeons of complacency to the bright hills of creative protest?"

Yes, these questions are still in my mind. In deep disappoint-   39
ment I have wept over the laxity of the church. But be assured that my tears have been tears of love. There can be no deep disappointment where there is not deep love. Yes, I love the church. How could I do otherwise? I am in the rather unique position of being the son, the grandson and the great-grandson of preachers. Yes, I see the church as the body of Christ. But, oh! How we have blemished and scarred that body through social neglect and through fear of being nonconformists.

There was a time when the church was very powerful—in the   40
time when the early Christians rejoiced at being deemed worthy to suffer for what they believed. In those days the church was not merely a thermometer that recorded the ideas and principles of popular opinion; it was a thermostat that transformed the mores of society. Whenever the early Christians entered a town, the people in power became disturbed and immediately sought to convict the Christians for being "disturbers of the peace" and "outside agitators." But the Christians pressed on, in the conviction that they were "a colony of heaven," called to obey God rather than man. Small in number, they were big in commitment. They were too God-

intoxicated to be "astronomically intimidated." By their effort and example they brought an end to such ancient evils as infanticide and gladiatorial contests.

Things are different now. So often the contemporary church is a weak, ineffectual voice with an uncertain sound. So often it is an archdefender of the status quo. Far from being disturbed by the presence of the church, the power structure of the average community is consoled by the church's silent—and often even vocal—sanction of things as they are. 41

But the judgment of God is upon the church as never before. If today's church does not recapture the sacrificial spirit of the early church, it will lose its authenticity, forfeit the loyalty of millions, and be dismissed as an irrelevant social club with no meaning for the twentieth century. Every day I meet young people whose disappointment with the church has turned into outright disgust. 42

Perhaps I have once again been too optimistic. Is organized religion too inextricably bound to the status quo to save our nation and the world? Perhaps I must turn my faith to the inner spiritual church, the church within the church, as the true *ekklesia* and the hope of the world. But again I am thankful to God that some noble souls from the ranks of organized religion have broken loose from the paralyzing chains of conformity and joined us as active partners in the struggle for freedom. They have left their secure congregations and walked the streets of Albany, Georgia, with us. They have gone down the highways of the South on tortuous rides for freedom. Yes, they have gone to jail with us. Some have been dismissed from their churches, have lost the support of their bishops and fellow ministers. But they have acted in the faith that right defeated is stronger than evil triumphant. Their witness has been the spiritual salt that has preserved the true meaning of the gospel in these troubled times. They have carved a tunnel of hope through the dark mountain of disappointment. 43

I hope the church as a whole will meet the challenge of this decisive hour. But even if the church does not come to the aid of justice, I have no despair about the future. I have no fear about the outcome of our struggle in Birmingham, even if our motives are at present misunderstood. We will reach the goal of freedom in Birmingham and all over the nation, because the goal of America is freedom. Abused and scorned though we may be, our destiny is tied up with America's destiny. Before the pilgrims landed at Plymouth, we were here. Before the pen of Jefferson etched the majestic words of the Declaration of Independence across the pages of history, we were here. For more than two centuries our forebears labored in this country without wages; they made cotton king; they built the 44 homes of their masters while suffering gross injustice and shameful humiliation—and yet out of a bottomless vitality they continued to thrive and develop. If the inexpressible cruelties of slavery could not stop us, the opposition we now face will surely fail. We will win our freedom because the sacred heritage of our nation and the eternal will of God are embodied in our echoing demands.

Before closing I feel impelled to mention one other point in your 45 statement that has troubled me profoundly. You warmly commended the Birmingham police force for keeping "order" and "preventing violence." I doubt that you would have so warmly commended the police force if you had seen its dogs sinking their teeth into unarmed, nonviolent Negroes. I doubt that you would so quickly commend the policemen if you were to observe their ugly and inhumane treatment of Negroes here in the city jail; if you were to watch them push and curse old Negro women and young Negro girls; if you were to see them slap and kick old Negro men and young boys; if you were to observe them, as they did on two occasions, refuse to give us food because we wanted to sing our grace together. I cannot join you in your praise of the Birmingham police department.

It is true that the police have exercised a degree of discipline in 46 handling the demonstrators. In this sense they have conducted themselves rather "nonviolently" in public. But for what purpose? To preserve the evil system of segregation. Over the past few years I have consistently preached that nonviolence demands that the means we use must be as pure as the ends we seek. I have tried to make clear that it is wrong to use immoral means to attain moral ends. But now I must affirm that it is just as wrong, or perhaps even more so, to use moral means to preserve immoral ends. Perhaps Mr. Connor and his policemen have been rather nonviolent in public, as was Chief Pritchett in Albany, Georgia, but they have used the moral means of nonviolence to maintain the immoral end of racial injustice. As T. S. Eliot has said: "The last temptation is the greatest treason: To do the right deed for the wrong reason."

I wish you had commended the Negro sit-inners and demon- 47 strators of Birmingham for their sublime courage, their willingness to suffer and their amazing discipline in the midst of great provocation. One day the South will recognize its real heroes. They will be the James Merediths, with the noble sense of purpose that enables them to face jeering and hostile mobs, and with the agonizing loneliness that characterizes the life of the pioneer. They will be old, oppressed, battered Negro women, symbolized in a seventy-two-year-old woman in Montgomery, Alabama, who rose up with a sense of dignity and with her people decided not to ride segregated buses, and who responded with ungrammatical profundity to one who inquired about her weariness: "My feets is tired, but my soul is at rest." They will be the young high school and college students, the young ministers of the gospel and a host of their elders, courageously and nonviolently sitting in at lunch counters and willingly going to jail for conscience' sake. One day the South will know that when these disinherited children of God sat down at lunch counters, they were in reality standing up for what is best in the American dream and for the most sacred values in our Judaeo-Christian heritage, thereby bringing our nation back to those great wells of democracy which were dug deep by the founding fathers in their formulation of the Constitution and the Declaration of Independence.

Never before have I written so long a letter. I'm afraid it is much 48 too long to take your precious time. I can assure you that it would have been much shorter if I had been writing from a comfortable desk, but what else can one do when he is alone in a narrow jail cell, other than write long letters, think long thoughts and pray long prayers?

If I have said anything in this letter that overstates the truth and 49 indicates an unreasonable impatience, I beg you to forgive me. If I have said anything that understates the truth and indicates my having a patience that allows me to settle for anything less than brotherhood, I beg God to forgive me.

I hope this letter finds you strong in the faith. I also hope that 50 circumstances will soon make it possible for me to meet each of you, not as an integrationist or a civil-rights leader but as a fellow clergyman and a Christian brother. Let us all hope that the dark clouds of racial prejudice will soon pass away and the deep fog of misunderstanding will be lifted from our fear-drenched communities, and in some not too distant tomorrow the radiant stars of love and brotherhood will shine over our great nation with all their scintillating beauty.

Yours for the cause of Peace and Brotherhood,

Martin Luther King, Jr.

QUESTIONS OF CONTENT

1. In responding to his fellow clergymen's charge that he is an outsider, what three reasons does King give for his presence? What point does he make about *any* person living in the United States? How realistic or idealistic in his statement there?

2. What are the four basic steps in a nonviolent campaign against injustices, according to King? How carefully had King and his followers apparently adhered to those steps in Birmingham in 1963?
3. How does King respond to the suggestion that the Birmingham direct-action campaign was not "well timed," and that he and his followers should "Wait"?
4. How does King differentiate between "just" and "unjust" laws? What historical examples does he use for support, and how appropriate are they?
5. King says that he is disappointed with white moderates (paragraphs 23–32) and with the white church and its leaders (33–44); why do you suppose he focuses on these two groups, and by what varied means does he support his claims of value regarding them?

QUESTIONS OF FORM

1. You will notice that King frequently refers to the Bible and to religious authorities. Which of his allusions did you find most valuable or convincing? Why are such uses especially appropriate in terms of his primary intended audience? What effect(s) might they have on his general audience?
2. After listing the four basic steps in a nonviolent campaign, where and how does King show that his group fulfilled those in Birmingham? What does his argument gain from this support?
3. What is the value of the rhetorical effect created in paragraph 14 by King's repetition of phrases beginning with "when you"? Where else do you notice his use of repetition for rhetorical effect?
4. King often uses figurative language to heighten the appeal of his argument. Where are three such uses, and how effective are they?
5. King's argument is long and complex, making a variety of claims, supporting those in many ways, and using all three sorts of appeals. Which appeal seems most prominent: logical, ethical, or emotional? Be prepared to point out an effective example of each of the three sorts in this essay.
6. Why do you suppose King included his essay's last three paragraphs? How do they fit into his overall argument?

SUGGESTIONS FOR WRITING

1. Argue for or against one of King's assertions listed below. Use a news event or (events) to support your claim.
   a. "Injustice anywhere is a threat to justice everywhere." (Paragraph 4)
   b. "... groups tend to be more immoral than individuals." (Paragraph 12—attributed to the theologian Reinhold Niebuhr)

c. "Sometimes a law is just on its face and unjust in its application." (Paragraph 19)

d. ". . . the time is always ripe to do right." (Paragraph 26)

e. "Oppressed people cannot remain oppressed forever." (Paragraph 30)

2. Choose the paragraph in King's essay which appeals to you the most, and in an organized paper discuss the key factors in its appeal for you, with particular attention to the accuracy of his language and the strength of his examples.

3. Assume you are one of the white Birmingham religious leaders to whom King's letter was directed. Respond to him in a letter of your own, being sure to identify your assumed religion. (Your instructor may want you to do some background research, especially in newspapers and magazines of the time, so that you can manage this assignment better.)

APPENDIX

A Short Guide to Material and Formal Fallacies

Fallacies are various types of deceptive or erroneous or false reasoning; they cause an argument to be logically flawed, even though that argument may be emotionally persuasive and may appear to be true. A fallacious argument may contain one or several fallacies.

The value of being able to recognize fallacies may already be clear, even before you read the brief descriptions that appear below. For instance, since all of us are consumers, we are confronted every day with fallacious media advertisements and salespersons' propositions. As citizens, we must often consider explanations from officials, pronouncements from government agencies, and speeches from politicians; any of these may contain fallacies. Finally, we can expect, as employees and employers, to have to contend with fallacies in the public and private communications that help business, industry, and professions operate. Therefore, at home and at work, we need to be alert for and ready to resist conscious or unconscious fallacies, in others' arguments or our own. After all, fallacies hinder or even prevent honest, rational discussions and the making of correct, logical decisions.

As an aid to understanding, fallacies are often divided into two broad categories: material and formal. *Material fallacies* (sometimes called informal fallacies) result from errors in the content or wording of arguments, and thus could be separated into two groups (although they overlap in places): emotional and language. These sorts of fallacies tend to be present in arguments that we intuitively recognize as wrong but whose flaws we have trouble explaining.

Formal fallacies (sometimes called structural fallacies) result from errors in the form or structure of deductive arguments. Their conclusions are unacceptable because of those flaws in reasoning, and you should be able to learn to pick out those flaws.

You will see in what follows that some fallacies have several names. They may also be best known by their traditional Latin names, dating from an earlier time when fallacies were a familiar part of rhetorical study in schools. You will need to learn the various names and definitions for fallacies in order to understand and to participate in class discussions and other course exercises.

Material Fallacies

Material fallacies result either from: (1) imprecise or improper use of language, or from (2) appeals to emotion rather than to reason. Here are short discussions, with examples, of some of the most common material fallacies.

Appeal to Force. This emotion-based fallacy can cause people to act in inappropriate ways, or not to act in appropriate ways. Either real force or the threat of force is used in an attempt to cause the acceptance of a conclusion. The threat may be veiled and nonphysical, as in a threat to withhold votes from one politician or to deliver them to an opponent, based on government actions that the politician may influence or control. In contrast, an open threat might include beatings, the brandishing of weapons, kidnappings, bombings, or even war. Appeals to force are the staples of gang warfare and revolutions.

This fallacy is very closely related to another emotion-based fallacy, the *appeal to fear,* which plays upon its audience's sense of danger; you may have seen useful but still fallacious examples in anti-drug and anti-drunk driving public service advertisements. The appeal to fear is a particular favorite of insurance companies, which capitalize upon our legitimate worries concerning potential losses of property, health, or even life itself.

Appeal to the People (ad Populum). This fallacy is the "my friends and fellow Americans" (or New Yorkers or teachers or Presbyterians or whatever group is being addressed) approach especially favored by some politicians, who hope to hide the flimsiness of an idea or an argument behind a verbal screen that emphasizes attitudes or beliefs that are presumably shared. But emotional language will not suffice as supporting evidence.

Appeal to Pity (ad Misericordiam). This emotional approach tries to arouse the sympathy or pity of a person or group in order to influence a decision. For instance, a defense attorney may put her client's family prominently on display in the courtroom in an attempt to persuade the jury or judge that the future welfare and happiness of that family depends wholly on lenient treatment of the accused. A student might be using a similar approach when, having missed a class—or wanting to miss one—she or he tells an instructor about the illness, accident, or death of a relative or close friend. If the story is false, the student is both lying and appealing to pity; if the student is telling the truth, then this would be an instance of an appeal to pity only if the student was actually unmoved by the other person's misfortune and using it as an excuse.

Appeal to Tradition.   This rather transparent fallacy is based on the assumption that whatever has existed for a long time, or has been repeated fairly regularly for a number of times, is somehow made legitimate by its history. But historical maltreatment of others, for instance as members of a minority group, certainly cannot justify continuation of that bad behavior; it should be easy enough to think of examples of the appearance of this fallacy in arguments involving civil rights, women's rights, animal rights, and the like. The person proposing to maintain a tradition that is dangerous or oppressive should be made to provide reasons or backing, beyond the mere fact of historical precedent, as support for the continuation of that tradition.

Argument ad Hominem (at the Person).   This emotional fallacy occurs when someone attacks an adversary's character in the course of an argument. One familiar and open form of the fallacy involves *name calling,* which occurs when a person's ideas are criticized because she or he has some apparent background flaw, such as being a reformed alcohol or drug abuser, or having flunked out of college, or even having served a prison sentence. At other times the fallacy may be more subtle, for instance through the use of familiar psychological labels for neuroses, such as inferiority complex, compulsive behavior, Oedipus complex, and so forth. However, such criticisms, even if true (frequently they are not, or else they are overstated), are generally irrelevant to the points at issue, to which attention must be directed to neutralize this fallacy.

The *genetic* or *stereotypical fallacy* is closely related. In this case, a person's ideas are criticized because of his or her race, sex, religion, nationality, and the like. But even if suspect because of possible self-interest, a feminist's ideas about abortion or a police officer's ideas on capital punishment may be perfectly sound. Certainly in fairness we ought to try to keep the background of a person separate from the ideas she or he supports, and ought to accept or reject them on logical, not emotional, grounds.

A pernicious subvariety of these two fallacies is labeled *poisoning the well*. In this case, an attack is made on a person's background or character, or on a person or group originating an idea, before the argument has actually begun.

Bandwagon.   This familiar fallacy is really a variety of the appeal to fear, for it profits from our desire to be part of a group, or "in the parade." Thus, because we don't want to be left out, we "jump on the bandwagon." Accordingly, we are often fallaciously encouraged to buy a product because it is the most popular (or so its commercials claim), or we may be urged to support a candidate that polls show is ahead in a political race. Yet we should depend first on logical, not emotional, reasons for the choices we make. The teenager's familiar claim, "Everyone else has one," is not a logical reason; "Everyone else" can be wrong again, just as they have often been before.

Begging the Question (Circular Reasoning).   This fallacy might be classed as formal rather than material, for in it the conclusion of a deductive argument is contained among the deductive argument's premises: "Of course cocaine users lack will power. That's why they're cocaine users." This fallacy is very difficult to notice when buried in a lengthy argument or when it is expressed in difficult language, as in this example: "To allow every person unrestricted freedom of speech must always be, on the whole, advantageous to the state; for it is highly conducive to the interests of the society at large when each individual citizen enjoys the liberty, perfectly unlimited, of expressing his or her sentiments." In simpler words: "Free speech is good for the state because it's good for the state when there is free speech." Taking an argument through a full circle does not prove anything.

Dicto Simpliciter (Unqualified Generalization).   This fallacy results when an argument is based upon a generalization that is completely inclusive and presented as unequivocally true in all circumstances. "Milk is good for you" is simply not true for everybody; neither is "Alcohol is bad for your health" (physicians sometimes recommend an occasional glass of beer for nursing mothers, to aid their milk flow, and may suggest a daily moderate amount of alcohol for some aged patients).

Either/or (False Dilemma).   This fallacy denies that there is any intermediate possibility between two extremes. Examples include:

"Ms. Franklin must be a communist; she won't join the other local business owners in the Chamber of Commerce." "Mary has become an atheist since she went off to college; she hasn't been to church all semester." "Jason wants to become a killer; he just enlisted in the Army." Unfortunately, because such statements too often appeal to our prejudices and ignorance, we sometimes accept them as true without considering any probable alternative explanations.

Equivocation.   This language fallacy is produced by accidental or deliberate misuse of two or more meanings of the same word or phrase in a statement. The ambiguous results may be amusing, sometimes in a grim way, as in these sample newspaper headlines: "Mass Murderer Receives Last Rights Before Execution," "Eastern Airlines Drops Union Pilots From Flights," "Doctors to Offer Poor Examinations." Equivocation can also occur in serious contexts, thereby causing critical disagreements. This is particularly so when abstract words such as "right," "guarantee," and "natural" are involved. Consider, for instance, the commonly used phrase "lifetime warranty." Without any qualifying information, how can you tell what either word means? Whose "lifetime"? What is covered by the "warranty"? The best policy in such cases is to be sure that all equivocal words are explained or defined, thus greatly reducing the possibility of misunderstandings that may be personally or financially damaging.

Faulty Analogy.   This fallacy results when two subjects are compared, and while the two share certain similarities, their differences may be so important that they negate the value of the comparison; a familiar statement used to point out faulty analogy is "You're comparing apples and oranges." Of course, comparing the current world political situation to one 20, 50, or 100 years back may be interesting and even enlightening. But many factors have changed in the intervening time spans, so any conclusions based on this analogy are liable to be imperfect.

A related fallacy is *faulty metaphor,* which makes a comparison based on a few resemblances (or just one), usually to criticize. The language is sometimes lively and colorful, as in this example: "Knee-jerk, milktoast-eating liberals always want to confiscate our guns, leaving us red-blooded American patriots nothing but our teeth and nails as protection for the living treasures of our homes against a host of drug-crazed perverts." But such metaphor-laden statements offer little basis for rational understanding or logical choice.

Hasty (Faulty, Sweeping) Generalization.   This fallacy occurs when a proposed inductive conclusion is based on either a too limited sample or number of examples or else is based on unrepresentative examples. For instance, while you and most of your neighbors may prefer a certain presidential candidate or brand of soft drink, that sample is so small and localized that it is of questionable value; neither the candidate or the soft drink company would be wise to use the results as the basis for important decisions about the success of the candidate's campaign or the likelihood that Pepsi and Coke can be displaced as leading brands.

Hypostatization.   This language fallacy results from the failure to differentiate between abstract and concrete words, speaking of abstractions such as *nature, justice, science,* and the like as though they were concrete. Although such abstract words can convey and create emotion, they are not specific enough to convey useful, precise information that will help in reaching a rational decision. "Have you thanked nature today?" is one example of hypostatization, as are "Love conquers all" and "Science puts industry to work."

Hypothesis Contrary to Fact.   In this fallacy a hypothesis (a proposition offered as an explanation for the occurrence of some event or phenomenon) that is not true is used as the starting place for a deductive argument. "If Albert Einstein had stayed in Germany, the Nazis would have had an atomic bomb before the United States did" is one such fallacious argument, for Einstein did not stay in Germany, and even if he had, various other factors might well have prevented the Nazis from producing an atomic bomb before the United States did.

Irrelevance (Red Herring).   This fallacy results when the argument or discussion deliberately or accidentally strays off the subject and begins to deal with another, even an unrelated, subject, just as dragging smoked (red) herring across a trail will divert hunting dogs from following their prey and lead them off in another direction. Thus, opponents of gun registration may display bumper stickers which read "If guns are outlawed, only outlaws will have guns." This slogan has emotional appeal (its ending assertion uses the *appeal to fear* fallacy), but it has fallaciously changed the point of contention from *registering* guns to *outlawing* them, thus misrepresenting the gun registration supporters' position.

Labored Hypothesis.   This fallacy results when a hypothesis drawn from one body of evidence is more complex, unlikely, or unusual than an alternative one; for example, "Dozens of laboratory animals were released from their cages at University Medical Center during the night, and they escaped through an outside door whose lock was broken; there were no witnesses, but Medical Center personnel must have done it in order to get the local animal rights activist group in trouble with the police."

Non Sequitur.   This fallacy's Latin phrase means "It does not follow." The conclusion in such an argument lacks a connection to the premises: "I grew up in Miami; therefore I have always wanted to be a movie star." This example is clearly nonsense, but sometimes the argument may go astray in a less obvious way: "Free enterprise is being undermined by the federal government, which tells all companies how to operate, has taken over management of our farms, and even forces managers to cooperate with union organizers. Democracy is almost extinct in the United States." Perhaps this argument has quite a bit of emotional appeal for you and seems convincing. But you then must not have noticed how the argument shifted, for free enterprise is an economic system and democracy is a political system; thus there is no connection between the premises and the conclusion.

Post Hoc, Ergo Propter Hoc (False Cause).   Latin words that translate as "after this, therefore because of this" commonly identify this fallacy. The problem occurs when a person assumes that a cause and effect relationship exists just because one event follows another. But there must be a demonstrable causal link between the two events before such reasoning can be considered sound. An example familiar to us all is assuming that bad luck will occur if a black cat crosses our path. It's clear that we are being led astray by our superstitious natures, but most of us too often resort to similar fallacious reasoning, assigning our good and bad experiences to some questionably-related causes.

Reductio ad Absurdum.   This is another fallacy with a Latin name, here meaning "reduction to absurdity." An effective means of refuting another argument, frequently with a satirical effect, this approach, though fallacious, makes an idea or an attitude seem to be irrational by exaggerating or extending its logical consequences, sometimes to the point of ridiculousness. The classic example of this approach is Jonathan Swift's essay, "A Modest Proposal," reprinted in the "Selected Classic Arguments" section of this book. Swift ironically recommends that, to solve the terrible poverty in eighteenth century Ireland, the poor should sell their children to be used as food.

Slippery Slope (Domino Theory).   This fallacy, like *post hoc, ergo propter hoc,* has its basis in the fallacious linking of causes and effects. A slippery slope argument hypothetically links a series of events, asserting that if the first event takes place, then the others will follow, just as one false step on an icy hill may result in an injured person at the hill's bottom, and just as a row of closely spaced dominoes placed on their ends will topple, one after another, if the end one is pushed over. But often events are not as closely linked as those carefully placed dominoes (a *faulty analogy* is also present here), and therefore bans on automatic weapons and cheap handguns need not lead inevitably to the confiscation of Great Grandpa's hunting rifle that has been passed down in the family for generations. Stopping places usually exist along the way, and pointing those out is one appropriate way to refute such fallacies.

Special Pleading (Card Stacking).   This inductive fallacy results when certain evidence, generally numerical or statistical, is emphasized, while other evidence, equally or even more pertinent, is suppressed or minimized. When we are told by the local power company's news release that its coal-burning smokestack has new pollution control devices that have reduced its sulphur dioxide emissions (the key ingredient in acid rain) to one-half of one percent, that may seem commendable; but then we realize we haven't been told what that "percent" is part of. Eventually we learn that the percent is of the total volume of emissions, which amount to 10 tons per day, so that annually the plant is still producing over 18 tons of sulphur dioxide, or enough to form quite a few railroad tank cars of sulfuric acid. Twain indirectly referred to just this fallacy when he said, "There are three kinds of lies: lies, damn lies, and statistics." News media can be guilty of this fallacy in a modified form if they feature the activities of certain political figures or government programs that they favor and ignore or give abbreviated coverage to those that they do not.

Syntactic Ambiguity   This language fallacy is the result of faulty sentence structure. Sometimes parts are misplaced: "Sam cut firewood with his best friend"; "The students couldn't understand why Shakespeare was so well liked in high school"; "The professor explained why plagiarism is wrong on Monday." Sometimes multiple or complex questions are phrased so they are self-incriminating whether answered yes or no: "Have you stopped spending all of your money on beer?" or "Are you still cheating on tests?" Similarly, because pauses and emphasis on words can create different meanings, they can result in deliberate or accidental misunderstandings.

If you repeat this short sentence, "She slapped him," three times and emphasize a different word each time, the potential for ambiguity will be obvious.

Transfer (False Authority). This fallacy is based on the principle of favorable association, even though there may be little or no logical connection. In one variety, the subject is identified with some idea or entity that is inherently pleasing or attractive. Any viewer of television or reader of popular magazines is constantly bombarded with advertisements or commercials that use transfer. The association may be with having a good time (see soft drink, liquor, and cigarette ads) or with pleasant memories (food and telephone) or with looking better (clothing and personal care products, always featuring attractive models).

Another variety of transfer, also favored by advertisers, is related to the use of authority in an argument, except here the prestige or reputation of a respected or admired person or institution is used to support an idea or product. This *false authority* fallacy occurs when the person featured is removed from his or her area of expertise; thus Ray Charles and Joe Montana are great stars in their respective fields of popular music and professional football, but their claims of value regarding soft drinks are not likely to be any more accurate than the average person's—and furthermore they are being paid considerable sums for their promotional efforts. In a related way, Biblical references may be used fallaciously to support political or other ideas. In any case, the association or identification should certainly be examined for a logical connection; if there is none, the fallacy of transfer or false authority is present.

Tu Quoque. This Latin term for "you also" or "you're another" identifies a fallacy that avoids the subject or deflects questions or accusations by making similar accusations against an opponent. For instance, a person being criticized for eating a second candy bar might reply to the critic, "Well, you're *already* too fat or you'd take a *third* one!" or "If you weren't on a diet, you'd be reaching for a Snickers yourself!" Neither of these responses provides logical reasons for eating a second candy bar, but each instead attempts to divert attention elsewhere.

Formal Fallacies

Formal fallacies result from the improper construction of syllogisms, which form the frameworks of deductive arguments. Such

fallacies are therefore errors of structure or form. In order to understand formal fallacies, you will also need to have a working knowledge of the simple syllogism. A *syllogism* is a series of three statements arranged according to this formula:

> All humans are mortal.   (First or major premise)
> Jill is a human.   (Second or minor premise)
> _____
> Therefore, Jill is mortal.   (Conclusion)

The syllogism must meet certain standards of construction and
arrangement in order to be *valid*, or logically consistent. First, the
syllogism must consist of three two-term statements: two propositions (*premises*) and a *conclusion*, as in the example just given.

Second, it must consist of three different *terms* ("humans,"
"mortal," and "Jill" in the above example); one term must appear in
both premises but not in the conclusion, and each of the other two
terms must appear in one premise and in the conclusion. The term
that appears in both premises but not in the conclusion ("human") is
called the *middle term;* the other terms ("mortal" and "Jill") are
called *end terms.*

Third, in order to be valid a syllogism must conform to three
simple rules, the first and most important being that the middle
term must be *distributed* only once. To be distributed, a term,
whether middle or end, must appear *either* as the subject of a universal statement (one that by means of such words as "every," "all," or
"no" totally includes or totally excludes all members of a class or
group) *or* as the predicate term of a negative statement. (For our
purposes, a predicate term is one that completes either the verb "to
be" or some other linking verb—as, for example, "eater of plants"
does in this negative statement: "Fido is not an eater of plants.")

A term is *undistributed* if it is the subject of a particular statement or the predicate term of a positive statement. For instance, in
this syllogism,

> All Italians are fans of opera.   (First premise)
> Susie is not a fan of opera.   (Second premise)
> _____
> Susie is not an Italian.   (Conclusion)

the middle term, "fan(s) of opera," is undistributed in the first premise, since it is the predicate term of a positive statement, and distributed in the second premise as the predicate term of a negative state-

ment. The end term "Susie" is undistributed in both of its positions, being the subject of a particular statement, while "Italians" is distributed twice, once as the subject of a universal statement ("*All* Italians . . .") and once as the predicate term of a negative statement (". . . is *not* an Italian").

The case of the end term "Italian" also illustrates rule two: No end term may be distributed only once in a valid syllogism. The third and final rule, as you will see demonstrated later, is that no valid syllogism can have two negative premises.

Either to understand why this last rule is necessary or to determine the validity of any syllogism, you will probably find it useful to draw circles to represent the various classes or groups and individuals named. For example, draw a large circle to represent the class consisting of fans of opera. Then, since all Italians are fans of opera, draw a small circle within the large circle to represent all Italians (you must, of course, leave room for fans of opera from other countries). Now, where does Susie's small individual circle go? Outside both larger circles, of course (see Figure A.1). But what happens if you then give the syllogism two negative premises, like this:

No Italians are fans of opera.
Susie is not a fan of opera.

What can you conclude? By drawing the circles you will see the you cannot really say anything exclusively and positively about Susie's nationality, for you do not know exactly where to place her circle (see Figure A.2). Susie may or may not be an Italian, which is not a useful conclusion. Now you should understand why rule three is important. By using the circles you should also be able to determine why the rest of the standards and rules for validity are important.

So far we have been concentrating on the question of the *validity* of the deductive syllogism. A quick glance at the sample

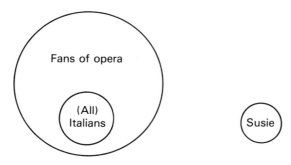

FIGURE A.1

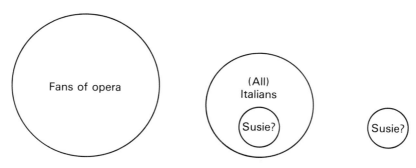

FIGURE A.2

syllogisms and circles, however, will suggest that the question of *truth* in a deductive syllogism is a separate one, for while it is commonly known that many Italians are indeed fans of opera, we can also be reasonably sure that at least some Italians prefer rock, jazz, or other musical entertainment. However, and this is a point that you must understand about deductive arguments, *if* a syllogism meets the standards of *validity*, and *if* the premises are accepted as true propositions, whether intuitively, inductively, or even deductively as conclusions of other syllogisms, then the conclusion of the syllogism in question is logically and undeniably true. Of course, few of us consciously use deductive syllogisms in the formal sense, although we do use deductive logic daily, often in an abbreviated form called an enthymeme.

An *enthymeme* is a syllogism with one of its three statements missing or unstated, and perhaps with its conclusion preceding its premise(s), as in this case: "Susie's not Italian. She doesn't like opera." Clearly the first premise, "All Italians are fans of opera," is absent, perhaps because the speaker thinks it is too obvious to need mentioning. Yet the speaker's audience, if they are critical thinkers, might realize the problem with the *truth* of the unstated first premise and reject the speaker's conclusion about Susie's nationality. (They could also reject the conclusion without really knowing exactly why, perhaps on the basis of "common sense.") Similarly, another speaker might state, "Dr. Green probably eats meat, since she is a veterinarian." But this conclusion might also be false, perhaps because the syllogism is invalid:

Most veterinarians eat meat.
Dr. Green is a veterinarian.

Dr. Green eats meat.   X

Here the middle term ("veterinarian") is not distributed, for "most" is not a word that includes or excludes all of a class or group. Or even if in valid form, with "all" substituted for "most," the first premise or proposition could be rejected as inductively false by a person who knows of one or more veterinarians who are vegetarians.

This is not to suggest, though, that all enthymemes are either invalid or false. Instead, you should be aware when they are being used and examine the total syllogism for validity and for true, acceptable propositions before you agree with or reject any deductive conclusion.

The five most common formal fallacies are discussed below. If you care to do so, you can use scratch paper to draw and appropriately label circles for each argument, in order to determine its invalidity.

1. *The four-term argument.*

All persons who drink to excess are alcoholics.
Sandra drinks beer.

Therefore, Sandra is an alcoholic.

The four terms here are "persons who drink to excess," "Sandra," "drinkers of beer," and "alcoholics." To make the argument a valid one, it must be shown that Sandra drinks to excess, thus eliminating the fourth term and providing a properly distributed middle term, "persons who drink to excess."

2. *Improperly distributed middle term.* This fallacy results when the middle term of a deductive syllogism is distributed more or less than once. For instance, in this invalid syllogism the middle term, "fans of opera," is not distributed at all:

All Italians are fans of opera.
Wolfgang is a fan of opera.

Wolfgang is an Italian.   X

Nothing prevents people of other nationalities from joining the class of fans of opera, since the middle term is not distributed. So Wolfgang may well be of some nationality other than Italian. If the middle term is distributed more than once, this invalid syllogism results:

All Italians are fans of opera.
All Italians are friendly.

?

When the middle term drops out, as it always does in a valid syllogism, we are left with no conclusion at all, for some fans of opera are not Italian and some friendly people are not Italians; we can assert nothing validly or positively about the friendliness of non-Italian fans of opera.

3. *Unequal distribution.* In this fallacy, an end term is distributed only once, as in this example:

All Italians are fans of opera.
No Germans are Italians.

No Germans are fans of opera.   X

Here, since the end term "fans of opera" is distributed in the conclusion (as the predicate of a negative statement) yet not distributed in the premise (as the predicate of a universal statement), it violates the basic rule of deduction that no end term may be distributed only once.

4. *Two particular premises.* No valid conclusion may be drawn from two particular premises. Consider this example:

Some tall persons are awkward.
Jim is a tall person.

Therefore, Jim is awkward.

Maybe he is, and maybe he isn't; no positive or negative conclusion can be reached.

5. *Two negative premises.* This fallacy results because no valid syllogism may have two negative premises, for then no exclusive and no positive conclusion can be drawn. For example,

No Australians have ever lived in my neighborhood.
Kathleen has never lived in my neighborhood.

?

Kathleen may be an Australian or not; we can't say for sure either way.

You have now finished this short discussion of material and formal fallacies. You will probably find it useful to turn back now and then to this section and to review it, just to maintain your ability to detect fallacies in arguments created by you and by others.

Glossary of Useful Terms

The following list provides brief definitions of key logical, rhetorical, and stylistic terms arranged alphabetically. Italics show that a word or phrase found in a definition also has its own definition in this glossary.

abstract words: Words expressing intangible feelings, ideas, or generalities (anger, religion, summer), as opposed to *concrete words*, which stand for tangible objects or things.

allusion: A brief reference to a person, place, thing, or event, or to a literary work or passage. Sometimes classified as historical, literary, or topical, allusions are comparisons used by writers to expand upon or to clarify ideas.

analogy: A comparison of two things which share some but not all qualities. By helping an *audience* comprehend the unfamiliar in terms of the familiar, analogy is one useful means of supporting a *claim.*

argument: The systematic process of providing proof to support a conclusion; the support for a *claim.*

argumentation: One of the basic modes of prose discourse, the others being *description, narration,* and *exposition. Purpose* is a key determinant in differentiating between these modes, with the writer of argumentative prose setting out to change the minds of the intended *audience.*

assertion: A specific declarative statement (*claim, proposition*) expressing a belief or opinion which the writer or speaker must support with *evidence* in order to gain the approval of an *audience.*

assumption: A statement or idea accepted or supposed true without demonstration or substantial proof.

478

audience: The person(s) who will read or hear an *argument*. The best writers have a particular audience in mind as they compose their work, taking into account the intended audience's knowledge of the subject, its opinions or biases, and the like. Although the real audience may differ from the intended one, the writer seeking success must select and organize the material, determine *purpose*, and adjust *tone* with his or her perceived audience in mind.

authority: A person or a source of information presumed or known to be reliable. An appeal to authority, made by referring to such a person, or to that person's findings or work, is one way to support a *claim*.

backing: The support for a *warrant* or *assertion*.

bibliography: A list of works, usually on a specific subject or by a specific person or group of persons, normally appearing at the end of a research paper, scholarly article, or book.

cause and effect: An important *method of development* used in supporting a *claim* by analyzing the connection(s) between the effects (results) and the causes of (reasons for) those effects.

claim: A statement or *assertion* that the writer of an *argument* must successfully support or prove. These can be classified as one of three types: claims of fact, claims of policy, claims of value.

classification: A *method of development* that can be used to support a *claim* by showing the connections between classes or types of ideas, persons, and things because of shared features or attributes.

cliché: A worn-out idea or expression, usually a comparison, which is so familiar that it no longer causes thought or calls to mind a visual image. "Good as gold," "beginner's luck," "happy as a lark" are examples; their use by a writer suggests mental dullness or laxity.

coherence: One desired goal of effective prose composition, wherein all of the parts of the written piece fit together clearly and logically. (Also see *transition* and *unity*.)

comparison/contrast: A *method of development* used to support a *claim* by focusing on the similarities (comparison) and/or differences (contrast) of two or more members of the same group of ideas or things.

concession: A rhetorical tactic whereby the writer acknowledges conflicting or differing views, *claims, warrants,* and the like on a subject, thereby attempting not only to neutralize those opposing points but also to indicate that the subject has been considered fully.

conclusion: (1) Structurally, the closing sentence, paragraph, or other section of a piece of writing, whose function is to add a sense of unity and finality to the composition; (2) in an *argument*, the specific statement or *assertion* being proven by a line of reasoning.

concrete words: Words which stand for tangible objects or things, ones which can be perceived by the human senses. Due to their sensory appeal, concrete words (in contrast to *abstract words*) help a writer's *audience* to imagine the object or thing, thereby adding clarity of expression while reducing ambiguity.

connotation: The secondary or associational meanings that most words have, due either to their contexts or to their emotional overtones for readers. (Compare to *denotation*.)

deduction: A traditional method of *logical argument* in which a *conclusion* (specific statement or *assertion*) is derived from *premises* (general or inclusive statement or *assertions*). (Compare to *induction*.)

definition: Normally, a synonym for or a statement of the exact meaning(s) of a word, such as can be found in a dictionary. Also a *method of development* used to support a *claim* by clarifying or demonstrating the meaning of a word or concept.

denotation: The literal or dictionary meaning of a word, as opposed to its *connotation*.

description: A form of writing relying mainly on *concrete words* to convey exact sensory impressions of persons, places, and things, and therefore often valuable in supporting a *claim*; frequently used in conjunction with *narration*.

diction: The selection of words in writing or speaking, with emphasis on accuracy, appropriateness, and *level of usage*. (See also *tone*.)

documentation: The references a writer provides in order to show the source(s) of any borrowed or adapted information. (See also *bibliography*.)

editing: The process of correcting writing problems of *diction*, grammar, or phrasing. (See also *proofreading, revising*.)

enthymeme: A *syllogism* with an unstated or implied *premise*.

essay: A *prose* composition that attempts to explain something, discuss a topic, express an attitude, or persuade an *audience* to accept a *proposition*.

evidence: Facts, statistics, or other data used to support a *claim* or *thesis*.

exemplification: The most important *method of development*, especially useful for supporting a *claim*, it is based on the use of examples to clarify a subject or support a *thesis*.

exposition: One of the basic *modes of discourse* or forms of *prose*, which are classified according to *purpose*. The writer of exposition attempts to explain a subject, or to inform the intended *audience* about it.

fact: Something accepted as true based on experience or observation, and which all reasonable persons normally will accept as true (wood comes from trees; seat belts save lives; milk contains calcium). A *claim* of fact is usually not debatable. Contrary to fact is *opinion*.

fallacy: Any of various types of deceptive, erroneous, or false reasoning that cause an *argument* to be logically flawed, even though the fallacy may be psychologically persuasive and seem to be true. (A complete discussion is provided in "A Short Guide to Material and Formal Fallacies," beginning on p. 463.)

figurative language: Writing or speaking that includes brief comparisons (figures of speech) based on the purposeful departure from the literal or common meanings of words in order to create clarity, freshness, or additional special meanings. Familiar figures of speech include *allusion, metaphor,* and *simile*.

focus: Confining a subject to a single point of view. In order to provide appropriate and steady focus, a writer must especially keep in mind the intended *audience,* the *purpose,* and the *subject*.

hypothesis: A *claim* presented as an explanation for some event or set of phenomena; also the *premise* for an *argument*.

induction: A method of *logical argument* in which a *hypothesis* or generalization is proposed, based on observation of representative actions, specific instances, statistical data, or other evidence.

introduction: The beginning of a piece of writing, varying in length from a single sentence to several pages or even a chapter, depending on the complexity of the subject and approach and on the work's length. An effective introduction identifies the subject, limits the subject, interests the *audience,* and may indicate the work's overall organization.

invalid: Not following the rules of *logical argument,* especially in the case of *deduction*. An invalid *argument* is not in the proper form, so its *conclusion* does not necessarily follow from its *premises*.

irony: A manner of writing or speaking so as to present one surface meaning while also presenting one or more veiled, contrasting meanings. Sometimes used quite effectively for argumentation, as in the case of Jonathan Swift's "A Modest Proposal," it may use such specific techniques as exaggeration, sarcasm, or understatement.

level of usage: The kind of language, especially in terms of *diction* and *syntax,* most suitable for the intended *audience*. The normal categories are these: (1) general; (2) informal; (3) formal; (4) nonstandard. Most undergraduate academic writing is done at the general level, a blend of the formal and informal.

logical argument: A kind of *argumentation* relying on appeals to reason, it features a reserved and detached *tone* and tends to avoid or limit appeals to emotion.

metaphor: A figure of speech suggesting an unstated comparison between one object and another, basically different object.

method of development: Those organizational techniques used in *paragraphs* or larger pieces of *prose*, especially *argumentation* and *exposition*, with the intent of achieving the best rhetorical effect on the intended *audience*. The most common methods are *cause and effect, classification, comparison/contrast, definition,* and *exemplification;* several or even all of these methods may be used at once in a piece of writing.

modes of discourse: The three *prose* forms, *argumentation, description–narration, exposition,* which may appear separately or in various combinations in a piece of writing.

narration: The process of telling about events, as in story form. Combined with *description*, this is one of the three basic *prose* forms (or *modes of discourse*). Often used for purposes of *argumentation* or *exposition,* it may also exist separately for its own sake.

objective: Expressing opinions or ideas based on detached observation, undistorted by personal feelings. (See *subjective.*)

opinion: A belief confidently held but not necessarily shared by other reasonable persons (city life is better than rural life; no dessert tastes better than blueberry cheesecake; skydiving is fun). Compare to *fact.*

paradox: A statement that on its face seems self-contradictory or in conflict with general belief, yet nevertheless contains some truth. "No news is good news" is a familiar example.

paragraph: A separate portion of a composition, usually marked by indentation of its first written line, it expresses a thought or point related to the whole work but is essentially complete by itself. Varying in length from one sentence to many, paragraphs may function as *introduction, conclusion,* and *transition* elements of an *essay;* other paragraphs form the main body of the essay and are used to develop or present the subject.

paraphrase: Restating another person's words either (1) to make them more understandable or concise or else (2) to show how those words are understood. In contrast with a *summary*, a paraphrase more closely approximates the length of the original version.

persuasion: A kind of *argumentation* that relies primarily on appeal to the emotions of an *audience* (compare to *logical argument*). Featuring a personal, even a friendly, *tone*, persuasion depends minimally, if at all, on *fact* and other elements of logical argument.

plagiarism: Presenting the words or ideas of another person as one's own, or without proper *documentation.*

premise: The *claim* or *proposition* on which an *argument* is based.

proofreading: The correcting of a piece of writing for errors of mechanics (spelling, punctuation, capitalization, and the like) and of typing and transcription. (See also *editing, revising.*)

proposition: A statement or *claim* that is to be proven or disproven.

prose: Written (or spoken) language that lacks metrical structure (as opposed to poetry or verse). It appears in three basic forms (or *modes of discourse*): argumentation, description–narration, and exposition.

purpose: A writer's intended goal, which may be to describe (*description*), to tell a story (*narration*), to explain (*exposition*), to change the *audience's* opinion (*argumentation*), or some combination of these.

qualifier: A word or words used to limit a *claim* or *assertion*, indicating that it may not always be true as stated. Familiar examples of qualifying words include "often," "normally," "in general," "with few exceptions," and the like.

refutation: Examining *arguments* or any of their parts and showing logical reasons for rejecting them.

revising: The major reworking of a piece of writing, including changes in organization, development, approach to the subject, point of view, and the like. (See also *editing* and *proofreading.*)

rhetoric: Written or spoken language consciously composed to influence the thought and conduct of an *audience.*

rhetorical question: A question posed mainly for effect, with either no answer expected or an obvious answer implied. Usually a rhetorical question is presented to gain the assent of the *audience* to something the writer assumes is obvious.

simile: A figure of speech in which a similarity between two things is directly expressed, most often by using *like, as,* or *than* to create the comparison.

slanting: Using *diction* (especially the *connotation* of words) and choosing *facts* so as to make the writer's *argument* seem better than it is. This practice may result in a *fallacy.*

style: The distinctive features of a piece of writing, especially as created by the writer's *diction, syntax, tone,* and arrangement of material.

subjective: Expressing opinions or ideas based on personal feelings or interests rather than on detached, disinterested observation. (See *objective.*)

summary: A concise statement of the major points or ideas of a piece of writing.

support: Anything used to prove a *claim*, including not only *evidence* but also appeals to the values and emotions of the *audience.*

syllogism: The basic formula or pattern of *deduction*, consisting of a major premise (general proposition), a minor premise (specific proposition), and a conclusion drawn from terms or parts of each premise. (See also *enthymeme.*)

syntax: The arrangement and relationship of words, phrases, and sentences.

thesis: A writer's assumption or specific statement, usually expressed in the *introduction*, which he or she then attempts to validate. A thesis statement or sentence (in a paragraph, called a topic sentence) often reveals the writer's *purpose.*

tone: The apparent attitude of the writer toward both subject and *audience*, especially as revealed by *diction*, selection of details and examples, and *syntax*. (See also *style.*)

transition: Any of various means of linking one topic (or aspect of a topic) to another. The most basic means of achieving effective transitions is logical organization, but a writer may also use such tactics as transitional words and phrases, repetition of key words and phrases, and repetition of sentence structure.

unity: The desirable quality found in a piece of writing that is limited to and focused on a single idea or topic.

valid: Following the rules of *logical argument*. A valid deductive argument adheres to the correct form, and thus its *conclusion* necessarily follows from its *premises.*

warrant: An underlying assumption or general principle that provides a connection between the *claim* and its *support.*

Index of Authors and Titles

Y